Human Performance Optimization

Human Performance Optimization

The Science and Ethics of Enhancing Human Capabilities

EDITED BY MICHAEL D. MATTHEWS

AND

DAVID M. SCHNYER

OXFORD
UNIVERSITY PRESS

Oxford University Press is a department of the University of Oxford. It furthers
the University's objective of excellence in research, scholarship, and education
by publishing worldwide. Oxford is a registered trade mark of Oxford University
Press in the UK and certain other countries.

Published in the United States of America by Oxford University Press
198 Madison Avenue, New York, NY 10016, United States of America.

CIP data is on file at the Library of Congress
ISBN 978–0–19–045513–2

9 8 7 6 5 4 3 2 1

Printed by Sheridan Books, Inc., United States of America

In memory of Dr. Victor M. Agruso. A great teacher, mentor, and friend.
His influence on psychology is manifested through his impact on the hundreds
of students he educated and inspired as Professor of Psychology at Drury University.

—MDM

CONTENTS

FOREWORD

As Chief of Staff of the United States Army, it was my responsibility to recruit, train, and field an Army capable of responding quickly and effectively to a full range of exigencies, from humanitarian assistance to full-scale combat. Including the Reserve Component and the National Guard, the Army is comprised of 1 million uniformed soldiers. This is supplemented by a workforce of more than 300,000 dedicated civilian employees who serve in a wide array of jobs and represent an integral part of the Army's capabilities. To those without military experience, this may seem like a sufficiently large force. However, with ongoing military operations in the Middle East, the growing threat on the Korean Peninsula, and increasing tensions with Russia and China, the Army needs every single soldier and civilian in order to meet current and future mission requirements.

The challenges faced by the Army are compounded by the nature of twenty-first-century warfare. With sophisticated technology, the speed of military operations is significantly faster than in previous centuries. This places a greater demand on the cognitive capabilities of soldiers who now may have only seconds or minutes to decide how to respond to a particular threat. Moreover, our experience since September 11, 2001, is that our foes are often ideologically motivated networks of enemies, often geographically dispersed, rather than traditional nation-state enemies such as when we faced Germany and Japan in World War II. To effectively respond to such a threat, soldiers must now be culturally savvy and understand the nuances of religious ideology and political objectives. Advances in weapons technology have increased the cognitive skills needed to manage and employ these systems. Moreover, the emergence of cyberwarfare adds to the range of knowledge and skills that soldiers and civilians must possess.

To meet current and future threats, the Army must develop training and development strategies to help all members of the force, uniformed and civilian alike, to perform to their full potential. The Army has long valued physical fitness in its soldiers, and through the years has developed ways to take new recruits and, through training, build their endurance and make them stronger. We know how to optimize physical performance in soldiers. But given the complexities of contemporary war, we need to better understand how to optimize other capabilities, including decision-making, cultural competence, leadership skills, and rapid understanding of fluctuating operating environments.

As the Army Chief of Staff, I formed a Strategic Studies Group (SSG) to help inform me on future challenges the Army may face and on general solutions to solving those problems. A new SSG cohort, consisting of about 20 Army officers, non-commissioned officers, and Army civilians was formed each July and worked together for 11 months to address issues that I identified as being of strategic importance to the Army and the nation. In 2014, I assigned five SSG Fellows to study human performance optimization (HPO), with the goal of exploring state-of-the-art and emerging scientific breakthroughs in the area of novel and revolutionary approaches to enhancing soldier and civilian performance. After 11 months of study, they submitted a report to me that captured the results of their research. The purpose of this book, co-edited by Dr. Matthews (one member of the HPO SSG team) is to report to the scientific community the results of this work. As you will see, the topics covered in this volume are grounded on scientifically based approaches to improving human performance. They focus on cognitive, physical, and social aspects of performance, with a common theme being those measures that organizations may take to enhance and grow the capabilities of their members in these areas.

Optimizing human performance toward the goal of improving organizational effectiveness is important not just to the Army, but also to all public and private organizations and institutions who employ others in high-stakes, high-stress, and oft-times dangerous environments. Other public institutions, such as law enforcement agencies, face many of the same challenges as the Army in recruiting, training, and developing personnel who can consistently perform at their highest levels. Large corporations in a variety of economic sectors will also benefit by the emerging knowledge contained in this book on how to develop and "get the most" from their employees.

I close with an additional thought. While, as Chief of Staff of the Army, I was understandably interested in identifying ways to optimize the performance of our soldiers and civilians, I had another motive for sponsoring this inquiry by my SSG. The Army, like the other services, proudly accepts young people from across this nation into its ranks. They are a public trust, and I feel that the Army has a responsibility to help these young men and women grow and flourish so that, when they return to civilian life, they and the nation will benefit from their military experience. In my 40 years as a soldier, I have seen countless soldiers benefit in this way from their service. I hope that the scientific insights contained in this book provide a blueprint for both public and private organizations committed to improving the human potential of their respective workforces to achieve their goals of HPO and, at the same time, help scientists develop a vision for future research on how to achieve this goal effectively and ethically. If successful, the Army and the nation will benefit.

—General (Retired) Raymond T. Odierno
38th Chief of Staff of the United States Army

ACKNOWLEDGMENTS

First and foremost, the authors thank Gretchen Bain Matthews who served as the project manager for this book. She tracked the status of 19 chapters written by a total of 47 coauthors. Gretchen worked with chapter authors to ensure that they were aware of both content and formatting requirements. She maintained regular contact with all authors and helped them resolve issues with formatting, style, the creation of graphs and figures, and making sure everything was done according to the Oxford University Press publication standards. In addition, she provided technical editing for all chapters. It is no understatement to say that without Gretchen's contributions, this book could not have been completed.

We also thank the contributing authors. We learned a lot from working with you and reading the drafts of your chapters, and we are grateful to each of you for making time to write a chapter for this book. Each chapter is vital in extending our understanding of human performance optimization. The breadth and depth of this work is far beyond the capabilities of any one scientist to understand fully. Collectively, you have helped create a useful source for scientists and practitioners interested in the science of performance enhancement.

Michael Matthews also extends his appreciation to the US Army, the US Military Academy (West Point), and the Department of Behavioral Sciences and Leadership for creating a stimulating intellectual environment that is conducive to scholarship. Most importantly, he thanks the members of the Chief of Staff of the Army's Strategic Studies Group with whom he had the privilege of working on the original project in 2014 and 2015. COL David Bolduc, LTC Robert Green, CSM Craig Davis, and Dr. Jessica Gallus all contributed immensely to his project and served as a source of inspiration for the development of this book. He also thanks General Raymond T. Odierno, the 38th Chief of Staff of the US Army, for letting him be a part of his Strategic Studies Group.

David Schnyer would like to extend appreciation to the Department of Psychology and the College of Liberal Arts at the University of Texas (UT), Austin, for the continued support of his research and scholarly work. In addition, he would like to acknowledge the Clinically Applied Research and Rehabilitation Engineering (CARE) initiative at UT Austin. Dr. Schnyer serves as the Research & Development Chair for this initiative, and the activities of this group inspired a number of the chapter ideas and contributing authors for this volume.

ABOUT THE EDITORS

Michael D. Matthews is Professor of Engineering Psychology at the United States Military Academy. He served as President of the American Psychological Association Society for Military Psychology from 2007 to 2008 and is a Templeton Foundation Senior Positive Psychology Fellow. From 2014 to 2015, he served as a Fellow for the US Army Chief of Staff's Strategic Studies Group. He has authored more than 250 scientific papers and edited several books on military psychology, and he is the author of *Head Strong: How Psychology Is Revolutionizing War* (2014). His most recent book (coedited with David E. Rohall and Morten G. Ender), *Inclusion in the American Military: A Force for Diversity*, was published in 2017.

David M. Schnyer is a Professor in the Department of Psychology and the Institute for Neuroscience at the University of Texas, Austin. He completed a PhD in Clinical Neuropsychology from the University of Arizona. While at the Memory Disorders Research Center at Boston University School of Medicine he was awarded a National Institutes of Health (NIH) K-award in multimodal neuroimaging techniques and trained at the Martino's Center for Biomedical Imaging (MGH). His lab researches the cognitive and neural systems that support memory and attention control in young and old healthy individuals, as well as in persons suffering from mental illness and traumatic brain injury.

CONTRIBUTORS

Priyanshu Agarwal
Mechanical Engineering Department
The University of Texas at Austin
Austin, Texas

Hubert Annen
Head of Military Psychology and
   Military Pedagogy Studies
Swiss Military Academy at ETH Zurich
Birmensdorf, Switzerland

Natalia Henao Arango
Biomedical Engineer, Biophysics and
   Biomedical Modeling Division
US Army Research Institute of
   Environmental Medicine
Natick, Massachusetts

Mark J. Buller
Research Physiologist, Biophysics and
   Biomedical Modeling Division
US Army Research Institute of
   Environmental Medicine
Natick, Massachusetts

Joshua A. Carlisle
Assistant Professor of Philosophy
Department of English and Philosophy
US Military Academy
West Point, New York

Yin-Jui Chang
NERDLab
The University of Texas at Austin
Austin, Texas

Sandra B. Chapman
Founder and Chief Director, Center for
   BrainHealth
Dee Wyly Distinguished University
   Professor, School of Behavioral and
   Brain Sciences
The University of Texas at Dallas
Dallas, Texas

Revathy U. Chottekalapanda
Senior Research Associate
Laboratory of Molecular and Cellular
   Neuroscience
The Rockefeller University
New York, New York

Lori G. Cook
Director of Clinical Research, Center
   for BrainHealth
Senior Clinician, Brain Performance
   Institute
Adjunct Assistant Professor, School of
   Behavioral and Brain Sciences
The University of Texas at Dallas
Dallas, Texas

Jennifer L. Creamer
San Antonio Military Health System
Department of Sleep Medicine
Joint Base San Antonio
Lackland, Texas

Ashish D. Deshpande
Associate Professor
Mechanical Engineering Department
The University of Texas at Austin
Austin, Texas

Benito R. Fernández
Associate Professor
The University of Texas at Austin
Mechanical Engineering
Austin, Texas

Karl E. Friedl
Senior Research Scientist (ST),
   Physiology
US Army Research Institute of
   Environmental Medicine
Natick, Massachusetts

Erin Gaffney-Stomberg
Research Physiologist, Military
   Performance Division
US Army Research Institute of
   Environmental Medicine
Natick, Massachusetts

Stephen Goldberg
US Army Research Laboratory
Human Research & Engineering
   Directorate
SFC Paul Ray Smith Simulation &
   Training Technology Center
Orlando, Florida

Stephen J. Grate
US Army, Retired
Frederick, Maryland

Paul Greengard
Vincent Astor Professor, Laboratory of
   Molecular and Cellular Neuroscience
The Rockefeller University
New York, New York

Reed W. Hoyt
Chief, Biophysics and Biomedical
   Modeling Division
US Army Research Institute of
   Environmental Medicine
Natick, Massachusetts

Daniela Huepe-Artigas
Center for Social and Cognitive
   Neuroscience (CSCN)
School of Psychology
Universidad Adolfo Ibáñez
Santiago, Chile
and
School of Psychological Sciences
University of Melbourne, Australia

Gautam Krishna
NERDLab
The University of Texas at Austin
Austin, Texas

Janice H. Laurence
Professor
Adult & Organizational Development
College of Education
Temple University
Philadelphia, Pennsylvania

Richard M. Lerner
Bergstrom Chair in Applied
   Developmental Science
Director, Institute for Applied Research
   in Youth Development
Tufts University
Medford, Massachusetts

Constanza Levican
Institute of Biological and Medical
   Engineering, Laboratory of
   Brain-Machine Interfaces and
   Neuromodulation, and Department of
   Psychiatry and Section of Neuroscience
Pontificia Católica Universidad
   de Chile
Santiago, Chile

Valerie E. Martindale
International Research Program
   Manager for Synthetic Biology
US Army Research Office
Tokyo, Japan

Panagiotis Matsangas
Operations Research Department
Naval Postgraduate School
Monterey, California

Michael D. Matthews
Professor of Engineering Psychology
Department of Behavioral Sciences and
  Leadership
US Military Academy
West Point, New York

James P. McClung
Chief, Military Nutrition Division
US Army Research Institute of
  Environmental Medicine
Natick, Massachusetts

Juan Andrés Mucarquer
Department of Electronic Engineering
Universidad Técnica Federico
  Santa María
Valparaíso, Chile

Vincent Mysliwiec
San Antonio Military Health System
Department of Sleep Medicine
Joint Base San Antonio
Lackland, Texas

James Ness
Professor of Engineering Psychology
Department of Behavioral Sciences and
  Leadership
US Military Academy
West Point, New York

John F. Nestojko
Department of Psychological & Brain
  Sciences
Washington University in St. Louis
St. Louis, Missouri

Matías Ramírez
Institute of Biological and Medical
  Engineering, Laboratory of
  Brain-Machine Interfaces and
  Neuromodulation, and Department
  of Psychiatry and Section of
  Neuroscience
Pontificia Católica Universidad
  de Chile
Santiago, Chile

Ian H. Robertson
T Boone Pickens Distinguished
  Scientist
Center for BrainHealth
The University of Texas at Dallas
Dallas, Texas
and
Co-Director
Global Brain Health Institute
Trinity College Dublin and University
  of California at San Francisco

Henry L. Roediger, III
James S. McDonnell Distinguished
  University Professor
Department of Psychological & Brain
  Sciences
Washington University in St. Louis
St. Louis, Missouri

Yotam Sagi
Senior Research Associate
Laboratory of Molecular and Cellular
  Neuroscience
The Rockefeller University
New York, New York

Andrea Sánchez Corzo
Institute of Biological and Medical
  Engineering, Laboratory of
  Brain-Machine Interfaces and
  Neuromodulation, and Department
  of Psychiatry and Section of
  Neuroscience
Pontificia Católica Universidad
  de Chile
Santiago, Chile

David M. Schnyer
Professor, Psychology and
  Neuroscience
Department Liaison for Medical Affairs
Research & Development Chair for the
  CARE Initiative
University of Texas at Austin
Austin, Texas

Nita Lewis Shattuck
Professor
Human Systems Integration Program
Operations Research Department
Naval Postgraduate School
Monterey, California

Ranganatha Sitaram
Associate Professor
Institute of Biological and Medical
   Engineering, Laboratory of
   Brain-Machine Interfaces and
   Neuromodulation, and Department
   of Psychiatry and Section of
   Neuroscience
Pontificia Católica Universidad
   de Chile
Santiago, Chile

Nicole S. Smith
Department of Psychology
University of Southern Mississippi
Hattiesburg, Mississippi

Robert Sottilare
Associate Director for Training
   Technology
US Army Research Laboratory
Human Research & Engineering
   Directorate
Orlando, Florida

William J. Tharion
Research Psychologist, Biophysics and
   Biomedical Modeling Division
US Army Research Institute of
   Environmental Medicine
Natick, Massachusetts

Logan T. Trujillo
Assistant Professor
Department of Psychology
Texas State University
San Marcos, Texas

Asha K. Vas
Assistant Professor, School of
   Occupational Therapy
Texas Woman's University
Dallas, Texas

Josephine Q. Wojciechowski
Associate for Strategic Communication
US Army Research Laboratory
Human Research and Engineering
   Directorate
Aberdeen Proving Ground, Maryland

Lissa V. Young
Assistant Professor
Department of Behavioral Sciences and
   Leadership
US Military Academy
West Point, New York

Mariana Zurita
Institute of Biological and Medical
   Engineering, Laboratory of
   Brain-Machine Interfaces and
   Neuromodulation, and Department
   of Psychiatry and Section of
   Neuroscience
Pontificia Católica Universidad
   de Chile
and
Electrical Engineering Department and
   Biomedical Imaging Center
Pontificia Universidad Católica
   de Chile
Santiago, Chile

Optimizing Human Performance

MICHAEL D. MATTHEWS AND DAVID M. SCHNYER*

INTRODUCTION

Workers are increasingly being required to function under conditions of constant physical and/or mental stress. Continuous connectivity, a 24/7 news cycle, and the challenge of balancing the demands of work with personal life, often lead to burnout and compromised performance in the workplace. This is particularly the case in the military and among first responders and healthcare workers (Sweeney, Matthews, & Lester, 2011).

The purpose of this book is to present state-of-the-art scientific research in human performance optimization (HPO). Our aim is to provide a clearer understanding of the physical, psychological, and social effects on human functioning presented by the challenges of performing in extreme settings. At the same time, we seek to explore solutions for optimizing human performance in these settings. While the genesis for this book lay in military policymaking, the optimization of human performance through applied science and engineering will yield benefits to a broad spectrum of human activities. These topics are relevant for first responders, healthcare workers, and physically or mentally impaired individuals, for whom everyday functioning can be considered a version of operating in "extreme circumstances." We believe that the ideas included in this volume will provide the basis to develop a heuristic, inform future research, and guide policymakers on the most viable, practical, and ethical avenues to enhance performance. The overarching goal is to enhance the human experience by allowing everyone to match their own strengths with jobs that utilize those strengths, resulting in less stress and greater life satisfaction.

Understanding the genesis of the ideas for this volume is critical to framing the contribution it will make. Beginning in the summer of 2014, the first author of this chapter spent a year as a Fellow for the US Army Chief of Staff's (CSA) Strategic Studies Group (SSG). General Raymond T. Odierno, the 38th Chief of Staff of the United States Army, founded the SSG in 2012 in order to assist the CSA in identifying emerging threats and opportunities, and to provide guidance in how to mitigate

*The views expressed herein are those of the authors and do not reflect the position of the United States Military Academy, the Department of the Army, or the Department of Defense.

these future threats and to fully exploit future opportunities. In July, a new SSG co-hort of about 20 Army soldiers and civilians formed and spent the next 11 months intensively studying a handful of issues thought by the CSA to be of strategic impor-tance. Military members of the SSG included senior noncommissioned officers and commissioned officers of the rank from captain to colonel. Civilian members were mid-level to senior Army employees, often scientists or other technical specialists. Much care was taken in selecting both the military and civilian members of the SSG in order to ensure a diverse group. To facilitate creativity, the members of the SSG reported directly to the Army Chief of Staff, thus minimizing the chances of ideas being filtered or censored. The SSG was tasked with conducting "independent, un-conventional, and revolutionary" research and analysis, with the goal of providing the CSA with "unbiased recommendations for concerns and opportunities at the strategic and operational level" (Gallus & Green, 2015).

The idea for this volume is based on one of the topics from the author's year with the SSG. By 2014, the US Army had been at war in Afghanistan and Iraq for 13 years. At the time the SSG came together, the Army had about 500,000 ac-tive duty soldiers. This may sound like a large number, but when the worldwide scope of its mission is considered, including ongoing combat operations in Iraq, Afghanistan, and elsewhere, the ability of the Army to meet all of its potential missions was strained. These demands on the active duty military meant soldiers were fatigued and stressed by repeated combat deployments. The danger and stress of combat, coupled with frequent and lengthy periods of time away from home and family, was taking its toll on the Army (and the other services as well). Rates of suicide and combat-related psychological disorders such as posttraumatic stress disorder (PTSD), substance abuse problems, depression, and other stress-related conditions were rising (Ursano et al., 2014; Wagner & Jakupcak, 2012) and the ability of the army to meet its mission requirements was being severely taxed. The challenges of repeated combat deployments were taking a toll on military families as well, resulting in difficult to quantify but nevertheless substantial impacts on quality of family life. Given the situation, General Odierno tasked a small team of his 2014 SSG Fellows to spend a year studying ways of enhancing soldier performance, a goal he called "Human Performance Optimization" or HPO. The mission for the SSG/ HPO team was to thoroughly investigate scientifically valid strategies to improve soldier performance, with a focus on state-of-the-art approaches, and to identify novel methods that may become available in the future. The team was asked to de-velop a report that could guide current Army practice and training in this domain and to give direction to future research efforts.

For the next year, the HPO team conducted a thorough analysis of evidence-based, scientifically valid, and ethically acceptable methods of performance enhancement. Three broad and somewhat overlapping domains of human performance were examined. The first, *cognition*, included ways of improving memory, attention, per-ception, decision-making, and related cognitive skills. The second, *social*, included the influences of human interactions on performance, such as team dynamics, lead-ership, resilience, trust, and the roles of emotional and social intelligence. The third domain, *physical*, looked at ways of improving strength, coordination, endurance, health, and injury/illness prevention and recovery. The methodology used included

(1) an exhaustive literature review, (2) interviews with subject matter experts, and (3) site visits to a variety of private, military, and educational organizations to observe best practices within the cognitive, social, and physical domains. The interviews were structured and designed to solicit expert guidance on what current research is likely to develop into useful performance optimization protocols and to identify strategies that, while not applicable now, held promise to become so in the next decade and beyond. The HPO team also organized two workshops, one held at the US Military Academy (West Point) in February 2015 that focused on the cognitive and physical domains and the other the following month in Arlington, Virginia, that focused on the social domain. Table 1.1 shows the key contacts made by the HPO team over the course of its research.

The results of the HPO team's efforts yielded the following general suggestions (for more details, see Bolduc, Davis, Gallus, Green, & Matthews, 2015). Some of the recommendations for increased research and development focus included precision medicine, based in large measure on advances in genomics that would include a better understanding of the genetic bases of behaviors, such as sleep, cognitive function, and resilience, and include measurement of biomarkers, such as proteins or neuropeptides that may predict reaction to stress and adversity. Other areas of promise included brain–machine interfaces, proteomics, human–robot interactions, and next-generation simulation technologies such as virtual reality. In the social domain, the team recommended incorporating current and emerging psychological science into the talent management life cycle, ranging from recruitment and selection to training and leader development and including emerging research on noncognitive factors, such as grit (Duckworth, Peterson, Matthews, & Kelly, 2007) and hardiness (Maddi et al., 2017). We have attempted to address as many of these domains as possible in the compilation of this volume. We approached experts in their respective fields and asked them to consider the application of their work in the service of optimizing performance across a broad spectrum of human activities.

PURPOSE OF THE CURRENT VOLUME

A consistent theme throughout the history of war is that issues and solutions that are vital to the military are also important in other sectors. More often than not, the military as an institution serves as a "model" for the effects of extreme physical and mental stress on human performance. There are many examples of how, through developing solutions to their problems, the military has contributed to advances in society more broadly (Matthews, 2014). For instance, World War I spurred the development of aptitude and intelligence testing. Because of the number of soldiers deployed and affected by their experiences during World War II, advances were made in clinical psychology, leading to a better understanding of combat stress and treatment approaches for soldiers, veterans, and civilians alike. Furthermore, rapid advances in engineering and technology during World War II gave rise to the field of human factors engineering. The Vietnam War led to the formal inclusion of PTSD as a psychiatric condition. Today, it is well understood that PTSD and related stress disorders are not confined to combat veterans but may afflict anyone who has experienced significant trauma in their lives. More recently, the ongoing military

Table 1.1 HPO CONCEPT TEAM KEY CONTACTS

Army Capabilities Integration Center (ARCIC)
Army Center for Enhanced Performance (ACEP)
Army Center of Excellence for the Professional Military Ethic (ACPME)
Army Combined Arms Center (CAC)
Army Forces Command (FORSCOM)
Army Manpower Personnel Integration Program (MANPRINT)
Army Medical Department Center and School (AMEDD C&S)
Army Physical Fitness School (TRADOC)
Army Program Executive Office Soldier (PEO Soldier)
Army Research Institute (ARI)
Army Research Laboratory (ARL) Human Research and Engineering Directorate
  (HRED)
Asymmetric Warfare Group (AWG/TRADOC)
Maneuver Center of Excellence (MCOE)
Medical Research and Materiel Command (MRMC) Comprehensive medical research
Natick Soldier Research Development and Engineering Center (NSRDEC)
United States Army Research Institute for the Behavioral and Social Sciences
United States Army Research Institute for Environmental Medicine (USARIEM)
United States Army Recruiting Command
United States Army Simulation Training and Technology Center, Orlando, Florida
United States Army Special Operations Command (USASOC) Tactical Human
  Optimization Rapid Rehabilitation and Reconditioning Program (THOR3)
United States Military Academy (USMA), Engineering Psychology Lab
United States Special Operations Command (USSOCOM) Preservation of the Force
  and Families (POTFF)
Academia (University of Texas, Johns Hopkins University, University of Pennsylvania,
  University of Pittsburgh)
Industry (EDGE Innovations/ General Dynamics)
Industry (Human Longevity INC, Dr. Craig Ventner)
Office of the Surgeon General (OTSG)
75th Ranger Regiment
Naval Health Research Center
United States Army War College
Naval Special Warfare Group 4
Fire Department New York (FDNY)
Center for a New American Security (CNAS)
Air Force 711th Human Performance Wing
Defense Health Agency, Director Human Performance and Training Biosystems
Uniformed Services University, Consortium for Health and Military Performance
National Defense University, Director Health and Fitness
Booz Allen Hamilton, Human Dimension Capabilities Development Task Force
TRADOC G-2 Training Brain Operations

operations stemming from the September 11, 2001, attacks have impacted psychological science and practice. Whereas Vietnam spurred further understanding of PTSD, the current wars have led to an explosion of research into factors related to resiliency and posttraumatic growth.

Understanding and optimizing human performance is no exception. Danger, stress, and high stakes are not unique to the military. As Sweeney et al. (2011) describe, law enforcement officers, firefighters, and first responders also perform under conditions of uncertainty and threats to physical, social, and psychological well-being. And while they may lack the element of mortal danger, many healthcare and corporate settings share other characteristics in common with the military, including high stress, long hours away from the family, high stakes, and uncertainty. Like the military, other organizations are under pressure to "do more with less," which often involves reducing the workforce without reducing performance and productivity demands. Finally, individuals who live with physical and mental disability due to injury or disease struggle to cope with their situation in much the same manner as a healthy individual may be forced to under conditions of extreme physical and psychological stress. Therefore, the solutions we seek to optimize performance in extreme settings may have application to the impaired population, particularly in the domains of precision medicine, psychological resilience, and application of engineering solutions.

OVERVIEW

This volume focuses on a variety of themes and topics that can broadly be described as the work of behavioral and cognitive neuroscience. The topics touch on all three pillars of human performance optimization—physical, cognitive, and social. The physical domain, with a focus on brain and metabolic function, includes chapters on metabolic enhancement of performance (Chapter 2), the role of nutrition and genetics in human performance (Chapter 3), and the molecular and cellular bases of depression (Chapter 4). Chapters 5 (computational biology) and 6 (neurofeedback approaches) complement a chapter on emerging methods for monitoring physiological status (Chapter 7). Neuroprosethetics and human performance are addressed in Chapter 8. In the behavioral domain, Chapter 9 focuses on contemporary approaches to understanding and regulating stress, and Chapter 10 explores contemporary research on sleep, based on work with military populations that must respond optimally despite chronic sleep restriction and fatigue. Finally, developments in exoskeleton research and applications are reviewed in Chapter 11.

We also include several chapters on cognitive processes linked to human performance. Chapter 12 provides an overview of recent Department of Defense efforts to develop human cognitive capabilities through brain-based training. The genetic and epigenetic approaches to enhancing cognitive processes are reviewed in Chapter 13. In Chapter 14, a very promising approach to enhancing memory is reviewed, and suggestions for immediate implementation of the procedures are made. Increasingly, simulations provide a vehicle for improving human cognitive performance. Chapter 15 reviews the work of an Army laboratory in this domain and explores implications for other institutional contexts where performance optimization is critical. In Chapter 16, noncognitive amplifiers of human performance are explored. Humans rarely work alone, of course, and Chapter 17 provides a comprehensive review of leadership and organizational factors in enhancing human performance. Taken in totality, the volume provides a broad range of coverage to address critical issues in HPO, under both normal and extreme conditions.

In the work of the SSG, and of the editors in the process of developing this volume, it was clear that science might provide avenues for optimizing human performance that create complex ethical dilemmas. Chapter 18, written by a military psychologist and a US Army officer with a doctorate in philosophy, thoroughly explores ethical issues and constraints in HPO. This is a very important question, and one that must be addressed by any organization that sets out to improve performance by applying advances in cognitive and behavioral neuroscience—or any other discipline—toward this end. In the military context at least, other nations may not hesitate to develop and employ HPO strategies that the United States and many other countries would find objectionable on moral/ethical grounds. Thus, we have placed the ethics chapter near the end of this volume, so that readers may use the ideas discussed therein to evaluate the HPO science reviewed elsewhere in the book.

In summary, the intent of this book is to provide information on the current status of a wide variety of approaches to enhancing human performance and to project what may be the most viable avenues for future research and development. The reader will find recommendations for performance enhancement that are ready for immediate implementation and others that await further research and field tests but that may be useable in the not too distant future. Finally, some recommendations may help advance the understanding and optimization of human performance, but, due to ethical or other limitations, may not be useful in practice. Together, the knowledge reviewed herein is especially relevant to organizations that select, train, and develop members to work in what Kolditz (2007) calls *in extremis* settings. For all organizations, whether *in extremis* or not, optimizing human performance is a desirable goal. This volume provides insights into current practice and future possibilities in attaining this objective.

REFERENCES

Bolduc, D. R., Davis, C. Z., Gallus, J., Green, R. L., & Matthews, M. D. (2015, June). *Chief of Staff of the Army Strategic Studies Group Human Performance Optimization Concept Team Final Report.* Arlington, VA: CSA SSG.

Duckworth, A. L., Peterson, C., Matthews, M. D., & Kelly, D. R. (2007). Grit: Perseverance and passion for long-term goals. *Journal of Personality and Social Psychology, 92,* 1087–1101.

Gallus, J., & Green, R. L. (2015, October–December). Human-performance optimization: Social considerations for leadership and team cohesion. *Armor, 126*(4), 55–58. Retrieved from http://www.benning.army.mil/armor/eARMOR/content/issues/2015/OCT_DEC/

Kolditz, T. A. (2007). *In Extremis Leadership: Leading as If Your Life Depended on It.* San Francisco, CA: Jossey-Bass.

Maddi, S. R., Matthews, M. D., Kelly, D. R., Villarreal, B. J., Gundersen, K. K., & Savino, S. C. (2017). The continuing role of hardiness and grit on performance and retention in West Point cadets. *Military Psychology, 29,* 355–358. doi:10.1037/mil0000145

Matthews, M. D. (2014). *Head Strong: How Psychology Is Revolutionizing War.* New York: Oxford University Press.

Sweeney, P. J., Matthews, M. D., & Lester, P. B. (2011). *Leadership in Dangerous Situations: A Handbook for the Armed Forces, Emergency Services, and First Responders.* Annapolis, MD: Naval Institute Press.

Ursano, R. J., Colpe, L. J., Heeringa, S. G., Kessler, R. C., Schoenbaum, M., & Stein, M. B. (2014). The army study to assess risk and resilience in servicemembers (Army STARRS). *Psychiatry: Interpersonal and Biological Processes, 77*(2), 107–119.

Wagner, A. W., & Jakupcak, M. (2012). Combat-related stress reactions among US veterans of wartime service. In J. H. Laurence & M. D. Matthews (Eds.), *The Oxford Handbook of Military Psychology* (pp. 15–27). New York: Oxford University Press.

2

Metabolic Enhancement of the Soldier Brain

KARL E. FRIEDL* AND STEPHEN J. GRATE*

> The difficult is what takes a little time; the impossible is what takes a little longer.
>
> —FRIDTJOF NANSEN, *Norwegian explorer and neurobiologist*

INTRODUCTION

Human performance is limited in extreme conditions by central mechanisms affecting stress resilience, fatigue, and mental toughness. These limiters of the human operator can cause major mission failure. Emerging findings in neurobiology are beginning to explain how physiology affects brain function, pointing the way to interventions that optimize brain function. Specifically, personal habits involving exercise, nutrition, sleep, and emotional self-regulation have major effects on brain physiology. These metabolic influences on the brain, in turn, moderate health and performance, ranging from endurance to disease susceptibility (Friedl et al., 2016). The neurobiological bases of these effects involve an intricate set of processes, such as reward-seeking behaviors with dopaminergic responses, social neurotransmitters such as oxytocin, secretion of neurotrophic factors (e.g., brain derived neurotrophic factor [BDNF], and insulin-like growth factor-1 [IGF1]), and neurogenesis, affecting mood and cognition.

The allure of new technologies, such as genetic manipulation and electronic implants, has overshadowed these major influences on the brain from seemingly mundane, everyday habits. There is an assumption that surely we know everything there is to know about exercise, nutrition, sleep, and how we interact with other people and moderate our own behavior because these are such basic human functions. Management of these functions is typically relegated to long-accepted

*The opinions and assertions in this chapter are solely those of the authors and do not necessarily represent any official view or position of the Department of the Army or the Department of Defense.

traditions of culture, upbringing, and personal discipline. Advances in neurobiology have begun to challenge some of these long-held beliefs. The Dalai Lama has been a leader in testing and updating Tibetan beliefs with science that verifies important benefits of meditation and other practices on the human brain while rejecting traditions not supported in science (Begley, 2007). In western medicine, some purported "known knowns" have also turned out to be astoundingly wrong.

Only a few decades ago, it was "well-known" that individuals were born with a fixed number of neurons, and there was no process of neurogenesis in the mature brain. It was a surprise when experiments with rodents demonstrated that exercise triggered the development of new neurons in the dentate gyrus of the hippocampus. Even more remarkable was the finding that there are important functions for these new, maturing neurons that provide fine pattern discrimination in humans (Deng, Aimone, & Gage, 2010). This might be a critical capability for a soldier attempting to discern intent from the complex facial expressions of an approaching person. US Army research has also demonstrated that inadequate sleep reduces the capability to discern intent from facial expressions (Huck, Mcbride, Kendall, Grugle, & Killgore, 2008). Neurogenesis is acutely sensitive to the stress of sleep deprivation (Mirescu, Peters, Noiman, & Gould, 2006). These findings provide one example of the contributions of regular physical activity and good sleep discipline to militarily relevant performance.

Well-designed research targets testable hypotheses, but it also produces new questions. The complete mapping of the human genome resulted in breakthrough understanding of genetic determinants, but it now opens the door to many new questions about gene–environment interactions and the "epigenome." For example, energy intake involves an intricate system of genetically programmed appetite signals and drives, but in utero influences induce epigenetic changes that affect weight management later in life (Tobi et al., 2014). A cohort of overweight Dutch Army recruits turned out to have a common risk factor: mothers who had been semi-starved during their pregnancies during the 1944–45 Dutch "Hongerwinter" famine (Ravelli, Stein, & Susser, 1976). Animal studies have reproduced this effect. A mother underfed during early-stage pregnancy may birth an offspring with a hypothalamic lesion, which results in hyperphagia and obesity. This has direct relevance to nutrition and weight management guidance for pregnant soldiers and return-to-duty weight standards that could be harmful to the next generation of soldiers (Friedl, 2012).

The truly revolutionary advances in knowledge have come from serendipity, with completely unforeseen findings (i.e., "unknown unknowns"). A few years ago, it would have seemed inconceivable that gut microbes could exert major influences on the brain and behavior. Now it is becoming clear that the gut bacteria play a very significant role in moods and cognition, also influencing neurogenesis (Cryan & Dinan, 2012; Ogbonnaya et al., 2015). For example, animal studies demonstrate that gut bacteria moderate metabolism of adrenaline and dopamine and have marked effects on anxiety (Heijtz et al., 2011). In humans, a single meal of animal fat such as a typical steak, compared to a very lean game meat meal, produces an acute inflammatory response with high circulating levels of TNF-α and IL-6, cytokines associated with depression (Arya et al., 2010; Dowlati et al., 2010). At the opposite extreme, probiotics reduce gut inflammatory responses, along with a reduction in associated anxiety levels (Foster & Neufeld, 2013). Gut bacteria can secrete a wide variety of neurotransmitters, such as tryptophan and acetylcholine, that influence the brain, and neurons in the gut lining provide opportunities for direct gut signaling to the brain. Emerging research on the gut microbiome suggests that we may soon be taking a much more comprehensive view of how we feed the bacteria within us to manage our brain function and resilience, connecting everyday nutrition to fundamental brain and behavior effects.

This chapter highlights only a few of the interrelated effects of individual modifiable habits on brain metabolism and consequent effects on health and performance. The focus is on the soldier and US Army research, but this has broad applicability. Developing a science basis for these effects is important to being able to provide predictive models and prescriptions for personal habits to optimize brain function.

STRESS AND SURVIVAL MECHANISMS

Stress Concepts

The general concepts represented by activation of endocrine systems necessary for individual survival responses in the face of physiological challenges ("stress response") and the ability to rebound from a physiological insult ("resilience") are key to soldier health and performance. Challenges to an organism ("stressors") can activate the fight-or-flight response described by Walter Cannon (Cannon, 1915, 1932), and they may activate the *general adaptation syndrome* described by Hans Selye (Selye, 1946). Both of these stress activation pathways involve adrenal hormones that place individuals in a heightened state of alertness and alter metabolic status in preparation for internal and external physiological and psychological threats. An individual cannot survive without adrenal steroids. These responses have been well studied in soldiers in high-risk training and in operational missions, and this information is relevant to understanding stress problems and solutions that affect soldier health and performance.

John Wayne Mason, a US Army physiologist, advanced Selye's initial stress model, particularly by characterizing the role of emotional stressors. He also refuted the generalizability of the adrenal response to stressors. Mason was part of a team that directly measured stress hormone responses in combat and other military field settings. Compared to the typical stress responses of new military recruits, urinary 17-hydroxycorticosteroid (the principal metabolite of the adrenal stress steroid, cortisol) was lower in experienced air ambulance medics during combat missions (Bourne, Rose, & Mason, 1967). This stress adaptation appeared to reflect effective psychological defense mechanisms such as mindful rationalization and spirituality. Urinary stress steroids were elevated in the commanding officer and radioman but reduced in all other members of the special forces A-team on the day of an attack in a remote outpost in Vietnam, in this case, corresponding to specific roles and level of responsibility (Bourne, Rose, & Mason, 1968). Such observations led US Army researchers to the conclusion that psychological stress is highly individual, altered by the individual's perceptions and adaptation to threats. Androgen secretion was also highly sensitive to psychological stress perception and was suppressed in basic training and in combat when stress was high (Rose, 1969a, 1969b; Rose et al., 1969; Kreuz, Rose, & Jennings, 1972).

An elegant study following Norwegian soldiers through parachute training characterized the neuroendocrine changes in psychological stress perception (Ursin, Baade, & Levine, 1978). Holger Ursin and his colleagues showed dramatic stress responses with elevation of cortisol and catecholamines, and they showed reduction in testosterone within minutes of the first practice jump out of a training tower. With subsequent training jumps, the responses converted to a "eustress" response, reflecting a thrill instead of a stress. Cortisol no longer increased, but testosterone did actually demonstrate an increase instead of a decrease. Catecholamines and heart rate continued to be activated independently of the psychological stress perception. The same phenomenon was demonstrated in a slide-for-life event in Austrian soldiers, where the fear responses dissipated with subsequent trials (Wittels, Johannes, Enne, Kirsch, & Gunga, 2002). Changes in voice stress, using voice pitch measurements, demonstrated adaptation of the emotional response, while heart rate was consistently elevated in every trial. Subsequent studies have demonstrated that perceptions of success following a hunting kill or a soccer competition produce sizeable acute increases in salivary testosterone concentration in men (Trumble et al., 2012; Trumble et al., 2014).

Current concepts of stress physiology have the advantage of many breakthrough discoveries in neurobiology. Bruce McEwen has promoted the concept of "allostasis" to better explain adaptive stress responses in the context of modern neurobiology. Allostasis describes shifts of an entire network of interrelated responses to achieve homeostasis in response to a challenge. This assumes a baseline metabolic condition that is optimal for health and performance and that a homeostatic shift is beneficial to reoptimization in the face of a stressor. These allostatic changes can be maladaptive with long-term exposure to chronic stressors. There is a fundamental distinction between biologically adaptive stress responses that help an individual survive an emergency challenge and the adverse consequences associated with the chronic stressors of modern life. Thus, stress responses are good for health and performance, but chronic or overwhelming levels of stress produce maladaptive changes in the brain. McEwen and Wingfield have described two different forms of allostatic responses, one triggered by a threat to fundamental survival needs (e.g., inadequate energy resources) and the other triggered by intraspecific stressors in an environment with adequate energy reserves (McEwen & Wingfield, 2003). This latter form of chronic allostatic response contributes to the sequence of maladaptive responses that can result in type 2 diabetes, and it is reversed with lifestyle modifications (Özcan et al., 2004; Tuomilehto et al., 2001).

Brain Responses to Chronic Existence Needs

The US Army Ranger Course is an example of the first type of allostatic response involving severe metabolic stress challenges. An energy deficit produced by prolonged intensive work and inadequate energy intake triggers a series of survival responses involving mobilization of body energy stores. Ranger students have served as a model of the lowest measured body fat in healthy humans because of this extreme metabolic stressor (Friedl et al., 1994). Their sleep has also been well characterized and averages 4 hours per night for the 8-week course, with a period of recovery involving fragmented sleep during readjustment. Basic existential drives of hunger, prolonged work, and sleep deficit are the stressors (Friedl et al., 2000). Psychological stress is not a key factor during Ranger training for most soldiers; anxiety is a luxury in this environment, suppressed by more fundamental stressors. Norwegian military academy cadets experience an acute version of Ranger training involving 1 week of no food and no organized sleep (Opstad & Aakvaag, 1981; 1983). The parallels between the acute starvation/sleep deprivation and chronic semi-starvation/sleep restriction models are striking, although the metabolic responses are accelerated and more profound in the Norwegian training. One key observation from studies of both of these stress models is the impact on host defense responses (immunological responses) and susceptibility to disease (Friedl, 2004). This appears to be related to a threshold of energy intake, where a deficit between work demands and intake of greater than approximately 1,000 kcal/d causes a significant immune compromise, and a slight increase in intake can substantially correct it (Kramer et al., 1997). This energy balance effect may be mediated through a hypothalamic "glucostat" center, which also regulates other functions such as gonadal hormone secretion. This would explain observed reductions in testosterone secretion in male Ranger students and reduced LH pulsatility and estrogen secretion in exercising college women at energy deficits of about 1,000 kcal/d (Loucks & Thuma, 2003; Friedl et al., 2000). The reduction in testosterone may be adaptive in tradeoffs between reproductive success and disease resistance (Muehlenbein & Bribiescas, 2005).

Adrenal hormone responses are not elevated until the end of the course when fat reserves have been depleted and a more severe catabolism occurs, with increased reliance on muscle protein. At this stage, glucocorticoids play a catabolic role and help to mobilize remaining body energy stores. This is an example of Mason's challenge to the generalizability of Selye's general adaptation syndrome, where a gradual stress, such as the metabolic stress that evolves through Ranger training, does not trigger an immediate activation of the hypothalamic-pituitary-adrenal axis (Mason, 1971).

Brain Responses to Chronic Psychosocial Stress

Persistent psychological stress is an example of the second form of allostatic response. Individual factors may be isolated in research studies that attempt to determine specific effects of a particular factor such as sleep or exercise. However, allostasis by definition involves a network of interrelated responses. Co-variables such as sleep, exercise, and nutrition must be characterized and controlled, or the results may be uninterpretable. McEwen and his colleagues have traced the impact of chronic psychological stressors through neurophysiological mechanisms that explain increased, stress-related health risks such as cardiovascular disease. Persistent stress reduces slow wave sleep, and this affects brain metabolic processes (Buguet, Roussel, Angus, Sabiston, & Radomski, 1980; Arnal et al., 2016). Impaired restorative sleep affects frontal lobe decision-making produces a reduced capacity to make healthy food choices (Killgore, Schwab, Weber et al., 2013). Exercise habits compensate for some of these effects of impaired sleep, but sleep deprivation also affects mood status and reduces motivation to exercise (Arnal, 2015; Baron, Reid, & Zee, 2013; Chennaoui et al., 2015). Accumulated abdominal fat stores resulting from chronic underexercise and overnutrition provide a labile supply of free fatty acids via the portal vein, with a direct impact on hepatic metabolism to increase insulin resistance (Ahlberg et al., 2002; Bjorntorp, 1991). The resulting poor blood glucose regulation affects mood and cognition, increasing irritability and the ability to make higher level decisions (Allen, Frier, & Strachan, 2004; Gold, MacLeod, Frier, & Deary, 1995). Type 2 diabetes or metabolic syndrome is the ultimate stress-related disorder that promotes hippocampal damage and memory impairments (Gold et al., 2007). Markers of chronic stress include intraabdominal fat accumulation and the associated health outcomes, such as hypertension and hypercholesterolemia (McEwen, 1998).

Glucocorticoids further contribute to brain changes by inhibition of hippocampal neurogenesis in chronic stress conditions such as depression and posttraumatic stress disorder (PTSD) (Sapolsky, 2000). Smaller hippocampal volumes in chronically stressed individuals may be an indicator of this effect (or could be a preexisting risk factor for stress; Apfel et al., 2011). Chronic stress has other profound effects on the brain that influence immune function, wound healing, and other host-defense responses (Breivik et al., 1996; Glaser & Kiecolt-Glaser, 2005). In one classic study involving exposing healthy individuals to cold virus to test disease resistance, those individuals who became the sickest were the ones with the greatest number of recent stressful life events (Cohen, Tyrell, & Smith, 1991).

Chronic stress is a condition of modern society that is managed on a national level in various ways. Japan provides an interesting case study because stress-related overwork and sudden death (*karoshi*) is a recognized occupational hazard. *Karoshi* is characterized by chronic sleep deficit and anxiety about job performance and is the label for sudden cardiovascular accidents in relatively young people in a demanding work environment (Iwasaki, Takahashi, & Nakata, 2006). Japan is also the only country that mandates weight management for all citizens over age 50, with waist circumference limits. This "Metabo law" seeks to prevent obesity-related diseases such as type 2 diabetes through better exercise, sleep, and nutrition habits (Oda, 2010). More recently, Japan has instituted new regulations for employers mandating vacation time for employees. German-speaking countries have a long tradition of annual health holidays ("the *Kur*"), which, until recently, was a covered healthcare benefit (Pforr & Locher, 2012).

Acute Stress and Neuropsychological Performance

Another form of psychological resilience is the type of heroism displayed by Audie Murphy, our most decorated combat soldier, recognized for audacious action in the face of enemy fire. This behavior can be ascribed to catecholamines in the brain that combine effective aggressive action and clear presence of mind when confronted with an imminent threat or opportunity in a fight-or-flight activation. The adaptive value of some of the physiological changes, such as hemostasis in preparation for life-threatening hemorrhage, are well characterized (Austin, Wissmann, & von Kanel, 2013). However, repeated high-intensity stress challenges can exhaust physiological reserve, including even the availability of some neurotransmitters in the brain.

Navy studies of attack carrier pilots landing on the pitching deck of aircraft carriers at night demonstrated high levels of sympathetic activation consistent with high levels of performance (Austin Jr. et al., 1967). During their combat tours in Vietnam, pilots executed these acutely stressful events repeatedly, and there was a concerted effort to develop a method to monitor individuals reaching the limits of "psychophysiological reserve" to determine when to prescribe rest, as well as monitoring to determine when an individual, recovered from stress and fatigue, was ready for another mission. The Aeromedical Biodata Team collected data in 1966 on 27 combat pilots to try to establish biochemical profiles of stressful combat performance that can be distinguished from the profiles produced by other stressors such as sleep deprivation and acceleration (Austin Jr., 1969). The blood phospholipid responses distinguished various groups by psychophysiological stress but never matured into a pilot management tool. Forty-five years later, serum phospholipid profiles have again been found to discriminate brain states, including mild cognitive impairment, in a US Army-funded study (Mapstone et al., 2014).

The acute stress response with a surge of catecholamines and cortisol can enhance learning and memory but appears to depend on how the stress is perceived (Taverniers, Taylor, & Smeets, 2013; Taverniers & De Boeck, 2014). When it is a novelty stress with naïve subjects, such as parachute training, learning is impaired, compared to a control group (Taverniers, Van Ruysseveldt, Smeets, & von Grumbkow, 2010). In a realistic shoot-house training event with experienced police, the fear of being shot at (with attenuated ammunition) was associated with elevated cortisol, subjective stress responses, and decreased working memory performance. However, the fear was also associated with a greater self-perceived task learning effect (Taverniers, Smeets, Van Ruysseveldt, Syroit, & von Grumbkow, 2011).

In a very stressful environment, performance begins to fall off because catecholamines are actually depleted. This has been difficult to test in properly controlled human studies because of ethical concerns for the high level of stress required. In one study, a group of Marine Corps snipers conducting training operations in extreme cold and hypoxic conditions on the slopes of Mount Denali demonstrated an unexpected decline in their marksmanship performance (Ahlers, Thomas, Schrot, & Shurtleff, 1994). The performance decline appeared to reverse in men who received a nutritional supplement with tyrosine. Controlled laboratory studies involving cold air or cold water immersion have demonstrated improved performance in critical functions, such as working memory, with a tyrosine supplement (Shurtleff, Thomas, Schrot, Kowalski, & Harford, 1994; O'Brien, Mahoney, Tharion, Sils, & Castellani, 2007). The mechanism is well supported by animal studies. Rodent studies with brain microdialysis have demonstrated that the formation of catecholamines from a tyrosine precursor is the rate limiter, and catecholamine levels and neuropsychological performance can be restored with dietary supplementation (Yeghiayan, Luo, Shukitt-Hale, & Lieberman, 2001).

Adaptive neurocognitive changes occur in response to new stressor demands such as hypervigilance in a combat environment. For example, improvements in reaction times were measured in redeployed soldiers compared to pre-deployment testing, while other functions such as sustained attention and visual-spatial working memory declined (Vasterling et al., 2006). With psychologically traumatic exposures some individuals develop maladaptive conditions such as PTSD, with sleep disturbances, re-experiencing of the memory of the stress or trauma, and startle responses; the physiological basis for this risk is still unknown, but the effect of stress activation on the brain is an important component. This clearly produces biological changes that can even be passed on to offspring. Recent studies by Rachel Yehuda with Holocaust survivors demonstrated a previously unknown intergenerational effect of brain trauma with epigenetic effects transmitted in utero from parent to child (Yehuda, Daskalakis et al., 2015). The offspring of Holocaust survivors with PTSD demonstrate altered glucocorticoid regulation and increased susceptibility to traumatic stress (Lehrner et al., 2014; Yehuda, Flory et al., 2015). Researchers interpreted these findings to mean that individuals may be at greater risk for PTSD during military service through stress susceptibility passed on to them because of untreated stress conditions in the parent. The concept of stress susceptibility, improperly interpreted by some as "weak" individuals, is not a popular concept to many veterans. The science appears to support the transmission of stress sensitivity, and the concept can be interpreted as genetic heritage rather than pejorative interpretations of "weakness." However interpreted, it is important to discover how to identify affected individuals and moderate these effects.

A larger segment of service members with deployment history develop dysfunctional symptoms of PTSD without scoring high enough for a diagnosis. This has been highlighted in the large proportion of veterans reporting chronic multisymptom illnesses, including subclinical threshold scores for PTSD (Weiner et al., 2011). No brain changes were evident with magnetic resonance spectroscopy in this group. These individuals have difficulty accessing behavioral healthcare services without a diagnosis, and, in fact, some do not want a disease diagnosis. In a keynote address at the annual Brain at War symposium, Medal of Honor winner "Buddy" Bucha spoke from personal experience about the stigma associated with a disease label of PTSD, which prompted friends to treat him as if he had a terminal illness. All he wanted was "a little bit of help" for anger management and other deployment-related symptoms (Bucha, 2014). This is the concept of "soldier reset," providing improved social reintegration and neuropsychological support to healthy soldiers in redeployment. "Soldier reset" and brain health were advanced in 2010 as cornerstones of the successful Program Objective Memorandum that resulted in the largest increase of the military medical research budget since World War II (now established as the Defense Health Program R&D portfolio; Friedl, 2008).

One concept in preventive medicine—to prevent maladaptive consequences of traumatic exposures in the form of a "psychological first aid"—is to turn down sustained physiological activation that may occur after a high-stress event such as a firefight with the enemy (Pitman et al., 2002). This strategy has been investigated using propranolol and other β-blockers to inhibit extended activation, but with mixed results (Sijbrandij, Kleiboer, Bisson, Barbui, & Cuijpers, 2015). Another strategy explored involves electronic games as a calming influence (Russoniello, Fish, & O'Brien, 2013). Using simple smartphone technology, heart rate variability is monitored from a finger held over the phone camera, and the game provides a biofeedback reward as the individual calms his breathing (Russoniello et al., 2009; Russoniello, O'Brien, & Parks, 2009).

NEUROBIOLOGY OF EXERCISE: THE PATHOLOGY OF A SEDENTARY LIFESTYLE

One plausible theory of human evolution is that human cognitive capability is an artifact of incidental stimulation from growth factors that are part of the adaptation of hunter-gathers to support increased aerobic activity and physiologic demands (Raichlen & Polk, 2013). Many studies report associations between lifetime exercise activity and brain cortical thickness, implicating a role of growth factors such as IGF1, stimulated by aerobic exercise and known to be an important anabolic factor for bone, muscle, and brain (Carro, Trejo, Busiguina, & Torres-Aleman, 2001; Nokia et al., 2016). Regardless of the why, evidence is mounting in support of regular activity as an essential requirement for human brain health and performance. Some evidence for this comes from the "stress" changes that follow inactivity and sedentary behavior. Reorganization of motor cortex patterning occurs within 12 hours of immobilizing a normal arm, and the associated slow wave sleep activity in the same local regions is reduced (Huber et al., 2006). Cessation of regular exercise for just 1 week produces arthralgia, fatigue, and impaired cognition in at least one-third of habitual runners (Glass et al., 2004). Physical activity is, in fact, the first line of treatment for challenging diseases, such as fibromyalgia and symptoms associated with Gulf War service (Donta et al., 2003; Burckhardt, Mannerkorpi, Hedenberg, & Bjelle, 1994; Busch, Barber, Overend, Peloso, & Schachter, 2007). At least part of this benefit appears to be through a modification of abnormal sensory processing and pain sensitivity (Fontaine, Conn, & Clauw, 2010). While the mechanism is unknown, one of many potential explanations may be that exercise is another form of peripheral nerve stimulation that moderates pain perception in the arcuate nucleus, similar to acupuncture (Carr et al., 1981; Nakagawasai et al., 1999; Thorén, Floras, Hoffmann, & Seals, 1990; Bart-Knauer & Friedl, 2013). Other potential mechanisms in this phenomenon are the up-regulation of trophic factors, enhanced neurogenesis, and alteration of neurotransmitter activity.

Both exercise and slow wave sleep increase secretion of neurotrophic growth factors such as BDNF and IGF1 (Rothman & Mattson, 2013; Arnal, 2015). The interrelationship with sleep is an additional brain benefit of physical activity. Habitual exercise increases slow wave sleep, possibly through cytokine-mediated stimulation of somnogenic factors, such as nitric oxide, prostaglandin D2, and growth hormone releasing hormone (Cespuglio, Amrouni, Meiller, Buguet, & Gautier-Sauvigné, 2012; Krueger, Obál, Fang, Kubota, & Taishi, 2001). French military studies by Alain Buguet demonstrate that other environmental stressors, such as heat and cold exposure, also have this effect on slow wave sleep (Buguet, Cespuglio, & Radomski, 1998). Buguet also demonstrated differences in the relationship between exercise and sleep, moderated by whether or not exercise was perceived as stressful (Buguet et al., 1980). Slow wave sleep may be directly important to brain health because this is the only time when the blood–brain barrier increases in permeability and the brain glymphatic system removes metabolic products accumulated during normal activity (Iliff et al., 2014). The brain lacks a lymphatic system, and this is the primary mechanism for removal of waste products and proteins.

The discovery that exercise could stimulate neurogenesis was revolutionary. Yet the notion that a behavior so mundane as physical activity could have such importance to brain health and optimized metabolic function has had difficulty gaining traction in public schools and even for office-based cyberwarriors (van Praag, Kempermann, & Gage, 1999). Empirical studies have demonstrated the value of a modest aerobic exercise training program to learning and behavior (Voss, Nagamatsu, Liu-Ambrose, & Kramer, 2011). The mechanisms may differ between children, where brain development is still occurring, and mature adult brains, but benefits are evident for both groups (Colcombe et al., 2006). While activity enhances learning, learning itself produces measurable changes. For example, London taxi drivers demonstrate a measurable hypertrophy of the hippocampus after mastering "the knowledge," learning every street location in London to pass their test for licensing (Maguire et al., 2000). The interaction between the hippocampal effects of memory training and physical exercise may be synergistic, based on findings from controlled animal studies involving enriched environments (van Praag, Kempermann, & Gage, 2000; Fares et al., 2013). Physical activity affects brain plasticity and neurotransmitters through a variety of mechanisms (Cotman, Berchtold, & Christie, 2007). Different modes of exercise such as resistance exercise, aerobic exercise, and activity involving skill and balance may differentially affect brain physiology. This is suggested by the differential effect of exercise mode and dose on the balance of stimulated neurotrophic factors (e.g., BDNF, IGF1, and vascular endothelial growth factor [VEGF]) and differing effects on neurogenesis, neuronal plasticity, angiogenesis, and more (Carro et al., 2001; Cassilhas et al., 2012; Liu-Ambrose, Nagamatsu, Voss, Khan, & Handy, 2012; Voss, Vivar, Kramer, & van Praag, 2013; Nokia et al., 2016). This may produce different effects on behavior and cognition. For example, the effect on neurogenesis provides a very specific cognitive benefit from activity of the new neurons, enhancing fine pattern discrimination (Deng et al., 2010). A long-term exercise program demonstrated an association between aerobic exercise habits and performance on a visual pattern recognition task (Déry et al., 2013). High depression scores had an opposite effect on this task, consistent with data that show suppression of neurogenic activity in stressed animals (Déry et al., 2013).

Decreased activity is a marker of depression, and, conversely, exercise is a significant mood enhancer (Lawlor & Hopker, 2001). Modest levels of exercise treatment may be even more effective for some patients than pharmacological treatment (Babyak et al., 2000). β-endorphin secretion is just one of the better known effects of exercise (Thorén et al., 1990). Specific proteins or metabolites produced in exercising muscle may have direct effects on brain metabolism. As one example, peroxisome proliferator-activated receptor-γ co-activator is an important metabolic regulator stimulated by exercise and, among many other physiological roles, promotes effects to prevent kynurenine from reaching the brain (Agudelo et al.,

2014). Depression is associated with kynurenine and its metabolites, and stress and inflammation increase its effects (Capuron et al., 2003; Gulaj, Pawlak, Bien, & Pawlak, 2010; Swardfager et al., 2009). There are many biochemical pathways implicated in depression and affected by exercise that will eventually explain these empirical observations and provide a science-based exercise prescription of mode and intensity (Sartori et al., 2011). US Army-funded studies led to identification of key functions of the protein p11, which modulates serotonin receptor expression and is directly associated with depression (Svenningsson, Kim, Warner-Schmidt, Oh, & Greengard, 2013; Alexander et al., 2010). Additional work by the same investigators demonstrated that BDNF is involved in the metabolic pathway for p11. Furthermore, p11, in combination with SMARC3, acts as a transcription factor for neurogenesis in the hippocampus to promote neurogenesis. This has permitted discovery of interactions important to the military, such as the effect of ibuprofen (Motrin) in blocking the effectiveness of selective serotonin reuptake inhibitors (SSRIs) such as fluoxetine (i.e., Prozac; Warner-Schmidt, Vanover, Chen, Marshall, & Greengard, 2011). These two drugs are commonly used in military medicine for patients in need of both pain control and treatment of depression.

Several other lines of approach in exercise neurobiology are driven by clinical needs, notably Parkinson's disease (PD). Exercise has been one of the most effective treatments to delay and improve symptoms in PD patients (Fisher et al., 2008). The work of Giselle Petzinger and her colleagues to advance the neurobiology of exercise has resulted in an exercise prescription for PD. "Skilled exercise" involving some complexity and variation in movements, such as Tai chi or dancing, stimulates both motor and frontal lobes, moderating both movement deficits and cognitive impairment (Petzinger et al., 2010; Petzinger et al., 2013). Other benefits of exercise include measurable changes in neuroplasticity, such as dopaminergic signaling, in human studies (Fisher et al., 2013). Recovery of brain function in disease and following injury may be very activity-dependent (Kempermann, van Praag, & Gage, 2000), with a basis in science for the common perception among rehabilitation experts that early mobilization is important to a comprehensive patient recovery. Still to be discovered are many potential exercise interactions with nutrition, sleep, emotional status, and stress activation.

NEUROPROTECTIVE NUTRITION

Perhaps the single greatest physiological challenge for modern-day soldier readiness is weight management, with increasingly overweight recruits representing national obesity trends. Energy balance and weight management have specific effects on brain metabolism, with consequences to neuroplasticity and brain changes that, in turn, affect body energy metabolism (van Praag, Fleshner, Schwartz, & Mattson, 2014). Obesity is responsible for high rates of type 2 diabetes, defined by increased insulin resistance. Abdominal obesity is associated with higher fasting glucose levels (Krotkiewski, Björntorp, Sjöström, & Smith, 1983). The brain is highly dependent on glucose regulation, and mood and cognition are acutely sensitive to fluctuations in blood glucose (Gold et al., 1995; Sommerfield, Deary, McAulay, & Frier, 2003). Perhaps as many as half of all Alzheimer's disease cases may also be attributable to the metabolic consequences of obesity and its attendant insulin resistance and poorly controlled glucose (Yaffe, Hoang, Byers, Barnes, & Friedl, 2014). Many claims are made for macronutrient balance and specific dietary components that moderate energy balance. So far, the composition of dietary intake has not held up in scientific studies as an important modifier of energy balance (de Souza et al., 2012). The important aspect of weight management is overall energy balance, including intake and expenditure. On the other hand, BDNF, which is increased with exercise and slow wave sleep, increases peripheral metabolism, thus connecting exercise, sleep, and energy metabolism (Rothman, Griffioen, Wan, & Mattson, 2012).

Dietary supplements affecting appetite and metabolic activity tend to be dangerous products in the general class of sympathomimetics (Manore, 2012). A combination of caffeine and ephedra, found in certain plants such as a Chinese herb (Ma Huang), have been shown to be particularly important in stimulating whole-body metabolic rate and lipolysis, but ephedrine-containing products are now banned in the United States because of health risk concerns associated with misuse (Astrup, Breum, Toubro, Hein, & Quaade, 1992). Specific dietary supplements may also have important effects on brain biology. The US Army has investigated performance-enhancing supplements that showed promise for soldier performance and could be included in operational rations (Marriott, 1994). Military interests include performance sustainment and optimization. Military research on performance-enhancing dietary supplements has identified only a few products that can help to sustain soldier performance in stressful conditions. Notable winners are carbohydrate, caffeine, and tyrosine. The brain's dependence on glucose is apparent during chronic underfeeding or even prolonged fasting-exercise (e.g., endurance events without refeeding). The effects of chronic food and sleep deprivation on militarily relevant cognitive tasks are rapidly restored during the US Army Ranger course with a single feeding (Friedl, Mays, Kramer, & Shippee, 2001). This same kind of nutritional intervention with a carbohydrate supplement extends motivation during prolonged endurance exercise, extending time to exhaustion by 15% in a lab experiment with special forces soldiers (Murphy, Hoyt, Jones, Gabaree, & Askew, 1995). Additional observations support the findings that readily absorbed carbohydrate supplements during exercise increase endurance time; these studies point to central fatigue mechanisms (Place, Lepers, Deley, & Millet, 2004; Nybo, 2003). These observations are the basis for inclusion of a carbohydrate supplement ("Zapple sauce") in the First Strike Ration, a compact ration designed by the US Army for use during short-duration, mobile, high-intensity combat operations (Institute of Medicine of the National Academies, 2006).

Caffeine has been the single most effective cognitive stimulator for soldiers. Coffee has long been a key component of soldier diets, with performance benefits recognized by US Army researchers during the Civil War (Gould, 1869), and with detailed investigations during World War II and ever since (Penetar et al., 1993; Rasmussen, 2011; Lieberman, Tharion, Shukitt-Hale, Speckman, & Tulley, 2002). While coffee has long been a staple for US Army nutrition, other forms of caffeine, such as caffeinated gum, are now available to soldiers (e.g., in the First Strike Ration) because of its recognized importance to cognitive function and endurance. The rapid action of caffeinated gum, with 5 minutes to peak action from caffeine absorption directly across the oral mucosa, is particularly relevant for soldiers in overcoming the 20- to 30-minute lag in sleep inertia to full alertness (Kamimori et al., 2002). Cognitive performance and decision-making are enhanced for several hours after caffeine administration after 72–85 hours of sleep deprivation (Wesensten, Killgore, & Balkin, 2005; Lieberman et al., 2002). The benefits to mental performance have been demonstrated even in well-rested soldiers engaged in demanding vigilance tasks, such as several hours of sentry duty (Johnson & Merullo, 1999). Benefits to mood are well defined, with important antidepressant effects mediated through adenosine A2A receptors (Lucas et al., 2011; Yacoubi et al., 2001). The neuroprotective effects of coffee and caffeine have been intensively studied in the US Army's PD research (Ross et al., 2000; Schwarzschild, Chen, & Ascherio, 2002). It is still not clear if caffeine reverses effects in the hypometabolic regions of the sleep-deprived brain or if it activates compensatory mechanisms (Thomas et al., 2000). It is clear that caffeine works through different centers than amphetamines; compared directly to caffeine, amphetamines promote a sense of capability and increase risk-taking when decision-making is already impaired by sleep deprivation (Killgore, Grugle, Killgore, et al., 2008). A key mechanism of action for caffeine is its action on adenosine A2A receptors, increasing alertness and reducing the risk of neurodegenerative disease such as PD (Huang et al., 2005; Chen et al., 2001).

Some other candidate supplements with plausible mechanisms for neuroperformance have failed to demonstrate benefits in military studies. As one example, choline was carefully investigated in US Army Rangers as a precursor of acetylcholine, with the hypothesis that this should extend performance in endurance activities typical of the military or of marathon racing. This was more than a hypothesis, because Richard Wurtman had animal and human data suggesting its benefits in fatiguing exercise events (Sandage, Sabounjian, White, & Wurtman, 1992). The Boston Celtics even had a winning season while using a choline drink, a nice marketing ploy typical in the dietary supplement industry. In the field study conducted with a Ranger Battalion, high blood levels of choline were achieved with the supplement, but there was no benefit to any of the performance measures (Warber et al., 2000). Based on known biochemical pathways, Wurtman developed a cocktail of interdependent phosphatide precursors and cofactors (including three key constituents: uridine, choline, and docosahexaenoic acid) and demonstrated what appears to be a therapeutic nutritional support that has proved effective in randomized controlled trials for memory improvement in patients with mild cognitive impairment (Wurtman, 2014; Scheltens et al., 2012).

Omega-3 fatty acids have gained a great following as part of another hype cycle. Mothers and grandmothers have long pushed fish as "brain food." There appears to be a scientific basis for that, with omega-3 fatty acids forming the major fatty acid component of myelin nerve sheaths and other metabolic pathways in the brain. Omega-3 fatty acids have potentially important anti-inflammatory roles in the brain through protectins and resolvins (Serhan et al., 2002; Serhan, Chiang, & Van Dyke, 2008). Chronic inflammatory processes in the brain, perhaps triggered by exposure to blast or toxic chemical exposures during military service, have long-term consequences, notably neurodegenerative diseases such as PD and Alzheimer's

(Weiner et al., 2013; Phani, Loike, & Przedborski, 2012; Tanner, Goldman, Ross, & Grate, 2014). One leading theory is that long-term activation of brain microglia may promote these diseases (Jackson-Lewis et al., 2002). This chronic overresponse of microglia causes damage to neurons, especially in susceptible neuronal populations; thus, one proposed beneficial role for omega-3 fatty acids is mitigation of the in-flammatory overresponse (Serhan et al., 2002). Omega-3 fatty acids have also been proposed to reduce depression and suicide risk, but these effects have been difficult to demonstrate because of the complexities of fatty acid metabolism, interdepend-ence on many other variables, and the difficulty in measuring some of the claimed benefits (Sublette, Hibbeln, Galfalvy, Oquendo, & Mann, 2006). A study using samples from the Department of Defense serum repository analyzed stored sera from 800 service members who had committed suicide. Researchers found lower docosahexaenoic acid, an omega-3 fatty acid, in these samples compared to samples of 800 other service members (Lewis et al., 2011). The significance of such findings is unknown and certainly does not imply that increasing omega-3 fatty acids in soldiers' diets will prevent suicide (Hakkarainen et al., 2004). Nevertheless, studies like this have spurred many other studies on the effects of omega-3 fatty acids on high-risk behavior.

There is growing scientific support for some time-tested, empirically derived tra-ditional dietary practices. The basis for health and performance benefits of dietary components of Mediterranean diets, ayurvedic spices, and very specific components used in centuries-old practices are finally emerging from rigorous neurobiological investigations. Epidemiological studies of cultural differences in specific outcomes have led to new discoveries of biologically active components in some traditional practices. Norman Hollenberg, a cardiovascular physiologist, investigated the low incidence of hypertension in Kuna Indians (Hollenberg et al., 1997). Initially, he thought genetics, dietary salt intake, or psychosocial stress levels would explain the phenomenon, but he discovered that their health and longevity probably traced to a traditional cocoa-derived drink, based on the increased rates of hyper-tension in those who abandoned the traditional drink when they moved to urban communities (Hollenberg, Fisher, & McCullough, 2009). The resulting flurry of research by Mars, Inc. researchers and others have identified flavonoids in cocoa, most notably epicatechin, that promote nitric oxide production with a wide variety of potential health and performance benefits (Fisher, Hughes, Gerhard-Herman, & Hollenberg, 2003). Among other important effects, flavonols, such as epicatechin and epigallocatechin, components of dark chocolate and green tea, increase angi-ogenesis, neuronal spine density, and neurogenesis in animal studies (van Praag et al., 2007; Ortiz-López et al., 2016). This was associated with improved spatial memory, and the effect was increased in combination with exercise (van Praag et al., 2007). Epigallocatechin has been observed to elevate metabolic rate (Westerterp-Plantenga, 2010). Recent data suggest an interaction with cannabinoid receptors, and these pathways and mechanisms in metabolism and appetite drive are just be-ginning to be explored. It seems clear that at least one dietary supplement found in foods such as dark chocolate, green tea, and wine provides direct benefits to brain metabolism, but there is much more to be discovered about interactions with other factors such as exercise and sleep habits, dose and duration of effects, and the overall relative importance of the effects. Flavonoids continue to be investigated in US Army physiology research.

Other dietary components may be important sources of anti-inflammatory actions. One component of the Mediterranean diet, extra-virgin olive oil, has anti-inflammatory effects similar to ibuprofen. Extra virgin olive oil produces a detectable irritation in the back of the throat, similar to the effect of ibuprofen (Cicerale, Breslin, Beauchamp, & Keast, 2009). This effect led scientists at the Monell Chemical Senses Institute to the discovery of oleocanthal and its potent anti-inflammatory activity in amounts of olive oil typically ingested in a Mediterranean diet. This effect is comparable to ibuprofen, but the chemical compositions are completely different (Beauchamp et al., 2005). Among other benefits, oleocanthal appears to suppress the development of β amyloid and tau protein neurofibrillary tangles associated with Alzheimer's and chronic traumatic encephalopathies following head injury (Li et al., 2009).

Nutritional strategies to prevent or mitigate the severity of brain injury from military blast or toxic chemical exposures have been an active area of research since the 1960s. A ketogenic diet (high-fat, low-carbohydrate) has been long recognized as an effective mode of treatment for neurological disorders such as pediatric epilepsy, where the seizure activity is reduced by ketones produced from fat metabolism (Millichap, Jones, & Rudis, 1964). The mechanism of action may involve increasing brain γ-aminobutyric acid (GABA) production to inhibit seizure activity, but other mechanisms may also be important. The benefits could extend to other neurological disorders, including traumatic brain injury, neurotoxic chemical injury, and neurodegenerative diseases. US Army-funded PD research has examined the neuroprotective functions related to neurotoxic chemical damage to mitochondrial respiratory chain (Tieu et al., 2003). Ketones increase adenosine triphosphate (ATP) synthesis and bypass glutamate inhibition of complex I, thus reducing oxidative stress and cell damage (Kashiwaya et al., 2000; Massieu, Haces, Montiel, & Hernandez-Fonseca, 2003). After initial funding under the US Army PD program, the Defense Advanced Research Projects Agency (DARPA) funded studies to evaluate the safety, tolerability, pharmacokinetics, and performance effects of oral doses of D-β-hydroxybutyrate-R-1, 3-butanediol monoester. Results of the studies indicated that the compound is safe and well tolerated, and it may increase both physical and cognitive performance (Clarke et al., 2012; Murray et al., 2016; Cox et al., 2016; Pinckaers, Churchward-Venne, Bailey, & van Loon, 2016). The final report of a 25-year annual review process for the US Army nutrition research program was a very comprehensive assessment of research needs on the topic of neuroprotective nutrition (Bistrian et al., 2011; Erdman, Oria, & Pillsbury, 2011). While there are many promising nutritional interventions to protect the brain from injury, none has passed the test of rigorous randomized controlled trials. One difficulty is the cost of such experiments and the setbacks to additional study support every time a promising intervention fails in human studies.

There are nutritional factors that are important to brain metabolism and that have performance benefits. To date, the most important factor is weight management that sustains a healthy and appropriate glucose regulation. Specific components that sustain performance in extreme environments, especially relevant to soldier performance, include carbohydrate supplements during exhaustive performance, caffeine for sustained attention and mood, and tyrosine in very high-stress conditions. Many other supplements have interesting but still unproved potential benefits. Iron status is an example of nutritional balance proved effective in sustaining mood and cognition, but supplementation is only relevant in deficiency conditions (McClung et al., 2009; Karl et al., 2010). Iron is particularly important for young women undergoing initial military training, including West Point plebes and new recruits in basic training; studies on these populations have found a high prevalence of iron deficiency and iron deficiency anemia (McClung & Murray-Kolb, 2013). Psychobiotics, the types of foods that promote brain health and performance benefits through their interactions with gut bacteria, are currently among the most promising nutritional interventions on the horizon.

MODERATING MALADAPTIVE STRESS

The concept of emotional intelligence, a measure of the ability to regulate one's own emotions and the emotions of others, is useful in quantifying characteristics that are modified by training, significantly impact performance outcomes, and also correspond to measurable brain changes (Ciarrochi, Deane, & Anderson, 2002; Killgore et al., 2014; Killgore, Alkozei, Smith, Divatia, & Demers, 2016). Specifically, emotional intelligence involves perceiving, understanding, and solving emotional problems (Killgore, Schwab, Tkachenko et al., 2013). This ability is reflected in brain changes that enhance physiological and psychological resilience, expressed in a common slogan, "train the mind, change the brain" (Begley, 2007). Certain stressors, notably inadequate sleep, reduce emotional intelligence benefits (Killgore, Kahn-Greene, Lipizzi, et al., 2008). Emotional intelligence is also an important factor in the development of chronic multisymptom illnesses, including posttraumatic stress and undiagnosed Gulf War illness symptoms. Emotional intelligence is modifiable with training, as demonstrated by William "Scott" Killgore and his colleagues in a continuing series of studies on enhancement of mental resilience (Vanuk, Fridman, Demers, & Killgore, 2015; Killgore et al., 2016). The overarching basis has been referred to in some stress management courses as "training the wizard" (i.e., frontal cortex) to "tame the lizard" (i.e., more primitive brain including the limbic system; Lt. Col. Robert Carter, personal communications, 2016). Research in this area is on the path to discovering the neurobiological bases of emotional intelligence and the other characteristics that moderate individual and unit performance in stressful conditions, including mental toughness, leadership, social cooperation, and purposeful self-regulation.

Mental Toughness and Dopaminergic Systems

"Mental toughness" is an individual characteristic that can decide the outcome of a physical contest. David Costill spent his entire career studying the physiology of the distance runner. He summarized some of this work in a keynote lecture at an annual meeting of the American College of Sports Medicine, giving examples of each component of running that might differentiate winning performance in elite competition (Costill, 2002). For each class of characteristics, such as biomechanical running style, mix of muscle fiber types, metabolic efficiency, and cardiopulmonary capacity, he was able to provide examples of winners who departed from the expected rule; thus, he could not identify a physiological factor that distinguished winning performance between elite performers. He then showed video interviews with winners before their races who asserted with an irrational confidence that they knew they were going to win. After the race, they made statements such as, "I was looking over my shoulder not to see if I was ahead but just to see by how much I was going to beat them." Costill concluded, with a humble admission, that his sports psychology colleagues had been right all along and that, ultimately, it was what was in the performer's brain that determined success at the elite level. This example of the connectivity between the mind and performance physiology likely involves dopaminergic centers in the brain. Dopamine has been defined as the "go-and-get-it neurotransmitter," but there are good arguments for a modulatory role in the reward system that could be reframed as providing "adaptive behavioral flexibility" instead of blindly driving reward behavior (Beeler, Cools, Luciana, Ostlund, & Petzinger, 2015). Some of this is the result of personality traits, but there are also aspects of "mental toughness" that can be modified by PD drugs, amphetamines, androgenic anabolic steroids, and other pharmaceuticals.

The example of the endurance of the distance runner is directly relevant to the military. Physiological studies of special operators have generally described individuals who look very similar to their physically active peers. What differs may be nothing more than a bit more brain dopamine secretion that provides superior motivation and self-confidence but not so much that the line to psychosis is crossed. The resulting behavior, manifested in a refusal to accept defeat even in the face of seemingly insurmountable odds, is a working definition of "mental toughness" and one part of soldier resilience. In samples of seamen and Marines in survival training and in aviation training, mental toughness or "hardiness" was associated with measures of physical health, apparently mediated by mental health (Taylor, Pietrobon, Taverniers, Leon, & Fern, 2013). US Army neuroendocrine studies discovered that replacing the leader of a monkey colony resulted in elevated testosterone levels in the new leader by virtue of his new social dominance (Rose, Holaday, & Bernstein, 1971). This has never been tested with military units and individuals rotating through key leadership positions, but it might provide useful insights; more interesting would be to assess the behaviors and any parallel neuroendocrine responses in female leaders, where androgens also play important behavioral roles. There have been studies demonstrating an association between competitive success and testosterone in humans, albeit in a more complicated relationship than monkey colony conflict studies (Rose, Berstein, & Gordon, 1975; Bernhardt, Dabbs Jr., Fielden, & Lutter, 1998). However, in a large sample of Vietnam-era veterans, Dabbs found an inverse correlation between professional success and testosterone levels (Dabbs, 1992). The regulation of androgen secretion and the complex relationship with social roles and interactions is important because of the influence of androgen on dopaminergic systems, at least in animal studies. In high-dose testosterone administration to soldiers, effects on peripheral dopamine metabolism were not apparent, even though there were significant effects on self-confidence and aggression scales; further studies have been difficult to conduct because of legal and ethical restrictions (Hannan, Friedl, Zold, Kettler, & Plymate, 1991). A commonly cited reason for men to use anabolic-androgenic steroids is to improve self-confidence (a "brave" pill). For some individuals, this effect has been associated with irrational and dangerous behaviors (Vassallo & Olrich, 2010; Kanayama, Pope, Cohane, & Hudson, 2003; Pope & Katz, 1994).

Effect of Leadership and Unit Cohesion

Effective leadership under extreme conditions is an example of emotional intelligence. Ernest Shackleton brought his entire 27-man crew home alive from a 2-year ordeal after the Antarctic winter ice crushed their ship (very aptly named *Endurance*). A century later, Shackleton's leadership is an instructive model for executives and military officers (Morrell & Capparell, 2001), but more significant to this paper is the effect that leadership had on the group's outlook and survival. Group dynamics leading to strong social support have direct effects on immune competence, wound healing, and a variety of other physiological consequences (Uchino, Cacioppo, & Kiecolt-Glaser, 1996). One likely consequence of Shackleton's leadership was a beneficial set of brain responses in his men that sustained their physiological cold tolerance, musculoskeletal vigor, and resistance to disease. This would be attributable to a mental outlook instilled in his men that enhanced their physiological resilience, one mediated through adaptive neurochemical responses. Strong leadership has a direct impact on the ability of individuals and groups to cope with psychological stress. For example, there is a positive relationship between individual perception of unit cohesion and PTSD symptoms in US Marines (Breslau, Setodji, & Vaughan, 2016). Others have reported that perception of good leadership and unit cohesion is inversely associated with PTSD symptoms (Du Preez, Sundin, Wessely, & Fear, 2012). PTSD and related chronic multisymptom illnesses are one aspect of maladaptive responses to psychological stressors.

In similarly challenging conditions that ended in disaster, such as Robert Falcon Scott's Terra Nova Expedition, a sense of defeat and resultant maladaptive stress responses undoubtedly contributed to the opposite physiological effects, with motivational, cognitive, and physical failures (refer to Figure 2.1). A comparison between Amundsen's team that was quite satisfied by their successful "First at the South Pole" and the defeatist attitude of Scott's team—reeling from the discovery that they were not first—is a graphic illustration of the impact of leadership and emotional regulation. Scott's recorded notes were "The worst has happened"; "All the day dreams must go"; "Great God! This is an awful place." Neurobiological findings of the past few decades help to rationalize the basis of the very different outcomes of these two expeditions. In a psychosocial stress model, male tree shrews allowed to establish dominance and then caged next to each other result in prominent chronic adrenal stress and depression and can even result in the stress-related death of the defeated animal within a few weeks (Fuchs, 2005). In these animals, as in human contests for dominance, testosterone and cortisol responses move in opposite directions (Fuchs et al., 2001). The psychosocial stress effects are well characterized, with large effects on neurogenesis in the dentate gyrus, and these

Pride and success: South Pole "first"   Defeat, to be followed by breakdown and death

Figure 2.1 A notional estimate of testosterone (T) and cortisol (C) responses in Amundsen's team when they reached the South Pole (*left*), compared to Scott's team when they discovered the Norwegian flag already planted at the South Pole one month later (*right*). Findings on the stress responses from psychosocial interactions in male tree shrews suggest that psychological defeat can dramatically compromise brain health and physiological resilience.
Image on left adapted from a photo by Helmer Hanssen from the National Library of Norway (Nasjonalbiblioteket); image on right adapted from "The Great White South" (1922), by Herbert Ponting, sourced from Public Domain Review on Flickr under Creative Commons.

stress effects are suppressed by antidepressant drugs (Gould, McEwen, Tanapat, Galea, & Fuchs, 1997; Fuchs, Kramer, Hermes, Netter, & Hiemke, 1996).

Leadership affects group cohesion, but group affiliation also promotes a separate brain phenomenon best represented in oxytocin hormone responses, which may moderate motivations through interactions with dopaminergic networks (Love, 2014). The factors that influence oxytocin secretion range from pheromones to eye contact. Visual contact between individuals increases oxytocin and enhances social behavior (MacDonald & MacDonald, 2010). This is a well-known phenomenon for lactating mothers with effects on milk letdown (Fox & Knaggs, 1969). Human–dog eye gaze enhances the bond with canine pets, with a surge in oxytocin release in both (Nagasawa et al., 2015). This may be a basis for the therapeutic benefits of psychiatric therapy dogs currently being explored in the management of PTSD. Members of close-knit, small military units may share a common smell affiliation that positively affects brain and behavior. This phenomenon has yet to be experimentally demonstrated, but previous psychiatry researchers have suggested that an individual evacuated for stress-related problems might benefit from taking odoriferous t-shirts from some of their unit members for psychological comfort and stress reduction through postulated oxytocin-mediated calming effects. Studies using oxytocin hormone administered by insufflation suggest that this hormonal "socializing" of individuals can help manage PTSD symptoms (Feldman, Vengrober, & Ebstein, 2014; Koch et al., 2014). Early in the discovery of oxytocin's social effects, it was suggested that an oxytocin spray could be used at future political rallies to enhance trust and receptivity to a candidate's message (Kosfeld, Heinrichs, Zak, Fischbacher,

& Fehr, 2005). Contributions of oxytocin responses to brain responses to leadership and leader charisma have yet to be tested.

Biology of Mindfulness and Meditation

Traditional practices of emotional self-regulation and rejuvenation, such as meditation and mindfulness, have gained western credibility with an emerging neurophysiological scientific basis. Herbert Benson was instrumental in identifying transcultural commonalities of relaxation techniques that could significantly moderate blood pressure and cardiovascular health outcomes (Beary & Benson, 1974; Benson, Beary, & Carol, 1974). These involved clearing the mind of distracting thoughts, concentrating on a single mantra, and invoking a calming physiological rhythm such as concentration on deep breathing. The results of these simple relaxation methods are mental calmness and clarity of thought. Even the Sergeant Major of the US Army and some of his staff were impressed when Benson took them through a brief and impromptu relaxation exercise in the Pentagon. The science is beginning to fill in the "how" behind the empirical evidence for the effectiveness of soldier meditation. Benson's group and others have shown the biological effects of meditation on increased electroencephalogram (EEG) α wave activity, increased cortical thickness, and on gene activation (Lazar et al., 2000; Lazar et al., 2005; Bhasin et al., 2013). Some other military forces, such as the French Army, have successfully implemented mind, body, and stress-reactivity management training for high-stress first responders, such as the Paris firefighters (an arm of the French military; Trousselard, Dutheil, Ferrer, Babouraj, & Canini, 2015).

The effect of meditation on physiology can be profound. A study involving Benson and Ralph Goldman (US Army Research Institute of Environmental Medicine) with skilled Tibetan meditators demonstrated their ability to increase metabolic rate by an average 60% with a specialized form of meditation: Tum-mo yoga, meditating on the "eternal flame" (i.e., thinking warm thoughts; Benson et al., 1982; Benson, Malhotra, Goldman, Jacobs, & Hopkins, 1990). Core temperature and metabolism could also be reduced by a similar magnitude. Other variations on meditation include deep breathing training, purposeful exercise such as yoga and Tai-chi, and physiological challenges such as Native American sweat lodges and Finnish sauna (Silver & Wilson, 1988; Kukkonen-Harjula et al., 1989; Shore, Shore, & Manson, 2009; Carter & Carter, 2016). Investigation of the mechanisms of stress reduction point to common themes of the relaxation response, which Benson has described. These themes include clearing the brain of distracting thoughts with benefits of reduced stress hormones and inflammatory responses such as interleukin-6 and C-reactive protein (Kiecolt-Glaser et al., 2010).

Stress reduction strategies involve some aspect of training higher cortical regulation of the limbic system. Neuroimaging studies in Paris firefighters highlight these links to resilience characteristics (Reynaud et al., 2013; Reynaud et al., 2015). Individuals with stronger cortical–limbic links (e.g., better educated, mindful individuals) are more effective in compensating for these changes and managing emotions and behaviors. This association between education level and ability to rationally analyze and manage a stressful situation has been a repeated finding in studies of stress-related conditions, including Gulf War illness (Proctor, Harley, Wolfe, Heeren, & White, 2001; Wolfe, Erickson, Sharkansky, King, & King, 1999). Ultimately, chronic psychological stress adversely affects brain health and performance, but personal behaviors provide multiple moderators of this effect.

APPLICATION TO HUMAN PERFORMANCE OPTIMIZATION

In 2012, the new US Army Surgeon General, Major General Patricia Horoho, outlined a new concept for soldier readiness, focusing on personal responsibility and everyday health habits. These specifically identified the "Performance Triad" of nutrition, exercise, and sleep as modifiable personal habits that are key determinants of individual soldier readiness. Horoho stated that the US Army Medical Department has long been occupied with "healthcare" but had not adequately addressed more fundamental issues of "health." Horoho's focus on soldier health and performance readiness was well suited to the preventive medicine leadership role of the medical profession. By now, these "Triad" concepts seem self-evident and are discussed as if these have always been well-recognized, important priorities for soldiers. In fact, this was not the case. Before Horoho's leadership, the US Army was headed toward a repeat of the individual health and readiness decline of the post-Vietnam era that prompted President Carter to order the 1980 review of fitness in the services (US Department of Defense [DoD], 1981), resulting in the DoD Directive 1308.1 based on recommendations of the study. The Triad initiative also helped to move integrative medicine concepts into mainstream implementation. The Joint Chief of Staff, Admiral Michael Mullen, introduced an integrative medicine symposium sponsored by the US Army's innovation center (Telemedicine and Advanced Technology Research Center; TATRC), yet the final publication from this symposium belied the central theme by reporting interrelated behaviors as separate and distinct chapters organized by conventional disciplines. Horoho changed the US Army mindset by moving the focus to readiness outcomes, such as effective weight management, instead of single contributors, such as nutrition or exercise considered in isolation. A report on the initial results of the Triad campaign restates the key objectives as the "physical, emotional, and cognitive health and fitness to win in environments that are complex, unknown, and constantly changing" (US Department of the Army, 2015). Neurobiology research as outlined in this chapter continues to revalidate and strengthen the concepts underlying the Triad initiative.

Even with the increasingly technological roles of military cyberwarriors, physical fitness habits turn out to be important performance determinants. The effects of health behaviors on neurotrophins, neurogenesis, and other determinants of mood and cognition make these fitness habits as relevant to mental performance as physical performance.

CONCLUSION

This chapter briefly illustrated brain metabolic influences that relate to mental limits of performance. Personal health habit interventions may be the most effective tools to enhance soldier resilience. There is no need to invoke genetic manipulation or electronic brain implants. How we exercise, eat, rest, and manage our emotions has a major effect on brain metabolism and human performance. The specific "prescription" for individuals is not yet defined, but minimum thresholds can be proposed, including some form of daily physical activity, regular adequate sleep, and a balanced diet—possibly including components of the Mediterranean diet and other food traditions and strategies. The US Army is the primary US federal agency charged with a research mission in performance physiology. Current research by the Army will result in specific recommendations on mode and dose of exercise, restorative sleep strategies, and specific dietary components, with broad dual-use applications to healthy active Americans. The most important conclusion to date is that these self-moderating strategies can yield major benefits to brain health and performance, and this emphasizes the importance of personal responsibility.

ACKNOWLEDGMENTS

Stephen J. Grate contributed to this manuscript without compensation. We gratefully acknowledge the expert editing of this manuscript by Ms. Mallory Roussel.

REFERENCES

Agudelo, L. Z., Femenía, T., Orhan, F., Porsmyr-Palmertz, M., Goiny, M., Martinez-Redondo, V., . . . Pettersson, A. T. (2014). Skeletal muscle PGC-1α1 modulates kynurenine metabolism and mediates resilience to stress-induced depression. *Cell, 159*(1), 33–45.

Ahlberg, A. C., Ljung, T., Rosmond, R., McEwen, B., Holm, G., Åkesson, H. O., & Björntorp, P. (2002). Depression and anxiety symptoms in relation to anthropometry and metabolism in men. *Psychiatry Research, 112,* 101–110.

Ahlers, S. T., Thomas, J. R., Schrot, J., & Shurtleff, D. (1994). Tyrosine and glucose modulation of cognitive deficits resulting from cold stress. In B. M. Marriott (Ed.), *Food Components to Enhance Performance: An Evaluation of Potential Performance-enhancing Food Components for Operational Rations* (pp. 277–299). Washington, DC: National Academies Press.

Alexander, B., Warner-Schmidt, J., Eriksson, T. M., Tamminga, C., Arango-Lievano, M., Ghose, S., . . . Svenningsson, P. (2010). Reversal of depressed behaviors in mice by p11 gene therapy in the nucleus accumbens. *Science Translational Medicine, 2*(54), 54ra76–54ra76.

Allen, K. V., Frier, B. M., & Strachan, M. W. (2004). The relationship between type 2 diabetes and cognitive dysfunction: Longitudinal studies and their methodological limitations. *European Journal of Pharmacology, 490*(1), 169–175.

Apfel, B. A., Ross, J., Hlavin, J., Meyerhoff, D. J., Metzler, T. J., Marmar, C. R., . . . Neylan, T. C. (2011). Hippocampal volume differences in Gulf War veterans with current versus lifetime posttraumatic stress disorder symptoms. *Biological Psychiatry, 69,* 541–548.

Arnal, P. J. (2015). *Countermeasures to Prevent Performance Degradation and Modulation of Endocrine Responses Induced by Sleep Deprivation* (Doctoral thesis). Université Jean Monnet de Saint-Étienne and Institut de Recherche Biomédicale des Armées. Retrieved from http://www.theses.fr/s131327

Arnal, P. J., Drogou, C., Sauvet, F., Regnauld, J., Dispersyn, G., Faraut, B., . . . Chennaoui, M. (2016). Effect of sleep extension on the subsequent testosterone, cortisol and pro-lactin responses to total sleep deprivation and recovery. *Journal of Neuroendocrinology, 28*(2), 12346. doi:10.1111/jne.12346

Arya, F., Egger, S., Colquhoun, D., Sullivan, D., Pal, S., & Egger, G. (2010). Differences in postprandial inflammatory responses to a "modern" *v.* traditional meat meal: A prelim-inary study. *British Journal of Nutrition, 104*(5), 724–728.

Astrup, A., Breum, L., Toubro, S., Hein, P., & Quaade, F. (1992). The effect and safety of an ephedrine/caffeine compound compared to ephedrine, caffeine and placebo in obese subjects on an energy restricted diet: A double blind trial. *International Journal of Obesity and Related Metabolic Disorders, 16*(4), 269–277.

Austin, A. W., Wissmann, T., & von Kanel, R. (2013). Stress and hemostasis: An update. *Seminars in Thrombosis and Hemostasis, 39,* 902–912.

Austin, F. H., Jr. (1969). A review of stress and fatigue monitoring of naval aviators during aircraft carrier combat operations: Blood and urine biochemical studies. In P. G. Bourne (Ed.), *The Psychology and Physiology of Stress: With Reference to Special Studies of the Viet Nam War* (pp. 197–218). New York: Academic Press.

Austin, F. H., Jr., Gallagher, T. J., Brictson, C. A., Polis, B. D., Furry, D. E., & Lewis Jr., C. E. (1967). Aeromedical monitoring of naval aviators during aircraft carrier combat oper-ation. *Aerospace Medicine, 38*(6), 593–596.

Babyak, M., Blumenthal, J. A., Herman, S., Khatri, P., Doraiswamy, M., Moore, K., . . . Krishnan, K. R. (2000). Exercise treatment for major depression: Maintenance of therapeutic benefit at 10 months. *Psychosomatic Medicine, 62*(5), 633–638.

Baron, K. G., Reid, K. J., & Zee, P. C. (2013). Exercise to improve sleep in in-somnia: Exploration of the bidirectional effects. *Journal of Clinical Sleep Medicine, 9*(8), 819–824.

Bart-Knauer, B., & Friedl, K. E. (2013). When will acupuncture become a first-line treat-ment for acute pain management? *Military Medicine, 178*(8), 827–828.

Beary, J. F., & Benson, H. (1974). A simple psychophysiologic technique which elicits the hypometabolic changes of the relaxation response. *Psychosomatic Medicine, 36*(2), 115.

Beauchamp, G. K., Keast, R. S., Morel, D., Lin, J., Pika, J., Han, Q., . . . Breslin, P. A. (2005). Phytochemistry: Ibuprofen-like activity in extra-virgin olive oil. *Nature, 437*(7055), 45–46.

Beeler, J. A., Cools, R., Luciana, M., Ostlund, S. B., & Petzinger, G. (2015). A kinder, gentler dopamine: Highlighting dopamine's role in behavioral flexibility. *Frontiers in Neuroscience, 8.* doi:10.3389/frins.2014.00004

Begley, S. (2007). *Train Your Mind, Change Your Brain: How a New Science Reveals Our Extraordinary Potential to Transform Ourselves.* New York: Random House Digital.

Benson, H., Beary, J. F., & Carol, M. P. (1974). The relaxation response. *Psychiatry, 37*(1), 37–46.

Benson, H., Lehmann, J. W., Malhotra, M. S., Goldman, R. F., Hopkins, J., & Epstein, M. D. (1982). Body temperature changes during the practice of g Tum-mo yoga. *Nature, 295*(5846), 234–236.

Benson, H., Malhotra, M. S., Goldman, R. F., Jacobs, G. D., & Hopkins, P. J. (1990). Three case reports of the metabolic and electroencephalographic changes during advanced Buddhist meditation techniques. *Behavioral Medicine, 16*(2), 90–95.

Bernhardt, P. C., Dabbs Jr., J. M., Fielden, J. A., & Lutter, C. D. (1998). Testosterone changes during vicarious experiences of winning and losing among fans at sporting events. *Physiology & Behavior, 65*(1), 59–62.

Bhasin, M. K., Dusek, J. A., Chang, B. H., Joseph, M. G., Denninger, J. W., Fricchione, G. L., . . . Libermann, T. A. (2013). Relaxation response induces temporal transcriptome changes in energy metabolism, insulin secretion and inflammatory pathways. *PLoS One, 8*(5), e62817.

Bistrian, B. R., Askew, W., Erdman, J. W., & Oria, M. P. (2011). Nutrition and traumatic brain injury: A perspective from the Institute of Medicine report. *Journal of Parenteral and Enteral Nutrition, 35*(5), 556–559.

Björntorp, P. (1991). Metabolic implications of body fat distribution. *Diabetes Care, 14*(12), 1132–1143.

Bourne, P. G., Rose, R. M., & Mason, J. W. (1967). Urinary 17-OHCS levels: Data on seven helicopter ambulance medics in combat. *Archives of General Psychiatry, 17*(1), 104–110.

Bourne, P. G., Rose, R. M., & Mason, J. W. (1968). 17-OHCS levels in combat: Special forces "A" team under threat of attack. *Archives of General Psychiatry, 19*(2), 135–140.

Breivik, T., Thrane, P. S., Murison, R., & Gjermo, P. (1996). Emotional stress effects on immunity, gingivitis and periodontitis. *European Journal of Oral Sciences, 104*, 327–334.

Breslau, J., Setodji, C. M., & Vaughan, C. A. (2016). Is cohesion within military units associated with post-deployment behavioral and mental health outcomes? *Journal of Affective Disorders, 198*, 102–107.

Bucha, P. W. (2014, October). *Mending minds and wounds.* Keynote address presented at the 7th Annual Brain at War Conference, San Francisco, CA.

Buguet, A., Cespuglio, R., & Radomski, M. W. (1998). Sleep and stress in man: An approach through exercise and exposure to extreme environments. *Canadian Journal of Physiological Pharmacology, 76*, 553–561.

Buguet, A., Roussel, B., Angus, R., Sabiston, B., & Radomski, M. (1980). Human sleep and adrenal individual reactions to exercise. *Electroencephalography and Clinical Neurophysiology, 49*, 515–523.

Burckhardt, C. S., Mannerkorpi, K., Hedenberg, L., & Bjelle, A. (1994). A randomized, controlled clinical trial of education and physical training for women with fibromyalgia. *The Journal of Rheumatology, 21*,714–720.

Busch, A. J., Barber, K. A., Overend, T. J., Peloso, P. M. J., & Schachter, C. L. (2007). Exercise for treating fibromyalgia syndrome. *Cochrane Database of Systematic Reviews,* 4: CD003786. doi: 10.1002/14651858.CD003786.pub2

Cannon, W. B. (1915). *Bodily Changes in Pain, Hunger, Fear, and Rage: An Account of Recent Researches into the Function of Emotional Excitement.* New York: D. Appleton.

Cannon, W. B. (1932). *The Wisdom of the Body.* New York: Norton.

Capuron, L., Neurauter, G., Musselman, D. L., Lawson, D. H., Nemeroff, C. B., Fuchs, D., & Miller, A. H. (2003). Interferon-alpha-induced changes in tryptophan metabolism: Relationship to depression and paroxetine treatment. *Biological Psychiatry, 54*(9), 906–914.

Carr, D. B., Bullen, B. A., Skrinar, G. S., Arnold, M. A., Rosenblatt, M., Beitins, I. Z., . . . McArthur, J. W. (1981). Physical conditioning facilitates the exercise-induced secretion of beta-endorphin and beta-lipotropin in women. *New England Journal of Medicine, 305*(10), 560–563.

Carro, E., Trejo, J. L., Busiguina, S., & Torres-Aleman, I. (2001). Circulating insulin-like growth factor I mediates the protective effects of physical exercise against brain insults of different etiology and anatomy. *The Journal of Neuroscience, 21*(15), 5678–5684.

Carter, K. S., & Carter, R, III. (2016). Breath-based meditation: A mechanism to restore the physiological and cognitive reserves for optimal human performance. *World Journal of Clinical Cases, 4*(4), 99–102.

Cassilhas, R. C., Lee, K. S., Fernandes, J., Oliveira, M. G. M., Tufik, S., Meeusen, R., & De Mello, M. T. (2012). Spatial memory is improved by aerobic and resistance exercise through divergent molecular mechanisms. *Neuroscience, 202*, 309–317.

Cespuglio, R., Amrouni, D., Meiller, A., Buguet, A., & Gautier-Sauvigné, S. (2012). Nitric oxide in the regulation of the sleep-wake states. *Sleep Medicine Reviews, 16*(3), 265–279.

Chen, J. F., Xu, K., Petzer, J. P., Staal, R., Xu, Y. H., Beilstein, M., . . . Schwarzschild, M. A. (2001). Neuroprotection by caffeine and A2A adenosine receptor inactivation in a model of Parkinson's disease. *Journal of Neuroscience, 21*(10), RC143.

Chennaoui, M., Arnal, P. J., Sauvet, F., & Leger, D. (2015). Sleep and exercise: A reciprocal issue? *Sleep Medicine Reviews, 20*, 59–72.

Ciarrochi, J., Deane, F. P., & Anderson, S. (2002). Emotional intelligence moderates the relationship between stress and mental health. *Personality and Individual Differences, 32*(2), 197–209.

Cicerale, S., Breslin, P. A., Beauchamp, G. K., & Keast, R. S. (2009). Sensory characterization of the irritant properties of oleocanthal, a natural anti-inflammatory agent in extra virgin olive oils. *Chemical Senses, 34*(4), 333–339.

Clarke, K., Tchabanenko, K., Pawlosky, R., Carter, E., King, M. T., Musa-Veloso, K., . . . Veech, R. L. (2012). Kinetics, safety and tolerability of (R)-3-hydroxybutyl (R)-3-hydroxybutyrate in healthy adult subjects. *Regulatory Toxicology and Pharmacology, 63*(3), 401–408.

Cohen, S., Tyrrell, D. A., & Smith, A. P. (1991). Psychological stress and susceptibility to the common cold. *New England Journal of Medicine, 325*(9), 606–612.

Colcombe, S. J., Erickson, K. I., Scalf, P. E., Kim, J. S., Prakash, R., McAuley, E., . . . Kramer, A. F. (2006). Aerobic exercise training increases brain volume in aging humans. *The Journals of Gerontology Series A: Biological Sciences and Medical Sciences, 61*(11), 1166–1170.

Costill, D. L. (2002, May). *Distance running: A century on the treadmill.* D. B. Dill Historical Lecture presented at the American College of Sports Medicine, 49th Annual Meeting, St. Louis, MO.

Cotman, C. W., Berchtold, N. C., & Christie, L. A. (2007). Exercise builds brain health: Key roles of growth factor cascades and inflammation. *Trends in Neurosciences, 30*(9), 464–472.

Cox, P. J., Kirk, T., Ashmore, T., Willerton, K., Evans, R., Smith, A., . . . King, M. T. (2016). Nutritional ketosis alters fuel preference and thereby endurance performance in athletes. *Cell Metabolism, 24*(2), 256–268.

Cryan, J. F., & Dinan, T. G. (2012). Mind-altering microorganisms: The impact of the gut microbiota on brain and behaviour. *Nature Reviews Neuroscience, 13*(10), 701–712.

Dabbs, J. M. (1992). Testosterone and occupational achievement. *Social Forces, 70*(3), 813–824.

Deng, W., Aimone, J. B., & Gage, F. H. (2010). New neurons and new memories: How does adult hippocampal neurogenesis affect learning and memory? *Nature Reviews Neuroscience, 11*(5), 339–350.

Déry, N., Pilgrim, M., Gibala, M., Gillen, J., Wojtowicz, J. M., MacQueen, G., & Becker, S. (2013). Adult hippocampal neurogenesis reduces memory interference in humans: Opposing effects of aerobic exercise and depression. *Frontiers in Neuroscience, 7*, 66.

de Souza, R. J., Bray, G. A., Carey, V. J., Hall, K. D., LeBoff, M. S., Loria, C. M., . . . Smith, S. R. (2012). Effects of 4 weight-loss diets differing in fat, protein, and carbohydrate on fat mass, lean mass, visceral adipose tissue, and hepatic fat: Results from the POUNDS LOST trial. *The American Journal of Clinical Nutrition, 95*(3), 614–625.

Donta, S. T., Clauw, D. J., Engel Jr., C. C., Guarino, P., Peduzzi, P., Williams, D. A., . . . Sogg, S. (2003). Cognitive behavioral therapy and aerobic exercise for Gulf War veterans' illnesses: A randomized controlled trial. *The Journal of the American Medical Association, 289*(11), 1396–1404.

Dowlati, Y., Herrmann, N., Swardfager, W., Liu, H., Sham, L., Reim, E. K., & Lanctôt, K. L. (2010). A meta-analysis of cytokines in major depression. *Biological Psychiatry, 67*(5), 446–457.

Du Preez, J., Sundin, J., Wessely, S., & Fear, N. T. (2012). Unit cohesion and mental health in the UK Armed Forces. *Occupational Medicine, 62*(1), 47–53.

Erdman, J., Oria, M., & Pillsbury, L. (Eds.). (2011). *Nutrition and Traumatic Brain Injury: Improving Acute and Subacute Health Outcomes in Military Personnel.* Washington, DC: National Academies Press.

Fares, R. P., Belmeguenai, A., Sanchez, P. E., Kouchi, H. Y., Bodennec, J., Morales, A., . . . Bezin, L. (2013). Standardized environmental enrichment supports enhanced brain plasticity in healthy rats and prevents cognitive impairment in epileptic rats. *PLoS One, 8*(1), e53888.

Feldman, R., Vengrober, A., & Ebstein, R. P. (2014). Affiliation buffers stress: Cumulative genetic risk in oxytocin-vasopressin genes combines with early caregiving to predict PTSD in war-exposed young children. *Translational Psychiatry, 4*(3), e370.

Fisher, B. E., Li, Q., Nacca, A., Salem, G. J., Song, J., Yip, J., . . . Petzinger, G. M. (2013). Treadmill exercise elevates striatal dopamine D2 receptor binding potential in patients with early Parkinson's disease. *NeuroReport, 24*(10), 509–514.

Fisher, B. E., Wu, A. D., Salem, G. J., Song, J., Lin, C. H. J., Yip, J., . . . Petzinger, G. (2008). The effect of exercise training in improving motor performance and corticomotor excitability in people with early Parkinson's disease. *Archives of Physical Medicine and Rehabilitation, 89*(7), 1221–1229.

Fisher, N. D., Hughes, M., Gerhard-Herman, M., & Hollenberg, N. K. (2003). Flavanol-rich cocoa induces nitric-oxide-dependent vasodilation in healthy humans. *Journal of Hypertension, 21*(12), 2281–2286.

Fontaine, K. R., Conn, L., & Clauw, D. J. (2010). Effects of lifestyle physical activity on perceived symptoms and physical function in adults with fibromyalgia: Results of a randomized trial. *Arthritis Research & Therapy, 12*(2), 1. doi:10.1186/ar2967

Foster, J. A., & Neufeld, K. A. M. (2013). Gut–brain axis: How the microbiome influences anxiety and depression. *Trends in Neurosciences, 36*(5), 305–312.

Fox, C. A., & Knaggs, G. S. (1969). Milk-ejection activity (oxytocin) in peripheral venous blood in man during lactation and in association with coitus. *Journal of Endocrinology, 45*(1), 145–146.

Friedl, K. E. (2004). Military studies and nutritional immunology: Undernutrition and susceptibility to illness. In D. A. Hughes, L. G. Darlington, & A. Bendich (Eds.), *Diet and Human Immune Function* (pp. 381–396). New York: Humana Press.

Friedl, K. E. (2008). ["Soldier reset" and brain health as cornerstones of "2010 Program Objective Memorandum"]. Unpublished briefings.

Friedl, K. E. (2012). Body composition and military performance: Many things to many people. *The Journal of Strength & Conditioning Research, 26,* S87–S100.

Friedl, K. E., Breivik, T. J., Carter III, R., Leyk, D., Opstad, P. K., Taverniers, J., & Trousselard, M. (2016). Soldier health habits and the metabolically optimized brain. *Military Medicine, 181*(11), e1499–e1507.

Friedl, K. E., Mays, M. Z., Kramer, T. R., & Shippee, R. L. (2001). Acute recovery of physiological and cognitive function in US Army Ranger students in a multistressor field environment. In *The Effect of Prolonged Military Activities in Man. Physiological and Biochemical Changes. Possible Means of Rapid Recuperation* (Technical Report RTO-MP-042; pp. 6.1–6.10). Neuilly-sur-Seine Cedex, France: North Atlantic Treaty Organization, Research and Technology Organization.

Friedl, K. E., Moore, R. J., Hoyt, R. W., Marchitelli, L. J., Martinez-Lopez, L. E., & Askew, E. W. (2000). Endocrine markers of semistarvation in healthy lean men in a multistressor environment. *Journal of Applied Physiology, 88,* 1820–1830.

Friedl, K. E., Moore, R. J., Martinez-Lopez, L. E., Vogel, J. A., Askew, E. W., Marchitelli, L. J., Hoyt, R. W., & Gordon, C. C. (1994). Lower limit of body fat in healthy active men. *Journal of Applied Physiology, 77,* 933–940.

Fuchs, E. (2005). Social stress in tree shrews as an animal model of depression: An example of a behavioral model of a CNS disorder. *CNS Spectrums, 10*(3), 182–190.

Fuchs, E., Flügge, G., Ohl, F., Lucassen, P., Vollmann-Honsdorf, G. K., & Michaelis, T. (2001). Psychosocial stress, glucocorticoids, and structural alterations in the tree shrew hippocampus. *Physiology & Behavior, 73*(3), 285–291.

Fuchs, E., Kramer, M., Hermes, B., Netter, P., & Hiemke, C. (1996). Psychosocial stress in tree shrews: Clomipramine counteracts behavioral and endocrine changes. *Pharmacology Biochemistry and Behavior, 54*(1), 219–228.

Glaser, R., & Kiecolt-Glaser, J. K. (2005). Stress-induced immune dysfunction: Implications for health. *Nature Reviews Immunology, 5*(3), 243–251.

Glass, J. M., Lyden, A. K., Petzke, F., Stein, P., Whalen, G., Ambrose, K., . . . Clauw, D. J. (2004). The effect of brief exercise cessation on pain, fatigue, and mood symptom development in healthy, fit individuals. *Journal of Psychosomatic Research, 57*(4), 391–398.

Gold, A. E., MacLeod, K. M., Frier, B. M., & Deary, I. J. (1995). Changes in mood during acute hypoglycemia in healthy participants. *Journal of Personality and Social Psychology, 68*(3), 498.

Gold, S. M., Dziobek, I., Sweat, V., Tirsi, A., Rogers, K., Bruehl, H., . . . Convit, A. (2007). Hippocampal damage and memory impairments as possible early brain complications of type 2 diabetes. *Diabetologia, 50*(4), 711–719.

Gould, B. A. (1869). *Investigations in the Military and Anthropological Statistics of American Soldiers.* New York: Hurd and Houghton.

Gould, E., McEwen, B. S., Tanapat, P., Galea, L. A., & Fuchs, E. (1997). Neurogenesis in the dentate gyrus of the adult tree shrew is regulated by psychosocial stress and NMDA receptor activation. *The Journal of Neuroscience, 17*(7), 2492–2498.

Gulaj, E., Pawlak, K., Bien, B., & Pawlak, D. (2010). Kynurenine and its metabolites in Alzheimer's disease patients. *Advances in Medical Sciences, 55*(2), 204–211.

Hakkarainen, R., Partonen, T., Haukka, J., Virtamo, J., Albanes, D., & Lönnqvist, J. (2004). Is low dietary intake of omega-3 fatty acids associated with depression? *American Journal of Psychiatry, 161*(3), 567–569.

Hannan, C. J., Friedl, K. E., Zold, A., Kettler, T. M., & Plymate, S. R. (1991). Psychological and serum homovanillic acid changes in men administered androgenic steroids. *Psychoneuroendocrinology, 16*(4), 335–343.

Heijtz, R. D., Wang, S., Anuar, F., Qian, Y., Björkholm, B., Samuelsson, A., . . . Pettersson, S. (2011). Normal gut microbiota modulates brain development and behavior. *Proceedings of the National Academy of Sciences, 108*(7), 3047–3052.

Hollenberg, N. K., Fisher, N. D., & McCullough, M. L. (2009). Flavanols, the Kuna, cocoa consumption, and nitric oxide. *Journal of the American Society of Hypertension, 3*(2), 105–112.

Hollenberg, N. K., Martinez, G., McCullough, M., Meinking, T., Passan, D., Preston, M., . . . Vicaria-Clement, M. (1997). Aging, acculturation, salt intake, and hypertension in the Kuna of Panama. *Hypertension, 29*(1), 171–176.

Huang, Z. L., Qu, W. M., Eguchi, N., Chen, J. F., Schwarzschild, M. A., Fredholm, B. B., . . . Hayaishi, O. (2005). Adenosine A2A, but not A1, receptors mediate the arousal effect of caffeine. *Nature Neuroscience, 8*(7), 858–859.

Huber, R., Ghilardi, M. F., Massimini, M., Ferrarelli, F., Riedner, B. A., Peterson, M. J., & Tononi, G. (2006). Arm immobilization causes cortical plastic changes and locally decreases sleep slow wave activity. *Nature Neuroscience, 9*(9), 1169–1176.

Huck, N. O., Mcbride, S. A., Kendall, A. P., Grugle, N. L., & Killgore, W. D. (2008). The effects of modafinil, caffeine, and dextroamphetamine on judgments of simple versus complex emotional expressions following sleep deprivation. *International Journal of Neuroscience, 118*(4), 487–502.

Iliff, J. J., Chen, M. J., Plog, B. A., Zeppenfeld, D. M., Soltero, M., Yang, L., . . . Nedergaard, M. (2014). Impairment of glymphatic pathway function promotes tau pathology after traumatic brain injury. *Journal of Neuroscience, 34*, 16180–16193.

Institute of Medicine of the National Academies. (2006). *Nutrient Composition of Rations for Short-Term, High-Intensity Combat Operations.* Washington, DC: National Academies Press. https://doi.org/10.17226/11325

Iwasaki, K., Takahashi, M., & Nakata, A. (2006). Health problems due to long working hours in Japan: Working hours, workers' compensation (Karoshi), and preventive measures. *Industrial Health, 44*(4), 537–540.

Jackson-Lewis, V., Vila, M., Tieu, K., Teismann, P., Vadseth, C., Choi, D. K., . . . Przedborski, S. (2002). Blockade of microglial activation is neuroprotective in the 1-methyl-4-phenyl-1, 2, 3, 6-tetrahydropyridine mouse model of Parkinson disease. *The Journal of Neuroscience, 22*(5), 1763–1771.

Johnson, R. F., & Merullo, D. J. (1999). Friend-foe discrimination, caffeine, and sentry duty. *Proceedings of the Human Factors and Ergonomics Society Annual Meeting* (Vol. 43, No. 23, 1348–1352). Thousand Oaks, CA: SAGE.

Kamimori, G. H., Karyekar, C. S., Otterstetter, R., Cox, D. S., Balkin, T. J., Belenky, G. L., & Eddington, N. D. (2002). The rate of absorption and relative bioavailability of caffeine administered in chewing gum versus capsules to normal healthy volunteers. *International Journal of Pharmaceutics, 234*(1), 159–167.

Kanayama, G., Pope, H. G., Cohane, G., & Hudson, J. I. (2003). Risk factors for anabolic-androgenic steroid use among weightlifters: A case-control study. *Drug and Alcohol Dependence, 71*(1), 77–86.

Karl, J. P., Lieberman, H. R., Cable, S. J., Williams, K. W., Young, A. J., & McClung, J. P. (2010). Randomized, double-blind, placebo-controlled trial of an iron-fortified food product in female soldiers during military training: Relations between iron status, serum hepcidin, and inflammation. *The American Journal of Clinical Nutrition*, *92*(1), 93–100.

Kashiwaya, Y., Takeshima, T., Mori, N., Nakashima, K., Clarke, K., & Veech, R. L. (2000). d-β-Hydroxybutyrate protects neurons in models of Alzheimer's and Parkinson's disease. *Proceedings of the National Academy of Sciences*, *97*(10), 5440–5444.

Kempermann, G., van Praag, H., & Gage, F. H. (2000). Activity-dependent regulation of neuronal plasticity and self repair. *Progress in Brain Research*, *127*, 35–48.

Kiecolt-Glaser, J. K., Christian, L., Preston, H., Houts, C. R., Malarkey, W. B., Emery, C. F., & Glaser, R. (2010). Stress, inflammation, and yoga practice. *Psychosomatic Medicine*, *72*(2), 113–121.

Killgore, W. D., Alkozei, A., Smith, R., Divatia, S., & Demers, L. (2016, August). *Enhancing emotional intelligence skills with a brief internet-based program: A pilot study*. Presentation at the Military Health System Research Symposium, Kissimmee, FL.

Killgore, W. D., Britton, J. C., Schwab, Z. J., Price, L. M., Weiner, M. R., Gold, A. L., . . . Rauch, S. L. (2014). Cortico-limbic responses to masked affective faces across PTSD, panic disorder, and specific phobia. *Depression and Anxiety*, *31*(2), 150–159.

Killgore, W. D., Grugle, N. L., Killgore, D. B., Leavitt, B. P., Watlington, G. I., McNair, S., & Balkin, T. J. (2008). Restoration of risk-propensity during sleep deprivation: Caffeine, dextroamphetamine, and modafinil. *Aviation, Space, and Environmental Medicine*, *79*(9), 867–874.

Killgore, W. D., Kahn-Greene, E. T., Lipizzi, E. L., Newman, R. A., Kamimori, G. H., & Balkin, T. J. (2008). Sleep deprivation reduces perceived emotional intelligence and constructive thinking skills. *Sleep Medicine*, *9*(5), 517–526.

Killgore, W. D., Schwab, Z. J., Tkachenko, O., Webb, C. A., DelDonno, S. R., Kipman, . . . Weber, M. (2013). Emotional intelligence correlates with functional responses to dynamic changes in facial trustworthiness. *Social Neuroscience*, *8*(4), 334–346.

Killgore, W. D., Schwab, Z. J., Weber, M., Kipman, M., DelDonno, S. R., Weiner, M. R., & Rauch, S. L. (2013). Daytime sleepiness affects prefrontal regulation of food intake. *Neuroimage*, *71*, 216–223.

Koch, S. B., van Zuiden, M., Nawijn, L., Frijling, J. L., Veltman, D. J., & Olff, M. (2014). Intranasal oxytocin as strategy for medication-enhanced psychotherapy of PTSD: Salience processing and fear inhibition processes. *Psychoneuroendocrinology*, *40*, 242–256.

Kosfeld, M., Heinrichs, M., Zak, P. J., Fischbacher, U., & Fehr, E. (2005). Oxytocin increases trust in humans. *Nature*, *435*, 673–676.

Kramer, T. R., Moore, R. J., Shippee, R. L., Friedl, K. E., Martinez-Lopez, L., Chan, M. M., & Askew, E. W. (1997). Effects of food restriction in military training on T-lymphocyte responses. *International Journal of Sports Medicine*, *18*(S 1), S84–S90.

Kreuz, M. L. E., Rose, R. M., & Jennings, C. J. R. (1972). Suppression of plasma testosterone levels and psychological stress: A longitudinal study of young men in officer candidate school. *Archives of General Psychiatry*, *26*(5), 479–482.

Krotkiewski, M., Björntorp, P., Sjöström, L., & Smith, U. (1983). Impact of obesity on metabolism in men and women. Importance of regional adipose tissue distribution. *Journal of Clinical Investigation*, *72*(3), 1150–1162.

Krueger, J. M., Obál, F., Fang, J., Kubota, T., & Taishi, P. (2001). The role of cytokines in physiological sleep regulation. *Annals of the New York Academy of Sciences*, *933*(1), 211–221.

Kukkonen-Harjula, K., Oja, P., Laustiola, K., Vuori, I., Jolkkonen, J., Siitonen, S., & Vapaatalo, H. (1989). Haemodynamic and hormonal responses to heat exposure in a Finnish sauna bath. *European Journal of Applied Physiology and Occupational Physiology*, 58(5), 543–550.

Lawlor, D. A., & Hopker, S. W. (2001). The effectiveness of exercise as an intervention in the management of depression: Systematic review and meta-regression analysis of randomised controlled trials. *The BMJ*, 322(7289), 763.

Lazar, S. W., Bush, G., Gollub, R. L., Fricchione, G. L., Khalsa, G., & Benson, H. (2000). Functional brain mapping of the relaxation response and meditation. *NeuroReport*, 11(7), 1581–1585.

Lazar, S. W., Kerr, C. E., Wasserman, R. H., Gray, J. R., Greve, D. N., Treadway, M. T., . . . Rauch, S. L. (2005). Meditation experience is associated with increased cortical thickness. *NeuroReport*, 16(17), 1893–1897.

Lehrner, A., Bierer, L. M., Passarelli, V., Pratchett, L. C., Flory, J. D., Bader, H. N., . . . Yehuda, R. (2014). Maternal PTSD associates with greater glucocorticoid sensitivity in offspring of Holocaust survivors. *Psychoneuroendocrinology*, 40, 213–220.

Lewis, M. D., Hibbeln, J. R., Johnson, J. E., Lin, Y. H., Hyun, D. Y., & Loewke, J. D. (2011). Suicide deaths of active-duty US military and omega-3 fatty-acid status: A case-control comparison. *The Journal of Clinical Psychiatry*, 72(12), 1585–1590.

Li, W., Sperry, J. B., Crowe, A., Trojanowski, J. Q., Smith, A. B., III, & Lee, V. M. Y. (2009). Inhibition of tau fibrillization by oleocanthal via reaction with the amino groups of tau. *Journal of Neurochemistry*, 110(4), 1339–1351.

Lieberman, H. R., Tharion, W. J., Shukitt-Hale, B., Speckman, K. L., & Tulley, R. (2002). Effects of caffeine, sleep loss, and stress on cognitive performance and mood during US Navy SEAL training. *Psychopharmacology*, 164(3), 250–261.

Liu-Ambrose, T., Nagamatsu, L. S., Voss, M. W., Khan, K. M., & Handy, T. C. (2012). Resistance training and functional plasticity of the aging brain: A 12-month randomized controlled trial. *Neurobiology of Aging*, 33(8), 1690–1698.

Loucks, A. B., & Thuma, J. R. (2003). Luteinizing hormone pulsatility is disrupted at a threshold of energy availability in regularly menstruating women. *The Journal of Clinical Endocrinology & Metabolism*, 88(1), 297–311.

Love, T. M. (2014). Oxytocin, motivation and the role of dopamine. *Pharmacology Biochemistry and Behavior*, 119, 49–60.

Lucas, M., Mirzaei, F., Pan, A., Okereke, O. I., Willett, W. C., O'Reilly, É. J., . . . Ascherio, A. (2011). Coffee, caffeine, and risk of depression among women. *Archives of Internal Medicine*, 171(17), 1571–1578.

MacDonald, K., & MacDonald, T. M. (2010). The peptide that binds: A systematic review of oxytocin and its prosocial effects in humans. *Harvard Review of Psychiatry*, 18(1), 1–21.

Maguire, E. A., Gadian, D. G., Johnsrude, I. S., Good, C. D., Ashburner, J., Frackowiak, R. S., & Frith, C. D. (2000). Navigation-related structural change in the hippocampi of taxi drivers. *Proceedings of the National Academy of Sciences*, 97(8), 4398–4403.

Manore, M. M. (2012). Dietary supplements for improving body composition and reducing body weight: Where is the evidence? *International Journal of Sport Nutrition and Exercise Metabolism*, 22(2), 139–154.

Mapstone, M., Cheema, A. K., Fiandaca, M. S., Zhong, X., Mhyre, T. R., MacArthur, L. H., . . . Nazar, M. D. (2014). Plasma phospholipids identify antecedent memory impairment in older adults. *Nature Medicine*, 20(4), 415–418.

Marriott, B. M. (Ed.). (1994). *Food Components to Enhance Performance: An Evaluation of Potential Performance-enhancing Food Components for Operational Rations.* Washington, DC: National Academies Press.

Mason, J. W. (1971). A re-evaluation of the concept of "non-specificity" in stress theory. *Journal of Psychiatric Research, 8*, 323–333.

Massieu, L., Haces, M. L., Montiel, T., & Hernandez-Fonseca, K. (2003). Acetoacetate protects hippocampal neurons against glutamate-mediated neuronal damage during glycolysis inhibition. *Neuroscience, 120*(2), 365–378.

McClung, J. P., Karl, J. P., Cable, S. J., Williams, K. W., Nindl, B. C., Young, A. J., & Lieberman, H. R. (2009). Randomized, double-blind, placebo-controlled trial of iron supplementation in female soldiers during military training: Effects on iron status, physical performance, and mood. *The American Journal of Clinical Nutrition, 90*(1), 124–131.

McClung, J. P., & Murray-Kolb, L. E. (2013). Iron nutrition and premenopausal women: Effects of poor iron status on physical and neuropsychological performance. *Annual Review of Nutrition, 33*, 271–288.

McEwen, B. S. (1998). Protective and damaging effects of stress mediators. *New England Journal of Medicine, 338*(3), 171–179.

McEwen, B. S., & Wingfield, J. C. (2003). The concept of allostasis in biology and biomedicine. *Hormones and Behavior, 43*(1), 2–15.

Millichap, J. G., Jones, J. D., & Rudis, B. P. (1964). Mechanism of anticonvulsant action of ketogenic diet: Studies in animals with experimental seizures and in children with petit mal epilepsy. *American Journal of Diseases of Children, 107*(6), 593–604.

Mirescu, C., Peters, J. D., Noiman, L., & Gould, E. (2006). Sleep deprivation inhibits adult neurogenesis in the hippocampus by elevating glucocorticoids. *Proceedings of the National Academy of Sciences, 103*(50), 19170–19175.

Morrell, M., & Capparell, S. (2001). *Shackleton's Way: Leadership Lessons from the Great Antarctic Explorer.* London: Penguin Books.

Muehlenbein, M. P., & Bribiescas, R. G. (2005). Testosterone-mediated immune functions and male life histories. *American Journal of Human Biology, 17*(5), 527–558.

Murphy, T. C., Hoyt, R. W., Jones, T. E., Gabaree, C. L., & Askew, E. W. (1995). *Performance Enhancing Ration Components Program: Supplemental carbohydrate Test.* (Technical Report No. USARIEM-T95-2). Natick, MA: US Army Research Institute of Environmental Medicine.

Murray, A. J., Knight, N. S., Cole, M. A., Cochlin, L. E., Carter, E., Tchabanenko, K., . . . Deacon, R. M. (2016). Novel ketone diet enhances physical and cognitive performance. *The FASEB Journal, 30*(12), 4021–4032.

Nagasawa, M., Mitsui, S., En, S., Ohtani, N., Ohta, M., Sakuma, Y., . . . Kikusui, T. (2015). Oxytocin-gaze positive loop and the coevolution of human–dog bonds. *Science, 348*(6232), 333–336.

Nakagawasai, O., Tadano, T., Tan-No, K., Niijima, F., Sakurada, S., Endo, Y., & Kisara, K. (1999). Changes in b-endorphin and stress induced analgesia in mice after exposure to forced walking stress. *Methods and Findings in Experimental and Clinical Pharmacology, 21*, 471–476.

Nokia, M. S., Lensu, S., Ahtiainen, J. P., Johansson, P. P., Koch, L. G., Britton, S. L., & Kainulainen, H. (2016). Physical exercise increases adult hippocampal neurogenesis in male rats provided it is aerobic and sustained. *The Journal of Physiology, 594*(7), 1855–1873.

Nybo, L. (2003). CNS fatigue and prolonged exercise: Effect of glucose supplementation. *Medicine and Science in Sports and Exercise, 35*(4), 589–594.

O'Brien, C., Mahoney, C., Tharion, W. J., Sils, I. V., & Castellani, J. W. (2007). Dietary tyrosine benefits cognitive and psychomotor performance during body cooling. *Physiology & Behavior, 90*(2), 301–307.

Oda, B. T. (2010). An alternative perspective to battling the bulge: The social and legal fallout of Japan's anti-obesity legislation. *Asian-Pacific Law & Policy Journal, 12*, 249–294.

Ogbonnaya, E. S., Clarke, G., Shanahan, F., Dinan, T. G., Cryan, J. F., & O'Leary, O. F. (2015). Adult hippocampal neurogenesis is regulated by the microbiome. *Biological Psychiatry, 78*(4), e7–e9.

Opstad, P. K., & Aakvaag, A. (1981). The effect of a high calory diet on hormonal changes in young men during prolonged physical strain and sleep deprivation. *European Journal of Applied Physiology and Occupational Physiology, 46*, 31–39.

Opstad, P. K., & Aakvaag, A. (1983). The effect of sleep deprivation on the plasma levels of hormones during prolonged physical strain and calorie deficiency. *European Journal of Applied Physiology and Occupational Physiology, 51*, 97–107.

Ortiz-López, L., Márquez-Valadez, B., Gómez-Sánchez, A., Silva-Lucero, M. D. C., Torres-Pérez, M., Téllez-Ballesteros, R. I., . . . Ramírez-Rodríguez, G. B. (2016). Green tea compound epigallo-catechin-3-gallate (EGCG) increases neuronal survival in adult hippocampal neurogenesis in vivo and in vitro. *Neuroscience, 322*, 208–220.

Özcan, U., Cao, Q., Yilmaz, E., Lee, A. H., Iwakoshi, N. N., Özdelen, E., . . . Hotamisligil, G. S. (2004). Endoplasmic reticulum stress links obesity, insulin action, and type 2 diabetes. *Science, 306*(5695), 457–461.

Penetar, D., McCann, U., Thorne, D., Kamimori, G., Galinski, C., Sing, H., . . . Belenky, G. (1993). Caffeine reversal of sleep deprivation effects on alertness and mood. *Psychopharmacology, 112*(2-3), 359–365.

Petzinger, G. M., Fisher, B. E., McEwen, S., Beeler, J. A., Walsh, J. P., & Jakowec, M. W. (2013). Exercise-enhanced neuroplasticity targeting motor and cognitive circuitry in Parkinson's disease. *The Lancet Neurology, 12*(7), 716–726.

Petzinger, G. M., Fisher, B. E., Van Leeuwen, J. E., Vukovic, M., Akopian, G., Meshul, C. K., . . . Jakowec, M. W. (2010). Enhancing neuroplasticity in the basal ganglia: The role of exercise in Parkinson's disease. *Movement Disorders, 25*(S1), S141–S145.

Pforr, C., & Locher, C. (2012). The German spa and health resort industry in the light of health care system reforms. *Journal of Travel & Tourism Marketing, 29*(3), 298–312.

Phani, S., Loike, J. D., & Przedborski, S. (2012). Neurodegeneration and inflammation in Parkinson's disease. *Parkinsonism & Related Disorders, 18*, S207–S209.

Pinckaers, P. J., Churchward-Venne, T. A., Bailey, D., & van Loon, L. J. (2016). Ketone bodies and exercise performance: The next magic bullet or merely hype? *Sports Medicine*, 1–9.

Pitman, R. K., Sanders, K. M., Zusman, R. M., Healy, A. R., Cheema, F., Lasko, N. B., . . . Orr, S. P. (2002). Pilot study of secondary prevention of posttraumatic stress disorder with propranolol. *Biological Psychiatry, 51*(2), 189–192.

Place, N., Lepers, R., Deley, G., & Millet, G. Y. (2004). Time course of neuromuscular alterations during a prolonged running exercise. *Medicine and Science in Sports and Exercise, 36*, 1347–1356.

Pope, H. G., & Katz, D. L. (1994). Psychiatric and medical effects of anabolic-androgenic steroid use: A controlled study of 160 athletes. *Archives of General Psychiatry, 51*(5), 375–382.

Proctor, S. P., Harley, R., Wolfe, J., Heeren, T., & White, R. F. (2001). Health-related quality of life in Persian Gulf War veterans. *Military Medicine, 166*(6), 510–519.

Raichlen, D. A., & Polk, J. D. (2013). Linking brains and brawn: Exercise and the evolution of human neurobiology. *Proceedings of the Royal Society of London B: Biological Sciences, 280*(1750), 20122250.

Rasmussen, N. (2011). Medical science and the military: The Allies' use of amphetamine during World War II. *Journal of Interdisciplinary History, 42*(2), 205–233.

Ravelli, G. P., Stein, Z. A., & Susser, M. W. (1976). Obesity in young men after famine exposure in utero and early infancy. *New England Journal of Medicine, 295*(7), 349–353.

Reynaud, E., Guedj, E., Souville, M., Trousselard, M., Zendjidjian, X., El Khoury-Malhame, M., . . . Khalfa, S. (2013). Relationship between emotional experience and resilience: An fMRI study in fire-fighters. *Neuropsychologia, 51*(5), 845–849.

Reynaud, E., Guedj, E., Trousselard, M., El Khoury-Malhame, M., Zendjidjian, X., Fakra, E., . . . Khalfa, S. (2015). Acute stress disorder modifies cerebral activity of amygdala and prefrontal cortex. *Cognitive Neuroscience, 6*, 39–43.

Rose, R. M. (1969a). Androgen responses to stress: I. Psychoendocrine relationships and assessment of androgen activity. *Psychosomatic Medicine, 31*(5), 405–417.

Rose, R. M. (1969b). Androgen excretion in stress. In P. G. Bourne (Ed.), *The Psychology and Physiology of Stress: With Reference to Special Studies of the Viet Nam War* (pp. 117–147). New York: Academic Press.

Rose, R. M., Berstein, I. S., & Gordon, T. P. (1975). Consequences of social conflict on plasma testosterone levels in rhesus monkeys. *Psychosomatic Medicine, 37*(1), 50–61.

Rose, R. M., Bourne, P. G., Poe, R. O., Mougey, E. H., Collins, D. R., & Mason, J. W. (1969). Androgen responses to stress: II. Excretion of testosterone, epitestosterone, androsterone and etiocholanolone during basic combat training and under threat of attack. *Psychosomatic Medicine, 31*(5), 418–436.

Rose, R. M., Holaday, J. W., & Bernstein, I. S. (1971). Plasma testosterone, dominance rank and aggressive behaviour in male rhesus monkeys. *Nature, 231*(5302), 366–368.

Ross, G. W., Abbott, R. D., Petrovitch, H., Morens, D. M., Grandinetti, A., Tung, K. H., . . . Popper, J. S. (2000). Association of coffee and caffeine intake with the risk of Parkinson disease. *The Journal of the American Medical Association, 283*(20), 2674–2679.

Rothman, S. M., Griffioen, K. J., Wan, R., & Mattson, M. P. (2012). Brain-derived neurotrophic factor as a regulator of systemic and brain energy metabolism and cardiovascular health. *Annals of the New York Academy of Sciences, 1264*(1), 49–63.

Rothman, S. M., & Mattson, M. P. (2013). Activity-dependent, stress-responsive BDNF signaling and the quest for optimal brain health and resilience throughout the lifespan. *Neuroscience, 239*, 228–240.

Russoniello, C. V., Fish, M., & O'Brien, K. (2013). The efficacy of casual videogame play in reducing clinical depression: A randomized controlled study. *GAMES FOR HEALTH: Research, Development, and Clinical Applications, 2*(6), 341–346.

Russoniello, C. V., Fish, M., Parks, J., Rhodes, J., Stover, B., & Patton, H. (2009). Training for optimal performance biofeedback program: A cooperative program between East Carolina University and the United States Marine Corps Wounded Warrior Battalion East. *Biofeedback, 37*, 12–17.

Russoniello, C. V., O'Brien, K., & Parks, J. M. (2009). The effectiveness of casual video games in improving mood and decreasing stress. *Journal of Cybertherapy and Rehabilitation, 2*, 53–66.

Sandage, B. W., Sabounjian, L. A., White, R., & Wurtman, R. J. (1992). Choline citrate may enhance athletic performance. *Physiologist, 35*:236a.

Sapolsky, R. M. (2000). Glucocorticoids and hippocampal atrophy in neuropsychiatric disorders. *Archives of General Psychiatry, 57*(10), 925–935.

Sartori, C. R., Vieira, A. S., Ferrari, E. M., Langone, F., Tongiorgi, E., & Parada, C. A. (2011). The antidepressive effect of the physical exercise correlates with increased levels of mature BDNF, and proBDNF proteolytic cleavage-related genes, p11 and tPA. *Neuroscience, 180*, 9–18.

Scheltens, P., Twisk, J. W., Blesa, R., Scarpini, E., von Arnim, C. A., Bongers, A., . . . Wurtman, R. J. (2012). Efficacy of Souvenaid in mild Alzheimer's disease: Results from a randomized, controlled trial. *Journal of Alzheimer's Disease, 31*(1), 225–236.

Schwarzschild, M. A., Chen, J. F., & Ascherio, A. (2002). Caffeinated clues and the promise of adenosine A2A antagonists in PD. *Neurology, 58*(8), 1154–1160.

Selye, H. (1946). The general adaptation syndrome and the diseases of adaptation 1. *The Journal of Clinical Endocrinology & Metabolism, 6*(2), 117–230.

Serhan, C. N., Chiang, N., & Van Dyke, T. E. (2008). Resolving inflammation: Dual anti-inflammatory and pro-resolution lipid mediators. *Nature Reviews Immunology, 8*(5), 349–361.

Serhan, C. N., Hong, S., Gronert, K., Colgan, S. P., Devchand, P. R., Mirick, G., & Moussignac, R. L. (2002). Resolvins: A family of bioactive products of omega-3 fatty acid transformation circuits initiated by aspirin treatment that counter proinflammation signals. *The Journal of Experimental Medicine, 196*(8), 1025–1037.

Shore, J. H., Shore, J. H., and Manson, S. M. (2009). American Indian healers and psychiatrists. In M. Incayawar, R. Wintrob, & L. Bouchard (Eds.), *Psychiatrists and Traditional Healers: Unwitting Partners in Global Mental Health* (pp. 123–134). Chichester, UK: John Wiley & Sons.

Shurtleff, D., Thomas, J. R., Schrot, J., Kowalski, K., & Harford, R. (1994). Tyrosine reverses a cold-induced working memory deficit in humans. *Pharmacology Biochemistry and Behavior, 47*(4), 935–941.

Sijbrandij, M., Kleiboer, A., Bisson, J. I., Barbui, C., & Cuijpers, P. (2015). Pharmacological prevention of post-traumatic stress disorder and acute stress disorder: A systematic review and meta-analysis. *The Lancet Psychiatry, 2*, 413–421.

Silver, S. M., & Wilson, J. P. (1988). Native American healing and purification rituals for war stress. In J. P. Wilson, Z. Harel, & B. (Eds.), *Human Adaptation to Extreme Stress: From the Holocaust to Viet Nam* (pp. 337–355). New York: Plenum Publishing.

Sommerfield, A. J., Deary, I. J., McAulay, V., & Frier, B. M. (2003). Moderate hypoglycemia impairs multiple memory functions in healthy adults. *Neuropsychology, 17*, 125–132.

Sublette, M. E., Hibbeln, J. R., Galfalvy, H., Oquendo, M. A., & Mann, J. J. (2006). Omega-3 polyunsaturated essential fatty acid status as a predictor of future suicide risk. *American Journal of Psychiatry, 163*, 1100–1102.

Svenningsson, P., Kim, Y., Warner-Schmidt, J., Oh, Y. S., & Greengard, P. (2013). p11 and its role in depression and therapeutic responses to antidepressants. *Nature Reviews Neuroscience, 14*(10), 673–680.

Swardfager, W., Herrmann, N., Dowlati, Y., Oh, P. I., Kiss, A., Walker, S. E., & Lanctôt, K. L. (2009). Indoleamine 2, 3-dioxygenase activation and depressive symptoms in patients with coronary artery disease. *Psychoneuroendocrinology, 34*(10), 1560–1566.

Tanner, C. M., Goldman, S. M., Ross, G. W., & Grate, S. J. (2014). The disease intersection of susceptibility and exposure: Chemical exposures and neurodegenerative disease risk. *Alzheimer's & Dementia, 10*(3), S213–S225.

Taverniers, J., & De Boeck, P. (2014). Force-on-force handgun practice: An intra-individual exploration of stress effects, biomarker regulation, and behavioral changes. *Human Factors, 56*, 403–413.

Taverniers, J., Smeets, T., Van Ruysseveldt, J., Syroit, J., & von Grumbkow, J. (2011). The risk of being shot at: Stress, cortisol secretion, and their impact on memory and perceived learning during reality-based practice for armed officers. *International Journal of Stress Management, 18*(2), 113–132.

Taverniers, J., Taylor, M. K., & Smeets, T. (2013). Delayed memory effects after intense stress in Special Forces candidates: Exploring path processes between cortisol secretion and memory recall. *Stress, 16*, 311–320.

Taverniers, J., Van Ruysseveldt, J., Smeets, T., & von Grumbkow, J. (2010). High-intensity stress elicits robust cortisol increases, and impairs working memory and visuo-spatial declarative memory in special forces candidates: A field experiment. *Stress, 13*, 323–33.

Taylor, M. K., Pietrobon, R., Taverniers, J., Leon, M. R., & Fern, B. J. (2013). Relationships of hardiness to physical and mental health status in military men: A test of mediated effects. *Journal of Behavioral Medicine, 36*(1), 1–9.

Thomas, M., Sing, H., Belenky, G., Holcomb, H., Mayberg, H., Dannals, R., . . . Welsh, A. (2000). Neural basis of alertness and cognitive performance impairments during sleepiness. I. Effects of 24 h of sleep deprivation on waking human regional brain activity. *Journal of Sleep Research, 9*(4), 335–352.

Thorén, P., Floras, J. S., Hoffmann, P., & Seals, D. R. (1990). Endorphins and exercise: Physiological mechanisms and clinical implications. *Medicine and Science in Sports and Exercise, 22*(4), 417–428.

Tieu, K., Perier, C., Caspersen, C., Teismann, P., Wu, D. C., Yan, S. D., . . . Przedborski, S. (2003). D-β-Hydroxybutyrate rescues mitochondrial respiration and mitigates features of Parkinson disease. *The Journal of Clinical Investigation, 112*(6), 892–901.

Tobi, E. W., Goeman, J. J., Monajemi, R., Gu, H., Putter, H., Zhang, Y., . . . van Zwet, E. W. (2014). DNA methylation signatures link prenatal famine exposure to growth and metabolism. *Nature Communications, 5*, 5592. doi:10.1038/ncomms6592

Trousselard, M., Dutheil, F., Ferrer, M. H., Babouraj, N., & Canini, F. (2015). Tactics to optimize the potential and cardiobiofeedback in stress management: The French experience. *Medical Acupuncture, 27*(5), 367–375.

Trumble, B. C., Cummings, D., von Rueden, C., O'Connor, K. A., Smith, E. A., Gurven, M., & Kaplan, H. (2012). Physical competition increases testosterone among Amazonian forager-horticulturalists: A test of the 'challenge hypothesis'. *Proceedings of the Royal Society B: Biological Sciences, 279*(1739), 2907.

Trumble, B. C., Smith, E. A., O'Connor, K. A., Kaplan, H. S., & Gurven, M. D. (2014). Successful hunting increases testosterone and cortisol in a subsistence population. *Proceedings of the Royal Society B: Biological Sciences, 281*(1776), 20132876.

Tuomilehto, J., Lindström, J., Eriksson, J. G., Valle, T. T., Hämäläinen, H., Ilanne-Parikka, P., . . . Salminen, V. (2001). Prevention of type 2 diabetes mellitus by changes in lifestyle among subjects with impaired glucose tolerance. *New England Journal of Medicine, 344*(18), 1343–1350.

Uchino, B. N., Cacioppo, J. T., & Kiecolt-Glaser, J. K. (1996). The relationship between social support and physiological processes: A review with emphasis on underlying mechanisms and implications for health. *Psychological Bulletin, 119*(3), 488.

US Department of the Army. (2015). *Health of the force report.* Retrieved from https://www.army.mil/e2/c/downloads/419337.pdf

US Department of Defense. (1981). *Study of the Military Services Physical Fitness.* Washington, DC: Office of the Assistant Secretary of Defense for Manpower, Reserve Affairs and Logistics.

Ursin, H., Baade, E., & Levine, S. (Eds.). (1978). *Psychobiology of Stress: A Study of Coping Men.* New York: Academic Press.

van Praag, H., Fleshner, M., Schwartz, M. W., & Mattson, M. P. (2014). Exercise, energy intake, glucose homeostasis, and the brain. *The Journal of Neuroscience, 34*(46), 15139–15149.

van Praag, H., Kempermann, G., & Gage, F. H. (1999). Running increases cell proliferation and neurogenesis in the adult mouse dentate gyrus. *Nature Neuroscience, 2*(3), 266–270.

van Praag, H., Kempermann, G., & Gage, F. H. (2000). Neural consequences of environmental enrichment. *Nature Reviews Neuroscience, 1*(3), 191–198.

van Praag, H., Lucero, M. J., Yeo, G. W., Stecker, K., Heivand, N., Zhao, C., . . . Gage, F. H. (2007). Plant-derived flavanol (-)epicatechin enhances angiogenesis and retention of spatial memory in mice. *The Journal of Neuroscience, 27*(22), 5869–5878.

Vanuk, J. R., Fridman, A., Demers, L., & Killgore, W. D. (2015). Engaging in meditation and internet-based training as a means of enhancing emotional intelligence. *Biological Psychiatry, 77*(9), 389S–390S.

Vassallo, M. J., & Olrich, T. W. (2010). Confidence by injection: Male users of anabolic steroids speak of increases in perceived confidence through anabolic steroid use. *International Journal of Sport and Exercise Psychology, 8*(1), 70–80.

Vasterling, J. J., Proctor, S. P., Amoroso, P., Kane, R., Heeren, T., & White, R. F. (2006). Neuropsychological outcomes of Army personnel following deployment to the Iraq war. *Journal of the American Medical Association, 296*(5), 519–529.

Voss, M. W., Nagamatsu, L. S., Liu-Ambrose, T., & Kramer, A. F. (2011). Exercise, brain, and cognition across the life span. *Journal of Applied Physiology, 111*(5), 1505–1513.

Voss, M. W., Vivar, C., Kramer, A. F., & van Praag, H. (2013). Bridging animal and human models of exercise-induced brain plasticity. *Trends in Cognitive Sciences, 17*(10), 525–544.

Warber, J. P., Patton, J. F., Tharion, W. J., Zeisel, S. H., Mello, R. P., Kemnitz, C. P., & Lieberman, H. R. (2000). The effects of choline supplementation on physical performance. *International Journal of Sport Nutrition and Exercise Metabolism, 10*(2), 170–181.

Warner-Schmidt, J. L., Vanover, K. E., Chen, E. Y., Marshall, J. J., & Greengard, P. (2011). Antidepressant effects of selective serotonin reuptake inhibitors (SSRIs) are attenuated by antiinflammatory drugs in mice and humans. *Proceedings of the National Academy of Sciences, 108*(22), 9262–9267.

Weiner, M. W., Friedl, K. E., Pacifico, A., Chapman, J. C., Jaffee, M. S., Little, D. M., . . . Yaffe, K. (2013). Military risk factors for Alzheimer's disease. *Alzheimer's & Dementia, 9*(4), 445–451.

Weiner, M. W., Meyerhoff, D. J., Neylan, T. C., Hlavin, J., Ramage, E. R., McCoy, D., . . . Chu, P. W. (2011). The relationship between Gulf War illness, brain N-acetylaspartate, and post-traumatic stress disorder. *Military Medicine*, *176*(8), 896–902.

Wesensten, N. J., Killgore, W. D., & Balkin, T. J. (2005). Performance and alertness effects of caffeine, dextroamphetamine, and modafinil during sleep deprivation. *Journal of Sleep Research*, *14*(3), 255–266.

Westerterp-Plantenga, M. S. (2010). Green tea catechins, caffeine and body-weight regulation. *Physiology & Behavior*, *100*(1), 42–46.

Wittels, P., Johannes, B., Enne, R., Kirsch, K., & Gunga, H. C. (2002). Voice monitoring to measure emotional load during short-term stress. *European Journal of Applied Physiology*, *87*(3), 278–282.

Wolfe, J., Erickson, D. J., Sharkansky, E. J., King, D. W., & King, L. A. (1999). Course and predictors of posttraumatic stress disorder among Gulf War veterans: A prospective analysis. *Journal of Consulting and Clinical Psychology*, *67*(4), 520.

Wurtman, R. J. (2014). A nutrient combination that can affect synapse formation. *Nutrients*, *6*(4), 1701–1710.

Yacoubi, M. E., Ledent, C., Parmentier, M., Bertorelli, R., Ongini, E., Costentin, J., & Vaugeois, J. M. (2001). Adenosine A2A receptor antagonists are potential antidepressants: Evidence based on pharmacology and A2A receptor knockout mice. *British Journal of Pharmacology*, *134*(1), 68–77.

Yaffe, K., Hoang, T. D., Byers, A. L., Barnes, D. E., & Friedl, K. E. (2014). Lifestyle and health-related risk factors and risk of cognitive aging among older veterans. *Alzheimer's & Dementia*, *10*(3), S111–S121.

Yeghiayan, S. K., Luo, S., Shukitt-Hale, B., & Lieberman, H. R. (2001). Tyrosine improves behavioral and neurochemical deficits caused by cold exposure. *Physiology & Behavior*, *72*(3), 311–316.

Yehuda, R., Daskalakis, N. P., Bierer, L. M., Bader, H. N., Klengel, T., Holsboer, F., & Binder, E. B. (2015). Holocaust exposure induced intergenerational effects on FKBP5 methylation. *Biological Psychiatry*, *80*(5), 372–380.

Yehuda, R., Flory, J. D., Bierer, L. M., Henn-Haase, C., Lehrner, A., Desarnaud, F., . . . Meaney, M. J. (2015). Lower methylation of glucocorticoid receptor gene promoter 1 F in peripheral blood of veterans with posttraumatic stress disorder. *Biological Psychiatry*, *77*(4), 356–364.

3

Nutrition, Genetics, and Human Performance During Military Training

ERIN GAFFNEY-STOMBERG AND JAMES P. MCCLUNG*

INTRODUCTION

Military personnel train and conduct operations in austere environments that have profound effects on cognitive and physical performance. The military operational environment results in exposure to multiple stressors, such as sleep deprivation, caloric deficit, dehydration, environmental exposure (i.e., heat, cold, and altitude), psychological strain (i.e., fear and anxiety), and increased energy expenditure. For example, the cognitive effects of exposure to combat stress, often described as the "fog of war," result in the degradation of both simple and complex cognitive functions such as reaction time, vigilance, memory, and logical reasoning (Lieberman, Bathalon, Falco, Morgan et al., 2005). In fact, cognitive deficits observed during combat-like stress have been compared to the effects of alcohol intoxication, treatment with sedating drugs, and clinical hypoglycemia. Military training and operations also have effects on physical performance as caloric deprivation and increased energy demands result in the loss of lean body mass and may result in injury. Studies have characterized decrements in both aerobic and anaerobic performance as a result of military operational stress, including reductions in lifting strength, peak power, and maximal oxygen consumption (Guezennec, Satabin, Legrand, & Bigard, 1994; Nindl et al., 2007). Furthermore, musculoskeletal injury is a leading cause of lost duty days in military personnel, and one study characterized nearly 750,000 injury-related musculoskeletal conditions requiring treatment among nondeployed active duty service members in 1 year alone (Hauret, Jones, Bullock, Canham-Chervak, & Canada, 2010).

Nutritional status and genetic factors may contribute to the impact of military stressors on cognitive and physical performance. Furthermore, the optimization of nutritional status or the identification of genetic factors affecting physiological

*The opinions or assertions contained herein are the private views of the author(s) and are not to be construed as official or as reflecting the views of the US Army or the Department of Defense.

health and cognitive function may serve as targets for interventions aimed at optimizing military performance and improving injury resistance.

This chapter draws on the peer-reviewed literature as a means to detail the contribution of nutrition and genetics to human performance to include resistance to or protection from injury. Laboratory experiments, applied field studies, and controlled trials conducted in the military training environment will be utilized to detail relevant research outlining the relative contribution of nutrition and genetics to military performance and the prevention of injury. Controlled laboratory experiments assessing metabolic homeostasis and appetite regulation during severe energy deprivation, similar to conditions experienced by military personnel during training and operational deployment, will be utilized to detail the effects of diminished interstitial glucose concentrations and hypoglycemia on cognitive performance and mood. Applied field studies will be reviewed to outline the effects of simulated captivity during military training on stress hormones, heart rate, nutritional status, and cognitive function. Controlled trials conducted in the initial military training environment will be utilized to review the role of nutritional status and genetic factors in preventing injury and sustaining cognitive performance in military recruits. Finally, evidence gleaned from the literature reviewed in this chapter will be synthesized to provide perspective regarding the application of nutrition and genetic factors to human performance optimization.

UNDERNUTRITION, MILITARY STRESS, AND COGNITIVE PERFORMANCE

Controlled Laboratory Experiments

Negative energy balance is encountered during military training and operations as a result of increased energy expenditure and inadequate energy intake. Increased energy expenditure is often the result of physically demanding occupational tasks, such as marching with protective equipment, including body armor, while carrying mission-essential military materiel. Inadequate energy intake may be the result of a suboptimal logistical supply of food items, limited time to eat and prepare food, and diminished appetite. Studies have documented a range of total energy expenditure in warfighters from various units engaged in diverse missions ranging from approximately 3,100–7,100 kcal/day in male warfighters and 2,300–5,600 kcal/day in female warfighters (Tharion et al., 2005). These levels of energy expenditure may require the provision of energy (food) at levels more than threefold greater than typical civilian requirements and result in a significant logistical burden, often resulting in underfeeding.

The historic Minnesota Starvation Experiment, the work of Dr. Ancel Keys and his colleagues at the University of Minnesota, was among the first scientific studies assessing the effects of undernutrition on psychological outcomes (Keys, 1950). In this landmark study, volunteers were provided with approximately 1,560 kcal/day for a period of 6 months, resulting in the loss of approximately 25% of their starting body weight. Conclusions from the study describe depression, hysteria, hypochondriasis, and a preoccupation with food lasting into a rehabilitation phase during which controlled methods for refeeding were investigated. As noted in reports characterizing the Minnesota experiment, the use of human volunteers for the study of caloric deprivation is notoriously difficult. When not carefully controlled, such studies may result in significant deviations from prescribed diets and levels of physical activity, thus affecting the quality of outcome data.

Laboratory studies provide the opportunity to control both diet and physical activity through the careful monitoring of human volunteers. Until recently, the inability to formulate calorie-free feeding regimens (including placebo foods) mimicking energy-balanced conditions restricted the ability to design double-blind, randomized, controlled studies assessing the effects of caloric deprivation on cognitive performance. The development of test diets varying in energy content formulated with the use of hydrocolloid-based gels and artificial colors and sweeteners, was first reported in 2008 (Lieberman et al., 2008). A critical element of studies utilizing such test diets is the assurance that energy-containing meals remain nearly indistinguishable from "placebo" meals with regards to sensory properties (taste, texture, volume, and appearance), thereby limiting treatment bias through the inclusion of an appropriately blinded placebo group.

In the first experiment assessing the effects of caloric deprivation on cognitive performance utilizing such diets, Lieberman et al. enrolled 27 volunteers (male and female) for a 48-hour inpatient study including an energy-restricted or fully fed state during which behavioral testing was assessed concomitantly with the continuous assessment of interstitial glucose (Lieberman et al., 2008). The study utilized a crossover design and resulted in the intake of approximately 313 kcal/day in the calorie deprivation phase and 2,294 kcal/day in the full feeding phase. Energy expenditure was carefully controlled and did not differ between treatment conditions. As expected, interstitial glucose levels were reduced during caloric deprivation as compared to fully fed conditions. Interestingly, and perhaps contrary to study hypotheses, caloric deprivation did not affect any aspect of cognitive performance, including psychomotor and visual vigilance, logistical reasoning, or working memory. Similarly, mood was not degraded as a result of energy restriction. The authors concluded that the preservation of cognitive performance during short-term caloric restriction may represent an adaptive mechanism sustaining the ability to seek food, which may be a desirable outcome from a survival or military performance perspective.

In a second laboratory study utilizing similar hydrocolloid-based gels as placebo foods, Lieberman and colleagues (Lieberman et al., 2017) investigated the effects of greater levels of energy deficit induced by increased energy expenditure through physical activity on physical performance and mood. In this case, 23 male and female volunteers participated in a 51-hour inpatient study using a crossover design similar to the initial study. However, in this study, volunteers participated in exercise sessions for 4 hours per day at a prescribed intensity. As a result, in the calorically deprived phase, volunteers consumed approximately 266 kcal/day, whereas in the fully fed state energy consumption was approximately 3,935 kcal/day. Notably, the energy deficit experienced in the study that included 4 hours per day of controlled physical activity was more than 1,500 kcal/day greater than in the initial study. As expected, interstitial glucose levels were reduced in the calorically deprived state as compared to the fed state (Smith et al., 2016). Notably, energy deficit resulted in robust declines in mood state, including increased tension, fatigue, and total mood disturbance. However, cognitive performance, including psychomotor and visual vigilance, working memory, and grammatical reasoning, were not affected. Importantly, findings from this study indicate that although mood declined, degradations in cognitive performance did not occur in response to 2 days of near complete starvation in human volunteers. This reinforces the assertion that the maintenance of cognitive performance may be an adaptive mechanism to promote survival during short-term caloric deprivation.

Field Studies

Although laboratory experiments provide exquisite control over many of the factors that may confound the ability to assess individual variables affecting cognitive performance, such studies may not entirely reflect the realities of combat stress. Combat stress is complex; psychological stressors such as fear, uncertainty, and information overload may be experienced on the battlefield but are not easily replicated in controlled laboratory experiments or applied field settings. In an effort to characterize the effects of combat stress and associated factors (such as caloric deprivation) on cognitive performance without collecting data on the battlefield (due to obvious constraints), investigators have gained access to a series of military training activities that most closely mimic combat stress. These training activities include sustained training operations, simulated combat, and participation in special forces training schools and courses, such as Survival, Evasion, Resistance, and Escape (SERE) school. Collecting data during such training activities allows for some control for experimental variables, such as sleep, nutrition, and physical activity, as these factors are typically prescribed by the training leadership, while including many of the factors associated with combat stress, such as uncertainty and information overload.

Early efforts to assess the effects of military stress on cognitive and physical performance began in the late 1970s and characterized the effects of combat training (Opstad, Ekanger, Nummestad, & Raabe, 1978). Subsequently, Haslam characterized the effects of sustained operations and sleep loss on military performance; primary findings indicated that the exercise resulted in decrements in cognitive performance whereas physical performance was maintained (Haslam, 1984). More recent studies have allowed for the collection of more comprehensive assessment of cognitive and physiological markers of stress. In one such study, Lieberman et al. characterized cognitive performance, mood, physical activity, sleep, body composition, and a series of biomarkers in experienced (averaging >9 years of service) elite US Army infantry officers undergoing a 53-hour simulated combat mission (Lieberman, Bathalon, Falco, Kramer et al., 2005). Soldier volunteers engaged in a variety of combat tasks, including parachuting, travel in small boats, sustained off-road patrolling with heavy load carriage, and exposure to explosions and gunfire. Participants experienced significant caloric deficit: throughout the entire training exercise, only one combat ration containing 1,250 kcal of energy was provided. The effects of the simulated training exercise on study outcomes was stark: soldiers slept only 3 hours during the exercise; lost more than 10 pounds of body weight on average; experienced severe degradations in cognitive performance, including vigilance, reaction time, attention, and memory; and demonstrated significant deteriorations in mood, including diminished vigor, increased fatigue, confusion, depression, and tension. This study contributed significantly to the understanding of the cognitive and physical performance responses to combat-like stress because it was the first to include comprehensive measures of both physiological health and cognitive performance. Notably, severe decrements in cognitive performance and mood were observed during the relatively short exposure to a simulated combat period even in a group of elite, experienced officers. Although the independent effects of caloric deprivation cannot be parsed from the multistressor environment, it is likely that undernutrition contributed to observed declines in cognitive performance and mood.

In recent years, military personnel participating in SERE training have served as volunteers in studies assessing the effects of military stress on cognitive performance and physiological outcomes. This course offers a unique opportunity for the collection of data because the exposure to real-world stress occurs in a highly controlled manner. Furthermore, the course generally occurs over a 2- or 3-week period, thereby allowing for the collection of data beyond 2- or 3-day laboratory experiments or acute operational studies. During SERE school, students (i.e., military personnel serving in roles that may place them in jeopardy of capture) begin the course with an academic period providing training detailing survival, evasion, resistance, and escape techniques, followed by a field exercise requiring navigation through hostile territory, locating water and food sources (hunting and gathering), and evading mock enemy forces. In the final phase, students are captured and endure a series of stressful mock interrogations while residing in a mock prisoner of war camp. Notably, there is variation in the activities that occur during SERE school such that students experience significant uncertainty and fatigue coupled with severe caloric deprivation. In one study characterizing the effects of SERE school on a series of biomarkers including cognitive function, Lieberman et al. (2016) detailed significant declines in grammatical reasoning, sustained attention, working memory, and a series of mood state indicators, particularly during the simulated captivity and mock interrogation portions of the course. Declines in cognitive performance were coupled with negative physiological effects, such as increased heart rate, elevated levels of stress hormones, and decreased levels of sex hormones.

Investigators have utilized SERE and survival schools as an environment to assess the impact of nutrition interventions on cognitive performance and mood state. In one study, Morgan, Hazlett, Southwick, Rasmusson, and Lieberman (2009) tested the effects of carbohydrate administration on recovery from deficits in cognitive function observed in response to the mock captivity phase of a military survival training course. In this double-blind, placebo-controlled study, volunteers were provided with varying levels of carbohydrate or a placebo beverage following mock captivity and prior to a night of recovery sleep. In comparison to data collected following mock captivity and prior to treatment administration, consumption of the carbohydrate beverages resulted in significantly improved performance on a complex cognitive task involving concentration as compared to the placebo group, suggesting that nutritional interventions may offer the opportunity to enhance the recovery of cognitive performance in response to a multistressor environment. In a second double-blind, placebo-controlled trial conducted at SERE school, Lieberman et al. (2015) administered food bars containing supplemental levels of tyrosine, a catecholamine neurotransmitter precursor, approximately 60 minutes prior to mock interrogations. Similar to other studies in the SERE or survival training environment, interrogations resulted in significant negative effects on mood and stress hormones. Interestingly, tyrosine increased anger, as measured using the Profile of Mood States, following interrogation. Similar to studies demonstrating the efficacy of carbohydrate to promote recovery from military stress, this finding highlights the potential use of a nutrient to affect mood, particularly anger, which may be an appropriate response to severe physical and psychological stress.

NUTRITION AND PHYSICAL PERFORMANCE DURING INITIAL MILITARY TRAINING

Iron Status

Initial military training (IMT), the approximately 10-week training course in which civilians joining the military are indoctrinated into military service, is a period of dynamic physical and psychological stress. During this time recruits encounter many unfamiliar tasks within a new environment that results in unique physical and cognitive demands (Simpson et al., 2013). Similar to other military environments, recruits may experience sleep disturbances or deficits, increased energy expenditure, and restricted access to energy intake in the context of the psychological and physical stressors of military training. Performance during IMT is impacted by starting nutritional status as well as nutrient intake during training.

Perhaps one of the most consistently observed nutritional responses to IMT is a decrement in iron status (McClung, Karl, Cable, Williams, Young et al., 2009; Yanovich et al., 2015). Iron is an essential micronutrient that contributes to a number of biological functions, including oxygen storage and delivery. Men are at reduced risk of poor iron status due to the lack of regular iron excretion through menstruation, although decrements in iron status are still observed during IMT. However, premenopausal women are at high risk of negative iron balance due to monthly menstrual losses combined with inadequate dietary intake and physical training which may impart even greater risk (Ashenden, Martin, Dobson, Mackintosh, & Hahn, 1998; Blum, Sherman, & Boileau, 1986; Harvey et al., 2005). Negative iron balance can lead to iron deficiency (ID), in which iron stores are depleted, and eventually iron deficiency anemia (IDA), in which persistently diminished iron stores result in reduced circulating hemoglobin. Iron deficiency anemia results in well-characterized decrements in physical and cognitive performance (Gardner, Edgerton, Senewiratne, Barnard, & Ohira, 1977; Tufts, Haas, Beard, & Spielvogel, 1985). While not as well defined, ID may also affect performance. In a randomized double-blind placebo-controlled trial of iron supplementation, McClung and colleagues determined that daily supplementation with 15 mg of elemental iron improved iron status in females who started IMT with IDA (McClung,

Karl, Cable, Williams, Nindl et al., 2009) and prevented decrements in iron status associated with IMT. The improvement in iron status due to iron supplementation in women beginning the course with IDA was associated with performance as run times and indicators of mood improved as compared to the placebo group.

The cause of reduced iron status during IMT is likely multifactorial and may be due to inadequate dietary intake, inflammatory responses to training, gastrointestinal bleeding, increased whole-body iron turnover, exercise-induced hematuria, and/or iron loss through sweat. Recent studies have assessed the effects of inflammation on iron status, including studies detailing the inflammatory response to military training. The effects of inflammation on iron status are mediated through the acute phase protein, hepcidin, which is a master regulator of iron status. Hepcidin exerts its effects on iron status by reducing membrane expression of the iron exporter ferroportin, thereby reducing intestinal iron absorption and sequestering iron in peripheral cells. Recent findings indicate that hepcidin is positively associated with other inflammatory markers and with iron status at both the start and end of IMT and that hepcidin increases in response to both acute exercise and a multiday sustained military training exercise (Pasiakos et al., 2016).

Calcium, Vitamin D, and Bone Health

Injuries, including stress fractures, are one common reason for attrition from military training. Up to 6% of males and 18% of females undergoing IMT may sustain a stress fracture during training (Jones, Thacker, Gilchrist, Kimsey, & Sosin, 2002). Stress fractures are incomplete fractures of the bone that occur due to repeated use/overuse. The most commonly fractured sites are bones of the lower extremities, such as the tibia. Military trainees are at higher risk than their active duty counterparts: fractures are 18 times more frequent during IMT, likely due to unaccustomed, repeated physical activity. Because stress fractures are painful and treatment requires rest and unloading of the affected bone, these injuries significantly impact physical performance and military readiness. It is estimated that up to 60% of trainees who sustain a stress fracture during training will attrite from military service (Friedl, Evans, & Moran, 2008).

The etiology of stress fractures is multifactorial and includes both modifiable and nonmodifiable factors (McClung & Karl, 2010). For example, increasing age, a history of smoking, menstrual disturbances, low physical fitness, and female sex each increase the risk of stress fracture. In addition, bone structure and function, nutritional status, and genetics also modulate risk.

The two primary micronutrients that affect bone health are calcium and vitamin D. The evidence for a role of these micronutrients in skeletal health is of such magnitude that bone health outcomes were used by the US Institute of Medicine (IOM) when reviewing existing research in order to set dietary reference intakes (DRI) for calcium and vitamin D (Ross et al., 2011). Calcium is the major mineral found in the inorganic phase of bone, and vitamin D facilitates intestinal calcium absorption and bone mineralization. Vitamin D is a unique nutrient in that it can be synthesized endogenously from cholesterol precursors in response to ultraviolet B (UVB) radiation of the skin as well as consumed in the diet. Hepatic 25-hydroxylation of both endogenous and dietary vitamin D result in 25-hydroxyvitamin D (25OHD), which is the major circulating form of vitamin D. Circulating 25OHD is further hydroxylated in the kidney to produce 1,25-dihydroxyvitmain D $(1,25(OH)_2D_3)$, the active hormonal form of vitamin D. Deficiency of either calcium or vitamin D results in impaired bone mineralization, known as *osteomalacia* in adults or *rickets* in children.

A recent meta-analysis of eight studies of stress fracture in military personnel confirmed a link between circulating 25OHD, both at start of training as well as at the time of diagnosis, and stress fracture risk (Dao et al., 2015). However, the nature of this relationship differed by sex when subgroup analyses were performed. In males, 25OHD at start of training was lower in those who went on to sustain a stress fracture as compared to controls (mean difference and 95% confidence interval: -4.69 ng/mL $[-8.73, -0.65]$), whereas no difference was found in females. In contrast, serum 25OHD at time of fracture diagnosis was lower in females compared to nonfractured controls (mean difference and 95% confidence interval: -2.26 ng/mL $[-3.89, -0.63]$), while no such difference was found in males. Subsequently, another prospective trial was conducted in male Royal Marine recruits undergoing a 32-week training program (Davey et al., 2015). In this trial, 25OHD at the start of training was not different in those who sustained a fracture compared to nonfractured controls; however, baseline 25OHD less than 20 ng/mL (50 nmol), the level used by the IOM to set the DRI, was associated with a 1.6-fold increased risk of fracture. While these observational trials support a relationship between vitamin D status and injury risk, further research is needed to determine whether race- and sex-specific cutoffs exist for predicting fracture risk.

The next tier of evidence to support a protective effect of calcium and vitamin D on bone health fracture risk during IMT emanated from randomized controlled trials (RCTs) of calcium and vitamin D supplementation (Gaffney-Stomberg et al., 2014; Lappe et al., 2008). In a foundational RCT with more than 5,000 female Navy recruits, Lappe and colleagues (2008) reported a 20% reduction in stress fracture incidence in those randomized to daily calcium and vitamin D supplements as compared to placebo. This critical study indicated that a relatively low-cost nutrition intervention can reduce injury during IMT. However, this study only included females, and, as blood samples were not collected, it was not possible to determine circulating 25OHD concentrations that may have contributed to injury prevention. To address some of these limitations, Gaffney-Stomberg and colleagues conducted an RCT in males and females undergoing Army IMT. They reported that twice-daily consumption of calcium and vitamin D-fortified energy bars by males and females undergoing Army IMT resulted in greater increases in volumetric bone mineral density (vBMD) of the distal tibia compared with consumption of placebo bars (Gaffney-Stomberg et al., 2014). As vBMD is one important component of bone strength, it was concluded that greater increases in vBMD in response to calcium and vitamin D supplementation may be a mechanism for the lower injury risk observed in the study by Lappe and colleagues.

GENETIC FACTORS AND INJURY PREVENTION

While the preceding evidence clearly outlines effects of nutrition on skeletal health, twin and family studies indicate that 50–85% of the variability in BMD is heritable, while the remaining can be attributed to lifestyle factors such as nutritional status and physical activity (Peacock, Turner, Econs, & Foroud, 2002). The impact of genetics on bone is complex because genetic control of BMD and fracture risk involves common variants of many genes. These variants are commonly due to single nucleotide polymorphisms (SNPs) that may result in changes in gene expression level and/or protein function depending on the location of the SNP within the DNA. While there are some monogenic bone diseases involving rare SNPs, most of the genetic variability in BMD is polygenetic with fairly small individual contributions of many different relatively common SNPs. Over the past decade or so, several genome-wide association studies (GWAS) were conducted with tens of thousands of volunteers in order to identify loci related to BMD and fragility fractures in older adults. To date, approximately 63 loci have been reported to be associated with BMD with only 14 loci associated with fragility fracture risk, as summarized in a recent meta-analysis including data from 17 separate GWAS (Duncan et al., 2011; Estrada et al., 2012; Richards et al., 2008; Rivadeneira et al., 2009; Styrkarsdottir et al., 2009). Many of the SNPs at these loci are located in or near genes with known biological functions in bone tissue, with the strongest evidence for genes within three key pathways: (1) the RANK-RANKL-OPG pathway, which is involved in osteoclast function; (2) the mesenchymal stem cell differentiation pathway, which impacts osteoblastogenesis; and (3) the bone anabolic Wnt-signaling pathway. While BMD is still the best individual predictor of fracture risk, few of the SNPs associated with BMD were also associated with fracture risk. In addition, some genes not associated with BMD were independently associated with fracture risk. Of note, a recent report by Ho-Le and colleagues, in which a genetic risk score (GRS) was calculated as the sum of BMD-lowering loci, found that while those with higher GRS had lower femoral neck BMD, GRS explained less than 2% of the total variance in BMD (Ho-Le, Center, Eisman, Nguyen, & Nguyen, 2017). These results underscore the polygenic nature of BMD and, ultimately, fracture risk and point to potential gene–environment interactions that were not evaluated. However, despite the relatively small contribution to overall BMD variability, inclusion of the GRS in fracture prediction models improved prediction accuracy. These findings provide evidence of the need to identify genetic determinants of fracture risk—both fragility and stress fractures—in future trials.

Similar large-scale GWAS have not been conducted with stress fracture as an outcome; the limited knowledge regarding interactions between genetics and stress fracture risk has come from smaller studies using a candidate gene approach (Chatzipapas et al., 2009; Friedman, Moran, Ben-Avraham, Yanovich, & Atzmon, 2014; Valimaki et al., 2005; Varley et al., 2016; Varley et al., 2015; Yanovich et al., 2012; Zhao, Chang, Huang, & Huang, 2016). In the first exploration of this kind, the Israeli Defense Force (IDF) genotyped 454 soldiers, 171 with stress fractures and 283 with normal bone scans, for the androgen receptor gene in order to detect the number of CAG repeats (Yanovich, Milgrom, Friedman, & Moran, 2011). The authors concluded that stress fracture cases had a higher prevalence of a low number of androgen repeats (<16) as compared to controls. However, the total number of repeats varied from 6 to 31 in cases and from 11 to 32 in controls, making androgen receptor repeats analysis an insensitive and impractical tool for determining stress fracture risk. Subsequently, the IDF conducted an analysis of 17 candidate genes containing 268 SNPs. Of note, the majority of SNPs evaluated were not on the list of SNPs associated with BMD identified by prior BMD GWAS. Of the 17 genes interrogated, 9 showed significant differences between cases (n = 182 soldiers with stress fracture) and controls (n = 203 nonfractured controls); however, none of these findings remained significant after controlling for false discovery rate due to the relatively small sample size compared to the number of SNPs evaluated. Despite this limitation, the study identified SNPs in the CALCR (calcitonin receptor) and VDR (vitamin D receptor) genes which show potential for future study. Two other reports using the candidate gene approach yielded significant associations between RANK and RANKL SNPs and stress fracture in elite athletes (Varley et al., 2015) and in the P2X7 gene in a combined sample of elite athletes and IDF soldiers (Varley et al., 2016). The RANK pathway is commonly identified in BMD GWAS studies and is of likely importance for stress fracture. The P2X7 gene encodes a polymorphic purinergic receptor (P2X7R), which was previously associated with response to estrogen treatment for fragility fracture and bone mechanotransduction; it is thus another potential candidate involved in the pathophysiology of stress fracture (Li, Liu, Ke, Duncan, & Turner, 2005; Ohlendorff et al., 2007). Finally, in an attempt to perform an unbiased screen of potential genes involved in stress fracture pathogenesis, IDF researchers performed whole-exome sequencing of high-grade stress fracture cases (n = 34) and ethnically matched controls (n = 60; Friedman et al., 2014). This study identified six SNPs associated with stress fractures, none of which was identified in prior studies evaluating genetic determinants of stress fracture, BMD, fragility fracture, microarchitecture, or bone geometry.

In addition, few studies in children and adolescents have sought to determine whether genes associated with BMD and fracture risk in later life are related to BMD accrual (Medina-Gomez et al., 2012; Mitchell et al., 2015; Mitchell et al., 2016). In one such study, higher overall adult BMD GRS, Wnt signaling GRS, and fracture GRS were associated with lower BMD z-scores in children (Mitchell et al., 2016). In another, overall adult BMD GRS was associated with lower BMD, lower bone mineral content (BMC), and a reduced rate of bone accrual between 13 and 17 years of age (Warrington, Kemp, Tilling, Tobias, & Evans, 2015). As IMT is an anabolic environment where many individuals graduate the course with higher fitness levels and lean mass as compared to entry, genes involved in bone mass accrual could be important candidates to evaluate for relationships with stress fracture risk. In sum, the research on genetic contributions to stress fracture risk is limited and the data are inconsistent due at least in part to the rather limited sample sizes. Larger trials are needed to replicate existing findings from the stress fracture trials as well as to test the genetic traits identified in the larger GWAS as contributing to BMD and fragility fracture.

Since both genetics and environment contribute to bone strength and fracture, one limitation in the field is a paucity of trials assessing the relative contribution of key environmental factors, in particular nutrition and physical activity, and their interactions with genes involved in skeletal metabolism. One example of this is the VDR, as polymorphisms in this gene are known to impact BMD, stress fracture risk, and circulating 25OHD (Chatzipapas et al., 2009; Gaffney-Stomberg et al., 2016; Thakkinstian, D'Este, Eisman, Nguyen, & Attia, 2004). In a recent study in Army and Air Force recruits, VDR and vitamin D binding protein (DBP) SNPs were each independently associated with circulating 25OHD at the start of training. When a composite GRS was calculated as the sum of 25OHD-lowering alleles in these SNPs, this, too, was associated with 25OHD status as well as with change in 25OHD in response to vitamin D intake during training (Gaffney-Stomberg et al., 2016). This was the first study to detect a gene-by-diet interaction in military recruits, and results suggested that those at the greatest risk required the highest intake of vitamin D (approximately twice the DRI for this age group) in order to improve 25OHD status. Importantly, these results indicate that a nutrition intervention targeted to those at highest risk could potentially overcome the genetic predisposition toward lower 25OHD status. However, whether this GRS is independently associated with measures of bone strength, such as BMD or fracture risk, was not evaluated. Thus the functional consequence of this GRS on bone tissue and injury risk is a critical piece of evidence that is needed before GRS could be considered for use as a screening tool for preventing injury in military personnel.

APPLICATION TO HUMAN PERFORMANCE OPTIMIZATION

As detailed throughout this chapter, nutrition and genetic factors contribute significantly to cognitive and physical performance during military training and operations. Evidence collected through studies in the military environment has significant application to human performance optimization in both military personnel during training and operations and to civilian populations engaging in athletics and physically demanding occupations.

Studies assessing the effects of undernutrition on cognition indicate that short periods of underfeeding (up to 2 days) may have minimal impact on cognitive performance and mood, although mood becomes significantly degraded as negative energy balance becomes severe due to the effects of increased physical activity. These findings indicate that short-term underfeeding may not degrade cognitive performance during tasks requiring minimal physical activity. However, as the duration and energy requirements of particular tasks increase, the importance of providing nutritional sustainment becomes paramount. These findings have implications for the planning of military training and operations as command staff and leadership work to minimize logistical demands while optimizing performance. Although limited in scope, studies assessing the effects of single nutrients, such as carbohydrate and tyrosine, may hold promise for tailored nutritional solutions for individuals enduring demanding occupational activities. An applied solution may be the provision of minimal footprint eat-on-the-go items composed of nutritional elements tailored to the demands of short-term tasks followed by full replenishment of energy and nutrient needs during periods of recovery, such that the loss of lean body mass and the development of nutritional deficiencies may be avoided.

Evidence indicates that particular nutrients are of importance for the optimization of physical performance and avoidance of injury during longer term military or athletic training. Female military personnel and athletes are at risk of poor iron status due to increased nutritional requirements and declines that may occur due to physical training. Solutions include improved nutritional education highlighting the importance of consuming iron-rich foods. In some cases, consumption of iron-fortified foods or iron-containing multivitamins may be recommended to avoid ID and IDA. As the inflammatory response to physical activity, particularly unaccustomed activity, appears to affect the absorption of iron and other nutrients, future research should focus on the potential benefits of attenuating the inflammatory response to activity, including improved methods of introducing unaccustomed activities. Similarly, future research may assess the efficacy of anti-inflammatory diets or pharmacologics for the prevention of declines in nutritional status.

Calcium and vitamin D are essential for the optimization of bone health and the prevention of stress fracture in military personnel and athletes. Evidence indicates that calcium and vitamin D requirements may be greater in individuals engaging in unaccustomed activities, such as marching with a load, or in repeated activities, such as distance running. Populations exposed to such activities should consider increased consumption of these nutrients, including the potential use of dietary supplements or fortified foods at doses within safe limits as designated by the IOM. Emerging scientific evidence suggests that genetic factors contribute significantly to the absorption of nutrients and injury risk. Although the study of nutrient–gene interactions is at an early stage, the use of SNPs and GRS as potential tools for providing tailored, personalized solutions for the optimization of human performance and avoidance of injury holds great promise for the future. A potential application of such technologies may be the rapid assessment of genetic profiles and propensity for injury, coupled with tailored solutions to meet individual nutritional needs.

CONCLUSION

Military training and operations result in exposure to a multistressor environment. Many of these stressors, including caloric deficit, unaccustomed physical activity, and increased energy expenditure, have profound effects on cognitive and physical performance. This chapter includes a review of relevant evidence gleaned from a range of environments detailing the associations among nutrition, genetic factors, and cognitive and physical performance. Energy deficit and the relative contribution of single nutrients, such as carbohydrate, tyrosine, iron, calcium, and vitamin D, have each been linked to performance outcomes. Finally, the emerging role of nutrient–gene interactions in maintaining nutrient homeostasis and injury prevention has been highlighted. In summary, nutrition and genetic factors hold great promise as intervention targets for the future development of tailored solutions to optimize human performance during both military and occupationally demanding tasks.

REFERENCES

Ashenden, M. J., Martin, D. T., Dobson, G. P., Mackintosh, C., & Hahn, A. G. (1998). Serum ferritin and anemia in trained female athletes. *International Journal of Sport Nutrition and Exercise Metabolism, 8*(3), 223–229.

Blum, S. M., Sherman, A. R., & Boileau, R. A. (1986). The effects of fitness-type exercise on iron status in adult women. *The American Journal of Clinical Nutrition, 43*(3), 456–463.

Chatzipapas, C., Boikos, S., Drosos, G. I., Kazakos, K., Tripsianis, G., Serbis, A.,... Stratakis, C. A. (2009). Polymorphisms of the vitamin D receptor gene and stress fractures. *Hormone and Metabolic Research, 41*(8), 635–640. doi:10.1055/s-0029–1216375

Dao, D., Sodhi, S., Tabasinejad, R., Peterson, D., Ayeni, O. R., Bhandari, M., & Farrokhyar, F. (2015). Serum 25-Hydroxyvitamin D levels and stress fractures in military personnel: A systematic review and meta-analysis. *The American Journal of Sports Medicine, 43*(8), 2064–2072. doi:10.1177/0363546514555971

Davey, T., Lanham-New, S. A., Shaw, A. M., Hale, B., Cobley, R., Berry, J. L.,... Fallowfield, J. L. (2015). Low serum 25-hydroxyvitamin D is associated with increased risk of stress fracture during Royal Marine recruit training. *Osteoporosis International, 27*(1), 171–179. doi:10.1007/s00198-015-3228-5

Duncan, E. L., Danoy, P., Kemp, J. P., Leo, P. J., McCloskey, E., Nicholson, G. C.,... Brown, M. A. (2011). Genome-wide association study using extreme truncate selection identifies novel genes affecting bone mineral density and fracture risk. *PLoS Genetics, 7*(4), e1001372. doi:10.1371/journal.pgen.1001372

Estrada, K., Styrkarsdottir, U., Evangelou, E., Hsu, Y. H., Duncan, E. L., Ntzani, E. E.,... Rivadeneira, F. (2012). Genome-wide meta-analysis identifies 56 bone mineral density loci and reveals 14 loci associated with risk of fracture. *Nature Genetics, 44*(5), 491–501. doi:10.1038/ng.2249

Friedl, K. E., Evans, R. K., & Moran, D. S. (2008). Stress fracture and military medical readiness: Bridging basic and applied research. *Medicine & Science in Sports & Exercise, 40*(11 Suppl), S609–622. doi:10.1249/MSS.0b013e3181892d53

Friedman, E., Moran, D. S., Ben-Avraham, D., Yanovich, R., & Atzmon, G. (2014). Novel candidate genes putatively involved in stress fracture predisposition detected by whole-exome sequencing. *Genetics Research, 96*, e004. doi:10.1017/S001667231400007X

Gaffney-Stomberg, E., Lutz, L. J., Rood, J. C., Cable, S. J., Pasiakos, S. M., Young, A. J., & McClung, J. P. (2014). Calcium and vitamin D supplementation maintains parathyroid hormone and improves bone density during initial military training: A randomized, double-blind, placebo controlled trial. *Bone, 68*, 46–56. doi:10.1016/j.bone.2014.08.002

Gaffney-Stomberg, E., Lutz, L. J., Shcherbina, A., Ricke, D. O., Petrovick, M., Cropper, T. L.,... McClung, J. P. (2016). Association between single gene polymorphisms and bone biomarkers and response to calcium and vitamin D supplementation in young adults undergoing military training. *Journal of Bone and Mineral Research, 32*(3), 498–507. doi:10.1002/jbmr.3008

Gardner, G. W., Edgerton, V. R., Senewiratne, B., Barnard, R. J., & Ohira, Y. (1977). Physical work capacity and metabolic stress in subjects with iron deficiency anemia. *The American Journal of Clinical Nutrition, 30*(6), 910–917.

Guezennec, C. Y., Satabin, P., Legrand, H., & Bigard, A. X. (1994). Physical performance and metabolic changes induced by combined prolonged exercise and different energy intakes in humans. *European Journal of Applied Physiology and Occupational Physiology, 68*(6), 525–530.

Harvey, L. J., Armah, C. N., Dainty, J. R., Foxall, R. J., John Lewis, D., Langford, N. J., & Fairweather-Tait, S. J. (2005). Impact of menstrual blood loss and diet on iron deficiency among women in the UK. *British Journal of Nutrition, 94*(4), 557–564.

Haslam, D. R. (1984). The military performance of soldiers in sustained operations. *Aviation, Space, and Environmental Medicine, 55*(3), 216–221.

Hauret, K. G., Jones, B. H., Bullock, S. H., Canham-Chervak, M., & Canada, S. (2010). Musculoskeletal injuries description of an under-recognized injury problem among military personnel. *American Journal of Preventive Medicine, 38*(1 Suppl), S61–70. doi:10.1016/j.amepre.2009.10.021

Ho-Le, T. P., Center, J. R., Eisman, J. A., Nguyen, H. T., & Nguyen, T. V. (2017). Prediction of bone mineral density and fragility fracture by genetic profiling. *Journal of Bone and Mineral Research, 32*(2), 285–293. doi:10.1002/jbmr.2998

Jones, B. H., Thacker, S. B., Gilchrist, J., Kimsey, C. D., Jr., & Sosin, D. M. (2002). Prevention of lower extremity stress fractures in athletes and soldiers: A systematic review. *Epidemiologic Reviews, 24*(2), 228–247.

Keys, A. (1950). The residues of malnutrition and starvation. *Science, 112*(2909), 371–373.

Lappe, J., Cullen, D., Haynatzki, G., Recker, R., Ahlf, R., & Thompson, K. (2008). Calcium and vitamin d supplementation decreases incidence of stress fractures in female navy recruits. *Journal of Bone and Mineral Research, 23*(5), 741–749. doi:10.1359/jbmr.080102

Li, J., Liu, D., Ke, H. Z., Duncan, R. L., & Turner, C. H. (2005). The P2X7 nucleotide receptor mediates skeletal mechanotransduction. *Journal of Biological Chemistry, 280*(52), 42952–42959. doi:10.1074/jbc.M506415200

Lieberman, H. R., Bathalon, G. P., Falco, C. M., Kramer, F. M., Morgan, C. A., 3rd, & Niro, P. (2005). Severe decrements in cognition function and mood induced by sleep loss, heat, dehydration, and undernutrition during simulated combat. *Biological Psychiatry, 57*(4), 422–429. doi:10.1016/j.biopsych.2004.11.014

Lieberman, H. R., Bathalon, G. P., Falco, C. M., Morgan, C. A., 3rd, Niro, P. J., & Tharion, W. J. (2005). The fog of war: Decrements in cognitive performance and mood associated with combat-like stress. *Aviation, Space, and Environmental Medicine, 76*(7 Suppl), C7–14.

Lieberman, H. R., Bukhari, A. S., Caldwell, J. A., Wilson, M. A., Mahoney, C. R., Pasiakos, S. M., . . . Smith, T. J. (2017). Two days of calorie deprivation induced by underfeeding and aerobic exercise degrades mood and lowers interstitial glucose but does not impair cognitive function in young adults. *The Journal of Nutrition, 147*(1), 110–116. doi:10.3945/jn.116.238246

Lieberman, H. R., Caruso, C. M., Niro, P. J., Adam, G. E., Kellogg, M. D., Nindl, B. C., & Kramer, F. M. (2008). A double-blind, placebo-controlled test of 2 d of calorie deprivation: Effects on cognition, activity, sleep, and interstitial glucose concentrations. *The American Journal of Clinical Nutrition, 88*(3), 667–676.

Lieberman, H. R., Farina, E. K., Caldwell, J., Williams, K. W., Thompson, L. A., Niro, P. J., . . . McClung, J. P. (2016). Cognitive function, stress hormones, heart rate and nutritional status during simulated captivity in military survival training. *Physiology & Behavior, 165*, 86–97. doi:10.1016/j.physbeh.2016.06.037

Lieberman, H. R., Thompson, L. A., Caruso, C. M., Niro, P. J., Mahoney, C. R., McClung, J. P., & Caron, G. R. (2015). The catecholamine neurotransmitter precursor tyrosine increases anger during exposure to severe psychological stress. *Psychopharmacology, 232*(5), 943–951. doi:10.1007/s00213-014-3727-7

McClung, J. P., & Karl, J. P. (2010). Vitamin D and stress fracture: The contribution of vitamin D receptor gene polymorphisms. *Nutrition Reviews, 68*(6), 365–369. doi:10.1111/j.1753-4887.2010.00295.x

McClung, J. P., Karl, J. P., Cable, S. J., Williams, K. W., Nindl, B. C., Young, A. J., & Lieberman, H. R. (2009). Randomized, double-blind, placebo-controlled trial of iron supplementation in female soldiers during military training: Effects on iron status, physical performance, and mood. *The American Journal of Clinical Nutrition, 90*(1), 124–131. doi:ajcn.2009.27774

McClung, J. P., Karl, J. P., Cable, S. J., Williams, K. W., Young, A. J., & Lieberman, H. R. (2009). Longitudinal decrements in iron status during military training in female soldiers. *British Journal of Nutrition, 102*(4), 605–609. doi:S0007114509220873

Medina-Gomez, C., Kemp, J. P., Estrada, K., Eriksson, J., Liu, J., Reppe, S., . . . Rivadeneira, F. (2012). Meta-analysis of genome-wide scans for total body BMD in children and adults reveals allelic heterogeneity and age-specific effects at the WNT16 locus. *PLoS Genetics, 8*(7), e1002718. doi:10.1371/journal.pgen.1002718

Mitchell, J. A., Chesi, A., Elci, O., McCormack, S. E., Kalkwarf, H. J., Lappe, J. M., . . . Grant, S. F. (2015). Genetics of bone mass in childhood and adolescence: Effects of sex and maturation interactions. *Journal of Bone and Mineral Research, 30*(9), 1676–1683. doi:10.1002/jbmr.2508

Mitchell, J. A., Chesi, A., Elci, O., McCormack, S. E., Roy, S. M., Kalkwarf, H. J., . . . Zemel, B. S. (2016). Genetic risk scores implicated in adult bone fragility associate with pediatric bone density. *Journal of Bone and Mineral Research, 31*(4), 789–795. doi:10.1002/jbmr.2744

Morgan, C. A., 3rd, Hazlett, G., Southwick, S., Rasmusson, A., & Lieberman, H. R. (2009). Effect of carbohydrate administration on recovery from stress-induced deficits in cognitive function: A double-blind, placebo-controlled study of soldiers exposed to survival school stress. *Military Medicine, 174*(2), 132–138.

Nindl, B. C., Barnes, B. R., Alemany, J. A., Frykman, P. N., Shippee, R. L., & Friedl, K. E. (2007). Physiological consequences of US Army Ranger training. *Medicine & Science in Sports & Exercise, 39*(8), 1380–1387. doi:10.1249/MSS.0b013e318067e2f7

Ohlendorff, S. D., Tofteng, C. L., Jensen, J. E., Petersen, S., Civitelli, R., Fenger, M., . . . Jorgensen, N. R. (2007). Single nucleotide polymorphisms in the P2X7 gene are associated to fracture risk and to effect of estrogen treatment. *Pharmacogenetics and Genomics, 17*(7), 555–567. doi:10.1097/FPC.0b013e3280951625

Opstad, P. K., Ekanger, R., Nummestad, M., & Raabe, N. (1978). Performance, mood, and clinical symptoms in men exposed to prolonged, severe physical work and sleep deprivation. *Aviation, Space, and Environmental Medicine, 49*(9), 1065–1073.

Pasiakos, S. M., Margolis, L. M., Murphy, N. E., McClung, H. L., Martini, S., Gundersen, Y., . . . McClung, J. P. (2016). Effects of exercise mode, energy, and macronutrient interventions on inflammation during military training. *Physiological Reports, 4*(11). doi:10.14814/phy2.12820

Peacock, M., Turner, C. H., Econs, M. J., & Foroud, T. (2002). Genetics of osteoporosis. *Endocrine Reviews, 23*(3), 303–326. doi:10.1210/edrv.23.3.0464

Richards, J. B., Rivadeneira, F., Inouye, M., Pastinen, T. M., Soranzo, N., Wilson, S. G., . . . Spector, T. D. (2008). Bone mineral density, osteoporosis, and osteoporotic fractures: A genome-wide association study. *Lancet, 371*(9623), 1505–1512. doi:10.1016/S0140-6736(08)60599-1

Rivadeneira, F., Styrkarsdottir, U., Estrada, K., Halldorsson, B. V., Hsu, Y. H., Richards, J. B., . . . Uitterlinden, A. G. [for the Genetic Factors for Osteoporosis (GEFOS) Consortium]. (2009). Twenty bone-mineral-density loci identified by large-scale meta-analysis of genome-wide association studies. *Nature Genetics, 41*(11), 1199–1206. doi:10.1038/ng.446

Ross, A. C., Manson, J. E., Abrams, S. A., Aloia, J. F., Brannon, P. M., Clinton, S. K., . . . Shapses, S. A. (2011). The 2011 report on dietary reference intakes for calcium and vitamin D from the Institute of Medicine: What clinicians need to know. *The Journal of Clinical Endocrinology & Metabolism, 96*(1), 53–58. doi:jc.2010-2704

Simpson, K., Redmond, J. E., Cohen, B. S., Hendrickson, N. R., Spiering, B. A., Steelman, R., . . . Sharp, M. A. (2013, Oct-Dec). Quantification of physical activity performed during US Army Basic Combat Training. *US Army Medical Department Journal*, 55–65.

Smith, T. J., Wilson, M. A., Karl, J. P., Austin, K., Bukhari, A., Pasiakos, S. M., . . . Lieberman, H. R. (2016). Interstitial glucose concentrations and hypoglycemia during 2 days of caloric deficit and sustained exercise: A double-blind, placebo-controlled trial. *Journal of Applied Physiology, 121*(5), 1208–1216. doi:10.1152/japplphysiol.00432.2016

Styrkarsdottir, U., Halldorsson, B. V., Gretarsdottir, S., Gudbjartsson, D. F., Walters, G. B., Ingvarsson, T., . . . Stefansson, K. (2009). New sequence variants associated with bone mineral density. *Nature Genetics, 41*(1), 15–17. doi:10.1038/ng.284

Thakkinstian, A., D'Este, C., Eisman, J., Nguyen, T., & Attia, J. (2004). Meta-analysis of molecular association studies: Vitamin D receptor gene polymorphisms and BMD as a case study. *Journal of Bone and Mineral Research, 19*(3), 419–428. doi:10.1359/JBMR.0301265

Tharion, W. J., Lieberman, H. R., Montain, S. J., Young, A. J., Baker-Fulco, C. J., Delany, J. P., & Hoyt, R. W. (2005). Energy requirements of military personnel. *Appetite, 44*(1), 47–65. doi:10.1016/j.appet.2003.11.010

Tufts, D. A., Haas, J. D., Beard, J. L., & Spielvogel, H. (1985). Distribution of hemoglobin and functional consequences of anemia in adult males at high altitude. *The American Journal of Clinical Nutrition, 42*(1), 1–11.

Valimaki, V. V., Alfthan, H., Lehmuskallio, E., Loyttyniemi, E., Sahi, T., Suominen, H., & Valimaki, M. J. (2005). Risk factors for clinical stress fractures in male military recruits: A prospective cohort study. *Bone, 37*(2), 267–273. doi:S8756-3282(05)00152-3

Varley, I., Greeves, J. P., Sale, C., Friedman, E., Moran, D. S., Yanovich, R., . . . Gallagher, J. A. (2016). Functional polymorphisms in the P2X7 receptor gene are associated with stress fracture injury. *Purinergic Signalling, 12*(1), 103–113. doi:10.1007/s11302-016-9495-6

Varley, I., Hughes, D. C., Greeves, J. P., Stellingwerff, T., Ranson, C., Fraser, W. D., & Sale, C. (2015). RANK/RANKL/OPG pathway: Genetic associations with stress fracture period prevalence in elite athletes. *Bone, 71*, 131–136. doi:10.1016/j.bone.2014.10.004

Warrington, N. M., Kemp, J. P., Tilling, K., Tobias, J. H., & Evans, D. M. (2015). Genetic variants in adult bone mineral density and fracture risk genes are associated with the rate of bone mineral density acquisition in adolescence. *Human Molecular Genetics, 24*(14), 4158–4166. doi:10.1093/hmg/ddv143

Yanovich, R., Friedman, E., Milgrom, R., Oberman, B., Freedman, L., & Moran, D. S. (2012). Candidate gene analysis in israeli soldiers with stress fractures. *Journal of Sports Science and Medicine, 11*(1), 147–155.

Yanovich, R., Karl, J. P., Yanovich, E., Lutz, L. J., Williams, K. W., Cable, S. J., ... McClung, J. P. (2015, Apr-Jun). Effects of basic combat training on iron status in male and female soldiers: A comparative study. *US Army Medical Department Journal*, 67–73.

Yanovich, R., Milgrom, R., Friedman, E., & Moran, D. S. (2011). Androgen receptor CAG repeat size is associated with stress fracture risk: A pilot study. *Clinical Orthopaedics and Related Research, 469*(10), 2925–2931. doi:10.1007/s11999-011-1805-2

Zhao, L., Chang, Q., Huang, T., & Huang, C. (2016). Prospective cohort study of the risk factors for stress fractures in Chinese male infantry recruits. *The Journal of International Medical Research, 44*(4), 787–795. doi:10.1177/0300060516639751

4

Molecular and Cellular Aspects of Major Depressive Disorder

REVATHY U. CHOTTEKALAPANDA, PAUL GREENGARD, AND YOTAM SAGI*

INTRODUCTION

Over the past two decades, major depressive disorder (MDD) has become a leading cause of disability worldwide (Lopez & Murray, 1998). The economic burden of depression was estimated to be US$83.1 billion in 2000 (Greenberg et al., 2003). MDD is the most common psychiatric illness, with high levels of morbidity and mortality. It is estimated that 10–15% of the general population will experience clinical depression during their lifetime (Tsuang, Taylor, & Faraone, 2004), and 5% of men and 9% of women will experience a depressive disorder in a given year, according to the World Health Organization (Kessler, Chiu, Demler, Merikangas, & Walters, 2005).

Depression is often associated with chronic illnesses or other mood disorders such as comorbid anxiety and posttraumatic stress disorder (PTSD; Mitchell, Vaze, & Rao, 2009). Both PTSD and traumatic brain injury (TBI) are associated with MDD and cognitive impairment (Krishnan & Nestler, 2010). Symptoms of MDD include "core" and "non-core" symptoms. "Depressed mood" and "loss of interest or pleasure in nearly all activities" are core features of a major depressive episode. Other symptoms include fatigue, sleep disturbance, anxiety, and neurocognitive and sexual dysfunction. When left untreated, these symptoms may lead to suicidal thoughts and attempts (Kupfer, Frank, & Phillips, 2012). The diagnosis of MDD is only based on self-report. Physiological biomarker or diagnostic measures have not been well established. Although meta-analyses concluded that general practitioners correctly exclude depression in most individuals who are not depressed, over-detections (false positives) can outnumber missed cases, whereas insufficient self-report increases the measures of undiagnosed subjects. The presence of comorbidities, including anxiety or PTSD with depression, contributes to the difficulties in diagnosis and treatment of the disease (Das-Munshi et al., 2008; Kessler et al., 2005; Mitchell et al., 2009), whereas special populations, including

*Revathy U. Chottekalapanda (rchottekal@rockefeller.edu), Paul Greengard (greengard@rockefeller.edu), Yotam Sagi (ysagi@rockefeller.edu).

soldiers, limit self-report and may require additional outreach and screening to decrease suicidal ideation and attempts (Ramsawh et al., 2014).

The etiology of MDD remains unknown. Genetic factors may play important roles in the development of MDD, as indicated in family, twin, and adoption studies. Twin studies suggest a heritability of 40–50%, and family studies indicate a two- to threefold increase in lifetime risk of developing MDD among first-degree relatives. This degree of familial aggregation, coupled with the high heritability from twin studies, generated early optimism that molecular genetic techniques would reveal genes of substantial influence on MDD risk (Lohoff, 2010). However, as with other complex psychiatric disorders, recent genetic studies revealed that there is not a universal susceptibility gene for MDD. It can also be expected that multiple genes with small effect sizes contribute to depression. Genetic studies have been extensively used recently to identify genetic markers. A recent study revealed that synapse-related as well as histone methylation and immune and neuronal signaling pathways are implicated in the susceptibility for MDD (Psychiatric Genomics Consortium, 2015). However, recent genome-wide association studies from larger cohorts have failed to reproduce these initial results (Psychiatric Genomics Consortium, 2015; Tansey et al., 2012). Several candidate genes initially showed promising preliminary results, including the genes encoding the serotonin receptor 5-HT2A (*HTR2A*), norepinephrine transporter gene (*SLC6A2*), glucocorticoid receptor (*NR3C1*), and the brain-derived neurotrophic factor (*BDNF*). Variation in genes encoding HTR2A, SLC6A2, and NR3C1 was associated with outcome of antidepressant treatment, whereas variation in the BDNF gene influences susceptibility to depression (McMahon et al., 2006; Uher et al., 2009; Hashimoto, 2010). This latter finding may be of particular importance as stress and immune response seem to be highly linked to the pathophysiology of MDD. Accumulating data point to a role for pro- and anti-inflammatory molecules, including BDNF and other cytokines, in the etiology of MDD and for antidepressant response. Correlation studies associate increased blood concentrations of pro-inflammatory cytokines with depression severity (Howren, Lamkin, & Suls, 2009). Furthermore, inflammation markers in the periphery were also found to be strongly associated with nonresponsiveness to antidepressant treatment (Cattaneo et al., 2013).

Further insight into the neuropathology of MDD is derived from postmortem studies which identified subtle differences, including smaller neuronal size, fewer glial cells, shorter dendrites, and lower levels of trophic factors in cortical and hippocampal regions (Hercher, Turecki, & Mechawar, 2009; Karege et al., 2005; Soetanto et al., 2010). These studies have helped to formulate a "glutamatergic hypothesis of depression" which is grossly simplistic and only fuels inaccurate public misconceptions of depression's "chemical imbalance" since more than one-half of all neurons in the brain utilize glutamate as a neurotransmitter. An important insight gained from everyday clinical practice is the observation that monoamine reuptake inhibitors and other modulators of monoaminergic function improve symptoms in about 50% of depressed patients and produce a remission in 30–40% of patients (Trivedi et al., 2006). Since monoamine enhancers improve depressive symptoms, it was suggested that depression is caused by deficits in monoaminergic transmission. This "monoamine hypothesis" continues to be a prominent preoccupation in the field.

REVIEW AND ANALYSIS

Current Therapeutic Strategies and Classification of Antidepressant Drug Therapies

As discussed, MDD is characterized by symptoms of emotional, motivational, cognitive, and physiological domains, which make it a complex disease to treat. Pharmacotherapy and manual-based psychotherapy are both effective treatments for unipolar depression, either as monotherapies or in combination. Interpersonal psychotherapy alone or in combination with pharmacotherapy is effective for the acute treatment of depression (Cuijpers, Dekker, Hollon, & Andersson, 2009; Cuijpers, van Straten, van Oppen, & Andersson, 2008). Patients with psychotic depression (presence of delusions or hallucinations) are often difficult to treat and need several interventions. Although new pharmacological strategies are being tested, electroconvulsive therapy is frequently used and is an effective treatment (Kupfer et al., 2012). The drugs approved by the US Food and Drug Administration (FDA) that effectively improve depressive symptoms for MDD are monoamine enhancers (refer to Table 4.1).

Among antidepressants, selective serotonin reuptake inhibitors (SSRIs) that increase synaptic transmission at serotonergic synapses are the most clinically effective antidepressants for the treatment of MDD (Rush et al., 2004). The large Sequenced Treatment Alternatives to Relieve Depression (STAR*D) study, which enrolled 4,041 adult outpatients with MDD, found that SSRI treatment response and remission rates were 48.6% and 36.8%, respectively. It is therefore estimated that fewer than 50% of depressed patients are responsive to currently available antidepressant treatments (Rush et al., 2006). Taken together, the body of evidence indicates that currently available treatments for depression are modestly effective for many patients and are unfortunately ineffective for a substantial proportion of patients.

The Link Between the Molecule p11, Serotonin Signaling, and MDD

p11 is a member of the S100 proteins, which have no known enzymatic activity and exert their intracellular effects via interaction with and regulation of the activity of other proteins, termed *target proteins*. This interaction between S100 members and their targets is mediated in both a calcium-dependent and -independent manner (Zimmer, Wright Sadosky, & Weber, 2003). Some of the downstream targets of p11, which were identified by the Greengard laboratory at Rockefeller University and by other groups, include ion channels and metabotropic receptors (Donier, Rugiero, Okuse, & Wood, 2005; Kilisch, Lytovchenko, Schwappach, Renigunta, & Daut, 2015; Lee et al., 2015; Svenningsson et al., 2006). S100 binding sites on target proteins are limited to only a few target proteins; annexins (Oh et al., 2013); the

Table 4.1 CLASSES OF ANTIDEPRESSANTS APPROVED BY THE US FOOD AND DRUG
ADMINISTRATION (FDA)

Class	Drugs	Proposed mechanism of action	Efficacy/Tolerability
Selective serotonin reuptake inhibitors	Citalopram Escitaloprm Fluoxetine Fluvoxamine Paroxetine Sertaline	Selective inhibition of reuptake of serotonin	Modest efficacy, have side effects; usually are first choice
Tricyclic antidepressants	Amitrptyline Desipramine Imipramine Maprotyline Nortripytiline	Inhibition of reuptake of serotonin, noradrenaline and dopamine	Modest efficacy and pronounced side effects
Norepinephrine-dopamine reuptake inhibitor	Bupropion	Inhibition of reuptake of noradrenaline and dopamine	Modest efficacy; side effects include risk of seizures at high doses
Serotonin modulators	Nefazodone Trazodone	Primarily antagonizes 5-HT2R	Low efficacy and fewer side effects
Serotonin - Norepinephrine reuptake inhibitors	Desvenlafaxine Duloxetine Venlafaxine	Inhibition of reuptake of serotonin and noradrenaline	Low efficacy; side effects include liver failure and may increase blood pressure (duloxetine)
Noradrenergic and specific serotonergic modulator	Mirtazapine	Primarily antagonizes α2R and 5-HT2cR	Low efficacy and higher risk of weight gain
Serotonin reuptake inhibitor and 5-HT1A partial agonist	Vilazodone	Inhibition of reuptake of serotonin and acts as a partial agonist of the 5-HT1A receptor	Low efficacy and fewer side effects

actin-binding protein, CapZ (Ivanenkov, Jamieson, Gruenstein, & Dimlich, 1995); and myoD (Baudier et al., 1995). Most S100 family members bind four ions of free calcium per dimer (two calcium ions per monomer); each calcium molecule binds to a motif called EF-hand. Importantly, p11 is the exception of the S100 protein family due to alterations in both EF hands that render it incapable of binding calcium (Gerke & Weber, 1985). Another major difference between p11 and all other S100 members lies in the cellular and molecular mechanisms by which their gene expression is regulated during depression and antidepressant responses (Anisman, Du, et al., 2008; Svenningsson et al., 2006; Warner-Schmidt et al., 2010). The increase in p11 levels during antidepressant treatment appears to enable it to interact with its target proteins, induce their shuttling to the cell membrane, and promote their function.

To understand the role of the serotonergic system in depression, the Greengard laboratory has studied serotonin (5-HT) receptor signaling and has identified several molecular mechanisms underlying this disorder. Recently, p11 (the protein product of the *S100A10* gene) was found to be an important factor mediating antidepressant responses and depression-like states (Svenningsson et al., 2006), making it a possible therapeutic and a diagnostic target for MDD and for cognitive impairment. p11 is an adaptor protein that is highly expressed in the central nervous system (CNS) (Egeland, Warner-Schmidt, Greengard, & Svenningsson, 2011). The distribution of p11 mRNA in the brain resembled that of 5-HT1B receptor mRNA (Svenningsson et al., 2006). p11 regulates serotonin signaling by binding to serotonin receptors 1B, 1D, and 4 and stabilizing the localization of these receptors at the cell surface (Svenningsson et al., 2006; Warner-Schmidt et al., 2009).

Studies in cell lines have shown that overexpression of p11 leads to an enhanced number of 5-HT1B receptors at the cell surface. For example, an experiment with COS-7 cells found a twofold increase in the level of the 5HT-1B receptors in the cell surface following transfection with p11. Chronic antidepressant treatment, electroconvulsive therapy, and BDNF treatment all result in increased p11 expression in the cerebral cortex (Svenningsson et al., 2006; Warner-Schmidt et al., 2010). To study the interdependence of depressive states and p11 levels, transgenic mice with doxycycline-regulatable overexpression of p11 under the calcium/calmodulin-dependent protein kinase II (CamKII) promoter were generated. Mice overexpressing p11 were generally hyperactive and acted as if they were treated with antidepressants (Svenningsson et al., 2006). These mice had increased functional 5-HT1B receptors in the substantia nigra and exhibited reduced thigmotaxis (an index of anxiety-related distress) and increased horizontal activity in the open-field test. They also showed a decreased immobility in the tail suspension test (an index of a depression-like state). These results prove the interdependence between p11 expression and depressive-like states. Decreased p11 levels were found in the cortex of MDD patients, suicide victims, and in a mouse model of depression (Anisman, Du et al., 2008; Svenningsson et al., 2006). Importantly, mice lacking p11 exhibit depressive-like behaviors, increased anxiety, and a blunted behavioral response to antidepressant treatment (Svenningsson et al., 2006; Warner-Schmidt et al., 2009). p11 knockout mice have reduced responsiveness to stimulation of 5-HT1B receptors in biochemical and electrophysiological tests, as well as to the behavioral action of imipramine in the tail suspension test. Increased p11 expression (e.g., induced by antidepressant therapies) up-regulates the number of 5-HT1B receptors and their activity at the cell membrane, increasing serotonergic neurotransmission and increasing antidepressant efficacy. Decreased p11 expression correlates with a reduced number of 5-HT1B receptors at the cell surface, decreasing serotonergic neurotransmission and leading to depression-like symptomatology. Together, these studies suggest a relationship among p11, serotonin, 5-HT1B receptors, and depression-like states.

Cell Type-Specific Expression of p11 in the Central Nervous System

Our understanding of the current pathogenesis and treatments for depression and the development of more specific therapies is limited by the complexity of the circuits controlling mood and the distributed actions of antidepressants. Although the therapeutic efficacy of antidepressant treatment is correlated with increases in cortical activity, the cell types mediating their action remain unknown. Furthermore, it is crucial that we determine which neuronal cell types regulate depressive-like behaviors or antidepressive treatment to eventually develop highly targeted antidepressants that could be both faster acting and with fewer off-site effects. We observed that p11 expression is enriched in the layer 5a pyramidal neurons of the prefrontal cortex (PFC), in mossy and basket interneuronal populations in the hippocampus, and in the cholinergic interneurons in the nucleus accumbens (NAc) as shown in Figure 4.1. Using mice in which p11 was selectively depleted from a defined group of neurons, we have found that depressive-like behavior (anhedonia) is

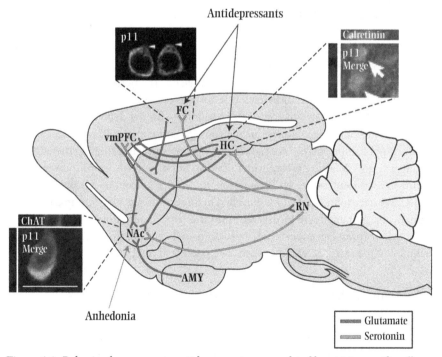

Figure 4.1 Behavioral responses to antidepressants are regulated by p11 in specific cells types in distinct brain regions. p11 in cholinergic interneurons of the nucleus accumbens (NAc, expressing the protein ChAT) contributes to experience of pleasure, whereas neurons lacking p11 cause anhedonia, a core symptom of MDD. p11-expressing cells in the hippocampus (HC) and the layer 5a of the frontal cortex (FC) contribute to antidepressant efficacy. Also shown: AMY: amygdala; vmPFC, ventral medial prefrontal cortex; serotonergic neurons of the dorsal raphe nucleus (RN).
Image courtesy of the authors.

encoded in a subtype of neurons while the response to antidepressants is mediated by another subtype (Figure 4.1).

Recent advances in mouse genetics enable us to manipulate the expression levels of genes in two principal fashions: global and selective. *Global* or *constitutive knockout* of a gene refers to an animal in which a specific gene is deleted from all somatic cells of the body. A *selective* or *conditional knockout* of a gene refers to an animal in which a gene is deleted only in a specific subset of cells with a common function and defined gene expression characteristics. While constitutive deletion of p11 from all cells result in a depressed phenotype and a failure to respond to antidepressants, mice with a selective deletion of p11 from cholinergic neurons of the subcortical nucleus accumbens (NAc) showed a depressed phenotype but responded normally to antidepressant therapy. We have found that although the basal level of p11 in the NAc of mice is relatively low, p11 is exceptionally enriched in cholinergic neurons. Remarkably, the p11 levels in human brains showed an identical expression pattern, suggesting that vulnerability to depression-like behavior is conserved in humans. Importantly, selective restoration of p11 to cholinergic neurons of the NAc restores normal behavior to p11 knockout mice (Warner-Schmidt et al., 2012).

In contrast to the NAc, mice in which p11 is specifically removed from the projecting neurons in the layer 5a of the cerebral cortex manifest a blunted response to antidepressants. In several cortical areas including the motor, sensory, and visual cortices, we found that p11 expression is restricted to a subpopulation of pyramidal neurons localized to layer 5a. While antidepressant therapy elevates the levels of p11 in this brain area, depletion of p11 abolishes the behavioral effect of these drugs. Importantly, the basal behavior of cortical-depleted p11 mice is normal, in contrast to the depressive-like phenotype in mice with the depletion of p11 in the entire body or only from cholinergic neurons (Schmidt et al., 2012).

The hippocampus plays a central role in cognition and in mediating the effects of antidepressants. We have recently identified an important role for p11 in regulating neurogenesis, depression, and cognition in the hippocampus (Eriksson et al., 2013). We have found that p11 is enriched in three groups of hippocampal neurons; namely, the glutamatergic mossy cells and the two γ-aminobutyric acid (GABA) ergic cells expressing either cholecystokinin or parvalbumin (Egeland, Warner-Schmidt, Greengard, & Svenningsson, 2010; Oh et al., 2013).

Elucidating Molecular and Cellular Functions of p11 in the Central Nervous System

We recently elucidated the roles of p11 and 5-HT in the function of the NAc, a brain area associated with reward and anhedonia. We found that 5-HT hyperpolarizes (inhibits) cholinergic neurons of the NAc. We characterized the receptors for 5-HT in these cells and found that 5-HT1A and 5-HT1B are highly expressed and synergistically inhibit the excitability and synaptic transmission of cholinergic neurons. The inhibitory modulation of acetylcholine release by 5-HT1B is mediated by p11, whereas the expression level of 5-HT1B in these cells is not, thus confirming previous findings that p11 regulates 5-HT1B receptor function in neurons but not its expression (Figure 4.2A). We also found that specific deletion of 5-HT1B receptors

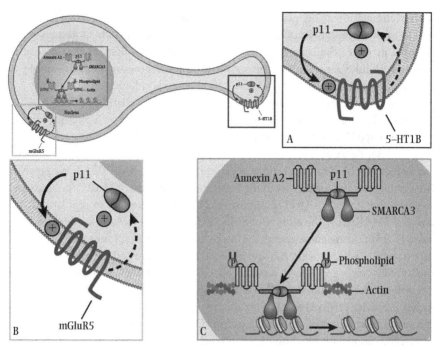

Figure 4.2 A model for p11 function in central nervous system neurons. Three established mechanisms may be involved in occluding depressive-like behavior and in mediating the action of antidepressants (*top left*). A. Presynaptically, serotonin activates the 5-HT1B receptor. p11 positively regulates the surface expression and function of 5-HT1B and modulates cholinergic neurotransmission (*top right inset*). B. p11 positively regulates postsynaptic glutamatergic signaling by modulating mGluR5 receptor function. mGluR5 and p11 mutually facilitate their accumulation at the plasma membrane (*bottom left inset*). C. Nuclear function of the p11 complex regulates the activity of the chromatin remodeling factor SMARCA3 and enables de novo transcription of target genes (*bottom right inset*). Adapted from P. Svenningsson, Y. Kim, J. Warner-Schmidt, Y. S. Oh, & P. Greengard, p11 and its role in depression and therapeutic responses to antidepressants, *Nature Reviews Neuroscience, 14*(10), 673–680, 2013.

from cholinergic neurons results in anhedonic-like behavior in mice, a phenotype that is similar to mice with specific deletion of p11 from cholinergic neurons (Virk et al., 2016). We also gained insight into a novel functional role of p11 in regulating 5-HT4 receptor expression levels. Layer 5 corticostriatal pyramidal cells expressing p11 are strongly and specifically responsive to chronic antidepressant treatment. This response requires p11 and includes a specific increase of 5-HT4 receptor expression. Cortex-specific deletion of p11 abolishes behavioral responses to SSRIs but does not lead to increased depression-like behaviors (Schmidt et al., 2012).

This role of p11 in regulating surface levels of G-protein-coupled receptors may not be exclusive to 5-HT receptors. We recently found that p11 can also regulate depression-like behaviors via regulation of glutamatergic metabotropic receptors (mGluRs; refer to Figure 4.2B). p11 directly binds to the cytoplasmic tail of the mGluR5 receptor (Lee et al., 2015). In cells, p11 and mGluR5 mutually facilitate their accumulation at the plasma membrane, and p11 increases cell surface avail-ability of the receptor. Knockout of mGluR5 or p11 specifically in glutamatergic neurons in mice results in depression-like behaviors. In light of the interest in utilizing mGluR5 receptor antagonists as future antidepressants, this action of p11 may contribute to the clinical response to fast-acting antidepressants.

We proposed a molecular mechanism by which p11 mediates its effects on gene expression by antidepressants. This mechanism is dependent on a physical interac-tion between p11 and the protein annexin-A2, in a heterotetramer protein complex (Figure 4.3). Two molecules of p11 and two molecules of annexin-A2 interact with each other and bind to the chromatin-remodeling factor, SMARCA3. We resolved the crystal structure of this protein complex and found that SMARCA3 binds to a hydrophobic pocket of (p11)2(annexin A2)2 heterotetramer, to regulate the ac-tivity of SMARCA3. The affinity of SMARCA3 to bind DNA molecules and regu-late transcription are enhanced by the interaction with (p11)2(annexin A2)2. In the hippocampus, p11, annexin A2, and SMARCA3 are expressed in the glutamatergic mossy cells and GABAergic basket cells. The SMARCA3 interaction with the heterotetramer is required for fluoxetine-induced antidepressive effects. The p11-induced activity of SMARCA3 is believed to regulate genes that mediate behavioral changes during an antidepressant response (Oh et al., 2013; refer to Figure 4.2C).

Another important function of p11, annexin A2, and SMARCA3 is in the regula-tion of hippocampal neurogenesis. Neurogenesis refers to the process that involves the differentiation, proliferation, and integration of newly born neurons in the CNS of the adult brain. Normal neurogenesis is restricted only to the subgranular zone (SGZ) in the hippocampus and the subventricular zones (SVZs) of the cerebellar cortex, and it was shown to be reduced under several pathological conditions (Ming & Song, 2011). The role for neurogenesis in depression is still unknown, but it is clear that hippocampal neurogenesis is induced during all forms of antidepressant

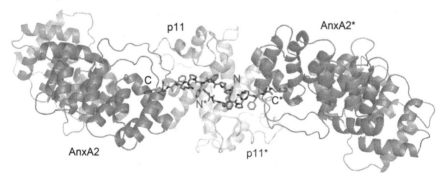

Figure 4.3 Structure of full-length p11 and AnxA2 bound to the SMARCA3 peptide solved at 2.8 A° resolution. The interaction between p11, Annexin A2, and SMARCA3 is implicated in mediating gene expression changes that underlie the action of antidepressants.

Reprinted from Y. S. Oh, P. Gao, K. W. Lee, I. Ceglia, J. S. Seo, X. Zhang, . . . P. Greengard, SMARCA3, a chromatin-remodeling factor, is required for p11-dependent antidepressant action, *Cell, 152*(4), 831–843, 2013.

treatments (Malberg, Eisch, Nestler, & Duman, 2000). Importantly, the stimulatory effects of fluoxetine on cell proliferation, neurogenesis, cell survival, and apoptosis in the hippocampus are reduced in p11-knockout mice (Egeland et al., 2010). Similarly, chronic fluoxetine-induced proliferation of neural progenitors is abolished, and survival of newborn neurons is partially reduced in constitutive SMARCA3 knockout mice (Oh et al., 2013). These findings suggest that the p11–annexin A2–SMARCA3 complex regulates the multiple aspects of antidepressant-stimulated neurogenesis. This complex probably acts in a non–cell-autonomous fashion as p11 expression is increased by chronic fluoxetine in the hippocampus, specifically in GABAergic basket cells and glutamatergic hilar mossy cells in the dentate gyrus (where p11 is colocalized with SMARCA3 in both these cell types), but not in the newborn cells of this region (Egeland et al., 2010). The exact mechanism by which the p11–annexin A2–SMARCA3 protein complex regulates chromatin remodeling is still unclear. An intriguing possibility is that the localization of this protein complex to the nuclear matrix fraction is controlled by the intrinsic phospholipid- and actin-binding properties of annexin A2. As the complex nears the nuclear matrix, critical nuclear events, such as gene expression, replication, and repair, processing can occur (Figure 4.2C).

Another important molecule involved in the role of p11 in mediating neurogenesis is the key BDNF. We also found a role for p11 in the antidepressant activity of BDNF (Warner-Schmidt et al., 2010). BDNF modulates synaptic plasticity, promotes neuronal cell survival, and influences adult hippocampal neurogenesis. We found that BDNF stimulates p11 expression through BDNF receptor and a specific cellular signaling pathway. In neuronal cultures treated with BDNF, a dose-dependent increase in p11 expression was observed. The change in p11 levels in mouse brains induced by BDNF correlated with changes in ligand binding to the 5-HT1B receptor and its subcellular localization. Behavioral studies have also demonstrated that p11 knockout mice are insensitive to the antidepressant actions of BDNF (Warner-Schmidt et al., 2010).

BIOMARKERS FOR DEPRESSION AND ANTIDEPRESSANT RESPONSES

The genetic architecture of depression is poorly understood due to its phenotypic heterogeneity indicating involvement of multiple genes. The *Diagnostic and Statistical Manual of Mental Disorders* (DSM-IV; DSM_IV_CODE, 2000) defines 227 different symptom combinations broadly described as psychomotor/cognitive, mood, and neurovegetative symptoms. These symptoms of MDD reflect different subtypes of genetic contributions with respect to onset, course, and response to treatment. Genome-wide association studies (GWAS) are most widely used to identify risk loci using 1 million or more common variants known as *single nucleotide polymorphisms* (SNPs) to examine their association with a disease (Balding, 2006; Corvin, Craddock, & Sullivan, 2010; McCarroll, Feng, & Hyman, 2014). Among the GWAS studies conducted for (Welter et al., 2014) for MDD or depressive symptoms, very few SNPs reached genome-wide significance, and the effects of most SNPs were found to be small in magnitude and had poor reproducibility (Dunn et al., 2015). For example, there are reduced levels of SLC6A15 (solute carrier family 6, neutral amino acid transporter member 15) involved in transporting neutral amino acids. In addition, 11 of the top 200 SNPs were found in a 167 kb region that overlaps with the gene PCLO (piccolo presynaptic cytomatrix protein) and an intronic SNP in the RORA gene (retinoid-related orphan receptor α gene). A recent study indicated that risk variants for psychiatric disorders aggregate in particular biological pathways involving histone methylation and immune and neuronal signaling (Psychiatric Genomics Consortium, 2015). GWAS studies have limited success as they simply examine "depressed" cases versus controls, which may decrease the signal-to-noise ratio by combining multiple disorder subtypes that vary in their genetic etiology. The advent of new genome-scale experimental tools, data resources, and unbiased approaches to data collection and analysis is likely to achieve the scale necessary to screen and identify disease-associated DNA sequences in the future. Recent studies have focused largely on candidate genes implicated in the neurobiology of depression, such as those regulating 5-HT, dopamine (DA), and glutamate neurotransmission, given the involvement of these neurotransmitters in the pathophysiology of depression and as targets of current antidepressant measures (Gerhard, Wohleb, & Duman, 2016; Kavalali & Monteggia, 2015; Krishnan & Nestler, 2011). Pharmacogenetic studies have focused on identifying key genes involved in antidepressant mechanisms of action and those involved in serotonergic neurotransmission (*SLC6A4* and *HTR2A*), neuroprotection and neuroplasticity (*BDNF*), second-messenger cascades (*GNB3*), glucocorticoid signaling (*FKBP5*), antidepressant transport, metabolism (*ABCB1, CYP2D6*, and *CYP2C19*), and inflammation (Fabbri & Serretti, 2015).

The Role of Inflammatory Molecules in Depression

The search for biomarkers in psychiatric disorders has primarily focused our attention on inflammatory cytokines and their role in neuromodulation, neurotransmitter-like function, and direct/indirect regulation of neurogenesis (Audet & Anisman, 2013; Irwin & Miller, 2007; Maes, 1995; Stuart & Baune, 2014; Wohleb, Franklin, Iwata, & Duman, 2016). Cytokines are pleiotropic, immunomodulatory signaling molecules which include interleukins (IL), interferons (IFN), tumor necrosis factors (TNF), and chemokines that are generally associated with inflammation, immune activation, and cell differentiation or death (Taniguchi, 1995). They have diverse actions; most have little or no known function in healthy tissues but are rapidly induced in response to tissue injury, infection, or inflammation (Perry, Bell, Brown, & Matyszak, 1995). Cognitive impairment, depression, and inflammation co-occur across many conditions such as infectious diseases (HCV, HIV, malaria), cardiovascular diseases and risk factors (stroke, ischemia, high cholesterol, diabetes, bypass surgery), inflammatory conditions (arthritis), autoimmune disorders (lupus, multiple sclerosis), cytokine-based therapies (IFNα for HCV), and substance abuse disorders (Loftis, Huckans, & Morasco, 2010). Also, administration of cytokines for the treatment of infectious diseases and cancer is associated with depressive side effects in 20–50% of patients (Capuron et al., 2002; Wood et al., 2006).

Cytokines in the CNS are constitutively expressed and have functions of neuroprotection and neurodegeneration (Barone & Parsons, 2000; del Zoppo et al., 2000). Their involvement in CNS disease is a rapidly growing area of biological and clinical research that has been increasingly implicated in neuropsychiatric disorders. Bidirectional pathways of neuroimmune communication have emphasized unique interactions between the two systems (Irwin & Miller, 2007; Sternberg, 2006). For example, during an immune and inflammatory response, acute activation of TNFα leads to chronic increases in brain levels of pro-inflammatory cytokines (Qin et al., 2007). Administration of IFNα activates expression of several IFN-stimulated genes in the brain as well as in the peripheral organs. IFNγ participates in the death of dopaminergic neurons by regulating microglial activity. Peripheral cytokines are able to access the brain and affect function via vagal nerve activation, a leaky or compromised blood–brain barrier (BBB), active transport across the BBB, or binding to cell surface proteins on brain endothelial cells (Erickson, Dohi, & Banks, 2012; Quan, 2008). Psychosocial and environmental stress promotes activation of the hypothalamic pituitary adrenal (HPA) axis and the sympathetic nervous system (SNS), releasing glucocorticoids (GCs) and catecholamines (noradrenaline [NA] and adrenaline), thus influencing the development, trafficking, and activation of central and peripheral immune cells (Garcia-Bueno, Caso, & Leza, 2008; Hodes, Kana, Menard, Merad, & Russo, 2015; Irwin & Miller, 2007; Wohleb et al., 2016). Exposure to a psychosocial stressor greatly augments the effects of immune activation on sickness, plasma corticosterone, and hippocampal norepinephrine, as well as on the levels of circulating IL-6, TNFα, and IL-10 (Anisman, Poulter, Gandhi, Merali, & Hayley, 2007; Anisman, Prakash, Merali, & Poulter, 2007; Gibb, Hayley, Gandhi, Poulter, & Anisman, 2008; Zunszain, Anacker, Cattaneo, Carvalho, & Pariante, 2011). MDD patients with HPA axis hyperactivity show a dramatic increase in the production of pro-inflammatory cytokines IL-1 and IL-6 (Maes, Bosmans, Meltzer, Scharpe, & Suy, 1993; Maes, Bosmans, Scharpe, D'Hondt, & Desnyder, 1995). There is considerable overlap between MDD, sickness behavior and major depressive episode (idiopathic depression, which is a hallmark of deployed Army personnel). The similarities are thought to result partly from an overproduction of endogenous pro-inflammatory cytokines and a dysregulation of the HPA axis (Dantzer, O'Connor, Freund, Johnson, & Kelley, 2008; Maes et al., 1993).

Several groups have documented the importance of anti-inflammatory therapy in depression, including observations of aspirin synergizing with fluoxetine, as well as celecoxib facilitating antidepressant actions (Chen, Tzeng, & Chen, 2010; Muller et al., 2006). The TNFα antagonist etanercept (Enbrel) is associated with diminished depression in patients receiving the drug for treatment of psoriasis (Bayramgurler et al., 2013). These discrepancies may reflect the complexity of the large body of cytokines expressed in different cell populations in the periphery and the brain with differing functions.

Cytokine Regulation of p11

Neuroinflammation is an established process that has both detrimental and beneficial effects differing between acute and delayed phases after injury and during psychosocial and environmental stress (Kyritsis et al., 2012; Monje, Toda, & Palmer, 2003).

Antidepressants induce serum levels of many cytokines (Alboni, Benatti, Montanari, Tascedda, & Brunello, 2013; Cattaneo et al., 2013). Our studies show a link between p11 and inflammatory molecules. We demonstrated that antidepressant treatment was ineffective when taken together with nonsteroidal anti-inflammatory drugs (NSAIDs). We observed that the SSRI antidepressant citalopram increases brain cytokine levels and that ibuprofen blocks this effect, leading to diminished antidepressant response (Figure 4.4). We found that administering IFNγ or TNFα increases brain levels of p11, thus providing evidence for the beneficial effect of cytokines in the brain. The augmentation of p11 elicited by SSRIs is abolished in mice with the genetic deletion of receptors for the cytokines IFNγ and TNFα. These data delineate a pathway where SSRIs increase brain cytokines, stimulate p11 expression, and regulate antidepressant response. Also actions of the SSRIs on cytokines are presumably mediated by the potentiation of serotonin as other antidepressants that do not affect serotonergic systems fail to influence cytokines and p11. Likewise, ibuprofen specifically inhibits antidepressant action of SSRIs and not other antidepressants that act via norepinephrine or other mechanisms such as tranylcypromine, bupropion, and desipramine (Figure 4.4).

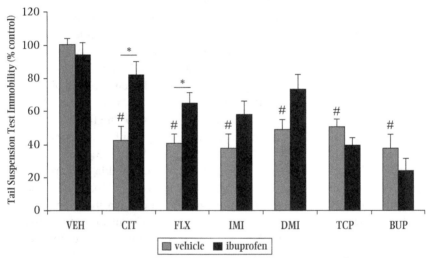

Figure 4.4 Nonsteroidal anti-inflammatory drugs (NSAIDs) and other analgesics attenuate the behavioral response to selective serotonin reuptake inhibitors (SSRIs). Ibuprofen (IBU) (5–7 d treatment) diminished the behavioral response citalopram (CIT) and fluoxetine (FLX), was less effective in altering behavioral responses to the tricyclic antidepressants imipramine (IMI) and desipramine (DMI), but did not affect responses to other classes of antidepressants, including the monoamine oxidase inhibitor tranylcypromine (TCP) and the atypical antidepressant bupropion (BUP) in tail suspension test. All data are presented as means ± SEM. Statistically significant effects of antidepressants (#P < 0.05) or NSAIDs/analgesics (*P < 0.05, **P < 0.01) are noted. $n = 8–16$ per group.
Reprinted from J. L. Warner-Schmidt, K. E. Vanover, E. Y. Chen, J. J. Marshall, & P. Greengard, Antidepressant effects of selective serotonin reuptake inhibitors (SSRIs) are attenuated by antiinflammatory drugs in mice and humans, *Proceedings of the National Academy of Sciences, 108*(22), 9262–9267, 2011.

This observation of NSAIDs preventing antidepressant response in animal studies has also been extended to humans by analysis of clinical data from the STAR*D study, a large-scale investigation of antidepressant therapy in treatment-resistant patients (Rush, 2006). The analysis showed reduced remission rates and increased treatment resistance when citalopram was taken together with NSAIDs (Warner-Schmidt, Vanover, Chen, Marshall, & Greengard, 2011). Based on the evidence that neuroimmune regulation contributes to the neurobiology of neuropsychiatric disorders (Psychiatric Genomics Consortium, 2015), identifying and understanding the dynamics of peripheral and central immune targets mediating behavioral consequences is critical to designing novel drug strategies to treat subsets of MDD patients. Specifically, our studies could become more relevant when treating traumatic brain injury (TBI) patients who have suffered injury and trauma when a cascade of inflammatory mediators is produced (Helmy, De Simoni, Guilfoyle, Carpenter, & Hutchinson, 2011), contributing to the pathological consequences of CNS injury. The key to developing potential treatment for TBI is to minimize the detrimental and neurotoxic effects of neuroinflammation while promoting their beneficial neurotrophic effects, thereby creating optimal conditions for regeneration and recovery.

Expression Levels of p11 in Peripheral Immune Cells as a Predictor of Antidepressant Response

The prediction of treatment response in many neuropsychiatric disorders could be facilitated by easily accessible biomarkers. Our studies show that p11 in white blood cells could serve as a biomarker of antidepressant response using the SSRI citalopram (Svenningsson et al., 2014) in two separate cohorts of MDD patients.

Flow cytometry analysis on peripheral blood mononuclear cells (PBMCs) was performed, and the results revealed that p11 is enriched in a cell type–specific manner in CD3−CD56+ natural killer cells (NK cells), all CD14+ monocytes, and most CD3+ T cells (refer to Figure 4.5). Monocytes had the highest enrichment of p11. Twenty-six patients with MDD with a major depressive episode were recruited at the National Institute of Mental Health (NIMH), screened, and diagnosed using DSM-IV. Severity of depression was assessed using the Montgomery–Åsberg Depression Rating Scale (MADRS) and the Quick Inventory of Depressive Symptomatology-C16 (QIDS). Participants were given a daily dosage of citalopram and evaluated on a weekly basis for 8 weeks. PBMCs were prepared at baseline and after 2 and 8 weeks of citalopram treatment. The study participants were treated with citalopram and had blood collected at baseline and after 1 and 12 weeks. Clinical evaluations showed that most patients in the NIMH cohort responded to citalopram. p11 was reduced in NK cells and monocytes after 2 weeks of citalopram; this reduction correlated with clinical improvements on MADRS and QIDS as assessed after 8 weeks of citalopram. Correlations were found when comparing p11 reductions and clinical improvements after 8 weeks of citalopram. A second group of nine patients with MDD was recruited at the University of Texas, Southwestern, in Dallas and assessed using QIDS. Similar to the NIMH cohort, p11 was reduced in NK cells and monocytes after 1 week of citalopram in these patients; this reduction correlated with clinical improvements on QIDS as assessed after 12 weeks of

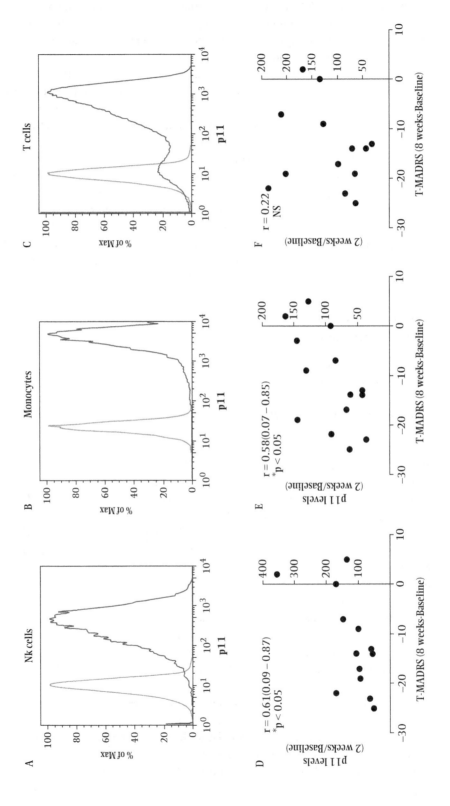

Figure 4.5 p11 expression in immune cells and its regulation by selective serotonin reuptake inhibitor (SSRI) antidepressant citalopram in depressed individuals. Flow cytometry analysis of peripheral blood mononuclear cells with primary antibody against p11 (*black lines*) or IgG1 isotype antibody as negative control (*gray lines*) showing fluorescent intensity (horizontal axis) against the number of events detected (vertical axis). Enriched p11 expression observed in (A) CD56$^+$CD3$^-$ NK cells and (B) CD14$^+$ monocytes and (C) CD3$^+$ T cells. (D–F) Graphs showing median fluorescence intensity of p11 (percentage of baseline values) in (D) NK cells, (E) monocytes, and (F) T cells after 2 weeks of citalopram treatment and correlations to improvements in total Montgomery–Åsberg Depression Rating Scale score after 8 weeks of citalopram treatment. Each dot represents an individual patient. Pearson's correlation test was used for statistical analyses and determined 95% confidence intervals. Statistical significance was defined as P < 0.05.

Reprinted from P. Svenningsson, L. Berg, D. Matthews, D. F. Ionescu, E. Richards, M. Niciu, . . . P. Greengard, Preliminary evidence that early reduction in p11 levels in natural killer cells and monocytes predicts the likelihood of antidepressant response to chronic citalopram, *Molecular Psychiatry, 19*(9), 962–964. 2014.

citalopram. Taken together, these data suggest that early reduction in p11 levels in NK cells and monocytes in response to citalopram predicts the likelihood of a later antidepressive response. As animal studies have shown that antidepressants increase p11 in most classes of neurons in the brain, it appears paradoxical that a decrease in p11 in white blood cells should be associated with antidepressant response. Future studies are needed to examine whether antidepressants regulate p11 in microglia in the brain, which, like monocytes, are derived from myeloid precursors.

RELEVANCE OF P11 STUDIES TO HUMAN PERFORMANCE OPTIMIZATION

MDD is generally recognized to be among the most burdensome of all disorders, with strong adverse effects on personal and social functioning (Kessler, Nock, & Schoenbaum, 2014; Luppa, Heinrich, Angermeyer, Konig, & Riedel-Heller, 2007). Although genetic factors confer some heritable risk of developing MDD, it is evident that exposure to traumatic or repeated psychosocial and environmental stressors can increase the vulnerability to MDD. MDD has a persistent and debilitating symptomatology that impairs the return of affected individuals to full-time work, adversely affects post-deployment welfare, causes PTSD, and leads to alcohol and drug abuse. Victims become prone to suicidal ideation, with some attempting suicide (Wolf, Mitchell, Koenen, & Miller, 2014). Research shows that mTBI and PTSD are comorbid with MDD, disrupting the complex sensorimotor pathways and cognition and causing long-term anxiety and depression (Jackson et al., 2016; Jorge et al., 1993). MDD and other associated psychiatric disorders are of significant military concern (Adams et al., 2016; Fann, Hart, & Schomer, 2009; Forbes et al., 2012; Garber, Rusu, & Zamorski, 2014). Not all individuals with MDD respond to current treatment practices, such as the SSRIs that target serotonergic systems (Stahl, Lee-Zimmerman, Cartwright, & Morrissette, 2013), with only 50–70% of treated patients having complete remission of symptoms. Moreover, frequent and long-term treatments cause several side effects (Berton & Nestler, 2006; Racagni & Popoli, 2008). These drawbacks justify an effort to develop more effective and rapid-acting treatment strategies allowing for a faster and fuller recovery after depression, a quicker return to active duty, and an improved post-deployment functioning.

Our studies have established a direct link between reduced levels of p11 (S100a10) in specific neurons and increased depressive- and anxiety-like states in rodents and humans (Svenningsson & Greengard, 2007). Mice that lack p11 exhibit depressive-like behavior and do not respond to antidepressant treatment, whereas mice that overexpress p11 show an antidepressant phenotype. Moreover, p11 mRNA and protein are down-regulated in brain regions from depressed individuals and in suicide victims (Anisman, Merali, & Stead, 2008; Svenningsson et al., 2006; Tzang et al., 2008; Ursano et al., 2009). Indeed, recent studies show that p11 can be measured from blood-derived extracts and that it may function as a viable biomarker for PTSD, bipolar (BP) disorder, MDD, and suicide (Ursano et al., 2009; Zhang, Li, Benedek, Li, & Ursano, 2009; Zhang et al., 2011; Zhang, Ursano, & Li, 2012). Additionally, it has been shown that serum BDNF levels were negatively correlated with the severity of depression and that they recovered to normal levels after antidepressant treatment (Molendijk et al., 2014; Taniguchi, 1995). In addition to neuropsychological self-assessments, informative biomarkers can serve as useful indicators for an unbiased assessment of the affected person's health. The use of p11 and BDNF as biomarkers could be optimized and used to guide treatment to reduce PTSD-like symptoms and suicide, reducing the risk through early screening and early intervention and thereby improving human performance in the military.

We have observed that p11 levels are reduced in the circulating immune cells in patients responding to antidepressants. Hence p11 could serve as a potential biomarker for antidepressant response prediction. Based on these studies, we will be able to optimize treatment where p11 levels could now be monitored in the peripheral immune cells. This will enable us to rapidly identify and predict which patients are likely to respond to antidepressants. This would tremendously benefit in the treatment of military personnel by allowing a rapid change in medications when the patient is unresponsive and provide faster relief from behavioral despair.

Other strategies that may normalize dysregulation in MDD are nonpharmacological interventions, such as exercise, environmental enrichment, and social interaction, which will improve physical and psychological domains and overall quality of life (Ota & Duman, 2013; Schuch, Dunn, Kanitz, Delevatti, & Fleck, 2016; Schuch, Vancampfort, et al., 2016). Clinical studies show the antidepressive effects of exercise (Hillman, Erickson, & Kramer, 2008), and animal research corroborates such evidence (Creer, Romberg, Saksida, van Praag, & Bussey, 2010; Voss, Vivar, Kramer, & van Praag, 2013). Physical exercise and enrichment promote better cognitive performance by influencing brain structure and plasticity, inducing neurotrophic factors, and enhancing neurogenesis and vasculature. As to neurobiological mechanisms, BDNF mRNA is increased in the mouse cerebellum, caudal cortex (analogous to the entorhinal and visual cortex in humans), and hippocampus after exercise (Berchtold, Chinn, Chou, Kesslak, & Cotman, 2005; Neeper, Gomez-Pinilla, Choi, & Cotman, 1995; Sartori et al., 2011; Vaynman, Ying, & Gomez-Pinilla, 2004), similar to chemical antidepressant treatment (Saarelainen et al., 2003). Both BDNF gene and protein expression are increased in the hippocampus after short (2–7 days) or long (1–8 months) periods of exercise, and they remain elevated at least 2 weeks after exercise has ended (Berchtold et al., 2005; Sartori et al., 2011). Interestingly, many genes that are upregulated with exercise have a recognized interaction with BDNF, supporting a central role for this neurotrophin in brain plasticity (Binder & Scharfman, 2004; Poo, 2001). BDNF utilizes the tropomyosin receptor kinase B (TrkB) receptor to activate signal transduction cascades (Cowansage, LeDoux, & Monfils, 2010). Indeed, exercise increases both BDNF and TrkB receptor levels in the hippocampus (Gomez-Pinilla, Ying, Roy, Molteni, & Edgerton, 2002). We have demonstrated that p11 can be stimulated directly by BDNF (Warner-Schmidt et al., 2010), and several studies have shown the exercise-dependent modulation of p11 expression (Sartori et al., 2011; Tsai, 2007). These changes in BDNF and p11 regulation observed in response to both pharmacological treatment and physical exercise/enrichment highlight the mechanisms common to these two different modes of treatment. This underscores the importance of using physical exercise as a treatment strategy and intervention to reduce stress-related dysfunctions to optimize and enhance human performance during and after deployment.

CONCLUSION

MDD is an invalidating neuropsychiatric disease of significant military concern due to the risk of stressful life experiences during deployment. Best estimates of recent prevalence are 12% among those currently deployed, 13.1% among those previously deployed, and 5.7% among those never deployed (Gadermann et al., 2014). Not all individuals with MDD and comorbid mTBI and PTSD respond to current treatment, and only 50–70% of treated patients have complete remission of symptoms. There is an unmet need to optimize treatments and strategies. Studies in our laboratory have identified p11 as an important regulator of depression and antidepressant responses. The mRNA and protein levels of p11 are relatively low in the brain regions (NAc, basolateral amygdala, hippocampus, and PFC) of depressed humans and animals, but are induced following antidepressant treatment. The protein p11 appears to affect mood by regulating neuronal cell surface expression of the serotonin receptors 5-HT1B, 5-HT1D, and 5-HT4 and by mediating changes in gene expression critical to the antidepressant role of neurons in the described regions. The p11 protein also functions by mediating changes in gene expression critical to the antidepressant role of neurons. Recent studies from other groups have shown that p11 can be measured from peripheral blood and that it may function as a viable biomarker for PTSD and suicide. We have also measured p11 levels in the peripheral blood and observed that antidepressant treatment effectiveness is linked to p11 downregulation. With this discovery, clinicians are now able to identify and prescribe an effective antidepressant treatment faster than ever before. We propose novel strategies based on this work that will help the military in early intervention and screening to reduce risk and respond adequately. Specifically, BDNF and p11 are induced by chemical antidepressants and physical exercise and are likely important for promoting cognitive performance in humans and rodents. We propose that implementing adequate physical exercise and enhancing cognitive function is a promising potential antidepressant therapeutic strategy as well as a precaution that can be implemented during deployment and post-deployment to maintain overall mental health and human performance.

Studying p11 regulation alone could be argued as a very focused study while considering the complex neural circuitry and the involvement of the immune, endocrine, and neural systems in the pathophysiology of depression. However, p11 function has been established as an important mediator of depression and antidepressant efficacy. We are able to understand more about stress-induced depression and about the serotonin signaling pathway, thus providing avenues to unravel potential therapeutic targets to improve the temporal aspects of drug action. The three major p11-enriched cell types of focus in our studies—within the PFC, hippocampus, and NAc, as shown in Figure 4.1—are part of a highly interacting circuit, which the field has shown is crucial for mood regulation under normal and pathological conditions. We have dissected the key neuronal cell types and brain region circuitry involved in depression and antidepressant efficacy, going beyond the understanding of p11 signaling. Moreover, reduced p11 expression levels in specific immune cells from the peripheral blood in patients responding to antidepressants serve as a potential diagnostic tool to perform screening in patients. We are in a better position now to identify new therapeutic targets that are unique in action by utilizing the inflammatory molecules (those stimulating p11 expression) that will facilitate the antidepressant response. We have thus mined the p11 signaling hub and have unraveled unique insights into depression-related behavioral abnormalities and antidepressant mechanisms of action, advancing the search for improved antidepressant medications and the discovery of potential diagnostic tools. We hope to further explore research with novel approaches that will benefit military personnel and civilians over the coming decades in ameliorating neuropsychiatric deficits and enhancing cognitive function to optimize human performance.

REFERENCES

Adams, R. S., Larson, M. J., Corrigan, J. D., Ritter, G. A., Horgan, C. M., Bray, R. M., & Williams, T. V. (2016). Combat-acquired traumatic brain injury, posttraumatic stress disorder, and their relative associations with postdeployment binge drinking. *Journal of Head Trauma Rehabilitation, 31*(1), 13–22. doi:10.1097/HTR.0000000000000082

Alboni, S., Benatti, C., Montanari, C., Tascedda, F., & Brunello, N. (2013). Chronic antidepressant treatments resulted in altered expression of genes involved in inflammation in the rat hypothalamus. *European Journal of Pharmacology, 721*(1-3), 158–167. doi:10.1016/j.ejphar.2013.08.046

Anisman, H., Du, L., Palkovits, M., Faludi, G., Kovacs, G. G., Szontagh-Kishazi, P., . . . Poulter, M. O. (2008). Serotonin receptor subtype and p11 mRNA expression in stress-relevant brain regions of suicide and control subjects. *Journal of Psychiatry and Neuroscience, 33*(2), 131–141.

Anisman, H., Merali, Z., & Stead, J. D. (2008). Experiential and genetic contributions to depressive- and anxiety-like disorders: Clinical and experimental studies. *Neuroscience & Biobehavioral Reviews, 32*(6), 1185–1206. doi:10.1016/j.neubiorev.2008.03.001

Anisman, H., Poulter, M. O., Gandhi, R., Merali, Z., & Hayley, S. (2007). Interferon-alpha effects are exaggerated when administered on a psychosocial stressor backdrop: Cytokine, corticosterone and brain monoamine variations. *Journal of Neuroimmunology, 186*(1-2), 45–53. doi:10.1016/j.jneuroim.2007.02.008

Anisman, H., Prakash, P., Merali, Z., & Poulter, M. O. (2007). Corticotropin releasing hormone receptor alterations elicited by acute and chronic unpredictable stressor challenges in stressor-susceptible and resilient strains of mice. *Behavioural Brain Research, 181*(2), 180–190. doi:10.1016/j.bbr.2007.04.002

Audet, M. C., & Anisman, H. (2013). Interplay between pro-inflammatory cytokines and growth factors in depressive illnesses. *Frontiers in Cellular Neuroscience, 7*, 68. doi:10.3389/fncel.2013.00068

Balding, D. J. (2006). A tutorial on statistical methods for population association studies. *Nature Reviews Genetics, 7*(10), 781–791. doi:10.1038/nrg1916

Barone, F. C., & Parsons, A. A. (2000). Therapeutic potential of anti-inflammatory drugs in focal stroke. *Expert Opinion on Investigational Drugs, 9*(10), 2281–2306. doi:10.1517/13543784.9.10.2281

Baudier, J., Bergeret, E., Bertacchi, N., Weintraub, H., Gagnon, J., & Garin, J. (1995). Interactions of myogenic bHLH transcription factors with calcium-binding calmodulin and S100a (alpha alpha) proteins. *Biochemistry, 34*(24), 7834–7846.

Bayramgurler, D., Karson, A., Yazir, Y., Celikyurt, I. K., Kurnaz, S., & Utkan, T. (2013). The effect of etanercept on aortic nitric oxide-dependent vasorelaxation in an unpredictable chronic, mild stress model of depression in rats. *European Journal of Pharmacology*, *710*(1-3), 67–72. doi:10.1016/j.ejphar.2013.04.007

Berchtold, N. C., Chinn, G., Chou, M., Kesslak, J. P., & Cotman, C. W. (2005). Exercise primes a molecular memory for brain-derived neurotrophic factor protein induction in the rat hippocampus. *Neuroscience*, *133*(3), 853–861. doi:10.1016/j.neuroscience.2005.03.026

Berton, O., & Nestler, E. J. (2006). New approaches to antidepressant drug discovery: Beyond monoamines. *Nature Reviews Neuroscience*, *7*(2), 137–151. doi:10.1038/nrn1846

Binder, D. K., & Scharfman, H. E. (2004). Brain-derived neurotrophic factor. *Growth Factors*, *22*(3), 123–131.

Capuron, L., Ravaud, A., Neveu, P. J., Miller, A. H., Maes, M., & Dantzer, R. (2002). Association between decreased serum tryptophan concentrations and depressive symptoms in cancer patients undergoing cytokine therapy. *Molecular Psychiatry*, *7*(5), 468–473. doi:10.1038/sj.mp.4000995

Cattaneo, A., Gennarelli, M., Uher, R., Breen, G., Farmer, A., Aitchison, K. J., . . . Pariante, C. M. (2013). Candidate genes expression profile associated with antidepressants response in the GENDEP study: Differentiating between baseline 'predictors' and longitudinal 'targets'. *Neuropsychopharmacology*, *38*(3), 377–385. doi:10.1038/npp.2012.191

Chen, C. Y., Tzeng, N. S., & Chen, Y. C. (2010). Maintenance therapy of celecoxib for major depression with mimicking neuropsychological dysfunction. *General Hospital Psychiatry*, *32*(6), 647 e647–649. doi:10.1016/j.genhosppsych.2010.07.001

Corvin, A., Craddock, N., & Sullivan, P. F. (2010). Genome-wide association studies: A primer. *Psychological Medicine*, *40*(7), 1063–1077. doi:10.1017/S0033291709991723

Cowansage, K. K., LeDoux, J. E., & Monfils, M. H. (2010). Brain-derived neurotrophic factor: A dynamic gatekeeper of neural plasticity. *Current Molecular Pharmacology*, *3*(1), 12–29.

Creer, D. J., Romberg, C., Saksida, L. M., van Praag, H., & Bussey, T. J. (2010). Running enhances spatial pattern separation in mice. *Proceedings of the National Academy of Sciences*, *107*(5), 2367–2372. doi:10.1073/pnas.0911725107

Cuijpers, P., Dekker, J., Hollon, S. D., & Andersson, G. (2009). Adding psychotherapy to pharmacotherapy in the treatment of depressive disorders in adults: A meta-analysis. *Journal of Clinical Psychiatry*, *70*(9), 1219–1229. doi:10.4088/JCP.09r05021

Cuijpers, P., van Straten, A., van Oppen, P., & Andersson, G. (2008). Are psychological and pharmacologic interventions equally effective in the treatment of adult depressive disorders? A meta-analysis of comparative studies. *Journal of Clinical Psychiatry*, *69*(11), 1675–1685; quiz 1839-1641. doi:ej07m04112 [pii]

Dantzer, R., O'Connor, J. C., Freund, G. G., Johnson, R. W., & Kelley, K. W. (2008). From inflammation to sickness and depression: When the immune system subjugates the brain. *Nature Reviews Neuroscience*, *9*(1), 46–56. doi:10.1038/nrn2297

Das-Munshi, J., Goldberg, D., Bebbington, P. E., Bhugra, D. K., Brugha, T. S., Dewey, M. E., . . . Prince, M. (2008). Public health significance of mixed anxiety and depression: Beyond current classification. *British Journal of Psychiatry*, *192*(3), 171–177. doi: 10.1192/bjp.bp.107.036707

del Zoppo, G., Ginis, I., Hallenbeck, J. M., Iadecola, C., Wang, X., & Feuerstein, G. Z. (2000). Inflammation and stroke: Putative role for cytokines, adhesion molecules and iNOS in brain response to ischemia. *Brain Pathology*, *10*(1), 95–112.

Donier, E., Rugiero, F., Okuse, K., & Wood, J. N. (2005). Annexin II light chain p11 promotes functional expression of acid-sensing ion channel ASIC1a. *Journal of Biological Chemistry*, *280*(46), 38666–38672. doi: 10.1074/jbc.M505981200

DSM_IV_CODE. (2000). *Diagnostic and Statistical Manual of Mental Disorders (DSM IV)*. Washington, DC: American Psychiatric Association.

Dunn, E. C., Brown, R. C., Dai, Y., Rosand, J., Nugent, N. R., Amstadter, A. B., & Smoller, J. W. (2015). Genetic determinants of depression: Recent findings and future directions. *Harvard Review of Psychiatry, 23*(1), 1–18. doi:10.1097/HRP.0000000000000054

Egeland, M., Warner-Schmidt, J., Greengard, P., & Svenningsson, P. (2010). Neurogenic effects of fluoxetine are attenuated in p11 (S100A10) knockout mice. *Biological Psychiatry, 67*(11), 1048–1056. doi:10.1016/j.biopsych.2010.01.024

Egeland, M., Warner-Schmidt, J., Greengard, P., & Svenningsson, P. (2011). Co-expression of serotonin 5-HT(1B) and 5-HT(4) receptors in p11 containing cells in cerebral cortex, hippocampus, caudate-putamen and cerebellum. *Neuropharmacology, 61*(3), 442–450. doi:10.1016/j.neuropharm.2011.01.046

Erickson, M. A., Dohi, K., & Banks, W. A. (2012). Neuroinflammation: A common pathway in CNS diseases as mediated at the blood-brain barrier. *Neuroimmunomodulation, 19*(2), 121–130. doi:10.1159/000330247

Eriksson, T. M., Alvarsson, A., Stan, T. L., Zhang, X., Hascup, K. N., Hascup, E. R., . . . Svenningsson, P. (2013). Bidirectional regulation of emotional memory by 5-HT1B receptors involves hippocampal p11. *Molecular Psychiatry, 18*(10), 1096–1105. doi:10.1038/mp.2012.130

Fabbri, C., & Serretti, A. (2015). Pharmacogenetics of major depressive disorder: Top genes and pathways toward clinical applications. *Current Psychiatry Reports, 17*(7), 50. doi:10.1007/s11920-015-0594-9

Fann, J. R., Hart, T., & Schomer, K. G. (2009). Treatment for depression after traumatic brain injury: A systematic review. *Journal of Neurotrauma, 26*(12), 2383–2402. doi:10.1089/neu.2009.1091

Forbes, H. J., Jones, N., Woodhead, C., Greenberg, N., Harrison, K., White, S., . . . Fear, N. T. (2012). What are the effects of having an illness or injury whilst deployed on post deployment mental health? A population based record linkage study of UK army personnel who have served in Iraq or Afghanistan. *BMC Psychiatry, 12*, 178. doi:10.1186/1471-244X-12-178

Gadermann, A. M., Heeringa, S. G., Stein, M. B., Ursano, R. J., Colpe, L. J., Fullerton, C. S., . . . Army, S. C. (2014). Classifying US Army Military Occupational Specialties using the Occupational Information Network. *Military Medicine, 179*(7), 752–761. doi:10.7205/MILMED-D-13-00446

Garber, B. G., Rusu, C., & Zamorski, M. A. (2014). Deployment-related mild traumatic brain injury, mental health problems, and post-concussive symptoms in Canadian Armed Forces personnel. *BMC Psychiatry, 14*, 325. doi:10.1186/s12888-014-0325-5

Garcia-Bueno, B., Caso, J. R., & Leza, J. C. (2008). Stress as a neuroinflammatory condition in brain: Damaging and protective mechanisms. *Neuroscience & Biobehavioral Reviews, 32*(6), 1136–1151. doi:10.1016/j.neubiorev.2008.04.001

Gerhard, D. M., Wohleb, E. S., & Duman, R. S. (2016). Emerging treatment mechanisms for depression: Focus on glutamate and synaptic plasticity. *Drug Discovery Today, 21*(3), 454–464. doi:10.1016/j.drudis.2016.01.016

Gerke, V., & Weber, K. (1985). The regulatory chain in the p36-kd substrate complex of viral tyrosine-specific protein kinases is related in sequence to the S-100 protein of glial cells. *EMBO Journal, 4*(11), 2917–2920.

Gibb, J., Hayley, S., Gandhi, R., Poulter, M. O., & Anisman, H. (2008). Synergistic and additive actions of a psychosocial stressor and endotoxin challenge: Circulating and brain cytokines, plasma corticosterone and behavioral changes in mice. *Brain, Behavior, and Immunity, 22*(4), 573–589. doi:10.1016/j.bbi.2007.12.001

Gomez-Pinilla, F., Ying, Z., Roy, R. R., Molteni, R., & Edgerton, V. R. (2002). Voluntary exercise induces a BDNF-mediated mechanism that promotes neuroplasticity. *Journal of Neurophysiology, 88*(5), 2187–2195. doi:10.1152/jn.00152.2002

Greenberg, P. E., Kessler, R. C., Birnbaum, H. G., Leong, S. A., Lowe, S. W., Berglund, P. A., & Corey-Lisle, P. K. (2003). The economic burden of depression in the United States: How did it change between 1990 and 2000? *Journal of Clinical Psychiatry, 64*(12), 1465–1475.

Hashimoto, K. (2010). Brain-derived neurotrophic factor as a biomarker for mood disorders: An historical overview and future directions. *Psychiatry and Clinical Neurosciences, 64*(4), 341–357. doi:10.1111/j.1440-1819.2010.02113.x

Helmy, A., De Simoni, M. G., Guilfoyle, M. R., Carpenter, K. L., & Hutchinson, P. J. (2011). Cytokines and innate inflammation in the pathogenesis of human traumatic brain injury. *Progress in Neurobiology, 95*(3), 352–372. doi:10.1016/j.pneurobio.2011.09.003

Hercher, C., Turecki, G., & Mechawar, N. (2009). Through the looking glass: Examining neuroanatomical evidence for cellular alterations in major depression. *Journal of Psychiatric Research, 43*(11), 947–961. doi:10.1016/j.jpsychires.2009.01.006

Hillman, C. H., Erickson, K. I., & Kramer, A. F. (2008). Be smart, exercise your heart: Exercise effects on brain and cognition. *Nature Reviews Neuroscience, 9*(1), 58–65. doi:10.1038/nrn2298

Hodes, G. E., Kana, V., Menard, C., Merad, M., & Russo, S. J. (2015). Neuroimmune mechanisms of depression. *Nature Neuroscience, 18*(10), 1386–1393. doi:10.1038/nn.4113

Howren, M. B., Lamkin, D. M., & Suls, J. (2009). Associations of depression with C-reactive protein, IL-1, and IL-6: A meta-analysis. *Psychosomatic Medicine, 71*(2), 171–186. doi:10.1097/PSY.0b013e3181907c1b

Irwin, M. R., & Miller, A. H. (2007). Depressive disorders and immunity: 20 years of progress and discovery. *Brain, Behavior, and Immunity, 21*(4), 374–383. doi:10.1016/j.bbi.2007.01.010

Ivanenkov, V. V., Jamieson, G. A., Jr., Gruenstein, E., & Dimlich, R. V. (1995). Characterization of S-100b binding epitopes. Identification of a novel target, the actin capping protein, CapZ. *Journal of Biological Chemistry, 270*(24), 14651–14658.

Jackson, C. E., Green, J. D., Bovin, M. J., Vasterling, J. J., Holowka, D. W., Ranganathan, G., . . . Marx, B. P. (2016). Mild traumatic brain injury, PTSD, and psychosocial functioning among male and female US OEF/OIF veterans. *Journal of Traumatic Stress.* doi:10.1002/jts.22110

Jorge, R. E., Robinson, R. G., Arndt, S. V., Forrester, A. W., Geisler, F., & Starkstein, S. E. (1993). Comparison between acute- and delayed-onset depression following traumatic brain injury. *J Neuropsychiatry Clin Neurosci, 5*(1), 43–49. doi:10.1176/jnp.5.1.43

Karege, F., Bondolfi, G., Gervasoni, N., Schwald, M., Aubry, J. M., & Bertschy, G. (2005). Low brain-derived neurotrophic factor (BDNF) levels in serum of depressed patients probably results from lowered platelet BDNF release unrelated to platelet reactivity. *Biological Psychiatry, 57*(9), 1068–1072. doi:10.1016/j.biopsych.2005.01.008

Kavalali, E. T., & Monteggia, L. M. (2015). How does ketamine elicit a rapid anti-depressant response? *Current Opinion in Pharmacology, 20,* 35–39. doi:10.1016/j.coph.2014.11.005

Kessler, R. C., Chiu, W. T., Demler, O., Merikangas, K. R., & Walters, E. E. (2005). Prevalence, severity, and comorbidity of 12-month DSM-IV disorders in the National Comorbidity Survey Replication. *Archives of General Psychiatry, 62*(6), 617–627. doi: 10.1001/archpsyc.62.6.617

Kessler, R. C., Nock, M. K., & Schoenbaum, M. (2014). Mental health and the army—Reply. *JAMA Psychiatry, 71*(8), 967–968. doi:10.1001/jamapsychiatry.2014.716

Kilisch, M., Lytovchenko, O., Schwappach, B., Renigunta, V., & Daut, J. (2015). The role of protein-protein interactions in the intracellular traffic of the potassium channels TASK-1 and TASK-3. *Pflugers Archive, 467*(5), 1105–1120. doi:10.1007/s00424-014-1672-2

Krishnan, V., & Nestler, E. J. (2010). Linking molecules to mood: New insight into the biology of depression. *American Journal of Psychiatry, 167*(11), 1305–1320. doi:10.1176/appi.ajp.2009.10030434

Krishnan, V., & Nestler, E. J. (2011). Animal models of depression: Molecular perspectives. In J. Hagan (Ed.), *Molecular and Functional Models in Neuropsychiatry. Current Topics in Behavioral Neurosciences* (Vol. 7, pp. 121–147). Berlin, : Springer. doi:10.1007/7854_2010_108

Kupfer, D. J., Frank, E., & Phillips, M. L. (2012). Major depressive disorder: New clinical, neurobiological, and treatment perspectives. *Lancet, 379*(9820), 1045–1055. doi:10.1016/S0140-6736(11)60602-8

Kyritsis, N., Kizil, C., Zocher, S., Kroehne, V., Kaslin, J., Freudenreich, D., . . . Brand, M. (2012). Acute inflammation initiates the regenerative response in the adult zebrafish brain. *Science, 338*(6112), 1353–1356. doi:10.1126/science.1228773

Lee, K. W., Westin, L., Kim, J., Chang, J. C., Oh, Y. S., Amreen, B., . . . Greengard, P. (2015). p11 regulates the surface localization of mGluR5. *Molecular Psychiatry, 20*(12), 1485. doi:10.1038/mp.2015.171 mp2015171

Loftis, J. M., Huckans, M., & Morasco, B. J. (2010). Neuroimmune mechanisms of cytokine-induced depression: Current theories and novel treatment strategies. *Neurobiology of Disease, 37*(3), 519–533. doi:10.1016/j.nbd.2009.11.015

Lohoff, F. W. (2010). Overview of the genetics of major depressive disorder. *Current Psychiatry Reports, 12*(6), 539–546. doi:10.1007/s11920-010-0150-6

Lopez, A. D., & Murray, C. C. (1998). The global burden of disease, 1990–2020. *Nature Medicine, 4*(11), 1241–1243. doi:10.1038/3218

Luppa, M., Heinrich, S., Angermeyer, M. C., Konig, H. H., & Riedel-Heller, S. G. (2007). Cost-of-illness studies of depression: A systematic review. *Journal of Affective Disorders, 98*(1-2), 29–43. doi:10.1016/j.jad.2006.07.017

Maes, M. (1995). Evidence for an immune response in major depression: A review and hypothesis. *Progress in Neuro-Psychopharmacology and Biological Psychiatry, 19*(1), 11–38.

Maes, M., Bosmans, E., Meltzer, H. Y., Scharpe, S., & Suy, E. (1993). Interleukin-1 beta: A putative mediator of HPA axis hyperactivity in major depression? *American Journal of Psychiatry, 150*(8), 1189–1193. doi:10.1176/ajp.150.8.1189

Maes, M., Bosmans, E., Scharpe, S., D'Hondt, P., & Desnyder, R. (1995). Plasma soluble interleukin-2-receptor in depression: Relationships to plasma neopterin and serum IL-2 concentrations and HPA-axis activity. *European Psychiatry, 10*(8), 397–403. doi:10.1016/0924-9338(96)80345-2

Malberg, J. E., Eisch, A. J., Nestler, E. J., & Duman, R. S. (2000). Chronic antidepressant treatment increases neurogenesis in adult rat hippocampus. *Journal of Neuroscience, 20*(24), 9104–9110. doi:20/24/9104

McCarroll, S. A., Feng, G., & Hyman, S. E. (2014). Genome-scale neurogenetics: Methodology and meaning. *Nature Neuroscience, 17*(6), 756–763. doi:10.1038/nn.3716

McMahon, F. J., Buervenich, S., Charney, D., Lipsky, R., Rush, A. J., Wilson, A. F., . . . Manji, H. (2006). Variation in the gene encoding the serotonin 2A receptor is associated with outcome of antidepressant treatment. *American Journal of Human Genetics, 78*(5), 804–814. doi:10.1086/503820

Ming, G. L., & Song, H. (2011). Adult neurogenesis in the mammalian brain: Significant answers and significant questions. *Neuron, 70*(4), 687–702. doi:10.1016/j.neuron.2011.05.001

Mitchell, A. J., Vaze, A., & Rao, S. (2009). Clinical diagnosis of depression in primary care: A meta-analysis. *Lancet, 374*(9690), 609–619. doi:10.1016/S0140-6736(09)60879-5

Molendijk, M. L., Spinhoven, P., Polak, M., Bus, B. A., Penninx, B. W., & Elzinga, B. M. (2014). Serum BDNF concentrations as peripheral manifestations of depression: Evidence from a systematic review and meta-analyses on 179 associations (N=9484). *Molecular Psychiatry, 19*(7), 791–800. doi:10.1038/mp.2013.105

Monje, M. L., Toda, H., & Palmer, T. D. (2003). Inflammatory blockade restores adult hippocampal neurogenesis. *Science, 302*(5651), 1760–1765. doi:10.1126/science.1088417

Muller, N., Schwarz, M. J., Dehning, S., Douhe, A., Cerovecki, A., Goldstein-Muller, B., . . . Riedel, M. (2006). The cyclooxygenase-2 inhibitor celecoxib has therapeutic effects in major depression: Results of a double-blind, randomized, placebo controlled, add-on pilot study to reboxetine. *Molecular Psychiatry, 11*(7), 680–684. doi:10.1038/sj.mp.4001805

Neeper, S. A., Gomez-Pinilla, F., Choi, J., & Cotman, C. (1995). Exercise and brain neurotrophins. *Nature, 373*(6510), 109. doi:10.1038/373109a0

Oh, Y. S., Gao, P., Lee, K. W., Ceglia, I., Seo, J. S., Zhang, X., . . . Greengard, P. (2013). SMARCA3, a chromatin-remodeling factor, is required for p11-dependent antidepressant action. *Cell, 152*(4), 831–843. doi:10.1016/j.cell.2013.01.014

Ota, K. T., & Duman, R. S. (2013). Environmental and pharmacological modulations of cellular plasticity: Role in the pathophysiology and treatment of depression. *Neurobiology of Disease, 57*, 28–37. doi:10.1016/j.nbd.2012.05.022

Perry, V. H., Bell, M. D., Brown, H. C., & Matyszak, M. K. (1995). Inflammation in the nervous system. *Current Opinion in Neurobiology, 5*(5), 636–641.

Poo, M. M. (2001). Neurotrophins as synaptic modulators. *Nature Reviews Neuroscience, 2*(1), 24–32. doi:10.1038/35049004

Psychiatric Genomics Consortium, Network and Pathway Analysis Subgroup. (2015). Psychiatric genome-wide association study analyses implicate neuronal, immune and histone pathways. *Nature Neuroscience, 18*(2), 199–209. doi:10.1038/nn.3922

Qin, L., Wu, X., Block, M. L., Liu, Y., Breese, G. R., Hong, J. S., . . . Crews, F. T. (2007). Systemic LPS causes chronic neuroinflammation and progressive neurodegeneration. *Glia, 55*(5), 453–462. doi:10.1002/glia.20467

Quan, N. (2008). Immune-to-brain signaling: How important are the blood-brain barrier-independent pathways? *Molecular Neurobiology, 37*(2-3), 142–152. doi:10.1007/s12035-008-8026-z

Racagni, G., & Popoli, M. (2008). Cellular and molecular mechanisms in the long-term action of antidepressants. *Dialogues in Clinical Neuroscience, 10*(4), 385–400.

Ramsawh, H. J., Fullerton, C. S., Mash, H. B., Ng, T. H., Kessler, R. C., Stein, M. B., & Ursano, R. J. (2014). Risk for suicidal behaviors associated with PTSD, depression, and their comorbidity in the US Army. *Journal of Affective Disorders, 161*, 116–122. doi:10.1016/j.jad.2014.03.016

Rush, A. J., Bernstein, I. H., Trivedi, M. H., Carmody, T. J., Wisniewski, S., Mundt, J. C., . . . Fava, M. (2006). An evaluation of the quick inventory of depressive symptomatology and the hamilton rating scale for depression: A sequenced treatment alternatives to relieve depression trial report. *Biological Psychiatry, 59*(6), 493–501. doi:10.1016/j.biopsych.2005.08.022

Rush, A. J., Fava, M., Wisniewski, S. R., Lavori, P. W., Trivedi, M. H., Sackeim, H. A., . . . Niederehe, G. (2004). Sequenced treatment alternatives to relieve depression (STAR*D): Rationale and design. *Controlled Clinical Trials, 25*(1), 119–142. doi:10.1016/S0197-2456(03)00112-0

Saarelainen, T., Hendolin, P., Lucas, G., Koponen, E., Sairanen, M., MacDonald, E., . . . Castren, E. (2003). Activation of the TrkB neurotrophin receptor is induced by antidepressant drugs and is required for antidepressant-induced behavioral effects. *Journal of Neuroscience, 23*(1), 349–357.

Sartori, C. R., Vieira, A. S., Ferrari, E. M., Langone, F., Tongiorgi, E., & Parada, C. A. (2011). The antidepressive effect of the physical exercise correlates with increased levels of mature BDNF, and proBDNF proteolytic cleavage-related genes, p11 and tPA. *Neuroscience, 180*, 9–18. doi:10.1016/j.neuroscience.2011.02.055

Schmidt, E. F., Warner-Schmidt, J. L., Otopalik, B. G., Pickett, S. B., Greengard, P., & Heintz, N. (2012). Identification of the cortical neurons that mediate antidepressant responses. *Cell, 149*(5), 1152–1163. doi:10.1016/j.cell.2012.03.038

Schuch, F. B., Dunn, A. L., Kanitz, A. C., Delevatti, R. S., & Fleck, M. P. (2016). Moderators of response in exercise treatment for depression: A systematic review. *Journal of Affective Disorders, 195*, 40–49. doi:10.1016/j.jad.2016.01.014

Schuch, F. B., Vancampfort, D., Rosenbaum, S., Richards, J., Ward, P. B., & Stubbs, B. (2016). Exercise improves physical and psychological quality of life in people with depression: A meta-analysis including the evaluation of control group response. *Psychiatry Research, 241*, 47–54. doi:10.1016/j.psychres.2016.04.054

Soetanto, A., Wilson, R. S., Talbot, K., Un, A., Schneider, J. A., Sobiesk, M., . . . Arnold, S. E. (2010). Association of anxiety and depression with microtubule-associated protein 2- and synaptopodin-immunolabeled dendrite and spine densities in hippocampal CA3 of older humans. *Archives of General Psychiatry, 67*(5), 448–457. doi:10.1001/archgenpsychiatry.2010.48 67/5/448

Stahl, S. M., Lee-Zimmerman, C., Cartwright, S., & Morrissette, D. A. (2013). Serotonergic drugs for depression and beyond. *Current Drug Targets, 14*(5), 578–585.

Sternberg, E. M. (2006). Neural regulation of innate immunity: A coordinated nonspecific host response to pathogens. *Nature Reviews Immunology, 6*(4), 318–328. doi:10.1038/nri1810

Stuart, M. J., & Baune, B. T. (2014). Chemokines and chemokine receptors in mood disorders, schizophrenia, and cognitive impairment: A systematic review of biomarker studies. *Neuroscience & Biobehavioral Reviews, 42*, 93–115. doi:10.1016/j.neubiorev.2014.02.001

Svenningsson, P., Berg, L., Matthews, D., Ionescu, D. F., Richards, E. M., Niciu, M. J., . . . Greengard, P. (2014). Preliminary evidence that early reduction in p11 levels in natural killer cells and monocytes predicts the likelihood of antidepressant response to chronic citalopram. *Molecular Psychiatry, 19*(9), 962–964. doi:10.1038/mp.2014.13

Svenningsson, P., Chergui, K., Rachleff, I., Flajolet, M., Zhang, X., El Yacoubi, M., . . . Greengard, P. (2006). Alterations in 5-HT1B receptor function by p11 in depression-like states. *Science, 311*(5757), 77–80. doi:10.1126/science.1117571

Svenningsson, P., & Greengard, P. (2007). p11 (S100A10)--an inducible adaptor protein that modulates neuronal functions. *Current Opinion in Pharmacology, 7*(1), 27–32. doi:10.1016/j.coph.2006.10.001

Taniguchi, T. (1995). Cytokine signaling through nonreceptor protein tyrosine kinases. *Science, 268*(5208), 251–255.

Tansey, K. E., Guipponi, M., Perroud, N., Bondolfi, G., Domenici, E., Evans, D., . . . Uher, R. (2012). Genetic predictors of response to serotonergic and noradrenergic antidepressants in major depressive disorder: A genome-wide analysis of individual-level data and a meta-analysis. *PLoS Med, 9*(10), e1001326. doi:10.1371/journal.pmed.1001326

Trivedi, M. H., Rush, A. J., Wisniewski, S. R., Nierenberg, A. A., Warden, D., Ritz, L., . . . Fava, M. (2006). Evaluation of outcomes with citalopram for depression using measurement-based care in STAR*D: Implications for clinical practice. *American Journal of Psychiatry, 163*(1), 28–40. doi:10.1176/appi.ajp.163.1.28

Tsai, S. J. (2007). The P11, tPA/plasminogen system and brain-derived neurotrophic factor: Implications for the pathogenesis of major depression and the therapeutic mechanism of antidepressants. *Medical Hypotheses, 68*(1), 180–183. doi:10.1016/j.mehy.2006.06.005

Tsuang, M. T., Taylor, L., & Faraone, S. V. (2004). An overview of the genetics of psychotic mood disorders. *Journal of Psychiatric Research, 38*(1), 3–15. doi:S0022395603000967

Tzang, R. F., Hong, C. J., Liou, Y. J., Yu, Y. W., Chen, T. J., & Tsai, S. J. (2008). Association study of p11 gene with major depressive disorder, suicidal behaviors and treatment response. *Neuroscience Letters, 447*(1), 92–95. doi:10.1016/j.neulet.2008.09.063

Uher, R., Huezo-Diaz, P., Perroud, N., Smith, R., Rietschel, M., Mors, O., . . . Craig, I. (2009). Genetic predictors of response to antidepressants in the GENDEP project. *Pharmacogenomics Journal, 9*(4), 225–233. doi:10.1038/tpj.2009.12 tpj200912

Ursano, R. J., Zhang, L., Li, H., Johnson, L., Carlton, J., Fullerton, C. S., & Benedek, D. M. (2009). PTSD and traumatic stress from gene to community and bench to bedside. *Brain Research, 1293*, 2–12. doi:10.1016/j.brainres.2009.03.030

Vaynman, S., Ying, Z., & Gomez-Pinilla, F. (2004). Hippocampal BDNF mediates the efficacy of exercise on synaptic plasticity and cognition. *European Journal of Neuroscience, 20*(10), 2580–2590. doi:10.1111/j.1460-9568.2004.03720.x

Virk, M. S., Sagi, Y., Medrihan, L., Leung, J., Kaplitt, M. G., & Greengard, P. (2016). Opposing roles for serotonin in cholinergic neurons of the ventral and dorsal striatum. *Proceedings of the National Academy of Sciences*, doi:10.1073/pnas.1524183113

Voss, M. W., Vivar, C., Kramer, A. F., & van Praag, H. (2013). Bridging animal and human models of exercise-induced brain plasticity. *Trends in Cognitive Sciences, 17*(10), 525–544. doi:10.1016/j.tics.2013.08.001

Warner-Schmidt, J. L., Chen, E. Y., Zhang, X., Marshall, J. J., Morozov, A., Svenningsson, P., & Greengard, P. (2010). A role for p11 in the antidepressant action of brain-derived neurotrophic factor. *Biological Psychiatry, 68*(6), 528–535. doi:10.1016/j.biopsych.2010.04.029

Warner-Schmidt, J. L., Flajolet, M., Maller, A., Chen, E. Y., Qi, H., Svenningsson, P., & Greengard, P. (2009). Role of p11 in cellular and behavioral effects of 5-HT4 receptor stimulation. *Journal of Neuroscience, 29*(6), 1937–1946. doi:10.1523/JNEUROSCI.5343-08.2009 29/6/1937

Warner-Schmidt, J. L., Schmidt, E. F., Marshall, J. J., Rubin, A. J., Arango-Lievano, M., Kaplitt, M. G., . . . Greengard, P. (2012). Cholinergic interneurons in the nucleus accumbens regulate depression-like behavior. *Proceedings of the National Academy of Sciences, 109*(28), 11360–11365. doi:10.1073/pnas.1209293109 1209293109

Warner-Schmidt, J. L., Vanover, K. E., Chen, E. Y., Marshall, J. J., & Greengard, P. (2011). Antidepressant effects of selective serotonin reuptake inhibitors (SSRIs) are attenuated by antiinflammatory drugs in mice and humans. *Proceedings of the National Academy of Sciences, 108*(22), 9262–9267. doi:10.1073/pnas.1104836108 1104836108

Welter, D., MacArthur, J., Morales, J., Burdett, T., Hall, P., Junkins, H., . . . Parkinson, H. (2014). The NHGRI GWAS Catalog, a curated resource of SNP-trait associations. *Nucleic Acids Research, 42*(Database issue), D1001–1006. doi:10.1093/nar/gkt1229

Wohleb, E. S., Franklin, T., Iwata, M., & Duman, R. S. (2016). Integrating neuroimmune systems in the neurobiology of depression. *Nature Reviews Neuroscience, 17*(8), 497–511. doi:10.1038/nrn.2016.69

Wolf, E. J., Mitchell, K. S., Koenen, K. C., & Miller, M. W. (2014). Combat exposure severity as a moderator of genetic and environmental liability to posttraumatic stress disorder. *Psychological Medicine, 44*(7), 1499–1509. doi:10.1017/S0033291713002286

Wood, L. J., Nail, L. M., Perrin, N. A., Elsea, C. R., Fischer, A., & Druker, B. J. (2006). The cancer chemotherapy drug etoposide (VP-16) induces proinflammatory cytokine production and sickness behavior-like symptoms in a mouse model of cancer chemotherapy-related symptoms. *Biological Research for Nursing, 8*(2), 157–169. doi:10.1177/1099800406290932

Zhang, L., Li, H., Benedek, D., Li, X., & Ursano, R. (2009). A strategy for the development of biomarker tests for PTSD. *Medical Hypotheses, 73*(3), 404–409. doi:10.1016/j.mehy.2009.02.038

Zhang, L., Li, H., Hu, X., Li, X. X., Smerin, S., & Ursano, R. (2011). Glucocorticoid-induced p11 over-expression and chromatin remodeling: A novel molecular mechanism of traumatic stress? *Medical Hypotheses, 76*(6), 774–777. doi:10.1016/j.mehy.2011.02.015

Zhang, L., Ursano, R. J., & Li, H. (2012). P11: A potential biomarker for posttraumatic stress disorder. In F. Kobeissy (Ed.), *Psychiatric Disorders. Methods in Molecular Biology (Methods and Protocols)* (Vol. 829, pp. 453–468). Springer Protocols, Springer Nature, Switzerland. doi:10.1007/978-1-61779-458-2_29

Zimmer, D. B., Wright Sadosky, P., & Weber, D. J. (2003). Molecular mechanisms of S100-target protein interactions. *Microscopy Research and Technique, 60*(6), 552–559. doi:10.1002/jemt.10297

Zunszain, P. A., Anacker, C., Cattaneo, A., Carvalho, L. A., & Pariante, C. M. (2011). Glucocorticoids, cytokines and brain abnormalities in depression. *Progress in Neuro-Psychopharmacology and Biological Psychiatry, 35*(3), 722–729. doi:10.1016/j.pnpbp.2010.04.011

5

Computational Approaches to Human Performance in Moderate and Extreme Settings

LOGAN T. TRUJILLO

INTRODUCTION

This chapter is an introduction to the use of computational modeling, simulation, and analysis techniques in human factors research, with an eye toward how such methods may be used to optimize human performance in extreme settings. Human factors research studies the interaction between humans and technological systems in order to optimize human–system performance (Proctor & Van Zandt, 2008). Originating during the Industrial Revolution of the nineteenth century from a practical need to increase human work efficiency and safety, human factors emerged as a field of its own during World War II, when technology had developed to the point of exceeding human abilities to adapt to poor technological design. Thus, the field focuses on the capabilities and limitations of human physical and cognitive abilities and how this informs the design and use of technology. Human factors practitioners also study sociotechnical systems, such as human organizational structures (military, law enforcement, business, and academic) composed of personnel subsystems interacting with each other via a technical base. Major subfields of human factors include ergonomics (focused on user performance with equipment and in workspaces), engineering psychology (the use of psychological principles and research to improve human performance), usability engineering (focused on maximizing ease of use of technology), and user experience design (concerned with enhancing user satisfaction and positive emotional responses to technology).

Traditionally, the study of human factors has been empirical, with a focus on observation and experiment in laboratory and real-world settings. However, the field has utilized computational models of human performance since the 1950s (Byrne & Pew, 2009). This use has increased with the advent of modern computer technology, which now enables the development and testing of sophisticated quantitative theories of human–technology performance. This has led to the relatively recent emergence of the new multidisciplinary subfield of *human performance modeling* (Gray & Pew, 2004), with its foundations in psychology, neuroscience, engineering, computer science, applied mathematics, and statistics. Human performance modeling involves the development and application of mathematical models, computer simulation techniques, and computational data analysis methods to the study of human performance. Topics of investigation include (1) computational tests of human factors theories; (2) computer modeling and simulation of human performance and human interaction with virtual environments; (3) digital human anthropometric, biomechanical, kinesthetic, and physiological modeling and simulation; and (4) advanced statistical and signal-processing analysis of neurocognitive indices of human information processing (Inderscience Enterprises Ltd., 2014; Gray & Pew, 2004).

As will be evident in this chapter, human performance modeling is an effective tool for studying human performance. It can ascertain specific physical or information processing characteristics that affect human performance yet are not directly identifiable based on empirical information alone (Byrne & Pew, 2009). Human performance modeling can suggest ways to overcome performance limitations via relevant skill training, protocol and procedure changes, and usable technology. Computational techniques can be used in technology and behavioral protocol design to investigate the effect of parameter changes before time- and resource-intensive training of human operators or the production of physical prototypes. Moreover, human performance modeling provides a virtual laboratory to quantitatively investigate human performance in extreme or dangerous settings that are difficult to replicate or study empirically due to a high probability of human physical/emotional injury or loss of life (Hugo & Gertman, 2012).

MODELS AND SIMULATIONS OF HUMAN PERFORMANCE

Much of human performance modeling research involves the development and application of computational models and simulations of human performance. However, there is a distinction between a model and a simulation (Maria, 1997). A *model* is an abstract conceptual or mathematical representation of a real-world system that approximates the system's most important features. *Conceptual models* are simplified verbal-analytic or block diagram-based descriptions used to produce qualitative predictions of a system's behavior. *Mathematical models*, with their more precise specifications, allow quantitative description and prediction of system behavior typically via direct analytic calculation. In either case, there is a tradeoff between realism and simplicity in model specification, with more realistic models being less simple (more complex) and vice-versa. A *simulation* is the use of a model to analyze the behavior and performance of the real-world system by systematic manipulation of system variables. Simulations may be implemented via direct analytical calculation for simple models or via computer approximation for complex models. Moreover, simulations allow the manipulation of variables that cannot be controlled in a real-world system and enable the exploration of system states that would be unlikely or impossible in the real world. Importantly, simulations allow the determination of model parameters that optimize a system's performance, parameters that can then be implemented in the real-world system.

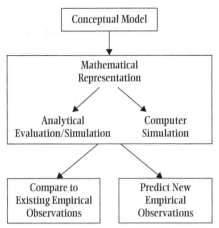

Figure 5.1 Three-tiered approach to human performance modeling. Image courtesy of author.

Thus, human performance modeling typically follows a three-tiered approach (Figure 5.1). First, develop a conceptual model to gain a qualitative understanding of human performance. Although human performance modelers ultimately work with "models based on abstractions that involve explicit mathematical or computer-based formalisms and that have an executable or computable representation" (Gray & Pew, 2004, p. 2110), here the view is taken that some kind of initial structured conceptualization of a system of interest is needed upon which to base a relevant mathematical or computer formalism. Second, create a mathematical representation of the conceptual model to quantitatively simulate human performance. If highly detailed quantitative understanding is needed or if the human performance scenario is too complex to be simulated analytically, then implement a computer simulation of the mathematical model. Third, compare the simulation results to empirical data if they are available; if they are not, then use the results to predict the outcome of new empirical studies.

There are some important issues to consider when using human performance modeling (Byrne & Pew, 2009). First, the goal is not to explain human behavior but to characterize performance in order to predict and optimize it. Thus, models may be derived from known neurocognitive processes or observed relationships between behavior and environmental or task parameters, depending on required accuracy and difficulty in implementing a model. Second, human performance may be modeled at different abstraction levels that omit particular details. Thus, models may sometimes provide approximate predictions, but they do so for a wider set of circumstances than more precise models; this can be useful in certain human factors contexts and detrimental in others. Third, human performance models often require the use of free parameters that must be set from empirical data, which can limit a model's usefulness. Moreover, models with free parameters are sometimes flexible enough to "overfit" data; that is, the models capture spurious characteristics of a dataset that do not generalize to new data and thus yield poor predictive performance.

The Human-Machine System Model

Most computational models of human performance are rooted in the conceptual model of a *human-machine system* (HMS; Card, Moran, & Newell, 1983; Proctor & Van Zandt, 2008). The rationale for it lies in the fact that efficient human performance requires the coordinated implementation of multiple human information processing and physical abilities that must be appropriately interfaced with external technology. The HMS model consists of a closed loop of human and machine subsystems responsible for information input, processing, and output (Figure 5.2). The human subsystems are perception (the input of information), cognition (the processing of that information, in which the information is transformed in some way), and action (the output of the internal transformation of information in terms of physical activity). The machine components of the HMS mirror the human components, with human actions being input into the machine via the controls, which are then transformed by internal machine operations to output the results via a display (visual, auditory, tactile) or to produce a mechanical action/event. The HMS is embedded within a work environment, which consists of external factors (physical, social, organizational, cultural) and factors internal to the human operator (stress-related emotional and physiological states, mental models). Thus, HMS performance is dependent on the individual performance of the human operator and the machine in the context of the environment in which they interact.

The HMS model was originally formulated to describe human interaction with technology. However, the model is also applicable to human interaction with the

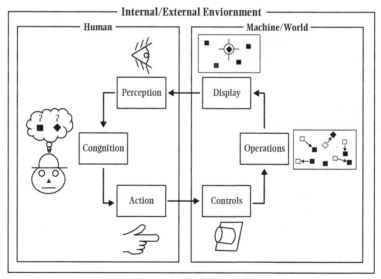

Figure 5.2 The human-machine system (HMS) model. A closed-loop of interacting human subsystems (perception, cognition, action) and machine/world subsystems (controls, operations, display) embedded within an environment consisting of external (physical, social, organizational, cultural) and internal factors (stress-related emotional and physiological states, mental models).
Image courtesy of author.

world more generally. For example, consider a solider under heavy fire scanning a landscape for enemy combatants (Figure 5.2). The soldier sees the landscape via ambient light in the environment that presents visual images to the soldier's eyes (perception). The soldier attends to the landscape's multiple visual elements in order to locate and identify the enemy (perception and cognition). If an enemy combatant appears, then the soldier must decide to act or not (cognition) before selecting and executing the decided course of action (e.g., fire a gun, signal an alert, take cover or retreat) via the soldier's interface with the environment (world control; i.e., the gun, alert button, body). This action induces some kind of change in the world (world operation; i.e., change in enemy or soldier position) that impinges itself upon the soldier's sensory systems (world display). This change is detected by the soldier, and the cycle continues. Importantly, this cycle takes place rapidly and under conditions of high stress of the soldier (internal environment) and a chaotically changing world environment.

The utility of the HMS model is that it allows researchers to isolate and analyze the activity of specific human information processing stages in order to see where performance limitations may arise, the factors that give rise to them, and the effect this has on performance as a whole. From the perspective of human performance modeling, this amounts to formulating a specific mathematical or computer model of the relevant human or human–machine interface component(s) or stage(s), simulating the model's behavior, and then analyzing the results in terms of reliability, efficiency of operation, and/or degree of performance error. The next few sections will follow the HMS framework and briefly overview some influential computational models of perceptual, cognitive, and action performance. A complete review of such models is beyond the scope of this chapter (for more comprehensive reviews, see Byrne & Pew, 2009; Laughery, Plott, Matessa, Archer, & Leblere, 2012; Fisher, Schweickert, & Drury, 2012; Pew & Mavor, 1998). Instead, the goal here is to show how key aspects of human–machine systems can be computationally modeled in order to provide a backdrop for a later discussion of how computational modeling can be used to understand human performance in extreme settings. Summaries of the specific representative HMS performance domain models discussed in the next sections are given in Table 5.1.

Perceptual Performance

Consider the real-world HMS example of the soldier scanning a landscape for enemy combatants. The first step of this process is the soldier's detection of salient sensory information in the visual environment (i.e., seeing the landscape). One useful model of the ability to detect sensory stimuli is *signal detection theory* (SDT; Tanner & Swets, 1954; see Figure 5.3A). SDT models a scenario where a human operator has to make a binary yes–no decision about the presence or absence of a sensory signal against a background of sensory or environmental noise. SDT assumes two possible world states: the signal was present, or it was absent. This creates four possible signal response combinations: hits (H), where the operator correctly detects a present signal; false alarms (FA), where the operator indicates that a signal was present when the signal was absent; correct rejections (CR), where the operator

Table 5.1 Representative Models of Human–Machine System (HMS) Performance Domains

Performance domain	Representative model	Brief description
Perception	Signal Detection Theory (Tanner & Swets, 1954)	Models the detection of sensory signals embedded in the context of sensory or environmental noise
Cognition		
Visual attention	Itti & Koch (2000) Exogenous Search Model	Models visual search as a function of the saliency of objects in the visual environment
	Meloy et al. (2006) Endogenous Search Model	Models visual search as a function of the most recent semisystematic deployment of visual fixations
	VDM 2000 Model Witus & Ellis (2003)	Models visual search as an interaction between bottom-up and top-down visual processes
	Visual Scanning Salience, Effort, Expectancy, & Value (SEEV) model Wickens et al. (2003)	Models visual scanning behavior as a process in which operators sequentially sample their visual environment in discrete units.
Decision-making	Lens Model of Decision Making (Brunswik, 1952; Cooksey, 1996)	Models decision-making as a linear, weighted function of multiple evidentiary cues and information streams
Mental workload	Multiple Resource Theory of Mental Workload (Horrey & Wickens, 2003) Automatic vs. Controlled Processing Tomlin et al. (2015)	Models the effects of finite mental resource allocation on human information processing.
Action		
Response selection	Hick-Hyman Law of Choice Response Time (Hick, 1952; Hyman, 1953)	Models choice response time as a linear function of the amount of information contained within a task
	Evidence Accumulation Model of Speed-Accuracy Tradeoff (Van Zandt et al., 2000)	Models speed-accuracy tradeoff as a function of the accumulation of perceptual evidence toward an internal decision threshold
Response control	Fitt's Law for Aimed Movements Fitt's law (Fitts, 1954)	Models the time to perform aimed movements as a linear function of movement difficulty
	Optimal Control Model for Target-Tracking (Pew & Baron, 1978)	Models human target-tracking behavior as a function of the error-minimizing feedback signals

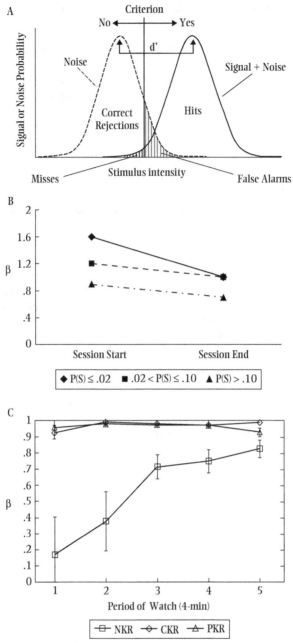

Figure 5.3 Signal detection theory. (A) Decision variable distribution for noise (*dashed curve*) and signal + noise (*solid curve*). Hits, correct rejections, misses, and false alarms are quantified by the indicated areas created by the intersection of the two distributions with each other and a line extending vertically from the criterion point. Sensitivity, d′, quantifies the separation between the two distributions; bias, β, is quantified as the ratio of the signal + noise distribution to the noise distribution at the criterion point. (B) Graphical representation of tabular data presented by Craig (1978) showing mean signal detection bias, β, decrement across a simple attentional vigilance task for low (*filled diamonds, solid*

correctly indicates the absence of a signal; and a miss (M), when the operator fails to detect the presence of a signal. The model assumes probability distributions (typically a normal distribution) for the signal and noise, which can then be used to compute two important performance parameters for an ideal observer: sensitivity (d') to signals, operationally defined as the distance between the signal and noise distributions, and response bias (β), a measure of an observer's tendency to be liberal or conservative in deciding the presence or absence of a signal according to some internal criterion threshold. Both quantities can be computed from actual human performance data to assess how a real human observer compares to an ideal observer as determined by the model.

SDT has been applied to multiple research problems in psychology, including memory, recognition, and perception. In the human factors field, it has been used to study *attentional vigilance*, the ability to detect infrequent signals over prolonged periods of time (Davies & Parasuraman, 1982). Vigilance is important for many tasks, such as sentry duty, security screenings, air traffic control, industrial quality control, power plant monitoring, and medical monitoring. Decrements in vigilance are related to a reduction in sensitivity and/or a conservative shift in response bias over time (Broadbent & Gregory, 1965; See, Howe, Warm, & Dember, 1995); see Figure 5.3B. Shifting response bias is a strategy used by operators when they become aware that signals are relatively rare (Craig, 1978). The SDT model has been used to show that the vigilance decrement can be reduced or eliminated by appropriate training and/or feedback about an individual's pattern of hits and false alarms (Szalma, Hancock, Warm, Dember, & Parsons, 2006); see Figure 5.3C.

Cognitive Performance

VISUAL ATTENTION

Returning to the real-world HMS example, once the landscape is seen, the soldier must then search through it in order to locate and identify the enemy. This process is called *visual search* and involves the allocation of visuospatial attention to different locations in the visual landscape and the identification of the objects found there. Visuospatial attention can be divided into two categories: reflexive shifts of attention driven by salient stimuli in the environment (exogenous attention) and voluntary shifts of attention driven by factors internal to an individual (endogenous attention;

---

line), medium (*filled squares, dashed line*), and high (*filled triangles, dash-dot line*) signal probabilities.(C) The vigilance decrement can be minimized when operators are given computer feedback or "knowledge of results" (e.g., "correct response," "miss," or "false alarm") during vigilance task performance. The figure shows mean across-task signal detection bias, β, changes when subjects are given partial knowledge of results (PKR; *open triangles*), continuous knowledge of results (CKR, *open diamonds*), and no knowledge of results (NKR, *open squares*). Note that subjects are highly biased throughout their watch session when given PKR or CKR.

A, B images courtesy of author. C, reprinted from J. L. Szalma, P. A. Hancock, J. S. Warm, W. N. Dember, & K. S. Parsons, Training for vigilance: using predictive power to evaluate feedback effectiveness. *Human Factors, 48,* 682–692, 2006.

Jonides, 1981). Either of these attentional processes can drive visual search. For example, Itti and Koch (2000) report a computational model of exogenously driven visual search based on the notion of an explicit mapping of the saliency or prominence of objects in the visual environment. In contrast, Melloy, Das, Gramopadhye, and Duchowski (2006) conceptualized visual search as a semi-systematic deployment of endogenous attention. This was modeled as a discrete-time Markov chain, a nonstationary random process in which future visuospatial fixations of attention are determined by the most recent fixations. It is also possible to model visual search as a combination of exogenous and endogenous attention. Witus and Ellis (2003) present a model called the VDM2000 in which visual search is modeled as a cascading sequence of equations representing bottom-up vision and top-down perceptual organization, evidence accumulation, and psychophysical signal detection. They successfully used this model to detect ground vehicles in complex images and validated the model against human performance data.

In the HMS example given earlier, the soldier was searching for a target at uncertain spatial locations. Consider instead the scenario where the soldier may be driving a vehicle or flying a helicopter, a situation where the soldier has to supervise and scan among a series of dynamic processes (e.g., vehicle gauges and movements) at consistent spatial locations. One model that describes this situation is the *salience, effort, expectancy, and value* (SEEV) model of visual scanning behavior (Wickens, Goh, Helleberg, Horrey, & Talleur, 2003; Wickens et al., 2008). The SEEV model conceptualizes visual scanning behavior as a process in which operators sequentially sample their visual environment in discrete units. The main goal of the model is to describe the probability that a given area of the visual field will attract attention to it. The SEEV model is expressed by the equation,

$$p(A) = s \times S - ef \times EF + (ex \times EX) \times (v \times V),$$

where $p(A)$ is the probability a particular visual area will be sampled, S is the salience (or degree of prominence) for that area, EF represents the physical distance from the currently attended location to the sampled area, EX represents the expected rate at which dynamic events occur, and V represents the value of the information in the scanned area. The lowercase values in the equation are the model's free parameter constants. Values of these constants may be derived for optimal and normative operator behavior, as well as actual (i.e., nonoptimal or non-normative) operator behavior. A variant of the model allows for relative rather than absolute estimation of the free parameters for the environment (Wickens et al., 2008).

DECISION-MAKING

Once the soldier attends to the potential location in the landscape, a decision must be made concerning whether the perceived object is important or not and whether an action should be made. Decision-making is a cognitive ability that has long been of interest to psychologists, human factors researchers, and economists. It requires operators to make judgments under conditions of uncertainty of choice outcome. Most models of decision-making are either concerned with the process by which humans reach decisions or describe optimal behavior that acts as a baseline of comparison with real-world human behavior (Kahneman & Tversky, 1979; Payne, Bettman, and Johnson, 1993; Tversky, 1972).

In many domains, it is unclear what counts as optimal behavior or what cognitive processes are involved in decision-making. One useful model for this situation is the *lens model* (Brunswik, 1952; Cooksey, 1996), which has been used to study decision-making in aviation (Bisantz & Pritchett, 2003), command and control (Bisantz et al., 2000), physicians' diagnoses (LaDuca, Engel, & Chovan, 1988), and other areas. The lens model employs multiple regression analysis to weight the many cues or information streams that an individual utilizes to reach a judgment. Cues with large weights are the ones that most likely contribute to the decision-maker's judgment, whereas cues with low or zero weights are contributing less or being ignored by the judge. Moreover, the lens model quantifies the consistency of a decision-maker's judgment policy via the multiple correlations between the cues and judgments. Highly consistent judges will have a robust multiple correlation in the model and are said to exert cognitive control. Furthermore, the lens model can be expanded by introducing a second regression (using the same cues) that models the influences of environment on the situation or outcomes to be judged. This allows the determination of which cues actually predict relationships of interest and thus provides a criterion by which a decision-maker's judgments can be evaluated in terms of predictive accuracy and available information. Decision-makers can then be trained to attend to objectively predictive cues while disregarding nonpredictive cues. Although relatively unsophisticated, the lens model shows that human judgments can be captured by a simple linear model of weighted sums and suggests that many human decisions are made utilizing only a few cues.

MENTAL WORKLOAD

Mental workload may be defined as "the relation between the function relating the mental resources demanded by a task and those resources available to be supplied by the human operator" (Parasuraman, Sheridan, & Wickens, 2008, pp. 145–146). This definition reflects the empirical observation that human operators have certain information processing limitations that degrade performance when exceeded. Mental workload limitations are studied by examining the degree to which multiple simultaneously performed tasks interfere with each other. For example, Horrey and Wickens (2003) examined the extent to which a secondary task interferes with driving performance via a computational model based on multiple resource theory (Wickens, 2002; 2008). The theory proposes that perceptual, cognitive, and action processes each have their own resource pools; interference occurs when the simultaneously performed tasks rely on the same (or overlapping) resource pools; see Figure 5.4A. Such interference has also been modeled at the more general level of automatic versus controlled cognitive processing (Tomlin, Rand, Ludvig, & Cohen, 2015).

The model of Horrey and Wickens involves several general stages. First, a *demand vector* is created whose element magnitudes reflect the dependence of each task on a given resource. The summation of the demand vector elements yields a *demand scalar*, which reflects the overall degree of task difficulty; the sum of the demand scalar of both tasks is called the *demand score*. The resource overlap of the tasks is

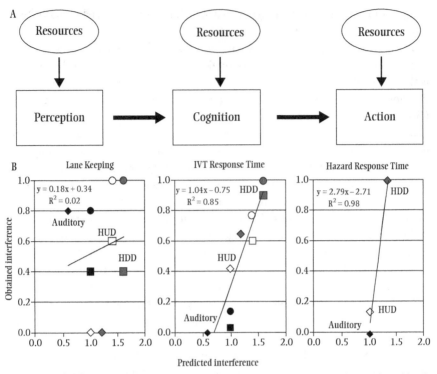

Figure 5.4 (A) Simple representation of the multiple resources model of mental workload. Each mode of information processing (perceptual, cognitive, motor) is supplied by separate pools of mental resources. Image courtesy of author. (B) Application of the multiple resources model to dual-task performance during simulated driving (Horrey & Wickens, 2003). Human drivers in a driving simulator (primary task) engaged in a secondary phone number read-back task presented using different display modalities. Figure panels show the observed task interference as a function model's predicted interference for the main driving (lane keeping) task (left column), the secondary phone number read-back task presented via the in-vehicle technology interfaces (IVT), and response times to discrete road hazards (right column) that occurred throughout the experimental session. Phone numbers were presented in three modalities: a visual head-up display (HUD) 7 degrees below the horizon line (white markers) and a visual head-down display (HDD) 38 degrees offset from the forward horizon (gray markers), and an auditory display (black markers). Diamond markers indicate simulated driving through straight rural roads, circles represent driving though curved rural roads, and squares represent straight urban roads.
Image adapted from Horrey & Wickens (2003) with permission from the University of Iowa Public Policy Center.

coded as a *conflict matrix* whose elements reflect task conflict values for each model dimension. The conflict matrix and the demand vectors are then compared with each other to determine a *resource conflict score*. Finally, the total demand score and resource conflict scores are summed to produce a *total interference score,* which is distributed between the two tasks "depending on the extent to which one or the other is treated as 'primary' or 'secondary'" (p. 9). The model successfully predicted performance decrements across several dual-task conditions involving simulated driving (primary task) and a phone number read-back task (secondary task); see Figure 5.4.

Action Performance

After a decision to act has been made, the soldier must then select a response to make and execute it in a controlled manner. Different aspects of response selection that have been modeled include choice response time and speed–accuracy tradeoff (Hick, 1952; Hyman, 1953; Osman et al., 2000; Van Zandt, Colonius, & Proctor, 2000). Aspects of response control that have been modeled include aimed movements and target-tracking behavior (Accot & Zhai, 1997; Drury, 1975; Fitts, 1954; Pew & Baron, 1978).

RESPONSE SELECTION: CHOICE RESPONSE TIME
The Hick-Hyman law for choice response time (Hick, 1952; Hyman, 1953) models response time as a linear function of task entropy (H), a measure of the amount of information contained within a task,

$$RT = a + b \times H,$$

where a and b are the linear regression intercept and slope constants, respectively. In the case that each response alternative is equally probable, then

$$RT = a + b \times \log_2 (n+1),$$

where n is the number of choice alternatives. This expression captures the intuition that the greater uncertainty an operator has regarding which response should be made, the longer time it takes to respond. Although the Hick-Hyman law has not been widely used in human performance modeling (Seow, 2005), it is useful in situations where operator expertise is stable and response alternatives are well defined (Byrne & Pew 2009; see Figure 5.5 for an example application). One area where the Hick-Hyman law has proved useful is in the modeling of human interaction with computer menus (Cockburn, Gutwin, & Greenberg, 2007).

RESPONSE SELECTION: SPEED–ACCURACY TRADEOFF
Another feature of choice-response time that is important for understanding human behavioral performance is the speed–accuracy tradeoff. This is the situation where slower response times are more accurate than faster response-times (Osman et al., 2000). This tradeoff is well-described by information accumulation computational models (Van Zandt et al., 2000), which assume that certain stimulus conditions require specific responses, and information for a particular stimulus type accumulates over time until a critical threshold is reached and a response is selected and executed. More information, and thus more time, is needed to reach large thresholds, and the operator will be less likely to accumulate a large amount of erroneous information. This leads to slower but more accurate responses by the operator. In

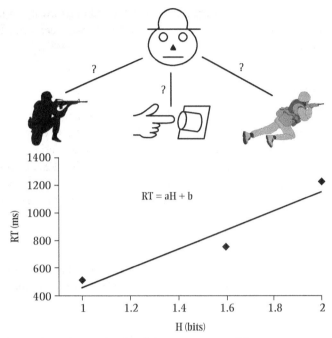

Figure 5.5 Hypothetical example of Hick-Hyman Law. A solider encountering an enemy combatant must select one out of what may be several courses of action (e.g., fire a gun, signal an alert, take cover). The time it takes the solider to select a response (RT) is a linear function of the entropy (H) of response choices. In the case of equiprobable responses, H is a logarithmic function of the number of response choices.
Image courtesy of author.

contrast, small thresholds require less information and time to reach, and thus an operator will be more likely to accumulate erroneous information. This produces faster yet less accurate responses. The free parameters of these models include the rate of information accumulation and response threshold level, each of which may be affected by task demands and internal or external environmental variables (Rundell & Williams, 1979).

RESPONSE CONTROL: AIMED MOVEMENTS
Aimed hand movements to stationary targets, such as the alarm button in the soldier example, have been modeled by Fitt's law (1954), which models aimed movement time (MT) as a linear function of the index of difficulty (ID), a measure of the difficulty to make a movement,

$$MT = a + b \times ID.$$
$$ID = log_2(2 \times D / W),$$

where D is the distance to a target and W is the width of the target. Fitt's law has been extended to encompass aimed movements to moving targets (Accot & Zhai, 1997) and aimed movements made with the feet (Drury, 1975). One very influential application of Fitt's law was the adoption of the computer mouse as the preferred pointing device for graphic user interfaces (Card, English, and Burr, 1978).

RESPONSE CONTROL: TARGET-TRACKING

Human target-tracking behavior is a complex motor task that is necessary for the continuous, stable control of technology that utilizes massive servomechanisms (e.g., radar antennas, gun turrets, tank controls, ships and aircraft, manufacturing machinery). Stabilization is achieved via feedback control signals that minimize the difference between required and actual behavior. Thus, there is a closed loop between the human and the technology, a hallmark of the HMS model.

The basic structure of modern control theory models is achieved by estimating the functions describing human inputs and machine outputs in response to those inputs (Byrne & Pew, 2009). In one-dimensional tracking, for example, these functions might be represented by periodic sinusoidal functions. The model alters the amplitude (strength) and phase (timing) of the input function to convert the input function to an approximation of the output function. The two main parameters of these models are *gain* (amplitude ratio of the input-to-output function) and the *lag* (input–output phase difference). *Crossover control theory* models assume a closed-loop HMS structure, with a human operator (H) inputting responses (I) to a machine (M) and observing the output (O). Differences between the technological system input and output are interpreted by human operators as error (E). The operator's goal is to adapt to the machine's dynamics to achieve stability of the total HMS.

An important aspect of control theory model analysis is the determination of overall HMS stability. This occurs when the system crossover points—the function frequencies at which the gain and lag are zero—are such that the gain crossover is lower than the lag crossover. Otherwise, the system is unstable and the operator is more likely to lose control. Extensions of the crossover model include the *optimal control model* (Pew & Baron, 1978), which addresses the human portion of the HMS in more detail. This includes formal modeling of the human operator's ability to mentally represent system dynamics and minimize the error between input and output, and the noise in operator error signal estimation and motor output.

Integrative Models

One major drawback of the models reviewed so far is that they are mostly limited to describing the performance of individual human information processing and psychomotor abilities in isolation. However, real-world human performance relies on the coordinated implementation of several such capabilities. Some of the models reviewed thus far have explicitly included multiple processes in their formalisms. For example, SDT is ostensibly a model of basic human perception, yet it incorporates aspects of decision-making (in the β parameter used to determine operator bias). Stronger efforts have been made to model the integration of multiple human information processing domains. There are two dominant integrative modeling approaches in contemporary human factors work, *reductionist models* and *first-principle models*

(Laughery et al., 2012). Reductionist models decompose large-scale HMS tasks into sequences of elemental human–system behaviors. The local scale of this representation is determined by the smallest task element at which human performance can be reasonably estimated. Two widely used examples of reductionist models are the *goals, operators, methods, and selection (GOMS) framework* and *task network modeling*. In contrast, first-principle models represent human performance in terms of fundamental principles and mechanisms of human information processing and behavior. Such models directly represent elemental perceptual, cognitive, and motor processes and how these processes interact among themselves, with the technological system under human control, and in the task environment. Examples of first-principle models are *cognitive architectures*. Summaries of these integrative models are given in Table 5.2.

Table 5.2 REPRESENTATIVE REDUCTIONIST AND FIRST-PRINCIPLE INTEGRATIVE MODELS OF HUMAN PERFORMANCE

Reductionist	Representative models	Brief description
Goals, Operators, Methods, and Selection (GOMS)	Keystroke Level Model (KLM) (Card, Moran, & Newell, 1980) Cognitive, Perceptual, & Motor (CPM)-GOMS (John & Kieras, 1996a)	Models human performance as an open-loop sequence of mental and physical operations that change an operator's mental state or task environment in order to realize a goal
Task Network Modeling	Systems Analysis of Integrated Networks of Tasks (SAINT) programming language (Wortman et al., 1974; Archer, Headley, & Allender, 2003). US Army-sponsored Improved Performance Research Integration Tool (IMPRINT) (Archer, Headley, & Allender, 2003) C3TRACE (Command, Control, and Communication—Techniques for Reliable Assessment of Concept Execution) (Hansberger & Barnett, 2005)	Models HMS task structure as sequences of discrete subtasks (perceptual, cognitive, motor) that are conceptually-represented as nodes in a global task network
First-Principle		
Cognitive Architectures	EPIC system (Kieras & Meyer, 1997) Queuing Network-Model Human Processor (Wu & Liu, 2007; 2008) Cognitive Modeling Framework (Bernard et al., 2005) Adaptive Control of Thought-Rational (ACT-R) (Anderson, 1993; Anderson & Lebiere, 1998)	Models human performance as the interaction of different information processing modules that represent a cognitive model of the task and implement task production rules

GOALS, OPERATORS, METHODS, AND SELECTION FRAMEWORK

This approach models human performance as an open-loop sequence of mental (perceptual, cognitive) and physical (action) operations that change an operator's mental state or task environment in order to realize a goal (Card, Moran, & Newell, 1983; John & Kieras, 1996a, 1996b).[1] A specific operation sequence constitutes a method for realizing a goal, and there are rules to select among different possible methods. Operation sequences are implemented in serial or parallel, with different levels of dependencies among operations. Each operation takes a specific amount of time to implement, with total task time estimated as the summation of individual operation times (taking into account any parallel operations). Different methods are more efficient at realizing particular goals than others, which can be assessed by comparing their estimated execution times.

GOMS models are most useful for modeling the acquisition, execution, and transfer of routine cognitive skill (Card et al., 1983; Gong & Kieras, 1994). This is the situation where an operator is an expert at performing a task to the point that it is routine and thus she must simply execute that task. In addition, GOMS models can be implemented across a range of scales. At the simplest scale is the keystroke-level model (KLM; Card et al., 1980) that represents the physical actions of computer user input behavior (keystrokes, button presses, mouse clicks, etc.) as goal-realizing operations that occur over a time scale of hundreds of milliseconds. At a more complex scale is the cognitive, perceptual, and motor GOMS model (John & Kieras, 1996a) that implements finely detailed descriptions of cognitive and procedural processes operating on a timescale of tens to hundreds of milliseconds. This flexibility in scale of analysis is useful for analyzing cases where relatively small time differences to perform given operations have a disproportionate impact on task outcome (Byrne & Pew, 2009). Some disadvantages of GOMS are an inability to account for novice operators, effects of mental fatigue or workload, and individual differences among operators. Furthermore, GOMS cannot explicitly model operator error, although the framework can be used to identify errors and reduce their frequency (Woods & Kieras, 2002).

TASK NETWORK MODELING

This approach is similar to GOMS in that it uses task analysis to decompose a global HMS task structure into sequences of discrete subtasks (Laughery et al., 2012); these subtasks can be conceptually represented as nodes in a global task network. Some subtasks may represent perceptual, cognitive, or action processes, whereas others may represent particular combinations of the three. Each subtask is characterized by two statistical distributions, one describing the time to task completion and the other describing the probability of completion. Subtask node sequences are networked in serial and/or parallel path organizations with a logical gating structure that controls the flow of information throughout the network. Monte Carlo computer simulations of the task network are then used to create combined statistical distributions of relevant performance measures.

For the task network modeling to be successful, the modeler must select the appropriate abstraction level at which to represent the network nodes and paths. The modeler must also correctly estimate the network statistics from previous data, theory, or first principles, which can be difficult. Nonetheless, task network models are well validated across a variety of task scenarios, are relatively straightforward to implement, and have the ability to incorporate human and machine hardware/software elements into a closed-loop representation of an HMS. Modern software packages to conduct task analysis include Micro Saint Sharp, originating from the US Air Force-sponsored Systems Analysis of Integrated Networks of Tasks (SAINT) programming language, and the US Army-sponsored Improved Performance Research Integration Tool (IMPRINT; Archer, Headley, & Allender, 2003; Wortman, Pritsker, Seum, Seifert, & Chubb, 1974). Both software packages allow the modeling of a variety of HMS performance scenarios.

Task network models can also be used to study the interactive effects of social and sociotechnical environments on performance. For example, the US Army Research Laboratory's C3TRACE (Command, Control, and Communication—Techniques for Reliable Assessment of Concept Execution) task network model represents "different organizational structures, individuals within those structures, the tasks and functions performed within a task, and the communication patterns between individuals in an organizational structure" (Hansberger & Barnett, 2005, p. 1183). C3TRACE has been used to evaluate the effects of different global and local organization architectures on multiple performance variables (communication, decision-making quality, workload, situation awareness, time-on-task; Hansberger & Barnett, 2005; Swoboda, Kilduff, & Katz, 2005).

COGNITIVE ARCHITECTURES

This first-principle modeling approach integrates theories of human perception, cognition, and action into a unified computational framework called a *cognitive architecture* that encompasses time- and task-independent features of human cognition (Byrne & Pew, 2009; Gray, Young, & Kirschenbaum, 1997; Laugherty et al., 2012; Ritter & Young, 2001). In general, cognitive architectures are composed of interacting modules implementing different domains of human information processing. The architectures are also structured to represent *procedural* ("how to do it") knowledge via *production rules*—a set of if-then rules the architecture uses to perform a task (Kieras & Meyer, 2000). These procedural rules allow different tasks to be implemented within the same cognitive architecture and are determined via empirical human factors techniques, such as task analyses of the modeled activity (Kieras & Meyer, 2000). Cognitive architectures are designed to implement a *cognitive model*, which is a general model of a particular category of task that can be reprogrammed as necessary to implement specific task instances. Prominent cognitive architectures include the EPIC system (Kieras & Meyer 1997), the Queuing Network-Model Human Processor (Wu & Liu, 2007; 2008; Lin, Wu, & Chaovalitwongsec, 2014), Sandia National Laboratories' Cognitive Modeling Framework (Bernard et al., 2005), and the ACT-R (Anderson, 1993;

Anderson & Lebiere, 1998; Anderson et al., 2004). Although their general organizational principles are the same, these models differ in terms of the particular information processes that are included and the detail with which they are modeled.

The ACT-R architecture is the most well known and widely used in the human factors field (Byrne & Pew, 2009); see Figure 5.6. It consists of several modules that reflect the anatomical localization of different human brain functions, including vision (occipital/parietal cortex), memory for *declarative* ("what is it") knowledge (temporal cortex/hippocampus), motor control (motor cortex and cerebellum), and the representation of goals and intentions (frontal cortex). These modules are all integrated via a central production module (basal ganglia subcortex) that selects *productions*—basic units of procedural knowledge. Production selection is driven by input from the current state of each of the architecture modules. In turn, productions signal the modules to carry out an operation, which may be internal (shifting attention, retrieving information from memory) or external (executing a manual response). The module states are changed as a result (i.e., attention is

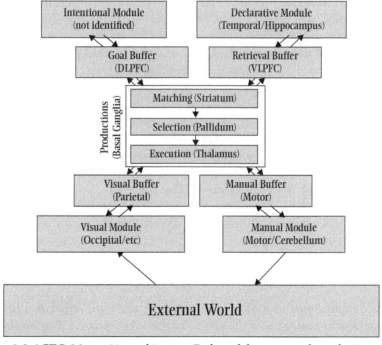

Figure 5.6 ACT-R 5.0 cognitive architecture. Each module corresponds to a brain region known to implement specific cognitive and perceptual operations (DLPFC, dorsolateral prefrontal cortex; VLPFC, ventrolateral prefrontal cortex). Module buffer information is acted on and modulated by production rules originating from the production module associated with the basal ganglia brain region.

Image from J. R. Anderson, D. Bothell, M. D. Byrne, S. Douglass, C. Lebiere, & Y. Qin, An integrated theory of the mind, *Psychological Review, 111,* 1036–1060, 2004, reprinted with permission.

shifted, information retrieved, or manual response executed) and a new sequence is initiated.

An important feature of the ACT-R architecture is that procedural and declarative knowledge is represented at a symbolic level, but access to that knowledge is determined by neural-like subsymbolic processes; the latter also allow the architecture to statistically learn the characteristics of its environment in a graded fashion (Laugherty et al., 2012). This is useful when the architecture is interfaced with a simulated complex task environment or with the actual software or hardware used in task performance. Although implementing the model–environment interface is often a challenge, ACT-R has been used to successfully model and simulate multiple human performance scenarios (Byrne & Pew, 2009; Laughery et al. 2012), such as driving while dialing a mobile phone, process monitoring, and aircraft maneuvering and taxiing (see Figure 5.7).

COMPUTATIONAL ANALYSIS OF HUMAN PERFORMANCE DATA

In contrast to the model-based approaches to human performance outlined so far, another computational methodology has recently emerged that is data-driven. Here, advanced computer-implemented mathematical and statistical techniques are used to quantify and predict human performance data. These methods allow the precise extraction and quantification of information from data that are not available via conventional descriptive and null-hypothesis inferential statistics. Examples include wavelet analysis and genetic algorithms (Lew, Dyre, Soule, Ragsdale, & Werner, 2010), chaos theory (Karwowski, 2012), catastrophe models (Guastello et al., 2012; 2014), Bayesian analysis (Lawton, Miller, & Campbell, 2005; Regens, Mould, Jensen, Graves, & Edger, 2015; Rong, Luo, Chen, Sun, & Wang, 2014), and statistical meta-analysis (Sebok, Wickens, Sargent, & Alion Science and Technology, 2013). However, the most promising of these approaches for human performance are those designed to assess multivariate data sets. Such techniques can be used to single out the most important variable(s) that contribute to human performance in a given context or identify patterns and regularities across multiple performance variables. Single examples of each use are, respectively, *blind source separation* and *multivariate pattern recognition*.

Blind Source Separation

These computational methods isolate source signals from mixed signals using little or no information about the sources or the mixing process. Two well-known examples include *principal component analysis (PCA)* and *independent component analysis (ICA)*, which decompose multivariate signals into additive subcomponents. In PCA, this is achieved by transforming the mixed signals into a set of linearly un-correlated stationary Gaussian signals. In contrast, ICA identifies statistically independent non-Gaussian source signals that may or may not be stationary. Example applications of PCA include the study of workspace ergonomics (Kecek, Çakmak, & Yildirim, 2010) and the understanding of human error contributing to aircraft

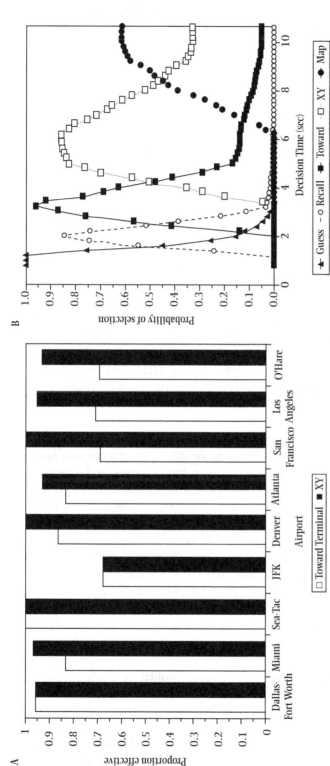

Figure 5.7 Comparison of a human pilot subject matter expert (SME) and ACT-R model performance during taxiing of a simulated commercial jet airliner at several major US airports. The task was to taxi the aircraft from landing touchdown to the disembarking terminal using one of five heuristic strategies to make turn decisions. (A) Accuracy of two of the most accurate decision strategies: make turns toward the airline gates ("Toward Terminal" strategy) or turn the aircraft in the direction that decreases the larger of the X or Y distance between the gate and the current aircraft location ("XY" strategy). Plotted is the strategy effectiveness at reproducing the likely or expected taxi routes as indicated by the SME. (B) The probability that the ACT-R model selected a particular decision strategy as a function of the time-limit to make turn decisions. Additional decision strategies included random guessing ("Guess"), making turn decisions based off of a map or spatial knowledge ("Map"), and basing turn decisions from the memory of correct taxiway clearance instructions relayed from ground-based air traffic controllers ("Recall").

Reprinted from M. D. Byrne & A. Kirlik, Using computational cognitive modeling to diagnose possible sources, *The International Journal of Aviation Psychology*, 15, 135–155, 2005.

accidents (O'Hare, Wiggins, Batt, & Morrison, 2007). ICA has been success-fully used in electroencephalographic (EEG)-based drowsiness estimation during driving (Lin et al., 2005).

Multivariate Pattern Recognition

This refers to computer-implemented statistical techniques that can ex-tract patterns and regularities across multiple variables. Pattern recognition is realized via machine learning algorithms that allow computers to identify data regularities via general learning principles rather than programming them in exact and minute detail (Samuel, 2000). Identified data patterns can then be used by a computer to perform predictive analyses (Kohavi & Provost, 1998). For known patterns, learning algorithms may be supervised by proper labeling of the training data; other algorithms can implement unsupervised learning to uncover previously unidentified patterns. Perhaps the best known example of pattern recognition is classification, where a computer algorithm assigns input data to one of a given set of categories. For example, classifiers may be applied to a range of behavioral, physical, and physiological variables to categorize dif-ferent levels or kinds of operator functional state (Fong, Sibley, Cole, Baldwin, & Coyne, 2010; Wilson, Russell, Monnin, Estepp, & Christensen, 2010). This as-signment is not exact, however; instead, the inputs are probabilistically matched to the categories in a manner that accounts for sources of statistical variation (i.e., intrinsic variability of HMS behavior and/or measurement noise). Widely used classifier algorithms include support vector machines, artificial neural networks, and genetic algorithms.

Pattern recognition has proved to be a very useful tool for understanding and optimizing human performance. In addition to identifying general operator func-tional states, it has also been used to study changes in team cognition and communi-cation (Gorman et al., 2016; Stevens, Galloway, Berka, & Behneman, 2010), human errors in numerical data entry (Lin et al., 2014), and mental fatigue during simu-lated air traffic control tasks (Dasari, Crowe, Ling, & Ding, 2010). Perhaps the most promising application of pattern recognition is its use in *neuroergonomics*, a branch of ergonomics that uses real-time assessment of human brain function to con-trol and adapt human–machine interaction (Parasuraman, 2003; Parasuraman & Wilson, 2008). For example, pattern recognition algorithms can be used to identify loads on human information processing bottlenecks and to assess the effectiveness of human–system augmentation strategies designed to alleviate those loads (such as changes in task presentation, sequencing, pacing, or delegation; Schmorrow et al., 2012).

As an example of the promise of this approach, consider the study of Wilson and Russell (2007) that used a neural network classifier of psychophysiolog-ical signals to monitor human mental workload during an uninhabited aerial vehicle (UAV) task (Figure 5.8). In this task, human operators monitored four preplanned UAV bombing missions via computer screens. The operators were given radar images of the target areas (Figure 5.8A), for which they visually

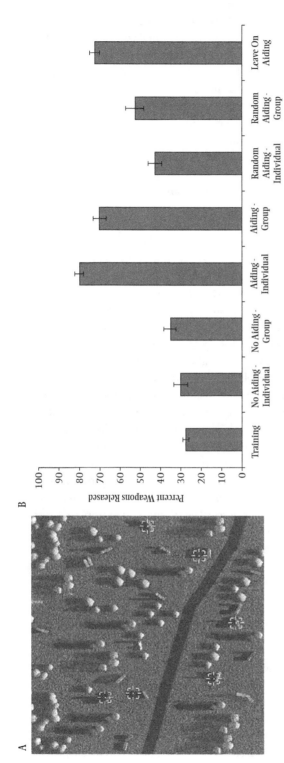

Figure 5.8 Adaptive aiding guided by psychophysiological pattern recognition. (A) Example radar image used during the difficult UAV task of Wilson and Russell (2007); six targets are designated by crosshairs. (B) Mean successful weapons release during a difficult UAV task. Training = ANN training only; No aiding-individual = no aid to task performance, with UAV speeds determined by individual operator difficulty level; No aiding-group = no aid to task performance, with UAV speeds determined by group operator difficulty level; Aiding-individual = aiding during high mental workload using ANNs trained with individual UAV speeds; Aiding-group = aiding during high mental workload using ANNs trained with mean group UAV speeds; Random aiding-individual = random task assistance with total aiding time equal to an individual operator's aiding-individual total aid time; Random aiding-group = random task assistance with total aiding time equal to an individual operator's aiding-group total aid time; Leave on aiding = continuous aiding using ANNs trained with individual UAV speeds.

Reprinted from G. F. Wilson & C. A. Russell, Performance enhancement in an uninhabited air vehicle task using psychophysiologically determined adaptive aiding, *Human Factors, 49,* 1005–1018, 2007.

identified six bombing targets for the UAVs. Operators had to select and identify targets according to a predetermined set of priorities and then give a weapons release command before the vehicles reached a predetermined waypoint. Operators also had to simultaneously monitor the current states of the vehicles. Task difficulty was manipulated in the form of modulations of vehicle speed, image complexity, and the insertion of distractor messages within a stream of regular vehicle status updates. Operator working memory was highly engaged in this task because the radar images could not be viewed in their entirety, so operators had to pan around the images and remember target types and locations. Memory was further strained by requiring operators to remember vehicle status problems messages until a command was given that identified when the problem reached critical status in a particular vehicle. At that point, an operator could take steps to fix the problem.

High difficulty levels were determined for individual participants in an initial task session, during which EEG, electrooculographic (EOG), and heart rate variability measures were recorded. These data were then used to train an artificial neural network (ANN) to identify specific psychophysiological patterns associated with periods of low and high mental workload, as indexed by behavioral performance and subjective estimates of mental workload obtained via the NASA Task Load Index (NASA-TLX; Hart & Staveland, 1988). In a second testing session, the ANN then monitored an operator's psychophysiological data in order to estimate his mental workload level in a real-time manner. When the ANN identified a period of high mental workload, the difficulty of the UAV task was either temporarily reduced (*adaptive aiding condition*) or continuously reduced (*leave on aiding*) by decreasing UAV speed and using an enhanced mode of vehicle status messages. For comparison, a third condition was employed in which task assistance was given at random intervals (*random aiding condition*), whereas no assistance was given in a fourth condition (*no adaptive aiding condition*). These conditions were further divided according to whether the aiding times, ANN training data, and UAV speeds were determined on the basis of individual operator performance or mean performance across the group of operators that were tested. The study found that UAV task performance was highest in the adaptive and leave-on aiding conditions (Figure 5.8B). This demonstrates the potential utility of combining pattern and psychophysiological techniques to augment human performance in complex task scenarios.

APPLICATION TO HUMAN PERFORMANCE
IN EXTREME SETTINGS

Most of the computational approaches discussed so far have been used to predict human performance in moderate settings, but human performance modeling has already proved useful for understanding performance in situations that may be considered "extreme," such as space exploration (Chua & Feigh, 2014; Gacy, Wickens, Sebok, Gore, & Hooey, 2011; Gore, 2014; Kaiser, Allen, Barshi, Billman, & Holden, 2010; Matessa & Remington, 2005; Sebok, Wickens, Clegg, & Sargent, 2014; Wong, Walters, & Fairey, 2010), emergency evacuations (Dutt,

Yu, & Gonzalez, 2011; Pan, Han, Dauber, & Law, 2006), and air traffic control (Lee, Kolling, & Lewis, 2011). Yet, despite their usefulness, many of these models are limited to describing the performance of particular human–machine components of the HMS and do not explicitly incorporate the effects of the HMS environment (or only do so in limited detail). This dearth of explicit modeling of the environment is not specific to models of performance in extreme settings, but is a limitation of most human performance models in wide use (Byrne & Pew, 2009).[2]

Environmental factors are crucial influences on HMS performance in any context, but they are especially relevant to performance in extreme settings. Human operators must perceive, decide, and act under multiple extreme internal, external, and social factors including (1) excessive, highly dynamic, and/or chaotic physical parameters; (2) uncertain evidence and ambiguous information; (3) intense time pressure or long delays; (4) the triggering of large consequences by minor actions; (4) high operator stress and physical and mental workloads; and (5) conflicting operator goals due to unstable social and organizational factors (Worm, 2000). These powerful factors contribute much of the risk in human operations in extreme settings. Yet, though they may be uncontrollable in the real world, these factors can be controlled in the virtual world of computer models and simulations and then systematically assessed for their effects on human performance before the commencement of actual operations. This is where computational approaches can contribute the most toward understanding human performance in extreme environments. The explicit modeling of HMS environments (and, more importantly, the interaction of operator and environment—see later discussion) allows the study of human performance without exposing operators to actual risk or danger (Hugo & Gertman, 2012).

At present, there are few modeling approaches that attempt to directly incorporate the effects of operator environment. One approach is to directly link cognitive architectures like ACT-R to dynamic computer-simulated interactive environments such as flight and driving simulators or military systems (Allender, Archer, Kelley, & Lockett, 2005; Byrne & Kirlik, 2005; Gluck, Ball, Krusmark, Rodgers, & Purtee, 2003; Lawton et al., 2005). For example, Salvucci (2006) used an ACT-R architecture to drive a standard midsize vehicle on a simulated multilane highway with moderate traffic. Model performance was comparable to that of human drivers. Zemla et al. (2011) used an ACT-R cognitive architecture to successfully control the taxiing of a simulated commercial jetliner. The simulated runway environment was populated with aircraft whose behavior was based on recordings of real aircraft at a major airport.

A second approach is to model the interaction between an operator's internal and external environments. For example, in the performance construct of *situation awareness (SA)*, operators guide their behavior on the basis of a mental model that integrates "the perception of the elements in the environment within a volume of time and space, the comprehension of their meaning, and the projection of their status in the near future" (Endsley, 2006, p. 529). Thus, SA involves a general awareness of what is happening in one's environment and how current events and one's own actions will affect one's immediate and future goals.

The most well-known model of situation awareness is the *attention-situation awareness (A-SA)* model (Wickens et al., 2008). Here, the SEEV model of attention (Wickens et al., 2003) is incorporated into a perception/attention module that feeds information into a cognitive SA-updating module that constructs a mental model of the operator's situation. This mental model then guides future attentional scanning behavior via feedback to the perception/attention module. Wickens et al. (2008) used this model to predict taxiway errors and scanning behavior of commercial airline pilots. A second method to model SA utilizes structural equations modeling, in which networks of unobservable "latent" variables are fit to one or more observed variables, with the strength and direction of the relationships among the latent variables assigned by the model. Berggren, Prytz, Johansson, and Nählinder (2011) used structural equation statistical modeling to study SA during team interaction in a computer-simulated fire-fighting "microworld." The study found positive relationships between SA and teamwork and a negative effect of mental workload on SA and teamwork. A third approach to modeling SA involves fuzzy cognitive mapping (FCM), in which the relationships among elements of a mental model are quantified in order to compute the degree to which each element supports decision-making. FCM has been used to quantify the interactions between goals, decision-making, and SA during US Army operations (Bolstad et al., 2010).

Another example of the interaction between internal and external operator environments is the *human stress response,* defined as "the body's reaction or response to the imbalance caused between demands and resources available to a person" (Sharma & Gedeon, 2015, p. 191). Sharma and Gedeon developed a computational model in which an operator's physical, physiological, subjective, and behavioral responses are measured and analyzed via signal processing and statistical techniques (including ANNs) to identify global stress feature patterns (Figure 5.9). The model then uses computer pattern recognition algorithms to compare observed stress patterns to a knowledge base that is used to recognize or evaluate the presence or absence of stress in the human observer. Sharma and Gedeon used this approach to successfully model and detect stress patterns in human observers immersed in abstract virtual environments (reading of stressful content), virtual environments (watching stressful visual media), and real environments (interview setting and meditation setting).

The integration of human performance models with models of performance environment is an important direction for future efforts to optimize human performance in extreme settings. Nonetheless, future models must address certain theoretical obstacles that arise from the modeling of real-world performance more generally (Kirlik, 2007). A limitation of most human performance models is that they are based on noninteractive laboratory tasks that do not change during task performance and in which perception is a passive process. These circumstances are much different from the dynamic and interactive real-world environments in which cognition is typically embedded. Thus, human performance models cannot simply simulate an HMS as a passive receiver of input from the environment. Models must take an active perception approach that views the perception of an environment in terms of the opportunities it affords (Gibson, 1979; Norman, 2013). On the other

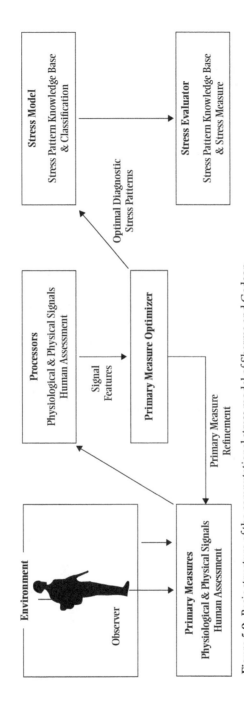

Figure 5.9 Basic structure of the computational stress model of Sharma and Gedeon. Image courtesy of author, based on research described in Sharma & Gedeon (2015).

hand, models can also no longer consider the environment as a static and passive context within which humans and technology interact. Instead, models must consider the environment as an active component of the HMS that plays a functional role in cognition. This view of an active, functional interplay between humans, technology, and the environment is similar to that put forward by ecological psychology (Barker, 1968; Gibson, 1979) and schools of thought on enactive, embedded, and extended cognition (Rosch, Thompson, & Varela, 1991; Rowlands, 2010). Finally, most laboratory subjects are task-naïve, whereas in real-world contexts human operators (e.g., firefighters, pilots, military personnel, law enforcement, etc.) are skilled in their jobs and highly experienced with their respective technological tools and operating environments. Thus accurate models also require extensive empirical study of a to-be-modeled task and the human expertise necessary to perform it (Foyle et al., 2005; Gray & Kirschenbaum, 2000; Kirlik, 2007).

CONCLUSION

It should be clear from this chapter that computational modeling, simulation, and analysis techniques are very useful for understanding, predicting, and optimizing human performance across a broad range of performance settings. The HMS model provides a general conceptual framework for how humans interact with technology and the world and of the various factors that govern that interaction. The modeling and simulation of HMS components allows researchers to identify specific operator performance limitations and to suggest ways to overcome them via training, use of technology, and/or changes in task protocols and procedures. Computational analysis of human performance can also be used to identify these limits while providing a way to quantify the effects of HMS augmentation. Application of these computational methods to the study of human performance in extreme settings has already proved useful. It will become more useful as new models are developed that explicitly incorporate the direct, interactive effects of an operator's environment (internal, external, social) and expertise.

NOTES

1.   Note that some authors (e.g., Byrne & Pew, 2009) consider the GOMS framework to be a cognitive architecture, but here it is placed in the reductionist integrative model category because its basic architecture involves task sequences of elemental human–system behaviors.
2.   Although there are some exceptions, including the SEEV model of visual attention reviewed earlier in this chapter, as well as models tailored to the specific performance demands and environmental characteristics of space flight (Gacy et al., 2011; Gore, 2014; Kaiser, Allen, Barshi, Billman, & Holden, 2010).

REFERENCES

Accot, J., & Zhai, S. (1997). Beyond Fitts' law: Models for trajectory-based HCI tasks. In *Human Factors in Computing Systems: Proceedings of the ACM SIGCHI Conference on Human Factors in Computing Systems* (pp. 295–302). New York: Association for Computing Machinery.

Allender, L., Archer, S., Kelley, T., & Lockett, J. (2005). Human performance modeling in the army: A long and winding road. In *Proceedings of the Human Factors and Ergonomics Society 49th Annual Meeting* (pp. 1191–1195). Santa Monica, CA: SAGE Publications.

Anderson, J. R. (1993). *Rules of the Mind*. Hillsdale, NJ: Lawrence Erlbaum Associates.

Anderson, J. R., & Lebiere, C. (1998). *The Atomic Components of Thought*. Mahwah, NJ: Erlbaum.

Anderson, J. R., Bothell, D., Byrne, M. D., Douglass, S., Lebiere, C., & Qin, Y. (2004). An integrated theory of the mind. *Psychological Review, 111,* 1036–1060.

Archer, S., Headley, D., & Allender, L. (2003). Manpower, personnel, and training integration methods and tools. In H. Booher (Ed.), *Handbook of Human Systems Integration* (pp. 379–431). New York: Wiley.

Barker, R. G. (1968). *Ecological Psychology: Concepts and Methods for Studying the Environment of Human Behavior*. Stanford, CA: Stanford University Press.

Berggren, P., Prytz, E., Johansson, B., & Nählinder, S. (2011). The relationship between workload, teamwork, situation awareness, and performance in teams: A microworld study. In *Proceedings of the Human Factors and Ergonomics Society 55th Annual Meeting* (pp. 851–855). Santa Monica, CA: SAGE Publications.

Bernard, M. L., Xavier, P., Wolfenbarger, P., Hart, D., Waymire, R., Glickman, M., & Gardner, M. (2005). Psychologically plausible cognitive models for simulating interactive human behaviors. In *Proceedings of the Human Factors and Ergonomics Society 49th Annual Meeting* (pp. 1205–1209). Santa Monica, CA: SAGE Publications.

Bisantz, A. M., Kirlik, A., Gay, P., Phipps, D. A., Walker, N., & Fisk, A. D. (2000). Modeling and analysis of a dynamic judgment task using a lens model approach. *IEEE Transactions on Systems, Man, and Cybernetics—Part A, Systems and Humans, 30,* 605–616.

Bisantz, A. M., & Pritchett, A. R. (2003).Measuring the fit between human judgments and automated alerting algorithms: A study of collision detection. *Human Factors, 45,* 266–280.

Bolstad, C. A., Cuevas, H. M. Connors, E. S., González, C., Foltz, P. W., Lau, N. K. C., & Warwick, W. J. (2010). Advances in modeling situation awareness, decision making, and performance in complex operational environments. In *Proceedings of the Human Factors and Ergonomics Society 54th Annual Meeting* (pp. 1047–1051). Santa Monica, CA: SAGE Publications.

Broadbent, D. E., & Gregory, M. (1965). Effects of noise and of signal rate upon vigilance analyzed by means of decision theory. *Human Factors, 7,* 155–162.

Brunswik, E. (1952). *The conceptual framework of psychology*. Chicago: University of Chicago Press.

Byrne, M. D., & Kirlik, A. (2005). Using computational cognitive modeling to diagnose possible sources of aviation error. *International Journal of Aviation Psychology, 15,* 135–155.

Byrne, M. D., & Pew, R. W. (2009). A history and primer of human performance modeling. *Reviews of Human Factors and Ergonomics 5,* 225–263.

Card, S. K., English, W. K., & Burr, B. J. (1978). Evaluation of mouse, rate-controlled isometric joystick, step keys, and text keys for text selection on a CRT. *Ergonomics, 21,* 601–613.

Card, S. K., Moran, T. P., & Newell, A. (1980). The keystroke-level model for user performance time with interactive systems. *Communications of the Association for Computing Machinery, 23,* 396–410.

Card, S. K., Moran, T. P., & Newell, A. (1983). *The Psychology of Human-Computer Interaction*. Hillsdale, NJ: Lawrence Erlbaum.

Chua, Z. K., & Feigh, K. M. (2014). Cognitive process model of astronaut decision making during lunar landing. In *Proceedings of the Human Factors and Ergonomics Society 58th Annual Meeting* (pp. 874–878). Santa Monica, CA: SAGE Publications.

Cockburn, A., Gutwin, C., & Greenberg, S. (2007). A predictive model of menu performance. In *Human Factors in Computing Systems: Proceedings of CHI 2007* (pp. 627–636). New York: Association for Computing Machinery.

Cooksey, R. W. (1996). *Judgment Analysis: Theory, Method, And Applications*. New York: Academic Press.

Craig, A. (1978). Is the vigilance decrement simply a response toward probability matching? *Human Factors, 20*, 441–446.

Davies, D. R., & Parasuraman, R. (1982). *The Psychology of Vigilance*. London: Academic Press.

Dasari, D., Crowe, C., Ling, C., Zhu, M., & Ding, L. (2010). EEG pattern analysis for physiological indicators of mental fatigue in simulated air traffic control tasks. In *Proceedings of the Human Factors and Ergonomics Society 54th Annual Meeting* (pp. 205–209). Santa Monica, CA: SAGE Publications.

Drury, C. G. (1975). Application of Fitts' law to foot-pedal design. *Human Factors, 17*, 368–373.

Dutt, V., Yu, M., & Gonzalez, C. (2011). Deciding when to escape a mine emergency: Modeling accumulation of evidence about emergencies through instance-based learning. In *Proceedings of the Human Factors and Ergonomics Society 55th Annual Meeting* (pp. 841–845). Santa Monica, CA; SAGE Publications.

Endsley, M. (2006). Situation awareness. In G. Salvendy (Ed.), *Handbook of Human Factors and Ergonomics* (3rd ed., pp. 528–542). New York: Wiley.

Fisher, D. L., Schweickert, R., & Drury, C. G. (2012). Mathematical models in engineering psychology: optimizing performance. In G. Salvendy (Ed.), *Handbook of Human Factors and Ergonomics* (4th ed., pp. 962–989). Hoboken, NJ: Wiley.

Fitts, P. M. (1954). The information capacity of the human motor system in controlling the amplitude of movement. *Journal of Experimental Psychology, 47*, 381–391.

Fong, A., Sibley, C., Cole, A., Baldwin, C., & Coyne, J. (2010). A comparison of artificial neural networks, logistic regressions, and classification tress for modeling mental workload in real-time. In *Proceedings of the Human Factors and Ergonomics Society 54th Annual Meeting* (pp. 264–268). Santa Monica, CA: SAGE Publications.

Foyle, D. C., Hooey, B. L., Byrne, M. D., Corker, K. M., Deutsch, S., Lebiere, C., Leiden, K., & Wickens, C. D. (2005). Human performance models of pilot behavior. In *Proceedings of the Human Factors and Ergonomics Society 49th Annual Meeting* (pp. 1109–1113). Santa Monica, CA; SAGE Publications.

Gacey, A. M., Wickens, C. D., Sebok, A., Gore, B. F., & Hooey, B. L. (2011). Modeling operator performance and cognition in robotic missions. In *Proceedings of the Human Factors and Ergonomics Society 55th Annual Meeting* (pp. 861–865). Santa Monica, CA; SAGE Publications.

Gibson, J. J. (1979). *The Ecological Theory of Perception*. Boston, MA: Houghton Mifflin.

Gluck, K. A., Ball, J. T., Krusmark, M. A., Rodgers, S. M., & Purtee, M. D. (2003). A computational process model of basic aircraft maneuvering. In F. Detje, D. Dörner, & H. Schaub (Eds.), *Proceedings of the Fifth International Conference on Cognitive Modeling* (pp. 117–122). Bamberg, Germany: Universitas-Verlag Bamberg.

Gong, R., & Kieras, D. E. (1994). A validation of the GOMS model methodology in the development of a specialized, commercial software application. In *Human Factors in Computing Systems: Proceedings of CHI 94* (pp. 351–357). New York: Association for Computing Machinery.

Gore, B. (2014). Using empirical research and human performance modeling to predict astronaut performance in long-duration space missions. In *Proceedings of the Human Factors and Ergonomics Society 58th Annual Meeting* (pp. 832–833). Santa Monica, CA; SAGE Publications.

Gorman, J. C., Martin, M. J., Dunbar, T. A., Stevens, R. H. Galloway, T. L., Amazeen, P. G., & Likens, A. D. (2016). Cross-level effects between neurophysiology and communication during team training. *Human Factors, 58*, 181–199.

Gray, W. D., & Kirschenbaum, S. S. (2000). Analyzing a novel expertise: An unmarked road. In J. M. C. Schraagen, S. F. Chipman & V. L. Shalin (Eds.), *Cognitive Task Analysis* (pp. 275–290). Mahwah, NJ: Lawrence Erlbaum Associates.

Gray, W. D., & Pew, R. W. (2004). Introduction to human performance modeling (HPM) & to this symposium on cognitive HPM. In *Proceedings of the Human Factors and Ergonomics Society 48th Annual Meeting* (pp. 2109–2110). Santa Monica, CA: SAGE Publications.

Gray, W. D., Young, R. M., & Kirschenbaum, S. S. (1997). Introduction to this special issue on cognitive architectures and human-computer interaction. *Human-Computer Interaction, 12*, 301–309.

Guastello, S. J., Boeh, H., Schimmels, M. J., Gorin, H., Huschen, S., Davis, E., Peters, N. E., Fabisch, M., & Poston, K. (2012). Cusp catastrophe models for cognitive workload and fatigue in verbally cued pictorial memory task. *Human Factors, 54*, 811–825.

Guastello, S. J., Malon, M., Timm, P., Weinberger, K., Gorin, H., Fabisch, M., & Poston, K. (2014). Catastrophe models for cognitive workload and fatigue in a vigilance dual task. *Human Factors, 56*, 737–751.

Hansberger, J. T., & Barnett, D. (2005). Human performance modeling for operational command, control, and communication. In *Proceedings of the Human Factors and Ergonomics Society 49th Annual Meeting* (pp. 1182–1185). Santa Monica, CA: SAGE Publications.

Hart, S. G., & Staveland, L. E. (1988). Development of the NASA-TLX (Task Load Index): Results of experimental and theoretical research. In P. A. Hancock & N. Meshkati (Eds.), *Human Mental Workload* (pp. 239–250). Amsterdam: North Holland Press.

Hick, W. E. (1952). On the rate of gain of information. *Quarterly Journal of Experimental Psychology, 4*, 11–26.

Horrey, B., & Wickens, C. D. (2003). Multiple resource modeling of task interference in vehicle control, hazard awareness and in-vehicle task performance. In *Proceedings of the Second International Driving Symposium on Human Factors in Driver Assessment, Training and Vehicle Design* (pp. 7–12). Iowa City; University of Iowa.

Hugo, J., & Gertman, D. I. (2012, July). *The use of computational human performance modeling as task analysis tool.* Paper presented at the Eighth American Nuclear Society International Topical Meeting on Nuclear Plant Instrumentation, Control, and Human–Machine Interface Technologies, NPIC & HMIT, San Diego, CA.

Hyman, R. (1953). Stimulus information as a determinant of reaction time. *Journal of Experimental Psychology, 45*, 188–196.

Itti, L., & Koch, C. (2000). A saliency-based mechanism for overt and covert shifts of visual attention. *Vision Research, 40,* 1489–1506.

Inderscience Enterprises Ltd. (2014). International Journal of Human Factors Modelling and Simulation Leaflet. Retrieved from http://www.inderscience.com/jhome.php?jcode=ijhfms.

John, B. E., & Kieras, D. E. (1996*a*). The GOMS family of user interface analysis techniques: Comparison and contrast. *ACM Transactions on Computer-Human Interaction, 3,* 320–351.

John, B. E., & Kieras, D. E. (1996*b*). Using GOMS for user interface design and evaluation: Which technique? *ACM Transactions on Computer-Human Interaction, 3,* 287–319.

Jonides, J. (1981). Voluntary versus automatic control over the mind's eye's movement. In J. B. Long & A. D. Baddeley (Eds.), *Attention and Performance IX* (pp. 187–203). Hillsdale, NJ: Lawrence Erlbaum Associates.

Kahneman, D., & Tversky, A. (1979). Prospect theory: An analysis of decision under risk. *Econometrica, 44,* 263–291.

Kaiser, M. K., Allen, C. S., Barshi, I., Billman, D., Holden, K. L. (2010). Human factors research for space exploration: Measurement, modeling, and mitigation. In *Proceedings of the Human Factors and Ergonomics Society 54th Annual Meeting* (pp. 136–139). Santa Monica, CA; SAGE Publications.

Karwowski, W. (2012). A review of human factors challenges of complex adaptive systems: discovering and understanding chaos in human performance. *Human Factors, 54,* 983–995.

Kecek, G., Çakmak, Z., & Yildirim, E. (2010). Determination of ergonomics dimension of production enterprises by principal component analysis. *Problems and Perspectives in Management, 8,* 72–81.

Kieras, D. E., & Meyer, D. E. (1997). An overview of the EPIC architecture for cognition and performance with application to human-computer interaction. *Human-Computer Interaction, 12,* 391–438.

Kieras, D. E., & Meyer, D. E. (2000). The role of cognitive task analysis in the application of predictive models of human performance. In J. M. Schraagen, S. F. Chipman, & V. L. Shalin (Eds.), *Cognitive Task Analysis* (pp. 237–260). Mahwah, NJ: Lawrence Erlbaum Associates.

Kirlik, A. (2007). Ecological resources for modeling interactive behavior and embodied cognition. In W. D. Gray (Ed.), *Integrated Models of Cognitive Systems* (pp. 194–210). New York: Oxford University Press.

Kohavi, R., & Provost, F. (1998). Glossary of terms: Special issue on applications of machine learning and the knowledge discovery process. *Machine Learning, 30,* 271–274.

LaDuca, A., Engel, J. D., & Chovan, J. D. (1988). An exploratory study of physicians' clinical judgment: An application of social judgment theory. *Evaluation and the Health Professions, 11,* 178–1200.

Laughery, K. R., Jr., Plott, B., Matessa, M., Archer, S., & Leblere, C. (2012). Modeling human performance in complex systems. In G. Salvendy (Ed.) *Handbook of Human Factors and Ergonomics* (4th ed., pp. 931–961). Hoboken, NJ: Wiley.

Lawton, C. R., Miller, D. P., & Campbell, J. E. (2005). *Human Performance Modeling for System of Systems Analytics: Soldier Fatigue* (SAND Report No. SAND2005-6569). Albuquerque, NM: Sandia National Laboratories.

Lee, P. J., Kolling, A., & Lewis, M. (2011). Workload modeling using time windows and utilization in an air traffic control task. In *Proceedings of the Human Factors and Ergonomics Society 55th Annual Meeting* (pp. 831–835). Santa Monica, CA: SAGE Publications.

Lew, R., Dyre, B. P., Soule, T., Ragsdale, S. A., & Werner, S. (2010). Assessing mental workload from skin conductance and pupillometry using wavelets and genetic programming. In *Proceedings of the Human Factors and Ergonomics Society 54th Annual Meeting* (pp. 254–258). Santa Monica, CA; SAGE Publications.

Lin, C. T., Wu, C., & Chaovalitwongsec, A. A. (2014). Integrating behavior modeling in data mining to improve human error prediction in numerical entry. In *Proceedings of the Human Factors and Ergonomics Society 58th Annual Meeting* (pp. 854–858). Santa Monica, CA: SAGE Publications.

Lin, C. T., Wu, R. C., Liang, S. F., Chao, W. H., Chen, Y. J., & Jung, T. P. (2005). EEG-based drowsiness estimation for safety driving using independent component analysis. *IEEE Transactions on Circuits and Systems I: Regular Papers, 52*, 2726–2738.

Matessa, M., & Remington, R. (2005). Eyemovements in human performance modeling of space shuttle operations. In *Proceedings of the Human Factors and Ergonomics Society 49th Annual Meeting* (pp. 1114–1118). Santa Monica, CA: SAGE Publications.

Maria, A. (1997). Introduction to modeling and simulation. In S. Andradóttir, K. J. Healy, D. H. Withers, & B. L. Nelson (Eds.), *Proceedings of the 29th Conference on Winter Simulation* (pp. 7–13). Washington, DC: IEEE Computer Science Society.

Melloy, B. J., Das, S., Gramopadhye, A. K., & Duchowski, A. T. (2006). A model of extended, semisystematic visual search. *Human Factors, 48*, 540–554.

Norman, D. (2013). *The Design of Everyday Things: Revised and Expanded Edition.* New York: Basic Books.

O'Hare, D., Wiggins, M., Batt, R., & Morrison, D. (2007). Cognitive failure analysis for aircraft accident investigation. *Ergonomics, 37*, 1855–1869.

Osman, A., Lou, L., Muller-Gethmann, H., Rinkenauer, G., Mattes, S., & Ulrich, R. (2000). Mechanisms of speed-accuracy tradeoff: Evidence from covert motor processes. *Biological Psychology, 51*, 173–199.

Pan, X., Han, C. S., Dauber, K., & Law, K. H. (2006). Human and social behavior in computational modeling and analysis of egress. *Automation in Construction, 15*, 448–461.

Parasuraman, R. (2003). Neuroergonomics: research and practice. *Theoretical Issues in Ergonomic Science, 4*, 5–20.

Parasuraman, R., Sheridan, T. B., & Wickens, C. D. (2008). Situation awareness, mental workload, and trust in automation: Viable, empirically supported cognitive engineering constructs. *Journal of Cognitive Engineering and Decision Making, 2*, 140–160.

Parasuraman, R., & Wilson, G. F. (2008). Putting the brain to work: Neuroergonomics past, present, and future. *Human Factors, 50*, 468–474.

Payne, J. W., Bettman, J., & Johnson, E. J. (1993). *The Adaptive Decision Maker.* London: Cambridge University Press.

Pew, R. W., & Baron, S. (1978). The components of an information processing theory of skilled performance based on an optimal control perspective. In G. E. Steinbach (Ed.), *Information Processing in Motor Control and Learning* (pp. 71–78). New York: Academic Press.

Pew, R. W., & Mavor, A. S. (Eds.). (1998). *Modeling human and Organizational Behavior: Application to Military Simulations.* Washington, DC: National Academy Press.

Proctor, R. W., & Van Zandt, T. (2008). *Human Factors in Simple and Complex Systems* (2nd ed.). Boca Raton, FL: CRC Press.

Regens, J. L., Mould, N., Jensen, C. J., Graves, M. A., & Edger, D. N. (2015). Probabilistic graphical modeling of terrorism threat recognition using Bayesian networks and Monte Carlo simulation. *Journal of Cognitive Engineering and Decision Making, 9*, 295–311.

Ritter, F. E., & Young, R. M. (2001). Embodied models as simulated users: Introduction to this special issue on using cognitive models to improve interface design. *International Journal of Human-Computer Studies, 55*, 1–14.

Rong, M., Luo, M., Chen, Y., Sun, C., & Wang, Y. (2014). Human factor quantitative analysis based on OHFAM and Bayesian network. In C. Stephanidis (Ed.), *HCI International 2014—Proceedings of the International Conference, HCI International, Part I* (pp. 533–539). Cham, Switzerland: Springer International.

Rosch, E., Thompson, E., & Varela, F. J. (1991). *The Embodied Mind: Cognitive Science and Human Experience.* Cambridge, MA: MIT Press.

Rowlands, M. (2010). *The New Science Of The Mind: From extended mind to Embodied Phenomenology.* Cambridge, MA: MIT Press.

Rundell, O. H., & Williams, H. L. (1979). Alcohol and speed-accuracy tradeoff. *Human Factors, 21*, 433–443.

Salvucci, D. D. (2006). Modeling driver behavior in a cognitive architecture. *Human Factors, 48*, 362–380.

Samuel, A. J. (2000). Some studies in machine learning using the game of checkers. *IBM Journal of Research and Development, 44*, 206–226

Schmorrow, D., Stanney, K. M., Hale, K. S., Fuchs, S., Wilson, G., & Young, P. (2012). Neuroergonomics in human–system interaction. In G. Salvendy (Ed.), *Handbook of Human Factors and Ergonomics* (4th ed., pp. 1057–1082). Hoboken, NJ: Wiley.

Sebok, A., Wickens, C., Clegg, B., Sargent, R., & Alion Science and Technology. (2014). Using empirical research and computational modeling to predict operator response to unexpected events. In *Proceedings of the Human Factors and Ergonomics Society 58th Annual Meeting* (pp. 834–838). Santa Monica, CA; SAGE Publications.

Sebok, A., Wickens, C., Sargent, R., & Alion Science and Technology. (2013). Using meta-analyses results and data gathering to support human performance model development. In *Proceedings of the Human Factors and Ergonomics Society 57th Annual Meeting* (pp. 783–787). Santa Monica, CA; SAGE Publications.

See, J. E., Howe, S. R., Warm, J. S., & Dember, W. N. (1995). Meta-analysis of the sensitivity decrement in vigilance. *Psychological Bulletin, 117*, 230–249.

Seow, S. C. (2005). Information theoretic models of HCI: A comparison of the Hick-Hyman law and Fitts' law. *Human-Computer Interaction, 20*, 315–352.

Sharma, N., & Gedeon, T. (2015). Modeling observer stress: A computational approach. *Intelligent Decision Technologies, 9*, 191–207.

Stevens, R. H., Galloway, T. L., Berka, C., & Behneman, A. (2010). Temporal sequences of neurophysiologic synchronies can identify changes in team cognition. In *Proceedings of the Human Factors and Ergonomics Society 54th Annual Meeting* (pp. 190–194). Santa Monica, CA: SAGE Publications.

Swoboda, J. C., Kilduff, P. W., & Katz, J. P. (2005). A platoon level model of communication flow and the effects on soldier performance. In *Proceedings of the Human Factors and Ergonomics Society 49th Annual Meeting* (pp. 1210–1214). Santa Monica, CA: SAGE Publications.

Szalma, J. L., Hancock, P. A., Warm, J. S., Dember, W. N., & Parsons, K. S. (2006). Training for vigilance: Using predictive power to evaluate feedback effectiveness. *Human Factors, 48*, 682–692.

Tanner, W. P., Jr., & Swets, J. A. (1954). A decision-making theory of visual detection. *Psychological Review, 6*, 401–409.

Tomlin, D., Rand, D. G., Ludvig, E. A., & Cohen, J. D. (2015). The evolution and devolution of cognitive control: The costs of deliberation in a competitive world. *Scientific Reports, 5*, Article number: 11002.

Tversky, A. (1972). Elimination by aspects: A theory of choice. *Psychological Review, 79*, 281–299.

Van Zandt, T., Colonius, H., & Proctor, R. W. (2000). A comparison of two response time models applied to perceptual matching. *Psychonomic Bulletin and Review, 7*, 208–256.

Wickens, C. D. (2002). Multiple resources and performance prediction. *Theoretical Issues in Ergonomics Science, 3*, 159–177.

Wickens, C. D. (2008). Multiple resources and mental workload. *Human Factors, 50*, 449–455.

Wickens, C. D., Goh, J., Helleberg, J., Horrey, W. J., & Talleur, D. A. (2003). Attentional models of multitask pilot performance using advanced display technology. *Human Factors, 45*, 360–380.

Wickens, C. D., McCarley, J. S., Alexander, A. L., Thomas, L. C., Ambinder, M., & Zheng, S. (2008). Attention-situation awareness (A-SA) model of pilot error. In D. C. Foyle & B. L. Hooey (Eds.), *Human Performance Modeling in Aviation* (pp. 213–239). New York: CRC Press.

Wilson, G. F., & Russell, C. A. (2007). Performance enhancement in an uninhabited air vehicle task using psychophysiologically determined adaptive aiding. *Human Factors, 49*, 1005–1018.

Wilson, G. F., Russell, C. A., Monnin, J. W., Estepp, J. R., & Christensen, J. C. (2010). How does day-to-day variability in psychophysiological data affect classifier accuracy? In *Proceedings of the Human Factors and Ergonomics Society 54th Annual Meeting* (pp. 264–268). Santa Monica, CA: SAGE Publications.

Witus, G., & Ellis R. D. (2003). Computational modeling of foveal target detection. *Human Factors, 45*, 47–60.

Wong, D., Walters, B., & Fairey, L. (2010). Validating human performance models of the future Orion crew exploration vehicle. In *Proceedings of the Human Factors and Ergonomics Society 54th Annual Meeting* (pp. 1002–1006). Santa Monica, CA; SAGE Publications.

Wood, S. D., & Kieras, D. E. (2002). Modeling human error for experimentation, training, and error-tolerant design. In *Proceedings of the Interservice/Industry Training, Simulation, and Education Conference* (pp. 1075–1085). Arlington, VA: National Training and Simulation Association.

Worm, A. (2000). Analysis of tactical missions: Integrating systems theory, systems engineering and psychophysiology. In *Proceedings of the Human Factors and Ergonomics Society 44th Annual Meeting* (pp. 274–277). Santa Monica, CA; SAGE Publications.

Wortman, D. R., Pritsker, A. A. B., Seum, C. S., Seifert, D. J., & Chubb, G. P. (1974). *SAINT: Vol. II. User's manual* (AMRL-TR-73–128).Wright-Patterson Air Force Base, OH: Aerospace Medical Research Laboratory.

Wu, C., & Liu, Y. (2007). Queuing network modeling of driver performance and workload. *IEEE Transactions on Intelligent Transportation Systems, 8*, 528–537.

Wu, C., & Liu, Y. (2008). Queuing network modeling of transcription typing. *Transactions on Computer-Human Interaction, 15*, 1–45.

Zemla, J. C., Ustun, V., Byrne, M. D., Kirlik, A., Riddle, K., & Alexander, A. L. (2011). An ACT-R model of commercial jetliner taxiing. In *Proceedings of the Human Factors and Ergonomics Society 55th Annual Meeting* (pp. 831–835). Santa Monica, CA: SAGE Publications.

6

Brain–Computer Interfaces and Neurofeedback for Enhancing Human Performance

RANGANATHA SITARAM, ANDREA SÁNCHEZ CORZO,
MARIANA ZURITA, CONSTANZA LEVICAN,
DANIELA HUEPE-ARTIGAS, JUAN ANDRÉS MUCARQUER,
AND MATÍAS RAMÍREZ

INTRODUCTION

It has long been thought, in the popular as well as scientific imagination, that signals from the brain could be used for communication and control. Converting thoughts into action has been the lore and imagination of fairy tales and science fiction (Wolpaw & Wolpaw, 2012). It is only in the past three decades that extensive research has begun, and it is only in the past 15 years that research in brain–computer interfaces (BCIs), also called brain–machine interfaces (BMIs), has emerged as a new field.

BCIs evolved from *biofeedback*, which is a group of experimental procedures in which an external sensor is used to provide information about a specific bodily process in order to change the measured quantity (Schwartz & Beatty, 1977). Proceeding from this definition, *neurofeedback* can be defined as a group of experimental procedures in which brain activity of a specific region or regions is measured and provided in the form of external sensory information for the purpose of changing specific brain activity. Neurofeedback can be used as a neuroscientific tool to understand the brain–behavior relationship by training individuals to modulate brain activity as an independent variable to test its effect on behavior. Neurofeedback has also shown promise as a clinical tool for the purpose of treatment or rehabilitation of neurological and psychiatric disorders.

The central nervous system (CNS) processes information about events in the outside world or inside the body and produces changes in the musculature and in the neural and hormonal systems of the body for serving the needs of the organism. A BCI is a system that produces new output, different from the neuromuscular and hormonal output of the body (Wolpaw & Wolpaw, 2012). BCI is a system that processes CNS activity and converts it into artificial output that replaces, restores, enhances, supplements, or improves the natural CNS output and thereby changes

the interactions between the CNS and the external as well as the internal environment in relation to the body.

CNS activity consists of (1) neuroelectric activity, including neural spikes or action potentials, multiunit activity, and synaptic potentials; (2) neurochemical activity, including the release of neurotransmitters and changes in other chemicals
and ions in the brain; and (3) metabolic activity, which includes the changes in
blood flow, oxygenation and deoxygenation, glucose metabolism, and other related
changes.

These changes in the CNS can be measured by placing sensors on the scalp, near
the vicinity of the head, on the surface as well as inside the CNS. These sensors could
be electrical (e.g., electroencephalography [EEG], electrocorticography [ECoG],
or intracortical electrodes); magnetic (e.g., magnetoencephalography [MEG]);
optical (e.g., functional near infrared spectroscopy [fNIRS] or two-photon imaging; or nuclear (e.g., functional magnetic resonance imaging [fMRI] and positron
emission tomography [PET]). These sensors are some of the most prominent and
widely used brain imaging systems in vogue today.

A BCI or a neurofeedback system acquires signals from the brain of a human or
an animal using any one or more of these sensors, then selects or extracts specific
features of interest from the signal and converts and then translates these into artificial output that can act on the body or the outside world. The process begins
with observation of neural activity using EEG, MEG, invasive electrodes, fMRI,
fNIRS, or imaging sensors (see Figure 6.1). The grids shown on the neural tissues
provide a qualitative reference for the relative spatial resolutions of the various imaging technologies. Univariate signal processing approaches extract signals from
a single channel or region of interest, such as an evoked potential or levels of the
blood oxygenation level–dependent response (BOLD). Calculation of coherence
or connectivity between two channels as a measure of functional connectivity is another common feedback method. Features from a set of sensors, such as the power
at a frequency window or the level of activation, can be classified as multivariate pattern analysis (MVPA). The calculated signal is then presented to the individual via
visual, auditory, haptic, or electrical stimulation feedback, allowing the user to alter
neural function and complete the loop with neural processing of feedback or translation of the signal features to commands, which then activate an external device.

A BCI may influence human performance by replacing, restoring, supplementing,
or enhancing the CNS function (Wolpaw & Wolpaw, 2012). A BCI output may replace a natural function that has been lost due to injury or disease (e.g., amyotrophic
lateral sclerosis [ALS]) by providing a communication system for conveying
messages to caregivers or for control of a wheelchair. A BCI/neurofeedback system
has the potential to restore lost or affected natural output, for example in a person
who is affected by spinal cord injury. A BCI/neurofeedback system may enhance
CNS function, such as perception, action, cognition, or emotion, through closed-
loop training/tuning of the appropriate and effective activation of the neural network involved in the function. A BCI may also supplement natural CNS output,
for example by providing an additional robotic arm for conducting a precision task.
In addition to these tasks, a BCI may improve the natural CNS function by closed-
loop neurofeedback training. For example, a person whose hand is weak due to a

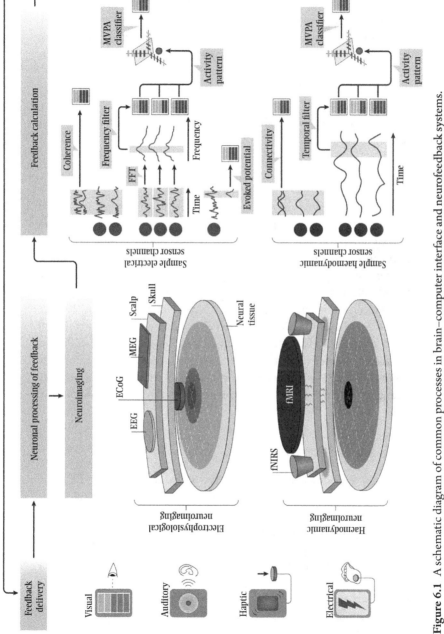

Figure 6.1 A schematic diagram of common processes in brain–computer interface and neurofeedback systems. Adapted with permission from Ranganatha Sitaram et al., Closed-loop brain training: The science of neurofeedback, *Nature Reviews Neuroscience, 18*, 86–100, 2017.

stroke in the motor cortex may recover his lost movement through BCI training involving electrical stimulation of muscles on his affected hand every time the BCI decodes his intention to move.

In this chapter, we discuss the extant research in terms of experimental work and neuroscience understanding of the application of BCIs and neurofeedback systems in influencing human performance in different CNS functions—namely, action, perception, cognition, and emotion—in healthy individuals, expert performers, and patients. This chapter is not intended to be a comprehensive review of the literature of this field, but rather to serve as an introduction to the field with representative examples. For a more detailed and comprehensive review of the literature, the reader is encouraged to refer to Sitaram et al. (2017); Ruiz, Buyukturkoglu, Rana, Birbaumer, and Sitaram (2014); and Birbaumer, Ruiz, and Sitaram (2013); or other similar reviews.

ACTION

Motor function can be affected for many reasons, including traumas, stroke, and diseases like Parkinson's disease (PD) and multiple sclerosis (MS). These brain disorders can eliminate or significantly reduce one's ability to perform certain movements. When a person has a significant motor impairment, especially in an environment that is not adequate or without proper care and aid, his or her quality of life is significantly affected. Even when physical and neurological therapies are available, some patients never achieve motor rehabilitation (Dimyan & Cohen, 2011).

The motor cortex shows functional and structural changes during learning of physical and abstract skills (Koralek, Jin, Long, Costa, & Carmena, 2012). This is why BCIs based on motor cortical signals have shown promise in learning new skills that could help people either recover a lost function or develop a new ability (e.g., controlling an external device to realize a specific task, such as moving an artificial arm).

Movement Recovery

There are a number of studies analyzing motor functional recovery using BCIs, especially in stroke survivors (Ang et al., 2011; Buch et al., 2008; Bundy et al. 2012; Mihara et al., 2013; Pichiorri et al., 2015; RamosMurguialday et al., 2013, to name a few), where neuroplasticity is of special importance (Dimyan & Cohen, 2011). Physical movements in stroke patients are in many cases not possible, which is why alternative paths formed by neuroplasticity can potentially achieve a better recovery (Ang et al., 2011).

Different approaches for training brain self-regulation using BCIs have been followed so far, including motor imagery and the use of orthopedic devices controlled by neural signals. There is a particular interest in motor imagery (i.e., the mental rehearsal of a physical movement; Ang et al., 2011) because it shows potential as a treatment for obtaining better functional outcomes in cases of severe motor impairment (Pichiorri et al., 2015). There is increasing evidence that motor imagery and motor execution share the same neural pathways (Mihara et al., 2013).

Subjects perform motor imagery and receive feedback based on their performance to learn to better control the activations of their motor areas.

An alternative for motor functional recovery is using BCI to help train movement with the aid of an orthosis. Birbaumer's group (Buch et al., 2008; Birbaumer et al., 2006; Birbaumer & Cohen, 2007) developed a MEG-controlled hand orthosis that helped patients with no residual hand movement to perform opening, closing, and grasping actions. The patients had two kinds of feedback: visual feedback that was correlated with the signal from the sensorimotor region of the brain and haptic feedback from the orthosis, which moved proportionately to the levels of brain activation in the targeted regions of the motor cortex.

Bundy et al. (2012) trained patients affected in one hemisphere to use the unaffected hemisphere to control the hand of that same side. The authors trained patients to control the EEG signal from the unaffected hemisphere to move a cursor, and they achieved ipsilateral motor activity with high accuracy. This approach could potentially be used to provide an alternative for traditional methods of rehabilitation of the affected side through physical therapy or pharmacological intervention.

Movement Replacement

Motor function replacement refers to giving the subject an alternate way to fulfill the action affected by the disease or trauma. This can be done, for example, by giving the subject a prosthesis or a wheelchair for movement. BCIs can be used to help the subject control those prostheses or even direct the movement of a wheelchair. Patients are trained to use their brain activity to control devices that can help them overcome their motor limitations.

One example of motor function replacement is presented in a study by Hochberg and colleagues who implanted a 96channel microelectrode array in the dominant M1 hand area to acquire extracellular action potentials (Hochberg et al., 2012). Subjects were able to control a robotic arm to reach and grasp small objects. One of the subjects, who had suffered a stroke 14 years earlier that left her tetraplegic, was even able to grab a bottle of coffee, bring it to her mouth to drink it, and then return it to the table for the first time since her stroke. In another study, Lee, Ryu, Jolesz, Cho, and Yoo (2009) trained subjects with real-time fMRI to modulate their motor cortical activity to control a robotic arm, which they could see through visual feedback. These two examples show that patients can be trained to regulate brain activity to perform motor tasks using external arms.

There are recent advances in developing an alternative approach for enabling movement in patients with motor impairment. One particular example is shown in a study carried out by Carlson and Millan (2013), where they developed a wheelchair controlled by a BCI system based on EEG.

Although the studies so far have shown promise for providing subjects greater opportunities of movement replacement, the methods are not yet ready for use in daily life. However, this area is advancing rapidly, and we are probably not far from a future where patients will be able to use some of these technologies to carry out daily tasks.

Sports Performance

There are potentially other applications of neurofeedback in addition to the recovery of movement lost in an accident or disease. Researchers have shown empirical evidence that it is possible to enhance motor abilities and performance in healthy individuals. In this regard, an interesting observation is that patterns of brain signals in professional athletes are different from amateur sport practitioners. It is proposed that identification and replication of EEG states of higher performance might help us enhance performance in sports at all competitive levels.

Research examining the psychophysiology of athletes has reported hemispheric asymmetries in the EEG prior to the execution of a skill. For instance, Hatfield, Landers, and Ray (1984) found that during the preparatory period of a skill, left-temporal EEG α activity (8–12 Hz) significantly increased. A similar finding was reported by Salazar et al. (1990), who found a significant increase in spectral power at 10 and 12 Hz in the left temporal region prior to the performance of a skill. This increase in the α frequency range allows the visual-spatial processes in the right hemisphere to become more dominant than the verbalization skills that are processed by the left temporal region. Researchers have wondered if it is possible to reduce left-temporal activity prior to skill execution movement in order to enhance physical activity via neurofeedback and training BCI systems.

There are also applications of neuroscience research and neurofeedback in sport. Pre-/post-measurements of EEG have been applied in boxers to discover the differences between pre-/post-combat electrocortical activity and also to evaluate long-term injuries due to repeated head hits. Football players have also been studied in this way to correlate brain damage and some disease symptoms such as headache, dizziness, irritability, and memory impairment. The most interesting research has been done in measuring EEG states of professional shooters. The pause in movement has provided sufficient scope to describe optimal patterns of cortical activity for taking aim in several sports: archery, golf, and rifle shooting.

Ring, Cooke, Kayussanu, McIntyre, and Masters (2015) reported that individuals who were trained with neurofeedback were capable of reducing the power of the α wave in their frontal regions, similar to the frontal brain activation of expert golfers before striking golf putts. However, this training did not strongly influence the subjects' golf performance. Neurofeedback training might improve concentration and focus, cognitive function, and emotional control, but there are still other variables implicated in enhancing sport performance that need to be understood and considered for it to be effective.

On the other hand, there are many emotional factors playing an important role in athletic performance. Graczyk et al. (2014) studied whether the intensive neurofeedback training of an athlete who has lost his performance confidence after a sports injury could change brain activity. They realized that, after a few sessions, the subject had increased the amplitude of the activity in the anterior cingulate cortex and the medial prefrontal cortex. They concluded that those changes could increase confidence in sport performance.

PERCEPTION

Perception relies on the interplay of ongoing spontaneous activity and stimulus-evoked activity in sensory cortices (Scharnowski, Hutton, Josephs, Weiskopf, & Rees, 2012). Neurofeedback studies have been developed to evaluate the effects of training on perception. The most extensive literature in perceptual learning with neurofeedback has been performed in visual perception. Scharnowski et al. (2012) evaluated the effect of training ongoing spontaneous activity in early retinotopic visual cortex and tested how this training could enhance perceptual sensitivity. Healthy volunteers were asked to up-regulate the level of activity in the visual cortex to a target level shown on the feedback display. Subjects learned self-regulation in a trial-and-error manner using a freely chosen mental strategy. Results showed a significant increase in the BOLD signal in the visual cortex as voluntarily controlled by learners. Post-training visual sensitivity tests showed an increase in the measure for stimuli presented at locations in the visual field that overlapped with the early retinotopic visual cortex in the learners. This study showed that training increases the brain activity in the visual cortex, which is associated with changes in the perception of visual stimuli.

Shibata, Watanabe, Sasaki, and Kawato (2011) addressed the question of whether the early visual cortex has sufficient plasticity to allow behavioral and/or sensitivity changes. To answer this question, the authors developed a neurofeedback method using a real-time fMRI decoder of activation patterns in V1/V2, corresponding to specific orientations (i.e., 70 degrees, 130 degrees) of Gabor gratings. First, gratings in three different orientations (10 degrees, 70 degrees, and 130 degrees) were presented to each participant. A decoder was implemented on fMRI signals evoked in the early visual cortex in response to the repeated trials of visual stimuli. After this, the same decoder was applied on the ongoing activity in the region to assess the likelihood of the activity to a target orientation that was selected from the three decoded orientations. Activation patterns were repeatedly induced with neurofeedback training without the participants knowing what they were learning. During the orientation discrimination task, participants were asked to report which of the three orientations of Gabor patches were presented to them in multiple trials. Results showed that after learning to induce activation patterns in V1/V2 corresponding to specific orientations chosen by the experimenter but not known to the participants, an increase in the mean likelihood of the target orientation was observed to be significantly higher than chance in comparison to the other nontarget orientations. This helped to demonstrate that the early visual cortex is amenable to neuroplastic changes brought about by neurofeedback training.

Salari, Büchel, and Rose (2014) studied neurofeedback training of visual perception using an electrophysiological approach. Knowing that γ band oscillations in the visual cortex play a functional role in perceptual processing (Tallon-Baudry & Bertrand, 1999), they aimed to investigate if γ band neurofeedback training affects perceptual processing. In a previous study, they had shown that neurofeedback training enhances ongoing activity in the γ band range over the lateral visual areas and that the presentation of images during the states of high γ band oscillation results in an increased perceptual processing of the stimulus (Salari, Büchel, &

Rose, 2012). Following this study, the authors hypothesized that neurofeedback training of γ band activity in the occipital cortex should also improve perceptual processing after training. To test this hypothesis, 24 volunteers were divided into two groups: a feedback group that was trained to modulate oscillations in the γ band and a control group with random feedback. Participants performed a perceptual object detection task and a spatial attention task before and after neurofeedback training. The behavioral tests revealed a very specific improvement related to the neurofeedback training. After the training, only the feedback group was able to enhance γ band activity and detected more objects correctly than the control group, thus demonstrating the perceptual enhancement in a specific manner due to neurofeedback training.

Cho, Kim, Lee, and Jung (2015) researched the effect of neurofeedback training on visual perception in stroke patients. The authors recruited 27 stroke patients who received occupational and physical therapy and divided them into two groups, a neurofeedback group ($n = 13$) who received neurofeedback training plus occupational and physical therapy and a control group ($n = 14$) who received only occupational and physical therapy. Participants received neurofeedback with auditory and visual reinforcement to increase the sensory motor rhythm (SMR, 12–15Hz) and decrease both the Δ (0.5–4Hz) and high-β (22–36 Hz) components of the EEG signal. A motor-free visual perception test (MVPT) was used to measure the visual discrimination, form constancy, visual memory, visual closure, and spatial relation. Analysis of the EEG signals before and after neurofeedback training revealed a statistically significant difference in the neurofeedback group for the SMR. The neurofeedback group had the most statistically significant differences in MVPT score, indicating the specific effect of neurofeedback on visual perception.

Other studies have focused on neurofeedback to modify perception in pathologies such as chronic pain and tinnitus. For example, deCharms et al. (2004) investigated whether learned manipulation of right anterior cingulate cortex (rACC) activation leads to effects on pain perception. In this study, healthy volunteer subjects were presented with nociceptive stimuli while receiving real-time fMRI feedback from the activation of rACC trained to be increased and then decreased. Results demonstrate that participants learned to control activation in the rACC and, after training, reported higher changes in intensity and unpleasantness in the perception of the stimuli. Increasing rACC activation was rated as significantly more painful compared to four independent control groups without valid rACC neurofeedback training. A group of chronic pain patients was also trained to control activation in the rACC; they reported reduction in the level of chronic pain after training.

Haller, Birbaumer, and Veit (2010) investigated whether patients suffering from tinnitus can learn to voluntarily reduce activation of the auditory cortices by real-time fMRI neurofeedback and whether learning improves tinnitus symptoms. In a sample size of six patients who suffered from continuous, nonpulsating tinnitus, the authors first identified the individual primary auditory cortices using a bilateral auditory stimulation with sinusoidal tone and then applied four neurofeedback training sessions of down-regulation. Five of the six subjects successfully learned to down-regulate their activations in the region of interest, showing significant linear decrease in the auditory activations over the training sessions. However, while subjects reported no change or mild improvement in tinnitus symptoms after the training, none of them reported increasing tinnitus symptoms.

COGNITION

Among the multitude of sensory information such as images, sounds, tastes, and smells coming to us, we can selectively attend to some information and ignore the rest. This ability or state of selectively processing simultaneously arriving information is called *attention* (Bear, Connors, & Paradiso, 2007). There have been attempts made at using BCI and neurofeedback to investigate the possibility of regulating brain regions involved in attentional processing and whether that would have a behavioral effect on attentional performance. In one such study, monkeys were trained to voluntarily increase or decrease the firing rate of neurons in the frontal eye field during fixation (Schafer & Moore, 2011). They were given auditory feedback and a reward when the desirable threshold was reached. Training led to improvement in the modulation of the neural activation of the frontal eye field and improvement in the behavioral measures of visual attention.

Another study investigated structural changes in gray matter volume and white matter connectivity after a neurofeedback training protocol to improve sustained attention. Subjects were trained to enhance the amplitude of EEG β waves in the range of 15–18 Hz (Ghaziri et al., 2013). Using diffusion tensor imaging, researchers found changes in the frontal and parietal regions of the brain after neurofeedback training. These structural changes were associated with improvements in visual and auditory sustained attention after training.

How can these approaches help in the investigation and treatment of problems related to attention? Individuals with attention deficit/hyperactivity disorder (ADHD) have shown anomalies in visual attention, specifically in θ and α oscillations of brain activity (Mazaheri et al., 2014). Indeed, a simultaneous EEG-fMRI imaging study (Ros et al., 2013) showed that neurofeedback training decreased the amplitude of the α rhythm, which was in turn associated with reduced mind-wandering, an experience in which thoughts do not persist long enough on one topic, particularly when an attention-demanding task is to be performed.

Other studies have looked at the modulation of slow cortical potentials (SCP), which are slow shifts in the direct-current levels of the EEG signal, considered to originate in the cell assemblies in the cortical layer. Neurofeedback training to increase the amplitude of the negative SCP amplitude was associated with improved clinical symptoms in ADHD (Gevensleben et al., 2014; Heinrich, Gevensleben, Freisleder, Moll, & Rothenberger, 2004).

Some researchers suggest that neurofeedback could be used to treat the elevated low-frequency synchronization in ADHD (Lubar & Lubar, 1984). Studies in children have shown that decreases in low-frequency amplitudes due to neurofeedback training were associated with improvements in ADHD symptoms (Janssen et al., 2016). Other studies have reported that the clinical effect of neurofeedback can be superior to computerized attention training carried out for 6 months (Gevensleben et al., 2009) or can even be similar to standard pharmacotherapy (Duric, Assmus, Gundersen, & Elgen, 2012; Meisel, Servera, Garcia-Banda, Cardo, & Moreno,

2013). As we can note, the voluntary modulation of neural activity can produce changes in cognitive functions; therefore neurofeedback training may be a therapeutic strategy for patients with ADHD (Gevensleben et al., 2009; Loo & Barkley, 2005).

In a study related to interception (i.e., attention toward one's own feelings and body sensations), participants were trained to gain control over the right anterior insular activity using real-time fMRI neurofeedback (Caria et al., 2007). To do this, subjects were provided with continuously updated information of the region's level of activation by visual feedback. Training led to up-regulation of this area and was associated with increased subjective ratings of the intensity of the aversive quality of negative images. As the right insula is related to subjective emotional responses, this increase in its activity might represent an increased attention to internal body sensations during subjective affective experience (Critchley, Wiens, Rotshtein, Öhman, & Dolan, 2004).

Neurofeedback training for ADHD using EEG is an alternative technique to pharmacotherapy that has been extensively studied in clinical environments. Although the underlying mechanisms of ADHD are not completely understood and definitive evidence of the efficacy of neurofeedback training for ADHD treatment is still lacking, there are a growing number of studies showing significant improvement of ADHD symptoms due to neurofeedback training. Some of these protocols have been extended to healthy subjects as well, in order to enhance attention and working memory.

Training protocols involving sensorimotor rhythm (SMR) and lower β EEG bands have shown enhancement in sustained attention in students of music (Egner & Gruzelier, 2003; 2004). The effectiveness of these protocols was measured by a Go-NoGo task showing a significant reduction in commission error. Similarly, SMR/θ and α/θ neurofeedback protocols have been used to optimize microsurgical skills (Ros et al., 2009) that are visuomotor skills under time constraints. The observed improvement after training was 26% less time, with an additional improvement in reduction of anxiety. SMR neurofeedback training produced better performance between training sessions in terms of more controlled and paced action. The α/θ training showed no significant difference between sessions, but a within-sessions effect was observed as a performance enhancement in the surgical technique.

Momentary loss of attention can have negative consequences, such as accidents. In a recent study, deBettencourt, Cohen, Lee, Norman, and Turk-Browne (2015) used real-time fMRI neurofeedback to train individuals to enhance sustained attention abilities and reduce the frequency of loss of attention. In the authors' laboratory, we built a novel real-time pattern classifier based on whole-brain neuroimaging data that could monitor the focus of attention. When the classifier indicated attentional lapses, the researchers gave human participants feedback by making the task more difficult. Behavioral performance improved after one training session relative to control participants who did not receive real or veridical feedback. This improvement was observed when the feedback was derived from a frontoparietal attention network. The findings from this study suggest that attention can be trained with appropriate feedback about neural signals.

EMOTION

Research of EEG-based neurofeedback signals has found that participants can learn to influence the amplitude or topography of specific components of scalp electric activity (Birbaumer et al., 2006). The development of real-time fMRI neurofeedback enabled the regulation of brain activity with much higher spatial precision (Weiskopf et al., 2004).

If neural bases of brain disorders are properly understood, it may be possible to create more effective interventions. Considering this, researchers have used real-time fMRI neurofeedback to train individuals to self-regulate brain areas that react to negative emotions and to determine whether these areas can be regulated voluntarily (Johnston, Boehm, Healy, Goebel, & Linden, 2010). Participants were trained to up-regulate such areas by looking at a thermometer that changed up or down according to the amplitude of the fMRI signal. With this approach, brain areas related to negative emotions can be regulated by means of neurofeedback. Participants used negative and positive imagery for regulation and needed only a brief training period to achieve a great degree of control over these networks. This study demonstrated the feasibility of real-time fMRI neurofeedback of emotion networks and its potential for therapeutic use in neuropsychiatric disorders (Johnston et al., 2010).

Falquez et al. (2014) also studied cognitive regulation of negative emotions but in a sample group of brain-injured patients. They propose that "self-focused reappraisal" (REAPPself) helps to decrease the relevance of negative events. This skill has been associated with neural activity in regions near the right medial prefrontal cortex. To know which area of the prefrontal cortex impairs this ability the most, they studied patients with damage in the frontal lobe. They presented neutral and negative affective pictures and also negative pictures where participants had to decrease the triggered negative emotions by means of REAPPself. Through fMRI analysis, they found that regions in the dorsolateral prefrontal cortex and the right dorsal anterior cingulate cortex were associated with a patient's impaired down-regulation of arousal. Therefore, a lesion in these areas might adversely affect the reappraisal ability necessary for affective and cognitive health (Falquez et al., 2014).

Positive emotions have been investigated with this approach as well. Johnston et al. (2011) implemented a method for identifying brain areas that are activated with positive stimulus. Participants were trained to up-regulate the insula and medial prefrontal cortex to attain reliable self-control of the target area, which led to activation of an extensive network of brain regions outside these targeted regions. However, self-control of the brain regions was not accompanied by clear changes in self-reported emotions, which led to the hypothesis that the benefits of self-control over emotion networks works only in people who display abnormal emotional regulation (Johnston et al., 2011).

Another group of researchers pointed out a key region of emotion regulation, the right anterior insula, which is involved in emotion processing and interoceptive awareness (Lawrence et al., 2014). Insular dysfunction has been noticed in several clinical conditions, and hence this research can have clinical applications. Researchers included a mindfulness-based strategy due to its feasibility for clinical populations. Participants were trained to increase right insular activation by real-time fMRI neurofeedback. Another group was shown feedback of activation levels from another brain area not directly involved in emotion processing. The results indicated a significant linear increase in right anterior insula activation in the group who received feedback from this region. This study showed that it is possible to regulate anterior insula using real-time fMRI neurofeedback, and such reward-learning is mediated by the dorsal anterior cingulate.

Some emotional dysregulation disorders during early stages of development can bring about a number of problems in adulthood. If clinicians can intervene in these problems in childhood or adolescence, then negative consequences might be diminished. A study tested the viability of training emotion regulation in children and adolescents (Cohen et al., 2016) by up-regulating the bilateral insula using real-time fMRI neurofeedback. Researchers found that all the subjects learned to increase activation during the up-regulation trials, contrary to down-regulation trials. After training, researchers observed functional connectivity between amygdala to the bilateral insula and to the left insula and the mid-cingulate cortex. This approach has potential use for shaping brain regions involved in social cognition during development.

Another approach that can have clinical implications is the prediction of emotional states from brain activity. Sitaram et al. (2011) showed a robust classification model to recognize emotional states in real time from fMRI signals. The objective was to demonstrate that multiple discrete emotional states, such as happiness, disgust, and sadness, could be classified and the information fed back to the participants. This approach could be potentially used in neuropsychiatric patients to modulate a whole network of brain regions involved in a complex brain function such as emotion for retuning the brain. The development of evidence-based neurofeedback trainings would be of great importance in patients suffering from disorders that involve emotional dysregulations, such as depression, anxiety, and other neuropsychiatric disorders.

Emotional disorders, such as social phobia or antisocial behavior, may be amenable to change through the modulation of brain activity in those regions related to emotion and attention (e.g., insula, anterior cingulate, and amygdala) through real-time fMRI training because these disorders are characterized by hyper- and hypoactivation in these brain regions.

CONCLUSION

Research in BCI and neurofeedback systems has enabled an alternate way of studying the relationship between brain and behavior and has led to improved knowledge of neural function by using brain activation as the independent variable and behavior and thought as dependent variables. Learned modulation of brain activity in specific regions, connections, and patterns can lead to specific functional and behavioral changes in action, perception, cognition, and emotion. Empirical and theoretical knowledge from BCI and neurofeedback studies could potentially be used to improve human performance by targeting training in healthy individuals, skilled performers, and patients. Technological and methodological developments in this field may accelerate this progress even further. However, there is much more that remains to be investigated, including the integration of the vast knowledge of neural mechanisms of learning and memory and training psychology into neurofeedback protocols. The levels and granularity of neural networks that can be modulated in neurofeedback, from single cells and connectivity between regions to multivariate patterns, is beginning to be understood. Clinical, therapeutic, and commercial use of BCIs and neurofeedback techniques is in its infancy, but there is a need for rigorous, well-controlled clinical trials and further understanding of the usability and ethical aspects of these techniques. BCIs and neurofeedback systems have the potential to be the harbingers of enhanced mental and physical performance in humans.

REFERENCES

Ang, K. K., Guan, C., Chua, K. S., Ang, B. T., Kuah, C. W., Wang, C., & Zhang, H. (2011). A large clinical study on the ability of stroke patients to use an EEGbased motor imagery braincomputer interface. *Clinical EEG and Neuroscience, 42*(4), 253258. doi:10.1177/155005941104200411

Bear, M. F., Connors, B. W., & Paradiso, M. A. (Eds.). (2007). *Neuroscience* (Vol. 2). Baltimore, MD: Lippincott Williams & Wilkins.

Birbaumer, N., & Cohen, L. G. (2007). Braincomputer interfaces: Communication and restoration of movement in paralysis. *The Journal of Physiology, 579*(3), 621–636. doi:10.1113/jphysiol.2006.125633

Birbaumer, N., Ruiz, S., & Sitaram, R. (2013). Learned regulation of brain metabolism. *Trends in Cognitive Sciences, 17*(6), 295–302. doi: 10.1016/j.tics.2013.04.009

Birbaumer, N., Weber, C., Neuper, C., Buch, E., Haapen, K., & Cohen, L. (2006). Physiological regulation of thinking: Brain–computer interface (BCI) research. *Progress in brain research, 159*, 369–391. doi:10.1016/S0079-6123(06)59024-7

Buch, E., Weber, C., Cohen, L. G., Braun, C., Dimyan, M. A., Ard, T., & Birbaumer, N. (2008). Think to move: A neuromagnetic braincomputer interface (BCI) system for chronic stroke. *Stroke, 39*(3), 910–917. doi:10.1161/strokeaha.107.505313

Bundy, D. T., Wronkiewicz, M., Sharma, M., Moran, D. W., Corbetta, M., & Leuthardt, E. C. (2012). Using ipsilateral motor signals in the unaffected cerebral hemisphere as a signal platform for brain–computer interfaces in hemiplegic stroke survivors. *Journal of Neural Engineering, 9*(3), 036011. doi:10.1088/17412560/9/3/036011

Caria, A., Veit, R., Sitaram, R., Lotze, M., Weiskopf, N., Grodd, W., & Birbaumer, N. (2007). Regulation of anterior insular cortex activity using real-time fMRI. *Neuroimage, 35*(3), 1238–1246. doi:10.1016/j.neuroimage.2007.01.018

Carlson, T., & Millan, J. D. (2013). Braincontrolled wheelchairs: A robotic architecture. *IEEE Robotics & Automation Magazine, 20*(1), 65–73. doi:10.1109/mra.2012.2229936

Cho, H. Y., Kim, K., Lee, B., & Jung, J. (2015). The effect of neurofeedback on a brain wave and visual perception in stroke: A randomized control trial. *Journal of Physical Therapy Science, 27*(3), 673–676. doi:10.1589/jpts.27.673

Cohen, K., Luo, Q., Burca, C. De, Sokunbi, M. O., Feng, J., Linden, D. E. J., & Lau, J. Y. F. (2016). Using real-time fMRI to influence effective connectivity in the developing emotion regulation network. *NeuroImage, 125,* 616–626. doi:10.1016/j.neuroimage.2015.09.070

Critchley, H. D., Wiens, S., Rotshtein, P., Öhman, A., & Dolan, R. J. (2004). Neural systems supporting interoceptive awareness. *Nature Neuroscience, 7*(2), 189–195. doi:10.1038/nn1176

deBettencourt, M. T., Cohen, J. D., Lee, R. F., Norman, K. A., & Turk-Browne, N. B. (2015). Closed-loop training of attention with real-time brain imaging. *Nature neuroscience, 18*(3), 470–475. doi:10.1038/nn.3940

deCharms, R., Christoff, K., Glover, G. H., Pauly, J. M., Whitfield, S., & Gabrieli, J. D. (2004). Learned regulation of spatially localized brain activation using real-time fMRI. *Neuroimage, 21*(1), 436–443. doi: 10.1016/j.neuroimage.2003.08.041

Dimyan, M. A., & Cohen, L. G. (2011). Neuroplasticity in the context of motor rehabilitation after stroke. *Nature Reviews Neurology, 7*(2), 76–85. doi:10.1038/nrneurol.2010.200

Duric, N. S., Assmus, J., Gundersen, D., & Elgen, I. B. (2012). Neurofeedback for the treatment of children and adolescents with ADHD: A randomized and controlled clinical trial using parental reports. *BMC Psychiatry, 12*(1), 107. doi:10.1186/1471-244X-12-107

Egner, T., & Gruzelier, J. H. (2003). Ecological validity of neurofeedback: Modulation of slow wave EEG enhances musical performance. *Neuroreport, 14*(9), 1221–1224. doi:10.1097/01.wnr.0000081875.45938.d1

Egner, T., & Gruzelier, J. H. (2004). EEG biofeedback of low beta band components: Frequency-specific effects on variables of attention and event-related brain potentials. *Clinical Neurophysiology, 115*(1), 131–139. doi:10.1016/S1388-2457(03)00353-5

Falquez, R., Couto, B., Ibanez, A., Freitag, M. T., Berger, M., Arens, E. A., . . . & Barnow, S. (2014). Detaching from the negative by reappraisal: The role of right superior frontal gyrus (BA9/32). *Frontiers in Behavioral Neuroscience, 8,* 165. doi:10.3389/fnbeh.2014.00165

Gevensleben, H., Albrecht, B., Lütcke, H., Auer, T., Dewiputri, W. I., Schweizer, R., . . . Rothenberger, A. (2014). Neurofeedback of slow cortical potentials: Neural mechanisms and feasibility of a placebo-controlled design in healthy adults. *Frontiers in Human Neuroscience, 8,* 990. doi:10.3389/fnhum.2014.00990

Gevensleben, H., Holl, B., Albrecht, B., Vogel, C., Schlamp, D., Kratz, O., & Heinrich, H. (2009). Is neurofeedback an efficacious treatment for ADHD? A randomised controlled clinical trial. *Journal of Child Psychology and Psychiatry, Psychiatry, 50*(7), 780–789. doi:10.1111/j.1469-7610.2008.02033.x

Ghaziri, J., Tucholka, A., Larue, V., Blanchette-Sylvestre, M., Reyburn, G., Gilbert, G., . . . Beauregard, M. (2013). Neurofeedback training induces changes in white and gray matter. *Clinical EEG and Neuroscience, 44*(4), 265–272. doi:10.1177/1550059413476031

Graczyk, M., Pachalska, M., Ziolkowski, A., Manko, G., Lukaszewska, B., Kochanowicz, K., . . . Kropotow, I. D. (2014). Neurofeedback training for peak performance. *Annals of Agricultural and Environmental Medicine, 21*(4),871–875. doi:10.5604/12321966.1129950

Haller, S., Birbaumer, N., & Veit, R. (2010). Real-time fMRI feedback training may improve chronic tinnitus. *European Radiology, 20*(3), 696–703. doi: 10.1007/s00330-009-1595-z

Hatfield, B. D., Landers, D. M., & Ray, W. J. (1984). Cognitive processes during self-paced motor performance: An electroencephalographic profile of skilled marksmen. *Journal of Sport Psychology, 6*(1), 42–59. doi:10.1123/jsp.6.1.42

Heinrich, H., Gevensleben, H., Freisleder, F. J., Moll, G. H., & Rothenberger, A. (2004). Training of slow cortical potentials in attention-deficit/hyperactivity disorder: Evidence for positive behavioral and neurophysiological effects. *Biological Psychiatry, 55*(7), 772–775. doi:10.1016/j.biopsych.2003.11.013

Hochberg, L. R., Bacher, D., Jarosiewicz, B., Masse, N. Y., Simeral, J. D., Vogel, J., & Donoghue, J. P. (2012). Reach and grasp by people with tetraplegia using a neurally controlled robotic arm. *Nature, 485*(7398), 372–375. doi:10.1038/nature11076

Janssen, T. W. P., Bink, M., Geladé, K., van Mourik, R., Maras, A., & Oosterlaan, J. (2016). A randomized controlled trial into the effects of neurofeedback, methylphenidate, and physical activity on EEG power spectra in children with ADHD. *Journal of Child Psychology and Psychiatry, 57*(5), 633–644. doi:10.1111/jcpp.12517

Johnston, S., Linden, D. E. J., Healy, D., Goebel, R., Habes, I., & Boehm, S. G. (2011). Upregulation of emotion areas through neurofeedback with a focus on positive mood. *Cognitive, Affective, & Behavioral Neuroscience, 11*(1), 44–51. doi:10.3758/s13415-010-0010-1

Johnston, S. J., Boehm, S. G., Healy, D., Goebel, R., & Linden, D. E. (2010). Neurofeedback: A promising tool for the self-regulation of emotion networks. *NeuroImage, 49*(1), 1066–1072. doi:10.1016/j.neuroimage.2009.07.056

Koralek, A. C., Jin, X., Long II, J. D., Costa, R. M., & Carmena, J. M. (2012). Corticostriatal plasticity is necessary for learning intentional neuroprosthetic skills. *Nature, 483*(7389), 331–335. doi:10.1038/nature10845

Lawrence, E. J., Su, L., Barker, G. J., Medford, N., Dalton, J., Williams, S. C., . . . Brammer, M. (2014). Self-regulation of the anterior insula: Reinforcement learning using real-time fMRI neurofeedback. *NeuroImage, 88*, 113–124. doi:10.1016/j.neuroimage.2013.10.069

Lee, J., Ryu, J., Jolesz, F. A., Cho, Z., & Yoo, S. (2009). Brain–machine interface via real-time fMRI: Preliminary study on thoughtcontrolled robotic arm. *Neuroscience Letters, 450*(1), 1–6. doi:10.1016/j.neulet.2008.11.024

Loo, S. K., & Barkley, R. A. (2005). Clinical utility of EEG in attention deficit hyperactivity disorder. *Applied Neuropsychology, 12*(2), 64–76. doi:10.1207/s15324826an1202_2

Lubar, J. O., & Lubar, J. F. (1984). Electroencephalographic biofeedback of SMR and beta for treatment of attention deficit disorders in a clinical setting. *Applied Psychophysiology and Biofeedback, 9*(1), 1–23. doi: 10.1007/BF00998842

Mazaheri, A., Fassbender, C., Coffey-Corina, S., Hartanto, T. A., Schweitzer, J. B., & Mangun, G. R. (2014). Differential oscillatory electroencephalogram between attention-deficit/hyperactivity disorder subtypes and typically developing adolescents. *Biological Psychiatry, 76*(5), 422–429. doi:10.1016/j.biopsych.2013.08.023

Meisel, V., Servera, M., Garcia-Banda, G., Cardo, E., & Moreno, I. (2013). Neurofeedback and standard pharmacological intervention in ADHD: A randomized controlled trial with six-month follow-up. *Biological Psychology, 94*(1), 12–21. doi:10.1016/j.biopsycho.2013.04.015

Mihara, M., Hattori, N., Hatakenaka, M., Yagura, H., Kawano, T., Hino, T., & Miyai, I. (2013). Nearinfrared spectroscopymediated neurofeedback enhances efficacy of motor imagerybased training in poststroke victims: A pilot study. *Stroke, 44*(4), 1091–1098. doi:10.1161/strokeaha.111.674507

Pichiorri, F., Morone, G., Petti, M., Toppi, J., Pisotta, I., Molinari, M., & Mattia, D. (2015). Braincomputer interface boosts motor imagery practice during stroke recovery. *Annals of Neurology, 77*(5), 851–865. doi:10.1002/ana.24390

RamosMurguialday, A., Broetz, D., Rea, M., Läer, L., Yilmaz, Ö., Brasil, F. L., & Birbaumer, N. (2013). Brainmachine interface in chronic stroke rehabilitation: A controlled study. *Annals of Neurology, 74*(1), 100–108. doi:10.1002/ana.23879

Ring, C., Cooke, A., Kavussanu, M., McIntyre, D., & Masters, R. (2015). Investigating the efficacy of neurofeedback training for expediting expertise and excellence in sport. *Psychology of Sport and Exercise, 16*, 118–127. doi:10.1016/j.psychsport.2014.08.005

Ros, T., Moseley, M. J., Bloom, P. A., Benjamin, L., Parkinson, L. A., & Gruzelier, J. H. (2009). Optimizing microsurgical skills with EEG neurofeedback. *BMC Neuroscience, 10*(1), 87. doi:10.1186/1471-2202-10-87

Ros, T., Theberge, J., Frewen, P. A., Kluetsch, R., Densmore, M., Calhoun, V. D., & Lanius, R. A. (2013). Mind over chatter: Plastic up-regulation of the fMRI salience network directly after EEG neurofeedback. *Neuroimage, 65*, 324–335. doi:10.1016/j.neuroimage.2012.09.046

Ruiz, S., Buyukturkoglu, K., Rana, M., Birbaumer, N., & Sitaram, R. (2014). Real-time fMRI brain computer interfaces: Self-regulation of single brain regions to networks. *Biological Psychology, 95*, 4–20. doi: 10.1016/j.biopsycho.2013.04.010

Salari, N., Büchel, C., & Rose, M. (2012). Functional dissociation of ongoing oscillatory brain states. *PloS One, 7*(5), e38090. doi:10.1371/journal.pone.0038090

Salari, N., Büchel, C., & Rose, M. (2014). Neurofeedback training of gamma band oscillations improves perceptual processing. *Experimental Brain Research, 232*(10), 3353–3361. doi:10.1007/s00221-014-4023-9

Salazar, W., Landers, D. M., Petruzzello, S. J., Han, M., Crews, D. J., & Kubitz, K. A. (1990). Hemispheric asymmetry, cardiac response, and performance in elite archers. *Research Quarterly for Exercise and Sport, 61*(4), 351–359. doi:10.1080/02701367.1990.10607499

Schafer, R. J., & Moore, T. (2011). Selective attention from voluntary control of neurons in prefrontal cortex. *Science, 332*(6037), 1568–1571. doi:10.1126/science.1199892

Scharnowski, F., Hutton, C., Josephs, O., Weiskopf, N., & Rees, G. (2012). Improving visual perception through neurofeedback. *Journal of Neuroscience, 32*(49), 17830–17841. doi:10.1523/JNEUROSCI.6334-11.2012

Schwartz, G., & Beatty, J. (1977). *Biofeedback, Theory and Research.* New York: Academic Press.

Shibata, K., Watanabe, T., Sasaki, Y., & Kawato, M. (2011). Perceptual learning incepted by decoded fMRI neurofeedback without stimulus presentation. *Science, 334*(6061), 1413–1415. doi:10.1126/science.1212003

Sitaram, R., Lee, S., Ruiz, S., Rana, M., Veit, R., & Birbaumer, N. (2011). Real-time support vector classification and feedback of multiple emotional brain states. *NeuroImage, 56*(2), 753–765. doi:10.1016/j.neuroimage.2010.08.007

Sitaram, R., Ros, T., Stoeckel, L., Haller, S., Scharnowski, F., Lewis-Peacock, J., . . ., Birbaumer, N. (2017). Closed-loop brain training: The science of neurofeedback. *Nature Reviews Neuroscience, 18*(2), 86–100. doi: 10.1038/nrn.2016.164

Tallon-Baudry, C., & Bertrand, O. (1999). Oscillatory gamma activity in humans and its role in object representation. *Trends in Cognitive Sciences, 3*(4), 151–162. doi:10.1016/S1364-6613(99)01299-1

Weiskopf, N., Scharnowski, F., Veit, R., Goebel, R., Birbaumer, N., & Mathiak, K. (2004). Self-regulation of local brain activity using real-time functional magnetic resonance imaging (fMRI). *Journal of Physiology-Paris*, 98(4–6), 357–373. doi:10.1016/j.jphysparis.2005.09.019

Wolpaw, J., & Wolpaw, E. W. (Eds.). (2012). *Brain–Computer Interfaces: Principles and Practice*. New York: Oxford University Press.

7

Evolution of Physiological Status Monitoring for Ambulatory Military Applications

WILLIAM J. THARION, KARL E. FRIEDL, MARK J. BULLER, NATALIA HENAO ARANGO, AND REED W. HOYT*

INTRODUCTION

While the information presented here is soldier-centric, the research and considerations are relevant to the health, safety, and performance monitoring of humans in a host of environments. The Army has sophisticated monitoring technologies for its vehicles and aircraft, but lacked a similar status monitoring strategy for soldiers. To help address this gap, concerted research and development efforts conducted by the US Army Research Institute of Environmental Medicine (USARIEM) and its partners have produced wearable physiological monitoring systems that can provide useful information to soldiers, medics, and small-unit leaders.

Ambulatory physiological monitoring of humans has been possible for more than 50 years. The invention of the Holter monitor in 1947 allowed continuous collection of electrocardiograms (ECGs), including off-the-body telemetry (NMAH, 2011). Norman "Jeff" Holter first demonstrated his system, which weighed about 82 pounds, while riding on a stationary bicycle. Early Holter monitors enabled the first ambulatory studies with continuous ECGs (Holter, 1961). Similar systems that are smaller, lighter, and consume less power were subsequently developed and remain the mainstay in cardiology diagnostics today. Patients using these systems can engage in normal activities for 24 hours or more while ECG data are collected and stored for use by cardiologists checking cardiac abnormalities. Clinical tools such

*The opinions or assertions contained herein are the private views of the authors and are not to be construed as official or as reflecting the views of the Army or the Department of Defense. The investigators have adhered to the policies for protection of human subjects as prescribed in Army Regulation 70-25 and SECNAVINST 3900.39D, and the research was conducted in adherence with the provisions of 32 CFR Part 219. Citations of commercial organizations and trade names in this report do not constitute an official Department of the Army endorsement or approval of the products or services of these organizations.

as the Holter monitor have inspired the development of a wide variety of wearable physiological monitoring systems/products for athletes, soldiers, and other healthy populations interested in tracking general health and performance.

The current heart rate and activity monitoring systems available today are used primarily for fitness applications. In contrast to the early Holter monitor development effort with its clear focus on the acquisition of ECG data, the needs of the Army are more diverse. Having a more comprehensive real-time physiological status monitoring (RT-PSM) system (Buller, Hoyt, Ames, Latzka, & Freund, 2005) allows individual soldiers, medics, and small-unit leaders to assess various physiological and cognitive indicators of soldier readiness and overall performance (Friedl et al., 2016).

The Department of Defense has envisioned a wide range of real-time physiological status monitoring applications, resulting in multiple development paths for useful wearable sensors/devices; this complicates the process of developing a RT-PSM system to meet soldier's needs. Furthermore, significant challenges are associated with this high level of interest as there would be in any large organization where (1) multiple stakeholders and priorities exist and (2) product development starts before the research and development process has been completed because of the urgency to reach the product phase. In addition, RT-PSM systems used in research have different characteristics than those required to meet operational needs for specified mission-based working groups. Despite these issues, the USARIEM-led work effort resulted in important research and development products and scientific findings in areas such as life signs monitoring and ballistic impact detection. Major challenges to this concept of monitoring soldiers on the battlefield for their readiness to perform the mission include the cost of mass production for warfighter use, the large scope of the effort, and the development of secure radio transmitters to send data as they are being collected. In spite of these significant challenges, the work effort to date has been successful because it resulted in a RT-PSM system with a well-defined use model for a specific group of military users: the National Guard Bureau's Weapons of Mass Destruction–Civil Support Teams (WMD-CSTs). The mission of the WMD-CSTs is primarily focused on the threats of chemical, biological, radiological, and/or nuclear attacks or accidents. Other civilian and military groups with similar missions, that could likely benefit from RT-PSM include the Coast Guard's Strike Teams, firefighters, police departments' Special Weapons and Tactic (SWAT) teams, and other first responders who deal with the same threats and hazards. Regardless of the user community, these types of systems must provide actionable real-time information to sustain health and performance in real time, often in austere environments.

After addressing RT-PSM needs for WMD-CSTs' individual use during simulated operations, a mature technology was implemented for use that provides accurate assessments of changing thermal work strain while wearing personal protective equipment to protect the individual from hazardous chemical, biological, radiological, and/or nuclear exposures. A map for this development is shown in Figure 7.1 and described in detail within this chapter. The RT-PSM product was developed through product characteristics articulated by the WMD-CSTs. This first breakthrough application, offers great opportunities for the engineering and biomedical

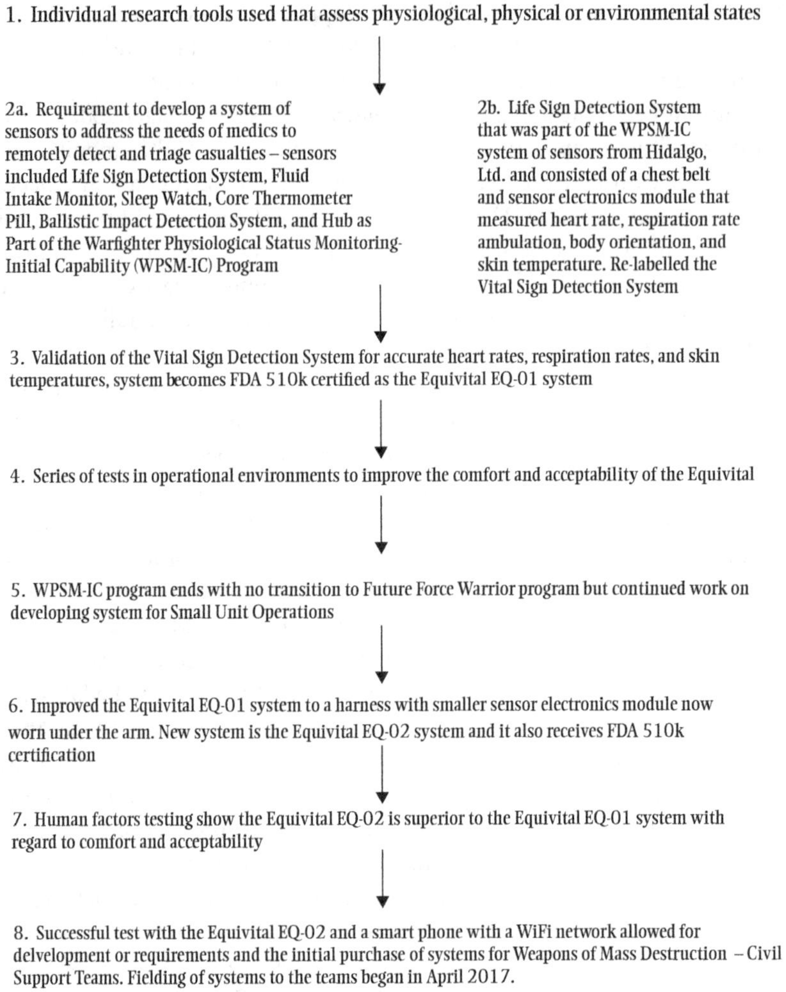

1. Individual research tools used that assess physiological, physical or environmental states

2a. Requirement to develop a system of sensors to address the needs of medics to remotely detect and triage casualties – sensors included Life Sign Detection System, Fluid Intake Monitor, Sleep Watch, Core Thermometer Pill, Ballistic Impact Detection System, and Hub as Part of the Warfighter Physiological Status Monitoring-Initial Capability (WPSM-IC) Program

2b. Life Sign Detection System that was part of the WPSM-IC system of sensors from Hidalgo, Ltd. and consisted of a chest belt and sensor electronics module that measured heart rate, respiration rate ambulation, body orientation, and skin temperature. Re-labelled the Vital Sign Detection System

3. Validation of the Vital Sign Detection System for accurate heart rates, respiration rates, and skin temperatures, system becomes FDA 510k certified as the Equivital EQ-01 system

4. Series of tests in operational environments to improve the comfort and acceptability of the Equivital

5. WPSM-IC program ends with no transition to Future Force Warrior program but continued work on developing system for Small Unit Operations

6. Improved the Equivital EQ-01 system to a harness with smaller sensor electronics module now worn under the arm. New system is the Equivital EQ-02 system and it also receives FDA 510k certification

7. Human factors testing show the Equivital EQ-02 is superior to the Equivital EQ-01 system with regard to comfort and acceptability

8. Successful test with the Equivital EQ-02 and a smart phone with a WiFi network allowed for delvelopment or requirements and the initial purchase of systems for Weapons of Mass Destruction – Civil Support Teams. Fielding of systems to the teams began in April 2017.

Figure 7.1 Roadmap of real-time physiological status monitoring (RT-PSM) system leading to operational use in the chemical, biological, radiological, and/or nuclear environment.
Image courtesy of the authors.

communities to improve the size, weight, power, and functionality to augment this initial capability with a full suite of readiness status indicators that are relevant to personnel in a number of different occupations (Friedl et al., 2016).

DEVELOPMENT OF REAL-TIME PHYSIOLOGICAL STATUS MONITORING (RT-PSM) FOR THERMAL WORK STRAIN MONITORING

In his 2015 State of the Union address, President Barack Obama announced a new national initiative in precision medicine. *Precision medicine* is the approach that considers individual responses based on genetics, environment, and lifestyle/health habits. Although the Army's mission planning tools currently comprise predictive models based on population means, RT-PSM and more individualized models (e.g., use of avatars and metabolic models, virtual reality scenario planning, personalized planning), are becoming a reality (Costanzo et al., 2014). The RT-PSM assessments of health, safety, and performance are made using validated sensor measurements of individual metrics, e.g., heart rate, motion patterns, and speech patterns.

An example of precision medicine was described in the Institute of Medicine book *Monitoring Metabolic Status* (Hoyt & Friedl, 2004), where two vastly different responses are recorded from two foot soldiers working together in the hot environment at Ft. Polk, Louisiana (ambient temperature, 32–34°C; relative humidity, 46–55%; solar load 800–875 W/m²; wind speed: 1–2 m/s⁻¹). One individual was a seasoned 509th Infantry[1] soldier who was heat acclimatized, weighed 68 kg with 13% body fat and had an estimated aerobic fitness (VO₂ max) of 53 ml·kg⁻¹·min⁻¹. The other was a military cadet who was not heat acclimatized, weighed 79 kg with 18% body fat, with an estimated VO₂ max of 47 ml·kg⁻¹·min⁻¹. The cadet was also carrying more weight (20.5 kg), than the 509th soldier (16.0 kg). The individuals were involved in the same physical activities but demonstrated different physiological responses. In Figure 7.2, it can be seen that, by early afternoon, the cadet's core temperature response to exercise as measured by an ingested thermometer pill was approaching unsafe levels, and this overheated individual was removed from the training exercise by medical staff for safety reasons. The basis for the differences in physiological responses and functional work capacities are multifaceted and not readily predicted. However, as seen in Figure 7.2, heat strain level is an overarching parameter that can be used for continuous monitoring by leaders and medical personnel to learn the limits of performance of the individual and the team.

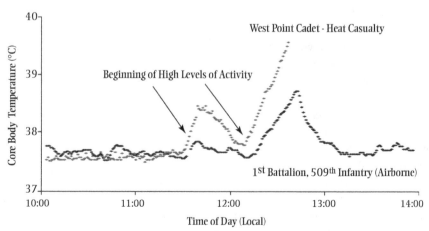

Figure 7.2 Thermal work strain differences in two individuals participating in simulated combat at the Joint Readiness Training Center, Fort Polk, Louisiana.
Image adapted from R. W. Hoyt & K. E. Friedl, Current status of field applications of physiological monitoring for the dismounted soldier, in *Monitoring Metabolic Status: Predicting Decrements in Physiological and Cognitive Performance* (pp. 247–257), Washington, DC: Institute of Medicine, 2004.

Smart sensor systems will aid small-unit leaders, similar to athlete or sport team coaches, efforts to maximize soldier training, ultimately pushing training unit limits while minimizing the risk of injuries. Real-time information regarding heat and work strain can be used to optimize march pace, load sharing, and work rate (Buller, Welles et al., 2015) increasing the likelihood of completing a physically challenging event. Team performance is not necessarily the sum of all individual task performances, but rather it is the coordinated effort of individuals all playing a part in the successful execution of a mission. For years, the idea of physiological monitoring, especially heat strain monitoring, has been advocated to improve the safety and performance of individuals in various stressful or harsh environments (Bernard & Kenney, 1994).

The military has developed PSM systems to meet the needs of the dismounted warfighter because commercially-available PSM systems were not available to meet those needs (Buller, Welles, Jenkins, & Hoyt, 2010). On the one hand, medical monitoring systems used in hospital or home healthcare settings provide the high-quality data required for medical decisions, but these systems have unfavorable size, weight, and power; lack durability; and may be uncomfortable or interfere with the normal physical activities that ambulatory warfighters need to perform for their jobs. On the other hand, there are monitoring systems primarily for use in the fitness arena that would be acceptable to wear, can be used in harsh environments, and do not interfere with job performance, but these do not provide the variety of accurate and precise physiological data needed to make mission or safety decisions. A suitable system must produce valid data, work reliably in the specific environment for which it is intended, be comfortable and easy to use, and not inhibit motion or job performance (Paradiso, Loriga, & Taccini, 2005). Furthermore, sensors must be of minimal weight and size, consume little power, and have negligible impact on the body (Patel, Park, Bonato, Chan, & Rodgers, 2012), and they must also provide accurate data that can be analyzed to provide actionable decision-making. To function in real time, wearable sensors must have reliable wireless body area network connections (Milenković, Otto, & Jonanov, 2006). Without connectivity, PSM use reverts to physiological data collection and storage for post hoc analysis.

For at least 25 years, USARIEM has collaborated with academic, commercial, and other government partners to develop stand-alone sensors primarily for use as research tools to assess the warfighter's health and performance in challenging operational environments. Tools such as heart rate monitors (Hoyt et al., 1997), global positioning systems (GPS; Hoyt et al., 1997), thermometer pills to assess core temperature (O'Brien, Hoyt, Buller, Castellani, & Young, 1998; Tharion & Hoyt, 2004), wrist-worn accelerometers to assess sleep performance and fatigue (Cole et al.,1992; Hursh et al., 2004), foot sensors to estimate movement and energy expenditures (Hoyt et al., 1994; Hoyt et al., 2004; Tharion, Yokota, Buller, DeLany, & Hoyt, 2004), and fluid intake monitors to assess hydration status/fluid intake (Tharion, Karis, & Hoyt, 2009) were all used to better understand the behavior and physiological status of soldiers and reduce the risk of heat casualties. As these wearable sensors became available, the need to develop a wireless body area network linking all the sensors became evident. A physiological monitoring system for warfighters was envisioned whereby the thermal, hydration, metabolic, environment, cognitive, and health safety status could be determined and communicated to decision-makers (e.g., a medic or squad leader) (Hoyt & Friedl, 2004).

THE WARFIGHTER PHYSIOLOGICAL STATUS MONITORING– INITIAL CAPABILITY (WPSM-IC) PROGRAM

Around 2000, the US Army Medical Research and Materiel Command, in a surge of interest, sought to develop a system of wearable sensors to help prevent soldiers from becoming casualties, enhance their physical and cognitive performance, and enable medics to remotely detect and triage casualties. The Warfighter Physiological Status Monitoring—Initial Capability (WPSM-IC) work effort sought to integrate a number of sensor systems to meet these goals (Buller et al., 2005). The sensors of the WPSM-IC system included:

- *Life sign detection system*: Measured heart rate and ECGs, respiration, ambulation, body orientation, and skin temperature;
- *Fluid intake monitor*: Flow meter attached to a soldier's bladder canteen to measure fluid consumed from the canteen;
- *Sleep watch*: Estimated apparent sleep from wrist motion;
- *Thermometer pill*: Measured core temperature by an ingested telemetry pill;
- *Ballistic impact detection system*: Measured an impact and location in the body of a projectile through vibration and acoustic signatures;
- *Hub*: Integrated the sensor signals and provided a central communications node for the array of sensors.

In addition to the sensors, five algorithms transformed raw data from the various sensors into information that the medic could use. The algorithms consisted of:

- *Life sign state*: Probability of individual being alive or dead;
- *Thermal state*: Individual's thermal response; normal or at risk of heat or cold injury;
- *Hydration state*: Individual's fluid consumption; euhydrated, underhydrated, or overhydrated;
- *Cognitive state*: Predicted cognitive function from individual sleep history;
- *Ballistic impact detection state*: Probability of an individual having been hit by a bullet or other projectile.

A depiction of the WPSM-IC system by components and the associated algorithms is shown in Figure 7.3.

This first integrated PSM system prototype collected and processed data from multiple sensors. The sensors aggregated, processed, and stored the data. Data from each of various sensor nodes were wirelessly transmitted to the hub where sensor data were further aggregated to provide the five categories of actionable information to be transmitted off the body (Buller, 2010). This aggregated actionable information was communicated via hard wire from the hub to a radio for transmission to a leader's or medic's Biomedical Information System-Tactical (BMIS-T), a

Figure 7.3 Warfighter physiological status monitoring (WPSM) system in 2005. Image adapted from M. J. Buller, R. W. Hoyt, J. Ames, W. Latzka, & B. Freund, Enhancing warfighter readiness through physiologic situational awareness: The warfighter physiological status monitoring: Initial capability," in *Proceedings of the 1st International Conference on Augmented Cognition* (p. 336), Mahwah, NJ: Erlbaum, 2005.

specialized personal digital assistant (PDA). This WPSM-IC system was part of a series of systems that would be layered into the Future Force Warrior[2] radio system. Alternatively, the WPSM-IC system could be used on a stand-alone basis with an off-body radio connection to transmit data to a remote computer for viewing. Key considerations for this system were:

- minimal size weight and power;
- open architecture to facilitate upgrades;
- simple design;
- minimal logistical tail; and
- economically reproducible in mass quantities.

The life sign detection system was the key component of the WPSM-IC system. It obtains ECG signals and heart rate, respiration rate, skin temperature, and body orientation and movement. An initial study with four prototype concept designs (a vest, rubber chest belt, textile chest belt, and an adhesive patch) were tested for user acceptability with soldiers who were taking part in the US Army Expert

Infantryman Badge course. Results from this test showed that a textile chest belt and an adhesive patch were most favorably rated (Beidleman et al., 2003). The next step was testing the system(s) for reliability and validity of measures. There were four candidate systems assessed: (1) the VivoMetrics Lifeshirt (Ventura, CA), (2) a soft chest strap from the Center for the Integration of Medicine and Innovative Technologies (CIMIT, Cambridge, MA), (3) a chest belt from Sarcos Research Company (Salt Lake City, UT), and (4) a thoracic sensor from Hidalgo Ltd. (Swavesey, Cambridge, UK). These candidate systems were compared to data collected at the same time from criterion gold standard devices: Schiller Cardiovit AT-6 ECG machine (Schiller Inc., Baer, Switzerland) for heart rate and a Sensor Medics 2900 metabolic cart (SensorMedics Corporation, Yorba Linda, CA) for respiration rate during a number of standard movements, such as lying down, sitting, standing, walking, running, and calisthenics. Results from this laboratory evaluation revealed that the VivoMetrics Lifeshirt and the CIMIT Soft Chest Strap were the most valid and reliable systems, whereas the Sarcos Integrated Sensor Unit and the Hidalgo Thoracic Sensor did not meet the criteria for valid measurements for heart rate or respiration (Beidleman, Tharion, Buller, Hoyt, & Freund, 2004). Although the Lifeshirt met the reliability and validity requirements, its form factor and comfort was not acceptable to soldiers in the field (Beidleman et al., 2003). It was heavy, not breathable and increased thermal strain in those who wore the system.

The Hidalgo prototype system (a pre-Equivital EQ-01 system) was redesigned from the thoracic sensor based on the results from the Beidleman et al. (2004) study to a chest strap with a detachable sensor electronics module. This system was then evaluated and improved through an iterative testing and development process. This new Hidalgo chest-belt system underwent a similar validity and reliability test, as was done for the previous four candidate systems in the Beidleman et al. (2004) study. This Hidalgo chest-belt system produced accurate heart rates for most activities, including walking and running, although some calisthenics activities with substantial upper body movements had increased numbers of invalid measurements (Tharion, Buller, Karis, & Mullen, 2008). Data from this study supplemented data collected by Hidalgo Ltd. and others were used to obtain Food and Drug Administration (FDA) 510k certification of the system (FDA #K061993).[3] This system, now termed the Equivital EQ-01, met the form and function attributes required for use by military personnel (Beidleman et al., 2003). As a result, the US Army funded further development of this system to meet the goals of the WPSM-IC program with a focus on a system for casualty detection and triage management.

The viewing interfaces for the WPSM-IC system were designed using feedback from US Army medics, the intended users of the system (Tharion & Kaushik, 2006; Kaushik & Tharion, 2009). Medics thought information on the BMIS-T PDA or computer screens should be color-coded into green ("good to go"), yellow ("look"), and red (an urgent "look now") to draw attention to an impending or apparent injury. A blue color was used to indicate that the information was not available or was unreliable. Medics did not want the system to determine the live/dead status of a soldier. Furthermore, there was no standard for remote death certification. They recommended seven screens one could navigate through to get information:

1. Map screen depicting geo-location and green, yellow, and red statuses of those soldiers a medic would be responsible for;
2. Summary of squad status;
3. Name list with top-level vital sign information displayed;
4. Individual warfighter information with detailed vital signs about a particular warfighter;
5. Treatment screen, where information on treatment administered to a particular warfighter could be added;
6. Electronic field medical card; and
7. Medical reference center where general medical information could be looked up.

Around 2006, the Life Sign Detection System was renamed the Vital Sign Detection System. This renaming was in part due to the information from medics, where they stated they did not want a machine determining live versus dead status. Therefore, the term "Life Sign" was changed to "Vital Sign." In 2007, the specifications for the on-body Vital Sign Detection System were provided to the Future Force Warrior program. However, the Future Force Warrior program ended, and the Vital Sign Detection System was never integrated into the Future Force Warrior System of Systems.

SMALL-UNIT OPERATIONS' PHYSIOLOGICAL STATUS MONITORING SYSTEM

Development of a RT-PSM system for small-unit operations continued, with the Equivital EQ-01 used as a research tool to collect data in field settings with minimal impact on warfighters' missions or training. Studies with the Ranger Training Brigade quantified thermal strain during a timed road march performed at different times of the year (Tharion, Karis, Potter, & Hoyt, 2014) and classified changes in gait pattern during the marches (Clements, Buller, Welles, & Tharion, 2012). Two important studies examined thermal strain experienced by Marine foot patrols in Iraq (Buller et al., 2008) and in Afghanistan (Welles et al., 2013). These studies documented thermal strain experienced by Marines when patrolling in hot environments (air temperatures higher than 39°C [102.2°F]) while wearing and carrying full combat loads. The data from the Iraq study indicated that there was at least a 50% risk of Marines succumbing to heat exhaustion (Buller et al., 2008). In Afghanistan, the heat problem was not as severe. These research studies showed how modeling of mission work rates, environmental conditions, and clothing and individual equipment worn or carried can be used to predict heat strain and the risk of heat illness during combat patrols (Buller et al., 2008; Welles, Buller, Richter, McCarthy & Hoyt, 2013). The high thermal strain associated with these patrols, the limited reserve capacity that was available if a higher work rate was needed to respond to a threat, and the rapid cooling that occurred with the removal of body armor were all documented. The US Marine Corps (USMC), seeking to mitigate the heat strain experienced in Marines working in hot environments, changed their doctrine to allow local field commanders to set the level of ballistic protection worn by their Marines based on the threat present and environmental conditions. In addition, simpler, cooler, and less encapsulating soft body armor was developed to reduce heat strain in hot environments.

In 2007, the Equivital EQ-01 PSM system was successfully commercialized. However, this system caused chafing, and the separate body area network hub component, which was typically carried in a pocket, was not ideal (Tharion, Buller, Karis, & Mullen, 2007). The Equivital EQ-01 system was incrementally improved based on results from a series of tests conducted during military training exercises (Figure 7.4). These tests were performed with military test volunteers training in (a) wooded and urban settings (Version 1); (b) urban operations (Version 2); (c) enclosed-space chemical, biological, radiological, and/or nuclear operations; (d) a Ranger Training Brigade road march (Version 3); and (e) during Special Forces Assessment School training in a primarily wooded environment (Version 4) (Tharion, Buller, Karis, & Hoyt, 2010). As shown in Figure 7.4, the Equivital EQ-01 Versions 1 and 2 would wirelessly send physiological data from the sensors to the hub. By Version 3, a separate hub was no longer needed as data processing and storage shifted from the hub to the sensor electronics module integrated onto the chest strap. These studies showed that the main human factors issues with the Equivital EQ-01 system were associated with the hard plastic sensor electronics module mounted to the chest strap in the middle of the chest. The sensor electronics module was uncomfortable and/or interfered with task performance when worn (1) under body armor; (2) during activities where a warfighter was performing a

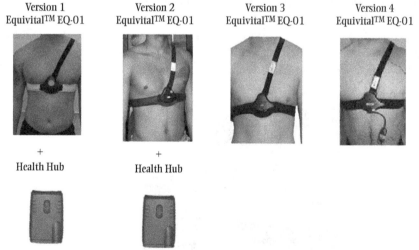

Figure 7.4 Vital sign detection systems tested under operational conditions.
Image adapted from W. J. Tharion, M. J. Buller, A. J. Karis, & R. W. Hoyt, Development of a remote medical monitoring system to meet soldier needs, in T. Marek, W. Karwowski, & V. Rice (Eds.), *Advances in Understanding Human Performance: Neuroergonomics, Human Factors, Design, and Special Populations* (p. 494), Boca Raton, FL: CRC Press, Taylor and Francis Group, 2010.

task in the prone position, such as shooting a rifle while prone or low crawling; and (3) while sleeping (Tharion et al., 2010).

As a result of the aforementioned studies, the Equivital EQ-01 system was redesigned from a chest belt with the sensor electronics module in the middle of the chest to an Equivital EQ-02 harness with a smaller sensor electronics module positioned under the left arm (Figure 7.5). The new Equivital EQ-02 system, which is FDA 510k-certified (FDA #K113054),[4] has proved to be a reliable and valid physiological monitor (Liu, Zhu, Wang, Ye, & Li, 2013). A study of US Army soldiers who were participating in infantry training exercises with and without body armor compared the Equivital EQ-02 system to the Equivital EQ-01 system. All volunteers (100%) reported the Equivital EQ-02 system would be acceptable to wear for 8 hours or longer, while only 70% of participants reported that the Equivital EQ-01 system would be acceptable to wear for that length of time (Tharion, Buller, Potter et al., 2013). Based on this study and the results of a study examining comfort and acceptability of the Equivital EQ-02 system when used in conjunction with chemical, biological, radiological, nuclear, and/or explosive personal protective equipment (Tharion, Buller, Clements et al., 2013), the Equivital EQ-02 system was deemed a candidate for a RT-PSM system by the National Guard Bureau to monitor heat strain levels in down-range WMD-CST personnel. The WMD-CST chemical-biological defense community now uses RT-PSM to monitor thermal strain in down-range operators.

Core temperatures measured directly through the use of rectal or esophageal probes or through the use of core thermometer pills can be used to monitor heat strain. However, probes are intrusive and ill-suited for use in the field and thermometer pills are not practical for routine use (Lim, Byrne, & Lee, 2008; Tharion & Hoyt, 2004). Specific issues with thermometer pills are that some individuals (e.g., those with gastrointestinal problems) should not ingest them, the pills are expensive (~$35–50 per pill), and they have a limited shelf life, creating logistical problems in their procurement and use. Thermometer pills may also be affected by cold water ingestion (Wilkinson, Carter, Richmond, Blacker, & Rayson, 2008).

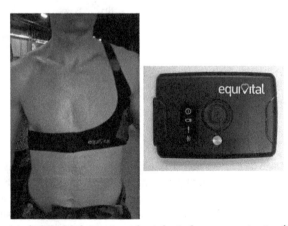

Figure 7.5 Equivital EQ-02 Life Monitor physiological status monitoring (PSM) system. Image courtesy of the authors.

Fortunately, core temperature can be accurately estimated from time series heart rate (Buller et al., 2013) where the developed algorithm/application can be incorporated into the PSM system's firmware. This algorithm has been shown to be reliable and valid when compared to core body temperature measured by an ingestible thermometer pill when used in a simulated chemical/biological environment (Buller, Tharion, Duhamel, & Yokota, 2015). Furthermore, this core temperature estimate can be used with instantaneous heart rate to calculate an easy-to-use index of thermal/work strain on the 1–10 physiological strain index (PSI) scale (Moran, Shitzer, & Pandolf, 1998). The advantage of using PSI is that it incorporates core temperature and work intensity heart rate into a single number. This enables the thermal/work strain on individual soldiers to be quickly assessed and the missions adjusted as needed to minimize the likelihood of heat casualties. However, it is also possible to simply show work strain, heart rate, and core temperatures/predicted core temperatures (i.e., from the heart rate algorithm) separately depending on user needs.

USE OF REAL-TIME PHYSIOLOGICAL STATUS MONITORING (RT-PSM) IN CHEMICAL, BIOLOGICAL, RADIOLOGICAL, NUCLEAR, AND EXPLOSIVE ENVIRONMENTS

Wearing body armor or personal protective equipment (e.g., chemical-biological suits) impedes evaporative cooling and can lead to increases in thermal strain and the risk of heat illnesses or injuries (Kenney et al., 1988). In a study of chemical, biological, radiological, and/or nuclear enclosed-space exercise almost 10 years ago (Buller et al., 2007), the Equivital EQ-01 system and a commercial Digi XTrend RF Modem (Maxstream Inc., Lindon, UT), were used to telemeter physiological data from down-range personnel in protective ensembles to a base station computer at the command post. This was one of the first demonstrations of real-time physiological data being transmitted off-body in a simulated chemical, biological, radiological, and/or nuclear environment. While the quality and accuracy of the data transmitted were not perfect, this demonstration with the Equivital EQ-01 system and a commercial-off-the-shelf radio system showed the practicality for RT-PSM.

As mentioned earlier, the National Guard Bureau is the first military group to acquire a RT-PSM system for use. Within the United States and its territories, the National Guard Bureau has 57 WMD-CSTs that serve as first responders to chemical, biological, radiological, and/or nuclear incidents. They assist law enforcement by gathering sample evidence and photographing chemical, biological, radiological, and/or nuclear material samples. To complete their missions, they are often encapsulated in Level A personal protective equipment with a self-contained breathing apparatus (SCBA). The impermeability of this personal protective equipment protects them from the chemical and biological agents, but it also creates a microenvironment that is thermally stressful primarily because heat dissipation through evaporation is dramatically compromised.

The WMD-CST missions typically involve a standardized sequence of actions once an incident takes place. A command post established at a safe distance from the incident site monitors and helps secure the site, and two-man survey teams are sent to investigate the contaminated zone. The command post monitors the health of the survey team typically with support from medical personnel who use verbal communication with the team members remotely via a radio system. Team members provide subjective assessments of each other's status and communicate that information to the medical team. The level of heat strain is a key point of concern, given that overheating is usually inevitable given the occlusive protective clothing. Mean work rates for these personnel range between 184 ± 66 W and 542 ± 142 W and total energy expenditure ranged from 1.2 ± 0.2 MJ to 2.6 ± 0.4 MJ (Welles, Tharion, Potter, & Buller, 2016). Work levels are important to understand because they are the basis for metabolic heat production. The use of RT-PSM systems allows the command and medical personnel to make judgments based on quantitative thermal work strain information rather than relying on subjective assessments of team members' health state.

Personnel performing chemical, biological, radiological, nuclear, and/or explosive missions are inherently at risk of overheating due to the encapsulating personal protective equipment they use for their missions. Tharion, Potter et al. (2013; see Figure 7.6) studied thermal work strain in chemical, biological, radiological, nuclear, and/or nuclear training environments and showed individual responses to heat stress varied widely. Specifically, seven WMD-CST

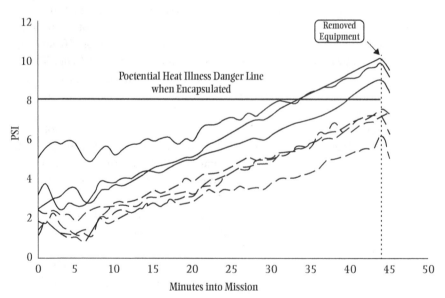

Figure 7.6 Estimated minute-by-minute physiological strain index (PSI) for seven soldiers simulating a 600 m approach march in Level A chemical biological personal protective equipment; solid lines represent three soldiers at a high risk for heat illness or injury, while the dashed lines represent the four soldiers who were at a low risk for a heat illness or injury near the end of the march.

Image adapted from W. J. Tharion, A. W. Potter, C. M. Duhamel, A. J. Karis, M. J. Buller, & R. W. Hoyt, Real-time physiological monitoring while encapsulated in personal protective equipment, *Journal of Sport and Human Performance*, 1(4), 18, 2013.

individuals performed a self-paced simulated approach march to a chemical/biological incident site. Prior to the end of the approach march and prior to removing their personal protective equipment, three individuals had elevated thermal work strain PSI values that put them at increased risk of becoming heat casualties.

Based on the successful demonstrations with the Equivitial EQ-02 RT-PSM system with the WMD-CST system (Tharion, Potter et al., 2013), the National Guard Bureau started the process of acquiring a RT-PSM system in 2013. However, radio communications were still an issue for the system to transmit data. In the demonstrations, a separate radio was required to be purchased and carried by down-range personnel to transmit their physiological information back to the command post. In addition, Bluetooth technology was used to transmit information from the sensor electronics module to the radio. Subsequently, during demonstrations with WMD-CSTs, a smartphone was attached to the outside of the personal protective equipment to display information to team members so they could monitor each other. Information from WMD-CST focus groups revealed that while the operators themselves viewed this smartphone—termed the "Buddy Display"—favorably, medical and leadership personnel did not. However, since all members carry smartphones, the decision was made within the WMD-CST working group to wire the sensor electronics module to the operator's smartphone and that it would be worn on the inside of the personal protective equipment. This decision was made to eliminate the need for any use of Bluetooth technologies, as systems using Bluetooth were excluded for purchase consideration by the WMD-CSTs. Therefore, information is transmitted by wire from the PSM harness to the smartphone and then is transmitted to the command post through a secure WiFi connection. Radio repeaters are used to send information over long distances or through enclosed spaces, like tunnels or concrete buildings. The Naval Air Command (NAVAIR, Patuxent River, MD) has been the lead integrator of getting the Equivital system to work with smartphones through the use of a secure WiFi network.

The National Guard Bureau's medical integrated product team developed a Medical Technical Directive (Autrey, Dominguez, Paquin, Sood, & Tharion, 2017) with suggested decision matrices for PSM system alerts that detail recommended actions for all users when various sensors indicate green (individual proceeds with mission activities), amber (medical provider or leader takes a look at the data or individual), or red (medical provider or leader makes a decision regarding the individual or mission activities) levels. These actions are, however, only recommendations as mission decision-making is left to the on-site medical or command person. Different personnel (e.g., command staff, medical staff, decontamination line, survey team members) all have different actions they take based on this sensor information. Finally, for use in the field, the term "physiological strain index" or PSI was changed to *heat strain index* or HSI because these WMD-CST personnel use the term PSI to refer to the pounds per square inch of air pressure in their SCBA tanks and a new acronym was needed (Tharion, Potter et al., 2013). However, the HSI equation used with these systems is identical to the PSI developed by Moran, Shitzer, and Pandolf (1998).

APPLICATION TO HUMAN PERFORMANCE OPTIMIZATION AND SAFETY

The National Guard Bureau developed requirements for PSM systems primarily focused on improving monitoring heat strain and its management for their operators. A "New Equipment Training" package that teaches proper use of the system and how to interpret the data from the system was developed, validated, and provided to the first four WMD-CSTs in the spring of 2017. In conjunction with the training, the Medical Technical Directive (Autrey et al., 2017) provides various team members suggested operating guidelines on what to do when various alarms or alerts from the system are triggered. Different data streams from the system go to different users, as well as different suggested courses of actions depending on job responsibility, as detailed in the Medical Technical Directive. For example, actual physiological data (heart rate, respiration, skin temperature) will be provided to the healthcare provider, whereas the command and operational staff gets a nonmedic view (fall alerts, an overall green-amber-red health status, etc.). This serves to provide the appropriate information to the right individuals and to have the system and the operation remain compliant with The Health Insurance Portability and Accountability Act of 1996 (HIPAA; The United States 104th Congress, 1996). Test results from the Army Test and Evaluation Command supported the procurement of this system (Figure 7.7) for all 57 WMD-CSTs. This initial purchase was completed, and, as of the summer of 2017, 12 of the 57 WMD-CSTs have received systems and their new equipment training on these systems and are using these systems in training and during actual missions. The schedule is that, by 2019, all 57 WMD-CSTs will have their systems and associated training on these systems. It is believed that continued experience using RT-PSM during chemical, biological, radiological, nuclear, and/or explosive missions should reduce the risk of heat illnesses or injuries. In turn, this knowledge will be valuable in advocating more widespread use of RT-PSM systems within the Department of Defense.

FUTURE OF PHYSIOLOGICAL STATUS MONITORING FOR MILITARY APPLICATIONS

Future use of PSM systems requires various users to determine how they will use the system, define their concept of operations, and articulate requirements. For example, the WMD-CSTs currently have missions that are less than 24 hours in duration and monitoring with a RT-PSM system only occurs with encapsulation in personal protective equipment, usually for less than 90 minutes. For these missions, power conservation is not a primary issue. However, for dismounted patrols that may last up to 72 hours, the size, weight, and power requirements of RT-PSM systems are great concerns. Systems that are dramatically smaller, lighter, and require less power are under development.

Future RT–PSM systems also need to provide accurate and reliable data for their intended use (e.g., valid time series heart rates are needed in order to derive valid predicted core temperatures) (Buller et al., 2013). Currently, chest-worn PSM systems are at a higher technical maturity level than non–chest-worn

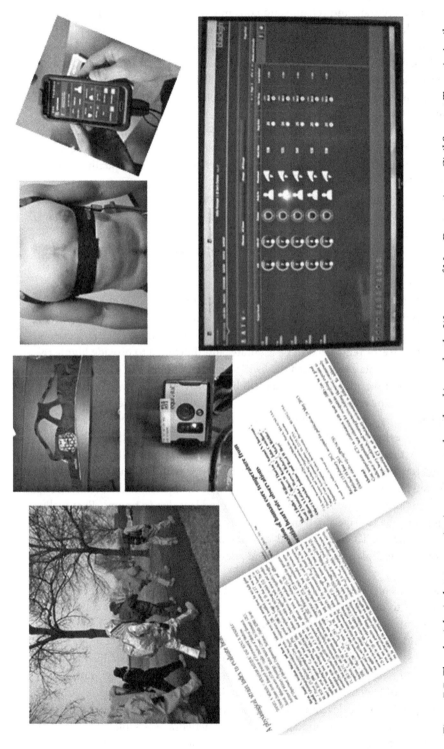

Figure 7.7 The physiological status monitoring system purchased and in use by the Weapons of Mass Destruction—Civil Support Teams in April 2017 including embedded algorithms described in the Moran et al. (1998) and Buller et al. (2013) papers. Image courtesy of the authors.

systems. That is to say that heart rate monitoring chest-based systems are generally more accurate and reliable and consume less power than optical sensors, enabling the systems to operate for longer time periods based on available battery power. It is also important to remember that any system, no matter how accurate the data it produces, must be worn for the system to be useful. Across user communities, there is a desire to transition to PSM systems that are wrist-watch–based, adhesive sensors, or embedded within clothing. Efforts to make systems as unobtrusive as possible (i.e., wear-and-forget) are necessary and welcomed. However, if chest-worn systems are comfortable enough to wear and do not impact job performance, they should only be replaced by other less cumbersome and more acceptable systems when those new systems produce equally or better accurate data.

Currently, the major development efforts for systems are divided between nonmedical systems that alert team members, leaders, or medics prior to an injury or in the event of a decrement in physical or cognitive performance and systems used to collect clinical information for medical diagnostics. Nonmedical systems are being developed to assess soldier readiness (Friedl et al., 2016) based on thermal status, physical readiness, alertness, wellness, and other parameters. This is likely to involve other sensors beyond heart rate, respiration rate, and accelerometer measures so that actions may take place to avoid fatigue and other problems. These are not medical systems and do not require FDA certification. However, these systems need to be accurate, and they need to provide highly reliable and valid data even though they will not be used to make a diagnosis of any medical condition. The ultimate goal will be to provide as accurate a prediction of soldier readiness for a particular mission as possible. This objective likely will be enhanced by examining other parameters in addition to thermal strain, such as sleep state, hydration state, emotional and cognitive state, and the like. In the meantime, there are separate efforts within the military to develop systems specifically for the combat casualty care community, where medical diagnoses and improved patient outcomes are the end goals. For example, a medical-grade PSM system could be used to assess and manage blood loss due to trauma. Eventually, the goal may be to have an all-in-one system or a modular system that will meet everyone's needs. To meet this goal, an open-architecture design is a necessity to allow a plug-and-play set of sensors as required for any particular set of needs or circumstances.

The close collaboration with industry and academia has proved to be an effective way to advance the development of PSM technologies that support the military's missions. This involvement of industry partners is also important because future PSM systems may utilize microsensors, such as temporary tattoos (Yang et al., 2015), sensors embedded in clothing, or other everyday wearable items like watches and necklaces (Patel et al., 2012), that are being developed outside the Department of Defense. New networked wireless, low-power "Internet of Things" technologies are being developed that allow sensors, both on the body and on local objects (e.g., unattended ground sensors), to be network assessable, readable, and controllable (Swan, 2012). Open architected Internet of Things–enabled sensors and applications will help service members and others more effectively manage their health, safety, and readiness for the demands of specific jobs. Examples include Internet of Things–enabled tools to manage body composition, physical activity, physical fitness, and metabolic fuel use. However, the development and use of Internet of Things–enabled technologies for personal healthcare and other applications is impeded by the proprietary systems that companies commonly produce.

Regardless of the sensor systems employed, algorithms will continue to be personalized to the unique individual combinations of physical, physiological, and mental attributes and to the specific mission tasks at hand. Concepts of operation and use will be needed for various missions where RT-PSM systems may be useful.

CONCLUSION

The research and development efforts described here have produced PSM systems sufficiently mature to use for specific military applications, most notably for personnel performing work in the chemical, biological, radiological, and/ or nuclear environments, where heat strain is a serious mission consideration and where direct visualization of the individuals on a down-range team may not be possible. Use of RT-PSM systems within training environments for the dismounted warfighter in nonhostile environments, especially within the United States, is ready to proceed. The early adopters of PSM technologies will provide useful knowledge regarding the efficacy and utility of these systems in improving training, mission performance, and reducing heat illness and heat injury events. The PSM systems, whether used in real-time or to collect data for post hoc analyses are valuable applied research tools that can be used to study warfighters and others in harsh environments without research procedures interfering with their missions or activities. To date, PSM systems have been used in operational and environmental medicine, physiology, psychology, human factors, biomedical engineering, mathematical modeling, and market research studies of soldier health and performance. It is expected that the development of advanced materiel solutions, such as clothing, individual equipment (e.g., packs and personal protective equipment), and communications systems, can all be enhanced through the collection and use of data using PSM technologies.

ACKNOWLEDGMENTS

The authors acknowledge all of the scientists, engineers, leaders, and key team members who have worked to make meaningful contributions in this area. Dr. Beth Beidleman was the principal investigator on two key early studies in the evaluation of the physiological status monitoring systems. Dr. Beau Freund (COL, U.S. Army, retired) and Dr. William Latzka (COL, U.S. Army, retired) provided outstanding leadership in their roles as the Science and Technology Objective Manager and the Development Team Leader, respectively. Other USARIEM individuals playing key roles as part of the PSM research, development, and test and evaluation team include Anthony Karis, Stephen Mullen, Dr. Sangeeta Kaushik, Dr. Miyo Yokota, and Cynthia Clements.

The authors thank Mallory Roussel, USARIEM Public Affairs, for assistance in preparing this manuscript and for editorial assistance. Special thanks to all the civilian and service men and women who have served as test volunteers and made personal heat strain monitoring technologies possible.

NOTES

1. The 509th infantry at Ft. Polk, Louisiana, serves as an experienced home-team training force for other units to compete against in simulated combat activities. As such, they are very experienced and highly proficient soldiers, both as individuals and as combat units.
2. The Future Force Warrior program was an Army program to integrate a number of new advanced technologies, including electronics, for soldiers who sought to enhance their fighting and protection capabilities.
3. https://www.accessdata.fda.gov/cdrh_docs/pdf6/K061993.pdf, accessed June 8, 2016.
4. https://www.accessdata.fda.gov/cdrh_docs/pdf11/K113054.pdf, accessed June 8, 2016.

REFERENCES

Autrey, A. W., Dominguez, D. A., Paquin, M. R., Sood, E., & Tharion, W. J. (2017, Marh 31). *Weapons of Mass Destruction—Civil Support Team (WMD-CST) Medical Community Technical Directive*. Arlington, VA: National Guard Bureau.

Beidleman, B. A., Hoyt, R. W., Pearce, F. J., Sims, N. M., Ditzler, D. T., Ames, J., . . . Freund, B. J. (2003). *User Acceptability of Design Concepts for a Life Sign Detection System* (Technical Report T-04-02). Natick, MA: United States Army Research Institute of Environmental Medicine. AD A421578.

Beidleman, B. A., Tharion, W. J., Buller, M. J., Hoyt, R. W., & Freund, B. J. (2004). *Reliability and Validity of Devices for a Life Sign Detection System* (Technical Report T-05-01). Natick, MA: United States Army Research Institute of Environmental Medicine. AD A428006.

Bernard, T. E., & Kenney, W. L. (1994). Rationale for a personal monitor for heat strain. *American Industrial Hygiene Association Journal, 55*(6), 505–514.

Buller, M. J. (2010). Systems architecture. In *HFM-132 Real-Time Physiological and Psycho-Physiological Status Monitoring. NATO RTG Technical Report*. (TR-HFM-132) (pp. 2.1–2.8). Paris: North Atlantic Treaty Organisation. AD A534283.

Buller, M. J., Hoyt, R. W., Ames, J., Latzka, W., & Freund, B. (2005). Enhancing warfighter readiness through physiologic situational awareness—The warfighter physiological status monitoring—Initial capability. In *Proceedings of the 1st International Conference on Augmented Cognition* (pp. 335–344). Mahwah, NJ: Erlbaum.

Buller, M. J., Tharion, W. J., Cheuvront, S. N., Montain, S. J., Hoyt, R. W., & Jenkins, O. C. (2013). Estimating human core temperature from heart rate. *Physiological Measurement, 34,* 781–798.

Buller, M. J., Tharion, W. J., Duhamel, C. M., & Yokota, M. (2015). Real-time core body temperature estimation from heart rate for first responders wearing different levels of personal protective equipment. *Ergonomics*, 58(11), 1830–1841.

Buller, M. J., Tharion W. J., Karis, A. J., Santee, W. R., Mullen, S. P., Blanchard, L. A., & Hoyt, R. W. (2007). *Demonstration of Real-time Physiological Status Monitoring of Encapsulated 1st Civil Support Team –Weapons of Mass Destruction (CST-WMD) Personnel* (Technical Report T-08-01). Natick, MA: United States Army Research Institute of Environmental Medicine. AD A473188.

Buller M. J., Welles, A., Jenkins, O. C., & Hoyt, R. W. (2010). Extreme health sensing: The challenges, technologies, and strategies for active health sustainment of military personnel during training and combat missions. In E. M. Carapezza (Ed.), *Proceedings of the SPIE, Sensors, and Command, Control, Communications, and Intelligence. (C3I) Technologies for Homeland Security and Homeland Defense IX*. Orlando, FL: International Society for Optics and Photonics (Vol. 7666, pp. 766610–766612).

Buller, M. J., Welles, A. P, Stevens, M., Leger, J., Gribok, A., Jenkins, O. C., Friedl, K. E., & Rumpler, W. (2015). Automated guidance from physiological sensing to reduce thermal-work strain levels on a novel task. In *2015 IEEE 12th International Conference on Wearable and Implantable Body Sensor Networks (BSN)* (pp. 1–6), Cambridge, MA: IEEE.

Buller, M. J., Wallis, D. C., Karis, A. J., Hebert, N., Cadarette, B. S., Blanchard, L. A., ... Richter, M. W. (2008). *Thermal Work Strain During Marine Rifle Squad Operations in Iraq (Summer, 2008)* (Technical Report T-09-01). Natick, MA: United States Army Research Institute of Environmental Medicine. AD B345494.

Clements, C. M., Buller, M. J., Welles, A. P., & Tharion, W. J. (2012). Real-time gait pattern classification from chest worn accelerometry. In *Proceedings of the 34th Annual International Conference of the IEEE EMBS* (pp. 364–367). San Diego, CA: Institute of Electrical and Electronics Engineers Engineering in Medicine and Biology Society.

Cole, R. J., Kripke, D. F., Gruen, W., Mullaney, D. J., & Gillin, J. C. (1992). Automatic sleep/wake identification from wrist activity. *Sleep*, 15(5), 461–469.

Costanzo, M. E., Leaman, S., Jovanovic, T., Norrholm, S. D., Rizzo, A. A., Taylor, P., and Roy, M. J. (2014). Psychophysiological responses to virtual reality and subthreshold posttraumatic stress disorder symptoms in recently deployed military. *Psychomatic Medicine*, 76, 670–677.

Friedl, K. E., Buller, M. J., Tharion, W. J., Potter, A. W., Manglapus, G. L., & Hoyt, R. W. (2016). *Real Time Physiological Status Monitoring (RT-PSM): Accomplishments, Requirements, and Research Roadmap*. (Technical Note TN-16-2). Natick, MA: United States Army Research Institute of Environmental Medicine. AD A630142.

Holter, N. J. (1961). New method for heart rate studies continuous electrocardiography of active subjects. *Science*, 134, 1214–1220.

Hoyt, R. W., Buller, M., Redin, M. S., Poor, R. D., Oliver, S. R., Matthew, W. T., ... Kearns, C. (1997). *Soldier Physiological Monitoring Results of Dismounted Battlespace Battle Lab Concept Experimentation Program Field Study* (Technical Report T-98-6). Natick, MA: United States Army Research Institute of Environmental Medicine. AD A332713

Hoyt, R. W., Buller, M. J., Santee, W. R., Yokota, M., Weyand, P. G., & DeLany, J. P. (2004). Total energy expenditure estimated using foot-ground contact pedometry. *Diabetes Technology and Therapeutics*, 6(1), 71–81.

Hoyt, R. W., & Friedl, K. E. (2004). *Monitoring Metabolic Status: Predicting Decrements in Physiological and Cognitive Performance* (pp. 247–257). Washington, DC: Institute of Medicine.

Hoyt, R. W., Knapik, J. J., Lanza, J. F., Jones, B. H., & Staab, J. S. (1994). Ambulatory foot contact monitor to estimate metabolic cost of human locomotion. *Journal of Applied Physiology, 76*(4), 1818–1822.

Hursh, S. R., Redmond, D. P., Johnson, M. L., Thorne, D. R., Belenky, G., Balkin, T. J., . . . Eddy, D. R. (2004). Fatigue models for applied research in warfighting. *Aviation, Space, and Environmental Medicine, 75*(3, Suppl), A44–A53.

Kenney, W. L., Lewis, D. A., Armstrong, C. G., Dykersterhouse, T. S., Fowler, S. R., & Williams, D. A. (1988). Psychometric limits to prolonged work in protective clothing ensembles. *American Industrial Hygiene Association Journal, 49*(8), 390–395.

Kaushik, S., & Tharion, W. J. (2009). US Army medic recommendations for a graphical user interface for a new battlefield medical monitoring system. *Military Medicine, 174,* 702–708.

Lim, C. L., Byrne, C., & Lee J. K. W. (2008). Human thermoregulation and measurement of body temperature in exercise and clinical settings. *Annals Academy of Medicine, 37,* 347–53.

Liu, Y., Zhu, S. H., Wang, G. H., Ye, F., & Li, P. Z. (2013). Validity and reliability of multiparameter physiological measurements recorded by the Equivital Lifemonitor during activities of various intensities. *Journal of Occupational and Environmental Hygiene, 10,* 78–85.

Milenković, A., Otto, C., & Jonanov, E. (2006). Wireless sensor networks for personal health monitoring: Issues and implementation. *Computer Communications, 29*(13–14), 2521–2533.

Moran, D. S., Shitzer, A., & Pandolf K. B. (1998). A physiological strain index to evaluate heat stress. *American Journal of Physiology Regulatory Integrative and Comparative Physiology, 275,* 129–134.

National Museum of American History (NMAH). (2011). *At the Heart of the Invention: Development of the Holter Monitor.* Washington, DC: Smithsonian National Museum of American History.

O'Brien, C., Hoyt, R. W., Buller, M. J., Castellani, J. W., & Young, A. J. (1998). Telemetry pill measurement of core temperature in humans during active heating and cooling. *Medicine and Science in Sports and Exercise, 30*(3), 468–472.

Paradiso, R., Loriga, G., & Taccini, N. (2005). A wearable health care system based on knitted integrated sensors. *IEEE Transactions on Information Technology in Biomedicine, 9*(3), 337–344.

Patel, S., Park, H., Bonato, P., Chan, L., & Rodgers, M. (2012). A review of wearable sensors and systems with application in rehabilitation. *Journal of Neuroengineering and Rehabilitation, 9*(21), 1–17.

Swan, M. (2012). Sensor mania! The Internet of Things, wearable computing, objective metrics and the quantified self 2.0. *Journal of Sensor Actuator Networks, 1,* 217–253.

Tharion, W. J., Buller, M. J., Clements, C. M., Dominguez, D., Sampsonis, C., Mullen, S. P., . . . Potter, A. W. (2013). *Human Factors Evaluation of the Hidalgo Equivital™ EQ-02 Physiological Status Monitoring System* (Technical Report T-14-2). Natick, MA: United States Army Research Institute of Environmental Medicine. AD A592523.

Tharion, W. J., Buller, M. J., Karis, A., & Hoyt, R. W. (2010). Development of a remote medical monitoring system to meet soldier needs. In T. Marek, W. Karwowski, & V. Rice (Eds.), *Advances in Understanding Human Performance: Neuroergonomics, Human Factors, Design, and Special Populations* (pp. 491–500). Boca Raton, FL: CRC Press, Taylor and Francis Group.

Tharion, W. J., Buller, M. J., Karis, A. J., & Mullen, S. P. (2007). Acceptability of a wearable vital sign detection system. In *Proceedings of the Human Factors and Ergonomics Society 51st Annual Meeting* (Vol. 51, pp. 1006–1010). Santa Monica, CA: Human Factors and Ergonomics Society.

Tharion, W. J., Buller, M. J., Karis, A. J., & Mullen, S. P. (2008). Reliability and validity of a wearable heart rate and respiration rate sensor system. *The FASEB Journal, 22,* 1175.7 (Abstract).

Tharion, W. J., Buller, M. J., Potter, A. W., Karis, A. J., Goetz, V., & Hoyt, R. W. (2013). Acceptability and usability of an ambulatory health monitoring system for use by military personnel. *IIE Transactions on Occupational Ergonomic and Human Factors, 1*(4), 204–214.

Tharion W. J., & Hoyt, R. W. (2004). *Ranger Medic Evaluation for Field Use of a Core Temperature Monitoring Unit* (Technical Report T-05-03). Natick, MA: United States Army Research Institute of Environmental Medicine. AD A429510.

Tharion, W. J., Karis, A. J., & Hoyt, R. W. (2009). *Reliability and Validity of Measurements of a Prototype Fluid Intake Monitor* (Technical Report T-09-04). Natick, MA: United States Army Research Institute of Environmental Medicine. AD A492057.

Tharion, W. J., Karis, A. J., Potter, A. W., & Hoyt, R. W. (2014). Seasonal differences in performance of the Ranger School qualifying road march. *Journal of Sport and Human Performance, 2*(2), 1–14.

Tharion, W. J., & Kaushik, S. (2006). *Graphical User Interface (GUI) for the Warfighter Physiological Status Monitoring (WPSM) system—US Army Medic Recommendations* (Technical Report T-07-04). Natick, MA: United States Army Research Institute of Environmental Medicine. AD A459019.

Tharion, W. J., Potter, A. W., Duhamel, C. M., Karis, A. J., Buller, M. J., & Hoyt, R. W. (2013). Real-time physiological monitoring while encapsulated in personal protective equipment. *Journal of Sport and Human Performance, 1*(4), 14–21.

Tharion, W. J., Yokota, M., Buller, M. J., DeLany, J. P., & Hoyt, R. W. (2004). Total energy expenditure using a foot-contact pedometer. *Medical Science Monitor, 10,* CR504-CR509.

The United States 104th Congress. (1996). Health Insurance Portability and Accountability Act of 1996. Public Law 104-191. Washington, DC: United States Government Printing Office.

Welles, A. P., Buller, M. J., Margolis, L., Economos, D., Hoyt, R. W., & Richter, M. W. (2013). Thermal-work strain during Marine rifle squad operations in Afghanistan. *Military Medicine, 178*(10), 1141–1148.

Welles, A. P., Buller, M. J., Richter, M. W., McCarthy, S., & Hoyt, R. W. (2013). *Thermal-work Strain and Energy Expenditure During Marine Rifle Squad Operations in Afghanistan (August 2013)* (Technical Report T-15-7). Natick, MA: United States Army Research Institute of Environmental Medicine. AD A620619.

Welles, A. P., Tharion, W. J., Potter, A. W., & Buller, M. J. (2016). *Estimation of Metabolic Rate from Core Temperature During Weapons of Mass Destruction-Civil Support Team*

(WMD-CST) Exercises. (Technical Report T-17-2). Natick, MA: United States Army Research Institute of Environmental Medicine. AD A1022691.

Wilkinson, D. M. L., Carter, J. M., Richmond, V. L., Blacker, S. D., & Rayson, M. P. (2008). The effect of cool water ingestion on gastrointestinal pill temperature. *Medicine and Science in Sports and Exercise, 40*(3), 523–528.

Yang, S., Chen, Y. C., Nicolini, L., Pasupathy, P., Sacks, J., Su, B., . . . Lu, N. (2015). "Cut and paste" manufacture of multiparmetric epidermal sensor systems. *Advanced Materials, Nov 27*(41), 6423–6430.

8

Neuroprosthetics for Human Performance Optimization

YIN-JUI CHANG, GAUTAM KRISHNA,
AND BENITO R. FERNÁNDEZ

INTRODUCTION

In 1973, after observing the modulation of electroencephalography (EEG) signals, the computer scientist Jacques Vidal proposed an idea in *Annual Review of Biophysics and Bioengineering*: "Can these observable electrical brain signals be served as carriers of information in human-computer communication or system inputs for controlling external [machinery]" (Vidal, 1973). Since then, the development of this field has grown rapidly. Generally, the brain generates signals carrying the information of intention; the signals are then transmitted through the spinal cord to human effectors, transforming the information signals that directly drive the skeletal muscular system. On some occasions, the signal transmission is degraded or blocked due to deterioration of the neuronal path, resulting in a reduction in performance. The neuroprosthetic is a bioengineering solution engineered to replace or assist unhealthy neurons with added electrical circuitry that allows the individual to compensate or overcome his neurological injury or disorder. Additionally, this approach could conceivably be designed to augment normal performance in an individual who is otherwise uncompromised.

A promising future for neuroprosthetics was recently demonstrated by a spinal cord-injured patient who was able to kick off the ball for the 2014 FIFA World Cup by using a brain-controlled prosthetic device. Neuroprosthetics can be formulated to transfer and manipulate information bidirectionally, either altering the input of information to the brain or altering the output of information from the brain. For instance, environmental stimuli can be captured and translated into specific code to be transmitted back into the human brain. In light of this technology, cochlear implants and functional retinal prostheses have been developed. Moreover, sensory feedback plays an important role in motion execution; it allows the human brain to receive sensory signals such as proprioception, touch, and pain from the body and to continuously modify the motor commands based on this sensory information. Clearly, once the technology of neural prosthetics is fully implemented, patients with neurological disorders or damage can experience improved quality of life, and normal individuals may even be able to augment their level of human performance.

This chapter describes neuroprosthetics-related research, development, and potential applications. Starting with a brief discussion of how a model neuroprosthetic system works, including the technology of sensing, decoding, and the stimulation interfaces for control action or performance augmentation, we then provide a brief description of the neuroprosthetic structure. We review previous and recent works in the field and point out the challenges that neuroprosthetic scientists meet when trying to widely apply this approach to human and clinical therapies. Finally, we introduce potential future applications of neuroprosthetics that could augment and improve a person's performance, thus increasing personal adjustment and quality of life. Although some obstacles need to be solved before neuroprosthetic systems are widely implemented, promising experimental results and rapidly growing technological developments show that such a future is imminent.

NEUROPROSTHETIC SYSTEM ARCHITECTURE

Neuroprosthetics is a multidisciplinary field involving neuroscience, engineering, computer science, surgery, pharmacology, and robotics. Generally, the system acquires signals from the brain, peripheral nerves, or muscles, then extracts useful bioinformation, and then translates it into input data streams and/or output commands for the purpose of recovery of normal functioning. Thus, neuroprosthetic architectures can be divided into four categories as shown in Figure 8.1: sensing interfaces, decoding, controllable devices, and stimulating interfaces.

Sensing Technology

The interface of the connection between human and system requires the technology of biosensing. Sensors detect the activity or events of targeting components and send information to a system for advanced signal conditioning, processing, and analysis. Brain activity can be detected from extracellular fields shaped by transmembrane current from several sources, including synaptic activity, fast action potentials, calcium spikes, intrinsic resonance, gap junctions (Buzsáki, Anastassiou, & Koch, 2012). Those electrical potentials can be recorded from many possible locations, including the scalp, on the surface of the cerebral cortex, deep in the brain, or on the surface of muscles.

EEG is one of the most commonly used approaches for detecting the electrical activity in the human brain (Niedermeyer & da Silva, 2005). It is a safe and convenient method to record signals because of its noninvasive approach. The recording electrodes are placed on the scalp and thus surgery is not required. However, due to the distortion effects of the tissues between the signal source and the recording electrodes, it is impossible to detect the firing patterns of individual neurons. Newer technologies for EEG recording such as dry electrodes, ball cap–like head arrays, and wireless transmission of signals have made this technology more field deployable.

Magnetoencephalography (MEG) is another noninvasive approach for recording neuron activity in the brain. The tiny magnetic fields outside the skull generated by

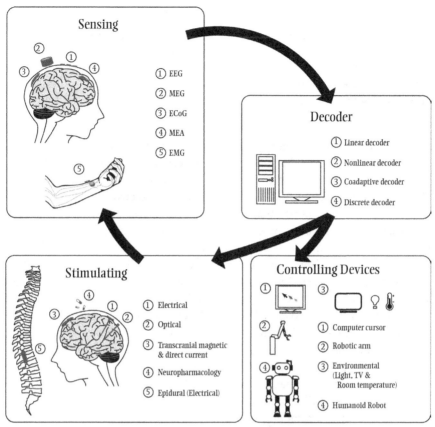

Figure 8.1 The structure of a neuroprosthetic system. Neurotechnology is divided into four categories: sensing, decoding, controlling devices, and stimulation. The bio-information informed from sensing technology is then processed through decoder algorithms. The output from decoders can serve as a control command for external devices or feedback to build a stimulation interface with the brain.
Image courtesy of the authors.

electrical currents in neurons can be measured by a superconducting quantum interference device (SQUID; Hämäläinen, Hari, Ilmoniemi, Knuutila, & Lounasmaa, 1993). Since MEG provides high spatial and temporal resolution, it is considered useful for investigating human neurophysiology and information processing. However, MEG is not yet field-deployable and requires expensive technologies and a highly shielded chamber.

Another way to improve the spatial resolution of recording is through electrocorticography (ECoG), or intracranial electroencephalography (iEEG; Buzsáki et al., 2012). This method uses stainless steel or platinum electrodes to record brain activity directly from the surface or depth of the cerebral cortex, which eliminates the distortion effect from the skull and intermediate tissue. Thus, ECoG provides better ability to map important functional areas of the brain.

Table 8.1 SIGNAL RESOLUTION OF DISPARATE SIGNAL RECORDINGS

	Electroen cephalogram (EEG)	Magnetoen cephalogram (MEG)	Electrocortico graphy (ECoG)	Multielec trode arrays (MEA)
Temporal resolution	1 (ms)	1 (ms)	1 (ms)	<1 (ms)
Spatial resolution	1 (cm)	1 (mm)	2 (mm)	0.1 (mm)

To obtain even higher signal fidelity (refer to Table 8.1), multielectrode arrays (MEAs), also called *microelectrode arrays*, have been developed. Generally, they can be divided into three categories: microwire, micromachined, and flexible arrays (Ghane-Motlagh & Sawan, 2013). Microwires are used to record individual neurons by applying them deep into the brain structure (Strumwasser, 1958). Micromachined arrays reduce the size of the array and provide higher spatial resolution. The "Michigan probe" is an example of micromachined arrays with electrodes placed on each shank for recording or stimulating in the central nervous system (CNS; Wise et al., 2008). Another type of micromachined arrays is the "Utah arrays" that consist of conductive silicon needles electrically isolated from each other (Campbell, Jones, Huber, Horch, & Normann, 1991). Due to its architecture, the Utah arrays are implanted easily into the cerebral cortex or peripheral nerves. However, most MEAs have a rigid structure, resulting in an undesired immune response and tissue encapsulation, which decreases signal quality over time (Sanchez, Alba, Nishida, Batich, & Carney, 2006). Flexible arrays hold the promise of being a solution to these issues. "Soft" materials provide high flexibility and good biocompatibility, which allow electrodes to fit on the surface of the brain for chronic recording.

Although brain signals contain a considerable amount of useful bioinformation, accurate control of prosthetics based only on a brain interface has proved difficult. Thus, combining information extracted from other sources such as peripheral nerves and muscle cells would be helpful to reach desired performance. The neuronal signals from peripheral nerves of an intact cortex may provide valuable motor control information to restore voluntary control of prosthetic limbs and recover the function of perceptual sensors (Wodlinger, Dweiri, & Durand, 2015).

Electromyography (EMG) is a technique for recording and evaluating the electrical potential generated by the muscle cells. There exists a close relationship between EMG and muscle force, allowing us to analyze how the muscles operate when performing tasks or natural movements (Hof, 1984). Accordingly, we can use EMG as a control input for a computer or other device to optimize human performance. Recording of muscle and peripheral nerve signals can be achieved by:

- extraneural electrodes, including cuff electrodes, which detect the electrical signals from the muscle at the surface of the skin; or
- intraneural electrodes, including:
  - longitudinally implanted intrafascicular electrodes (LIFE) that record longitudinal activation, and
  - transverse intrafascicular multichannel electrodes (TIME) that infer transverse activation (Kim & Romero-Ortega, 2012).

Decoding

In order to interpret the bioelectrical signals recorded from the human nervous system, suitable decoding algorithms are essential to translate the information into usable information. A transformation algorithm is applied to the recorded signals, which serve as inputs, to generate the output variables, which can serve to recover or optimize the function of neurons and control external apparatus.

In 1970, the reconstruction of the movement parameters such as displacement and velocity from the recording activities of multiple neurons in the motor cortex using linear regressions was demonstrated successfully (Humphrey, Schmidt, & Thompson, 1970). Since then, linear decoders used to compute the outputs have been introduced. The simplest and most popular decoding method uses a population vector approach, where each neuron contributes a so-called preferred direction vector (Shoham & Nagarajan, 2003). Georgopoulos used extracellular signals of single neurons in the contralateral motor cortex to derive the population vector $P\ (M)$ corresponding to the movement direction M (see Equation 8.1) and proved that the direction between arm motion and the population vector was similar (Georgopoulos, Schwartz, & Kettner, 1986). The equation is shown as follows:

$$P(M) = \sum w_i (M) C_i \qquad \text{(Eq. 8.1)}$$

where M represents the direction of the movement, C_i represents the preferred direction of the ith cell, and $w_i (M)$ is the magnitude of the contribution of the ith cell.

Another algorithm is the *Wiener filter*, which is commonly used for reducing the disturbance of signals and estimating desired outputs by minimizing the mean-square error (Wiener, 1949). This equation is shown as follows:

$$o_k = \sum_{i=0}^{N} h_i \, y_{k-i} \qquad \text{(Eq. 8.2)}$$

where o_k is estimated output, y_k is observed signal, h_k represents the impulse response parameter, and N is the filter length. Kim employed this filter to remove EEG signal noise to obtain better event-related potentials (ERPs), demonstrating that P300 components can be detected accurately (Kim & Kim, 2011).

The *Kalman filter*, also known as *linear quadratic estimation* (LQE), is another powerful algorithm for information decoding. It consists of two steps: predicting and updating. During the *prediction step* given by Equation 8.3, it estimates the next state $\hat{x}_{k|k-1}$ and error covariance matrix $P_{k|k-1}$ based on the previous state:

$$\hat{x}_{k|k-1} = F_k \, \hat{x}_{k-1|k-1} + B_k u_k$$

and

$$P_{k|k-1} = F_k P_{k-1|k-1} F_k^T + Q_k \qquad \text{(Eq. 8.3)}$$

where, F_k is the transition model, B_k is the control-input model, Q_k is the covariance of the process noise, and u_k represents the input.

The next step, called the *updating step*, converts the estimation of the next state into the estimation of the expected signals from the observation by adjusting the system parameters (Lebedev & Nicolelis, 2017). Let the measurement pre-fit residual $\underline{y}_k$ be

$$\underline{y}_k = z_k - H_k \, \hat{x}_{k|k-1}$$

and let the pre-fit residual covariance S_k be

$$S_k = R_k + H_k P_{k|k-1} H_k^T$$

where, z_k is the observed signal, H_k is the observation model, and R_k represents the covariance of observation noise. The optimal Kalman gain is then given by

$$K_k = P_{k|k-1} H_k^T S_k^{-1}$$

Next, the *state estimate* and *covariance* are updated as follows:

$$\hat{x}_{k|k} = \hat{x}_{k|k-1} + K_k \underline{y}_k$$

and

$$P_{k|k} = \left(I - K_k H_k \right) P_{k|k-1} \qquad\qquad \textbf{(Eq. 8.4)}$$

where, $\hat{x}_{k|k}$, and $P_{k|k}$ represent the updated state estimate and covariance respectively.

A group from Brown University has reported that the Kalman filter performed better than other linear decoders for reconstructing cursor motion using the spiking activity from the primary motor cortex (Wu et al., 2003).

Recently, the n-th order *unscented Kalman filter* (UKF) was proposed to improve the performance of the decoding algorithm. The UKF possesses two significant features: (1) the use of a nonlinear model that describes neural activity significantly better than the linear model and (2) augmentation of the state variables with a history of n − 1 recent states, which improves prediction of the desired command. Li and colleagues used the cortical activity recorded via MEAs to reconstruct the cursor movement and showed that the UKF outperformed both the Wiener filter and the standard Kalman filter (Li et al., 2009).

Other powerful decoding methods provide high accuracy as well. Krishna Shenoy's group (Sussillo et al., 2012) proposed a dynamic artificial neural network called the *recurrent neural network* (RNN) that has been proved to outperform the Kalman filter. Let the neuronal firing rate be:

$$r = tanh(x),$$

where x represents a vector of activation variables. The standard form of the dynamics of the activation vector is shown as follow

$$\tau\frac{dx}{dt}(t) = -x(t) + gJr(t) + hW_I u(t) + W_F z(t) + b \qquad \text{(Eq. 8.5)}$$

where τ represents neuronal time constant, g is a global parameter that controls the strength of the recurrent network's initial internal coupling, J represents the weights of recurrent connection, h is the scaling coefficients of the input, W_I and W_F represent the input and feedback weights, and $u(t)$ and b represent the input to and bias of the network, respectively. The output of the network is $z(t) = W_O^T r(t)$, where W_O represents the weights that govern the recurrent activity.

They first compared the performance of center-out reach tasks using neuronal activity in the motor cortex and showed that RNN was better, based on the assessment table including success rate, distance ratio, and average error angle. Then they tested for the more difficult task, a randomized point-to-point task, discovering that RNN could sustain performance for an hour while the Kalman filter couldn't.

Justin Sanchez's group (DiGiovanna, Mahmoudi, Fortes, Principe, & Sanchez, 2009) introduced reinforcement learning as a co-adaptive decoder that makes adjustments according to interactions with the environment to improve the decoder performance continuously. They exploited the user's neuronal activity to achieve a three-dimensional reaching task designed to increase the difficulty over the experiment using a prosthetic arm. The result demonstrated that all subjects could control the prosthetic arm better than expected at each level of difficulty.

A discrete classifier that converts the continuous signals into discrete choices is also a popular technique. Accurate decoding information has been produced with algorithms such as linear discriminant analysis with kernel trick (Mika, Ratsch, Weston, Scholkopf, & Mullers, 1999), artificial neural networks (Hiraiwa, Shimohara, & Tokunaga, 1990), support vector machine (Garrett, Peterson, Anderson, & Thaut, 2003), hidden Markov models (Rabiner, 1989), and nonlinear Bayesian classifiers (Denison, 2002).

Controllable Devices

Recently brain–computer interface (BCI) technology is being adapted for various practical real-life control applications, starting from two-dimensional control of a simple computer cursor to three-dimensional control of a robotic arm for assistive devices and rehabilitation engineering by using brain signals as a control command. In addition, Cincotti et al. integrated EEG-based BCI and a robotic platform in an environmental control system (Cincotti et al., 2008). For example, subjects could control devices such as a television, lights, and a thermostat. Inspired by EEG-based control, researchers are also developing control systems based on EMG or muscle activation signals to control prosthetic hands, legs, and more. These are popularly known as *myoelectric control systems*, where EMG signals are used as control signals to drive various prosthetics. Future developments in EEG-based control applications include humanoid robotic control and flight dynamics and armament delivery systems controlled by fighter plane pilots. BCI-based PC games or virtual reality are also becoming popular among regular users of virtual reality (VR) and gaming technologies.

In our lab at the University of Texas, Austin, we worked on a project to control a prosthetic hand using forearm EMG signals in the spring of 2017. The prosthetic hand was produced with a 3D printer. The framework was developed in National Instruments LabVIEW software for implementing real-time control. Epidermal electrodes were used to collect the forearm EMG signal data using Open BCI board. The collected raw EMG signals were processed by removing bias and applying digital filters to remove the noise, allowing us to get the data within a useful frequency range. Various statistical features like arithmetic mean, root mean square, zero crossing, and signal power were extracted from the processed EMG signals. An artificial neural network was used to classify the features for different finger movements. Based on the classifier's output, the servo motor connected to the fingers of the prosthetic hand is rotated, which in turn will result in the movement of the fingers of the prosthetic hand.

This framework can be extended to control a Kinova manipulator. We are currently working on interfacing the system for a Kinova manipulator, whereby it would be possible to develop a BCI for robots that could help paralyzed people grab objects. They could control the robotic arm using forearm EMG signals or EEG signals.

Stimulation Interfaces

With the decoding information, an interface for bioinformation translation should be designed to make the system work. Generally, stimulation interfaces are categorized into four approaches: electrical, optical, transcranial magnetic and direct current, and neuropharmacology.

Deep brain stimulation (DBS) is one of the most common electrical stimulation techniques currently in use for treating neurological disorders. It has a wide range of indications due to its reversibility, adaptability, and low morbidity. There is a frequency-dependent duality effect: low frequency excites both neurons and axons, while high frequency selectively inhibits clusters of neurons. DBS works through a brain–electrode–machine interface: it is achieved by implanting electrodes into the brain, and the electrodes are connected to a wireless implantable and programmable stimulator. It is widely used to treat Parkinson's disease (Gardner, 2013). Specific targets of implantation in Parkinson patients' brain are the thalamus, pallidum, subthalamic nucleus, and pedunculopontine nucleus. They are reached through a complex process of targeting, based on neuro navigation tools, including magnetic resonance imaging, atlases, and microrecording providing the signature of the recorded structure and allowing precise positioning of the electrode. During the surgery, it is possible at every level of the exploration to stimulate the traversed structure and to observe the effects of stimulation, which are frequency dependent.

In addition, it has been proved as well to be a standard and acceptable therapy for essential tremor, dystonia, and other disorders (Montgomery & Gale, 2008).

Unlike DBS which targets the brain, epidural stimulation (ES) is another electrical stimulation technique used to "reactivate neural circuits" by implanting an electrode array over the lower part of the spinal cord. A 23-year-old paraplegic patient recovered the neuromotor function of voluntary control of the lower limbs after 26 months of ES training sessions (Edgerton & Harkema, 2011).

Optical stimulation is a novel approach for artifact-free, damage-free, and contact-free neural activation (Wells et al., 2005). This approach promises to provide more selective stimulation and higher spatial resolution compared with electrical stimulation (Thompson, Stoddart, & Jansen, 2014). It uses light to evoke the action potentials of neurons and control and monitor the activities of individual neurons; this may lead to a treatment for blindness (Carter & de Lecea, 2011) and Parkinson's disease (Gradinaru, Mogri, Thompson, Henderson, & Deisseroth, 2009; Kravitz et al., 2010).

Transcranial magnetic stimulation (TMS) is seen as a powerful, noninvasive approach for neuronal stimulation. It generates current flow through a pulsed magnetic field based on the principle of electromagnetic induction (O'Shea & Walsh, 2007) to either excite or inhibit the neurons in a specific targeted area. It has been proved to produce a muscle movement when stimulating the motor cortex and to generate visual phosphenes and scotomas when stimulating the occipital cortex (Hallett, 2000). In addition, O'Reardon's group applied TMS to 301 medication-free patients with major depression and demonstrated that the depressive symptoms were significantly ameliorated after several weeks (O'Reardon et al., 2007). Although it is effective in dealing with depression (George & Post, 2011), TMS is expensive and may trigger some adverse effects (Fregni, Boggio, Nitsche, & Pascual-Leone, 2005). An alternative technique for noninvasive electrical stimulation of the brain is transcranial direct current stimulation (tDCS). tDCS uses weak direct currents through electrodes placed on the surface of the scalp and has shown potential for altering neuronal activity and behavior in humans (Nitsche et al., 2008).

Neuropharmacology is the study of how drugs act on neurons to influence human behavior. Since it can enhance or inhibit the action of targeted neuronal cells by altering neurotransmission, it can be regarded as another example of a stimulation interface. Several drugs have already been approved for treating mood disorder (Nemeroff & Owens, 2002) and Parkinson's disease (Jankovic & Aguilar, 2008). However, the researchers found the following challenges: the blood–brain barrier (BBB) that separates the blood from the extracellular fluid in the human brain, the probability of side effects, and nonspecificity, which requires preclinical trials to break down (Tallman, 1999). Fortunately, with recent developed chip technology such as blood–brain barrier on a chip (Griep et al., 2013), and neurons on a chip (Nagarah, 2011), we can simulate in vivo early clinical tests on a tiny chip. It is possible that so-called highly selective drugs are able to target a specific region of neural cells, thus optimizing their efficacy and minimizing adverse effects. Therefore, the idea of drugs that can cure neurological disorders or even maximize an individual's performance is no longer fiction.

Proprioception and Sensory Recovery

Every individual has five senses through which to receive information from the external environment: sight (vision), hearing (auditory), smell (olfaction), taste (gustation), and touch (somatosensation). In addition, proprioception, also called the "sixth sense," plays a critical role in daily activities. The sixth sense is the ability to integrate sensory signals from mechanoreceptors to determine the body's position, motion, and equilibrium (Han, Waddington, Adams, Anson, & Liu, 2016). Even if a person is blind, he or she is still aware that the arm is above the head or hanging by the side of the body. However, damage in the central or peripheral nervous system due to accidental brain injury or neurological disorder will cause impaired or loss of sensation, which significantly affects the patient's quality of life. With neuroprosthetic technology, it may be possible to recover the function of damaged senses. The technique used to accomplish this task is to design electrical signals that can mimic the sensory system's natural nerve impulses based on frequency and amplitude and then direct those signals to stimulate the sensory cortex in a manner that can distinguish disparate sensory input. In addition, it is possible to train the brain to classify particular signals with particular sensory information despite artifacts.

The bionic eye is another promising neuroprosthetic technology. Like cochlear implants that stimulate the auditory cortex to restore hearing (see Figure 8.2), such visual prostheses are designed to stimulate neurons in the retina, optical nerve, or the brain's visual cortex to restore vision (Ong & da Cruz, 2012; see Figure 8.3). For retinal prostheses, the device detects visual information and transforms this information into electrical signals that stimulate the surviving retinal neurons. It includes two types based on location: epiretinal (on the retina) and subretinal (behind the retina). The epiretinal approach transforms light captured from the external environment into electrical stimulation to stimulate retinal neurons (Javaheri, Hahn,

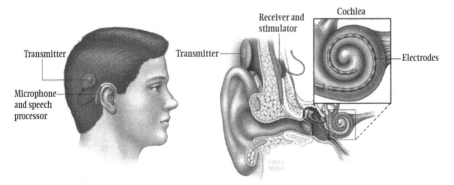

Figure 8.2 Schematic of a cochlear implant.

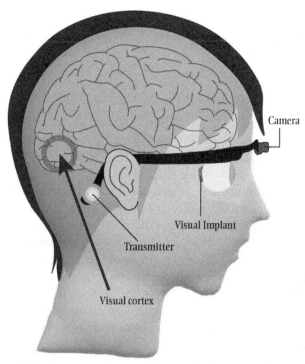

Figure 8.3 Schematic figure of bionic eye.
Image courtesy of the authors.

Lakhanpal, Weiland, & Humayun, 2006). Unlike epiretinal implants, which need an external camera to capture the images, subretinal implants placed between the pigmented epithelium and the outer layer of the retina stimulate retinal sensory neurons when light falls directly on the retina (Zrenner, 2002). This device then generates currents in the photodiodes and activates microelectrodes to stimulate receptors. Optical nerve stimulation is an alternative for blind patients with functional retinal ganglion cells. This approach produces phosphenes over a wide portion of the visual field by implanting multicontact electrodes (Veraart et al., 1998) onto the optic nerve, a paired nerve that transmits visual information from the retina to the brain. A cortical prosthesis is another approach to restore vision by directly stimulating the visual cortex. Although many challenges remain in this approach (since driving the cortex is much more complicated than driving the optic nerve or retina), it is starting to play an important role in future treatment of patients with damaged retinas or optic nerves.

In addition, cortical implants can restore not only auditory and visual functioning, but also other sensations such as smell, touch, and proprioception. Recently, Robert Gaunt and his colleagues (Flesher et al., 2016) demonstrated that, through intracortical multicontact microstimulation of the cerebral cortex, an individual with long-term spinal cord injury can restore tactile sensation. Until now, techniques for restoration of proprioception have not been demonstrated in humans. However, Lee Miller and his colleagues (Tomlinson & Miller, 2016) stimulated the part of the cortex responsible for proprioception. They recorded neural activity in the motor cortex and observed resulting movement simultaneously during their attempt to design patterns that can mimic proprioceptive signals.

HUMAN PERFORMANCE OPTIMIZATION USING BRAIN STIMULATION TECHNIQUES

Recently, several research groups have proved that human creativity can be improved through brain stimulation. Beginning at birth, experience results in the learning of rules about the structure of the world, and, automatically, these learned rules are applied to identifying new patterns. Such cognitive processes generated within the dorsolateral prefrontal cortex (DLPFC) are an efficient and reliable way to approach daily tasks, including working memory, planning, and rule-based learning (Jeon & Friederici, 2015). However, when encountering new problems which require a novel style of thinking, such processes might block a person's creative thinking because of the automatic application of learned rules from past experience (Thompson-Schill, Ramscar, & Chrysikou, 2009; Amer, Campbell, & Hasher, 2016). This blocking can be resolved by relaxing constraints so as to recover the ability to come up with new solutions or ideas to approach new tasks (Knoblich, Ohlsson, Haider, & Rhenius, 1999).

Researchers from Queen Mary University of London evaluated the performance of matchstick problem-solving ability before and after receiving anodal, cathodal, or sham tDCS to the left DLPFC. The result showed that individuals who received cathodal stimulation were more likely to solve the hardest matchstick problem. In other words, suppressing left DLPFC activity resulted in relaxing the influence of previously learned constraints thereby enhancing the ability to solve the difficult trials of a new problem (Luft, Zioga, Banissy, & Bhattacharya, 2017). In addition, other regions in the left inferior frontotemporal cortex such as the inferior frontal gyrus (IFG; Mayseless & Shamay-Tsoory, 2015), anterior temporal lobe (ATL; Chi & Snyder, 2011), and middle temporal gyrus (MTG) are responsible for inhibiting the generation of creative or new ideas. Applying cathodal tDCS to these regions can reduce excitability of the cortex, which increases the opportunity to generate new ideas and thus form a creative thought (Weinberger, Green, & Chrysikou, 2017).

Low-level light/laser treatment (LLLT) is a noninvasive brain stimulation technique that employs near-infrared light to stimulate targeted neurons. The 600–1,150 nm wavelengths light can penetrate through brain tissues and be absorbed by the photon acceptor, cytochrome oxidase, that is responsible for adenosine triphosphate (ATP) production (Gonzalez-Lima & Barrett, 2014). Wang et al. suggested that 1,064 nm laser stimulation causes cytochrome oxidase oxidation with the highest enzymatic activity (Wang et al., 2017). They discovered that continuous LLLT can up-regulate the amount of cytochrome oxidase and thereby increase neuronal capacity for metabolic energy production, which contributes important insight into cerebral physiological mechanisms. Due to its specificity and noninvasiveness, the US Food and Drug Administration (FDA) has approved LLLT for pain relief since 2002 (Fulop et al., 2010). Not only can it serve as a treatment for ischemic stroke (Lampl et al., 2007) and depressive disorder, but it can also increase cognitive performance.

Barrett and Gonzalez-Lima used transcranial 1,064 nm laser stimulation to demonstrate that the performance of cognitive and emotional function can be improved by LLLT (Barrett & Gonzalez-Lima, 2013). Their subjects completed several exercises: a psychomotor vigilance task (PVT, a test that assessed an individual's attention), a delayed match-to-sample (DMS, a memory task that involved remembering the visual stimulus through a delay), and the positive and negative affect schedule (PANAS-X, the questionnaires used to evaluate the emotional state). The results showed that the reaction time in PVT was decreased from 323 ms to 317 ms after laser treatment. In addition, the performance in DMS memory task was significantly enhanced with increasing corrected trials and decreasing memory retrieval latency. The emotional state was improved as well according to the questionnaires. In more recent studies, transcranial infrared laser stimulation has been proved to improve rule-based category learning evaluated by the classification accuracy of category tasks (Blanco, Saucedo, & Gonzalez-Lima, 2017) and executive function evaluated by Wisconsin Card Sorting Task (WCST), which relies on several cognitive processes (Blanco, Maddox, & Gonzalez-Lima, 2017). These studies all provide compelling evidence that LLLT is a promising technology that can be widely used to optimize human performance in the future.

BRAIN CHIP IMPLANTS

In recent years, electrical circuits implanted directly into the brain have become an active topic of scientific and engineering focus. Referred to as "brain chips," it is believed that, in the long term, they can help patients who suffer from a neurological disorder and that they will also enhance memory, intelligence, and other cognitive tasks in otherwise normal individuals. The futuristic idea of obtaining superhuman memory (once considered science fiction) is now ready to start trials in humans. Dr. Theodore Berger, who spent 20 years working on computer implants to mimic electrical activity in the brain, succeeded in designing electrical circuits that can enhance memory functioning. He demonstrated that the function of the hippocampus responsible for the formation of new long-term memories can be replaced with a very-large-scale integrated (VLSI) implant with a 1.1 mm^2 area by modeling the nonlinear dynamics of the subfield CA3 of the hippocampus (Hsiao et al., 2006). Berger first developed the single input/single output (SISO), third-order Volterra-Poisson model shown in Equation 8.6 to capture the signal dynamics of a single channel (Berger et al., 2005).

$$y(n_i) = A_i k_1 + A_i \sum_{n_i - \mu < n_j < n_i} A_j k_2 \left(n_i - n_j\right) +$$

$$A_i \sum_{n_i - \mu < n_{j_1} < n_i} \sum_{n_i - \mu < n_{j_2} < n_i} A_{j_1} A_{j_2} k_3 \left(n_i - n_{j_1}, n_i - n_{j_2}\right) \qquad \text{(Eq. 8.6)}$$

where A_i, A_j represent varying amplitudes of input, $y(n_i)$ represents output, k_1, k_2, k_3 are the $1st, 2nd, 3rd$ order kernel functions, respectively, n_i represents the time of current impulse, and n_j is the time of *jth* impulse prior to the present impulse within the kernel window μ. The multi-input/multi-output (MIMO) nonlinear model (Berger, Song, Chan, & Marmarelis, 2010; Berger et al., 2012) was developed to represent the dynamics of the different subpopulations of the ensemble. Berger demonstrated that the MIMO model not only improved performance on the memory task under normal conditions but also recovered the performance of subjects whose synaptic transmission of the hippocampal area was blocked by drugs (Berger et al., 2011). Such microchips can reconstruct neuron-to-neuron connection for memory formation so that, even without a functional hippocampus, a person will have the ability to produce long-term memories. Hence, it can not only help patients suffering from Alzheimer's or stroke to regain memory formation but could also improve the capacity to create long-term memories.

Another encouraging example of brain chip development is NeuroLife, a tiny brain chip that can help spinal cord injury patients regain control of their arms and hands. The first participant, Ian Burkhart, is a quadriplegic due to a diving accident in 2010. A Utah microelectrode array was implanted into his left primary motor cortex 4 years after his injury (Bouton et al., 2016). A stimulation sleeve designed to generate the pulse and transmit it through the cuff to invoke the movement was placed on his paralyzed forearm. Then he was trained to utilize his brain activity to control the neuromuscular electrical stimulator. The demonstration of such novel technology, called a *neural bypass system* (Friedenberg & Schwemmer, 2016), was displayed as he opened and closed his hand just by his thoughts. Now Burkhart is able to perform more sophisticated movements such as grasping and swiping a credit card or playing a guitar video game with his own fingers and hand. He can not only grasp a bottle, pour the contents into a glass, and put it back, but he can also pick up and hold a phone to his ear. These simple, everyday movements—and even more complex ones—that seem impossible for many paralyzed patients may someday be achievable through brain chip implants and continuous training and will significantly improve their quality of life.

Recently, technology entrepreneur Bryan Johnson created a new company called Kernel, which is creating an implantable brain chip that can treat neurodegenerative diseases. He claims that the "Kernel" can eventually make humans become a little "digital" by allowing them to interface, out-compete, or co-evolve with machines and thus improve human cognition. The CEO of SpaceX and Tesla, Elon Musk, has also started a brain–computer interface company, Neuralink, which focuses on building a brain-implantable device that integrates individuals with software and keeps pace with the development of artificial intelligence. The ultimate goal of Neuralink is to build direct interfacing with computing devices to improve human cognitive functions such as attention, knowledge, and memory, and enable humans to optimize their own individual performance. These two companies have begun combining their technologies to develop cutting-edge brain implants.

Researchers around the world are working on understanding neuronal activities more deeply, improving interface hardware such as recording or controlling devices and making brain chips easier to implant without brain surgery. With the development of such technology, we can imagine that in 5–10 years, brain chip implants will be available to the public and will change the world.

CONCLUSION

Brain damage due to illness or injuries can cause cognitive impairment or neurodegeneration, which in turn decreases human performance. Specifically, some occupations, such as soldier, may have a greater probability of head injuries, such as those sustained in combat. Mild traumatic brain injury (mTBI) is the most common brain injury suffered by soldiers, but it is also the most difficult to diagnose. These injuries increase the individual's risk of suffering neural diseases including Parkinson's disease, Alzheimer's disease, and motor neuron disease (McKee & Robinson, 2014). It is essential to explore the human brain more fully, to determine which areas of the brain are affected by these types of injuries, and to more accurately diagnosis these neurological disorders. We could then build a customized neuroprosthetic device to deal with such deteriorated cognitive performance. If this kind of development is successful, such technology may also help optimize behaviors such as attention, memory, vision, hearing, and decision-making. Certain neuroprosthetics under investigation have demonstrated encouraging results. Brain implants are the most promising because of being wireless, light, and convenient and because of their capacity for highly selective treatment. We expect to see brain–computer interfacing capable of controlling "assistive" prosthetics and neuroprostheses that mitigate some posttraumatic neurological impediments. It is foreseeable that, within 15 years, this technology will change lives in an excitingly diverse number of ways.

REFERENCES

Amer, T., Campbell, K. L., & Hasher, L. (2016). Cognitive control as a double-edged sword. *Trends in Cognitive Sciences, 20*(12), 905–915.

Barrett, D. W., & Gonzalez-Lima, F. (2013). Transcranial infrared laser stimulation produces beneficial cognitive and emotional effects in humans. *Neuroscience, 230,* 13–23.

Berger, T. W., Ahuja, A., Courellis, S. H., Deadwyler, S. A., Erinjippurath, G., Gerhardt, G. A., . . . LaCoss, J. (2005). Restoring lost cognitive function. *IEEE Engineering in Medicine and Biology Magazine, 24*(5), 30–44.

Berger, T. W., Hampson, R. E., Song, D., Goonawardena, A., Marmarelis, V. Z., & Deadwyler, S. A. (2011). A cortical neural prosthesis for restoring and enhancing memory. *Journal of Neural Engineering, 8*(4), 046017.

Berger, T. W., Song, D., Chan, R. H., & Marmarelis, V. Z. (2010). The neurobiological basis of cognition: Identification by multi-input, multioutput nonlinear dynamic modeling. *Proceedings of the IEEE, 98*(3), 356–374. doi:10.1109/JPROC.2009.2038804

Berger, T. W., Song, D., Chan, R. H., Marmarelis, V. Z., LaCoss, J., Wills, J., . . . Granacki, J. J. (2012). A hippocampal cognitive prosthesis: Multi-input, multi-output non-linear modeling, and VLSI implementation. *IEEE Transactions on Neural Systems and Rehabilitation Engineering, 20*(2), 198–211.

Blanco, N. J., Maddox, W. T., & Gonzalez-Lima, F. (2017). Improving executive function using transcranial infrared laser stimulation. *Journal of Neuropsychology, 11*(1), 14–25.

Blanco, N. J., Saucedo, C. L., & Gonzalez-Lima, F. (2017). Transcranial infrared laser stimulation improves rule-based, but not information-integration, category learning in humans. *Neurobiology of Learning and Memory, 139*, 69–75.

Bouton, C. E., Shaikhouni, A., Annetta, N. V., Bockbrader, M. A., Friedenberg, D. A., Nielson, D. M., . . . Morgan, A. G. (2016). Restoring cortical control of functional movement in a human with quadriplegia. *Nature, 533*(7602), 247–250.

Buzsáki, G., Anastassiou, C. A., & Koch, C. (2012). The origin of extracellular fields and currents—EEG, ECoG, LFP and spikes. *Nature Reviews Neuroscience, 13*(6), 407–420.

Campbell, P. K., Jones, K. E., Huber, R. J., Horch, K. W., & Normann, R. A. (1991). A silicon-based, three-dimensional neural interface: Manufacturing processes for an intracortical electrode array. *IEEE Transactions on Biomedical Engineering, 38*(8), 758–768.

Carter, M. E., & de Lecea, L. (2011). Optogenetic investigation of neural circuits in vivo. *Trends in Molecular Medicine, 17*(4), 197–206.

Chi, R. P., & Snyder, A. W. (2011). Facilitate insight by non-invasive brain stimulation. *PloS one, 6*(2), e16655.

Cincotti, F., Mattia, D., Aloise, F., Bufalari, S., Schalk, G., Oriolo, G., . . . Babiloni, F. (2008). Non-invasive brain–computer interface system: Towards its application as assistive technology. *Brain Research Bulletin, 75*(6), 796–803.

Denison, D. G. (2002). *Bayesian Methods for Nonlinear Classification and Regression* (Vol. 386). Chichester, UK: Wiley.

DiGiovanna, J., Mahmoudi, B., Fortes, J., Principe, J. C., & Sanchez, J. C. (2009). Coadaptive brain-machine interface via reinforcement learning. *IEEE Transactions on Biomedical Engineering, 56*(1), 54–64.

Edgerton, V. R., & Harkema, S. (2011). Epidural stimulation of the spinal cord in spinal cord injury: Current status and future challenges. *Expert Review of Neurotherapeutics, 11*(10), 1351–1353.

Flesher, S. N., Collinger, J. L., Foldes, S. T., Weiss, J. M., Downey, J. E., Tyler-Kabara, E. C., . . . Gaunt, R. A. (2016). Intracortical microstimulation of human somatosensory cortex. *Science Translational Medicine, 8*(361), 361ra141-361ra141.

Fregni, F., Boggio, P. S., Nitsche, M., & Pascual-Leone, A. (2005). Transcranial direct current stimulation. *The British Journal of Psychiatry, 186*(5), 446–447.

Friedenberg, D. A., & Schwemmer, M. A. (2016). Moving a paralyzed hand—A biomedical big data success story. *CHANCE, 29*(4), 4–13.

Fulop, A. M., Dhimmer, S., Deluca, J. R., Johanson, D. D., Lenz, R. V., Patel, K. B., . . . Enwemeka, C. S. (2010). A meta-analysis of the efficacy of laser phototherapy on pain relief. *The Clinical Journal of Pain, 26*(8), 729–736.

Gardner, J. (2013). A history of deep brain stimulation: Technological innovation and the role of clinical assessment tools. *Social Studies of Science, 43*(5), 707–728.

Garrett, D., Peterson, D. A., Anderson, C. W., & Thaut, M. H. (2003). Comparison of linear, nonlinear, and feature selection methods for EEG signal classification. *IEEE Transactions on Neural Systems and Rehabilitation Engineering, 11*(2), 141–144.

George, M. S., & Post, R. M. (2011). Daily left prefrontal repetitive transcranial magnetic stimulation for acute treatment of medication-resistant depression. *American Journal of Psychiatry, 168*(4), 356–364.

Georgopoulos, A. P., Schwartz, A. B., & Kettner, R. E. (1986). Neuronal population coding of movement direction. *Science,* 1416–1419.

Ghane-Motlagh, B., & Sawan, M. (2013). Design and implementation challenges of microelectrode arrays: A review. *Materials Sciences and Applications, 4*(08), 483.

Gonzalez-Lima, F., & Barrett, D. W. (2014). Augmentation of cognitive brain functions with transcranial lasers. *Frontiers in Systems Neuroscience, 8,* 36. doi:10.3389/fnsys.2014.00036

Gradinaru, V., Mogri, M., Thompson, K. R., Henderson, J. M., & Deisseroth, K. (2009). Optical deconstruction of parkinsonian neural circuitry. *Science, 324*(5925), 354–359.

Griep, L. M., Wolbers, F., De Wagenaar, B., Ter Braak, P. M., Weksler, B. B., Romero, I. A., . . . Van der Berg, A. (2013). BBB on a chip: Microfluidic platform to mechanically and biochemically modulate blood-brain barrier function. *Biomedical Microdevices, 15*(1), 145–150.

Hallett, M. (2000). Transcranial magnetic stimulation and the human brain. *Nature, 406*(6792), 147–150.

Hämäläinen, M., Hari, R., Ilmoniemi, R. J., Knuutila, J., & Lounasmaa, O. V. (1993). Magnetoencephalography-theory, instrumentation, and applications to noninvasive studies of the working human brain. *Review of Modern Physics, 65*(2), 413.

Han, J., Waddington, G., Adams, R., Anson, J., & Liu, Y. (2016). Assessing proprioception: A critical review of methods. *Journal of Sport and Health Science, 5*(1), 80–90.

Hiraiwa, A., Shimohara, K., & Tokunaga, Y. (1990). EEG topography recognition by neural networks. *IEEE Engineering in Medicine and Biology Magazine, 9*(3), 39–42.

Hof, A. L. (1984). EMG and muscle force: An introduction. *Human Movement Science, 3*(1), 119–153.

Hsiao, M. C., Chan, C. H., Srinivasan, V., Ahuja, A., Erinjippurath, G., Zanos, T. P., . . . Courellis, S. (2006). VLSI implementation of a nonlinear neuronal model: A "neural prosthesis" to restore hippocampal trisynaptic dynamics. *2006 International Conference of the IEEE Engineering in Medicine and Biology Society,* 4396–4399. doi:10.1109/IEMBS.2006.260138

Humphrey, D. R., Schmidt, E. M., & Thompson, W. D. (1970). Predicting measures of motor performance from multiple cortical spike trains. *Science, 170*(3959), 758–762.

Jankovic, J., & Aguilar, L. G. (2008). Current approaches to the treatment of Parkinson's disease. *Neuropsychiatric Disease and Treatment, 4*(4), 743.

Javaheri, M., Hahn, D. S., Lakhanpal, R. R., Weiland, J. D., & Humayun, M. S. (2006). Retinal prostheses for the blind. *Annals, Academy of Medicine, Singapore, 35*(3), 137.

Jeon, H. A., & Friederici, A. D. (2015). Degree of automaticity and the prefrontal cortex. *Trends in Cognitive Sciences, 19*(5), 244–250.

Kim, M. K., & Kim, S. P. (2011). Detection of P300 components using the Wiener filter for BCI-based spellers. *2011 8th Asian Control Conference (ASCC),* 892–896.

Kim, Y., & Romero-Ortega, M. I. (2012). Material considerations for peripheral nerve interfacing. *MRS Bulletin, 37*(06), 573–580.

Knoblich, G., Ohlsson, S., Haider, H., & Rhenius, D. (1999). Constraint relaxation and chunk decomposition in insight problem solving. *Journal of Experimental Psychology-Learning Memory and Cognition, 25*(6), 1534–1555.

Kravitz, A. V., Freeze, B. S., Parker, P. R., Kay, K., Thwin, M. T., Deisseroth, K., & Kreitzer, A. C. (2010). Regulation of parkinsonian motor behaviors by optogenetic control of basal ganglia circuitry. *Nature, 466*(7306), 622.

Lampl, Y., Zivin, J. A., Fisher, M., Lew, R., Welin, L., Dahlof, B., ... Ilic, S. (2007). Infrared laser therapy for ischemic stroke: A new treatment strategy. *Stroke, 38*(6), 1843–1849.

Lebedev, M. A., & Nicolelis, M. A. (2017). Brain-machine interfaces: From basic science to neuroprostheses and neurorehabilitation. *Physiological Reviews, 97*(2), 767–837.

Li, Z., O'Doherty, J. E., Hanson, T. L., Lebedev, M. A., Henriquez, C. S., & Nicolelis, M. A. (2009). Unscented Kalman filter for brain-machine interfaces. *PLOS One, 4*(7), e6243.

Luft, C. D., Zioga, I., Banissy, M. J., & Bhattacharya, J. (2017). Relaxing learned constraints through cathodal tDCS on the left dorsolateral prefrontal cortex. *Scientific Reports, 7*, 2916.

Mayseless, N., & Shamay-Tsoory, S. G. (2015). Enhancing verbal creativity: Modulating creativity by altering the balance between right and left inferior frontal gyrus with tDCS. *Neuroscience, 291*, 167–176.

McKee, A. C., & Robinson, M. E. (2014). Military-related traumatic brain injury and neurodegeneration. *Alzheimer's & Dementia, 10*(3), S242–S253.

Mika, S., Ratsch, G., Weston, J., Scholkopf, B., & Mullers, K. R. (1999, August). Fisher discriminant analysis with kernels. In *Neural Networks for Signal Processing IX, 1999. Proceedings of the 1999 IEEE Signal Processing Society Workshop* (pp. 41–48). Madison, WI: USA.

Montgomery, E. B., & Gale, J. T. (2008). Mechanisms of action of deep brain stimulation (DBS). *Neuroscience & Biobehavioral Reviews, 32*(3), 388–407.

Nagarah, J. M. (2011). Neurons on a chip: Toward high throughput network and pharmacology investigations. *Frontiers in Pharmacology, 2*(74).

Nemeroff, C. B., & Owens, M. J. (2002). Treatment of mood disorders. *Nature Neuroscience, 5*(11s), 1068–1070. Retrieved from http://link.galegroup.com/apps/doc/A185561714/SCIC?u=txshracd2598&xid=903f380b

Niedermeyer, E., & da Silva, F. L. (2005). *Electroencephalography: Basic Principles, Clinical Applications, and Related Fields* (5th ed.). Philadelphia, PA: Lippincott Williams & Wilkins.

Nitsche, M. A., Cohen, L. G., Wassermann, E. M., Priori, A., Lang, N., Antal, A., ... Pascual-Leone, A. (2008). Transcranial direct current stimulation: State of the art 2008. *Brain Stimulation, 1*(3), 206–223.

Ong, J. M., & da Cruz, L. (2012). The bionic eye: A review. *Clinical & Experimental Ophthalmology, 40*(1), 6–17.

O'Reardon, J. P., Solvason, H. B., Janicak, P. G., Sampson, S., Isenberg, K. E., Nahas, Z., ... Demitrack, M. A. (2007). Efficacy and safety of transcranial magnetic stimulation in the acute treatment of major depression: A multisite randomized controlled trial. *Biological Psychiatry, 62*(11), 1208–1216.

O'Shea, J., & Walsh, V. (2007). Transcranial magnetic stimulation. *Current Biology, 17*(6), R196-R199.

Rabiner, L. R. (1989). A tutorial on hidden Markov models and selected applications in speech recognition. *Proceedings of the IEEE, 77*(2), 257–286.

Sanchez, J. C., Alba, N., Nishida, T., Batich, C., & Carney, P. R. (2006). Structural modifications in chronic microwire electrodes for cortical neuroprosthetics: A case study. *IEEE Transactions on Neural Systems and Rehabilitation Engineering, 14*(2), 217–221.

Shoham, S., & Nagarajan, S. (2003). The theory of central nervous system recording. In K. W. Horch & G. S. Dhillon (Eds.), *Neuroprosthetics: Theory and Practice* (pp. 448–465). Singapore: World Scientific.

Strumwasser, F. (1958). Long-term recording from single neurons in brain of unrestrained mammals. *Science, 127*(3296), 469–470.

Sussillo, D., Nuyujukian, P., Fan, J. M., Kao, J. C., Stavisky, S. D., Ryu, S., & Shenoy, K. (2012). A recurrent neural network for closed-loop intracortical brain-machine interface decoders. *Journal of Neural Engineering, 9*(2), 026027.

Tallman, J. F. (1999). Neuropsychopharmacology at the new millennium: New industry directions. *Neuropsychopharmacology, 20*(2), 99–105.

Thompson, A. C., Stoddart, P. R., & Jansen, E. D. (2014). Optical stimulation of neurons. *Current Molecular Imaging, 3*(2), 162–177.

Thompson-Schill, S. L., Ramscar, M., & Chrysikou, E. G. (2009). Cognition without control: When a little frontal lobe goes a long way. *Current Directions in Psychological Science, 18*(5), 259–263.

Tomlinson, T., & Miller, L. E. (2016). Toward a proprioceptive neural interface that mimics natural cortical activity. In J. Laczko & M. L. Latash (Eds.), *Progress in Motor Control: Theories and Translations* (pp. 367–388). Cham, Switzerland: Springer International.

Veraart, C., Raftopoulos, C., Mortimer, J. T., Delbeke, J., Pins, D., Michaux, G., . . . Wanet-Defalque, M.-C. (1998). Visual sensations produced by optic nerve stimulation using an implanted self-sizing spiral cuff electrode. *Brain Research, 813*(1), 181–186.

Vidal, J. J. (1973). Toward direct brain-computer communication. *Annual Review of Biophysics and Bioengineering, 2*(1), 157–180.

Wang, X., Tian, F., Reddy, D. D., Nalawade, S. S., Barrett, D. W., Gonzalez-Lima, F., & Liu, H. (2017). Up-regulation of cerebral cytochrome-c-oxidase and hemodynamics by transcranial infrared laser stimulation: A broadband near-infrared spectroscopy study. *Journal of Cerebral Blood Flow & Metabolism, 37*(12), 3789–3802. doi:10.1177/0271678X17691783.

Weinberger, A. B., Green, A. E., & Chrysikou, E. G. (2017). Using transcranial direct current stimulation to enhance creative cognition: Interactions between task, polarity, and stimulation site. *Frontiers in Human Neuroscience, 11*, 246. doi:10.3389/fnhum.2017.00246

Wells, J., Kao, C., Mariappan, K., Albea, J., Jansen, E. D., Konrad, P., & Mahadevan-Jansen, A. (2005). Optical stimulation of neural tissue in vivo. *Optics Letters, 30*(5), 504–506.

Wiener, N. (1949). *Extrapolation, Interpolation, and Smoothing of Stationary Time Series* (Vol. 7). Cambridge, MA: MIT Press.

Wise, K. D., Sodagar, A. M., Yao, Y., Gulari, M. N., Perlin, G. E., & Najafi, K. (2008). Microelectrodes, microelectronics, and implantable neural microsystem. *Proceedings of the IEEE, 96*(7), 1184–1202.

Wodlinger, B., Dweiri, Y., & Durand, D. M. (2015). Biochips—electrical biosensors: Perceptual nerve sensors. In S. Bhunia, S. Majerus, & M. Sawan (Eds.), *Implantable Biomedical Microsystems: Design Principles and Applications* (pp. 203–214). Oxford: Elsevier.

Wu, W., Black, M. J., Gao, Y., Bienenstock, E., Serruya, M., Shaikhouni, A., & Donoghue, J. P. (2003). Neural decoding of cursor motion using a Kalman filter. In S. Becker, S. Thrun, & K. Obermayer (Eds.), *Advances in Neural Information Processing System 15: Proceedings of the 2002 NIPS Conference* (pp. 133–140). Cambridge, MA: MIT Press.

Zrenner, E. (2002). Will retinal implants restore vision? *Science, 295*(5557), 1022–1025.

9

Mitigating Stress Response to Optimize Human Performance

JAMES NESS AND JOSEPHINE Q. WOJCIECHOWSKI

INTRODUCTION

How do you optimize human performance? How do you define "optimal human performance?" These are questions that have been studied and reported on for decades. Common to these discussions are metaphors such as "Super Soldier" that guide research and thought into human performance optimization. In the context of human performance optimization, a Super Soldier is an attempt to increase the capabilities of soldiers, typically through performance-enhancing drugs, embedded technologies, or genetic alteration. While any or all of these may create a person more capable for a certain mission at a particular time, the possibility exists of affecting permanent changes that impoverish performance across other missions and contexts as well as impoverish the long-term health and well-being of the soldier.

This chapter provides perspective to the prevailing presupposition that the manifestation and stability of the phenotype is uniquely driven by endogenous factors. Much of the work on optimizing human performance is focused on fitting an engineered soldier to an invented niche to which the soldier is optimized. In this way, enhancing performance is seen in the hunt for a stable marker for health and performance and in the bioengineering ideas that essentially undermined the *wild type*[1] of the US service member. History has shown that ideas stemming from a tenacious belief (Peirce, 1887) in what future war will bring have had tragic endings for the very people who volunteered for service and who trust in the leadership advocating such measures (Wilson, 1977).

The thesis of this chapter is that mitigating stress and optimizing performance are only achievable through understanding the composite factors determining the biobehavioral system and the adaptations to be made within an effective environment. These factors not only include proximal influences, but also the system's ontogeny, which conditions the system to respond in particular ways. As a result, there is a considerable degree of variation with which individuals respond and adapt to an effective environment (Lickliter & Ness, 1990). An effective environment consists of those stimulus complexes to which the biobehavioral system responds or adapts.

The continuum of the influence of the effective environment on the biobehavioral system ranges from ephemeral (as in orienting responses) to relatively permanent changes (as in learning).

MAINTENANCE, FACILITATION, AND INDUCTION

Soldiers are accessed into service by selecting for biobehavioral function within normal limits as seen in a normal environment. Training is then employed to maintain and augment soldier health, well-being, and fitness, establishing the basis for unit readiness. At a minimum, to maintain readiness, the baseline pre-deployment function must be sustained in the context of the uncertain and life-threatening environments faced in deployment. To meet mission requirements, desired abilities can be maintained, facilitated, or induced from the soldiers' readiness posture. Maintaining, facilitating, or inducing desired abilities are sometimes associated with negative health and well-being consequences. Thus, in the short-term, optimizing human performance for desired abilities may achieve mission, but, in the mid-term, associated health and well-being consequences may impact readiness, and, in the long-term, associated consequences may persist throughout the service member's life. Health consequences are difficult to predict given the degree of variation conditioned by individual ontogenetic experience.

In general, the facilitation or maintenance of an exhibited or a latent functional ability is likely reversible since the ability is within the repertoire of the soldier's phenotype. Thus, the consequence to health and well-being are likely negligible. That said, at some point, quantity of sustainment of a desired function (e.g., hours of alertness) yields an irreversible qualitative change, as seen in the use of the drug Pervitin in the German Army during World War II (Hurst, 2013). Similarly, the induction of a new ability, particularly through biologically invasive means, is very likely irreversible since the ability does not, by definition, exist within the repertoire of the soldier's phenotype. The induction of a phenotypic expression through biologically invasive methods, although shown to be medically achievable, is done so in an abnormally functioning person within a normal environment. However, the inverse is the case for the soldier. The induction of a new phenotype in a soldier changes an otherwise normally functioning person into a uniquely defined performer designed to achieve a mission objective in an abnormal environment. Herein lies the very possibility of creating a hopeful monster rather than a Super Soldier (Castle, 2003).

In this discussion, human performance and health optimization are categorized as Gottlieb (1991) proposes, in the processes involved in the expression of phenotypes. These processes are maintenance, facilitation, and induction of a phenotypic expression as activated by *canalizing experiences*. This chapter focuses on optimizing in the sense of maintaining and facilitating human performance and does not discuss induction as it involves expressing supranormal phenotypes (Lickliter & Ness, 1990), which is beyond the scope of the current discussion. For the purposes of this chapter, human performance optimization is defined as facilitating the expression of desired, naturally expressed, or latent phenotypes. A *latent phenotype* is one within the biobehavioral system's repertoire, facilitated under conditions of strong environments. A *strong environment* pervasively and repeatedly prompts and reinforces particular biobehavioral attributes and discourages other attributes and associated behaviors. *Human performance maintenance* is defined as maintaining or sustaining the expression of desired naturally expressed phenotypes. The goal of maintaining and facilitating in the expression of a phenotype is to achieve optimal adaptations to a set of environmental conditions while mitigating negative consequences to health and well-being.

STRESS AND RESILIENCE: PERFORMANCE OPTIMIZATION ≠ HEALTH

An indicator of the consequences to health and well-being is stress. Selye (1950) defined stress as the "interplay between a force and the resistance offered to it." In this formulation, what are observable are changes in biologic systems and behavior in response to a load. A *load* is a stimulus event that produces a measurable effect on the biobehavioral system. That measurable effect is the degree and duration of deviation from an individual's homeostatic and behavioral normal limits. The deviations measured in biological systems and behavior are operationalized as *strains*. The sum total of the strains is *stress*, which is the construct that represents the force back on the load. In response to a load, biological systems respond with specific and general adaptations. Loads that elicit specific defensive reactions induce specific adaptations, such as formations of specific antibodies, adaptations to heat and cold, and tolerances to pharmacologic agents. General adaptation is defined as "non-load"–specific responses and typically involves preparatory "defensive" responses. These adaptations are governed by the hypothalamic, pituitary, and adrenal axis and are conditioned in some manner by preconditioning factors (e.g., heredity, diet, and previous exposures; Gunnar & Quevedo, 2007). The conditioning yields a considerable variation among individuals in the stress response.

The stress–strain relationships describe by Selye (1950) have recently been subsumed under the construct of *resilience* in the context of deployment-related health and well-being. Figure 9.1 depicts the results of an EBSCO search for deployment-related stress and resilience, excluding terms associated with engineering of materials. The graph shows an increase in primary source articles on health consequences of deployment-related stress in 2004 and steadily increasing through 2016. Resilience appears to be added to the lexicon of deployment-related stress around 2007 and parallels the number of primary source articles on posttraumatic stress (PTS). Across these articles, the construct of resilience is used as a metaphor for the capacity of a biobehavioral system to resist, recover from, or equilibrate to loads.

Resilience as resistance is used to convey the ability to accommodate to the load. *Resistance* is seen in the use of prophylaxes such as immunizations to prepare the body to resist strains of disease. Here the immune system accommodates to the inoculating effect of a vaccine such that the immune system builds antibodies in defense of some disease. The building of antibodies is a specific adaptation, as defined by Selye (1950). A similar specific adaptation is seen in the initial response to cold. The environmental thermal load facilitates accommodative physiologic responses

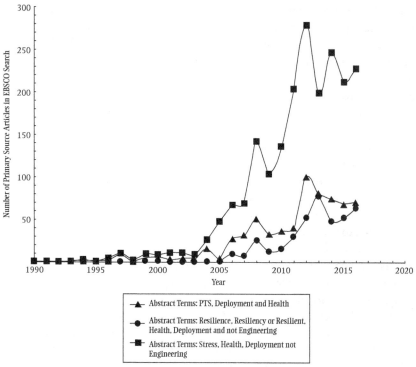

Figure 9.1 The number of articles per year in an EBSCO search engine search for primary sources whose abstract contained stress and resilience terms. Since engineers also use these terms, abstracts were excluded if they contained engineering references to limit stress and resilience to health and well-being.
Image courtesy of the authors.

such as cold-induced vasodilation, expressed within 10 minutes of cold exposure to an extremity. The response to cold is a pulsing of a constriction and expansion of capillaries in the extremities to limit the flow of cold blood to the core. Limiting flow reduces the load on the thermoregulatory system while maintaining peripheral blood flow to sustain the health of peripheral tissue (O'Brien et al., 2000).

Resilience in the "bounce back" or recovery sense is seen in a phenomenon described in medium to heavy conflict and called "battle fatigue." Fatigue was observed when units, upon receiving hostile fire, would flatten, meaning lying prone on the ground; then, once the threat abated, they would recover and continue moving. Universally, after three episodes of flattening on a mission, units were unable to go further even though the unit may have only covered a short distance and received no casualties. Two interventions served to improve resilience in this case. One was time to rest, allowing combat effectiveness to return. The other was re-establishing personal contact with each member of the team. The latter method was so effective that standing operating procedures (SOP) were established for the senior member of the unit to touch each soldier, speaking their name, and point out team members to their left and right (Operations Research Office, Johns Hopkins University, 1953).

The third connotation of the construct of resilience is *equilibration*. In this sense, resilience is reorganization of biological systems to render a new balance to reduce the strain on systems from strong environmental loads (McEwen & Wingfield, 2003). A study prompted in the mid-1990s by soldier deaths during the "Florida phase" of the US Army Ranger qualifying course revealed a caloric imbalance between the calories consumed during feeding and the calories expended for work and thermoregulatory maintenance (Young et al., 1998). The study showed that at the circadian nadir, core body temperatures of underfed and fatigued soldiers sleeping outside routinely drop to 35°C. This temperature is at the limit of thermoregulatory sufficiency. However, the soldiers were not in physiological distress. The physiological systems equilibrated in response to environmental loads, and, as a result, reduced overall physiological strain symptomatic of hypothermia. Over the course of Ranger School, the thermoregulatory system had adapted to the demands of the environment. Although the shift in core body temperature was found not to be symptomatic of thermoregulatory distress, the shift had the consequence of narrowing the margin between thermoregulation and thermoregulatory collapse. Soldiers were at greater risk for thermoregulatory collapse due to thermal conductance. Among the decisions to improve safety and maintain realism was the decision to feed the soldiers more calories so they could maintain a higher core temperature and could retain some fat to allow them to shiver. The canalizing experiential effect of underfeeding and fatigue facilitated a shift in core temperature. The shift from a normal 37°C to 35°C core temperature indicates resilience in the sense of equilibration. Equilibration means the facilitation of a latent phenotype, which in this case is that of a new thermoregulatory homeostasis. The change seen in the Rangers is reversible, with return of the core temperature to 37°C within 3–4 weeks of increased caloric intake and rest. This change demonstrates resiliency in that the equilibration reduced thermoregulatory stress and sustained soldier performance. However, the equilibration was at the cost of normal state resilience in that resistance to thermoregulatory threat was reduced. The phenotype of shivering became latent in that it could no longer be expressed, and the margin between thermoregulation and its collapse was reduced. This illustrates the point that there does not exist a reliable positive correlation between performance optimization and stress reduction and that of health and well-being.

STABILITY: DISPOSITIONAL AND STRONG ENVIRONMENT

There is little doubt that individuals tend to behave in a relatively stable manner (Siegal & Bergman, 2002). However, there is considerable debate as to the source of the stability (Mischel, 1977). Arguments generally emphasize either person variables, situational variables, or some combination of person and situational variables. Although analogous to nature–nurture dichotomies, the debate over the stability of personality has its roots in a learning theory debate over the specificity versus the generality of learning experience. The catalyst for the debate was a series of transfer of training studies led by Hartshorne (Hartshorne & May, 1928;

1929; Hartshorne, May, & Shuttleworth, 1930). The studies showed significant inconsistencies across situations in children's moral behavior. Notwithstanding, consistent but low intercorrelations across situations in behavior were also revealed.

Consistency of behavior of a dispositional nature is the presupposition under-lying aptitude tests for selection into a particular job. One of the larger efforts in the US Army was a Korean War study on attributes of a fighter versus a nonfighter (Egbert et al., 1957). A soldier was categorized as a fighter if two or more peers gave examples of good performance in battle or one peer gave a specific example of good performance and the soldier received or was recommended for an award. A soldier was categorized as a nonfighter if two or more peers gave specific instances of poor behavior in battle or if the soldier admitted poor performance. Assessments were conducted on 310 soldiers from September 21, 1953 to November 28, 1953. Assessments were made in central Korea at the 45th Division School of Standards and Replacement Center near Chu'unch'on, just below the 38th Parallel. The orig-inal pool was 345. Thirty-five soldiers were lost due to being killed or wounded in action, and others were rotated from theater. In the assessment, soldiers were interviewed about engagements that occurred from July through August 1953. These engagements included the Christmas Hill area, Kumhwa Valley, and Pork Chop Hill. The main findings over a large battery of assessments were that the fighter scored higher on the Aptitude Area I intelligence test than the nonfighter, was heavier ($\mu = 166$ lbs vs. $\mu = 157$ lbs) and taller ($\mu = 70$ in vs. $\mu = 69$ in), and was socially better adjusted than the nonfighter.

The mean Aptitude Area I intelligence test score for the nonfighter was 84 or about a standard deviation below the Army's average ($\mu = 100$, $\delta = 20$). The mean score for the fighter was 94. In the early 1950s, heavier and taller was actually healthier as many soldiers tended to be underweight and height tended to be as-sociated with developmental undernutrition. Socially well-adjusted meant growing up in a stable home life, having friends, and engaging in socially appropriate activ-ities. At the time, these were those activities that American culture associated with being masculine. In summary, these findings suggest that a person whose is of av-erage intelligence and is healthy and socially well-adjusted will perform well under fire. The findings are not profound other than to confirm that the underpinning of performance optimization and stress reduction is an individual who is well within normal limits of health and well-being.

More interesting and telling are the qualitative descriptions of fighters versus those of nonfighters. Table 9.1 shows the characteristics of a fighter versus a nonfighter when under fire (Egbert et al., 1957). The characteristics are recounted instances of behavior and do not suggest a stable dispositional trait. As shown in the Hartshorne studies cited earlier, it remains hard to predict on an individual level who will or will not do well under fire in a given instance and whether or not behaviors will remain consistent (Hartshorne & May, 1928; 1929; Hartshorne et al., 1930). Notwithstanding, at the unit level, cohesion does appear to be pre-dictive of how well units will perform (Egbert et al., 1957; Wieslogel, Flanagan, & Billingsley, 1953).

Table 9.1 FIGHTER AND NONFIGHTER BEHAVIORS

Fighter		Nonfighter	
Provides leadership in	• assaults & hazardous missions • getting soldiers into good firing positions • getting soldiers to fire weapons • calming & giving soldiers confidence	Withdraws or "bugs out" under fire	• stays in bunker or trench when should be moving • refuses direct order to fire at enemy • refuses direct order to evacuate wounded or dead • forced at gun point to obey an order
Takes aggressive action by	• advancing toward enemy & firing • firing effectively at enemy • volunteering for and performing hazardous missions	Malingers	• leaves, throws away, or purposely renders weapon inoperable • stops fighting when only slightly wounded • avoids fighting by carrying supplies or helping a wounded buddy • fails to fire for fear of giving position away • feigns illness or says he cannot take it
Performs supporting tasks under fire	• caring for & evacuating wounded • helping in body recovery • bringing up ammo • repairing weapons • laying communications wire & carrying messages	Hysterical	• imagines hearing and seeing things and fires weapon or throws grenades at them • trembles uncontrollably & cannot hold his weapon or fires wildly • Breaks down & cries • Shaky & nervous

As reported in "Fighter 1: An analysis of combat fighters and non-fighters (Technical Report 44)" by R. Egbert, T. Meeland, V. Cline, E. Forgy, M. Spickler, & C. Brown (1957). Monterey, CA: Human Resources Research Office, US Army Leadership Human Research Unit.

SOCIAL ANIMALS ARE HOMEOSTATIC OPEN SYSTEMS

The case for cohesion cannot be understated. In a summarization of his work on aggression, Cairns (1979) concluded that, contrary to widely held beliefs, the establishment of aggressive behavior does not require reinforcement or imitation, nor does it require the experience of frustration or pain. The absences of social experiences are associated with aggression from the withdrawn or isolated individual. Those with limited social experience tend not to regulate responses well in that they are more reactive to stimuli. Considering Cairn's finding of dysregulation, Hofer (1984) researched the physiological mechanisms that are regulated by the social environment, particularly those involved in separation and loss. He introduced the metaphor "homeostatically open system," which refers to the regulation of physiological and behavioral systems through the composite of stimuli provided by the social environment (Ness, Marshall, & Aravich, 1995; Lickliter, 2008). Specific physiological and behavioral systems open to regulation following separation from those with established emotional bonds stem from two independent phases: an acute "protest phase" and a chronic, slow developing "despair phase."

Behavioral and physiological changes associated with the acute phase of the separation response manifest themselves immediately and include increases in agitation, heart rate, and glucocorticoid and catecholamine (e.g., norepinephrine) levels. Behavioral and physiological changes associated with the despair phase are decreased and variable food intake, as well as decreased body weight, cardiac rate, growth hormone production, and T-cell activity. These two phases are independently developing in that the slower developing responses emerge after those of the acute phase but not as a result of or in response to acute phase responses. Thus, suppressing acute phase responses may have little effect on slower developing responses. In Selye's (1950) classification, these adaptations are general adaptations.

The concept of homeostatically open was implicitly understood by the warfighter in the establishment of the SOP to re-establish social contact after flattening. The concept is well understood by military psychiatry when a soldier presents with essentially nonfighter symptomatology. The therapy is to treat using the principles of immediacy, proximity, and expectancy (Jones, 1995). Immediacy is critical to mitigate the misattribution of the general adaptations of the physiologic system to rationalizations for the feelings based on prevailing health fears (Papez, 1995). Proximity is critical to retain the sense of belonging, thus preventing general adaptations associated with separation and loss. Proximity mitigates, in particular, the slow developing depressive-like symptomatology. Expectancy gives the soldier an understanding that reactions are normal in an abnormal environment, and normal function is quickly recovered. This is the counternarrative to the feelings of weakness, letting the team down, and poor mental health.

The war psychiatrist assesses not only the symptoms, but also the effective environment reinforcing the aberrant behaviors. Many of the treatments creatively remove the reinforcing quality of the symptoms. As reported by Jones (1995, p. 51), a rash of somnambulism broke out in a small engineering unit in Vietnam. The initial case had a childhood history of somnambulism, and the solution was to move the soldier's quarters from the perimeter of the camp to the camp's center. In this way the soldier would not wander under the cover of night into the minefield along the perimeter of the camp. The camp's perimeter was receiving sniper fire and had been infiltrated. Subsequent to the move of the initial case to the camp's center, a number of soldiers presented with somnambulism. Noting the reinforcement contingencies of moving quarters to the center of camp, the attending physician recommended a solution—night guard duty—so that the individuals would not sleep during the night, thus preventing the soldiers from wandering off under darkness into the minefield. Somnambulism complaints ceased.

The somnambulism case highlights several points. One is that the behavior is certainly a nonfighter behavior, but also that the behavior, in lieu of an ontogenetic history, is less a dispositional characteristic than it is a situational reinforced behavior. The other point is the considerable strength of the effective environment in facilitating and maintaining phenotypes. Within the Armed Forces, personnel perform duties in the context of strong environments. These environments present pervasive pressure on personnel whether as an environmental extreme, a malevolent environment, or as a high operations tempo environment. The loads experienced in these environments are often viewed as something to which personnel must be buffered. Approaching the environment from this perspective orients one toward mitigating the deleterious effects on personnel or protecting against exposure to deleterious situations. If strong environments have such effects. then they may also be used as a means to enhance performance through facilitating or maintaining desired characteristics. That is precisely how the attending physician dealt with the somnambulism cases. Through leveraging the reinforcement contingencies of the strong environment, this solution maintained fighter behavior in the soldiers presenting with nonfighter behavior (i.e., somnambulism).

PERSONALITY IS SOMETHING WE DO; IT IS NOT SOMETHING WE HAVE

Behavioral clusters describing personality, like those of all constructs, are conditioned by an ontogenetic history. Associated with personality is a biobehavioral shift in identity in the transition from adolescence to young adulthood. This shift entails forming identities and restructuring social and emotional attachments from parents to peers and significant others. During this period, personality factors are particularly mutable in the presence of a strong environment. Data from a longitudinal study of personality development in US Military Academy cadets showed a shift in personality traits toward an ideal that was not a result of self-selection or demand characteristic, but a result of an apparent canalization of Academy-desired traits within the cadet toward an ideal (Ness, Lewis, & Brazil, 2011).

The results support the idea that stability of the personality is as much a function of individuals seeking certain niches as it is adapting to those niches. In other words, personality was better understood as something one does rather than as something one has. For those who remained at the Academy, Neuroticism and Conscientious scores, as measured on the NEO-Personality-Inventory-Revised (NEO-PI-R), migrated reliably from freshman to junior year toward the "Ideal." Openness scores migrated reliably for females toward the Ideal from freshmen to junior year, which was toward the male Openness score. These factor scores were strongly agreed upon by the faculty, staff, and seniors as the Ideal and showed a large difference from that of cadet scores. This condition constitutes a "strong environment." The strong agreement establishes pervasiveness, and the difference between actual and ideal establishes the load on the cadet driving the adaptation. The staff deemed Agreeableness as an ideal trait, and Agreeableness showed a trend toward the Ideal but not a statistically significant change. The staff has the greatest contact with cadets, and the staff are responsible for military training, leadership grades, and summer assignments. However, Agreeableness did not fit the definition of a strong environment in that there was lack of agreement among faculty, staff, and seniors as to the Ideal for this factor. Thus, as hypothesized, there was only a nominal, nonsignificant shift toward the Ideal on this factor. In addition, as predicted, there was no shift in Extroversion because there was considerable overlap between Ideal and cadet scores. The condition of pervasiveness was met in that there was agreement on the Ideal. However, there was little difference between cadet and Ideal scores and thus no load. In this case, the environment served to maintain phenotypic expression.

The data bring into focus the findings in Table 9.1 and those of the somnambulism cases. The place where stimulus, reinforcement, and disposition meet and are integrated is in the brain. The data support a view of personality as something one does rather than as something one has (Ness, Kolditz, Lewis, & Lam, 2010). Personality is an activity, and thus even the prototypical "nonfighter" may turn out to be a hero. The recollection of General Marshall (ORO-T-185, 1953; p. 22) attests to this fact: "Getting back to your question, I thought during World War I that there was at least one category of individual that we could say would never work out in battle; that is the guy who was a social misfit, not liked by his squad, not liked by anybody around him, who in garrison was virtually ostracized, not because men didn't like him, but because he didn't like anybody else. He just didn't belong. I thought this was a pretty good rule. At Kwajalein Island, there was the case of a man who was put on the flamethrower by his company because the man was such a no-good that they wanted to destroy him. He was hated down to the last man, and he became one of the great heroes of the Kwajalein battle. There was nothing he would not do with a flamethrower. Oddly enough, it led to a total regeneration on his part. From that time on he was a good soldier. He had found a big job, something to challenge him. I have seen various other cases of the same sort."

Personality as something one does means that antecedents are seen as an active construction of the system, and the resulting personality is not uniquely understandable in terms of the structural preconditions of person, or environment, or both. Rather, the personality is understood in terms of the functions or goals of the individual or group. In this way personality is constructed by the present organization and the ongoing activity and is not predictable in terms of material entity whether stimuli, trait, or combination thereof. The logic of ascribing traits required of a Super Soldier is folly, as seen in recounting the hero (Super Soldier) of Kwajalein.

THE CHIMERA OF THE PHYSIOLOGICAL MARKER

Maintenance and facilitation of phenotypes is energetically taxing, and prolonged expression of a strong, environmentally evinced phenotype often results in disease (McEwen & Wingfield, 2003). In a prototypical strong environment as seen in the domestication of species, particularly those for food production, periods of rest are required to sustain a desired performance. For example, in milk production in ungulates a drying period is necessary to "rest" the mammary glands to reduce the probability of disease (Henderson, Hudson, Bradley, Sherwin, & Green, 2016; Church, Fox, Gaskins, Hancock, & Gay, 2008). In the strong environment described for the cadets, one of the things cadets seek are opportunities for respite from the strong environment. These respites come in the form of trip sections, which are opportunities to leave academy grounds, and "hides," which are places within academy grounds where cadets feel less of a pressure from the ideal. In the strong environment of the Korean War, battle fatigue would set in and the soldiers simply needed to rest.

The cause for the need for rest was explored in great detail during the Korean War because the fatigue was real, but not a unique result of physical exhaustion. The exhaustion was attributed to physiologic and hormonal strains associated with general adaptations of the body to combat (Davis & Taylor, 1954). On average, soldiers required 6 days of rest to fully recover to normal physiologic function. A measure of general adaptation in the physiologic studies of the warfighter during the Korean War was eosinophil counts, which are a type of leukocyte. Figure 9.2

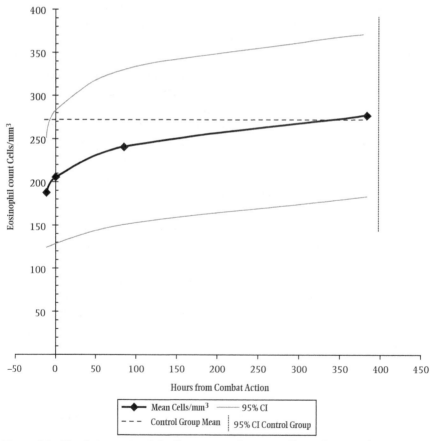

Figure 9.2 Circulating eosinophil cell counts as a function of hours from combat. Image courtesy of the authors, derived from data presented in Davis et al. (1953).

shows eosinophil count as a function of hours from combat action (Davis et al., 1953). Eosinophil counts prior to combat action indicate a preparatory preemptive response induced, ostensibly, by an affective load. The affective load can be an anticipatory learned response stemming from prior experiences, captured affect from other soldiers, or some other induced central nervous system–governed preemptive general adaptation. Prior to combat action, mean eosinophil circulating blood counts dropped to within 70% of baseline. The anti-inflammatory response (i.e., drop in circulating eosinophils) is associated with the release of adrenocorticotropic hormone (ACTH) in the activation of the hypothalamic-pituitary-adrenal axis (Selye, 1950; Renold, Quigley, Kennard, & Thorn, 1951). Eosinophil counts increased to baseline in the hours subsequent to combat action. Soldiers recovered to within a standard deviation of the control by 4 days. Notwithstanding, the figure does show a considerable individual variability, and the question remains as to the need for rest. Selye suggests an exhaustion phase, but that is based on a premise that opposing effectors cannot occur, which leaves the inference that exhaustion is a result of "using up" physiologic resources (Selye, 1946). However, if one considers the behavioral effector (motivation to drive on) and the physiologic effector (anticipation of threat to the system) in battle fatigue, these effectors are opposing. The opposition is energetically taxing in that the physiologic effector is overdriving in response to the opposing behavioral effector to continue. Herein lies an alternative hypothesis for the fatigue—that of an allostatic load explanation versus a homeostatic load explanation (Ramsey & Woods, 2014).

The variability in general adaptation across individuals, contexts, and times is such that the idea of a physiologic marker is likely to remain a chimera. Physiologic markers present an enigma not only due to individual variability but also due to the varied roles of a marker in response to loads. Eosinophils are granular leukocytes that respond in general and specific adaptations. Specific adaptations of the immune response that result in an increase in circulating eosinophils include allergic responses, asthma, and responses to multicellular parasites (Acharya & Ackerman, 2014). Moreover, eosinophils are implicated in multiple neurodegenerative diseases (Davis et al., 1953; Sharma et al., 2010). General adaptation in response to affective loads not only includes the anti-inflammatory response just discussed, but also includes a role of intestinal eosinophils in producing corticotrophin-releasing hormone (CRH). Corticotrophin-releasing hormone induces epithelial barrier degradation leading to ulceration (Zheng et al., 2009). Physiologic markers may thus be the wrong level of analysis in predicting stress-related health threats or as indicators of enhanced performance. A systems-level approach is likely a better approach, as has been advanced in the theory of allostasis (Goldstein & McEwen, 2002; McEwen & Wingfield, 2003).

HOMEOSTATIC ORIENTATION MAY FOCUS ON THE WRONG LEVEL OF ANALYSIS

There is a strong argument that the overgeneralization of engineering concepts in the life sciences (Werner, 2010) has generated presuppositions about living organisms such that a Super Soldier can be created. The presuppositions lack an isomorphism with biological reality. Homeostatically, biological systems are chaotically dynamic, with no real set point. The system organizes to optimize effective environment demands, with endogenous demands creating a constant flux. In this sense, homeostasis is an emergent property of a biological system. Within the system, opposing effectors can occur, which, in the case of battle fatigue, creates an allostatic load resulting in fatigue. When effectors are not in opposition, carrying laden rucksacks and marching away from battle present few if any symptoms of fatigue.

Since homeostasis is emergent, effectors are a functional construct and not an actual structure or fixed entity. There is an underlying discontinuity in biological organization, where lower order organization is foundational for higher order organization, but the functions of the higher order processes are not determined from lower order processes. Thus, identifying or influencing a structure or function to enhance performance or mitigate stress will likely be met with a self-righting at higher levels of organization. There is also a very real reversal of desired effects, as seen in pharmacological intervention. Here, there is the real possibility of a sign-reversal effect. One may want to create a pain-tolerant soldier and administer an analgesic prophylactically. Initially, there will be the desired effect, but after a period of time, the biological system will overshoot its response to the pharmacological agent and a hyperanalgesic state will ensue and will trigger a spiral of dysregulation (Bruins Slot, Pauwels, & Colpaert, 2002). The point is that reducing human performance to unique aspects of physiologic function may be the wrong level of analysis. Perhaps an understanding of the system in an allostatic sense rather than a homeostatic sense is a better approach to evincing functioning that enhances human performance.

CONCLUSION

This chapter began with a discussion of readiness since invasive performance enhancement essentially treats the soldier as expendable. Biologically invasive performance enhancements are often irreversible, and, although they may yield short-term tactical gains, they will result in diminishment of readiness and erosion of cohesion and trust with system dysregulation and in long-term negative health consequence. Thus, the chapter advocates for leveraging the natural diversity within the wild type rather than trying to force a lopsided performer in a narrowly defined context (as seen in domestication of species).

As discussed, the biological system has an allostatic quality which yields a large repertoire of available latent phenotypes. These can be facilitated and maintained through noninvasive yet strong environments. These latent phenotypes are manifest in the acclimatization to strong environments and are reversible (Ness, Kreim, Friedl, & Lyke, 2009). Other means to enhance performance are to mitigate the effects of opposing effectors. This is seen in the examples of the SOP to re-establish social contact among soldiers and in the psychiatrist re-establishing fighter behaviors through leveraging reinforcement contingencies and changing the valences of rewards by imposing night shift guard duties on soldiers presenting with somnambulism.

The breadth of possibilities is limited only by the creativity of the leadership and its scientific community. As cautioned, presuppositions are a limiting factor and one must not reify metaphors (Boring, 1953). For example, "set point" refers to a hypothetically optimal level of a parameter that is monitored, maintained, and defended, as in core body temperature. In actuality, body temperature is the consequence of multiple individual and independent thermo-effector loops, each with its own threshold (or set point) for activation, whose collective activity results in a value that reflects the current conditions and for which there is no central integrator that coordinates effector activity (Ramsay & Woods, 2014).

In summary, the best way to enhance performance and mitigate stress is to promote the diversity of the wild type to leverage its agile breadth of phenotypes. Note that Usain Bolt, by conventional wisdom, should not be the fastest human alive. Yet he is. We refer the reader to the *New York Times* article, "Something Strange in Usain Bolt's Stride" (Longman, 2017).

NOTE

1. The term "wild type" is used in the sense of species-typical, meaning a nonmutated genetic form or artificially engineered phenotype.

REFERENCES

Acharya, K. R., & Ackerman, S. J. (2014). Eosinophil granule proteins: Form and function. *The Journal of Biological Chemistry, 289*(25), 17406–7415.

Boring, E. (1953). The role of theory in experimental psychology. *The American Journal of Psychology, 64*(2), 169–184.

Bruins Slot, L. A., Pauwels, P. J., & Colpaert, F. C. (2002). Sign-reversal during persistent activation in mu-opioid signal transduction. *Journal of Theoretical Biology, 215*(2), 169–182. doi:10.1006/jtbi.2001.2509.

Cairns, R. (1979). Social *Development: The Origins and Plasticity of Interchanges*. W. H. Freeman & Co: San Francisco, CA.

Castle, D. (2003). Hopes against hopeful monsters. *The American Journal of Bioethics, 3*(3), 28–30.

Church, G., Fox, L., Gaskins, C., Hancock, D., & Gay, J. (2008). The effect of a shortened dry period on intramammary infections during the subsequent lactation. *Journal of Dairy Science, 91,* 4219–4225. doi:10.3168/jds.2008-1377

Davis, S. W, Elmadjian, F., Hanson, L. F., Liddell, H. S., Zilinsky, A. A., Johnston, M. E., . . . Longley, G. H. (1953). *A Study of Combat Stress Korea 1952* (Technical Memorandum ORO-T-41 [FEC]). Chevy Chase, MD: Johns Hopkins University Operations Research Office.

Davis, S. W., & Taylor, J. G. (1954). *Stress in Infantry Combat* (Technical Memorandum ORO-T-295). Chevy Chase, MD: Johns Hopkins University Operations Research Office.

Egbert, R., Meeland, T., Cline, V., Forgy, E., Spickler, M., & Brown, C. (1957). *Fighter 1: An Analysis of Combat Fighters and Non-Fighters* (Technical Report 44). Monterey, CA: Human Resources Research Office, US Army Leadership Human Research Unit.

Goldstein, D., & McEwen, B. (2002). Allostasis, homeostasis, and the nature of stress. *Stress, 5*(1), 55–58.

Gottlieb, G. (1991). Experiential canalization of behavioral development: Theory. *Developmental Psychology, 27*(1), 4–13.

Gunnar, M., & Quevedo, K. (2007). The neurobiology of stress and development. *Annual Review of Psychology, 58*(1), 145–173.

Hartshorne, H., & May, M. (1928). *Studies in the Nature of Character: Volume 1, Studies in Deceit.* New York: McMillian.

Hartshorne, H., & May, M. (1929). *Studies in the Nature of Character: Volume 2, Studies in Service and Self-Control.* New York: McMillian.

Hartshorne, H., May, M., & Shuttleworth, F. (1930). *Studies in the Nature of Character: Volume 3, Studies in the Organization of Character.* New York: McMillian.

Henderson, A., Hudson, C., Bradley, A., Sherwin, V., & Green, M. (2016). Prediction of intramammary infection status across the dry period from lifetime cow records. *Journal of Dairy Science, 99*, 5586–5595.

Hofer, M. (1984). Relationships as regulators: A psychobiologic perspective on bereavement. *Psychosomatic Medicine, 46*(3), 183–197.

Hurst, F. (2013, May 30). WWII drug: The German granddaddy of crystal meth. *Der Spiegel.* Translated from the German by Ella Ornstein. Retrieved from http://www.spiegel.de/international/germany/crystal-meth-origins-link-back-to-nazi-germany-and-world-war-ii-a-901755.html

Jones, F. (1995). Traditional warfare combat stress casualties. In F. D. Jones, L. R. Sparacino, V. L. Wilcox, J. M. Rothberg, & J. W. Stokes (Eds.), *War Psychiatry,* Washington, D.C.: Borden Institute, Office of the Surgeon General U.S.A.

Lickliter, R. (2008). Theories of attachment: The long and winding road to an integrative developmental science. *Integrative Psychological and Behavioral Sciences, 42*(4), 397–405.

Lickliter, R., & Ness, J. (1990). Domestication and comparative psychology: Status and strategy. *Journal of Comparative Psychology, 104*, 211–218.

Longman, J. (2017, July 20). Something strange in Usain Bolt's stride. *The New York Times.* https://www.nytimes.com/2017/07/20/sports/olympics/usain-bolt-stride-speed.html?_r=0.

McEwen, B., & Wingfield (2003). The concept of allostasis in biology and biomedicine. *Hormones and Behavior, 43*(1), 2–15.

Mischel, W. (1977). On the future of personality measurement. *American Psychologist, 32*, 246–254.

Ness, J., Kolditz, T., Lewis, P., & Lam, D. (2010). Development and implementation of the US Army Leader Self-Development Portfolio. In P. T. Bartone, R. H. Pastel, & M. A. Vaitkus (Eds.), *The 71-F Advantage: Applying Research Psychology For Health and Performance Gains.* Washington, DC: National Defense University Press.

Ness, J., Kreim, G., Friedl, K., & Lyke, D. (2009). US/German bilateral agreement on health status monitoring: Applications to cold environments. *NATO Science and Technology Organization, RTO-RT-HFM-168,* 08-1-08-9.

Ness, J., Lewis, P., & Brazil, D. (2011, October). *Building the total system: The effects of strong environments on personality development.* Paper presented at the American Society of Naval Engineers, Human Systems Integration Symposium, Vienna, Virginia.

Ness, J., Marshall, T., & Aravich, P. (1995). Effects of rearing condition on activity-induced weight loss. *Developmental Psychobiology, 28*(3), 165–173.

O'Brien, C., Young, A. J., Lee, D. T., Shitzer, A., Sawka, M. N., & Pandolf, K. B. (2000). Role of core temperature as a stimulus for cold acclimation during repeated immersion in 20°C water. *Journal of Applied Physiology, 89*(1), 242–250. http://jap.physiology.org/content/89/1/242.full

Operations Research Office, Johns Hopkins University. (March 17, 1953). Fatigue and Stress Symposium, *24–26 January 1952* (Technical Memorandum ORO-T-185). Chevy Chase, MD: Author.

Papez, J. (1995). A proposed mechanism of emotion. *Journal of Neuropsychiatry, 7*(1), 103–112.

Peirce, C. (1887). The fixation of belief. *Popular Science Monthly, 12* (Nov), 1–15. http://www.peirce.org/writings/p107.html

Ramsey, D., & Woods, S. (2014). Clarifying the roles of homeostasis and allostasis in physiological regulation. *Psychological Review, 121*(2), 225–247.

Renold, A. E., Quigley, T. B., Kennard, H. E., & Thorn, G. W. (1951). Reaction of the adrenal cortex to physical and emotional stress in college oarsmen. *The New England Journal of Medicine, 244*(20), 754–757.

Selye H. (1946). The general adaptation syndrome and the diseases of adaptation. *Journal of Clinical Endocrinology, 6,* 117–231. doi: 10.1210/jcem-6-2-117

Selye, H. (1950). Stress and the general adaptation syndrome. *British Medical Journal, June, 1*(4667), 1384–1392. https://www.jstor.org/stable/pdf/25357371.pdf

Sharma, A., Callahan, L., Sul, J., Kim, T., Barrett, L., Kim, M., . . . Eberwine, J. (2010). A neurotoxic phosphoform of Elk-1 associates with inclusions from multiple neurodegenerative diseases. *PLoS ONE, 5*(2): e9002. Retrieved from https://doi.org/10.1371/journal.pone.0009002

Siegal, M., & Bergman, A. (2002). Waddington's canalization revisited: Developmental stability and evolution. *Proceedings of the National Academy of Sciences, 99,* 10528–10532. Retrieved from http://www.pnas.org/cgi/content/full/99/16/10528

Werner, J. (2010). System properties, feedback control and effector coordination of human temperature regulation. *European Journal of Applied Physiology, 109*(1), 13–25.

Wieslogel, R., Flanagan, J., & Billingsley, S. (1953). *The Job of the Combat Infantryman* (Technical Memorandum ORO-T-250). Chevy Chase, MD: Operations Research Office, Johns Hopkins University.

Wilson, G. (March 9, 1977). Army conducted 239 secret, open-air germ warfare tests. *The Washington Post.* http://www.washingtonpost.com/archive/politics/1977/03/09/army-conducted-239-secret-open-air-germ-warfare-tests/b17e5ee7-3006-4152-acf3-0ad163e17a22/?tid=ss_mail&utm_term=.892221fc6b7e

Young, A., Castelllani, J., O'Brien, C., Shippe, R., Tikuisis, P., Meyer, L., . . . Sawka, M. (1998). Exertional fatigue, sleep loss, and negative energy balance increases susceptibility to hypothermia. *Journal of Applied Physiology, 85*(4): 1210–1217.

Zheng, P., Feng, B., Oluwole, C., Struiksma, S., Chen, X., Li, P., . . . Yang, P. (2009). Psychological stress induces eosinophils to produce corticotrophin releasing hormone in the intestine. *Gut, 58*(11), 1473–1479.

10

The Role of Sleep in Human Performance and Well-Being

NITA LEWIS SHATTUCK, PANAGIOTIS MATSANGAS,
VINCENT MYSLIWIEC, AND JENNIFER L. CREAMER

Sleep that knits up the ravell'd sleave of care, the death of each day's life, sore labour's bath, balm of hurt minds, great nature's second course, chief nourisher in life's feast.

—SHAKESPEARE, *Macbeth, Act II, Scene ii*

You must not needlessly fatigue the troops.

—NAPOLEON TO EUGENE DE BEAUHARNAIS, *July 29, 1806*

INTRODUCTION

In 1970, the futurist Alvin Toffler published a book entitled *Future Shock*, in which he describes the significant stress and individual dysfunction that results from accelerated rates of technological and social change (Toffler, 1970). Many of Toffler's predictions have come true: we now live in an ever changing, interconnected economic and socio-political global community. One byproduct of these changes is the infusion of a 24/7 tempo into our lives. For any occupation that requires continuous operations—for example, members of the military, emergency responders, and members of the transportation industry, news media, and police communities—this requirement to be awake at "unnatural" times of the day and night runs counter to our circadian biology. Although the requirement for sleep is frequently ignored—or at best, underestimated—sleep debt results in significant impacts to individual performance. Any volume that seeks to understand optimization of human performance must consider the critical roles of sleep and circadian rhythms on a wide range of human behaviors. In this chapter, we present compelling scientific evidence that has emerged over the past several decades that links sleep patterns and circadian rhythms to human performance and well-being.

This chapter provides the background for understanding both normal and abnormal sleep processes and reviews the causes and consequences of insufficient sleep. We begin with a discussion of the role of sleep, the homeostatic and the circadian systems, and the basic requirement for sleep in humans. We then provide a short description of sleep architecture and the functions served by various stages of sleep. We explore the causal factors of insufficient sleep, overview clinical aspects of sleep disorders, and inventory the known effects of sleep restriction on various kinds of human performance. As a major focus of this chapter, we then describe the special challenges of fatigue and sleep deprivation in the context of military service. The last section of the chapter addresses the efficacy of various fatigue countermeasures and alertness aids that are commonly used in the military. We conclude with an argument for more deliberate protection and promotion of sleep given its vital importance to all aspects of human performance and health. While the major focus of the chapter is on performance optimization in the military, this same information can be extended to that broad class of individuals outside the military who are required to work other than a normal nine-to-five routine.

NORMAL SLEEP

Sleep is a biological imperative for multicellular animals, a vital requirement for life (Savage & West, 2007). According to Carskadon and Dement (2016) "Sleep is a reversible behavioral state of perceptual disengagement from and unresponsiveness to the environment." Horne defined sleep as "the rest and recovery from the wear and tear of wakefulness" (Horne, 1988). Although studied for decades, the reason why we sleep still remains somewhat of a mystery. In an attempt to explore the enigma of sleep and its function, Krueger and colleagues recently identified and critiqued several candidate theories about why we sleep (Krueger, Frank, Wisor, & Roy, 2016). These theories include the following: sleep as a means to conserve caloric expenditure, the role of sleep in immune system response, sleep as a means to restore brain energy, the critical role of sleep in neuronal connectivity, sleep as a restorative for performance degradation that accrues with hours of wakefulness, and sleep serving to remove byproducts of waking activity through the glymphatic clearance of interstitial fluids in the central nervous system (Krueger et al., 2016). Each of these theories has strengths and limitations, and strong arguments have been made for each of them. At present, scientific research and debate continue to delve into the mysteries of sleep.

Humans are naturally diurnal: active and awake in the daytime and asleep at night. This pattern is modulated by two processes: homeostasis and circadian rhythms (Achermann & Borbély, 2003; Borbély, 1982; Borbély & Achermann, 1999). In the homeostatic process, the need for sleep, or "sleep propensity," increases linearly with cumulative wakefulness. Circadian rhythms are controlled by an internal oscillator, which resides in the suprachiasmatic nuclei of the hypothalamus in the brain (Brzezinski, 1997; Klein, Morre, & Reppert, 1991). This endogenous oscillator provides the approximately 24-hour circadian (*circa* = about, *dies* = day) pattern of sleep and wakefulness (Czeisler, Weitzman, Moore-Ede, Zimmerman, & Knauer, 1980).

The circadian oscillator, however, also affects many other human physiological functions. For example, core body temperature and hormones such as melatonin, cortisol, human growth hormone (HGH), leptin, and ghrelin are known to have circadian patterns of release and action. Together, these hormones mediate sleep and wakefulness and affect human performance, as well as growth and cellular repair, hunger, and satiation. Research conducted in temporal isolation facilities has shown that in the absence of other cues or external stimuli, humans have an innate 24.50- to 25-hour clock (Horne, 1988).

The phase of the circadian clock is not fixed, though, but can be aligned with the external environment through entrainment. *Zeitgebers* is the term given to behavioral patterns, mealtimes, daytime sounds, and, most importantly, light cues that help entrain and synchronize the body's internal rhythm with the environment (Cajochen, Chellappa, & Schmidt, 2014). Circadian entrainment, however, is not immediate; it can take at least a week to adjust from a diurnal to a nocturnal rhythm (Monk, 1986). Some researchers report it taking up to 12 or more days for full adaptation from days to nights (Colquhoun, Blake, & Edwards, 1969; Hockey, 1983).

Healthy adult humans require on average approximately 8 hours of sleep each night for full cognitive functioning (Anch, Browman, Mitler, & Walsh, 1988). However, there is considerable variability among individuals; some require more and some require less (Van Dongen & Dinges, 2000). The American Academy of Sleep Medicine (AASM) and Sleep Research Society (SRS) released a consensus report on the amount of sleep needed to promote optimal health in adults (Watson et al., 2015). Their report stated that adults should sleep 7 or more hours per night on a regular basis to promote optimal health. Sleeping longer, 9 hours or more per night on a regular basis, may be appropriate for young adults or for individuals recovering from sleep debt or illness. According to the consensus recommendation, sleeping less than 7 hours per night on a regular basis is associated with adverse health outcomes, including weight gain and obesity, diabetes, hypertension, heart disease and stroke, depression, and increased risk of death. Sleeping less than 7 hours per night is also associated with impaired immune function, increased pain, impaired performance, increased errors, and greater risk of accidents. It is evident that for anyone seeking to optimize human performance, sleep is vital.

Additionally, sleep patterns and sleep requirements are known to change over the course of a lifetime. The sleep patterns of newborns are polyphasic, characterized by little contiguous sleep, while children of 1 year of age typically are able to sleep through the night (Skeldon, Derks, & Dijk, 2016). Compared to adults, adolescents and young adults tend to have delayed bedtimes, later awakenings, and require approximately 0.5 to 1.25 hours more sleep per night (Carskadon, Wolfson, Tzischinsky, & Acebo, 1995; Wolfson & Carskadon, 1998; 2003). This finding is especially important for each of the branches of the military service or other career fields for which the preponderance of its members fall into this adolescent and young adult category. These younger service members actually require more sleep than fully grown adults; consequently, their levels of sleep deprivation are likely to be greater than the adults working alongside them.

Physiology of Normal Sleep

Sleep is comprised of non-REM (NREM) sleep and rapid eye movement (REM) sleep. NREM sleep is further divided into N1–N3 (N1 having the lowest arousal threshold, relatively easy to awaken from, and N3 the highest, or most difficult to awaken from). A polysomnogram (PSG) or sleep study utilizes electroencephalography (EEG) to evaluate brain waves, electrooculography to assess eye movements, and submental (chin) electromyography to determine muscle tone to provide the findings to determine sleep stages (Berry et al., 2015). NREM sleep has a synchronous EEG pattern with relatively low muscle tone, whereas the EEG in REM sleep is desynchronized with muscle atonia. Atonia, or skeletal muscle paralysis, is a defining feature of REM sleep. During a typical sleep episode, individuals normally start in N1 sleep and progress through N2 and N3 sleep prior to REM sleep. This ultradian rhythm occurs in approximately 90-minute intervals or cycles throughout the sleep period. N3 sleep occurs mostly in the first half of the sleep period, whereas REM sleep increases as the night progresses and is primary in the second half of the sleep period. Normal sleep duration in a young healthy adult is approximately 8 hours in length but varies with age, genetics, and other factors; N1 sleep compromises 2–5%, N2 sleep 45–55%, N3 sleep 10–20%, and REM 20–25% of the total sleep time (TST; Carskadon & Dement, 2016).

Brief arousals, which are not frank awakenings, occur throughout a sleep period and are considered a normal component of sleep. In a study evaluating healthy sleepers, the median arousal index (arousals/hour) for all sleepers was 13.3/hour (Mitterling et al., 2015). With increasing age, the number of arousals also increase along with the amount of time an individual is awake after falling asleep (Bonnet & Arand, 2007). An elevated arousal index potentially suggests an underlying sleep, medical, or psychiatric disorder. Of course, there are other non–disease related causes of elevated arousals such as ambient noise, temperature, light, or other disruptions to the sleep environment.

Overall sleep quality can be evaluated by looking at several different PSG parameters to include arousals, sleep onset latency (SOL), wakefulness after sleep onset (WASO), and sleep efficiency (SE). Disturbances in one or more of these parameters results in decreased sleep quality and/or quantity. Sleep efficiency is defined as the total sleep time (TST) divided by the time in bed spent trying to sleep. Normal sleep efficiency is around 90%. Sleep onset latency for a healthy adult is around 0–20 minutes and WASO is 0–25 minutes (Ohayon, Carskadon, Guilleminault, & Vitiello, 2004). Sleep efficiency can be decreased in patients with an increased SOL and WASO.

After one or more nights of insufficient sleep (i.e., sleeping less than 6 hours), there is a recovery sleep pattern with increased N3 sleep. When the time in bed is extended after sleep loss, TST increases, leading to increased SE (Banks, Van Dongen, Maislin, & Dinges, 2010). REM sleep will increase on the second or subsequent night of recovery sleep. Irregular sleep patterns or fragmented sleep can result in redistribution of sleep states, trending toward more light sleep (N1 and N2) and decreased N3 and/or REM sleep.

CAUSES OF INSUFFICIENT SLEEP

Normal sleep patterns can be interrupted by exogenous and endogenous factors. In these cases, at least one of the three requirements associated with normal sleep (i.e., timing, duration, and quality) is not met and sleep is considered insufficient. Insufficient sleep is the outcome of partial sleep deprivation (PSD) when humans receive less sleep than necessary, or when deprived of a specific sleep stage (N3/ slow wave sleep or REM sleep) in the controlled conditions of a sleep laboratory. When allowed to sleep following PSD, the sleep-deprived individual will tend to rebound into the sleep stage from which he or she was deprived.

Total sleep deprivation, or TSD, occurs when an individual is not allowed to sleep at all. After experiencing TSD, the individual has rebound sleep with increased N3/slow wave sleep. Immediately after awaking, sleep-deprived individuals may experience sleep inertia, a transitional state of lowered arousal and reduced cognitive functioning (Tassi & Muzet, 2000). Sleep inertia is a normal phenomenon which is most pronounced with an abrupt awakening from slow wave sleep (Bruck & Pisani, 1999). The duration of sleep inertia rarely exceeds 30 minutes in the absence of prolonged sleep deprivation; however, the decreased cognitive performance can last from 1 minute to 4 hours depending on the specific task (Burke, Scheer, Ronda, Czeisler, & Wright, 2015; Tassi & Muzet, 2000).

When an individual sleeps at inappropriate times, for example, during their biological day, the sleep they receive may be unsatisfactory and may result in "circadian misalignment or desynchrony" (Baron & Reid, 2014). In this situation, there is a conflict between the endogenous controlled circadian sleep–wake rhythm and the actual times an individual can sleep due to exogenous factors (i.e., patterns and rhythms that are imposed by the environment and thus cannot be controlled). This disruption of the internal circadian rhythm is accompanied by an alteration of melatonin production (Burch, Yost, Johnson, & Allen, 2005) and disturbance of the sleep–wakefulness cycle (Åkerstedt, 2003).

Multiple factors may disturb normal sleep patterns, making it difficult to either find adequate opportunity to sleep, to fall asleep, or to remain asleep. Psychological factors also disrupt normal sleep. Psychosocial stressors from work- or family-related issues, stressful life events, and physically or psychologically traumatic events may result in lighter sleep (Shattuck, Matsangas, & Brown, 2015). These sleep disturbances can be seen in PSG measures of sleep (i.e., decreases in N3 and REM sleep, deterioration of SE, and increases in sleep fragmentation with increased arousals and awakenings; Kim & Dimsdale, 2007).

The conditions necessary for optimal sleep may not be available in operational conditions. For example, sleep can be disrupted by noise from within or outside the sleeping quarters; ambient temperatures may be too hot or cold for sleep; light exposure from artificial or natural sources can disrupt sleep and circadian rhythms; and environmental motion, when severe, can serve to degrade sleep or conversely, serve as a soporific in the case of mild motion (Shattuck & Matsangas, 2014; Shattuck, Matsangas, & Brown, 2015; Shattuck, Matsangas, & Powley, 2015). Other factors may also contribute to poor sleep, such as lack of exercise, poor diet, irregular mealtimes, and the use of caffeine, nicotine, or alcohol.

Organizational factors such as irregular work commitments, long work hours, shiftwork, and traveling between different time zones leading to jet lag (a form of circadian misalignment) can result in poor sleep and chronic sleep debt (Shattuck & Matsangas, 2015*d*; Shattuck, Matsangas, & Powley, 2015). The term "shiftwork" denotes working other than the typical daytime work hours of 8:00 A.M. to 5:00 P.M. Shiftwork is an integral part of modern society, yet from the standpoint of human physiology, it is an abnormal behavior. Long duration shifts (e.g., workdays greater than 12 hours in length and work weeks greater than 55 hours) can result in short sleep duration (SSD), increased fatigue, and decreased alertness due to reduced sleep opportunities (Åkerstedt & Wright, 2009; Sallinen & Kecklund, 2010).

Many studies show that rotating shiftwork has a detrimental impact on the sleep–wake cycle (Colquhoun & Folkard, 1985; Goh, Tong, Lim, Low, & Lee, 2000; Hakola & Härmä, 2001). Yet there is disagreement about the benefit of fixed-shift systems compared to rotating systems (Åkerstedt, 2003; Folkard, 1992; Wedderburn, 1992; Wilkinson, 1992). Studies demonstrate that shiftwork can lead to performance degradation—as measured by sustained attention, vigilance, and simulated driving tasks—with shift workers having reaction times similar to individuals with 0.04–0.05% blood alcohol concentration levels (Arnedt, Owens, Crouch, Stahl, & Carskadon, 2005). Shiftwork is also associated with elevated levels of physical fatigue in manual tasks involving the upper extremities (Rosa, Bonnet, & Cole, 1998). Specifically, longer shifts (12 hours compared to 8 hours) and night shifts lead to increased fatigue.

In addition to circadian desynchrony, sleep deprivation, and performance impairment, shiftwork also has negative social consequences resulting from imbalances in work and home life. Scientific evidence suggests that shiftwork has a negative influence on family life, specifically, on children's well-being and on marital satisfaction (Albertsen, Rafnsdóttir, Grimsmo, Tómasson, & Kauppinen, 2008). Shift workers are more prone to developing medical disorders (e.g., obesity, gastrointestinal disorders, cardiovascular heart disease, compromised pregnancy outcome, breast cancer, prostate cancer, metabolic syndrome, and diabetes) (Drake & Wright, 2011; Folkard & Tucker, 2003; Harrington, 2001; Knutsson, 2003; Wang, Armstrong, Cairns, Key, & Travis, 2011). Notably, the International Agency for Research on Cancer has classified "shift work that involves circadian disruption" as a probable human carcinogen (Stevens et al., 2011, p. 764).

Shiftwork can have a substantial impact on organizational risk and safety rates. Epidemiological studies have shown that the relative risk of workplace accidents increases by approximately 15% during afternoon shifts and by 30% for night shifts compared to morning shifts (Folkard, Lombardi, & Spencer, 2006). Long work hours and shiftwork synergistically increase the risk of workplace accidents (Åkerstedt & Wright, 2009), with accident rates increasing between 50% and 100% (Wagstaff & Sigstad Lie, 2011). Work periods of greater than 8 hours carry an increased risk of accidents that is cumulative, so that the increased risk of accidents at 12 hours is twice the risk at 8 hours. These authors noted, however, that "pure" night work (i.e., nonrotating shifts) might bring some protection against the detrimental effects of shiftwork (Wagstaff & Sigstad Lie, 2011).

Sleep problems pose an increase in potential risk for work injuries. A recent meta-analysis of 27 observational studies with approximately 268,000 participants showed that workers with sleep problems have a higher risk (1.62 times greater) of being injured than workers without sleep problems (Uehli et al., 2014). This increased rate of injury is not the only consequence of poor sleep. Sleep deprivation also slows the rate of healing through the reduced secretion of growth hormone during deep sleep and elevated secretion of cortisol (Adam & Oswald, 1984).

Clinical Sleep Disorders

From a clinical viewpoint, medical and psychiatric disorders are frequently associated with impairments in sleep quality and quantity and ultimately can result in degraded cognitive and physical performance. Thus, in assessing insufficient sleep, one must not only consider the duration of sleep in terms of the length of time spent in bed, but also whether the sleep is of good quality. Individuals with clinical disorders that disrupt sleep quality tend to spend longer periods in bed (i.e., 8 or more hours) and, while appearing to obtain adequate sleep, they still manifest symptoms of insufficient sleep. In a study of nearly 7,000 firefighters, Barger et al. reported that 37.2% screened positive for a sleep disorder (primarily obstructive sleep apnea [OSA], followed by insomnia; Barger et al., 2015). Those who screened positive had an increased risk of motor vehicle accidents and were twice as likely to fall asleep while driving. Thus, it is important to understand how common sleep disorders result in sleep disturbances, insufficient sleep, and decreased human performance.

OSA is the most common sleep-related breathing disorder with a prevalence of 20–30% in males and 10–15% of females (Peppard et al., 2013; Young et al., 2009). Cardinal signs and symptoms of OSA include loud snoring, gasping and choking at night, and excessive daytime sleepiness (EDS). OSA results from collapsibility of the upper airway manifesting as apneas and hypopneas (complete or partial cessations in airflow, respectively) which cause arousals from sleep and/or intermittent hypoxia. The cortical arousals and hypoxia contribute to sleep fragmentation, resulting in decreased sleep quality and quantity. Sleepiness is a frequently reported symptom of OSA, although it is not universally present in patients with OSA (Gottlieb et al., 1999). Individuals with OSA often have deficits in sustained attention and vigilance (Lee et al., 2011). Additionally, cognitive impairments of monitoring, reaction time, processing capacity, and increased distractibility have been associated with OSA (Avalon, Ancoli-Israel, Aka, McKenna, & Drummond, 2009).

The neurocognitive deficits likely play a role in the two- to sevenfold increased risk for motor vehicle accidents as well as poor workplace performance and work-related injuries in patients with untreated OSA (Hirsch Allen, Bansback, & Ayas, 2015; Young, Blustein, Finn, & Palta, 1997). In commercial vehicle drivers where OSA is highly prevalent, adherence to continuous positive airway pressure (CPAP) therapy normalizes their risk of motor vehicle accidents; conversely, nonadherence results in a five times increased risk of preventable accidents (Burks et al., 2016). Similar effects of CPAP therapy resulting in improvements in excessive daytime sleepiness, memory, attention, executive function, and quality of life have also been reported (Canessa et al., 2011; McEvoy et al., 2016). OSA is a highly prevalent sleep disorder that impairs individual performance and contributes to increased risk of organizational accidents. Equally as important, treatment for OSA ameliorates the performance deficits associated with this disorder.

Insomnia is a sleep disorder characterized by impaired performance, fatigue, malaise, or sleepiness as a consequence of difficulty falling or staying asleep, or waking up early in the morning despite adequate opportunity to sleep (American Academy of Sleep Medicine, 2013). Insomnia is highly prevalent (12–20% of US adults) and accounts for more than 5 million office visits annually in the United States (Ford et al., 2014; Roth et al., 2011). Individuals with insomnia can have objective sleep impairments such as increased SOL and WASO, as well as decreased TST and SE on a sleep study (Stepanski, Zorick, Roehrs, & Roth, 2000). Multiple EEG studies have demonstrated that insomnia patients have higher cortical activation than normal sleepers during sleep and the wake–sleep transition period (Riemann et al., 2010). Common daytime symptoms include fatigue and mood disturbances as well as difficulty concentrating, making decisions, and memory problems (Linton & Bryngelsson, 2000; Roth & Ancoli-Israel, 1999). A meta-analysis of the cognitive effects of insomnia on daytime performance found an association between insomnia and impairment of working memory, episodic memory, and problem-solving (Fortier-Brochu, Beaulieu-Bonneau, Ivers, & Morin, 2012). Although insomnia can present as a primary disorder, a high rate of comorbidity exists between chronic insomnia and psychiatric and medical disorders (Hohagen et al., 1993; Ohayon & Reynolds III, 2009; Pearson, Johnson, & Nahin, 2006; Roth et al., 2006; Simon & VonKorff, 1997).

Disturbed sleep and daytime impairment are common complaints among individuals with mood disorders (Rumble, White, & Benca, 2015). Up to 90% of individuals in a depressive episode report disturbed sleep (Tsuno, Besset, & Ritchie, 2005). Major depressive disorder (MDD) is associated with insomnia symptoms (as just detailed) as well as with nonrestorative sleep with either increased or decreased TST and disturbing dreams (Yates et al., 2004). Polysomnography in individuals with MDD has demonstrated decreased TST and SE resulting from increased SOL, increased WASO, and early morning awakenings (Benca, Obermeyer, Thisted, & Gillin, 1992; Borbély et al., 1984). Individuals with mood disorders have increased rates of primary sleep disorders and vice versa. Patients with insomnia have been found to be four times more likely to develop new onset MDD and twice as likely to develop an anxiety disorder (Breslau, Roth, Rosenthal, & Andreski, 1996). Similarly, OSA is a risk factor for developing depression, and patients with depression have an increased prevalence of OSA (Peppard, Szklo-Coxe, Hla, & Young, 2006; Povitz et al., 2014).

Although sleep and psychiatric disorders are most frequently associated with decreased sleep quantity and quality, medical disorders can also cause substantial sleep disruption. Congestive heart failure; breathing disorders such as asthma, chronic obstructive pulmonary disease, and rhinosinusitis; and pain are all reported to negatively impact sleep quality (Bengtsson et al., 2016; Nunes et al., 2009; Redeker et al., 2010). Ultimately, there are multiple clinical disorders which, while not directly resulting in a shortened sleep, cause similar effects by decreasing overall sleep quality. The neurocognitive effects of fragmented and disrupted sleep have primarily been characterized in sleep disorders (such as OSA and insomnia); it is likely that similar negative effects on human performance would be present in other sleep, medical, and psychiatric disorders.

EFFECTS OF INSUFFICIENT SLEEP ON PERFORMANCE AND HEALTH

Insufficient sleep affects humans in various ways. First and foremost, insufficient sleep increases the need for sleep and the propensity to fall asleep. Consequently, sleep-deprived individuals may fall asleep unintentionally. A study calculated the prevalence of unintentional sleep to be 23.1% during leisure time and 7.0% during work hours (Åkerstedt et al., 2002). Interestingly, sleep-deprived humans often fail to accurately assess their level of sleepiness as compared to objective measures of their alertness state (Drake et al., 2001; Horne, 2010), and they are largely unaware of increasing cognitive deficits (Van Dongen, Maislin, Mullington, & Dinges, 2003). Therefore, sleep-deprived individuals may overestimate their ability to remain alert.

Beyond sleepiness, however, sleep and the circadian rhythm are important determinants of human physiological functions and behavioral expression, at both the individual and team levels (Baranski et al., 2007). Sleep, primarily slow wave and REM stages, is required for learning and has been shown to be crucial to both declarative and working memory. Sleep promotes the qualitative reorganization of memory and the quantitative strengthening of new memories (Broughton & Ogilvie, 1992; Landmann et al., 2014; Turner, Drummond, Salamat, & Brown, 2007). Sleep has been associated with creativity, innovative thinking, and strategic planning (Cai, Mednick, Harrison, Kanady, & Mednick, 2009; Harrison & Horne, 1999). Conversely, insufficient sleep leads to substantial deficits in various dimensions of neurobehavioral and cognitive performance (Babkoff, Mikelinder, Karlsson, & Kuklinski, 1988; Dinges & Kribbs, 1991; Durmer & Dinges, 2005). For example, sleep deprivation increases lapses in attention and vigilance performance (Van Dongen et al., 2003), deteriorates mood and affect (Dinges et al., 1997), and impairs the ability to integrate emotion and cognition to guide moral judgments (Killgore et al., 2007). According to Harrison and Horne (2000), sleep deprivation also impairs "real-world decision making; tasks which involve unique and unfamiliar circumstances, necessitating a wide range of other complex skills (e.g., assess difficult and rapidly changing situations; assess risk; anticipate the range of consequences; keep track of events-update the big picture; be innovative; develop, maintain, and revise plans; remember when events occurred; control mood and uninhibited behavior; show insight into one's own performance; communicate effectively; and avoid irrelevant distractions)." Furthermore, acceptance of risk for decision-making tasks is modulated by sleep deprivation (McKenna, Dickinson, Orff, & Drummond, 2007). Following 23 hours without sleep, individuals are willing to take more risk than they ordinarily would when considering a gain, but are more risk averse when considering a loss. Postural equilibrium, sensorimotor coupling, physical and athletic performance (e.g., speed and endurance) also deteriorate with sleep deprivation and circadian misalignment (Aguiar & Barela, 2014; Reilly & Edwards, 2007; Simpson, Gibbs, & Matheson, 2016).

Work environments that preclude healthy sleep practices not only affect individual human performance, but also can negatively impact long-term system-wide performance. Organizations that offer inadequate opportunities for quality sleep experience problems with employee retention. Recruiting and training replacement personnel is a costly proposition. In a 2014 study of US Navy Retention, sailors rated their quality of life more heavily than the quality of work when deciding whether to remain in uniform or transition to the private sector (Snodgrass & Kohlmann, 2014). In the same study, more than 70% of the sailors reported sleeping 6 hours or less per night—a figure that has been verified by multiple studies of sleep conducted on United States Navy ships.

Circadian Scarring and Increased Risk of Accidents

Shiftwork is prevalent throughout the military and first responder communities and is a major contributor to acute and chronic fatigue levels. The brain undergoes long-term changes when subjected to chronic sleep restriction (Belenky et al., 2003) altering neural function in a manner that precludes rapid recovery to baseline levels of alertness and performance even after sleep durations return to baseline levels. Workers often experience sleep disturbance and elevated levels of sleepiness after months or years of shiftwork (Drake & Wright, 2011). Research findings suggest that prior exposure to shiftwork is related to sleep problems during retirement (Monk et al., 2013). The term "circadian scarring" describes the sleep issues that are increasingly evident in individuals who have been exposed to periods of shiftwork and sleep deprivation. Mysliwiec and colleagues reported a case study of a 29-year-old sailor who developed a circadian sleep–wake disorder (Mysliwiec, Matsangas, Baxter, & Shattuck, 2015). Specifically, his sleep periods continually advanced through the 24-hour clock cycle, aligning with his prior 5 hours on/10 hours off military duty cycle. While this case highlights the development of a fulminant circadian disorder, many other shift workers develop less pronounced symptoms that are more consistent with insomnia. Irrespective of the shift system, night and early-morning shifts are associated with SSD and increased sleepiness (Sallinen & Kecklund, 2010). Shift workers experience increased sleep deprivation, shorter sleep episodes, greater sleep fragmentation, and higher levels of fatigue than their counterparts who do not work in shifts (Arendt, Middleton, Williams, Francis, & Luke, 2006).

Medical Consequences of Short Sleep Duration

As previously mentioned, SSD is associated with multiple medical disorders to include obesity, type 2 diabetes, coronary heart disease (CHD), hypertension, and stroke (St-Onge et al., 2016). A number of studies have described associations between long-term SSD and obesity. Short sleep duration has been associated with weight gain, obesity, and increased waist circumference, particularly in young adults (Grandner, Jackson, Gerstner, & Knutson, 2013; Sperry, Scully, Gramzow, & Jorgensen, 2015). A recent prospective study using data from the National Longitudinal Study of Adolescent to Adult Health found that individuals with cumulative exposure to SSD throughout adolescence and early adulthood are 1.45 times more likely to experience obesity and elevated waist circumference (Krueger, Reither, Peppard, Burger, & Hale, 2015). Other reports have found that the risk of obesity varied with sleep duration, noting the most pronounced effects among those reporting less than 5 hours of sleep per night (Altman et al., 2012).

Multiple theories exist to explain the SSD–obesity relationship. Sleep deprivation alters appetite-regulating hormones (i.e., decreased leptin), which increases appetite (Hanlon & Van Cauter, 2011). Insufficient sleep can cause neurocognitive changes that precipitate maladaptive food selections (Greer, Goldstein, & Walker, 2013). Observational studies have shown a variety of alterations in food choices with SSD to include eating a smaller variety of foods compared to normal sleepers (Grandner et al., 2013). In general, research shows an overall increase in 24-hour energy intake, with excess calories ranging from 182 to 559 kcal/day (Brondel, Romer, Nougues, Touyarou, & Davenne, 2010; Markwald et al., 2013). While data support the role of insufficient sleep on food intake, the effects of SSD on energy expenditure are mixed (St-Onge et al., 2016). At this time, studies evaluating the effect of sleep duration on resting metabolic rate have found either no difference or a lowered resting metabolic rate (Buxton et al., 2012; St-Onge et al., 2016).

In addition to altering appetite-regulating hormones, SSD is associated with impaired glucose metabolism (Hanlon & Van Cauter, 2011). Decreased insulin sensitivity was originally observed after 5 nights of partial sleep restriction and has since been observed in multiple experimental studies with varying degrees of sleep loss (Broussard, Ehrmann, Van Cauter, Tasali, & Brady, 2012; Spiegel, Leproult, & Van Cauter, 1999). While insufficient sleep has been connected with decreased insulin sensitivity, sleep extension in individuals with SSD can improve glucose tolerance (Leproult, Deliens, Gilson, & Peigneux, 2015). There is increasing evidence demonstrating a link between SSD and risk of developing type 2 diabetes (Arble et al., 2015). Two recent meta-analyses assessing this association had similar findings; the risk of diabetes increased approximately 30% with SSD (Cappuccio, D'Elia, Strazzullo, & Miller, 2010; Holliday, Magee, Kritharides, Banks, & Attia, 2013).

Short sleep duration has been associated with elevated blood pressure and hypertension in multiple cross-sectional and longitudinal epidemiological studies (Gangwisch, 2014). This relationship was substantiated by two meta-analyses across all populations evaluated, while a third study found the risk of hypertension was increased only among patients less than 65 years of age (Guo et al., 2013; Meng, Zheng, & Hui, 2013; Wang, Xi, Liu, Zhang, & Fu, 2012). Importantly, sleep extension in individuals with prehypertension or stage 1 hypertension has been shown to significantly reduce blood pressure (Haack et al., 2013). There is also an association of developing or dying of CHD with SSD and a modest association between SSD and incident stroke (Cappuccio, Cooper, D'Elia, Strazzullo, & Miller, 2011). Irrespective of CHD, SSD has been shown to be a significant predictor of all-cause mortality (Ferrie et al., 2007; Heslop, Smith, Metcalfe, Macleod, & Hart, 2002; Tamakoshi & Ohno, 2004). Whereas decreased performance and the increased risk of accidents due to SSD pose an immediate risk to individuals, there is mounting scientific evidence of multiple serious long-term medical sequelae of this preventable

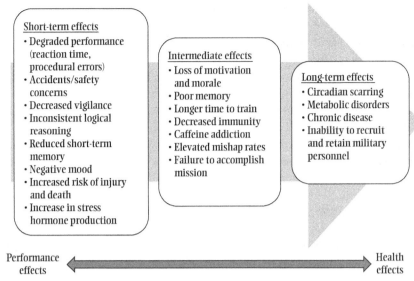

Short-term effects
- Degraded performance (reaction time, procedural errors)
- Accidents/safety concerns
- Decreased vigilance
- Inconsistent logical reasoning
- Reduced short-term memory
- Negative mood
- Increased risk of injury and death
- Increase in stress hormone production

Intermediate effects
- Loss of motivation and morale
- Poor memory
- Longer time to train
- Decreased immunity
- Caffeine addiction
- Elevated mishap rates
- Failure to accomplish mission

Long-term effects
- Circadian scarring
- Metabolic disorders
- Chronic disease
- Inability to recruit and retain military personnel

Performance effects   Health effects

Figure 10.1 Consequences of poor sleep practices.
Image courtesy of the authors.

maladaptive behavior. The medical consequences of sleep deprivation are shown in Figure 10.1.

SLEEP IN MILITARY POPULATIONS

As far back as war and human conflict can be traced, military life has been characterized by varying levels of fatigue and sleep deprivation. It should come as no surprise to learn that such is still the case. In fact, the around-the-clock, continuously connected operations of modern warfare have led to increasing demands on members of the military. Rather than reducing workload, the price of many military advancements—such as remotely piloted vehicles—comes at a steep cost: ever more work and longer hours demanded of their human operators. These demands almost always cut into the amount and quality of sleep that individual service members require, resulting in a cumulative sleep debt that poses grave dangers to the individual and jeopardizes the mission.

Approximately 35% of Americans report obtaining insufficient sleep (i.e., less than 7 hours per day; Liu et al., 2016). Based on the 2010 National Health Interview Survey (NHIS), short sleep duration of 6 hours or less per 24-hour period was reported by 30% of employed US adults (Centers for Disease Control and Prevention, 2012). The demographic structure of the United States military differs from the US population; the average age of the military population is younger. The active duty force average age is 28.7 years (officers = 34.7 years, enlisted personnel = 27.4 years), with nearly one-half (48.8%) of the enlisted personnel being 25 years old or younger (13.3% for officers) (DoD, 2015). For this age group, sleeping 9 hours or more per night on a regular basis is appropriate to promote optimal health (Watson et al., 2015).

Shiftwork is ubiquitous in the military, however, the rate of shiftwork varies by service. More than 90% of the crewmembers on US Navy ships are chronic shift workers as compared to approximately 15% of the civilian sector (US Bureau of Labor Statistics, 2005). In military units, the shift schedule depends on multiple factors such as the organizational culture, the prior experience of the command leadership, and the availability of personnel. This final factor is a critical consideration on ships with limited crew size. In the US Navy, it is the responsibility of the officer of the watch to ensure that individuals standing watch are able to stand an effective watch, presumably maintaining alertness throughout the watch period (Department of the Navy, 2012). Given the availability of personnel, the watch itself, and other daily activities, a number of fixed and rotating watch systems are used in the US Navy. These include schedules such as the 4 hours on/ 8 hours off (4/8), 6 hours on/6 hours off (6/6), the 12 hours on/12 hours off (12/12), the 6 hours on/18 hours off (6/18), and the 3 hours on/9 hours off (3/ 9). Some of these schedules result in days that are other than 24 hours in length. For example, the 5 hours on/10 hours off (5/10) generates a day that is either 15 or 30 hours in length, while the 5 hours on/15 hours off (5/15) results in a 20-hour day. Following a 1969 Naval Postgraduate School master's thesis by Stolgitis (1969), US Navy submarine crews adopted a 6 hours on/12 hours off (6/12), three-section watchstanding schedule that resulted in an 18-hour day. Of note, the typical workday of active duty service members generally includes many other activities in addition to standing watch. These other duties may prolong the work hours by up to 50%, with objective data indicating that some crewmembers on USN ships work up to 15 hours per day (Green, 2009; Haynes, 2007; Mason, 2009; Shattuck & Matsangas, 2016).

Multiple studies conducted at the Naval Postgraduate School have documented that sleep problems are prevalent in the military operational environment (Miller, Matsangas, & Kenney, 2012). Overall, these studies show that members of our military service are chronically sleep-deprived. They have insufficient opportunities to sleep due to operational commitments and find it difficult to sleep because the sleep opportunities afforded them often occur during circadian misaligned time periods. They accrue a cumulative sleep debt due to operational commitments and may experience chronic circadian desynchrony due to a combination of factors including poor quality of their sleep environment and working and sleeping at different times every day (Shattuck & Matsangas, 2015b, 2015c, 2015d; Shattuck, Matsangas, & Brown, 2015; Shattuck, Matsangas, & Powley, 2015; Shattuck, Waggoner, Young, Smith, & Matsangas, 2014).

Studies on naval vessels have shown that watch schedules traditionally used at sea lead to sleep deprivation, sleep fragmentation, suboptimal performance, and worrisome levels of alertness (Paul, Ebisuzaki, McHarg, Hursh, & Miller, 2012; Rutenfranz et al., 1988; Shattuck & Matsangas, 2014). Chronic pain from musculoskeletal injuries may also contribute to insufficient sleep. In a study of musculoskeletal injuries conducted on a US Navy aircraft carrier, crewmembers who self-identified as having experienced musculoskeletal injuries were also more likely to report elevated daytime sleepiness, increased fatigue level, shorter nighttime sleep duration, and to consume more caffeinated beverages compared to their asymptomatic peers (Brown, Matsangas, & Shattuck, 2015b; Shattuck, Matsangas, Moore, & Wegemann, 2016).

Chronic short sleep duration is clearly present in a case study of the commanding officer (CO) of an Arleigh Burke class destroyer (Shattuck & Matsangas, 2015d). Over the course of an entire 6-month period of the ship's deployment, the CO slept on average 5.2 hours per day. He received more than 8 hours of sleep on only 3 days over the whole deployment, which involved high-stakes decisions and dangerous activities on a daily basis.

The diagrams in Figures 10.2, 10.3 and 10.4 show the average daily sleep duration of 6,493 active duty service members whose sleep was assessed during operations, training and education, or deployments and combat missions between 2001 and 2016. The light grey bars denote sleep that was assessed with actigraphy, whereas dark grey bars denote self-reported sleep. On each bar, the number denotes the sample size in the corresponding study, whereas the horizontal black lines denote one standard deviation. For each study, we have included the ship and the year the data were collected. Depending on the study, data were collected for intervals ranging from 5 to 30 days.

In our studies, we routinely observed poor sleeping conditions which led to elevated levels of fatigue, degraded cognitive performance (slowed reaction times and increased errors), and poor crew morale (as indicated by standardized measures of mood) (Brown, Matsangas, & Shattuck, 2015a; Shattuck & Matsangas, 2015c; Shattuck, Matsangas, & Brown, 2015; Shattuck, Matsangas, Moore, & Wegemann, 2015; Shattuck, Matsangas, & Powley, 2015). These studies show the deleterious effect of sleep deprivation and circadian misalignment which are especially pronounced in psychomotor vigilance performance (i.e., decrements in average performance and in increased variability; Brown et al., 2015a; Shattuck & Matsangas, 2014, 2015b, 2015c, 2015d; Shattuck, Matsangas, & Brown, 2015; Shattuck, Matsangas, Moore, et al., 2015; Shattuck, Matsangas, & Powley, 2015). Chronic sleep deprivation also leads crewmembers to consume large amounts of caffeinated beverages; increasingly, their drinks of choice are energy drinks that may further contribute to unhealthy sleep patterns (Shattuck & Matsangas, 2015a). Refer to Figure 10.1 again to consider the short and long-term consequences of sleep deprivation.

To illustrate shipboard conditions, consider the wrist-worn actigraphic recordings ("actigrams") of two typical sleep patterns of crewmembers working on USN ships. In Figure 10.5, the first crewmember worked a rotating, noncircadian watchstanding schedule. Each row is a 24-hour period commencing at midnight. Black vertical bars represent activity. Periods with high levels of activity are considered periods of wakefulness. In contrast, periods of low activity (shown as gray bands) indicate rest periods within which the subject is sleeping. In a typical "good" sleep pattern, the individual would sleep for a contiguous period of around 8 hours, preferably during the nighttime hours, falling asleep and awakening consistently over consecutive days. As shown in the following actigram, the crewmember slept at different times every day with a sleep pattern iterating every 3 days. This sleep–wake pattern is common in individuals working the 5/10 watchstanding schedule.

The second actigram, Figure 10.6, is typical of a watchstander working on the fixed 3/9 schedule. The major sleep episodes are more stable compared to the 5/

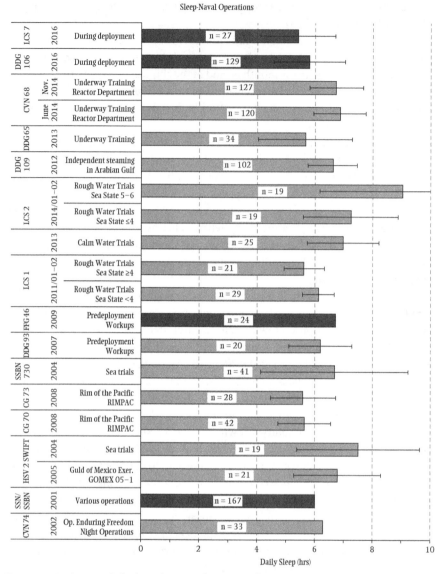

Figure 10.2 Average daily sleep duration during naval operations. Image courtesy of the authors.

10 and are located during the biological night. NPS studies in maritime operational environments have shown that fixed schedules like the 3/9 improve sleep quality and, consequently, psychomotor vigilance performance and mood (Shattuck & Matsangas, 2015b; Shattuck, Matsangas, & Brown, 2015; Shattuck, Matsangas, & Waggoner, 2014). Aligning the sleep period with the biological night ameliorates some of the deleterious effects of shiftwork, but it does not eliminate them altogether. Despite their documented benefits, even fixed watchstanding schedules are not without sleep-related issues. This point becomes obvious when comparing the

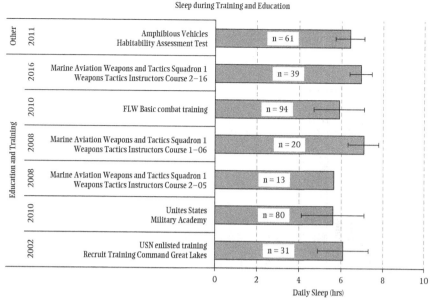

Figure 10.3 Average daily sleep duration during training and education. Image courtesy of the authors.

two actigrams. The sleep patterns of both crewmembers are characterized by polyphasic sleep patterns. Both crewmembers amassed a significant sleep debt, which they attempted to alleviate with napping.

Why do crewmembers receive insufficient sleep? While at sea, 24/7 operations and military duties contribute to insufficient and poor quality sleep that result in a substantial sleep debt. In our studies, we have observed that when faced with the choice between sleep and work duties, many crewmembers forfeit sleep. This sleep debt degrades cognitive performance and increases the risk for human error and mishaps.

Sleep Disorders in the Military

Active duty military personnel encounter multiple stressors that place them at risk for developing sleep disorders. They are subjected to rigorous schedules with frequent overnight and early-morning shiftwork that can cause fragmented and insufficient sleep. While deployed, poor sleeping conditions, noise, the inherent risk of harm, and 24-hour sustained operations are detrimental to overall sleep quantity and quality. Combat deployments are associated with sleep disruption, and, more recently, the increased potential for developing sleep disorders, such as insomnia and OSA, has been theorized (Mysliwiec, Walter, Collen, & Wesensten, 2016; Peterson, Goodie, Satterfield, & Brim, 2008).

Within the military, SSD is highly prevalent, with only 24% of active duty service members reporting adequate sleep duration of 7–8 hours/night (Bray et al., 2009). Self-reported sleep duration for service members, regardless of deployment status, ranges from 5.8 to 6.5 hours per night (Luxton et al., 2011; Peterson et al., 2008;

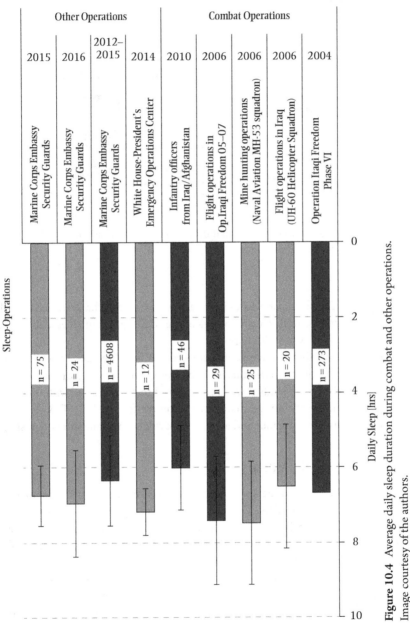

Figure 10.4 Average daily sleep duration during combat and other operations. Image courtesy of the authors.

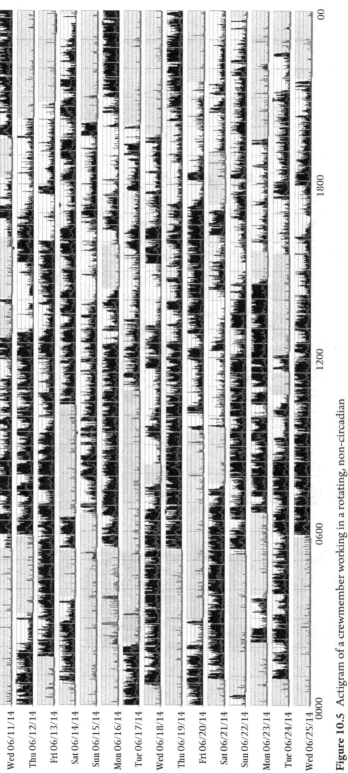

Figure 10.5 Actigram of a crewmember working in a rotating, non-circadian watchstanding schedule.

Image courtesy of the authors.

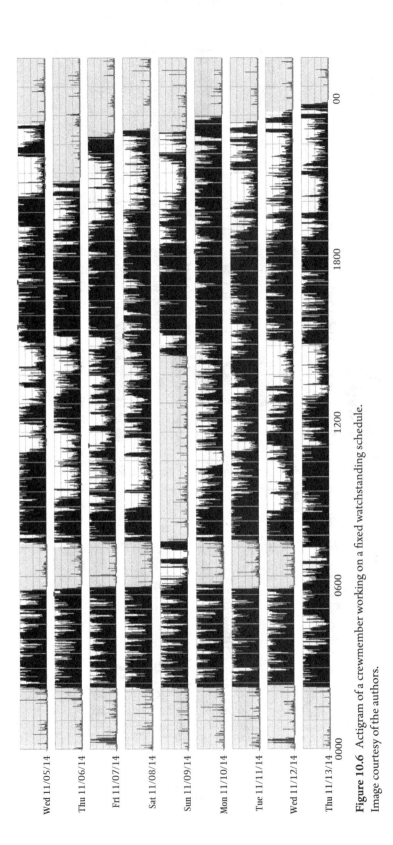

Figure 10.6 Actigram of a crewmember working on a fixed watchstanding schedule. Image courtesy of the authors.

Seelig et al., 2010). The extent of SSD has been associated with both deployment and comorbid illnesses. Sleep duration among active duty military personnel who have deployed or are currently deployed tends to be less than those who have not deployed. In a sample of 2,700 soldiers who recently returned from deployment, 72% reported sleeping 6 or less hours per night (Luxton et al., 2011). After controlling for combat exposure and compared to soldiers sleeping 7 or more hours/night, SSD was associated with depression, posttraumatic stress disorder (PTSD), tobacco and alcohol abuse, and suicide attempts. Additionally, sleep duration of less than 6 hours was found to be the strongest predictor of PTSD (Luxton et al., 2011). These findings were mirrored in a study of veterans that assessed self-reported sleep duration and comorbid illnesses in veterans of Operation Iraqi Freedom/Enduring Freedom (OIF/OEF). Overall, only 28% of participants reported obtaining 7 or more hours of sleep per night, with 49% reporting less than 6 hours of sleep per night. Veterans sleeping 6 hours or less had three times the rate of major depressive disorder and PTSD compared to those sleeping more than 7 hours per night (Swinkels, Ulmer, Beckham, Buse, & Calhoun, 2013). Another study assessing sleep in military veterans reported those with comorbid mental health diagnoses had significantly shorter sleep duration (4.9 vs. 5.9 hours/night) than those without (Ulmer et al., 2014). This study highlighted two major findings regarding military veterans: mental health disorders are associated with significantly shorter sleep duration, and veterans persist in having SSD after leaving military service irrespective of comorbid illnesses.

In addition, the prevalence of insomnia in US Army personnel was recently reported at 19.9% (Taylor et al., 2016). Since Operation Iraqi Freedom, Operation Enduring Freedom, and Operation New Dawn (OIF/OEF/OND), medical record reviews have shown a staggering 74-fold increase in the incident diagnosis of insomnia (Lewis, Emasealu, Rohrbeck, & Hu, 2014). Multiple factors related to military life contribute to sleep disturbances that can result in chronic insomnia. Stress, shiftwork, and frequent changes in duty stations contribute to sleep disruption in the nondeployed setting (Troxel et al., 2015). While deployed, there are additional precipitating factors for insomnia, including nighttime duties, poor sleeping conditions, high operations tempo, loud noises, and worry about family (Mental Health Advisory Team 9 (MHAT 9, 2013). In active duty military personnel, insomnia has been associated with traumatic brain injury (TBI), PTSD, depression, anxiety, and problem drinking (Bryan, 2013; Mysliwiec, McGraw, et al., 2013). The onset of sleep disturbances in susceptible military personnel is more than likely related to the stressful conditions they face, precipitating poor0quality sleep that is then further exacerbated by either deployment or ongoing work-related stress. These stressors can result in either persistently disturbed sleep or chronic insomnia.

OSA is a common diagnosis within the military population, although the exact prevalence remains unknown. Within the active duty population, OSA is frequently comorbid with TBI, PTSD, psychiatric disorders, and insomnia (Mysliwiec, McGraw, et al., 2013). Comorbid OSA and TBI have been associated with worsened clinical symptoms as well as impaired recovery and rehabilitation (Castriotta & Murthy, 2010). Similarly, service members with comorbid OSA and PTSD have decreased adherence to CPAP therapy, which likely contributes to their lower quality of life and increased symptomatology (Lettieri, Williams, & Collen, 2016). Additionally, there is an increased risk of depression and anxiety in both active duty military personnel and veterans with a diagnosis of OSA (Babson, Del Re, Bonn-Miller, & Woodward, 2013; Mysliwiec, McGraw, et al., 2013). In a study evaluating service members undergoing PSG after deployment, 38.2% were diagnosed with comorbid insomnia and OSA. Within this cohort, 71.4% met criteria for depression and 59.5% for PTSD (Mysliwiec, Gill, et al., 2013). In another investigation evaluating active duty service members with mild OSA, 81.1% had comorbid insomnia (Mysliwiec, Matsangas, et al., 2013). The etiology of sleep-disordered breathing in military personnel is not well established; however, it is notable that many young active duty military personnel are diagnosed with mild OSA. It is plausible that fragmented sleep of short duration contributes to ventilatory instability and the development of sleep disordered breathing in this unique population (Mysliwiec, Gill, et al., 2013).

COUNTERMEASURES FOR INSUFFICIENT SLEEP

As noted by Harrison and Horne (2000) "sleep is the best anodyne for the sleep-deprived decision maker." During prolonged operations lasting longer than 18 hours, human performance will suffer due to lack of sleep. The ideal solution is to obtain sleep when this occurs; however, sleep may not be possible due to mission requirements. Another aspect of sustained operations is that the effects of circadian rhythmicity are magnified by insufficient sleep; that is, there will be more pronounced performance degradation during the circadian nadir when carrying a sleep debt. However, some effective nonpharmacologic and pharmacologic countermeasures can help mitigate fatigue.

It is important to begin sustained operations fully rested; therefore, ensuring adequate sleep duration prior to an operation is imperative. Before commencing sustained operations, "sleep banking" (i.e., accruing excess sleep in reserve) may ameliorate the effects of an anticipated period of sleep deprivation (Axelsson & Vyazovskiy, 2015). Even though the practice has been somewhat controversial, recent studies support the notion that sleep banking may increase resilience to subsequent chronic sleep restriction and lead to faster recovery of neurobehavioral performance (Arnal et al., 2015; Rupp, Wesensten, Bliese, & Balkin, 2009). In operational environments, commanding officers should implement a sleep schedule that is operationally appropriate; that is, personnel should be allowed to sleep whenever possible given operational considerations. Even though long periods of sleep may not be possible in the operational environment, "prophylactic naps" (defined as sleep typically greater than 1 hour in duration that occurs on top of a regular night's sleep; Bonnet, 1991) have been demonstrated to increase alertness and improve performance (Driskell & Mullen, 2005) and decrease the risk of accidents (Garbarino et al., 2004).

In conjunction with sleep banking and napping, pharmacologic interventions may also be beneficial when appropriately implemented in the field. Both caffeine and modafinil have been studied to assess their ability to mitigate fatigue during periods of prolonged wakefulness. In a study at Walter Reed Army Institute of Research (WRAIR), Wesensten and colleagues found the optimal dose of modafinil was 400 mg and caffeine was 600 mg (Wesensten, Belenky, Thorne, Kautz, & Balkin, 2004) to sustain alertness during prolonged operations. Whereas most adults are accustomed to the effects of caffeine and a trial of therapy is not typically required, modafinil is a novel wakefulness-promoting agent that has the approval of the US Food and Drug Administration (FDA) for treating shiftwork sleep disorder and narcolepsy. The effects and potential side effects of modafinil vary depending on the individual. If the use of modafinil is contemplated, a trial of the medication should be given and monitored by an appropriately trained medical professional prior to its use in sustained operations.

At the organizational level, there is an increased recognition of the need for well-rested military service members. Numerous regulations and policy documents in all branches of the armed forces address sleep as an important factor of performance and safety (Troxel et al., 2015). The United States Army's Performance Triad is one example of a health promotion program that promotes sleep along with physical activity and nutrition as critical components of health, resilience, and readiness of service members. Improved performance being the goal, individual military members need to be properly educated about how to retain/restore their alertness when in the field by using optimal behavioral practices to promote sleep health. Even though a widely accepted definition of sleep health remains elusive, Buysse (2014) proposed the following definition: "Sleep health is a multidimensional pattern of sleep-wakefulness, adapted to individual, social, and environmental demands, that promotes physical and mental well-being. Good sleep health is characterized by subjective satisfaction, appropriate timing, adequate duration, high efficiency, and sustained alertness during waking hours."

CONCLUSION

Many occupations pose a threat to sleep and, as a result, optimal human performance. A starting point to mitigate degraded performance is to have organizational practices that assist individuals in obtaining quality sleep. Because the modern world considers time as "premium," short sleep duration will continue to plague mankind for the foreseeable future. It is incumbent on organizations to recognize this threat to optimal performance and make adjustments. Changing the sleep environment so that it is focused on optimal sleep would be one way to facilitate this organizational shift. Working with environmental and acoustic engineers to develop better sleeping environments, devoid of stimuli and distractions, could maximize an individual's time in bed resulting in enhanced individual performance. While pharmacologic agents to enhance sleep and wakefulness have been shown to have some benefit on human performance, until sleep itself is optimized, this practice should have limited use.

REFERENCES

Achermann, P., & Borbély, A. (2003). Mathematical models of sleep regulation. *Frontiers in Bioscience, 8,* s683-s693.

Adam, K., & Oswald, I. (1984). Sleep helps healing. *British Medical Journal, 289,* 1400–1401.

Aguiar, S. A., & Barela, J. A. (2014). Sleep deprivation affects sensorimotor coupling in postural control of young adults. *Neuroscience Letters, 574,* 47–52.

Åkerstedt, T. (2003). Shift work and disturbed sleep/wakefulness. *Occupational Medicine*, 53, 89–94.

Åkerstedt, T., Knutsson, A., Westerholm, P., Theorell, T., Alfredsson, L., & Kecklund, G. (2002). Work organisation and unintentional sleep: Results from the WOLF study. *Occupational and Environmental Medicine*, 59, 595–600.

Åkerstedt, T., & Wright, K. P. (2009). Sleep loss and fatigue in shift work and shift work disorder. *Sleep Medicine Clinics*, 4, 257–271.

Albertsen, K., Rafnsdóttir, G. L., Grimsmo, A., Tómasson, K., & Kauppinen, K. (2008). Workhours and worklife balance. *Scandinavian Journal of Work, Environment & Health, Supplements*, 5, 14–21.

Altman, N. G., Izci-Balserak, B., Schopfer, E., Jackson, N., Rattanaumpawan, P., Gehrman, P. R.,... Grandner, M. A. (2012). Sleep duration versus sleep insufficiency as predictors of cardiometabolic health outcomes. *Sleep Medicine*, 13(10), 1261–1270.

American Academy of Sleep Medicine. (2013). *International Classification of Sleep Disorders—Third Edition (ICSD-3)*. Darien, IL: American Academy of Sleep Medicine.

Anch, A. M., Browman, C. P., Mitler, M., & Walsh, J. K. (1988). *Sleep: A Scientific Perspective*. Englewood Cliffs, NJ: Prentice-Hall, Inc.

Arble, D. M., Bass, J., Behn, C. D., Butler, M. P., Challet, E., Czeisler, C. A.,... Wright, K. P. (2015). Impact of sleep and circadian disruption on energy balance and diabetes: A summary of workshop discussions. *Sleep*, 38(12), 1849–1860.

Arendt, J., Middleton, B., Williams, P., Francis, G., & Luke, C. (2006). Sleep and circadian phase in a ship's crew. *Journal of Biological Rhythms*, 21, 214–221.

Arnal, P. J., Sauvet, F., Leger, D., Van Beers, P., Bayon, V., Bougard, C.,... Chennaoui, M. (2015). Benefits of sleep extension on sustained attention and sleep pressure before and during total sleep deprivation and recovery. *Sleep*, 38(12), 1935–1943.

Arnedt, J. T., Owens, J., Crouch, M., Stahl, J., & Carskadon, M. A. (2005). Neurobehavioral performance of residents after heavy night call vs after alcohol ingestion. *JAMA*, 294, 1025–1033.

Avalon, L., Ancoli-Israel, S., Aka, A. A., McKenna, B. S., & Drummond, S. P. A. (2009). Relationship between obstructive sleep apnea severity and brain activation during a sustained attention task. *Sleep*, 32(3), 373–381.

Axelsson, J., & Vyazovskiy, V. V. (2015). Banking sleep and biological sleep need. *Sleep*, 38(12), 1843–1845.

Babkoff, H., Mikelinder, M., Karlsson, T., & Kuklinski, P. (1988). The topology of performance curves during 72 hours of sleep loss: A memory and search task. *Journal of Experimental Biology*, 40(737–756).

Babson, K. A., Del Re, A. C., Bonn-Miller, M. O., & Woodward, S. H. (2013). The comorbidity of sleep apnea and mood, anxiety, and substance use disorders among obese military veterans within the Veterans Health Administration. *Journal of Clinical Sleep Medicine*, 9(12), 1253–1258.

Banks, S., Van Dongen, H. P. A., Maislin, G., & Dinges, D. F. (2010). Neurobehavioral dynamics following chronic sleep restriction: Dose-response effects of one night for recovery. *Sleep*, 33(8), 1013–1026.

Baranski, J., Thompson, M., Lichacz, F. M. J., McCann, C., Gil, V., Pastó, L., & Pigeau, R. (2007). Effects of sleep loss on team decision making: Motivational loss or motivational gain? *Human Factors*, 49(4), 646–660.

Barger, L. K., Rajaratnam, S. M., Wang, W., O'Brien, C. S., Sullivan, J. P., Qadri, S.,... Czeisler, C. A. (2015). Common sleep disorders increase risk of motor vehicle crashes and adverse health outcomes in firefighters. *Journal of Clinical Sleep Medicine*, 11(3), 233–240.

Baron, K. G., & Reid, K. J. (2014). Cicradian misalignment and health. *International Review of Psychiatry, 26*(2), 139–154. doi: 10.3109/09540261.2014.911149

Belenky, G., Wesensten, N. J., Thorne, D. R., Thomas, M. L., Sing, H. C., Redmond, D. P., . . . Balkin, T. J. (2003). Patterns of performance degradation and restoration during sleep restriction and subsequent recovery: A sleep dose-response study. *Journal of Sleep Research, 12*, 1–12.

Benca, R. M., Obermeyer, W. H., Thisted, R. A., & Gillin, J. C. (1992). Sleep and psychiatric disorders. A meta-analysis. *Archives of General Psychiatry, 49*(8), 651–668.

Bengtsson, C., Lindberg, E., Jonsson, L., Holmström, M., Sundbom, F., Hedner, J., . . . Janson, C. (2017). Chronic rhinosinusitis impairs sleep quality: Results of the GA(2)LEN study. *Sleep, 40*(1).

Berry, R. B., Brooks, R., Gamaldo, C. E., Harding, S. M., Lloyd, R. M., Marcus, C. L., & Vaughn, B. V. (2015). *The AASM Manual for the Scoring of Sleep and Associated Events: Rules, Terminology and Technical Specification, Version 2.2.* Darien, IL: American Academy of Sleep Medicine.

Bonnet, M. H. (1991). The effect of varying prophylactic naps on performance, alertness and mood throughout a 52-hour continuous operation. *Sleep, 14*(4), 307–315.

Bonnet, M. H., & Arand, D. L. (2007). EEG arousal norms by age. *Journal of Clinical Sleep Medicine, 3*(3), 271–274.

Borbély, A. (1982). Two process model of sleep regulation. *Human Neurobiology, 1*, 195–204.

Borbély, A., & Achermann, P. (1999). Sleep homeostasis and models of sleep regulation. *Journal of Biological Rhythms, 14*(6), 557–568.

Borbély, A. A., Tobler, I., Loepfe, M., Kupfer, D. J., Ulrich, R. F., Grochocinski, V., . . . Matthews, G. (1984). All-night spectral analysis of the sleep EEG in untreated depressives and normal controls. *Psychiatry Research, 12*(1), 27–33.

Bray, R. M., Pemberton, M. R., Hourani, L. L., Witt, M., Olmsted, K. L., Brown, J. M., . . . Bradshaw, M. (2009). *Department of Defence Survey of Health Related Behaviors Among Active Duty Military Personnel* (Report No. RTI/10940-FR). Research Triangle Park, NC: RTI International.

Breslau, N., Roth, T., Rosenthal, L., & Andreski, P. (1996). Sleep disturbance and psychiatric disorders: A longitudinal epidemiological study of young adults. *Biological Psychiatry, 39*(6), 411–418.

Brondel, L., Romer, M. A., Nougues, P. M., Touyarou, P., & Davenne, D. (2010). Acute partial sleep deprivation increases food intake in healthy men. *American Journal of Clinical Nutrition, 91*(6), 1550–1559. doi: 10.3945/ajcn.2009.28523

Broughton, R. J., & Ogilvie, R. D. (1992). *Sleep, Arousal, and Performance.* Boston: Birkhauser.

Broussard, J. L., Ehrmann, D. A., Van Cauter, E., Tasali, E., & Brady, M. J. (2012). Impaired insulin signaling in human adipocytes after experimental sleep restriction: A randomized, crossover study. *Annals of Internal Medicine, 157*(8), 549–557.

Brown, S., Matsangas, P., & Shattuck, N. L. (2015a, October 26—30). *Comparison of a circadian-based and a forward rotating watch schedules on sleep, mood, and psychomotor vigilance performance.* Paper presented at the Human Factors and Ergonomics Society (HFES) Annual Meeting, Los Angeles, CA.

Brown, S., Matsangas, P., & Shattuck, N. L. (2015b). Is a sailor's life for you? Aches and pains of US Navy sailors. *Sleep, 38*(Abstract Supplement), A89.

Bruck, D., & Pisani, D. L. (1999). The effects of sleep inertia on decision-making performance. *Journal of Sleep Research, 8*(2), 95–103.

Bryan, C. J. (2013). Repetitive traumatic brain injury (or concussion) increases severity of sleep disturbance among deployed military personnel. *Sleep*, *36*(6), 941–946.

Brzezinski, A. (1997). Melatonin in humans. *New England Journal of Medicine*, *336*(3), 186–195.

Burch, J. B., Yost, M. G., Johnson, W., & Allen, E. (2005). Melatonin, sleep, and shift work adaptation. *Journal of Occupational and Environmental Medicine*, *47*(9), 893–901.

Burke, T. M., Scheer, F. A. J. L., Ronda, J. M., Czeisler, C. A., & Wright, K. P. (2015). Sleep inertia, sleep homeostatic and circadian influences on higher-order cognitive functions. *Journal of Sleep Research*, *24*(4), 364–371. doi: 10.1111/jsr.12291

Burks, S. V., Anderson, J. E., Bombyk, M., Haider, R., Ganzhorn, D., Jiao, X., . . . Kales, S. N. (2016). Nonadherence with employer-mandated sleep apnea treatment and increased risk of serious truck crashes. *Sleep*, *39*(5), 967–975.

Buxton, O. M., Cain, S. W., O'Connor, S. P., Porter, J. H., Duffy, J. F., Wang, W., . . . Shea, C. A. (2012). Adverse metabolic consequences in humans of prolonged sleep restriction combined with circadian disruption. *Science Translational Medicine*, *4*(129), 129ra143.

Buysse, D. J. (2014). Sleep health: Can we define it? Does it matter? *Sleep*, *37*(1), 9–17.

Cai, D. J., Mednick, S. A., Harrison, E. M., Kanady, J. C., & Mednick, S. C. (2009). REM, not incubation, improves creativity by priming associative networks. *PNAS*, *106*(25), 10130–10134.

Cajochen, C., Chellappa, S. L., & Schmidt, C. (2014). Circadian and light effect on human sleepiness-alertness. In S. Garbarino, L. Nobili, & G. Costa (Eds.), *Sleepiness and Human Impact Assessment* (pp. 9–22). Milan: Springer.

Canessa, N., Castronovo, V., Cappa, S. F., Aloia, M. S., Marelli, S., Falini, A., . . . Ferini-Strambi, L. (2011). Obstructive sleep apnea: Brain structural changes and neurocognitive function before and after treatment. *American Journal of Respiratory and Critical Care Medicine*, *183*(10), 1419–1426.

Cappuccio, F. P., Cooper, D., D'Elia, L., Strazzullo, P., & Miller, M. A. (2011). Sleep duration predicts cardiovascular outcomes: A systematic review and meta-analysis of prospective studies. *European Heart Journal*, *32*(12), 1484–1492.

Cappuccio, F. P., D'Elia, L., Strazzullo, P., & Miller, M. A. (2010). Quantity and quality of sleep and incidence of type 2 diabetes: A systematic review and meta-analysis. *Diabetes Care*, *33*(2), 414–420.

Carskadon, M. A., & Dement, W. C. (2016). Normal human sleep: An overview. In M. H. Kryger, T. Roth, & W. C. Dement (Eds.), *Principles and Practice of Sleep Medicine* (6th ed., pp. 15–25). Philadelphia, PA: Elsevier Saunders.

Carskadon, M. A., Wolfson, A. R., Tzischinsky, O., & Acebo, C. (1995). Early school schedules modify adolescent sleepiness. *Sleep Research*, *24*, 92.

Castriotta, R. J., & Murthy, J. N. (2010). Sleep disorders in patients with traumatic brain injury: A review. *CNS Drugs*, *25*(3), 175–185.

Centers for Disease Control and Prevention. (2012). Short sleep duration among workers—United States, 2010. *Morbidity and Mortality Weekly Report (MMWR)*, *61*(16), 281–285.

Colquhoun, W. P., Blake, M. J. F., & Edwards, R. S. (1969). Experimental studies of shift work III: Stabilized 12-hour shift systems. *Ergonomics*, *12*, 865–882.

Colquhoun, W. P., & Folkard, S. (1985). Scheduling watches at sea. In S. Folkard & T. H. Monk (Eds.), *Hours of Work: Temporal Factors in Work-Scheduling* (pp. 253–260). New York: John Wiley and Sons.

Czeisler, C. A., Weitzman, E. D., Moore-Ede, M. C., Zimmerman, J. C., & Knauer, R. S. (1980). Human sleep: Its duration and organization depend on its circadian phase. *Science, 210*(4475), 1264–1267.

Department of the Navy. (2012). *Standard Organization and Regulations of the US Navy— OPNAV Instruction 3120.32D*. Washington, DC: Department of the Navy.

Dinges, D. F., & Kribbs, N. B. (1991). Performing while sleepy: Effects of experimentally induced sleepiness. In T. H. Monk (Ed.), *Sleep, Sleepiness and Performance*. Chichester/ New York: Wiley.

Dinges, D. F., Pack, F., Williams, K., Gillen, K. A., Powell, J. W., Ott, G. E., . . . Pack, A. I. (1997). Cumulative sleepiness, mood disturbance, and psychomotor vigilance performance decrements during a week of sleep restricted to 4–5 hours per night. *Sleep, 20*(4), 267–277.

DoD. (2015). 2015 Demographics: Profile of the Military Community. Retrieved April 7, 2017, from www.militaryonesource.mil

Drake, C. L., Roehrs, T., Burduvali, E., Bonahoom, A., Rosekind, M. R., & Roth, T. (2001). Effects of rapid versus slow accumulation of eight hours of sleep loss. *Psychophysiology, 38*(6), 979–987.

Drake, C. L., & Wright, K. P. (2011). Shift work, shift-work disorder, and jet lag. In M. H. Kryger, T. Roth, & W. C. Dement (Eds.), *Principles and Practices of Sleep Medicine* (5th ed., pp. 784–798). St. Louis, MO: Elsevier Saunders.

Driskell, J. E., & Mullen, B. (2005). The efficacy of naps as a fatigue countermeasure: A meta-analytic integration. *Hum Factors, 47*(2), 360–377.

Durmer, J. S., & Dinges, D. F. (2005). Neurocognitive consequences of sleep deprivation. *Seminars in Neurology, 25*(1), 117–129.

Ferrie, J. E., Shipley, M. J., Cappuccio, F. P., Brunner, E., Miller, M. A., Kumari, M., & Marmot, M. G. (2007). A prospective study of change in sleep duration: Associations with mortality in the Whitehall II cohort. *Sleep, 30*(12), 1659–1666.

Folkard, S. (1992). Is there a 'best compromise' shift system? *Ergonomics, 35*, 1453–1463.

Folkard, S., Lombardi, D. A., & Spencer, M. B. (2006). Estimating the circadian rhythm in the risk of occupational injuries and accidents. *Chronobiology International, 23*(6), 1181–1192.

Folkard, S., & Tucker, P. (2003). Shift work, safety and productivity. *Occupational Medicine, 53*, 95–101.

Ford, E. S., Wheaton, A. G., Cunningham, T. J., Giles, W. H., Chapman, D. P., & Croft, J. B. (2014). Trends in outpatient visits for insomnia, sleep apnea, and prescriptions for sleep medications among US adults: Findings from the National Ambulatory Medical Care survey 1999–2010. *Sleep, 37*(8), 1283–1293.

Fortier-Brochu, E., Beaulieu-Bonneau, S., Ivers, H., & Morin, C. M. (2012). Insomnia and daytime cognitive performance: A meta-analysis. *Sleep Medicine Reviews, 16*(1), 83–94.

Gangwisch, J. E. (2014). A review of evidence for the link between sleep duration and hypertension. *American Journal of Hypertension, 27*(10), 1235–1242.

Garbarino, S., Mascialino, B., Penco, M. A., Squarcia, S., De Carli, F., Nobili, L., . . . Ferrillo, F. (2004). Professional shift-work drivers who adopt prophylactic naps can reduce the risk of car accidents during night work. *Sleep, 27*(7), 1295–1302.

Goh, V. H., Tong, T. Y., Lim, C. L., Low, E. C., & Lee, L. K. (2000). Circadian disturbances after night-shift work onboard a naval ship. *Military Medicine, 165*(2), 101–105.

Gottlieb, D. J., Whitney, C. W., Bonekat, W. H., Iber, C., James, G. D., Lebowitz, M., . . . Rosenberg, C. E. (1999). Relation of sleepiness to respiratory disturbance index: The Sleep Heart Health Study. *American Journal of Respiratory and Critical Care Medicine, 159*(2), 502–507.

Grandner, M. A., Jackson, N., Gerstner, J. R., & Knutson, K. L. (2013). Dietary nutrients associated with short and long sleep duration. Data from a nationally representative sample. *Appetite, 64,* 71–80.

Green, K. Y. (2009). *A Comparative Analysis Between the Navy Standard Workweek and the Actual Work/Rest Patterns of Sailors Aboard US Navy Frigates* (Master's thesis). Monterey, CA: Naval Postgraduate School.

Greer, S. M., Goldstein, A. N., & Walker, M. P. (2013). The impact of sleep deprivation on food desire in the human brain. *Nature Communications, 4,* 2259. doi: 10.1038/ncomms3259

Guo, X., Zheng, L., Wang, J., Zhang, X., Zhang, X., Li, J., & Sun, Y. (2013). Epidemiological evidence for the link between sleep duration and high blood pressure: A systematic review and meta-analysis. *Sleep Medicine, 14*(4), 324–332. doi: 10.1016/j.sleep.2012.12.001

Haack, M., Serrador, J., Cohen, D., Simpson, N., Meier-Ewert, H., & Mullington, J. M. (2013). Increasing sleep duration to lower beat-to-beat blood pressure: A pilot study. *Journal of Sleep Research, 22*(3), 295–304.

Hakola, T., & Härmä, M. (2001). Evaluation of a fast forward rotating shift schedule in the steel industry with a special focus on ageing and sleep. *Journal of Human Ergology, 30*(1–2), 315–319.

Hanlon, E. C., & Van Cauter, E. (2011). Quantification of sleep behavior and of its impact on the cross-talk between the brain and peripheral metabolism. *Proceedings of the National Academy of Science of the United States of America, 108*(Suppl. 3), 15609–15616.

Harrington, J. M. (2001). Health effects of shift work and extended hours of work. *Occupational and Environmental Medicine, 58,* 68–72.

Harrison, Y., & Horne, J. A. (1999). One night of sleep loss impairs innovative thinking and flexible decision making. *Organizational Behavior and Human Decision Processes, 78*(2), 128–145.

Harrison, Y., & Horne, J. A. (2000). The impact of sleep deprivation on decision making: A review. *Journal of Experimental Psychology, 6*(3), 236–249.

Haynes, L. E. (2007). *A Comparison Between the Navy Standard Workweek and the Actual Work and Rest Patterns of US Navy Sailors* (Master's thesis). Monterey, CA: Naval Postgraduate School.

Heslop, P., Smith, G. D., Metcalfe, C., Macleod, J., & Hart, C. (2002). Sleep duration and mortality: The effect of short or long sleep duration on cardiovascular and all-cause mortality in working men and women. *Sleep Medicine, 3*(4), 305–314.

Hirsch Allen, A. J., Bansback, N., & Ayas, N. T. (2015). The effect of OSA on work disability and work-related injuries. *Chest, 147*(5), 1422–1428.

Hockey, R. (Ed.). (1983). *Stress and Fatigue in Human Performance.* Durham: John Wiley & Sons.

Hohagen, F., Rink, K., Käppler, C., Schramm, E., Riemann, D., Weyerer, S., & Berger, M. (1993). Prevalence and treatment of insomnia in general practice. A longitudinal study. *European Archives of Psychiatry and Clinical Neuroscience, 242*(6), 329–336.

Holliday, E. G., Magee, C. A., Kritharides, L., Banks, E., & Attia, J. (2013). Short sleep duration is associated with risk of future diabetes but not cardiovascular disease: A prospective study and meta-analysis. *PLoS ONE, 8*(11), e82305.

Horne, J. A. (1988). *Why We Sleep*. New York: Oxford University Press.

Horne, J. A. (2010). Sleepiness as a need for sleep: When is enough, enough? *Neuroscience and Biobehavioral Reviews, 34*, 108–118.

Killgore, W. D., Killgore, D. B., Day, L. M., Li, C., Kamimori, G., & Balkin, T. (2007). The effects of 53 hours of sleep deprivation on moral judgment. *Sleep, 30*(3), 345–352.

Kim, E.-J., & Dimsdale, J. E. (2007). The effect of psychosocial stress on sleep: A review of polysomnographic evidence. *Behavioral Sleep Medicine, 5*(4), 256–278.

Klein, D. C., Morre, R. Y., & Reppert, S. M. (Eds.). (1991). *Suprachiasmatic Nucleus: The Mind's Clock*. New York: Oxford University Press.

Knutsson, A. (2003). Health disorders of shift workers. *Occupational Medicine, 53*, 103–108.

Krueger, J. M., Frank, M. G., Wisor, J. P., & Roy, S. (2016). Sleep function: Toward elucidating an enigma. *Sleep Medicine Reviews, 28*, 46–54. doi: 10.1016/j.smrv.2015.08.005

Krueger, P. M., Reither, E. N., Peppard, P. E., Burger, A. E., & Hale, L. (2015). Cumulative exposure to short sleep and body mass outcomes: A prospective study. *Journal of Sleep Research, 24*(6), 629–638.

Landmann, N., Kuhn, M., Piosczyk, H., Feige, B., Baglioni, C., Spiegelhalder, K.,... Nissen, C. (2014). The reorganisation of memory during sleep. *Sleep Medicine Reviews, 18*(6), 531–541.

Lee, I. S., Bardwell, W., Ancoli-Israel, S., Natarajan, L., Loredo, J. S., & Dimsdale, J. E. (2011). The relationship between psychomotor vigilance performance and quality of life in obstructive sleep apnea. *Journal of Clinical Sleep Medicine, 7*(3), 254–260.

Leproult, R., Deliens, G., Gilson, M., & Peigneux, P. (2015). Beneficial impact of sleep extension on fasting insulin sensitivity in adults with habitual sleep restriction. *Sleep, 38*(5), 707–715.

Lettieri, C. J., Williams, S. G., & Collen, J. F. (2016). OSA syndrome and posttraumatic stress disorder: Clinical outcomes and impact of positive airway pressure therapy. *Chest, 149*(2), 483–490.

Lewis, P. E., Emasealu, O. V., Rohrbeck, P., & Hu, Z. (2014). Risk of type II diabetes and hypertension associated with chronic insomnia among active component, US Armed Forces, 1998-2013. *MSMR, 21*(10), 6–13.

Linton, S. J., & Bryngelsson, I. (2000). Insomnia and its relationship to work and health in a working-age population. *Journal of Occupational Rehabilitation, 10*(2), 169–183.

Liu, Y., Wheaton, A. G., Chapman, D. P., Cunningham, T. J., Lu, H., & Croft, J. B. (2016). Prevalence of healthy sleep duration among adults—United States, 2014. *Morbidity and Mortality Weekly Report (MMWR), 65*(6), 137–141.

Luxton, D. D., Greenburg, D., Ryan, J., Niven, A., Wheeler, G., & Mysliwiec, V. (2011). Prevalence and impact of short sleep duration in redeployed OIF soldiers. *Sleep, 34*(9), 113–122.

Markwald, R. R., Melanson, E. L., Smith, M. R., Higgins, J., Perreault, L., Eckel, H., & Wright Jr., K. P. (2013). Impact of elinsufficient sleep on total daily energy expenditure, food intake, and weight gain. *Proceedings of the National Academy of Science of the United States of America, 110*, 5695–5700.

Mason, D. R. (2009). *A Comparative Analysis Between the Navy Standard Workweek and the Work/Rest Patterns Of Sailors Aboard US Navy Cruisers* (Master's thesis). Monterey, CA: Naval Postgraduate School.

McEvoy, R. D., Antic, N. A., Heeley, E., Luo, Y., Ou, Q., Zhang, X., . . . for the SAVE Investigators and Coordinators. (2016). CPAP for prevention of cardiovascular events in obstructive sleep apnea. *New England Journal of Medicine, 375*(10), 919–931.

McKenna, B. S., Dickinson, D. L., Orff, H. J., & Drummond, S. P. A. (2007). The effects of one night sleep deprivation on known-risk and ambiguous-risk decisions. *Journal of Sleep Research, 16,* 245–252.

Meng, L., Zheng, Y., & Hui, R. (2013). The relationship of sleep duration and insomnia to risk of hypertension incidence: A meta-analysis of prospective cohort studies. *Hypertension Research, 36*(11), 985–995. doi: 10.1038/hr.2013.70

Mental Health Advisory Team 9 (MHAT 9). (2013). *Operation Enduring Freedom (OEF):* Office of the Surgeon General, US Army, Fort Sam Houston, TX.

Miller, N. L., Matsangas, P., & Kenney, A. (2012). The role of sleep in the military: Implications for training and operational effectiveness. In J. H. Laurence & M. D. Matthews (Eds.), *The Oxford Handbook of Military Psychology* (pp. 262–281). New York: Oxford University Press.

Mitterling, T., Högl, B., Schönwald, S. V., Hackner, H., Gabelia, D., Biermayr, M., & Frauscher, B. (2015). Sleep and respiration in 100 healthy Caucasian sleepers— a polysomnographic study according to American Academy of Sleep Medicine Standards. *Sleep, 38*(6), 867–875.

Monk, T. H. (1986). Advantages and disadvantages of rapidly rotating shift schedules—A circadian viewpoint. *Human Factors, 28,* 553–557.

Monk, T. H., Buysse, D. J., Billy, B. D., Fletcher, M. E., Kennedy, K. S., Begley, A. E., . . . Beach, S. R. (2013). Shiftworkers report worse sleep than day workers, even in retirement. *Journal of Sleep Research, 22,* 201–208.

Mysliwiec, V., Gill, J., Lee, H., Baxter, T., Pierce, R., Barr, T. L., . . . Roth, B. J. (2013). Sleep disorders in US military personnel: A high rate of comorbid insomnia and obstructive sleep apnea. *Chest, 144*(2), 549–557.

Mysliwiec, V., Matsangas, P., Baxter, T., McGraw, L., Bothwell, N. E., & Roth, B. J. (2013). Comorbid insomnia and obstructive sleep apnea in military personnel: Correlation with polysomnographic variables. *Military Medicine, 179*(3), 294–300. doi: 10.7205/ MILMED-D-13-00396

Mysliwiec, V., Matsangas, P., Baxter, T., & Shattuck, N. L. (2015). An unusual circadian rhythm in an active duty service member. *Sleep and Biological Rhythms, 14*(1), 113–115.

Mysliwiec, V., McGraw, L., Pierce, R., Smith, P., Trapp, B., & Roth, B. J. (2013). Sleep disorders and associated medical comorbidities in active duty military personnel. *Sleep, 36*(2), 167–174.

Mysliwiec, V., Walter, R. J., Collen, J., & Wesensten, J. N. (2016). Military sleep management: An operational imperative. *US Army Medical Department Journal, Apr–Sep*(2– 16), 128–134.

Nunes, D. M., Mota, R. M., de Pontes Neto, O. L., Pereira, E. D., de Bruin, V. M., & de Bruin, P. F. (2009). Impaired sleep reduces quality of life in chronic obstructive pulmonary disease. *Lung, 187*(3), 159–163.

Ohayon, M. M., Carskadon, M. A., Guilleminault, C., & Vitiello, M. V. (2004). Meta-analysis of quantitative sleep parameters from childhood to old age in healthy individuals: Developing normative sleep values across the human lifespan. *Sleep, 27*(7), 1255–1273.

Ohayon, M. M., & Reynolds III, C. F. (2009). Epidemiological and clinical relevance of insomnia diagnosis algorithms according to the DSM-IV and the International Classification of Sleep Disorders (ICSD). *Sleep Medicine, 10*(9), 952–960.

Paul, M. A., Ebisuzaki, D., McHarg, J., Hursh, S. R., & Miller, J. C. (2012). *An Assessment of Some Watch Schedule Variants Used in Canadian Patrol Frigates* (Technical Report Report No. DRDC Toronto TR 2012-078). Toronto, Canada: Defence Research and Development.

Pearson, N. J., Johnson, L. L., & Nahin, R. L. (2006). Insomnia, trouble sleeping, and complementary and alternative medicine: Analysis of the 2002 national health interview survey data. *Archives of Internal Medicine, 166*(16), 1775–1782.

Peppard, P. E., Szklo-Coxe, M., Hla, K. M., & Young, T. (2006). Longitudinal association of sleep-related breathing disorder and depression. *Archives of Internal Medicine, 166*(16), 1709–1715.

Peppard, P. E., Young, T., Barnet, J. H., Palta, M., Hagen, E. W., & Hla, K. M. (2013). Increased prevalence of sleep-disordered breathing in adults. *American Journal of Epidemiology, 177*(9), 1006–1014.

Peterson, A. L., Goodie, J. L., Satterfield, W. A., & Brim, W. L. (2008). Sleep disturbance during military deployment. *Military Medicine, 173*(3), 230–235.

Povitz, M., Bolo, C. E., Heitman, S. J., Tsai, W. H., Wang, J., & James, M. T. (2014). Effect of treatment of obstructive sleep apnea on depressive symptoms: Systematic review and meta-analysis. *PLoS Medicine, 11*(11), e1001762.

Redeker, N. S., Jeon, S., Muench, U., Campbell, D., Walsleben, J., & Rapoport, D. M. (2010). Insomnia symptoms and daytime function in stable heart failure. *Sleep, 33*(9), 1210–1216.

Reilly, T., & Edwards, B. (2007). Altered sleep–wake cycles and physical performance in athletes. *Physiology & Behavior, 90*(2), 274–284.

Riemann, D., Spiegelhalder, K., Feige, B., Voderholzer, U., Berger, M., Perlis, M. L., & Nissen, C. (2010). The hyperarousal model of insomnia: A review of the concept and its evidence. *Sleep Medicine Reviews, 14*(1), 19–31.

Rosa, R. R., Bonnet, M. H., & Cole, L. L. (1998). Work schedule and task factors in upper-extremity fatigue. *Human Factors, 40*(1), 150–158.

Roth, T., & Ancoli-Israel, S. (1999). Daytime consequences and correlates of insomnia in the United States: Results of the 1991 National Sleep Foundation Survey. II.. *Sleep, 22*(Suppl.2), S354-S358.

Roth, T., Coulouvrat, C., Hajak, G., Lakoma, M. D., Sampson, N. A., Shahly, V., . . . Kessler, R. C. (2011). Prevalence and perceived health associated with insomnia based on DSM-IV-TR; International Statistical Classification of Diseases and Related Health Problems, Tenth Revision; and Research Diagnostic Criteria/International Classification of Sleep Disorders; Second Edition criteria: Results from the America Insomnia Survey. *Biological Psychiatry, 69*(6), 592–600.

Roth, T., Jaeger, S., Jin, R., Kalsekar, A., Stang, P. E., & Kessler, R. C. (2006). Sleep problems, comorbid mental disorders, and role functioning in the national comorbidity survey replication. *Biological Psychiatry, 60*(12), 1364–1371.

Rumble, M. E., White, K. H., & Benca, R. M. (2015). Sleep disturbances in mood disorders. *The Psychiatric Clinics of North America, 38*(4), 743–759.

Rupp, T. L., Wesensten, J. N., Bliese, P. D., & Balkin, T. (2009). Banking sleep: Realization of benefits during subsequent sleep restriction and recovery. *Sleep, 32*(3), 311–321.

Rutenfranz, J., Plett, R., Knauth, P., Condon, R., De Vol, D., Flethcher, N., . . . Colquhoun, W. P. (1988). Work at sea: A study of sleep, and circadian rhythms in physiological and psychological functions, in watchkeepers on merchant vessels. *International Archives of Occupational and Enivornmental Health, 60*(5), 331–339.

Sallinen, M., & Kecklund, G. (2010). Shift work, sleep, and sleepiness—differences between shift schedules and systems. *Scandinavian Journal of Work, Environment & Health, 36,* 121–133.

Savage, V. M., & West, G. B. (2007). A quantitative, theoretical framework for understanding mammalian sleep. *Proceedings of the National Academy of Sciences of the United States of America, 104*(3), 1051–1056.

Seelig, A. D., Jacobson, I. G., B., S., Hooper, T. I., Boyko, E. J., Gackstetter, G. D., . . . Millennium Cohort Study Team. (2010). Sleep patterns before, during, and after deployment to Iraq and Afghanistan. *Sleep, 33*(12), 1615–1622.

Shattuck, N. L., & Matsangas, P. (2014). *Work and Rest Patterns and Psychomotor Vigilance Performance of Crewmembers of the USS Jason Dunham: A Comparison of the 3/9 and 6/6 Watchstanding Schedules* (Technical Report Report No. NPS-OR-14-004). Monterey, CA: Naval Postgraduate School.

Shattuck, N. L., & Matsangas, P. (2015a). Caffeinated beverage consumption rates and reported sleep in a US Navy ship. *Proceedings of the Human Factors and Ergonomics Society Annual Meeting, 59*(1), 696–700.

Shattuck, N. L., & Matsangas, P. (2015b). A comparison of sleep and performance of US Navy sailors on four different shiftwork schedules. *Sleep, 38*(Abstract Supplement), A130.

Shattuck, N. L., & Matsangas, P. (2015c). Operational assessment of the 5-h on/10-h off watchstanding schedule on a US Navy ship: Sleep patterns, mood, and psychomotor vigilance performance of crew members in the nuclear reactor department. *Ergonomics, 59*(5), 657–664. doi: 10.1080/00140139.2015.1073794

Shattuck, N. L., & Matsangas, P. (2015d). A six-month assessment of sleep during naval deployment: A case study of a commanding officer. *Aerospace Medicine and Human Performance, 86*(5), 1–5.

Shattuck, N. L., & Matsangas, P. (2016). *Work and Rest Patterns in Marine Corps Embassy Security Guard Program: Promoting Health and Wellness Through Informed Work Schedules* (Technical Report No. NPS-OR-16-001R). Monterey, CA: Naval Postgraduate School.

Shattuck, N. L., Matsangas, P., & Brown, S. (2015). *A Comparison Between the 3/9 and the 5/10 Watchbills* (Technical Report Report No. NPS-OR-15-006). Monterey, CA: Naval Postgraduate School.

Shattuck, N. L., Matsangas, P., Moore, J., & Wegemann, L. (2015). *Prevalence of Musculoskeletal Symptoms, Excessive Daytime Sleepiness, and Fatigue in the Crewmembers of a US Navy Ship* (Technical Report No. NPS-OR-15-005). Monterey, CA: Naval Postgraduate School.

Shattuck, N. L., Matsangas, P., Moore, J., & Wegemann, L. (2016). Prevalence of musculoskeletal symptoms, excessive daytime sleepiness and fatigue in the crewmembers of a US Navy ship. *Military Medicine, 181*(7), 655–662.

Shattuck, N. L., Matsangas, P., & Powley, E. H. (2015). *Sleep Patterns, Mood, Psychomotor Vigilance Performance, and Command Resilience of Watchstanders on the "Five and Dime" Watchbill* (Technical Report No. NPS-OR-15-003). Monterey, CA: Naval Postgraduate School.

Shattuck, N. L., Matsangas, P., & Waggoner, L. (2014, October 27-31). *Assessment of a Novel Watchstanding Schedule on an Operational US Navy Vessel*. Paper presented at the Human Factors and Ergonomics Society (HFES) 58th Annual Meeting, Chicago, IL.

Shattuck, N. L., Waggoner, L. B., Young, R. L., Smith, C. S., & Matsangas, P. (2014). Shiftwork practices in the United States Navy: A study of sleep and performance in watchstanders aboard the USS Jason Dunham. *Sleep, 37*(Abstract Supplement), A78.

Simon, G. E., & VonKorff, M. (1997). Prevalence, burden, and treatment of insomnia in primary care. *American Journal of Psychiatry, 154*(10), 1417–1423.

Simpson, N. S., Gibbs, E. L., & Matheson, G. O. (2016). Optimizing sleep to maximize performance: Implications and recommendations for elite athletes. *Scandinavian Journal of Medicine and Science in Sports*. doi: 10.1111/sms.12703

Skeldon, A. C., Derks, G., & Dijk, D. J. (2016). Modelling changes in sleep timing and duration across the lifespan: Changes in circadian rhythmicity or sleep homeostasis? *Sleep Medicine Reviews, 28,* 96–107.

Snodgrass, G., & Kohlmann, B. (2014). 2014 Navy retention study. Retrieved February 10, 2014, from www.dodretention.org

Sperry, S. D., Scully, I. D., Gramzow, R. H., & Jorgensen, R. S. (2015). Sleep duration and waist circumference in adults: A meta-analysis. *Sleep, 38*(8), 1269–1276.

Spiegel, K., Leproult, R., & Van Cauter, E. (1999). Impact of sleep debt on metabolic and endocrine function. *Lancet, 354*(9188), 1435–1439.

St-Onge, M. P., Grandner, M. A., Brown, D., Conroy, M. B., Jean-Louis, G., Coons, M., . . . Stroke Council. (2016). Sleep duration and quality: Impact on lifestyle behaviors and cardiometabolic health: A scientific statement from the American Heart Association. *Circulation, 134,* e367-e386.

St-Onge, M. P., Roberts, A. L., Chen, J., Kelleman, M., O'Keeffe, M., Roy-Choudhury, A., & Jones, P. J. (2011). Short sleep duration increases energy intakes but does not change energy expenditure in normal-weight individuals. *American Journal of Clinical Nutrition, 94*(2), 410–416.

Stepanski, E. J., Zorick, F., Roehrs, T., & Roth, T. (2000). Effects of sleep deprivation on daytime sleepiness in primary insomnia. *Sleep, 23*(2), 1–5.

Stevens, R. G., Hansen, J., Costa, G., Haus, E., Kauppinen, T., Aronson, K. J., . . . Straif, K. (2011). Considerations of circadian impact for defining 'shift work' in cancer studies: IARC Working Group Report. *Occupational and Environmental Medicine, 68,* 154–162.

Stolgitis, W. C. (1969). *The Effects of Sleep Loss and Demanding Work/Rest Cycles: An Analysis of the Traditional Navy Watch System and a Proposed Alternative*. Monterey, CA: Naval Postgraduate School.

Swinkels, C., Ulmer, C., Beckham, J., Buse, N., & Calhoun, P. (2013). The association of sleep duration, mental health, and health risk behaviors among US Afghanistan/Iraq era veterans. *Sleep, 36*(7), 1019–1025.

Tamakoshi, A., & Ohno, Y. (2004). Self-reported sleep duration as a predictor of all-cause mortality: Results from the JACC study, Japan. *Sleep, 27*(1), 51–54.

Tassi, P., & Muzet, A. (2000). Sleep inertia. *Sleep Medicine Reviews, 4*(4), 341–353.

Taylor, D. J., Pruiksma, K. E., Hale, W. J., Kelly, K., Maurer, D., Peterson, A. L., . . . STRONG STAR Consortium. (2016). Prevalence, correlates, and predictors of insomnia in the US Army prior to deployment. *Sleep, 39*(10), 1795–1806.

Toffler, A. (1970). *Future Shock*: Random House.

Troxel, W. M., Shih, R. A., Pedersen, E., Geyer, L., Fisher, M. P., Griffin, B. A., . . . Steinberg, P. S. (2015). *Sleep in the Military: Promoting Healthy Sleep Among US Servicemembers.* Santa Monica, CA: RAND.

Tsuno, N., Besset, A., & Ritchie, K. (2005). Sleep and depression. *The Journal of Clinical Psychiatry, 66*(10), 1254–1269.

Turner, T. H., Drummond, S. P. A., Salamat, J. S., & Brown, C. G. (2007). Effects of 42 hr of total sleep deprivation on component processes of verbal working memory. *Neuropsychology, 21*(6), 787–795.

Uehli, K., Mehta, A. J., Miedinger, D., Hug, K., Schindler, C., Holsboer-Trachsler, E., . . . Künzli, N. (2014). Sleep problems and work injuries: A systematic review and metaanalysis. *Sleep Medicine Reviews, 18*(1), 61–73.

Ulmer, C. S., Van Voorhees, E., Germain, A. E., Voils, C. I., Beckham, J. C., & VA Mid-Atlantic Mental Illness Research Education and Clinical Center Registry Workgroup. (2014). A comparison of sleep difficulties among Iraq/Afghanistan theater veterans with and without mental health diagnoses. *Journal of Clinical Sleep Medicine, 11*(9), 995–1005.

US Bureau of Labor Statistics. (2005). Workers on flexible and shift schedules in May 2004 [Press release]. Retrieved from http://www.bls.gov/news.release/pdf/flex.pdf

Van Dongen, H. P. A., & Dinges, D. F. (2000). Circadian rhythms and fatigue alertness and performance. In M. H. Kryger, W. Dement, & T. Roth (Eds.), *Principles and Practice of Sleep Medicine* (3th ed., pp. 391–399). Philadephia, PA: W. B. Saunders.

Van Dongen, H. P. A., Maislin, G., Mullington, J. M., & Dinges, D. F. (2003). The cumulative cost of additional wakefulness: Dose-response effects on neurobehavioral functions and sleep physiology from chronic sleep restriction and total sleep deprivation. *Sleep, 26*(2), 117–126.

Wagstaff, A. S., & Sigstad Lie, J.-A. (2011). Shift and night work and long working hours: A systematic review of safety implications. *Scandinavian Journal of Work, Environment & Health, 37*(3), 173–185.

Wang, Q., Xi, B., Liu, M., Zhang, Y., & Fu, M. (2012). Short sleep duration is associated with hypertension risk among adults: A systematic review and meta-analysis. *Hypertension Research, 35*(10), 1012–1018. doi: 10.1038/hr.2012.91

Wang, X.-S., Armstrong, M. E. G., Cairns, B. J., Key, T. J., & Travis, R. C. (2011). Shift work and chronic disease: The epidemiological evidence. *Occupational Medicine, 61*, 78–89.

Watson, N. F., Badr, M. S., Belenky, G., Bliwise, D. L., Buxton, O. M., Buysse, D. J., . . . Tasali, E. (2015). Recommended amount of sleep for a healthy adult: A joint consensus statement of the American Academy of Sleep Medicine and Sleep Research Society. *Sleep, 38*(6), 843–844.

Wedderburn, A. A. I. (1992). How fast should the night shift rotate? A rejoinder. *Ergonomics, 35*, 1447–1451.

Wesensten, N. J., Belenky, G. L., Thorne, D. R., Kautz, M. A., & Balkin, T. J. (2004). Modafinil vs. caffeine: Effects on fatigue during sleep deprivation. *Aviation Space and Environmental Medicine, 75*(6), 520–525.

Wilkinson, R. T. (1992). How fast should the night shift rotate? *Ergonomics, 35*, 1425–1446.

Wolfson, A. R., & Carskadon, M. A. (1998). Sleep schedules and daytime functioning in adolescents. *Child Development, 69*(4), 875–887.

Wolfson, A. R., & Carskadon, M. A. (2003). Understanding adolescents' sleep patterns and school performance: A critical appraisal. *Sleep Medicine Reviews, 7*(6), 491–506.

Yates, W. R., Mitchell, J., Rush, A. J., Trivedi, M. H., Wisniewski, S. R., Hauger, R. B., ... Bryan, C. (2004). Clinical features of depressed outpatients with and without co-occurring general medical conditions in STAR*D. *General Hospital Psychiatry, 26*(6), 421–429.

Young, T., Blustein, J., Finn, L., & Palta, M. (1997). Sleep-disordered breathing and motor vehicle accidents in a population-based sample of employed adults. *Sleep, 20*(8), 608–613.

Young, T., Palta, M., Dempsey, J., Peppard, P. E., Nieto, F. J., & Hla, K. M. (2009). Burden of sleep apnea: Rationale, design, and major findings of the Wisconsin Sleep Cohort study. *WMJ, 108*(5), 246–249.

11

Exoskeletons

State-of-the-Art, Design Challenges, and Future Directions

PRIYANSHU AGARWAL AND ASHISH D. DESHPANDE

INTRODUCTION

Exoskeletons are wearable robotic devices that attach to the human body and work in synchrony with the limbs. These devices are designed to augment the user's performance, provide therapeutic exercises for rehabilitation, assist impaired individuals in performing activities of daily living, or be used as haptic devices for virtual reality applications. These devices make it possible to realize a coupled human–robot system that assists the human user with the capabilities and reliability of a machine while the wearer supervises the system using his intelligence and aptitude. Typical robots were originally developed for industrial applications to accomplish tedious and repetitive tasks in a structured environment (e.g., welding of automobile parts on an assembly line). These applications require robots to be fast and precise. The design challenges and opportunities for exoskeletons are fundamentally different. The most critical requirements for exoskeletons are safety, comfort, low encumbrance, and easy and seamless control.

The concept of exoskeletons, as we understand it today, dates back to 1883 when a pneumatically actuated body frame connected to the human lower limbs and controlled via neural impulses from the brain was proposed (Pons, 2008). The development of the modern exoskeleton prototypes started in the 1960s with the goal of augmenting human capability for military, earth-moving, and material-handling applications (Mosher, 1967). The use of exoskeletons for medical applications was first introduced in 1969 when lower limb exoskeletons were developed for the disabled to aid in realizing artificial gait (Vukobratovic, 2007).

EXOSKELETONS FOR MEDICAL APPLICATIONS

Stroke is the leading cause of serious long-term disability in United States, with an estimated total of 797,000 strokes per year—an average of 1 stroke every 40 seconds (Mozaffarian et al., 2015). Millions of individuals are left with serious disabilities after stroke and need weeks and sometimes months of physical and occupational therapy. Studies show that therapy is more effective when it is intense and the subject is more engaged and that the timing of therapy plays a critical role in how well the patient recovers. For example, therapy provided in the acute to subacute phase of stroke is much more effective than in the chronic phase. However, therapy is labor-intensive and costly, and many patients are left with limited recovery due to ineffective and insufficient therapy.

Exoskeletons present an appealing solution to this problem. These systems could move a patient's body through therapeutic exercises with an appropriate dosage of repetition and customized assistance. Especially for lower limb therapy, such as gait training, powered exoskeletons provide a convenient alternative to conventional therapy in that they reduce the physical burden on therapists while allowing for more intensive therapy. Modern technological advances, such as virtual reality and engaging games, could keep the subjects motivated to actively participate in therapy. In addition, sensors on the exoskeletons allow for quantitative assessment of recovery progress. All these potential benefits associated with exoskeletons led to gain in momentum in their research and development for neuromuscular rehabilitation since the late 1990s.

One of the first robots designed for upper limb rehabilitation was the Massachusetts Institute of Technology's MIT-MANUS that guided the motion of a patient's arm and hand in a plane. Since then, several robots for both upper and lower limbs have been developed for rehabilitation from various neuromuscular impairments such as stroke or spinal cord injury (Armeo®Power, 2017; Kim & Deshpande, 2017; Nef, Guidali, & Riener, 2009; Perry, Rosen, & Burns, 2007; see Figure 11.1). Exoskeletons have also shown potential in helping recover wrist and hands, but, so far, less attention has been focused on systems for hands, partially due to the difficulty in design challenges for powering complex movements in tight space (Agarwal, Fox, Yun, O'Malley, & Deshpande, 2015; Agarwal, Yun, Fox, Madden, & Deshpande, 2017; Asbeck, De Rossi, Holt, & Walsh, 2015; Hand of Hope, 2017; Ueki et al., 2012; see Figure 11.2).

There are numerous lower limb exoskeletons focused on the task of recovering walking (Asbeck et al., 2015; EksoGT, 2017; REX, 2017; Talaty, Esquenazi, & Briceno, 2013; Yan, Cempini, Oddo, & Vitiello, 2015; Zoss, Kazerooni, & Chu, 2006; see Figure 11.3). These exoskeletons attach to the lower limbs and were initially designed to assist individuals with spinal cord injury in walking (Sale, Franceschini, Waldner, & Hesse, 2012). Recently, exoskeletons are also being developed and used for gait rehabilitation as they allow for beneficial repetitive gait training and enable individuals to walk without overhead body weight support or a treadmill. The literature provides evidence that speed and endurance can be improved with traditional physical therapy (States, Salem, & Pappas, 2009), especially when performed in the subacute phase of stroke (Hornby et al., 2016). Several treadmill-based robots such as Lokomat, LOPES, and G-EO have been developed for this purpose. Studies suggest that these robotic devices could improve walking independence (Ada, Dean, Vargas, & Ennis, 2010; Mehrholz, Haedrich, Platz, Kugler, & Pohl, 2012) but result in limited improvement in speed or endurance (Hidler et al., 2009; Mehrholz, Elsner, Werner, Kugler, & Pohl, 2013). This is

Figure 11.1 Upper-limb exoskeletons for rehabilitation and assistive purposes.
(A) ARMin III. (B) EXO-UL7. (C) Harmony. (D) Armeo Power by Hocoma.
ARMin III is reprinted with permission from T. Nef, M. Guidali, and R. Riener, ARMin
III – arm therapy exoskeleton with an ergonomic shoulder actuation, *Applied Bionics
and Biomechanics*, 6(2), 127–142, 2009, Hindawi Publishing Corporation. EXO-UL7 is
copyright 2017 IEEE. Reprinted, with permission, from W. Yu, J. Rosen, J., & X. Li, PID
admittance control for an upper limb exoskeleton, *American Control Conference*, 1124–
1129, 2017; Harmony image is courtesy of the authors; Armeo Power is reprinted with
permission of Hocoma, Switzerland.

because these devices create an environment where subjects have less independence in step initiation due to predetermined belt speed and body weight compensation (Turchetti, Vitiello, Romiti, Geisler, & Micera, 2014). Furthermore,
the visuospatial flow does not vary in such a setting, which makes it difficult for
the subjects to cope with a variation in over-ground walking (Dobkin & Duncan,
2012). Some devices overcome these limitations by enabling over-ground walking,
allowing the user to more actively participate in both swing initiation and foot
placement and requiring them to maintain trunk and balance control. An exoskeleton called Hybrid Assistive Limb (HAL) has been developed by a Japanese company (CYBERDYNE) that can provide assistance to lower limbs in walking, sitting
down, and standing up (Kawamoto & Sankai, 2002). It is the only commercially
available exoskeleton that uses intention-based bioelectrical signals and generates
power-assist torque to realize the wearer's intended movement (Sankai, 2010).
Such devices have shown beneficial results as assistive devices for individuals
with spinal cord injury (Arazpour et al., 2015; Federici, Meloni, Bracalenti, & De

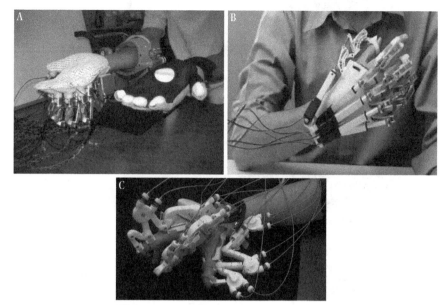

Figure 11.2 Hand exoskeletons designed for rehabilitation and assistive purposes (A). (B) Hand of Hope. (C) Maestro.
A is reprinted from S. Ito, H. Kawasaki, Y. Ishigure, M. Natsume, T. Mouri, & Y. Nishimoto, A design of fine motion assist equipment for disabled hand in robotic rehabilitation system, *Journal of the Franklin Institute, 348*(1), 79–89, 2011, with permission from Elsevier; Hand of Hope is copyright 2011 IEEE, reprinted, with permission, from Ho, N. S. K., Tong, K. Y., Hu, X. L., Fung, K. L., Wei, X. J., Rong, W., & Susanto, E. A., An EMG-driven exoskeleton hand robotic training device on chronic stroke subjects: task training system for stroke rehabilitation, *International Conference on Rehabilitation Robotics*, 1–5, 2011; Maestro image courtesy of the authors.

Filippis, 2015; Louie, Eng, & Lam, 2015) and stroke (Wall, Borg, & Palmcrantz, 2015). These initial studies suggest that exoskeleton-based gait training is as effective as conventional therapy for chronic stroke survivors and is more beneficial for subacute subjects.

Exoskeletons for Performance Augmentation

The idea of human augmentation in science fiction dates back to 1868, when a giant humanoid-shaped steam engine was depicted to tow its inventor in a cart at high speeds (Ellis, 2016). Exoskeletons for performance augmentation are designed and developed to amplify human strength and agility. These types of exoskeletons have primarily been pursued for military or industrial applications to enable soldiers and workers to perform physically exhausting tasks for longer durations (XOS 2, 2017; Sankai, 2010; Yamamoto, Hyodo, Ishii, & Matsuo, 2002; Ishii, Yamamoto, & Hyodo, 2005; see Figure 11.4).

The Defense Advanced Research Projects Agency (DARPA) funded a program called "Exoskeletons for Human Performance Augmentation" that focused on

Figure 11.3 Lower limb exoskeletons designed for capacity augmentation, rehabilitation, or assistance. (A) Berkeley lower extremity exoskeleton (BLEEX). (B) HAL: Hybrid assistive limb based on cybernics. (C) REX by REX Bionics. (D) Soft Exosuit. BLEEX copyright 2008 IEEE, image reprinted, with permission, from A. M. Dollar & H. Herr, Lower extremity exoskeletons and active orthoses: challenges and state-of-the-art," *IEEE Transactions on Robotics*, 24(1), 144–158, 2008; HAL reprinted with permission of Professor Sankai, University of Tsukuba and CYBERDYNE Inc.; REX copyright 2014 RexBionics Ltd; all rights reserved, reprinted with permission; Soft Exosuit reprinted from A. T. Asbeck, S. M. De Rossi, K. G. Holt, & C. J. Walsh, A biologically inspired soft exosuit for walking assistance, *The International Journal of Robotics Research*, 2015, SAGE.

Figure 11.4 Full-body exoskeletons designed for capacity augmentation. Reprinted with permission from M. Ishii, K. Yamamoto, & K. Hyodo, Stand-alone wearable power assist suit: Development and availability, *Journal of Robotics and Mechatronics*, 2005, Fuji Technology Press.

augmenting the capabilities of soldiers (Bogue, 2009; Garcia, Sater, & Main, 2002; Guizzo & Goldstein, 2005). The program resulted in the development of two major exoskeletons for human performance augmentation. The Berkeley Lower Extremity Exoskeleton (BLEEX) was developed to help soldiers carry heavy loads over large distances (Kazerooni, Strausser, Zoss, & Swift, 2011; Zoss et al., 2006). The device was designed such that the weight of the device and backpack is transferred to the ground through the exoskeleton frame. However, the device had a large mass, limited range of motion, and perceivable reaction lag time. The other exoskeleton was from Sarcos, which later evolved into a more energy-efficient version called XOS. The Sarcos exoskeleton was developed to support both the arms and legs to augment user strength and was powered by tethered hydraulic actuators. Unfortunately, limited information was published on this exoskeleton (Jacobsen et al., 2004).

STATE-OF-THE-ART IN CONSTITUTING SUBCOMPONENTS

The state-of-the-art in robotic exoskeletons has made rapid progress in the past decade with advances in technology enabling more capable, intuitive, and intelligent devices. Several key aspects of these devices define the state of the art. Design of these devices is governed by the availability of more compact, efficient, and powerful actuators; more reliable and accurate position and force (or torque) sensors; and more lightweight, strong, and durable materials. Another important aspect that significantly limits the performance of many state-of-the-art devices today is a lack of an intuitive and flexible user interface to control these devices. In this section, we discuss these design, actuation, and control aspects in detail.

Design

Traditionally, robots were designed with the philosophy of "stiffer is better" because high stiffness results in better precision, stability, and speed of response (Pratt & Williamson, 1995). This philosophy is applicable to environments where the tasks are structured and repetitious in nature. However, this notion is not applicable in the context of exoskeletons since safety and comfort are the most important requirements. Moreover, since humans are unpredictable, both in terms of body parameters and movement intentions, exoskeletons need to perform in an unstructured environment. To be effective in intimate contact with the user, there is a need to control the interaction forces between the device and human limb to ensure that these are within acceptable limits. Addressing these issues required a new paradigm of design that allows these devices to be force-controlled rather than position-controlled, which was achieved with advances in actuation and sensing technology. Furthermore, accurate force control requires physically rigid exoskeletons, which consist of stiff load-bearing structures and are actuated using mechanical linkages. Such exoskeletons are easier to design and manufacture and allow for easy transfer of power from body to the ground without significantly loading the human joints. However, rigid exoskeletons are bulky and therefore have high inertia, which could alter the natural motion of the wearer. Furthermore, rigid exoskeletons require either careful alignment of the biological joint with the exoskeleton joint or careful design of the exoskeleton mechanism to overcome joint axes misalignment problems, and they are difficult to customize for a specific user.

More recently, soft exoskeletons have been developed, drawing inspiration from biological systems to address some of the limitations of rigid exoskeletons. Soft exoskeletons have compliant materials and possess a flexible power transmission mechanism such as Bowden cables, air muscles, or shape memory alloys. Soft exoskeletons can be easily customized similar to clothing and can be worn underneath clothing, they are much smaller and lighter in weight, and they require less energy. Furthermore, soft exoskeletons do not significantly constrain the human user and could be significantly less expensive than a rigid exoskeleton. However, providing the needed assistance for movement with soft exoskeletons is a fundamental challenge. Also, soft exoskeletons are much more difficult to control due to their compliant nature and lack of accurate control over position or assistance. Soft exoskeletons have been developed for both the upper (O'Neill, Phipps, Cappello, Paganoni, & Walsh, 2017; Polygerinos, Wang, Galloway, Wood, & Walsh, 2015) and lower limbs (Asbeck et al., 2015) for both medical and performance augmentation applications. A soft robotic *exosuit* has recently been shown to improve walking in subjects post-stroke (Awad et al., 2017) and also to reduce the metabolic cost of running in healthy individuals (Lee et al., 2017).

Actuation

One of the most critical components of an exoskeleton system is the set of actuators that power the system. Actuators introduce a significant amount of weight and inertia to the exoskeleton system to produce the physiological torques needed for the various human joints. However, with improvements in technology and more optimized designs, portable and highly functional devices are being built. While geared electric motors suffer from high reflected inertia and striction and are difficult to backdrive, pneumatic and hydraulic systems suffer from high friction and are very difficult to backdrive. A majority of the current exoskeletons use electric motors, which can be much more accurately controlled for position than other types of actuators. Several existing exoskeletons employ brushless DC motors due to their high torque-to-weight ratio, reduced noise, and reliability. However, current off-the-shelf actuation technology is not directly suitable for force-controlled exoskeletons. Traditionally, force control was achieved with the current control of an electric motor using a direct drive, geared, or low-friction cable drive transmission load cell with force-feedback or with the fluid pressure control of a pneumatic or hydraulic actuator (Arumugom, Muthuraman, & Ponselvan, 2009). A direct drive system operates inefficiently in the low-speed and high-torque regions that are typically required for an exoskeleton system. Furthermore, gearing introduces significant nonlinear friction, which makes it difficult to accurately estimate motor torque using motor current. Also, low-friction cable drive often leads to large-sized pulleys to achieve the required reduction ratio when used with a direct drive motor. A system that uses a stiff load cell to measure the force and use this as feedback suffers from the problem of stability and shock loading.

More recently, series elastic actuators have been developed that introduce a compliant element into transmission, reduce output impedance, and allow for high backdrivability, greater shock tolerance, high fidelity, and stable force control and also the capability of energy storage that can reduce overall power requirements (Pratt & Williamson, 1995). Battery technology that is used to make these systems portable has also improved considerably with the introduction of lithium ion technology, which allows for higher power density with reduced size and weight. In industrial or military applications where heavy lifting is often required, hydraulic actuators are typically used, which allow for a higher power-to-weight ratio than pneumatic or electric actuators. Soft pneumatic actuators have relatively lower weight and also introduce compliance in the transmission.

Sensing

Sensors are essential for control of exoskeleton systems. They are used to measure various physical quantities such as position, force, or torque, and they help regulate the safety of the device and the control variable. Most exoskeletons use position sensing to estimate the configuration of the human limb and to control force or torque in cases where a series elastic actuator is used. Many lower limb exoskeletons use position sensors to accurately track joint angle trajectories for gait training. Some exoskeletons also use force sensors to help detect heel contact and toe-off motion. A few exoskeletons have also leveraged redundant sensing to achieve better estimates for difficult to measure human joint angles (Agarwal, Fox, et al., 2015). Hall effect sensors are used to commutate brushless DC motors for efficient and smooth operation. Accelerometers and gyroscopes are also used to estimate spatial orientation. Other mechanical sensors, such as limit switches, are also used to ensure safe operation of the device. Significant advances have also been made in sensing human intention using neural or muscular sensing. Several research exoskeletons have been developed that measure electromyographic signals from human muscles to detect human intent and then control the exo-skeleton based on this sensed intention using sophisticated control algorithms (Kawamoto, Lee, Kanbe, & Sankai, 2003). A few exoskeletons have also tapped into brain and neural signals to detect intent directly from the brain (Gancet et al., 2012; Kilicarslan, Prasad, Grossman, & Contreras-Vidal, 2013). However, due to the complexity of brain signals and the invasive nature of the sensors needed for reliable sensing, the use of such signals for controlling exoskeletons is very limited (Tucker et al., 2015).

Materials

Another important area that has seen major advancement over the years is the materials that are used to build these devices. The rigidity of the exoskeleton frame determines the accuracy with which the controllers can reliably track a desired trajectory. Most upper and lower body exoskeletons have metal frames. The load-bearing structure is usually created from some type of lightweight aluminum alloy. Titanium, although much more expensive, is a more ideal candidate due to its better strength and lower weight. Fiber-reinforced plastic (e.g., using carbon fiber) is another promising candidate. A few hand exoskeletons also use additive manufacturing, which allows for three-dimensional printing of complex shapes using plastic-, metal-, or rubber-based materials (Agarwal, Fox et al., 2015; Weiss et al., 1997). Additive manufacturing in general has also significantly reduced the time to build prototypes for quick testing due to its ability to rapidly prototype any complex shape when realized in the form of a three-dimensional computer model (Madden & Deshpande, 2015).

Controls

Versatility in the control of wearable exoskeletons is critical to make these devices suitable for operation under the environmental variability or uncer-tainty in which they are typically used. One major variability exists in the as-sistance required from these devices for each human subject. This variability in assistance stems from the fact that the physical characteristics of the human neuromuscular system significantly varies from subject to subject even within the healthy population and even more drastically in the impaired population based on the type and degree of impairment. Furthermore, devices developed specifically for medical applications (e.g., rehabilitation from stroke or spinal cord injury) require that their controller encourage the subject to actively recruit his own neuromuscular system to promote motor recovery. For these reasons, several assist-as-needed controllers have been developed both for upper (Agarwal, Fernandez, & Deshpande, 2015; Pehlivan, Losey, & O'Malley, 2016; Pehlivan, Sergi, & O'Malley, 2015; Wolbrecht, Chan, Reinkensmeyer, & Bobrow, 2008) and lower limb exoskeletons (Banala, Kim, Agrawal, & Scholz, 2009; Wu et al., 2014). Some of these controllers are adaptive in nature and learn subject-specific assistance requirements. They provide assistance according to the needs of the subject and encourage subject participation during training to facilitate motor recovery. A study conducted with chronic stroke survivors with moderate to severe deficit suggested that such controllers may make robotic training more effective than conventional therapy (Reinkensmeyer et al., 2012). Training with such controllers has been shown to help subjects perform better on training tasks (Mao, Jin, Dutta, Scholz, & Agrawal, 2015) and improve gait symmetry (Zanotto, Stegall, & Agrawal, 2014).

CASE STUDIES

Harmony

Approximately 795,000 stroke cases occur every year in the United States, and 84% of stroke survivors suffer from shoulder and arm dysfunction and pain. Recent research showed strong (AHA guideline, Level 1a) evidence that sensorimotor training with robotic devices improves upper extremity functional and motor outcomes for the shoulder and elbow. Rehabilitation hospitals have long been seeking a clinical intervention that would lead to a higher clinical efficacy than conventional care. However, the anatomy of the shoulder is a complex, multidimensional joint, and no commercially available robotic intervention exists to fully address its rehabilitation requirements.

We have developed one of the most sophisticated exoskeletons for shoulder and upper limb rehabilitation, called Harmony (Kim & Deshpande, 2017). The exoskeleton wraps around the subject's shoulders, arms, and wrists and has the capability to power the user's shoulder and arm joints through their natural motions during a wide range of dynamic movement tasks (see Figure 11.5). Specifically, the robot has the ability to move the user's shoulder complex through its natural mobility, including the ability to power the scapulohumeral rhythm (SHR; Kim & Deshpande, 2015).

The exoskeleton is equipped with a suite of sensors that collect motion data at a high speed (2 KHz); these data are fed into the robot's algorithm for instantaneous, responsive control. The data collected with Harmony also serve as biomarkers for monitoring patient progress. With the ability to control the force of its motors, Harmony can be programmed to power the user's motion either gently or firmly. So,

Figure 11.5 Harmony: an upper-body exoskeleton for shoulder and arm rehabilitation after stroke.
Image courtesy of the authors.

by modifying the human–robot interaction, we can make the subject feel varying levels of assistive or resistive forces (e.g., feeling weightless or feeling as if they are moving under water).

A unique and key advantage of Harmony is its ability to provide active assistance to the patient's coordinated movements including SHR around the shoulder, thus addressing a challenging shoulder rehabilitation problem related to flaccidity and spasticity after stroke (see Figure 11.6).

A DETAILED DESCRIPTION OF HARMONY

Harmony is a bilateral device that allows for a wide range of motion in both arms with a compact form factor. Each arm contains a five degrees of freedom (DOF) shoulder arrangement that can actively control both the elevation-depression and protraction-retraction of the shoulder girdle. Each joint of the exoskeleton uses series elastic actuators (Pratt & Williamson, 1995) for torque control with collocated feedback. The exoskeletal design allows us to control both single- and multijoint motions during therapy, including SHR.

Shoulder Biomechanics and Exoskeleton Kinematics. The human shoulder complex consists of four joints (Figure 11.7): (1) the sternoclavicular (SC) joint that connects the clavicle to the sternum, (2) the acromioclavicular (AC) joint that connects the scapula to the clavicle, (3) the scapulothoracic (ST) joint that describes the floating

Figure 11.6 Assistance with Harmony to achieve scapulohumeral rhythm (SHR), (A) healthy SHR, (B) reduced SHR in stroke, and (C) improved SHR.
Images courtesy of the authors.

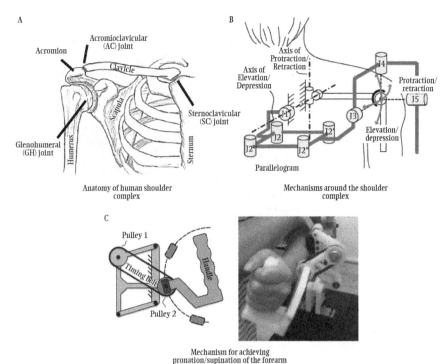

Figure 11.7 Exoskeleton design based on human anatomy to achieve safe, comfortable, and wide-ranging movements.
Reprinted from B. Kim, & A. D. Deshpande, An upper-body rehabilitation exoskeleton Harmony with an anatomical shoulder mechanism: design, modeling, control, and performance evaluation. *The International Journal of Robotics Research,* 2017, SAGE.

motion of scapula over the thoracic cage, and (4) the glenohumeral (GH) joint that connects the humerus (upper arm) to the scapula (or shoulder blade) (Nikooyan, Veeger, Chadwick, Praagman, & Helm, 2011).

The shoulder complex is cooperatively actuated by a number of muscle groups with a variety of insertion points. During arm movements, all four joints go through intricate coordinated motions. For example, when someone raises his arm, the scapula and clavicle rotate upward (van der Helm, 1994). This coordinated motion is SHR. The motion of the humerus accompanies the scapula's internal–external rotation, upward–downward rotation, and anterior–posterior tilt (Ludewig et al., 2009). The wide range of motion of the shoulder complex is a result of the ball-and-socket of the GH joint and rhythmic motion of the shoulder girdle. The coordinated motion of the shoulder girdle and humerus results in translational motion of the GH joint center. For kinematic compatibility with the user, the mechanisms of the exoskeleton around the shoulder must follow the translational motion of the GH joint. We have designed a novel mechanism consisting of two joints for the elevation–depression and protraction–retraction of the GH joint (see joints J1 and J2 in Figure 11.7). In order to avoid locating an actuator above the shoulder, we have designed a parallelogram mechanism located behind the user, which preserves the protraction–retraction motion of the GH joint. The ball-and-socket type motions of the GH joint is actuated by a serial chain of three joints (J3, J4, and J5) that are located at oblique angles to maximize the available range of motion and avoid locked positions.

Kinematics of Elbow and Forearm Mechanisms. We designed one active joint for elbow flexion–extension. With adjustable link lengths in the upper and lower arms, the axis of this joint can be matched precisely with that of the human elbow joint. To support pronation–supination of the forearm, we designed a novel mechanism that consists of a parallelogram and a transmission that transfers the rotation of one link in the parallelogram to the wrist mechanism (Figure 11.7). This results in an adjustable, light, and compact structure and is a better solution than the curved rail bearings used in other arm exoskeletons (Perry et al., 2007).

Kinematic Performance. Harmony is designed to provide a wide range of motion and natural movements of the shoulders, elbows, and wrists. We tested Harmony's performance by moving it through the full range of each joint and to the extremities of its workspace. We also tested the torque generation capabilities of each actuator. The results showed that the performance matches the design specification closely (Kim & Deshpande, 2017). We then tested Harmony's ability to follow natural movements by asking a user to don the exoskeleton and move his arms through their full range of motion. During these tests, the gravity compensation mode was turned on. The exoskeleton was connected to the user with custom cuffs at the wrist and upper arm. The user reported that the exoskeleton did not inhibit motions and that the movements were comfortable. The results show that Harmony supports almost the full range of motion necessary for daily activities, promising a sufficient range of motion in therapeutic training (Kim & Deshpande, 2017). The shoulder girdle mechanism was successfully tested in various movements of the upper arm, including independent shoulder girdle motion and coordinated rhythmic motion (Figure 11.8).

Hand Exoskeleton: Maestro

A disability of the upper extremity limits functional independence in activities of daily living (ADLs) and significantly deteriorates the quality of life of the affected

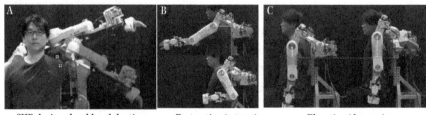

SHR during shoulder abduction   Protraction/retraction   Elevation/depression

Figure 11.8 Harmony achieves coordinated humerus and shoulder girdle movements. Reprinted from B. Kim, & A. D. Deshpande, An upper-body rehabilitation exoskeleton Harmony with an anatomical shoulder mechanism: design, modeling, control, and performance evaluation. *The International Journal of Robotics Research,* 2017, SAGE.

individual (Williams, Weinberger, Harris, Clark, & Biller, 1999). Maestro is an exoskeleton developed for rehabilitation of the hands from impairments caused by stroke and spinal cord injury (Figure 11.9; Agarwal, Fox et al., 2015; Agarwal, Yun, Fox, Madden, & Deshpande, 2017). Another variant of Maestro has been developed as an assistive device that could assist subjects in performing ADLs (Yun et al., 2017). Maestro consists of three exoskeleton modules to actively assist the index and middle fingers and the thumb. Each finger module has two actuated DOFs to assist the flexion–extension motion at the metacarpophalangeal (MCP) and proximal interphalangeal (PIP) joints of the finger (Figure 11.9B). In addition, a passive DOF for finger adduction–abduction motion is implemented in the MCP chain that allows for lateral movement of the index finger during flexion–extension motion. The thumb module has four actuated DOFs to actively assist the flexion–extension and abduction–adduction motion at the carpometacarpal (CMC) joint and flexion–extension motion at the MCP and interphalangeal (IP) joints of the thumb (Figure 11.9C). The kinematics of the device is designed to ensure low induced finger joint reaction forces during the operation of the device. Each active joint is actuated using a four-bar mechanism to avoid finger–exoskeleton axes misalignment. The kinematic mechanism of Maestro has been optimized to achieve large range of motion at both the finger and thumb joints for different hand sizes. Furthermore, the design has adjustable link lengths to further customize the mechanism for a specific hand size to maximize the range of motion for the hand digits.

One of the unique features of Maestro that distinguishes it from other hand exoskeletons is its capability to apply accurate pressure on the hand digits (torque control) similar to a therapist. Most of the other existing hand exoskeletons control the position of the hand digits without taking into account the amount of effort it takes to position the digit in the desired configuration (position control). These position-controlled devices can potentially be unsafe for rehabilitation and assistive applications because the method of control could lead to the application of too much force on the finger phalanges in the event of an occasionally stalled joint (Agarwal & Deshpande, 2015). A stalled joint is a potential risk during therapy due to the nature of impairment, such as spastic catch phenomena and the changing nature of spasms in spastic finger muscles (Dromerick, 2002) or due to inflammatory joint disease such as rheumatoid arthritis (Chillag & Greenberg, 2011). Furthermore, for effective rehabilitation, the literature suggests that the subject should actively participate in the therapy task for maximal recovery. Torque-controlled devices like Maestro allow for sharing of the effort required to perform the task since there is direct control over the amount of assistance provided by the device. Position-controlled devices, on the other hand, do not allow such sharing of the effort as the device has no control over the forces it applies on the hand digits. This makes the use of position-controlled devices less effective than torque-controlled devices for such applications. Furthermore, torque-controlled devices can implement more sophisticated control algorithms (e.g., assist-as-needed control) to further facilitate recovery of hand function using principles of motor learning (Agarwal & Deshpande, 2015; Agarwal, Fernandez, & Deshpande, 2015).

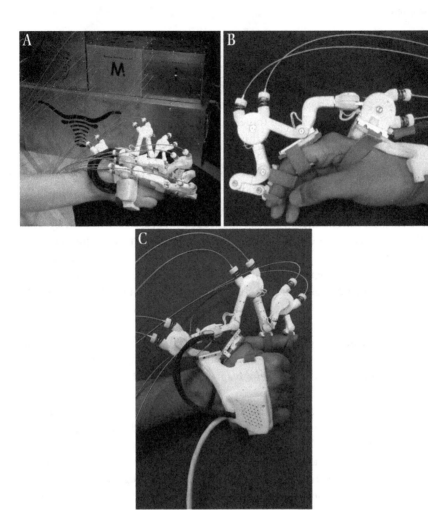

Figure 11.9 The full setup and two different modules of the hand exoskeleton system, Maestro. (A) Full setup of Maestro including the exoskeleton and the actuation and control units. (A) The small metal boxes at the top are the actuator boxes that house the motors that power the three digits of Maestro. The large metal box is the control box that houses the controller and power supplies for the motors. (B) The finger module of Maestro with two degrees of freedom (DOFs.) (C) The thumb module on Maestro with four actuated DOFs.

Torque control in Maestro is achieved using miniature Bowden cable–based series elastic actuators that are specifically developed to achieve bidirectional torque control in the limited space available on a hand exoskeleton (Agarwal et al., 2017). These actuators also make the device highly backdrivable while keeping the reflected inertia low. Each actuated joint consists of a pulley with a cable attached on the circumference of the pulley. The Bowden cable consists of a metal sheath with a stainless steel wire rope to allow for the transmission of required mechanical power to the device. There is a compression spring attached to the sheath at each end, connected to the joint pulley. When the motor actuates the pulley, it first compresses the spring. The introduction of the passive series elastic element in the transmission mechanism provides a means for accurately estimating cable tension using the joint displacement measurements obtained using the magnetic angle sensor mounted at the joint and the motor encoder. Performance characterization of the series elastic actuator shows that the actuator has adequate torque source quality (RMSE <10% of peak torque) with high fidelity (>97% at 0.5 Hz torque sinusoid), a force tracking bandwidth of 10 Hz (@ 0.5 Nm peak torque) and a peak torque of 0.7 Nm.

The various parts of Maestro are manufactured using an additive manufacturing technique called *selective laser sintering* (SLS), which allows for quick prototyping while providing the flexibility of further customizing the design for a specific subject. Remote actuation along with SLS using Nylon 11 significantly reduces the overall weight (~300 g) of the device. The design also allows for the easy replacement of its stiffness elements (for adjusting the achievable torque range specific to a subject) without having to remove the cables. The sliding and revolute joints were realized using ultra-miniature linear and rotary ball bearings. For components with significant loading, off-the-shelf steel parts (e.g., shafts) are used to reduce size and avoid excessive deformation. The entire chain is grounded on the exoskeleton base, which is attached to the wearer's hand with a Velcro strap. In addition, a high-density rubber foam is attached to the base to provide comfort for the wearer. Slots are provided on the base such that the attachment of the entire chain can be adjusted both in longitudinal and lateral directions as well as in angular positions to adapt to the index finger size and natural position of the wearer. A magnetoresistive angle sensor module (KMA210, NXP Semiconductors) with a diametrically magnetized ring magnet is used as a joint angle sensor. The ring magnet casing is built into the corresponding link with the sensor attached to the link moving relative to the previous one. The device has five angle sensors to collect data from five joint angles with one redundant sensor. This redundant information is used to estimate the kinematic parameters of the coupled finger–exoskeleton system in situ. Several controllers have also been developed for Maestro, including impedance control (Agarwal & Deshpande, 2015) and some subject-specific assist-as-needed controllers (Agarwal, Fernandez et al., 2015) for efficacious rehabilitation using the device.

ONGOING CHALLENGES AND FUTURE DIRECTIONS

Current Challenges in Exoskeleton Design

Despite great progress in the design and development of robotic exoskeletons, there are several challenges yet to be addressed. The major challenges lie in the areas of actuator design, brain-to-machine communication and intent detection, mechanical interface design, and intuitive control.

The actuators used to power these exoskeletons have limited torque and power density and are inefficient, which make these devices heavy, unnatural in shape, and noisy. There is a need to develop compact, efficient, and high power density actuators that could result in effective exoskeleton designs, especially for the lower extremity. Electroactive polymers are a promising technology that could act as artificial muscles; however, several technical challenges related to their durability, lifetime, and scalability need to be addressed before they can be implemented in these devices (Herr & Kornbluh, 2004; Mulgaonkar, Kornbluh, & Herr, 2008).

Another major challenge is the lack of direct communication between the user's nervous system and the device. Such an information exchange is needed for human intent detection and is essential for fluid and symbiotic interaction. Recent advances in brain–machine interface, EEG using electrodes placed on the scalp or neural implants in the motor cortex, and electromyographic sensors to measure muscle activity have recently begun to address this limitation (Kwak, Müller, & Lee, 2015; Soekadar et al., 2016).

The mechanical interface of current exoskeletons also limits the time for which these devices can be worn by the user due to discomfort. This is in part due to the challenging design, which either requires careful alignment of the human anatomical joint axes and the robot joint axes or by addressing the misalignment without overly complicating the design. The problem is further complicated by the fact that human joints do not behave like ideal primitive joints but rather have a complex kinematic nature in which nonstationary joint axes that are nonintersecting and nonorthogonal could be present. The physical interface that connects to the human body also contributes to discomfort due to the limited choice of materials that could reliably transfer the load through the interface without chafing the skin. This challenge is being addressed by designing user-specific custom interfaces. The rapid advancement in additive manufacturing technology has facilitated the development of such custom interfaces in recent years.

Another critical challenge is the design of controllers that allow for natural and intuitive control of these highly articulate robotic systems. The literature shows that, for rehabilitation robots, force control–based strategies can be more effective for recovery of both the upper (Blank, French, Pehlivan, & O'Malley, 2014; Colombo et al., 2005; Pehlivan et al., 2015) and lower limbs (Cai et al., 2006; Marchal-Crespo & Reinkensmeyer, 2009) than pure position-based control (Harwin, Rahman, & Foulds, 1995). This is because force control–based strategies allow for safe and comfortable interaction, and these can be designed to encourage subject involvement. Such a therapy is shown to be more effective than passive motor training even for a longer duration (Lotze, Braun, Birbaumer, Anders, & Cohen, 2003) and is considered to be essential for provoking motor plasticity (Perez, Lungholt, Nyborg, & Nielsen, 2004). Position control–based strategies, on the other hand, physically guide the movement of the impaired limb to strictly follow a predefined trajectory without enabling the subject to actively participate in the task (Bernhardt, Frey, Colombo, & Riener, 2005) or allowing for any subject-specific customization of the assistance (Meng et al., 2015). The guidance hypothesis in motor control research suggests that such a physically guided movement may decrease motor learning for some tasks due to the reduction in burden (motor output, effort, energy consumption, or attention) on the subject's motor system, which is needed to discover the principles necessary to perform the task successfully (Schmidt & Bjork, 1992). Furthermore, some impairments (e.g., spasticity) lead to uncertain motion of the limbs. This uncertainty requires that, during rehabilitation therapy, appropriate forces are applied on the limb rather than simply moving it through some predetermined positions, which can lead to the application of large forces and further harm the body. For lower limb exoskeletons, the more specific challenge is in developing an assistive strategy that could provide efficient and natural assistance while maintaining the balance of the wearer. None of the existing lower limb exoskeletons has so far demonstrated a significant decrease in the metabolic demands of walking or running (Herr, 2009).

Ethical, Social, and Legal Considerations

The use of exoskeletons raises several ethical and social concerns due to the nature of their being so closely integrated with the human body and becoming a part of life for an impaired individual (Greenbaum, 2016). The prohibitive costs of the currently commercialized exoskeletons for rehabilitation or assistive applications discourage insurers from covering the cost of such devices. This raises the question of unequal accessibility of this technology for different classes of society. The use of exoskeletons for military or industrial applications with the aim of augmenting human capability raises questions of treating humans like machines and has its own ethical concerns. The issues related to costs and ready accessibility of such technology will subside once devices are mass-produced and become cheaper. Nevertheless, the question of using devices capable of enhancing human performance raises complex and long-term questions about redefining humanity and self that need to be addressed by society as a whole. Currently, literature on the ethical, social, and legal aspects of this useful technology is scarce, and these issues are not addressed with due diligence.

One of the central ideas dealing with the various legal, social, and ethical issues related to exoskeletons is the definition of human enhancement. Currently, there is no legal definition of what is considered human enhancement. Specifically, it is unclear when an exoskeleton, integrated either externally or internally, should be considered an extension of the individual and therefore an enhancement rather than a mere external tool. Some arguments suggest that an "always on" feature or alterations for therapeutic reasons could be used to distinguish enhancement from a socially acceptable form of technology. However, corrective lenses might also be considered enhancement under the "always on" philosophy. In addition, therapeutic alterations could enhance an individual's ability beyond the norm, in which case the technology again moves into the questionable realm of an enhancement.

There are three main schools of thought regarding the nature of regulations on such technology. The group consisting of trans-humanists argue that limiting the use of technology to enhance one's body would discourage research and development of this new technology and would be in contradiction to the basic right to control one's own body. Those who are not a proponent of technology argue that strict regulations are needed for any technology related to human enhancement to avoid potential side effects and social disharmony. There are also those who stand in between and argue in favor of establishing regulations that abide by basic human rights. Among this ambiguity in the definition of human enhancement, it is difficult to understand where exoskeletons stand. However, being robotic devices, exoskeletons are regulated by the robot-specific laws that exist in several US states.

There are also several ethical concerns that arise in the use of exoskeletons, especially in the industrial and military domains, including the risk of dehumanizing the human workers and soldiers who are using exoskeletons. In these domains, supervisors could exploit workers or soldiers by overworking them under the impression that exoskeletons provide them with enhanced physical abilities. Furthermore, soldiers could be used to test these devices or be put into dangerous situation solely relying on their enhanced physical capabilities. The use of exoskeletons in sports have also raised concerns regarding the true ability of an athlete as opposed to that gained due to enhancement and the fair use of this technology to keep the spirit of the sport alive. It is also important to realize that most talented athletes perform well not only due to hard work and practice but also in part due to the naturally superior genes they are born with.

Among the social concerns, the primary one is that of equal opportunity to access this costly technology, which might only be available to those who could afford it. This raises the question of the right to technology as a social justice concern, especially for the disabled, to level the playing field. There are also concerns regarding readily available exoskeletons that could result in too much reliance on technology and concerns that their limited availability in certain scenarios could have psychosocial repercussions. Other concerns are related to defining ableness and disability in the context of humans enhanced with exoskeletons. Should such individuals still be considered disabled when they have regained the ability to walk or be mobile to some extent?

The use of exoskeletons also raises some interesting legal issues. For example, should an individual be charged with a crime if an accident occurs while the individual is using the device? The motivation behind the accident may be difficult to analyze due to the autonomous or semi-autonomous nature of the device. These issues will be further confounded as these devices integrate directly at the neural level where an unconscious or subconscious intention might result in a wrongful action. There are also privacy concerns regarding how the data collected by the device about a specific individual could be used. Furthermore, should workers using exoskeletons be compensated differently than those who do not use such devices?

Challenges in Exoskeleton Effectiveness

One of the challenges associated with the acceptance of exoskeletons, especially for rehabilitation and assistive purposes, is the fact that the conclusive demonstration of their effectiveness has yet not been established. Studies involving both upper and lower limb exoskeletons have shown that, even though robot-assisted therapy results in improvements similar to that of conventional therapy, no significant improvement in ADL function is observed with the use of these devices so far. One factor that might be responsible for this poor translation of improvement to functional scores is the fact that the ADL scales used in these studies are highly subjective, do not have the resolution to capture the improvement in function, and suffer from interrater reliability. The functional tests typically used to assess improvement in performance require performing ADLs, which require function not only at the muscular level but also at the neural level to achieve the level of coordination and skill required to perform these tasks. Often, these studies do not provide sufficient therapy to participating subjects due to the time and resources required to conduct experiments with impaired individuals on hardware-intensive research prototypes of these devices. Thus, there is need to develop more test scales that are objective and could quantitatively capture all the nuances of recovery.

THE FUTURE OF EXOSKELETONS

With advances in materials research, increased computational power, and better understanding of the neuromuscular system and neuromotor control of human movement, more advanced and sophisticated exoskeletons will be built that could fluidly support human motion and augment human capability beyond imagination. It would not be misleading to speculate that such devices could someday be ubiquitous. These sophisticated machines could transform today's disabled into tomorrow's super-abled.

ACKNOWLEDGMENTS

This work was supported, in part, by the National Science Foundation (NSF) grant CNS-1135949 and National Aeronautics and Space Administration (NASA) grant NNX12AM03G. The contents are solely the responsibility of the authors and do not necessarily represent the official views of the NSF or NASA.

REFERENCES

Ada, L., Dean, C. M., Vargas, J., & Ennis, S. (2010). Mechanically assisted walking with body weight support results in more independent walking than assisted overground walking in non-ambulatory patients early after stroke: A systematic review. *Journal of Physiotherapy, 56*(3), 153–161.

Agarwal, P., & Deshpande, A. D. (2015). Impedance and force-field control of the index finger module of a hand exoskeleton for rehabilitation. *2015 IEEE International*

Conference on Rehabilitation Robotics (ICORR), pp. 85–90. Retrieved from http://ieeexplore.ieee.org/abstract/document/7281180/

Agarwal, P., Fernandez, B., & Deshpande, A. D. (2015). Assist-as-needed controllers for index finger module of a hand exoskeleton for rehabilitation. *Proceedings of the ASME 2015 Dynamic Systems and Control Conference DSCC*. doi:10.1115/DSCC2015-9790

Agarwal, P., Fox, J., Yun, Y., O'Malley, M. K., & Deshpande, A. D. (2015). An index finger exoskeleton with series elastic actuation for rehabilitation: Design, control and performance characterization. *The International Journal of Robotics Research*, 34(14), 1747–1772.

Agarwal, P., Yun, Y., Fox, J., Madden, K., & Deshpande, A. D. (2017). Design, control, and testing of a thumb exoskeleton with series elastic actuation. *The International Journal of Robotics Research*, 36(3), 355–375.

Arazpour, M., Samadian, M., Bahramizadeh, M., Joghtaei, M., Maleki, M., Bani, M. A., & Hutchins, S. W. (2015). The efficiency of orthotic interventions on energy consumption in paraplegic patients: A literature review. *Spinal Cord*, 53(3), 168.

Armeo®Power [Apparatus]. (2017). Norwell, MA: Hocoma Inc., USA (https://www.hocoma.com/us/).

Arumugom, S., Muthuraman, S., & Ponselvan, V. (2009). Modeling and application of series elastic actuators for force control multi legged robots. *Journal of Computing*, 1(1), 26–33.

Asbeck, A. T., De Rossi, S. M., Holt, K. G., & Walsh, C. J. (2015). A biologically inspired soft exosuit for walking assistance. *The International Journal of Robotics Research*, 34(6), 744–762.

Awad, L. N., Bae, J., O'Donnell, K., De Rossi, S. M. M., Hendron, K., Sloot, L. H., . . . Walsh, C. J. (2017). A soft robotic exosuit improves walking in patients after stroke. *Science Translational Medicine*, 9(400), eaai9084. doi:10.1126/scitranslmed.aai9084

Banala, S. K., Kim, S. H., Agrawal, S. K., & Scholz, J. P. (2009). Robot assisted gait training with active leg exoskeleton (ALEX). *IEEE Transactions on Neural Systems and Rehabilitation Engineering*, 17(1), 2–8.

Bernhardt, M., Frey, M., Colombo, G., & Riener, R. (2005). Hybrid force-position control yields cooperative behaviour of the rehabilitation robot LOKOMAT. *ICORR 2005: 9th International Conference on Rehabilitation Robotics*, 536–539. doi:10.1109/ICORR.2005.1501159

Blank, A. A., French, J. A., Pehlivan, A. U., & O'Malley, M. K. (2014). Current trends in robot-assisted upper-limb stroke rehabilitation: Promoting patient engagement in therapy. *Current Physical Medicine and Rehabilitation Reports*, 2(3), 184–195.

Bogue, R. (2009). Exoskeletons and robotic prosthetics: A review of recent developments. *Industrial Robot: An International Journal*, 36(5), 421–427. https://doi.org/10.1108/01439910910980141

Cai, L. L., Fong, A. J., Otoshi, C. K., Liang, Y., Burdick, J. W., Roy, R. R., & Edgerton, V. R. (2006). Implications of assist-as-needed robotic step training after a complete spinal cord injury on intrinsic strategies of motor learning. *Journal of Neuroscience*, 26(41), 10564–10568.

Chillag, S. A., & Greenberg, S. (2011). An unusual cause of trigger finger. New England Journal of Medicine, 365(7), e14.

Colombo, R., Pisano, F., Micera, S., Mazzone, A., Delconte, C., Carrozza, M. C., . . . Minuco, G. (2005). Robotic techniques for upper limb evaluation and rehabilitation of stroke patients. *IEEE Transactions on Neural Systems and Rehabilitation Engineering, 13*(3), 311–324.

Dobkin, B. H., & Duncan, P. W. (2012). Should body weight–supported treadmill training and robotic-assistive steppers for locomotor training trot back to the starting gate? *Neurorehabilitation and Neural Repair, 26*(4), 308–317.

Dromerick, A. W. (2002). Clinical features of spasticity and principles of treatment. In Clinical evaluation and management of spasticity (pp. 13–26). Humana Press, Totowa, NJ.

Ellis, E. S. (2016). *The Steam Man of the Prairies*. Courier Dover Publications. Retrieved from https://books.google.com/books?hl=en&lr=&id=8WjiCwAAQBAJ&oi=fnd&pg=PA1&dq=The+Steam+Man+of+the+Prairies&ots=39f5iayJ2x&sig=vFZOv7brfTzlEDy_tfaSamGgaqY

EksoGT [Apparatus]. (2017). Richmond, CA: Ekso Bionics® (http://eksobionics.com/).

Federici, S., Meloni, F., Bracalenti, M., & De Filippis, M. L. (2015). The effectiveness of powered, active lower limb exoskeletons in neurorehabilitation: A systematic review. *NeuroRehabilitation, 37*(3), 321–340.

Gancet, J., Ilzkovitz, M., Motard, E., Nevatia, Y., Letier, P., de Weerdt, D., . . . Thorsteinsson, F. (2012). MINDWALKER: Going one step further with assistive lower limbs exoskeleton for SCI condition subjects. *4th IEEE RAS & EMBS International Conference on Biomedical Robotics and Biomechatronics*, 1794–1800. doi:10.1109/BioRob.2012.6290688

Garcia, E., Sater, J. M., & Main, J. (2002). Exoskeletons for human performance augmentation (EHPA): A program summary. *Journal of the Robotics Society of Japan, 20*(8), 822–826.

Greenbaum, D. (2016). Ethical, legal and social concerns relating to exoskeletons. *ACM SIGCAS Computers and Society, 45*(3), 234–239.

Guizzo, E., & Goldstein, H. (2005). The rise of the body bots. *IEEE SPECTRUM, 42*(10), 42.

Hand of Hope [Apparatus]. (2017). Hong Kong S. A. R., China: Rehab-Robotics (http://www.rehab-robotics.com/index.html).

Harwin, W. S., Rahman, T., & Foulds, R. A. (1995). A review of design issues in rehabilitation robotics with reference to North American research. *IEEE Transactions on Rehabilitation Engineering, 3*(1), 3–13.

Herr, H. (2009). Exoskeletons and orthoses: Classification, design challenges and future directions. *Journal of Neuroengineering and Rehabilitation, 6*(1), 21.

Herr, H., & Kornbluh, R. D. (2004). New horizons for orthotic and prosthetic technology: Artificial muscle for ambulation. In *Proceedings of SPIE* (Vol. 5385). Retrieved from http://proceedings.spiedigitallibrary.org/pdfaccess.ashx?url=/data/conferences/spiep/23310/1_1.pdf

Hidler, J., Nichols, D., Pelliccio, M., Brady, K., Campbell, D. D., Kahn, J. H., & Hornby, T. G. (2009). Multicenter randomized clinical trial evaluating the effectiveness of the Lokomat in subacute stroke. *Neurorehabilitation and Neural Repair, 23*(1), 5–13.

Hornby, T. G., Holleran, C. L., Hennessy, P. W., Leddy, A. L., Connolly, M., Camardo, J., . . . Roth, E. J. (2016). Variable Intensive early walking poststroke (VIEWS): A randomized controlled trial. *Neurorehabilitation and Neural Repair, 30*(5), 440–450.

Ishii, M., Yamamoto, K., & Hyodo, K. (2005). Stand-alone wearable power assist suit–development and availability. *Journal of Robotics and Mechatronics, 17*(5), 575–583.

Jacobsen, S. C., Olivier, M., Smith, F. M., Knutti, D. F., Johnson, R. T., Colvin, G. E., & Scroggin, W. B. (2004). Research robots for applications in artificial intelligence, teleoperation and entertainment. *The International Journal of Robotics Research, 23*(4–5), 319–330.

Kawamoto, H., Lee, S., Kanbe, S., & Sankai, Y. (2003). Power assist method for HAL-3 using EMG-based feedback controller. In *Systems, Man and Cybernetics, 2003. IEEE International Conference on* (Vol. 2, pp. 1648–1653). IEEE. Retrieved from http://ieeexplore.ieee.org/abstract/document/1244649/

Kawamoto, H., & Sankai, Y. (2002). Power assist system HAL-3 for gait disorder person. *Computers Helping People with Special Needs*, 19–29.

Kazerooni, H., Strausser, K., Zoss, A., & Swift, T. (2011). *Human Machine Interfaces for Lower Extremity Orthotics*. Google Patents.

Kilicarslan, A., Prasad, S., Grossman, R. G., & Contreras-Vidal, J. L. (2013). High accuracy decoding of user intentions using EEG to control a lower-body exoskeleton. In *Engineering in Medicine and Biology Society (EMBC), 2013 35th Annual International Conference of the IEEE* (pp. 5606–5609). IEEE. Retrieved from http://ieeexplore.ieee.org/abstract/document/6610821/

Kim, B., & Deshpande, A. D. (2015). Controls for the shoulder mechanism of an upper-body exoskeleton for promoting scapulohumeral rhythm. *2015 IEEE International Conference on Rehabilitation Robotics (ICORR)*, 538–542. IEEE. Retrieved from http://ieeexplore.ieee.org/xpls/abs_all.jsp?arnumber=7281255

Kim, B., & Deshpande, A. D. (2017). An upper-body rehabilitation exoskeleton Harmony with an anatomical shoulder mechanism: Design, modeling, control, and performance evaluation. *The International Journal of Robotics Research*, https://doi.org/10.1177/0278364917706743.

Kwak, N.-S., Müller, K.-R., & Lee, S.-W. (2015). A lower limb exoskeleton control system based on steady state visual evoked potentials. *Journal of Neural Engineering, 12*(5), 056009.

Lee, G., Kim, J., Panizzolo, F. A., Zhou, Y. M., Baker, L. M., Galiana, I., . . . Walsh, C. J. (2017). Reducing the metabolic cost of running with a tethered soft exosuit. *Science Robotics, 2*(6), eaan6708.

Lotze, M., Braun, C., Birbaumer, N., Anders, S., & Cohen, L. G. (2003). Motor learning elicited by voluntary drive. *Brain, 126*(4), 866–872.

Louie, D. R., Eng, J. J., & Lam, T. (2015). Gait speed using powered robotic exoskeletons after spinal cord injury: A systematic review and correlational study. *Journal of Neuroengineering and Rehabilitation, 12*(1), 82.

Ludewig, P. M., Phadke, V., Braman, J. P., Hassett, D. R., Cieminski, C. J., & LaPrade, R. F. (2009). Motion of the shoulder complex during multiplanar humeral elevation. *The Journal of Bone and Joint Surgery. American Volume, 91*(2), 378.

Madden, K. E., & Deshpande, A. D. (2015). On integration of additive manufacturing during the design and development of a rehabilitation robot: A case study. *Journal of Mechanical Design, 137*(11), 111417–111417. https://doi.org/10.1115/1.4031123

Mao, Y., Jin, X., Dutta, G. G., Scholz, J. P., & Agrawal, S. K. (2015). Human movement training with a cable driven arm exoskeleton (CAREX). *IEEE Transactions on Neural Systems and Rehabilitation Engineering, 23*(1), 84–92.

Marchal-Crespo, L., & Reinkensmeyer, D. J. (2009). Review of control strategies for robotic movement training after neurologic injury. *Journal of Neuroengineering and Rehabilitation, 6*, 20. https://doi.org/10.1186/1743-0003-6-20

Mehrholz, J., Elsner, B., Werner, C., Kugler, J., & Pohl, M. (2013). Electromechanical-assisted training for walking after stroke. *Stroke, 44*(10), e127–e128.

Mehrholz, J., Haedrich, A., Platz, T., Kugler, J., & Pohl, M. (2012). Electromechanical and robot-assisted arm training for improving generic activities of daily living, arm function, and arm muscle strength after stroke. *The Cochrane Library*. Retrieved from http://onlinelibrary.wiley.com/doi/10.1002/14651858.CD006876.pub3/full

Meng, W., Liu, Q., Zhou, Z., Ai, Q., Sheng, B., & Xie, S. S. (2015). Recent development of mechanisms and control strategies for robot-assisted lower limb rehabilitation. *Mechatronics, 31*, 132–145.

Mosher, R. S. (1967). *Handyman to hardiman*. SAE Technical Paper. Retrieved from http://papers.sae.org/670088/

Mozaffarian, D., Benjamin, E. J., Go, A. S., Arnett, D. K., Blaha, M. J., Cushman, M., Das, S. R., de Ferranti, S., Després, J. P., Fullerton, H. J., & Howard, V. J. (2015). Heart disease and stroke statistics—2015 update: A report from the American Heart Association. *Circulation, 131*(4), e29.

Mulgaonkar, A., Kornbluh, R., & Herr, H. (2008). A new frontier for orthotics and prosthetics: Application of dielectric elastomer actuators to bionics. *Dielectric Elastomers as Electromechanical Transducers: Fundamentals, Materials, Devices, Models and Applications of an Emerging Electroactive Polymer Technology*, 193–206.

Nef, T., Guidali, M., & Riener, R. (2009). ARMin III—Arm therapy exoskeleton with an ergonomic shoulder actuation. *Applied Bionics and Biomechanics, 6*(2), 127–142.

Nikooyan, A. A., Veeger, H. E. J., Chadwick, E. K. J., Praagman, M., & Helm, F. C. T. van der. (2011). Development of a comprehensive musculoskeletal model of the shoulder and elbow. *Medical & Biological Engineering & Computing, 49*(12), 1425–1435. https://doi.org/10.1007/s11517-011-0839-7

O'Neill, C., T., Phipps, N. S., Cappello, L., Paganoni, S., & Walsh, C. J. (2017). A soft wearable robot for the shoulder: Design, characterization, and preliminary testing. Presented at the IEEE International Conference on Rehabilitation Robotics (ICORR), London, UK. Retrieved from https://scholar.google.com/scholar?hl=en&as_sdt=0%2C44&q=A+soft+wearable+robot+for+the+shoulder%3A+Design%2C+characterization%2C+and+preliminary+testing&btnG=

Pehlivan, A. U., Losey, D. P., & O'Malley, M. K. (2016). Minimal assist-as-needed controller for upper limb robotic rehabilitation. *IEEE Transactions on Robotics, 32*(1), 113–124. https://doi.org/10.1109/TRO.2015.2503726

Pehlivan, A. U., Sergi, F., & O'Malley, M. K. (2015). A subject-adaptive controller for wrist robotic rehabilitation. *IEEE/ASME Transactions on Mechatronics, 20*(3), 1338–1350.

Perez, M. A., Lungholt, B. K., Nyborg, K., & Nielsen, J. B. (2004). Motor skill training induces changes in the excitability of the leg cortical area in healthy humans. *Experimental Brain Research, 159*(2), 197–205.

Perry, J. C., Rosen, J., & Burns, S. (2007). Upper-limb powered exoskeleton design. *IEEE/ASME Transactions on Mechatronics, 12*(4), 408–417.

Polygerinos, P., Wang, Z., Galloway, K. C., Wood, R. J., & Walsh, C. J. (2015). Soft robotic glove for combined assistance and at-home rehabilitation. *Robotics and Autonomous Systems, 73*, 135–143.

Pons, J. L. (2008). *Wearable Robots: Biomechatronic Exoskeletons*. West Sussex, UK: Wiley.

Pratt, G. A., & Williamson, M. M. (1995). Series elastic actuators. *Proceedings 1995 IEEE/ RSJ International Conference on Intelligent Robots and Systems, 1*, 399–406. doi:10.1109/ IROS.1995.525827

Reinkensmeyer, D. J., Wolbrecht, E. T., Chan, V., Chou, C., Cramer, S. C., & Bobrow, J. E. (2012). Comparison of 3D, assist-as-needed robotic arm/hand movement training provided with Pneu-WREX to conventional table top therapy following chronic stroke. *American Journal of Physical Medicine & Rehabilitation/Association of Academic Physiatrists, 91*(11 0 3), S232.

REX [Apparatus]. (2017). Auckland, New Zealand: Rex Bionics, Ltd (https://www. rexbionics.com/us/).

Sale, P., Franceschini, M., Waldner, A., & Hesse, S. (2012). Use of the robot assisted gait therapy in rehabilitation of patients with stroke and spinal cord injury. *European Journal of Physical and Rehabilitation Medicine, 48*(1), 111–121.

Sankai, Y. (2010). HAL: Hybrid assistive limb based on cybernics. In M. Kaneko & Y. Nakamura (Eds.), *Robotics Research*, Springer Tracts in Advanced Robotics (Vol 66, pp. 25–34). Berlin: Springer.

Schmidt, R. A., & Bjork, R. A. (1992). New conceptualizations of practice: Common principles in three paradigms suggest new concepts for training. *Psychological Science, 3*(4), 207–218.

Soekadar, S. R., Witkowski, M., Gómez, C., Opisso, E., Medina, J., Cortese, M., . . . Vitiello, N. (2016). Hybrid EEG/EOG-based brain/neural hand exoskeleton restores fully in-dependent daily living activities after quadriplegia. *Science Robotics, 1*(1), eaag3296.

States, R. A., Salem, Y., & Pappas, E. (2009). Overground gait training for individuals with chronic stroke: A Cochrane systematic review. *Journal of Neurologic Physical Therapy, 33*(4), 179–186.

Talaty, M., Esquenazi, A., & Briceno, J. E. (2013). Differentiating ability in users of the Rewalk™ powered exoskeleton: An analysis of walking kinematics. 2013 IEEE International Conference on Rehabilitation Robotics (ICORR), IEEE, pp 1–5.

Tucker, M. R., Olivier, J., Pagel, A., Bleuler, H., Bouri, M., Lambercy, O., . . . Gassert, R. (2015). Control strategies for active lower extremity prosthetics and orthotics: A re-view. *Journal of Neuroengineering and Rehabilitation, 12*(1), 1.

Turchetti, G., Vitiello, N., Romiti, S., Geisler, E., & Micera, S. (2014). Why effectiveness of robot-mediated neurorehabilitation does not necessarily influence its adoption. *IEEE Reviews in Biomedical Engineering, 7*, 143–153.

Ueki, S., Kawasaki, H., Ito, S., Nishimoto, Y., Abe, M., Aoki, T., . . . Mouri, T. (2012). Development of a hand-assist robot with multi-degrees-of-freedom for rehabilitation therapy. *IEEE/ASME Transactions on Mechatronics, 17*(1), 136–146.

van der Helm, F. C. T. (1994). Analysis of the kinematic and dynamic behavior of the shoulder mechanism. *Journal of Biomechanics, 27*(5), 527–550. https://doi.org/ 10.1016/0021-9290(94)90064-7

Vukobratovic, M. K. (2007). When were active exoskeletons actually born? *International Journal of Humanoid Robotics, 4*(03), 459–486.

Wall, A., Borg, J., & Palmcrantz, S. (2015). Clinical application of the Hybrid Assistive Limb (HAL) for gait training—a systematic review. *Frontiers in Systems Neuroscience, 9*. Retrieved from https://www.ncbi.nlm.nih.gov/pmc/articles/PMC4373251/

Weiss, L. E., Merz, R., Prinz, F. B., Neplotnik, G., Padmanabhan, P., Schultz, L., & Ramaswami, K. (1997). Shape deposition manufacturing of heterogeneous structures. *Journal of Manufacturing Systems, 16*(4), 239–248.

Williams, L. S., Weinberger, M., Harris, L. E., Clark, D. O., & Biller, J. (1999). Development of a stroke-specific quality of life scale. *Stroke, 30*(7), 1362–1369.

Wolbrecht, E. T., Chan, V., Reinkensmeyer, D. J., & Bobrow, J. E. (2008). Optimizing compliant, model-based robotic assistance to promote neurorehabilitation. *IEEE Transactions on Neural Systems and Rehabilitation Engineering, 16*(3), 286–297.

Wu, M., Landry, J. M., Kim, J., Schmit, B. D., Yen, S.-C., & MacDonald, J. (2014). Robotic resistance/assistance training improves locomotor function in individuals poststroke: A randomized controlled study. *Archives of Physical Medicine and Rehabilitation, 95*(5), 799–806. https://doi.org/10.1016/j.apmr.2013.12.021

XOS 2 [Apparatus]. (2017). Salt Lake City, UT: Sarcos (https://www.sarcos.com/).

Yamamoto, K., Hyodo, K., Ishii, M., & Matsuo, T. (2002). Development of power assisting suit for assisting nurse labor. *JSME International Journal Series C Mechanical Systems, Machine Elements and Manufacturing, 45*(3), 703–711.

Yan, T., Cempini, M., Oddo, C. M., & Vitiello, N. (2015). Review of assistive strategies in powered lower-limb orthoses and exoskeletons. *Robotics and Autonomous Systems, 64*, 120–136.

Yun, Y., Dancausse, S., Esmatloo, P., Serrato, A., Merring, C., Agarwal, P., & Deshpande, A. D. (2017). Maestro: An EMG-driven assistive hand exoskeleton for spinal cord injury patients. *IEEE International Conference on Robotics and Automation*, 2904–2910. doi:10.1109/ICRA.2017.7989337

Zanotto, D., Stegall, P., & Agrawal, S. K. (2014). Adaptive assist-as-needed controller to improve gait symmetry in robot-assisted gait training. *2014 IEEE International Conference on Robotics and Automation*, 724–729. doi:10.1109/ICRA.2014.6906934

Zoss, A. B., Kazerooni, H., & Chu, A. (2006). Biomechanical design of the Berkeley lower extremity exoskeleton (BLEEX). *IEEE/ASME Transactions on Mechatronics, 11*(2), 128–138. doi:10.1109/TMECH.2006.871087

12

Enhancing Human Cognitive Capital by Harnessing the Brain's Inherent Neuroplasticity

SANDRA B. CHAPMAN, LORI G. COOK, ASHA K. VAS, AND IAN H. ROBERTSON

INTRODUCTION

An unprecedented opportunity to strengthen our greatest asset—our human cognitive capital—is being pushed to the forefront as new discoveries unfold. Human cognitive capital is a dynamic rather than fixed capacity that has been defined as an "accumulating asset that can be drawn upon to create and to take advantage of opportunities and to sustain well-being, in response to environmental challenge and stress" (Richards & Deary, 2010). A fundamental motivation for advancing human performance optimization is to take advantage of the fact that our cognitive capacity is the engine that will drive mankind's ability to improve the world around us. The ability to expand human cognitive performance and related socioemotional capabilities will allow us to flourish, prosper, and solve the growing complexity of issues in a rapidly changing landscape of globalization, human conflict, constantly shifting corporate directions, and complex strategic military operations and in a successful adaptation to the profound influences of diverse cultural contexts.

A long-standing desire to raise mental agility and acumen for the average human has until recently resulted in false starts and failed attempts (Hurley, 2014). Moreover, the preponderant focus of current human brain performance research has previously targeted understanding how, why, and when it underperforms, declines, or fails. For example, measurement and diagnosis of the cognitive consequences of injury, insult, stress, depression, and disease on the brain has dominated the human brain performance (HBP) literature. Given the enormous personal, social, and economic costs of these negative outcomes, such crucially important work has to continue in the hands of dedicated, disability- and pathology- focused researchers and clinicians.

But to what extent does this research help us to understand whether and how it is possible to strengthen the capacity and performance of the *healthy* brain? This is an important question for at least two main reasons. First, normal, relatively unde-manding life and work may not require more than "ordinary" cognitive performance, yet individuals may be losing capacity that could be avoidable. Second, millions of people around the world daily face super-normal, highly demanding situations in which the "ordinary" level of mental performance simply will not suffice. This is par-ticularly true for those in "tip of the spear" roles or *in extremis* contexts, for whom every ounce of performance matters (Kolditz, 2007).

So the question arises: Can the healthy brain, which performs well in ordinary situations, be trained, strengthened, and optimized to perform better in hyper-normal situations of great complexity, demand, change, and stress? That is the defining question we pose and address in this chapter. In addressing the issue of ca-pability to enhance human cognitive performance, we describe emerging evidence from cognitive neuroscientific research that shows a real potential for the healthy brain to be improved and strengthened across the life span. This effort is opportune because the general public is becoming as concerned about brain health as heart health for the first time ever. As such, discovering ways to optimize human perfor-mance and to strengthen the defenses of the healthy brain against future decline and increase brain resilience against brain-related disorders or injuries becomes a research enterprise of paramount importance.

This book is a timely harvesting of the latest scientific evidence regarding what is known about human performance optimization and building a healthier brain capable of maintaining function in parallel with the equivalent search for enhanced physical fitness late in life. This chapter focuses on major efforts under way that are revealing ways to harness the inherent neuroplasticity of the brain to build its ca-pacity to be stronger, healthier, and more fit with increased resilience to combat the multitude of factors that can derail healthy brain function. We provide highlights from current evidence related to emerging metrics of brain health enhancement, a protocol that strongly implicates broad-based gains, and near-term future offerings that take advantage of the additive rather than destructive features of stress on per-formance. Thus, the key issues explored in this chapter on the state of the science of cognitive enhancement include:

- *What encompasses brain health?* In this chapter, we specify five core pillars/ components that contribute to brain health. We use the terms "brain health" and "cognitive capital" interchangeably throughout this chapter. Objective ways to measure these five components are rapidly being developed and translated so that they can be utilized to evaluate and inform whether new offerings—such as cognitive training, pharmacological approaches, or neural devices—enhance a person's cognitive capacity and elevate human performance optimization.
- *What are the different frameworks that motivate cognitive training approaches?* One way cognitive enhancement opportunities may be categorized is in regard to focus on improving component/specialized processes as well as targeting integrative, broad-based processes.
- *Can human cognitive capital be enhanced?* We describe evidence from cognitive training approaches that are showing efficacy in enhancing brain

health, highlighting a particular integrative approach that provides a vivid illustration of how combining measurements across the five pillars of brain health can expand our understanding of how cognitive strategies can strengthen higher order neural networks. The cognitive capacities targeted represent integrative processes used across multiple contexts and include abilities such as strategically blocking/inhibiting less relevant input while focusing on mission-critical input, rapidly absorbing complex information, thinking broadly while attending to specifics so that decisions reflect an effective combination of strategic thinking with tactical actions, efficiently updating ideas as information changes so as to embrace innovative problem-solving, and maintaining stability of goals despite contexts of uncertainty generated by high cognitive demands.

• *What are future opportunities to further enhance human cognitive capital in the near term?* One intriguing discovery is the potential to utilize stress to boost cognitive capacities. We present new research suggesting that individuals may soon be able to improve moment-to-moment self-monitoring of performance and thereby improve mental functions. Such self-awareness may allow individuals to more strategically harness their cognitive resources to achieve better overall performance in complex and stress-filled contexts.

PILLARS OF BRAIN HEALTH

The science that shapes our understanding of brain health and its fitness, though relatively complex, can be characterized in terms of at least five interdependent domains. We call these the "pillars" of brain health, and they include (1) neural health, including structure and function of brain systems; (2) cognitive performance; (3) psychological health status; (4) real-life functionality; and (5) socioemotional cognition. These factors are succinctly described in the next paragraphs.

Structure and Function of Brain Systems

Advances in magnetic resonance imaging (MRI) and sophisticated analytics now allow measurement of the brain's structure and function without major risks or exposure to radioactive tracers. In terms of brain structures, MRI allows a safe platform to measure the enhanced integrity of white matter connections and increases to cortical thickness. Functional measures include connectivity of neural networks, neural efficiency, and global/regional changes in cerebral blood flow and cerebrovascular reactivity. Evidence implicates that changes to certain brain regions could elevate the function of neural systems that support higher order cognitive capacity such as required for high performance under conditions of chaos and uncertainty. Two of the key networks which are being foregrounded for study are the cingulo-operculum (which supports cognitive processes that hold steady the endgame goal despite immense distractions and complexity) and the frontoparietal network (which allows a person to rapidly update actions with new data streaming into the senses) (Dosenbach, Fair, Cohen, Schlaggar, & Petersen, 2008; Dosenbach et al., 2007).

Cognitive Brain Health

Cognitive performance measures in the past have largely focused on component processes such as attention, memory, inhibition, and switching, to mention a few, that contribute to more integrative processes. There has recently been a shift to target more integrative, top-down cognitive processes, both in terms of assessment as well as training (Chapman & Mudar, 2014; Chen, Abrams, & D'Esposito, 2006; Chen & D'Esposito, 2010; D'Esposito & Chen, 2006; Vas, Chapman, & Cook, 2015). Integrative processes include strategic learning, integrated reasoning, and innovative thinking (Chapman et al., 2016). Findings reveal that when integrative cognitive processes are improved, there is often a transfer benefit to the component specialized functions such as memory, attention, and focus (Chapman & Mudar, 2014; Vas, Chapman, & Cook, 2015).

Psychological Brain Health

Enhancements to psychological health and emotional well-being would manifest in areas such as reducing or minimizing depressive symptoms, anxiety disorders, or stress-related problems including posttraumatic stress disorder (PTSD), to mention the most common ones (Max et al., 2015; Vas, Chapman, Aslan et al., 2016). In the past, cognitive capacity and psychological well-being have been addressed in separate silos of research undertakings. Newer findings implicate the potential that improved cognitive control may help to down-regulate heightened emotional response (Vas, Chapman, Aslan et al., 2016).

Functional Real-Life Performance

When human performance is optimized, it will be most effectively realized in improvements in everyday functions, responsibilities, and accomplishments. It is not enough to change brain and cognition—the litmus test is whether improvements are manifested in the competencies and complexities of life demands, whether in calm or chaos. All too often, research fails to address whether statistically significant cognitive gains have functional relevance to human performance in real-life contexts and especially in chaotic contexts of uncertainty. It is important that cognitive and brain enhancement is also expressed through progress in tackling more complex everyday life challenges, with continued growth in skills.

Socioemotional Cognitive Brain Health

Improving capacity to negotiate across the complexities of colleagues, peers, and team members and their diverse personalities and cultural contexts is central to advancing strategic brain performance in the context of global military, corporate, community, and educational operations. The evolving mix of cultures, changing family structures, and dynamically altering migration systems is motivating a major need to strengthen capacities to better relate to others across diverse cultural groups and generations. Moreover, human performance optimization is successful when individuals see clearly how to navigate the social complexities across multiple, ever-changing modalities/platforms.

Summary

In sum, we anticipate that the ability to optimize human performance and to strengthen human cognitive capital simultaneously engages and expands function across the five pillars of brain health, namely neural systems, top-down cognitive control processes, psychological well-being and quality of life, real-life performance, and social agility. Findings that show meaningful change across two or more of the five brain health domains, rather than isolated changes on single parameters, will offer the most convincing evidence that certain protocols offer promise in optimizing human cognitive performance. In particular, correspondence between changes in the supporting components of brain health will clarify the interplay and interdependence between these components. When positive findings converge across brain health domains, efforts should focus on translation and efficacy testing across demanding contexts, whether military, corporate, or educational.

DIFFERENT FRAMEWORKS FOR OPTIMIZING HUMAN COGNITIVE PERFORMANCE

Cognitive training programs to optimize performance, both in disease and health, have evolved over decades. Especially, the past decade, following 9/11, has brought unexpected challenges that led the military and scientific communities to redefine performance in a military context to go beyond a "shoot, move, and communicate" approach. The wars ensuing after 9/11 raised the fundamental question of soldier preparedness. Terms such as "human performance optimization" and "cognitive readiness" became focal issues to address and promote. Human performance optimization in military contexts is defined as the relatively "precise, controlled and combined application of certain substances and devices over the short and long-term to achieve optimization in a person or unit's performance overall" (Russell, Bulkley, & Grafton, 2005). Cognitive readiness refers to the mental capacity that an individual must establish and sustain in order to perform effectively in the complex and unpredictable environment of modern military operations. Cognitive readiness has been cited as one of five critical research areas by the Office of the Deputy Under Secretary of Defense for Science and Technology (Etter, 2002; Schatz et al., 2012). In essence, human cognition is considered the most important asset. Consequently, a health model—versus a medical model to remediate impairment or injury—is gaining prominence to foster cognitive and psychological readiness to adapt and optimize performance in stressful environments. Many military and non-military departments have undertaken this mission, including the Army Behavioral, Cognitive, and Neural Sciences (BCNS) program, which seeks a scientific under-standing of the factors that can enhance or diminish human performance. In corporate settings, brain training is becoming the new impetus in employee wellness, akin to company-paid gym memberships, with the goal of promoting employee engagement, productivity, and overall peak performance. For example, Aetna Health incorporated MyBrainSolutions (Brain Resource, Inc.), a program that provides employees online assessments and interactive games to improve brain performance across domains of emotion, thinking, feeling, and self-regulation. Increased focus on health versus disease/injury is also gaining ground with demand from the aging baby boomer generation. Brain training programs and "brain gyms" have proliferated and become widely available. Even at the youth level, franchised programs such as LearningRx (LearningRx, Inc.) are emerging which target strengthening of specific cognitive skills identified as weak in the individual student.

As previously mentioned, one way cognitive enhancement opportunities may be classified is in regard to whether the focus is on improving component/specialized process(es) or is instead targeting integrative top-down processes. This distinction motivates a neurobiological framework to help evaluate the differential impact of diverse trainings.

Specialized Process Training

Regarding the first training type, considerable efforts have previously focused on training specific cognitive processes such as working memory, attention, and inhibition (e.g., Jaeggi, Buschkuehl, Jonides, & Perrig, 2008; Takeuchi et al., 2013). These studies show promising results for improving these targeted bottom-up processes and potentially their supporting neural networks. Chen and colleagues (2006) referred to this bottom-up process-specific training approach as *functional specialization*, defined as targeting the basic cognitive processes that are localized to specific cortical regions.

Current cognitive training approaches are broadly categorized into neurocognitive and psychological fitness programs. Neurocognitive training (often referred to as cognitive/brain training) paradigms target cognitive processes (a) relevant to a specific task/context or (b) specific/individual processes that are part of human cognition. For example, programs such as the US Army's Basic Combat Training (Lieberman et al., 2014) focus on reaction time, vigilance, and anticipatory awareness that are directly applicable/critical in combat contexts. The other set of training programs employ repeated practice drills of tasks involving discrete processes such as memory, reaction time, language processing, and so on. The Dakim Brain Fitness program (Dakim, Inc.) provides exercises in memory, visual processing, language, and calculation using various stimuli, including video clips of movies, famous songs, and trivia. Lumosity (Lumos Labs, Inc.) provides exercises targeting memory, attention, speed, flexibility, and problem-solving. The CogMed (Pearson Education, Inc.) program specifically targets working memory capacity. The majority of these specialized cognitive process exercises are computerized and are practiced in relatively nonthreatening, non–real life contexts. In general, short-term post-training gains are reported from these training programs that target specific cognitive processes (e.g., Lampit, Hallock, & Valenzuela, 2014; Sullivan, Quinn, Pramuka, Sharkey, & French, 2012). Extension beyond targeted gains has been demonstrated by training programs such as Posit Science's BrainHQ (PositScience, Inc.), utilizing computerized games focused on improving accuracy and efficiency of auditory and visual processing skills, with generalized gains to other cognitive functions (e.g.,

Smith et al., 2009) and aspects of daily life functioning such as driving (e.g., Ball, Edwards, Ross, & McGwin, 2010) and health-related quality of life (e.g., Wolinsky et al., 2006).

Psychological fitness training approaches teach generalizable ways to develop mental fitness, regulate emotions, optimize emotional resilience for self and others, and deal with stress-related scenarios. Examples of these programs include the Comprehensive Soldier Fitness program (Cornum, Matthews, & Seligman, 2011), the Battlemind training program (Adler, Bliese, McGurk, Hoge, & Castro, 2009), and mindfulness trainings (e.g., Jha, Morrison, Dainer-Best, Parker, Rostrup, & Stanley, 2015). These programs provide multidimensional training on stress-related education, positive psychology, and emotional fitness. Teaching techniques include role play, virtual reality scenarios, biofeedback, repetitive mental exercises, progressive muscle relaxation techniques, and real-life scenarios. More research is needed to explore generalized benefits to other global cognitive functions or significant evidence of real-life improvement from these trainings.

Integrative Process Training

Chen and colleagues (2006) propose a neurobiological framework for top-down cognitive training approaches which they conceptualize as a *functional integration* approach due to the possibility that it may have a broad-based (therefore integrative) impact on key neural systems. They contrast the more generalized gains from a top-down functional integration approach with the more focal gains achieved through a functional specialization (or bottom-up) approach. The neurobiological distinction of integration versus specialization frameworks proposes that when one engages in integrative top-down cognitive control functions, the individual engages and strengthens the dynamic interactions of networks across broad-based cognitive control brain networks. Specifically, these networks have been shown to be pivotal for supporting higher order cognitive processing necessary for fast time scales for moment-to-moment adaptive responses (i.e., frontoparietal network) and those more analytical processes that operate over longer time scales for stable goal focus and task maintenance (i.e., cingulo-opercular network) (Dosenbach et al., 2008; Dosenbach et al., 2007; Zanto & Gazzaley, 2013).

Military training experts recognize the benefits of existing cognitive and psychological paradigms programs and the need for more integrative approaches that serve to benefit overall human performance in both combat and noncombat contexts (Schatz et al., 2012). To advance the way forward to enhance and optimize human cognitive capabilities, the Center for BrainHealth at the University of Texas at Dallas has developed, tested, and implemented a training program described in detail here and labeled SMART (a.k.a. Strategic Memory Advanced Reasoning Training). Ongoing research is accruing evidence that SMART provides a toolset of cognitive strategies to optimize human cognitive capital across brain health metrics. Additional studies are under way to determine training effectiveness in facilitating preparedness to successfully adapt to stressful circumstances and to strengthen resilience to avert or reduce long-term war-related cognitive and psychological sequelae.

The best approaches to optimize human cognitive performance will likely be derived by combining multiple neurocognitive therapeutics, such as those including both top-down and bottom-up approaches, among others. The testable concept would be to determine whether individuals become better equipped to handle the complexities of mental challenges in real time if the pillars of brain health are continuously strengthened as a habitual practice. The caution is that keeping the brain fit will not be a quick fix, single protocol, or "magic pill." The benefits are likely to be sustained only if multidimensional approaches and continued mental strategies continue to be implemented and practiced, similar to what is required for exercise regimens to maintain physical stamina, strength, and flexibility.

ENHANCING HUMAN COGNITIVE CAPITAL FROM THE TOP DOWN

To advance these important prior efforts that revealed improved performance in specific cognitive processes with targeted bottom-up training, we turn the approach right-side up and focus this chapter on the potential for top-down cognitive training to advance human performance optimization. Growing research findings support the potential for top-down strategy-based trainings to enhance cognitive brain health by building stronger, more resilient, and strategic cognitive performance (Chapman & Mudar, 2014; Vas, Chapman, & Cook, 2015). In this section, we summarize key findings from an exemplar of top-down strategy-based training that has recently been shown to enhance neural plasticity. The evidence shows that cognitive gains from a more functional integration approach benefit not only trained areas but also untrained domains of specific component processes. Additionally, we highlight evidence supporting the potential for top-down strategy-based trainings to be associated with dynamic improvements in neural networks, psychological health, and real-life functionality.

Strategic Memory Advanced Reasoning Training

In order to put forward a case that human cognitive capabilities can be strengthened, reinforced, and restored, we highlight evidence from multiple randomized trials. The training protocol investigated represents a specific example of a top-down, functional integrative approach to high performance brain training. The individual is made aware of how the integration of all mental strategies promotes increased productivity, lowered stress, elevated work efficiency, prioritized and maximized mental energy, diminished distractibility, increased flexibility in thinking, quicker information absorption, and enhanced decision-making. Adoption of these frontally mediated strategies has been shown to enhance brain structure and/or physiology at multiple levels—from blood flow and increased brain connectivity and efficiency, to expanding the physical connections across brain regions, facilitating generalized gains across cognitive, behavioral, and psychological domains.

The cognitive training program, namely, SMART trains top-down metacognitive strategies aimed at three pivotal processes that support clear, adaptive, and decisive thinking: strategic attention, integrative reasoning, and mental flexibility/

innovation. Strategies facilitate enhanced ability to calibrate mental effort to minimize brain fatigue and engage in deeper level processing as well as complex reasoning and strategic decision-making. The training is strategy-based rather than content-specific and provides practical ways to employ all of the strategies in a synergistic, integrated manner during real-life mental activities across multiple contexts, whether professional, academic, or social/relational. Participants are equipped to understand, practice, and identify ways to continually adopt the mental strategies that enhance core cognitive capabilities.

STRATEGIC ATTENTION

Strategic Attention provides mental tools that promote priming the brain to attend and efficiently manage time and cognitive resources, thus cultivating greater resilience. This is done by blocking distractions and inhibiting irrelevant input in order to prioritize the top two tasks to complete or ideas to communicate each day, intentionally single-tasking and building in regular mental breaks. The Strategic Attention strategies provide proactive tools to effectively deploy mental resources, beyond mere time management, and to consciously control information overflow. One of the most overwhelming challenges for individuals in modern society is processing the extraordinary volumes of information that must be taken in on a daily basis. The trainee is taught how to gauge a priori how much mental energy to spend on certain tasks. Specifically, they determine from the onset which tasks require expending analytical and deeper mental effort and when to go with quick, instinctual responses, expending less effort.

The Strategic Attention strategies empower individuals to take more control over their workload and provide tangible tools to reduce the chronic stress that often plagues the overtaxed, distractible brain, particularly in high-stakes circumstances. From student to top-tier professional, it is easy to become "stuck in the weeds" by overselecting unnecessary or irrelevant details based on the goal at hand. The result is wasted time in trying to absorb and learn indiscriminately, with a toll on mental capacity. When time is not used efficiently, the overwhelming feelings of information overload, intensifying stress, and burning-out can quickly follow. Individuals can use the strategies to hone inhibition skills, mitigate depletion of mental energy, improve focus, and use time efficiently to decompress, catalyzing those "a-ha" moments that motivate their next goal-oriented actions. The paradox of strategic attention habits is recognizing that the most effective leaders are talented at knowing at the outset the immense data/choices to ignore so they can better focus. They also limit multitasking when not absolutely necessary since dual-tasking can weaken neural pathways that support high performance. Elite performers know how to hyperfocus on one thing that is the most salient to task achievement.

INTEGRATIVE REASONING

Integrative Reasoning engages a deeper level of processing meanings rather than simply trying to register and encode as much data input as possible. Expanded integrative reasoning capacity facilitates the level of transformative thinking expected of high-level leaders across professional fields—whether business, medical, military, political, or academic. The ability to extract and implement strategic goals requires an ability to continually abstract the essence of information or target key goals/tasks being tackled. These core abilities build on and are interdependent on simultaneous implementation of strategic attention skills outlined earlier. Integrative reasoning utilizes mental tools to exert cognitive control to "zoom in" to quickly scan the critical details or steps to a goal. The rapid influx of information is then continuously updated and reprocessed into global ideas by "zoom out" strategies where one rapidly and continuously steps back and deciphers the "big picture." This strategy involves synthesizing and abstracting major ideas/goals. Synthesized processing is followed by "zooming deep and wide" to construct generalized interpretations, implications, and applications related to decisions and action at hand. For example, in "zooming deep and wide," individuals are trained to quickly consider the outcomes of their actions or decisions in light of a broader context.

Integrative Reasoning strategies are especially beneficial in overcoming personal obstacles to goal achievement and to down-regulating emotionally driven actions when necessary. When stress, frustrations, fear, and overwhelmed cognitive load arise, individuals are trained to employ tactical switching to shift mental mode to big-idea perspectives. Engaging frontal lobe reasoning capacity facilitates the fine-tuning of decision-making skills and actions to complete timely goals and respond effectively in rapidly changing and chaotic contexts. Utilizing top-down strategies helps one to identify the reoccurring sources of frustration and increases an individual's capacity to cut straight to the bigger-picture problem(s) in order to then tactically address hurdles (e.g., impaired focus, communication lines, decision-making authority, etc.).

INNOVATION

The mental facility of engaging in top-down processing to continually update new information while maintaining the goal at hand is further facilitated by Innovation strategies. Strategies of Innovation train fluid and flexible thinking and dynamic problem-solving. Innovation works hand in hand with integrative reasoning by stressing the need to rapidly consider and derive multiple interpretations, solutions, and approaches from divergent perspectives and outcome possibilities and to flexibly update ideas and perspectives to better understand the complexities and nuances of new situations/information. Practicing Innovation increases abstraction capacity and pushes individuals to recognize more expansive problem-solving opportunities so as to mitigate shallow thinking and becoming "stuck" in rote or status quo approaches or individually biased thinking that blinds one from the bigger context of the actions.

One key strategy practiced with Innovation is to engage stronger metacognitive skills to learn from both mistakes and successes by reviewing one's own and team behaviors, where revising decisions and actions could potentially lead to even better outcomes. By focusing on the positive upside of mistakes, the individual's dynamic problem-solving skills may become more flexible, honed, and sharpened. Additionally, Innovation strategies help to minimize the negative emotional toll of failure and self-inflicted disparaging self-talk to immediately engage the frontal lobe to develop proactive problem-solving and improved action determination.

Combined and Interdependent Strategies

To use a physical fitness analogy, the three core strategies just described represent a cognitive "toolkit" to promote increased endurance (Strategic Attention), strength (Integrative Reasoning), and flexibility (Innovation), and, when used together, cognitive fitness. Furthermore, to achieve measurable gains, adoption—incorporation into one's daily habits to transform status quo approaches and raise one's threshold for challenge—is key. These are not strategies meant solely for "drill" or practice during a particular block of time each day but rather are applied to accomplish and further goals and mental challenges faced throughout one's daily demands. The performance gains translate to allowing individuals to operate at a higher level, efficiently and optimally, even when faced with complex, chaotic, and unknown contexts.

Findings from Top-Down Cognitive Training

Neural Health Benefits

Since we are addressing how to leverage and optimize our greatest asset—human cognitive performance—evidence is needed to support the claims that the underlying brain systems supporting complex thinking can be enhanced. The notion that humans can change their brain by how it is used or misused is not new. Experience-driven neural plasticity was brought to the forefront of scientific discovery by Merzenich and colleagues decades ago (Merzenich, Recanzone, & Jenkins, 1991). This remarkable ability to be able to continuously modify and strengthen the brain or degrade its function by use has been documented through decades of research and is realized through enriched learning, education experiences, cognitive training, literacy, arts, scientific exploration, and even meditation, among others (e.g., Bavelier, Green, Pouget, & Schrater, 2012; Bennett, Diamond, Krech, & Rosenzweig, 1964; Merzenich et al., 1991; Mishra & Gazzaley, 2014). This principle of building fitness, not being born into it, has been widely accepted and put into practice for physical fitness. In contrast, the capacity to build brain health and its fitness has only recently begun to be given serious consideration to enhance human performance.

Advances in neuroimaging techniques such as functional MRI (fMRI) are providing scientists an objective methodology to directly view and measure whether or not the brain is changing in short time windows (Chapman, Aslan et al., 2015; Vas, Chapman, Aslan et al., 2016; Zanto & Gazzaley, 2013). Additionally, researchers realize the importance of carefully assessing whether the direction of changes is positive or negative. Herein, we highlight collaborating evidence across multimodal brain analyses to show that strategy-based, top-down cognitive training (i.e., SMART, in this case) significantly enhances and even repairs the brain's structural and functional systems. We feel optimistically confident that we can interpret our findings of brain changes as enhancement in brain function and structure since we found that improvements correlated with significant gains in cognitive performance.

In recent studies of healthy adults comparing gains in SMART cognitive training versus other control groups such as nonintervened controls or aerobic exercise control groups, we found evidence suggesting that the cognitive training enhanced two distinct frontal cognitive control networks: the frontoparietal network and the cingulo-opercular network identified by Dosenbach and colleagues (2007, 2008) (Chapman, Aslan et al., 2015, 2016). The significance of strengthening these networks is promising given evidence that the frontoparietal network operates at fast time scales, allowing moment-to-moment adaptive performance (Dosenbach et al., 2008). Simultaneously, improving the cingulo-opercular network is proposed to operate over longer time scales so that one can keep in mind the goal or task at hand as information is rapidly changing. As set forth, we proposed that one goal of cognitive enhancement is to increase the efficiency with which one is able to rapidly update ideas/solutions while maintaining stability of the goal at hand. This dual process is especially crucial to optimize human performance when operating in contexts of extreme uncertainty and chaos. The enhancement of the fronto-parietal neural system could be a gold mine of achievement toward the goal of optimizing human cognitive performance. This fronto-parietal network has been labeled the dynamic multinetwork *"flexible hub"* (Zanto & Gazzaley, 2013). As this flexible neural hub becomes stronger, scientists have speculated that the networks are fortified to rapidly reorganize in response to changes in input, resolve conflicting data, sort through complex input, and rapidly tackle new learning to guide behaviors (Zanto & Gazzaley, 2013). Considering the complexity of corporate issues, medical and financial decisions, immensely polarizing political crises, wartime conflicts, and global geopolitical concerns—whether immigration, refugees, world hunger or disease—we need immense mental capital and capacity to perform at optimal levels. Training to keep the goal in mind when confronted with extensive and often conflicting data and then fluidly and flexibly update our strategies and solutions with new input will serve to optimize human cognitive performance.

The possibility to partake of this capacity for enhanced brain systems may be within the realm of probabilities if we train our brain to engage these networks in dealing with complex circumstances and issues. Strengthening the dual *stability* (goal-maintained) and *adaptability* (flexible-hub) neural systems requires continual utilization of top-down mental strategies to harness the brain's neuroplastic potential. These top-down strategies may be used in concert with other neurocognitive therapeutics such as drug developments, mindfulness training, physical exercise, or targeted brain stimulation to optimize human performance.

In addition to showing nodes within these two networks (i.e., fronto-parietal and cingulo-opercular) were strengthened, the potential to harness the brain's neuroplastic potential was also manifested by evidence across multiple SMART training trials showing significant increases in global and regional cerebral blood flow (CBF) following SMART training in healthy adults (Chapman, Aslan et al., 2015; Chapman, Aslan et al., 2016) as well as in those with prior brain injuries (Vas, Chapman, Aslan et al., 2016) and in those with mental disorders such as bipolar disease (Venza, Spence, & Chapman, 2015). In the healthy adults, the increases to CBF were attributable to improved neural health but not attributable to changes in the neurovascular mechanisms (Chapman, Aslan et al., 2016). This conclusion was based on the lack of changes to cerebrovascular response in the first known study to address both brain blood flow and cerebrovascular reactivity. The evidence that mental training can increase neural health through increased CBF supports experienced-induced capacity to enhance neural plasticity. There is a well-accepted coupling between brain activity and cerebrovascular flow. Since brain blood flow increased without changes to the cerebrovascular system, the evidence indicates that neural health was enhanced by adoption of the SMART strategies. In addition to functional brain changes, we found evidence of enhancement in structural brain networks as measured by an expanded white matter uncinate fiber tract linking the memory and learning center to the abstraction area (Chapman, Aslan et al., 2015). Strengthening this major fiber tract has previously been associated with the capacity for individuals to think broadly while at the same time attending to specifics (Chapman, Aslan et al., 2015). Adding to the potential to enhance brain function with advanced reasoning training, Yezhuvath and colleagues (Yezhuvath, Motes, Aslan, Spence, & Chapman, 2016) found SMART training improved neural efficiency in the prefrontal cortex, increasing linearly with more training as compared to a control group in normally aging adults. The ability to increase neural efficiency suggests that the neural engine was *tuned up* to work faster to support performance (Yezhuvath et al., 2016). The end goal of optimizing human performance will likely require that the brain's operating systems are working as fast as "humanly" possible.

In a chronic-stage group of individuals with persistent mild brain injury deficits, brain function was strengthened not only in prefrontal brain regions—associated with cognitive control in becoming better at strategically inhibiting too much irrelevant input as well as linked to rapidly absorbing complex information (Vas, Chapman et al., 2016). These same individuals showed improvement in neural health in a region, namely the precuneus, associated with impaired psychological health such as PTSD and poor emotional regulation (Yan et al., 2013).

COGNITIVE BENEFITS

The top-down multidimensional SMART strategies facilitate and strengthen critical reasoning abilities to harness immense cognitive capacities in both healthy and clinical populations. In multiple randomized trials in healthy and clinical populations, participants demonstrated significant cognitive gains following SMART, at both short-term (immediate post-training) and longer periods (3–6 months post-training) (Chapman & Mudar, 2014). Cognitive gains were evident both on integrated, trained cognitive domains (i.e., strategic attention, integrated reasoning, and innovation) and in untrained, specific cognitive processes. Generalized gains (in varying degrees) in untrained processes included working memory, inhibition, switching, and memory for facts in adults with traumatic brain injuries (TBI) with persistent moderate functional deficits (Vas, Chapman, Cook, Elliott, & Keebler, 2011), mild functional deficits (Vas, Chapman, Aslan et al., 2016), and in adolescents with TBI (Cook, Chapman, Elliott, Evenson, & Vinton, 2014). Generalized gains of improved concept abstraction and verbal fluency were also reported in healthy senior adults (Anand et al., 2011). Studies also showed significant improvements in normally developing adolescents' academic performance on state-mandated critical thinking tests post-SMART (Gamino, Chapman, Hull, & Lyon, 2010; Gamino et al., 2014). Evidence supports the potential to enhance human cognitive capital when individuals utilize top-down processing, improving both integrative and specialized/isolated cognitive processes.

Whereas top-down integrated cognitive training shows a transfer benefit to specific processes, it remains unclear whether *strengthening specific processes* shows generalized benefits to higher order thinking abilities. For example, Gamino and colleagues (2010) found that typically developing teenagers who were trained to improve memorization skills did not improve on integrated reasoning or problem-solving despite showing improved memory for details. On the other hand, students who improved integrated reasoning (following SMART) also showed comparable gains in fact recall to those students who received memorization training (Gamino et al., 2010). Additionally, in a recent randomized trial of SMART versus a memory training protocol, adolescents with TBI showed significant gains in integrated reasoning as well as generalization to untrained executive functions of working memory and inhibition and improved memory for facts, whereas no such gains were demonstrated in the memory-trained group (Cook et al., 2014). Furthermore, recent evidence has shown that performance on specific processes (e.g., switching, working memory, and inhibition) only partially predicts integrated cognitive functions (Vas, Chapman, Aslan et al., 2016). The question remains as to whether or not cognitive trainings designed to improve specific bottom-up processes such as working memory, immediate memory, delayed memory, or switching promote generalized gains in improved top-down reasoning processes needed for human performance optimization. There is limited evidence from working memory training trials in healthy adults that suggests it may be possible to generalize benefits from specific processes to integrative functions (Buschkuehl, Hernandez-Garcia, Jaeggi, Bernard, & Jonides, 2014). More research is needed to explore the potential for bidirectional benefit from either bottom-up–focused cognitive training programs or top-down–focused integrative training protocols. Our series of studies support our proposal that training top-down integrative cognitive functions will achieve bidirectional gains with generalization to specific component cognitive processes. The SMART approach is an example of utilizing top-down metacognitive strategies to provide adoptable learning and task management tools to harness the vast neuroplastic nature of human cognition.

PSYCHOLOGICAL HEALTH GAINS

Cognitive and psychological health go hand-in-hand. Consequently, improved cognition could lead to resilient psychological well-being (Stanley, Schaldach, Kiyonaga, & Jha, 2011). In the past decade, emerging evidence of mutual benefits of cognitive and psychological therapies in adults with TBI are increasing, especially with comorbidity of depression and PTSD in chronic TBI (Corrigan, Selassie, & Orman, 2010; Ho & Bennett, 1997; Miller & Mittenberg, 1998; Tiersky et al., 2005). Recent findings from our work demonstrated generalized benefits of SMART extended to improved psychological health. The SMART program gains were evident as a reduced number of self-reported symptoms associated with depression and stress-related behaviors in adults with chronic TBI who were experiencing mild to moderate levels of depressive symptoms prior to training. We speculate a positive impact of SMART strategies on psychological functioning, especially in daily real-life situations. For example, repeated use of strategies of ignoring less relevant input (especially when faced with chaotic, unknown, and personally irritating dilemmas), focusing on the big picture/goal, flexible thinking, and examining the context from multiple perspectives may habituate an individual to consciously making an effort to be strategic in seeking solutions for major issues/contexts. These strategies engage cognitive control and serve to mitigate against being stuck in minutiae which can increase emotional distress and lower mood. These habits thus have the potential to down-regulate stressful emotions, improve mood, and reduce the intensity of symptoms related to depression. This finding of positive impact of strengthened integrative functions on psychological functions highlights the potential for a bidirectional flow of benefits between improved cognition and psychological health, although further research is needed to verify these pre- liminary findings.

FUNCTIONAL REAL-LIFE GAINS

An individual's optimal performance and participation in daily life activities reflects cognitive and psychological functioning. Likewise, impaired/weakened cognition and poor sense of well-being can significantly limit optimal integration at home, work/school, and community. Investigations using SMART have demonstrated generalized effects such as improved participation and performance in daily func- tionality. Adults with chronic TBI with moderate functional deficits (at the time of initiating the SMART program) reported improved participation in social and leisure activities and improved performance at home and community (Vas et al., 2011). Interestingly, these training benefits continued to improve over a 6-month follow-up post-training assessment, indicating that sustained effort of implementing the strategies is critical to witness tangible/palpable changes in daily function. Recent evidence also showed significant gains in awareness in adults with chronic TBI with mild functional deficits (Vas, Chapman, Aslan et al., 2016). We predict continuous use of SMART strategies may play a critical role in improved participa- tion and performance in daily activities. For example, the strategies promoting fo- cusing on key points during conversations (versus dwelling on less relevant details), adaptable approaches to problem-solving, and better understanding of complex in- formation may aid in improved (a) communication with family, friends, employers or colleagues; (b) planning meaningful family events; or (c) developing new leisure interests (e.g., sports, church-related activities). Furthermore, improved awareness of one's strengths and weaknesses guides adoption of strategies to accomplish a goal. That is, improved cognition and psychological health could have a positive impact on foundational quality of life aspects such as self-confidence and a sense of well-being and self-worth.

Future Approaches to Optimize Human Performance

CO-ENHANCEMENT OF COGNITIVE AND EMOTIONAL CAPITAL

Cognitive capital depends to a certain extent on emotional capital. The overlap be- tween cognitive and emotional processing becomes very large and almost insepa- rable in high-demand situations. For instance, take a common problem following

TBI—distractibility—where the individual experiences significant difficulty maintaining attentional focus in the face of competing, irrelevant information such as background conversation or noise. People suffering from TBI or with a diagnosis of attention deficit hyperactivity disorder commonly complain of this problem. They also report that maintaining focus in highly distracting environments is a source of significant stress for them, often leading them to avoid social and other situations where such distractions exist. Such compensatory avoidance is detrimental to their social and work lives and, consequently, to their psychological health. This is an example of a cognitive failure—impaired selective attention—leading to a negative emotional consequence, namely stress and/or irritability. This emotional state further decreases attentional and other cognitive functions (Arciniegas et al., 1999; Rao & Lyketsos, 2002). Similar challenges appear in healthy individuals under extreme time or environmental pressures. That is, when the cognitive demands of dealing with the pressure reduces available attentional resources to inhibit distracting stimuli, these situations elicit stress and impaired performance in a way that would not be apparent in situations of lower demand.

A common approach to reducing such pressure-elicited stress and its negative cognitive consequences has been to teach stress-management methods (e.g., Lewis et al., 2015). But, increasingly, interventions have been developed that target cognitive control processes which potentially can boost control over negative emotions, thereby reducing the handicapping effect of stress on cognitive function. Among individuals with TBI who reported problems of distractibility in the face of background noise, for instance, their attentional control could be improved by training them to listen to spoken text in one ear while ignoring competing text in the other. Findings reveal that those who showed the highest levels of perceived stress showed the greatest improvement following training (Dundon et al., 2015). Rather than training to improve attention, this training targeted integrative processes of strategic attention. Other attentional processes can also be trained, resulting in dual benefits to cognitive and emotional performance. These include cognitive bias modification, where anxious individuals are trained to avoid automatic orienting of attention toward threat stimuli, thereby reducing overall exposure to negative emotional stimuli through a cognitive manipulation (e.g., Hertel & Mathews, 2011).

Increasingly, future goals aim to co-enhance cognitive and emotional capital using training programs that focus both on stress management and cognitive training methods (e.g., Rose et al., 2013) such as goal-setting (Locke & Latham, 2006) and problem-solving. The advances in cognitive training, on the one hand, and stress-management methods on the other, are largely progressing relatively independently of each other. Hence, a considerable opportunity exists, in the near term, to bring the latest and best methods from each domain together. The fact that cognitive and emotional capital are so closely linked means that if these approaches are combined, the resulting performance enhancement is likely to be additive as compared to gains achieved by either approach alone.

EXPLOITING AROUSAL IN COGNITIVE CAPITAL

Optimal performance requires optimal arousal (Yerkes & Dodson, 1908), and norepinephrine (NE) is a key neurotransmitter mediating the arousal response

(Aston-Jones & Cohen, 2005). NE plays a critical role in memory performance (Sterpenich et al., 2006) as well as in other cognitive functions such as working memory (Chamberlain, Mueller, Blackwell, Robbins, & Sahakian, 2006), and both too low and too high levels of NE can disrupt human performance (Aston-Jones & Cohen, 2005). Animal models of stroke rehabilitation show enhancement of plasticity-based recovery of function through stimulation of the vagus nerve, which greatly increases NE availability and, because of its neuromodulatory properties, enhances plasticity during rehabilitative input (Hays et al., 2014). Future human studies, therefore, may see enhanced effects of cognitive training on human performance by temporarily increasing brain plasticity during key training inputs using vagus nerve stimulation or other less invasive methods such as noninvasive brain stimulation (e.g., Harty et al., 2014).

Perhaps the most ubiquitous source of NE activation is stress (George et al., 2013). While severe stress can impair cognitive function and deplete cognitive capital (Yuen et al., 2012), it is less commonly appreciated that moderate levels of stress may *improve* some cognitive functions (Broadbent, 1971). Certain stressors in older people, such as conflict with family or serious illness of a spouse, also are associated with better cognitive function over a 2-year period compared to where no stresses have been experienced (Comijs, van den Kommer, Minnaar, Penninx, & Deeg, 2011; Rosnick, Small, McEvoy, Borenstein, & Mortimer, 2007). Remarkably, objective performance can be increased by requiring performers in a very stressful situation to verbally label their arousal symptoms as "excitement" as opposed to "anxiousness" (Brooks, 2014). This pattern suggests that people can "use" their arousal in high-demand situations to enhance their performance by top-down changes in interpretation of arousal symptoms. Such methods may be incorporated with cognitive training in the future, potentially allowing high-level cognitive strategies to become more resilient to stress and hence capable of execution in extreme situations. Self-regulation of arousal has been shown to improve executive function in a number of populations, including TBI (Manly, Hawkins, Evans, Woldt, & Robertson, 2002), adult attention deficit hyperactivity disorder (O'Connell et al., 2008; Salomone et al., 2015), and normal aging (Milewski-Lopez et al., 2014). The strategic management of stress, therefore, is likely to play an increasing part in developing and implementing programs that optimize human performance. The possibility exists that enhancing brain plasticity at key moments in training is also very likely to emerge as a completely new approach to enhancing cognitive capital.

EMBEDDING COGNITIVE TRAINING IN REAL-LIFE SITUATIONS

As mentioned earlier in this chapter, the biggest challenge for cognitive training is generalization to real life. This roadblock is also true of therapies for emotional problems and stress. Trainings such as SMART, described in this chapter, have the advantage of using materials that are ubiquitous in daily life—daily tasks and responsibilities, correspondence, articles, broadcasts, and reports, for instance— and training cognitive skills in the actual environment in which they will ultimately be deployed, thus greatly increasing generalization to these skills. Commonly available technologies make it possible to offer other types of training in situ, for instance using smartphones to offer on-the-job stress management help to oncology nurses (Villani et al., 2013). A number of stress inoculation programs, particularly in the military, also train stress-management and related strategies in the context of very realistic high-demand simulated situations.

DEVELOPMENT OF MULTILEVEL INDICES OF COGNITIVE AND EMOTIONAL CAPITAL

Among the best validated forms of cognitive training are those which have demonstrated effects on fMRI-measured neural function, as such evidence is crucial for persuading both individuals considering embarking on the training, as well as policymakers choosing the best procedures. Psychological processes not only alter brain network function, but they may also have effects through all levels of central nervous system function down to the cellular and molecular. Exam stress, for instance, has been demonstrated to alter activity of the interleukin-2 receptor gene in medical students during exam periods as compared with nonstressful times when they had no exams (Glaser et al., 1990), resulting in lower immune function. Another study showed that the stress of performing mental tasks under time pressure led to altered function of the interleukin-1β gene that contributes to atherosclerosis (Brydon et al., 2005). The men most stressed by the tasks showed the biggest increase in this gene's activity, with the effects lasting 2 hours or more after it had ended. If mental processes can alter molecular function in negative emotional states, it is certainly plausible that positive states can have comparable effects in a positive direction. We can therefore confidently expect to be able to demonstrate molecular consequences of cognitive training—and at least one study of working memory training in humans has actually shown alterations in dopamine D1 receptor binding in prefrontal cortex (McNab et al., 2009). The challenge, therefore, is to develop and test robust markers of brain health that, if possible, can include indices of cellular and molecular change consequent to behavioral interventions and other forms of treatment that are showing positive outcomes. Once such measures are developed, then new and existing training methods can be tested against such crucial markers.

APPLICATION TO HUMAN COGNITIVE PERFORMANCE OPTIMIZATION

Never has it been more possible or as pressing a time than the present to harness the brain's inherent neuroplasticity and to optimize our human cognitive performance. Cognitive neuroscience is beginning to show that brain fitness trainings can reinforce neural health, enhance higher order reasoning capacity, mitigate psychological suffering by reducing depression and stress, elevate everyday life functionality and perhaps promote social-emotional resilience to optimize human performance and effective leadership in the face of extreme complexity and stress. In the near-term, *we believe that emerging research methodologies will allow us to elucidate the potential to determine the degree to which exercising healthy brain habits will have molecular benefits.* These molecular benefits may be manifested at the level of microstructural neural systems such as white matter integrity or cerebral blood flow, metabolic brain function such as energy metabolism, neurotransmitters, and epigenetics, to mention a few. What is needed now is to find ways to curate and implement proven healthy brain habits. The eminent (and imminent) question is how research findings can be effectively translated to benefit the public at large. The approaches need to be practical and accessible to students, educational systems, corporations, medical practice, political institutions, and military training programs, at the very least. Which of us would not benefit by enhanced cognitive capacities in these areas that should optimize our human performance?

- Improve focus by ramping up inhibitory processes.
- Learn complex information faster.
- Hold the big goal in mind while simultaneously flexibility updating action, decision and perspectives.
- Embrace risk with balanced state of mind by expanding our capacity to be innovators of new ideas, solutions, and outcomes as well as knowledge creators.

Educational Application: Repress Robotic Thinking

According to the Kennedy Forum (O'Brien & McCormack, 2015), a concentrated focus on brain fitness in our educational system will help restore our nation's status as a global frontrunner to ensure prosperity for citizens and our country. We agree that the application of high-performance brain training to educational environments provides particular promise. Equipping individuals throughout their educational years with proactive thinking tools can enhance not only their learning success but also bears potential for improving resilience to later stresses and/or injury at both a physiological and cognitive level. For education settings, the cognitive endgame should be to energize future discoverers and inspired thinkers and repress rote learners. Students taught in a mechanistic, rote style of stuffing away facts for a test will build a very different, less forward-thinking brain than those trained to abstract, synthesize, and connect meaning to their world, past, present and future (Chapman, 2013). The neural systems that support complex thinking and problem-solving are undergoing rapid maturation during the teen years through the twenties, so it is vital to take advantage of this crucial and protracted developmental stage for complex reasoning. Enhancing cognitive capital in our students encourages them to become life-long learners and dedicated problem-finders and solution-setters, preparing the next generation to solve the complexity of problems that are perhaps not yet even realized.

Military Application: Empower Brain Health at Early Stages by Reducing Stigma

For military contexts, one key aspiration should be to promote the importance of taking one's own brain performance seriously—in terms of both gains and losses—in order to reduce stigma around mental/cognitive aspects. Putting brain health into fitness regimens from early stages of training will promote service members who are always seeking to gain a mental edge and/or regain lost function, thus facilitating more long-standing adoption. With this in mind, proactively implementing cognitive training in the context of early military training (e.g., ROTC programs, military academies, basic training, etc.) would pay the greatest long-term dividends.

At the opposite end of the spectrum, another potential application is in the context of leadership training programs. One advantage the US Armed Forces has derives from the ability to develop the right leader—enlisted, officer, and civilian—who can think in this very complex world. The rapidly changing landscape in military situations, with its complex technology and massive information input, necessitates exploiting potential to improve cognitive readiness in our service members. Our military leaders draw on their cognitive capacities to deal with multiple scenarios and to make strategic, operational, and tactical decisions. This cognitive prowess facilitates the ability to anticipate change and creates agile, adaptive leaders.

For example, the University of Texas at Dallas Center for BrainHealth and Brain Performance Institute have been conducting training with Special Operation Forces, with the SMART program being delivered as part of the initial training courses as well as during Inter-Deployment Training Cycles. Special operators are often recognized for their ability to be innovative, dynamic problem-solvers. Operators want to be well-equipped to articulate the decision-making process and to optimize their effectiveness as instructors. Training leaders to engage these metacognitive strategies has the potential to facilitate personal cognitive enhancement, to suppress nonessential input, to down-regulate heightened response to stress (coolness in leading under stress), and reboot mental grit as well as to inspire team innovative problem-solving and focus.

Corporate Application: Stave Off Stagnation

For corporate settings, rather than approaching cognitive training through a narrow lens focused solely on enhancing productivity aspects, another major impetus should be staving off stagnation. When corporations embrace that they are building brain performance for all of their employees, they will rethink how both newer and experienced employees are being mentored and challenged. One key area of concern is how much innovation leadership and employees practice in running of meetings, conference calls, and project assignments/demands and responsibilities. This, in turn, can have a marked impact on corporate bottom-line and overall well-being, making it a powerful return on investment.

Because technology is such a fundamental aspect of day-to-day business, future efforts should leverage technology tools to provide individuals additional opportunities to strengthen and optimize their cognitive performance using highly accessible formats and modalities beyond desktop-bound platforms. Technology developers should be engaged to create innovative, user-friendly applications that could facilitate monitoring of one's own daily brain-healthy and brain-toxic habits both on and off the job, as well as provide remote access to collaborative "booster" sessions as frequently as desired or needed.

CONCLUSION

Every ounce of mental advantage leads to superior performance toward a mission of improving the world around us. What used to be science fiction with a seemingly far off vision to increase the brain's capacity is now becoming reality. Today, cognitive neuroscience is on the cusp of dramatic advances in understanding research-based ways to exploit the immense potential of our cognitive capital, making it stronger, healthier, and more fit. The overriding goals to optimize human cognitive performance need to continuously advance development, testing, and implementation of protocols that build mental resilience and foster the regenerative capacity of the brain. These goals will require large-scale, multidimensional efforts with scientists working together across disciplines. The efforts will advance more rapidly if they are outcome-focused and show benefits across the five pillars of brain health.

The vision for "smarter" individuals is obvious as this goal is foundational to how we educate future leaders, build a nimble workforce, advance scientific discoveries, develop more effective medical treatments, develop humanitarian policies, and train strategic military command to embrace the cognitive and cognitive-emotional skills required to be dynamic and adaptive thinkers across contexts, including situations of great change and stress. As noted in the introduction, operating in dynamically varying situations is becoming increasingly commonplace, not just in extreme settings such as military or civil conflict. These conditions are also prevalent in corporate, educational, governmental, law enforcement, athletic, and first-responder contexts, to mention major areas of concern. The demands of increasingly sophisticated technology and an ever-growing, rapid influx of new information to absorb and manage necessitates proactive approaches to promote optimal cognitive performance.

Frontline personnel, whether corporate executives, political leaders, technology innovators, scientists, warriors in combat zones or unfamiliar cultural contexts, or those in academic settings, must learn strategies to invest in their cognitive capital. Individuals need to be trained from early stages how to embrace their inherent potential and to recognize that their capacities are not fixed nor permanently broken when setbacks occur. *Rather, our human cognitive capital remains highly modifiable, trainable, and adaptable throughout our lifetime.* Humans can strengthen their abilities to deal with multiple scenarios at the same time, discern diverse perspectives of conflicting individuals/factions, design possible solutions while holding opposing ideas in mind, construct ways to better negotiate with or out-think their competition or opposition forces, maintain a proper balance of gut-level and analytic response to guide behavior, and make strategic, timely, and far-sighted decisions that address broader contexts of public impact and concern.

The continuous building of cognitive fortitude by training individuals how to maximize cognitive capacity will be a noble humanitarian achievement across the world. These efforts will facilitate the ability to achieve proactive agility over reactive adaptation, anticipate change in this rapidly changing world, and to create resilient personnel who can calmly lead and perform, not only when faced with life-threatening problems and in novel and chaotic environments. Our efforts to solve the complexities of issues/problems that are yet to exist lie within our human cognitive capital. Empowering everyone to realize their cognitive potential throughout their life will provide the momentum to propel our future prosperity and well-being.

REFERENCES

Adler, A. B., Bliese, P. D., McGurk, D., Hoge, C. W., & Castro, C. A. (2009). Battlemind debriefing and Battlemind training as early interventions with soldiers returning from Iraq: Randomization by platoon. *Journal of Consulting and Clinical Psychology, 77*(5), 928–940.

Anand, R., Chapman, S. B., Rackley, A., Keebler, M., Zientz, J., & Hart, J. (2011). Gist reasoning training in cognitively normal seniors. *International Journal of Geriatric Psychiatry, 26*, 961.

Arciniegas, D., Adler, L., Topkoff, J., Cawthra, E., Filley, C. M., & Reite, M. (1999). Attention and memory dysfunction after traumatic brain injury: Cholinergic mechanisms, sensory gating, and a hypothesis for further investigation. *Brain Injury, 13*(1), 1–13.

Aston-Jones, G., & Cohen, J. D. (2005). An integrative theory of locus coeruleus-norepinephrine function: Adaptive gain and optimal performance. *Annual Review of Neuroscience, 28*, 403–450.

Ball, K., Edwards, J. D., Ross, L. A., & McGwin, G., Jr. (2010). Cognitive training decreases motor vehicle collision involvement among older drivers. *Journal of the American Geriatrics Society, 58*(11), 2107–2113.

Bavelier, D., Green, C. S., Pouget, A., & Schrater, P. (2012). Brain plasticity through the life span: Learning to learn and action video games. *The Annual Review of Neuroscience, 35*, 391–416.

Bennett, E. L., Diamond, M. C., Krech, D., & Rosenzweig, M. R. (1964). Chemical and anatomical plasticity of the brain. *Science, 146*(3644), 610–619. doi: 10.1126/science.146.3644.610

Broadbent, D. E. (1971). *Decision and Stress*. London: Academic Press.

Brooks, A. W. (2014). Get excited: Reappraising pre-performance anxiety as excitement. *Journal of Experimental Psychology: General, 143*(3), 1144.

Brydon, L., Edwards, S., Jia, H., Mohamed-Ali, V., Zachary, I., Martin, J. F., & Steptoe, A. (2005). Psychological stress activates interleukin-1β gene expression in human mononuclear cells. *Brain, Behavior, and Immunity, 19*(6), 540–546.

Buschkuehl, M., Hernandez-Garcia, L., Jaeggi, S. M., Bernard, J. A., & Jonides, J. (2014). Neural effects of short-term training on working memory. *Cognitive, Affective, and Behavioral Neuroscience, 14*(1), 147–160. doi: 10.3758/s13415-013-0244-9

Chamberlain, S. R., Mueller, U., Blackwell, A. D., Robbins, T. W., & Sahakian, B. J. (2006). Noradrenergic modulation of working memory and emotional memory in humans. *Psychopharmacology, 188*, 397–407.

Chapman, S. B. (2013). *Make Your Brain Smarter: Increase Your Brain's Creativity, Energy, and Focus*. New York: Simon & Schuster.

Chapman, S. B., Aslan, S., Spence, J. S., Hart, J. J., Bartz, E. K., Didehbani, N., . . . Lu, H. (2015). Neural mechanisms of brain plasticity with complex cognitive training in healthy seniors. *Cerebral Cortex, 25*(2), 396–405. doi: 10.1093/cercor/bht234

Chapman, S. B., Aslan, S., Spence, J., Keebler, M. W., DeFina, L. F., Didehbani, N., . . . D'Esposito, M. (2016). Distinct brain and behavioral benefits from cognitive versus physical training: A randomized trial in aging adults. *Frontiers in Human Neuroscience, 10*, 338. doi: 10.3389/fnhum.2016.00338

Chapman, S. B., & Mudar, R. A. (2014). Enhancement of cognitive and neural functions through complex reasoning training: Evidence from normal and clinical populations. *Frontiers in Systems Neuroscience*. doi: 10.3389/fnsys.2014.00069

Chen, A. J. W., & D'Esposito, M. (2010). Traumatic brain injury: From bench to bedside to society. *Neuron, 66*, 11–14.

Chen, A. J. W., Abrams, G. M., & D'Esposito, M. (2006). Functional reintegration of prefrontal neural networks for enhancing recovery after brain injury. *Journal of Head Trauma Rehabilitation, 21*, 107.

Comijs, H. C., van den Kommer, T. N., Minnaar, R. W. M., Penninx, B. W. J. H., & Deeg, D. J. H. (2011). Accumulated and differential effects of life events on cognitive decline in older persons: Depending on depression, baseline cognition, or ApoE ε4 status? *The Journals of Gerontology Series B: Psychological Sciences and Social Sciences, 66B* (suppl 1), i111–i120.

Cook, L. G., Chapman, S. B., Elliott, A. C., Evenson, N. N., & Vinton, K. (2014). Cognitive gains from gist reasoning training in adolescents with chronic-stage traumatic brain injury. *Frontiers in Neurology, 5*. doi: 10.3389/fneur.2014.00087

Cornum, R., Matthews, M. D., & Seligman, M. E. P. (2011). Comprehensive soldier fitness: Building resilience in a challenging institutional context. *American Psychologist, 66*(1), 4–9.

Corrigan, J. D., Selassie, A. W., & Orman, J. A. (2010). The epidemiology of traumatic brain injury. *The Journal of Head Trauma Rehabilitation, 25*(2), 72–80.

D'Esposito M., & Chen, A. J. (2006). Neural mechanisms of prefrontal cortical function: Implications for cognitive rehabilitation. *Progress in Brain Research, 157*, 123–139.

Dosenbach, N. U., Fair, D. A., Cohen, A. L., Schlaggar, B. L., & Petersen, S. E. (2008). A dual-networks architecture of top-down control. *Trends in Cognitive Science, 12*, 99–105.

Dosenbach, N. U., Fair, D. A., Miezin, F. M., Cohen, A. L., Wenger, K. K., Dosenbach, R. A., . . . Petersen, S. E. (2007). Distinct brain networks for adaptive and stable task control in humans. *Proceedings of the National Academy of Sciences of the United States of America, 104*, 11073–11078.

Dundon, N. M., Dockree, S. P., Buckley, V., Merriman, N., Carton, M., Clarke, S., . . . Dockree, P. M. (2015). Impaired auditory selective attention ameliorated by cognitive training with graded exposure to noise in patients with traumatic brain injury. *Neuropsychologia, 75*, 74–87.

Etter, D. M. (2002). Cognitive readiness: An important research focus for national security. In M. C. Roco & W. S. Bainbridge (Eds.), *Converging Technologies for Improving Human Performance: Nanotechnology, Biotechnology, Information Technology and Cognitive Science* (pp. 330–336). Arlington, VA: National Science Foundation.

Gamino, J. F., Chapman, S. B., Hull, E. L., & Lyon, R. (2010). Effects of higher-order cognitive strategy training on gist reasoning and fact learning in adolescents. *Frontiers in Educational Psychology, 1.* doi:10.3389/fpsyg.2010.00188

Gamino, J. F., Motes, M. M., Riddle, R., Lyon, G. R., Spence, J. S., & Chapman, S. B. (2014). Enhancing inferential abilities in adolescence: New hope for students in poverty. *Frontiers in Human Neuroscience, 8,* 924. doi: 10.3389/fnhum.2014.00924

George, S. A., Knox, D., Curtis, A. L., Aldridge, J. W., Valentino, R. J., & Liberzon, I. (2013). Altered locus coeruleus–norepinephrine function following single prolonged stress. *European Journal of Neuroscience, 37*(6), 901–909.

Glaser, R., Kennedy, S., Lafuse, W. P., Bonneau, R. H., Speicher, C., Hillhouse, J., & Kiecolt-Glaser, J. K. (1990). Psychological stress-induced modulation of interleukin-2 receptor gene expression and interleukin-2 production in peripheral blood leukocytes. *Archives of General Psychiatry, 47*(8), 707–712.

Harty, S., Robertson, I. H., Miniussi, C., Sheehy, O. C., Devine, C. A., McCreery, S., & O'Connell, R. G. (2014). Transcranial direct current stimulation over right dorsolateral prefrontal cortex enhances error awareness in older age. *The Journal of Neuroscience, 34*(10), 3646–3652.

Hays, S. A., Khodaparast, N., Hulsey, D. R., Ruiz, A., Sloan, A. M., Rennaker, R. L., & Kilgard, M. P. (2014). Vagus nerve stimulation during rehabilitative training improves functional recovery after intracerebral hemorrhage. *Stroke, 45*(10), 3097–3100.

Hertel, P. T., & Mathews, A. (2011). Cognitive bias modification: Past perspectives, current findings, and future applications. *Perspectives on Psychological Science, 6,* 521–536.

Ho, M. R., & Bennett, T. L. (1997). Efficacy of neuropsychological rehabilitation for mild-moderate traumatic brain injury. *Archives of Clinical Neuropsychology, 12*(1), 1–11.

Hurley, D. (2014). *Smarter: The New Science of Building Brain Power.* New York: Hudson Street Press.

Jaeggi, S. M., Buschkuehl, M., Jonides, J., & Perrig, W. J. (2008). Improving fluid intelligence with training on working memory. *Proceedings of the National Academy of Sciences of the United States of America, 105,* 6829–6833.

Jha, A. P., Morrison, A. B., Dainer-Best, J., Parker, S., Rostrup, N., & Stanley, E. A. (2015). Minds "at attention": Mindfulness training curbs attentional lapses in military cohorts. *PLoS ONE, 10*(2): e0116889. doi:10.1371/journal.pone.0116889

Kolditz, T. A. (2007). *In Extremis Leadership: Leading as If Your Life Depended on It.* San Francisco: Jossey-Bass

Lampit, A., Hallock, H., & Valenzuela, M. (2014). Computerized cognitive training in cognitively healthy older adults: A systematic review and meta-analysis of effect modifiers. *PLoS Medicine, 11*(11), e1001756. doi: 10.1371/journal.pmed.1001756

Lewis, G. F., Hourani, L., Tueller, S., Kizakevich, P., Bryant, S., Weimer, B., & Strange, L. (2015). Relaxation training assisted by heart rate variability biofeedback: Implication for a military predeployment stress inoculation protocol. *Psychophysiology, 52*(9), 1167–1174.

Lieberman, H. R., Karl J. P., Niro, P. J., Williams, K. W., Farina, E. K., Cable, S. J., & McClung, J. P. (2014). Positive effects of basic training on cognitive performance and mood of adult females. *Human Factors, 56*(6), 1113–1123.

Locke, E. A., & Latham, G. P. (2006). New directions in goal-setting theory. *Current Directions in Psychological Science, 15*(5), 265–268.

Manly, T., Hawkins, K., Evans, J., Woldt, K., & Robertson, I. H. (2002). Rehabilitation of executive function: Facilitation of effective goal management on complex tasks using periodic auditory alerts. *Neuropsychologia, 40,* 271–281.

Max, J. E., Lopez, A., Wilde, E. A., Bigler, E. D., Schachar, R. J., Saunders, A., . . . Levin, H. S. (2015). Anxiety disorders in children and adolescents in the second six months after traumatic brain injury. *Journal of Pediatric Rehabilitation Medicine, 8*(4), 345–355.

McNab, F., Varrone, A., Farde, L., Jucaite, A., Bystritsky, P., Forssberg, H., & Klingberg, T. (2009). Changes in cortical dopamine D1 receptor binding associated with cognitive training. *Science, 323*(5915), 800–802.

Merzenich M. M., Recanzone G. H., & Jenkins W. (1991). How the brain functionally rewires itself. In M. Arbib & J. A. Robinson (Eds.), *Natural and Artificial Parallel Computations* (pp. 177–210). New York: MIT Press.

Milewski-Lopez, A., Greco, E., vandenBerg, F., McAvinue, L. P., McGuire, S., & Robertson, I. H. (2014). An evaluation of alertness training for older adults. *Frontiers in Aging Neuroscience, 6*(67). doi: 10.3389/fnagi.2014.00067

Miller, L. J., & Mittenberg, W. (1998). Brief cognitive behavioral interventions in mild traumatic brain injury. *Applied Neuropsychology, 5*(4), 172–183.

Mishra, J., & Gazzaley, A. (2014). Harnessing the neuroplastic potential of the human brain and the future of cognitive rehabilitation. *Frontiers in Human Neuroscience, 8*(218), 1–4. doi.org/10.3389/fnhum.2014.00218

O'Brien, C., & McCormack, H. (2015, June). Brain health and brain fitness: A national call for action. (An issue brief released by the Kennedy Forum). Retrieved from The Kennedy Forum website: https://www.thekennedyforum.org/vision/brainhealth

O'Connell, R. G., Bellgrove, M. A., Dockree, P. M., Lau, A., Fitzgerald, M., & Robertson, I. H. (2008). Self-Alert training: Volitional modulation of autonomic arousal improves sustained attention. *Neuropsychologia, 46*(5), 1379–1390.

Rao, V., & Lyketsos, C. G. (2002). Psychiatric aspects of traumatic brain injury. *The Psychiatric Clinics of North America, 25*(1), 43–69.

Richards, M., & Deary, I. (2010). Cognitive capital in the British birth cohorts: An introduction. *Longitudinal and Life Course Studies, 1*(3), 197–200.

Rose, R. D., Buckey, J. C., Zbozinek, T. D., Motivala, S. J., Glenn, D. E., Cartreine, J. A., & Craske, M. G. (2013). A randomized controlled trial of a self-guided, multimedia, stress management and resilience training program. *Behaviour Research and Therapy, 51*(2), 106–112.

Rosnick, C. B., Small, B. J., McEvoy, C. L., Borenstein, A. R., & Mortimer, J. A. (2007). Negative life events and cognitive performance in a population of older adults. *Journal of Aging and Health, 19*(4), 612–629.

Russell, A., Bulkley, B., & Grafton, C. (2005). *Human Performance Optimization and Military Missions: Final Report.* Washington, DC: United States Department of Defense Office of Net Assessment (ONA), GS-10F-0297K.

Salomone, S., Fleming, G. R., Shanahan, J. M., Castorina, M., Bramham, J., O'Connell, R. G., & Robertson, I. (2015). The effects of a Self-Alert Training (SAT) program in adults with ADHD. *Frontiers in Human Neuroscience, 9.* doi:10.3389/fnhum.2015.00045

Schatz, S., Bartlett, K., Burley, N., Dixon, C. D., Knarr, K., & Gannon, L. K. (2012). Making good instructors great: USMC cognitive readiness and instructor professionalization initiatives. In *The Interservice/Industry Training, Simulation & Education Conference (I/ITSEC)* (Paper No. 12185). Arlington, VA: National Training and Simulation Association.

Smith, G. E., Housen, P., Yaffe, K., Ruff, R., Kennison, R. F., Mahncke, H. W., & Zelinski, E. M. (2009). A cognitive training program based on principles of brain plasticity: Results from the Improvement in Memory with Plasticity-based Adaptive Cognitive Training (IMPACT) study. *Journal of the American Geriatrics Society, 57*(4), 594–603.

Stanley, E. A., Schaldach, J. M., Kiyonaga, A., & Jha, A. P. (2011). Mindfulness-based mind fitness training: A case study of a high-stress predeployment military cohort. *Cognitive and Behavioral Practice, 18*(4), 566–576.

Sterpenich, V., D'Argembeau, A., Desseilles, M., Balteau, E., Albouy, G., Vandewalle, G., . . . Maquet, P. (2006). The locus ceruleus is involved in the successful retrieval of emotional memories in humans. *The Journal of Neuroscience, 26*(28), 7416–7423.

Sullivan, K. W., Quinn, J. E., Pramuka, M., Sharkey, A. A., & French, L. M. (2012). Outcomes from a pilot study using computer-based rehabilitative tools in a military population. *Annual Review of Cybertherapy and Telemedicine, 10,* 71–77

Takeuchi, H., Taki, Y., Nouchi, R., Hashizume, H., Sekiguchi, A., Kotozaki, Y., . . . Kawashima, R. (2013). Effects of working memory-training on functional connectivity and cerebral blood flow during rest. *Cortex, 49,* 2106–2125. doi: 10.1016/j.cortex.2012.09.007

Tiersky, L. A., Anselmi, V., Johnston, M. V., Kurtyka, J., Roosen, E., Schwartz, T., & Deluca, J. (2005). A trial of neuropsychologic rehabilitation in mild-spectrum traumatic brain injury. *Archives of Physical Medicine and Rehabilitation, 86*(8), 1565–1574.

Vas, A., Chapman, S., Aslan, S., Spence, J., Keebler, M., Rodriguez-Larrain, G., . . . Krawczyk, D. (2016). Reasoning training in veteran and civilian traumatic brain injury with persistent mild impairment. *Neuropsychological Rehabilitation 26*(4), 502–531. doi: 10.1080/09602011.2015.1044013

Vas, A. K., Chapman, S. B., & Cook, L. G. (2015). Language impairments in traumatic brain injury: A window into complex cognitive performance. In A. Salazar & J. Grafman (Eds.), *Handbook of Clinical Neurology: Traumatic Brain Injury Part II* (Vol. 128, pp. 497–510). Amsterdam: Elsevier.

Vas, A. K., Chapman, S. B., Cook, L. G., Elliott, A. C., & Keebler, M. (2011). Higher-order reasoning training years after traumatic brain injury in adults. *Journal of Head Trauma Rehabilitation, 26*(3), 224–239.

Venza, E., Spence, J., & Chapman, S. B. (2016, April). Enhancing brain and behavior in adults with bipolar disorder through advanced reasoning training. Abstract presented at the 23rd Annual Meeting of the Cognitive Neuroscience Society in New York, NY.

Villani, D., Grassi, A., Cognetta, C., Toniolo, D., Cipresso, P., & Riva, G. (2013). Self-help stress management training through mobile phones: An experience with oncology nurses. *Psychological Services, 10*(3), 315.

Wolinsky, F. D., Unverzagt, F. W., Smith, D. M., Jones, R., Stoddard, A., & Tennstedt, S. L. (2006). The ACTIVE cognitive training trial and health-related quality of life: Protection that lasts for 5 years. *The Journals of Gerontology. Series A, Biological Sciences and Medical Sciences, 61*(12), 1324–1329.

Yan, X., Brown, A. D., Lazar, M., Cressman, V. L., Henn-Haase, C., Neylan, T. C., . . . Marmar, C. R. (2013). Spontaneous brain activity in combat related PTSD. *Neuroscience Letters, 547,* 1–5. doi:10.1016/j.neulet.2013.04.032

Yerkes, R. M., & Dodson, J. D. (1908). The relation of strength of stimulus to rapidity of habit-formation. *Journal of Comparative and Neurological Psychology, 18,* 459–482.

Yezhuvath, U., Motes, M. A., Aslan, S., Spence, J. S., & Chapman, S. B. (2016, April). Enhanced prefrontal neural efficiency in healthy agers following advanced reasoning training. Abstract presented at the annual Reprogramming the Human Brain to Health Symposium in Dallas, TX.

Yuen, E. Y., Wei, J., Liu, W., Zhong, P., Li, X., & Yan, Z. (2012). Repeated stress causes cognitive impairment by suppressing glutamate receptor expression and function in prefrontal cortex. *Neuron, 73*(5), 962–977.

Zanto, T. P., & Gazzaley, A. (2013). Fronto-parietal network: Flexible hub of cognitive control. *Trends in Cognitive Sciences, 17*(12), 602–603.

13

Optimizing Cognitive Performance

Genetic and Epigenetic Techniques

VALERIE E. MARTINDALE

GENES AND COGNITION

In order to consider genetic and epigenetic techniques for optimizing human cognitive performance, we must first consider to what extent cognitive performance is the product of genetic and epigenetic forces. Do we have evidence that genes drive cognitive performance, at least to some degree?

The best evidence of the role of genes in any trait, physical, cognitive, or behavioral is the degree to which that trait is heritable. Heritability in this sense is a technical term referring to traditional studies of family trees and monozygotic and dizygotic twins and now augmented with techniques that compare chunks of genetic material directly. These techniques determine just how much of the variability in a specific phenotype (trait, whether desirable or undesirable) is associated with the inheritance of specific DNA (a chromosome, haplotype, or even a single gene). The trait must be defined and measured, and then the pattern of its appearance in related individuals can be followed (Shikishima, Hiraishi, Yamagata, Ando, & Okada, 2015). Familiar examples that we will refer to as we proceed are sickle-cell trait (a gene-dose-dependent phenotype with deleterious effects), eye color (a simple, dominant, single gene inheritance), and height (a multigenic trait with heritability around 0.50).

The term "heritability" used in this way describes the amount of observed variation that is accounted for by hereditary mechanisms.[1] The amount of variation that is not explained by hereditary mechanisms is said to be due to the environment. Toward the end of the chapter, we will look at what that catchall term, "environment," encompasses.

For now, a quick look at what heritability encompasses will be helpful. A current biology textbook (Brooker, 2015) can provide more in-depth background, but here are the basics.

The field of genetics began with Gregor Mendel's observations of inheritance. He could see in his pea plants the passage from one generation to the next of specific traits, like the color of a flower or the smoothness of the ripe pea. He called the heritable units that were passed from one generation to the next "genes." He had no way to know what they consisted of.

The next great leap forward was understanding what has been called the central dogma of biology: DNA contains the instructions (genes) for making proteins, and proteins in turn provide the structural and functional machinery of living organisms (traits). Heritability has therefore been considered synonymous with "coded in the DNA." *Epigenetics* refers to another layer of genetic information, consisting of controls on the expression of DNA that do not affect the code itself. There is ample evidence that epigenetic differences affect cognition and behavior (Benevento, van de Molengraft, van Westen, van Bokhoven, & Nadif Kasri, 2015; Haas et al., 2016; Peter et al., 2016). Most such controls are mechanisms of "silencing," rendering a specific stretch of DNA inert by refusing access to the copy machinery. *Imprinting* is a particularly interesting form, in which a large stretch of DNA is silenced by mechanisms that typically silence only one copy, either always the maternally inherited copy or always the paternally inherited copy, of a specific stretch of DNA. When one copy of a gene is defective, and the other copy is imprinted, the defective copy becomes manifest. Prader-Willi syndrome is an example in humans, the first to be elucidated, of the silencing of a good maternally inherited chromosome 15 copy due to imprinting, revealing a defective or absent copy of the corresponding stretch of the paternally inherited chromosome 15 (see Butler, 2009, for more on imprinting in humans). Epigenetic changes can be considered a refinement on the central dogma. They are not often inherited, in most cases being cleared during the formation of sperm and ova (Probst, Dunleavy, & Almouzni, 2009), but they can have effects on the next generation (Ciabrelli et al., 2017) and, as noted, can imprint or otherwise affect inherited alleles, thereby masking or revealing inherited genes.

We are still coming to grips with the third leap in understanding heritability: the completion of the Human Genome Project revealed that less than 2% of the genome codes for proteins. The central dogma is much less central than we thought. Heritability presumably covers the functions of the noncoding DNA, even if we do not yet know what many of those functions are. We think the other 98% contains the instructions for exactly where, when, for how long, under what conditions, and to what extent those better-understood protein-coding genes are expressed (Taft, Pheasant, & Mattick, 2007). Genetic and epigenetic optimization of human cognitive performance therefore refers to optimizing that which is heritable, the DNA, and thereby the proteins and other functions[2] coded in DNA.

DEFINING OPTIMUM

In the discussion that follows, consideration of the actual method of implementing any optimization will be left to the very end, but it might be helpful to define, in general terms, what implementation means. To implement an optimization via genetic and/or epigenetic mechanisms means controlling the expression of genetic material, thereby forcing overexpression, underexpression, or expression of an altered product, or a combination of those. In order to proceed on any implementation, we must first understand the effects, intentional and unintentional, of altering genetic expression.

Let's consider an exemplar, a potential candidate for optimization. Catechol-O-methyltransferase (COMT) is an enzyme that degrades catecholamines and is the product of the COMT gene (Stein, Newman, Savitz, & Ramesar, 2006). The gene codes for two isoforms. One is soluble and widely distributed in tissues, and the other is membrane-bound and most active in the central nervous system (CNS). We will focus on the effects of the second one, the membrane-bound isoform in the CNS.

COMT has been dubbed the "warrior gene" and even the "warrior/worrier gene," to emphasize the effect that appears to result from alternate alleles that differ by a single nucleotide polymorphism at codon 158, resulting in alternate amino acid incorporation at position 158 in the expressed protein (Dickinson & Elvevåg, 2009). Codon 158 may code for a valine residue (most common) or a methionine residue. Val158 has a higher enzymatic activity than the less common met158 allele and therefore degrades the common neurotransmitter, dopamine, more rapidly, thereby affecting neural processes that depend on dopamine.

To employ a more familiar gene as an analogy, the gene for eye color exists in brown and blue alleles. COMT exists in one of two[3] states: val158 and met158. An individual will have one copy inherited from the mother and one from the father. Thus an individual may be val/val (high activity and low dopamine), val/met heterozygous (midlevels of activity and of dopamine), or met/met (low activity and high dopamine). Although neither allele is fully dominant in the way that brown eye color is dominant, the met158 (lower activity) form is partially dominant, so that heterozygotes are closer to met/met than to val/val. The warrior allele, val158, is a more effective enzyme, resulting in less dopamine in the CNS and, in particular, in the prefrontal cortex, as compared to the alternate allele, met158, which might be called the worrier allele for the state of lower activation and therefore indecisiveness associated with it (Stein et al., 2006). The worrier state may be considered dominant, like brown eyes, and the warrior state recessive, like blue eyes. Dominance is not the same as prevalence: the warrior allele is the more prevalent. The story sounds appealing and straightforward when told this way. The next section discusses the limitations on this story.

THE IMPORTANCE OF CONTEXT

First, let's consider the desired state. Which should be called optimal, the state of high aggression and rapid action, or the state of increased concentration and anxiety? The early research on the warrior/worrier gene offers the suggestion that a soldier may benefit from the warrior allele, while an analyst may benefit from the worrier allele (Dickinson & Elvevåg, 2009; Stein et al., 2006). The other side of the coin is the advantage of the met allele most of the time: when stress is low, rapid aggressive action is less desirable than calm deliberation. This demonstrates the role and the importance of context in any discussion of performance.

Environmental Context of Behavior

Optimizing performance requires context. What is the goal of "optimization?" Increasing aggression is clearly not an optimal response to curing disease, engaging in diplomacy, or doing meticulous research. Yet soldiers, in common with firefighters, rescue workers, and emergency response teams, can benefit from the self-confident and action-oriented warrior allele, rather than the more caution-inducing worrier allele. And what of police forces, which must be restrained in most circumstances, but prepared to use force and react rapidly in life-threatening situations? If an optimum could be determined, it might be better accomplished by choosing those best at the job and then surveying them for their genotypes. A host of problems attends this approach, not least of which is defining those who are best at the job.

While implementation of optimization strategies is left to a later section, it is worth pointing out here that temporary means of effecting an optimum may be beneficial, if for no other reason than the fact that context is not constant, or even necessarily predictable, for most of us in our daily lives.

The foregoing suggests that the two alleles vary in their effects in a dependable way. In fact, studies subsequent to the eye-catching warrior/worrier papers do not agree (Qayyum et al., 2015). The use of eye color, with its two distinct states, is therefore a misleading comparison. There are several interrelated reasons for the discrepancy.

Genetic Context of Expression

First, genes are always expressed within the context of other genes. While the expression of COMT within the context of autism or schizophrenia may not be relevant to the discussion of optimization of the norm, it illustrates the fact that a particular allele may have little or no effect, or even a contradictory effect, in an alternate genetic environment (Qayyum et al., 2015). If natural levels of the substrate, dopamine, are low, the met158 allele may be entirely sufficient to degrade them, or if the receptor is high-affinity and easily saturated, the val158 allele may make little difference in the ultimate strength of a dopamine signaling cascade. Alternately, a rare allele of a different enzyme may confer a compatible methyltransferase activity on another enzyme in the prefrontal cortex, or some other altered pathway may result in failure of the COMT enzyme itself to be degraded or inhibited, effectively resulting in greater enzyme activity.

Effect Size

Second, an effect size large enough to be reliably measured may still not be large enough to make a difference in an operational setting. In medicine, a distinction is made between statistical significance and clinical significance. A drug that reliably lowers blood pressure by 2 points, for example, is statistically significant, but such a small effect is not clinically significant in reducing the harmful effects of high blood pressure. Similarly, the increase in aggression due to the val158 allele may not be sufficient to be noticeable in the chaotic and fluid environment of military or rescue operations, and the improved memory and concentration provided by the met158 allele may be so diluted by other advantages and disadvantages as to be without effect.

Off-Target Effects

Third, in addition to tradeoffs inherent in the concept of optimization (i.e., the ability to optimize for speed or accuracy but not both), there are tradeoffs at the genetic level due to the pleiotropic nature of biochemical signals. Dopamine is a signaling molecule used in many ways other than aggressive versus cautious state changes. It also contributes to neural control of muscles, pleasure and reward, memory formation, and emotional experience. While the membrane-bound form of COMT is expressed primarily in the prefrontal cortex, it may also be expressed at low levels in other tissues. In addition to its high-affinity activity in metabolizing dopamine, epinephrine, and norepinephrine, it may also have a low but measurable activity in degrading related substrates, and its alteration may therefore produce what might be considered off-target effects. It may be instructive to consider that alleles that are less common but not rare may be maintained in the population precisely because they confer an advantage in some limited circumstances. The gene for sickle cell trait illustrates this. Heterozygotes, with one normal and one sickle-cell gene, have some increased resistance to infection by the malaria parasite. This advantage is enough to maintain the gene in the population despite the severe disadvantage of sickle cell disease in homozygotic individuals. Thus, both the surrounding genetic environment and the external environment determine whether a specific allele of a specific gene is advantageous, or even optimal.

THE CHALLENGE OF MULTIGENIC GENETIC TRAITS

A different picture is presented by the trait known as G, or general intelligence. G is difficult to define, although to paraphrase Justice Potter Stewart, we know it when we see it. G, like any complex trait, is best defined, at least for the purpose of investigation, by the means used to measure it. There are generally accepted standard measures of G, most notably the Stanford Binet test and the Wechsler Adult Intelligence Scale. For this discussion, we will assume G is what is measured by what are called standardized intelligence tests, recognizing that these are imperfect, as reflected in their within-subject variability.

Genetics of intelligence has long been an active area of investigation, fueled by observations that academic success and occupational success appear to run in families more than chance would dictate (Beam, Turkheimer, Dickens, & Davis, 2015; Shakeshaft et al., 2015). Many studies of the heritability of intelligence have converged on roughly 0.5 as the approximate value, with a range from 0.2 to 0.8. While 0.5 sounds equivalent to a coin flip, it is considered a high degree of heritability by geneticists. The fly in the ointment, however, is that there is no one gene for intelligence. Rather, there are hundreds, each contributing to less than 0.2% of observed variation (Plomin & Deary, 2015). The situation is quite comparable to the study of height as a heritable trait. Height, like intelligence, is a continuous variable with a limited range and also shows heritability around 0.5, with dozens of genes contributing. In both height and intelligence, a whopping 50% of variation remains to be accounted for by the environment.

Optimizing intelligence therefore raises some questions we have already investigated and some that are new. The first questions have to do with context and goal. When it comes to intelligence, is more always better? Our first inclination may be to say yes, and, in the modern world dominated by rapid-fire data, rapidly changing circumstances, and the need to understand complex causal chains, this may well be true. Has it always been true? Perhaps in a world dominated by routine and repetitive tasks, intelligence could be a burden. It is difficult to say, and even more difficult, should we find the means to reliably increase intelligence, to determine the reasoning by which we might dole out such a gift.

A new set of questions arises, having to do with the multigenic nature of intelligence that did not apply to consideration of COMT. To what extent do the genetic underpinnings of intelligence reflect the genetic control of the development of the nervous system? In other words, is G an effect of early genetic expression, which, once completed, is no longer amenable to alteration? Although intellectual disability does not appear to share the same genetic basis as exceptional cognitive ability (Franić et al., 2015; Hill et al., 2016), it can provide some insight on the role of development. The FOXP2 gene has been called a "gene for speech" or "gene for grammar" (Estruch, Graham, Chinnappa, Deriziotis, & Fisher, 2016). As the authors make clear, the appellation is incorrect, or at least incomplete, because the protein product, FOXP2, is necessary for brain (and lung) development, and the deficiencies in grammar caused by mutations in FOXP2 are therefore the effects of altered brain development. Members of family pedigrees demonstrating a mutant FOXP2 do indeed demonstrate distinctive speech aberrations, but affected individuals may also demonstrate impaired motor skills unrelated to speech and language, memory deficits, and autism spectrum symptoms. Speech, as a highly demanding synthesis of cognitive and motor activities, is in this case an indicator of widespread alterations, rather than a specific phenotype (Garcia-Calero, Botella-Lopez, Bahamonde, Perez-Balaguer, & Martinez, 2016; Lieberman, 2009).

G, like speech, is also a demanding synthesis of activities and may be expected to be sensitive to developmental conditions. Therefore, any gene that has an effect during development may influence G. This does not mean such genes are only active during embryonic development—far from it. Human nervous system development undergoes several critical periods of rapid growth and rearrangement—particularly in utero, in infancy, childhood, and in adolescence. Neural plasticity has been demonstrated in adults, and stem cells are now believed to be present in neural tissue even in the elderly, albeit at reduced numbers (Knudsen, 2004). Thus, processes that call upon the genes that influence G are active throughout life. G seems to be most variable early in life and to converge to relatively higher association with parental G values later in life, possibly pointing to continued genetic involvement in the adult nervous system (Plomin & Deary, 2015).

This pattern suggests that the most effective way of optimizing G may call for alteration of developmental processes. However, alteration at the adult phase should not be discounted. The induction of color vision in adult monkeys, following administration of genes for color vision receptor formation, raises the possibility of extreme plasticity even in the fully differentiated adult nervous system (Mancuso et al., 2009).

ENVIRONMENT: A NEW INTERPRETATION

The role of heredity in intelligence leaves a large fraction of variability unaccounted for. What is the role of environment, and what makes up the mechanisms by which environment affects intelligence?

Many factors have been hypothesized, and some are well understood, such as nutritional deficiencies, sensory stimulation, and variety of experience. But the most exciting new avenue of inquiry is the role of the *microbiome*, the assortment of microorganisms that colonize us from before birth and throughout life (Guzman, Bereza-Malcolm, De Groef, & Franks, 2015). These include viruses, bacteria, phages (viruses that prey on bacteria), fungi, archaea, and even protozoa. To describe the microbial denizens as parasites is much too limited. Some are definitely beneficial (Hoban et al., 2016); many, perhaps most, are neutral. Some are beneficial in some circumstances and harmful in others. Different, closely related strains of the same organism can have very different effects on health and well-being (Parashar & Udayabanu, 2016; Savignac, Tramullas, Kiely, Dinan, & Cryan, 2015).

The phenomenon of "horizontal gene transfer" makes it especially difficult to define a particular microbiome (Opstal & Bordenstein, 2015). Horizontal gene transfer is a collective term for the various mechanisms by which genetic material from one organism can become part of the genetic material of another organism. This is a fascinating subject in its own right, but, for our purposes, it may be best to consider the microbiome as a loosely defined collection of organisms whose genetic makeup can vary. Each individual has a unique microbiome at any given time. Unlike the nuclear genetic makeup of each individual, the genetic makeup of each individual's microbiome is subject to change over time. Illnesses and antibiotics can cause rapid and extensive changes, which are usually temporary (Langdon, Crook, & Dantas, 2016; Shreiner, Kao, & Young, 2015). Changes in diet and exercise and other environmental factors can also change the makeup of a particular microbiome (Clarke et al., 2014; David et al., 2013; Kang et al., 2014; Lyte et al., 2016).

How would the microbiome affect cognitive performance? Why would we think the organisms living in our guts and on our skin could change the way we think or perceive the world?

As it turns out, there are multiple possible mechanisms of action. Here are the three that appear the strongest.

1. There is a well-established two-way interaction between the gut and the CNS, termed the "gut-brain axis." The mechanisms are still not understood, but are likely to include the production of neurochemicals or their precursors by

gut bacteria (e.g. dopamine; de Araujo, Ferreira, Tellez, Ren, & Yeckel, 2012; Mayer, 2011) and potential transport of microorganisms or their products by retrograde transport in the vagus nerve (Bravo et al., 2011; Forsythe, Bienenstock, & Kunze, 2014; Galland, 2014).

2. The uptake of microorganisms by the lymphatic system with transport via the recently discovered lymphatic drainage of the brain (Carare, 2014).

3. Possible transport of intact microorganisms directly into neural tissue by circulating macrophages (Rosenberger & Finlay, 2003).

There is reason to believe that normal, healthy, immunocompetent brains are colonized at a low level by bacteria and probably other members of the microbiome as well (Branton et al., 2013). Pathogenic invaders known to seek out the nervous system and survive there, doing great damage in the process, include the bacterium responsible for syphilis and the virus responsible for rabies. We have assumed for a long time that any organism taking up residence in the nervous system would be a pathogen and cause obvious damage similar to these pathogens, and we have conversely assumed that a healthy brain is aseptic. That now appears to be far too simple a model.

Regardless of whether the microbiome has outposts in the CNS or acts entirely by transport of its products across the blood–brain barrier, the clear influence of the microbiome on the CNS opens up a whole new line of enquiry into optimization of human cognition. How much of the "environmental" influence responsible for variations in G, for example, is due to the microbiome? What is the influence of the microbiome during development? Even the intrauterine environment is not sterile (Aagaard et al., 2014). An unanswered question is the extent to which the microbiome itself is heritable. Because it is initially populated in the first hours and days of life, it is likely to be heavily populated by (inherited from) the mother's microbiome, and the microbiome is assumed to be strongly influenced by the immune system, which is also highly heritable (Opstal & Bordenstein, 2015). On the other hand, the composition of the microbiome can change dramatically within hours in response to change in diet, for example (Kang et al., 2014). Research into the effects on cognition of diet, exercise, and even sleep, may be mediated by changes in the microbiome. This is a new frontier, one with a potentially very high payoff.

While genetic manipulation is risky and fraught with ethical concerns, and epigenetic manipulation is still difficult and its effects largely speculative, manipulation of the microbiome is easily within our grasp. We do it ourselves, in fact, when enjoying natural products of fermentation (cheese, beer, wine) and foods with live bacterial cultures (yoghurt, kefir). We do it with fasting, with exercise, with pharmaceuticals, and with washing. It is highly likely that before we look at changing our nuclear or mitochondrial DNA to achieve optimization, we will first work via genetic alteration of the microbiome. This may include understanding the microbiome load of the CNS itself.

IMPLEMENTING GENETIC/EPIGENETIC OPTIMIZATION

With this foundation, it is time to look at implementation of genetic/epigenetic optimization. To implement an optimization via genetic and/or epigenetic mechanisms means controlling the expression of genetic material, whether it be by forcing overexpression, underexpression, or expression of an altered product, or a combination of those. When considering genetic or epigenetic means, gene editing is the first thing most people think of, so let's investigate that first.

Gene Editing and Plasmid Transfection

Let us suppose that we have decided to edit an individual who is a met/met ("worrier") homozygote with respect to COMT to produce the val158 ("warrior") gene product instead. Remember that met158 is partially dominant, so we will have to replace more than 50% of the met158 genes with val158 genes. Remember also that every cell contains two copies. To be effective, editing will have to change the majority of cells completely over to val158 genes. What are the ways this can be done?

There are two primary methods: introduce genetic material in addition to the host genetic material (plasmid insertion is often used this way in animal models) or introduce genetic material to replace some amount of host genetic material (true editing).

A *plasmid* is a floating bit of DNA that must be introduced into a host cell to be expressed. For our purposes, the mechanism by which the plasmid is targeted and taken up into a cell is unimportant, but some of the limitations of targeting and uptake are important. These include the potential for the plasmid to integrate into the host chromosome in an undesirable location, the difficulty of targeting the plasmid to specific cell and tissue types, and limitations on control of the plasmid once it is taken up.

Let's assume that we have a plasmid that will not integrate into the genome, will be targeted to cells of interest at a high efficiency, and contains appropriate controls. To effect the changeover from met158 to val158 using plasmid insertion, it is necessary to supply the val158 gene *and* to inactivate the met158 gene. A plasmid may easily be constructed to contain the desired val158 gene. Silencing by plasmid is a little trickier. The most direct and reliable way might be to produce an anti-sense RNA, or a specifically targeted inhibitory protein, to prevent the native gene from being expressed. By using a nonintegrating plasmid, the host DNA is not changed, but a new gene is added to the cell and a native gene is effectively removed. This method can be engineered to be reversible, provided the plasmid has a "kill switch" that will result in its internal destruction or rejection by the host cell, in response to some particular condition. For example, the plasmid may be designed to code for a gene that produces a protein that cuts the plasmid, thereby inactivating it, upon exposure to a particular drug.

There are currently drawbacks to using plasmids to accomplish our optimization. At this point, we are not very good at well-targeted, tissue-specific, high-efficiency plasmid introduction into animals. Ideally, we want only the target cells to receive and express the plasmid, and we want all, or at least a majority, of the target cells to receive and express the plasmid. We also run the risk of the plasmid integrating into the host genome, and the position of integration is not very controllable. This can lead to the disruption of important genes and, worse, to the induction of cancers caused when cellular regulation of growth and division is altered by disruption of the genes involved.

True gene editing, on the other hand, has become surprisingly precise. It is still not 100%, so the risk of off-target effects and even cancer induction is still present, but our abilities in this area are improving rapidly. However, true editing is much more difficult, if not impossible, to reverse. How can that be? If a gene can be edited from A to B, why not from B back to A? The problem arises because the editing efficiency is never 100%; 80% effectiveness is considered very high. In this case, some cells will have both copies edited, some will have one edited, and a few will have neither edited. The reversal is also only 80% effective, so that of the edited cells, some with one copy of the new gene will not have that copy reverted, some with two copies of the new gene will have only one reverted, and a few with two copies of the new gene will have neither copy reverted. In other words, the original state cannot be regained.

This failure to reverse gene editing might be averted by making use of cell types that have short lives, such as intestinal lining or circulating blood cells. Nerve cells are very long-lived, so direct editing of nerve cells must be carefully considered. Circulating white blood cells on the other hand have much shorter lives, so if the desired effect can be attained by editing circulating white blood cells, no reversal is needed—the unedited stem cells will produce new white blood cells over time, using the host's original DNA. In order to make use of this approach to genetic modification, the cells to be edited must be accurately targeted, and the edited cells must be able to produce the desired result. Changing COMT in circulating blood cells will not affect the desired processes in the prefrontal cortex, so while the principle holds, it is not always usable in a specific application.

There are a growing number of highly sophisticated techniques that can be used in cultured cells and even in animals to achieve desired results. The risk–benefit ratio, an essential ethical principle used to weigh the advisability of research and treatment involving humans, will not favor enhancement of healthy humans for some time. However, for treatment of certain genetic illnesses, gene therapy is already a reality, and more medical applications are on the way. Research on human gene therapy has come a long way, and in the summer of 2017 the US Food and Drug Administration (FDA), acting on the unanimous recommendation of its Oncology Drugs Advisory Committee, approved the first gene therapy available as treatment in the United States (Chustecka, 2017; FDA, 2017a; Grady, 2017). The treatment uses blood collected from the patient. The patient's own T cells are separated out and genetically engineered, then infused back into the patient, post-chemotherapy. The engineered T cells very specifically attack the patient's leukemic B cells with remarkable clinical results in research trials. A second therapy, also using modified T-cells, was approved two months later (FDA, 2017b), and a third genetic therapy was approved in December of 2017 to directly treat an inherited genetic disorder (FDA, 2017c), the first of its kind in the U.S. More information on how sophisticated methods are being applied to further the realization of medical gene editing can be found in the references (Suzuki et al., 2016; Yin et al., 2017).

THE FUTURE FOR GENETIC OPTIMIZATION OF HUMAN COGNITION?

As a comparison, here is a quick look at laser eye surgery. In 1972, the development of the excimer laser prompted Dr. Stephen Trokel to experiment with it on the eyes of animal cadavers. In 1983, 11 years later, he performed the first medical photorefractive keratectomy treatment on a patient. Improvements in lasers, surgical techniques, and underlying theory led to the development of successive techniques, so that by 1999, the procedure was so well tolerated and the risks so well understood that laser eye surgery could be performed on any adult whose vision would benefit and who did not have certain corneal diseases. In other words, the medical procedure had become a performance enhancement available to healthy individuals.

It is reasonable to expect that the same progression will happen with genetic techniques. Already the sophistication of genetic constructs and the efficiency and efficacy of genetic delivery techniques have advanced dramatically from the difficult laboratory procedures they once were. The zinc finger method began the precision editing era, first published in 1991, followed by TALENS in 2009, and most recently CRISPR in 2012. When the risk becomes as well understood and controlled as the risk of laser eye surgery, the enhancement of healthy humans becomes easy.

What will we choose to do in the cognitive arena? Poor vision used to be part of normal human variation, but it is safe to say individuals with poor vision did not desire that particular variation, and, when improvements became available, that variation began to seem more of a disability. It is likely we will begin with improvement of those traits that are considered less than "average," like poor vision. Poor reading skills, poor memory, poor planning skills (the list goes on) may be normal variations that individuals will wish to have improved if the means become available. It is unlikely that physical attributes will be left unimproved when genetic means are available, so we may be enhancing cognitive skills in order to cope with improved reflexes, vision in additional wavelengths, or the ability to live a few extra decades. We may also be trying to keep up with artificial intelligence, another field that is progressing rapidly.

It is an interesting irony to contemplate that we will be enhancing our ability to contemplate, and deciding what to enhance while still in our unenhanced state. I have the luxury as I write this of knowing that another chapter in this volume will be dedicated to ethical issues, but it is obvious that our grasp of the humanities and our exercise of moral philosophy has never been more important.

NOTES

1. Saying "the amount of variation" is not the same as saying "the amount of the trait itself." It is common to fall into the habit of using phrases like "a gene for height," but it is important to understand that we mean "a gene found to account for some of the variation in height."

2. DNA is known to code for RNA machines, such as the ribosomal components necessary to synthesize proteins, and for regulatory RNAs. DNA code contains binding sites for enhancers, suppressors, and transcription factors that alter the timing and degree of expression of RNAs and proteins. DNA structure affects cell division and gene expression. Thus there are many known functions of DNA that are not affected by the mechanism of coding for proteins but are still inherited inasmuch as they are dependent on the sequence of DNA bases.

3. COMT is a large protein and displays alleles with alternate bases at multiple sites. We will simplify here to the comparison of only the two most common and most studied alleles, those at codon 158.

REFERENCES

Aagaard, K., Ma, J., Antony, K. M., Ganu, R., Petrosino, J., & Versalovic, J. (2014). The placenta harbors a unique microbiome. *Science Translational Medicine*, 6(237), 237ra65-237ra65. https://doi.org/10.1126/scitranslmed.3008599

Beam, C. R., Turkheimer, E., Dickens, W. T., & Davis, D. W. (2015). Twin differentiation of cognitive ability through phenotype to environment transmission: The Louisville twin study. *Behavior Genetics*, 45(6), 622–634. https://doi.org/10.1007/s10519-015-9756-0

Benevento, M., van de Molengraft, M., van Westen, R., van Bokhoven, H., & Nadif Kasri, N. (2015). The role of chromatin repressive marks in cognition and disease: A focus on the repressive complex GLP/G9a. *Neurobiology of Learning and Memory*, 124, 88–96. https://doi.org/10.1016/j.nlm.2015.06.013

Branton, W. G., Ellestad, K. K., Maingat, F., Wheatley, B. M., Rud, E., Warren, R. L., . . . Power, C. (2013). Brain microbial populations in HIV/AIDS: α-Proteobacteria predominate independent of host immune status. *PLoS ONE*, 8(1), e54673. https://doi.org/10.1371/journal.pone.0054673

Bravo, J. A., Forsythe, P., Chew, M. V., Escaravage, E., Savignac, H. M., Dinan, T. G., . . . Cryan, J. F. (2011). Ingestion of Lactobacillus strain regulates emotional behavior and central GABA receptor expression in a mouse via the vagus nerve. *Proceedings of the National Academy of Sciences*, 108(38), 16050–16055. https://doi.org/10.1073/pnas.1102999108

Brooker, R. J. (2015). *Biology* (4th edition). New York: McGraw-Hill.

Butler, M. G. (2009). Genomic imprinting disorders in humans: a mini-review. *J Assist Reprod Genet*, 26, 477–486. doi 10.1007/s10815-009-9353-3

Carare, R. (2014). Afferent and efferent immunological pathways of the brain: anatomy, function and failure (84.1). *The FASEB Journal*, 28(1 Supplement). Retrieved from http://www.fasebj.org/content/28/1_Supplement/84.1.abstract

Chustecka, Z. (2017, July 12). A new dawn: First CAR T cell recommended for FDA Approval—Medscape. Retrieved from http://www.medscape.com/viewarticle/882858

Ciabrelli, F., Comoglio, F., Fellous, S., Bonev, B., Ninova, M., Szabo, Q., . . . Cavalli, G. (2017). Stable Polycomb-dependent transgenerational inheritance of chromatin states in Drosophila. *Nature Genetics*, 49(6), 876–886. https://doi.org/10.1038/ng.3848

Clarke, S. F., Murphy, E. F., O'Sullivan, O., Lucey, A. J., Humphreys, M., Hogan, A., . . . Cotter, P. D. (2014). Exercise and associated dietary extremes impact on gut microbial diversity. *Gut*, 63(12), 1913–1920. https://doi.org/10.1136/gutjnl-2013-306541

David, L. A., Maurice, C. F., Carmody, R. N., Gootenberg, D. B., Button, J. E., Wolfe, B. E., . . . Turnbaugh, P. J. (2013). Diet rapidly and reproducibly alters the human gut microbiome. *Nature, 505*(7484), 559–563. https://doi.org/10.1038/nature12820

de Araujo, I. E., Ferreira, J. G., Tellez, L. A., Ren, X., & Yeckel, C. W. (2012). The gut–brain dopamine axis: A regulatory system for caloric intake. *Physiology & Behavior, 106*(3), 394–399. https://doi.org/10.1016/j.physbeh.2012.02.026

Dickinson, D., & Elvevåg, B. (2009). Genes, cognition and brain through a COMT lens. *Neuroscience, 164*(1), 72–87. https://doi.org/10.1016/j.neuroscience.2009.05.014

Estruch, S. B., Graham, S. A., Chinnappa, S. M., Deriziotis, P., & Fisher, S. E. (2016). Functional characterization of rare FOXP2 variants in neurodevelopmental disorder. *Journal of Neurodevelopmental Disorders, 8*(1). https://doi.org/10.1186/s11689-016-9177-2

FDA News Release (2017a). FDA approval brings first gene therapy to the United States. 30 Aug 2017. https://www.fda.gov/NewsEvents/Newsroom/PressAnnouncements/ucm574058.htm

FDA News Release (2017b). FDA approves CAR-T cell therapy to treat adults with certain types of large B-cell lymphoma. 18 Oct 2017. https://www.fda.gov/NewsEvents/Newsroom/PressAnnouncements/ucm581216.htm

FDA News Release (2017c). FDA approves novel gene therapy to treat patients with a rare form of inherited vision loss. 19 Dec 2017 https://www.fda.gov/NewsEvents/Newsroom/PressAnnouncements/ucm589467.htm

Forsythe, P., Bienenstock, J., & Kunze, W. A. (2014). Vagal pathways for microbiome-brain-gut axis communication. In M. Lyte & J. F. Cryan (Eds.), *Microbial Endocrinology: The Microbiota-Gut-Brain Axis in Health and Disease* (pp. 115–133). New York: Springer New York. https://doi.org/10.1007/978-1-4939-0897-4_5

Franić, S., Dolan, C. V., Broxholme, J., Hu, H., Zemojtel, T., Davies, G. E., . . . Boomsma, D. I. (2015). Mendelian and polygenic inheritance of intelligence: A common set of causal genes? Using next-generation sequencing to examine the effects of 168 intellectual disability genes on normal-range intelligence. *Intelligence, 49*, 10–22. https://doi.org/10.1016/j.intell.2014.12.001

Galland, L. (2014). The gut microbiome and the brain. *Journal of Medicinal Food, 17*(12), 1261–1272. https://doi.org/10.1089/jmf.2014.7000

Garcia-Calero, E., Botella-Lopez, A., Bahamonde, O., Perez-Balaguer, A., & Martinez, S. (2016). FoxP2 protein levels regulate cell morphology changes and migration patterns in the vertebrate developing telencephalon. *Brain Structure and Function, 221*(6), 2905–2917. https://doi.org/10.1007/s00429-015-1079-7

Grady, D. (2017). FDA Approves first gene-altering leukemia treatment, costing $475,000. *New York Times*, August 30, 2017, https://www.nytimes.com/2017/08/30/health/gene-therapy-cancer.html?rref=collection%2Ftimestopic%2FFood%20and%20Drug%20Administration&action=click&contentCollection=timestopics&region=stream&module=stream_unit&version=latest&contentPlacement=1&pgtype=collection

Guzman, C. E., Bereza-Malcolm, L. T., De Groef, B., & Franks, A. E. (2015). Presence of selected methanogens, fibrolytic bacteria, and proteobacteria in the gastrointestinal tract of neonatal dairy calves from birth to 72 hours. *PLOS ONE, 10*(7), e0133048. https://doi.org/10.1371/journal.pone.0133048

Haas, B. W., Filkowski, M. M., Cochran, R. N., Denison, L., Ishak, A., Nishitani, S., & Smith, A. K. (2016). Epigenetic modification of OXT and human sociability. *Proceedings of the National Academy of Sciences, 113*(27), E3816–E3823. https://doi.org/10.1073/pnas.1602809113

Hill, W. D., Davies, G., Liewald, D. C., Payton, A., McNeil, C. J., Whalley, L. J., . . . Deary, I. J. (2016). Examining non-syndromic autosomal recessive intellectual disability (NS-ARID) genes for an enriched association with intelligence differences. *Intelligence, 54*, 80–89. https://doi.org/10.1016/j.intell.2015.11.005

Hoban, A. E., Stilling, R. M., Ryan, F. J., Shanahan, F., Dinan, T. G., Claesson, M. J., . . . Cryan, J. F. (2016). Regulation of prefrontal cortex myelination by the microbiota. *Translational Psychiatry, 6*(4), e774. https://doi.org/10.1038/tp.2016.42

Kang, S. S., Jeraldo, P. R., Kurti, A., Miller, M. E., Cook, M. D., Whitlock, K., . . . Fryer, J. D. (2014). Diet and exercise orthogonally alter the gut microbiome and reveal independent associations with anxiety and cognition. *Molecular Neurodegeneration, 9*(1), 36. https://doi.org/10.1186/1750-1326-9-36

Knudsen, E. I. (2004). Sensitive periods in the development of the brain and behavior. *Journal of Cognitive Neuroscience, 16*(8), 1412–1425. https://doi.org/10.1162/0898929042304796

Langdon, A., Crook, N., & Dantas, G. (2016). The effects of antibiotics on the microbiome throughout development and alternative approaches for therapeutic modulation. *Genome Medicine, 8*(1). https://doi.org/10.1186/s13073-016-0294-z

Lieberman, P. (2009). FOXP2 and human cognition. *Cell, 137*(5), 800–802. https://doi.org/10.1016/j.cell.2009.05.013

Lyte, M., Chapel, A., Lyte, J. M., Ai, Y., Proctor, A., Jane, J.-L., & Phillips, G. J. (2016). Resistant starch alters the microbiota-gut brain axis: Implications for dietary modulation of behavior. *PLoS ONE, 11*(1), e0146406. https://doi.org/10.1371/journal.pone.0146406

Mancuso, K., Hauswirth, W. W., Li, Q., Connor, T. B., Kuchenbecker, J. A., Mauck, M. C., . . . Neitz, M. (2009). Gene therapy for red–green colour blindness in adult primates. *Nature, 461*(7265), 784–787. https://doi.org/10.1038/nature08401

Mayer, E. A. (2011). Gut feelings: The emerging biology of gut–brain communication. *Nature Reviews Neuroscience, 12*(8), 453–466. https://doi.org/10.1038/nrn3071

Opstal, E. J. v., & Bordenstein, S. R. (2015). Rethinking heritability of the microbiome. *Science, 349*(6253), 1172–1173. https://doi.org/10.1126/science.aab3958

Parashar, A., & Udayabanu, M. (2016). Gut microbiota regulates key modulators of social behavior. *European Neuropsychopharmacology, 26*(1), 78–91. https://doi.org/10.1016/j.euroneuro.2015.11.002

Peter, C. J., Fischer, L. K., Kundakovic, M., Garg, P., Jakovcevski, M., Dincer, A., . . . Akbarian, S. (2016). DNA methylation signatures of early childhood malnutrition associated with impairments in attention and cognition. *Biological Psychiatry, 80*(10), 765–774. https://doi.org/10.1016/j.biopsych.2016.03.2100

Plomin, R., & Deary, I. J. (2015). Genetics and intelligence differences: Five special findings. *Molecular Psychiatry, 20*(1), 98–108. https://doi.org/10.1038/mp.2014.105

Probst, A. V., Dunleavy, E., & Almouzni, G. (2009). Epigenetic inheritance during the cell cycle. *Nature Reviews Molecular Cell Biology, 10*(3), 192–206. https://doi.org/10.1038/nrm2640

Qayyum, A., C. Zai, C., Hirata, Y., K. Tiwari, A., Cheema, S., Nowrouzi, B., . . . Kennedy, L. (2015). The role of the catechol-o-methyltransferase (COMT) geneval158met in aggressive behavior, a review of genetic studies. *Current Neuropharmacology, 13*(6), 802–814. https://doi.org/10.2174/1570159X13666150612225836

Rosenberger, C. M., & Finlay, B. B. (2003). Phagocyte sabotage: Disruption of macrophage signalling by bacterial pathogens. *Nature Reviews Molecular Cell Biology, 4*(5), 385–396. https://doi.org/10.1038/nrm1104

Savignac, H. M., Tramullas, M., Kiely, B., Dinan, T. G., & Cryan, J. F. (2015). Bifidobacteria modulate cognitive processes in an anxious mouse strain. *Behavioural Brain Research, 287*, 59–72. https://doi.org/10.1016/j.bbr.2015.02.044

Shakeshaft, N. G., Trzaskowski, M., McMillan, A., Krapohl, E., Simpson, M. A., Reichenberg, A., . . . Plomin, R. (2015). Thinking positively: The genetics of high intelligence. *Intelligence, 48*, 123–132. https://doi.org/10.1016/j.intell.2014.11.005

Shikishima, C., Hiraishi, K., Yamagata, S., Ando, J., & Okada, M. (2015). Genetic factors of individual differences in decision making in economic behavior: A Japanese twin study using the Allais Problem. *Frontiers in Psychology, 6*. https://doi.org/10.3389/fpsyg.2015.01712

Shreiner, A. B., Kao, J. Y., & Young, V. B. (2015). The gut microbiome in health and in disease. *Current Opinion in Gastroenterology, 31*(1), 69–75. https://doi.org/10.1097/MOG.0000000000000139

Stein, D. J., Newman, T. K., Savitz, J., & Ramesar, R. (2006). Warriors versus worriers: the role of COMT gene variants. *CNS Spectrums, 11*(10), 745–748.

Suzuki, K., Tsunekawa, Y., Hernandez-Benitez, R., Wu, J., Zhu, J., Kim, E. J., . . . Belmonte, J. C. I. (2016). In vivo genome editing via CRISPR/Cas9 mediated homology-independent targeted integration. *Nature, 540*(7631), 144–149. https://doi.org/10.1038/nature20565

Taft, R. J., Pheasant, M., & Mattick, J. S. (2007). The relationship between non-protein-coding DNA and eukaryotic complexity. *BioEssays, 29*(3), 288–299. https://doi.org/10.1002/bies.20544

Yin, C., Zhang, T., Qu, X., Zhang, Y., Putatunda, R., Xiao, X., . . . Hu, W. (2017). In vivo excision of HIV-1 provirus by saCas9 and multiplex single-guide RNAs in animal models. *Molecular Therapy, 25*(5), 1168–1186. https://doi.org/10.1016/j.ymthe.2017.03.012

14

Strategies to Improve Learning and Retention During Training

HENRY L. ROEDIGER, III, JOHN F. NESTOJKO,
AND NICOLE S. SMITH

INTRODUCTION

Training is one of the most critical operations of every organization. However, training is more critical in military service than in practically any other endeavor. Proper training is critical to national security and can be a life and death matter for those being trained. If some members of a unit are poorly trained, all members of the unit may be endangered.

In the US military services, Navy SEALs have the longest and most arduous process of training. The basic training lasts for more than a year, and around 75% of those beginning training drop out along the way. To be allowed to begin training, a person must pass a challenging set of physical and mental tests, so only the hardy and prepared even begin SEAL training. The first step to becoming a SEAL is to complete 8 weeks at the Naval Warfare Preparatory School at Great Lakes, Illinois. Those who make it through this course then begin real SEAL training. The next phase involves 24 weeks of Basic Underwater Demolition/SEAL (or BUD/S) training: 3 weeks of indoctrination training, then 7 weeks of physical conditioning, then 7 weeks of combat diving, then 7 weeks of land warfare. Those making it through this first phase of SEAL training (and many do not), then go on to Parachute Jump School (3 weeks). After that, they have 26 weeks of SEAL Qualification Training. Graduating from this course earns the prized Navy SEAL Trident. Only after this step is a SEAL assigned to a unit (e.g., SEAL Team 4). However, training has not ended. Navy SEALS continue higher level training throughout their career. Anyone interested in how Navy SEALS are trained should read Dick Couch's two fascinating books (2004, 2009) on the subject; a quicker overview can be found in the Wikipedia entry on Navy SEAL selection and training at https://en.wikipedia.org/wiki/United_States_Navy_SEAL_selection_and_training.

Because of the rigors of SEAL training, the public, as well as every branch of military service, regard the training of SEALs as the pinnacle of military training in the entire world. Their motto is "The only easy day was yesterday." Their training is the most difficult, as well as the longest, of any military organization.

Given this backdrop, the first author of this chapter was stunned to receive an email message from Carl Czech, one of the men responsible for selecting and training Navy SEALs, directed to the authors of *Make It Stick: The Science of Successful Learning* (Brown, Roediger, & McDaniel, 2014). With permission, we provide his note (from July, 2016) here:

Gentlemen,

I'm an instructional systems specialist and advisor at the Naval Special Warfare Center in Coronado, California. We and our subordinate commands are responsible for the selection and training of Navy SEALs. Our programs encompass everything from basic combat skills to advanced special operations.

Since I joined the SEAL community a decade ago, my professional colleagues and I have endeavored to make research-based instructional design a central tenet of Naval Special Warfare training. I write to tell you how much your work has helped us progress along that path. Shortly after "Make it Stick" was published, my Commanding Officer at the time came to me and said, "You keep telling me about research on learning and instruction. Is there something you could give me to read? Something that summarizes it in a straightforward way?" Luckily, I had a copy of your book on my desk. I never saw it again. He read it, talked about it, and then passed it on to the commander who succeeded him a few months later.

Subsequently, we obtained and distributed dozens of more copies and have made it a touchstone for our instructors and support staff. In a community that depends a great deal on apprenticeship and craft knowledge, we're beginning to develop a new appreciation for serious learning research. By communicating solid cognitive psychology principles in elegant and meaningful ways, we've begun to improve our instructional designs and delivery. This is no mean feat, since the vast majority of our instructors are assigned from the operating forces for only a couple of years at a time.

Last month, we convened an informal, one-day meeting of instructional designers, instructors and staff leaders. As we brainstormed improvement ideas, "Make it Stick" provided sturdy scaffolding for lively and focused discussion. Our plan is to continue the process with follow-on meetings that will extend to the larger Naval Special Warfare organization, including the training cadres who prepare SEAL Teams for deployment.

I'd personally appreciate any advice you may have for us as we move forward. In turn, we'd be happy to share our experience in how we're trying to gain real advantage for our learners as they tackle some of the toughest work in the world. Your work has been a recent part of that. Thanks again, from the guys in the field.

Best Regards,
Carl
Dr. Carl Czech
Senior Instructional Systems Specialist/Advisor
Naval Special Warfare Center
Coronado, CA 92155

Really? The commanders and trainers of the Navy SEALs are reading our book explaining principles of cognitive psychology and finding that they are useful in changing the procedures by which Navy SEALs are trained? The answer was *yes*. What ensued were numerous email exchanges and several telephone calls in which we learned what advice in our book was most useful in changing SEAL training. Eventually the first author of this chapter and Mark McDaniel, the other cognitive psychologist author of *Make It Stick*, flew to San Diego and spent 2 days on Coronado Island meeting with Navy SEAL trainers. We made a presentation to perhaps 60 trainers, many of whom were themselves SEALs, as well as to Commander Jay Hennessey. The visit was enlightening on both sides.

In reflecting on the issues that were facing Navy SEAL trainers, we see that they are ones that are common to practically all forms of training, not just military training. The principles occur in sports training, in musical training, in business training, and in learning in educational settings.

In this chapter, we provide three central strategies to improve training. These were all ones that the SEAL trainers began implementing, where possible, after reading our book, and they are ones that are not commonly incorporated into training in the military, in sports, or in education. Before we get to the new strategies, though, we consider typical means of training and discuss reasons why trainers see it as more effective than it is. We will use a sports analogy—learning to hit a baseball—as an example.

A TYPICAL TRAINING REGIME

Training of complex skills and procedures of any sort occurs over an extended period. A college baseball player must learn to hit the baseball, field his position, run the bases, and learn the rules of the game. Obviously, anyone who can make a college team has already played baseball for many years and achieved a certain level of success. How to improve?

The commonly used technique is repetition, practicing the same skill over and over until a greater level of proficiency is achieved. If a batter has trouble hitting a curve ball, he can expect the coach to throw him perhaps 30 curve balls in a row in practice. Sure enough, he gets better at hitting the curve. Similarly, a third baseman who has trouble fielding bunts will get a long series of bunts to field. These techniques are called *massed training,* and they are routinely used in training of every sort. The reason is that this technique supports rapid learning; if someone practices the same skill over and over, he or she is thought to build up "muscle memory" so that the skill will become more automatic. (Muscle memory is not a term cognitive psychologists endorse, but it is widely used in training.) And massed repetition does build up fast learning, but it leads to a major problem: skills learned this way decay rapidly; forgetting is as rapid as learning in some cases.

What should be done instead? Training on a particular skill should be spaced out in time—*spaced practice*—not bunched up all at once. After all, pitchers do not telegraph their pitches; there will never be a case where a batter knows that every pitch in his at bat will be a curve ball. The third baseman never knows when the bunt is coming. Besides spacing, the other principle that is useful in training is interleaving. A baseball hitter never knows what is coming next (fastball? change up? slider?). A batting practice pitcher should interleave the types of pitches that a batter receives, just as will happen in a game. The mantra in sports is often, "Practice like you play, and you will play like you practice." However, this bit of (good) advice would indicate that many techniques used in practice—doing the same thing over and over—should be discontinued because that will never happen in a game.

To formalize the preceding points using the language of cognitive psychology, we can say that trainers should emphasize *transfer appropriate processing* (e.g., Roediger, Gallo, & Geraci, 2002)—that is, the type of process during learning or training should match the way the skill will be used after training. This term captures the "practice like you play" phrase. The trainer should always keep in mind how the skill to be learned will be deployed in the field and have the trainee practice that way, especially in later stages of training. If the processes used in training mimic those that will be needed after training, in a game or in combat, then that is the way they should be practiced. Once this is pointed out, it is easy to nod in agreement. However, most training regimes violate this principle because they emphasize massed practice.

As we shall see, evidence from much research supports the principles of spaced and interleaved training as producing good long-term retention. Why don't trainers use these techniques as a matter of course? The answer is that these strategies of training slow learning and make it feel (for both the trainer and the learner) that not much progress is being made. Massed practice is much more satisfying because the learner gets better faster, but these gains are often short-lived and illusory, fading rapidly and failing to support good long-term performance. When learners experience rapid acquisition that does not stick in the long-term, they suffer from illusions of competence—they believe their training was effective and that their performance will remain high in the long run, when in fact it only appeared effective during training (Bjork, 1994).

Why do learners—and trainers—believe in and continue to use training methods that fail to produce lasting results? A helpful distinction is between *performance* during acquisition and *learning* in the long run. Army recruits must learn the Soldier's Creed to perfection and are expected to recite it at critical points, such as when they graduate from basic training (a quick search online uncovers discussion forums full of new soldiers agonizing over how to learn the Soldier's Creed to avoid embarrassment during basic training). Now imagine a soldier who simply studies the words over and over, hoping they will sink in. After enough exposure, he finally finds that he can get it right. Satisfied with his apparent learning, the soldier puts it aside to focus on other training. A week later, his drill sergeant calls on him suddenly to recite the Soldier's Creed and the young recruit finds that the words simply won't come. What went wrong? Why can he no longer remember what he knew just a week ago? In this situation, the soldier mistook performance during acquisition (correctly reciting the Soldier's Creed once after crammed study) as an indicator of durable learning. The soldier neglected to consider a fundamental property of memory: forgetting over time. Learners often fail to consider how strongly forgetting will reduce performance in the future, assuming that if they know something at one point it will continue into the future. This is why performance during training can often be a poor indicator of long-term mastery (Soderstrom & Bjork,

2015). Massed practice, as noted earlier, gives the illusion of mastery, but other techniques are needed to make learning stick. It is exactly this misplaced trust in performance measured during acquisition—as opposed to evaluations that take place long after training—that explains why ineffective training strategies remain popular.

Let us introduce another term from cognitive psychology that helps us to understand this situation: *Desirable difficulties in learning* (Bjork, 1994). This idea captures the fact that in several situations, techniques that produce good short-term learning lead to poor long-term retention. Massed practice is an example. Rather, other strategies for training that are more difficult, feel bad to the learner (and trainer), and slow learning actually lead to better performance in the long term. Spaced practice, interleaved practice, and retrieval practice (e.g., via tests) are three of these desirable difficulties. All three feel somewhat unnatural or difficult when used during learning, but they lead to good retention when measured after a delay. We will present evidence supporting these claims in the next sections of the chapter.

Training also occurs in the classroom, for soldiers being trained, for athletes, and, of course, for traditional students. Baseball players go over rules for many game situations that happen infrequently (e.g., the infield fly rule). Or infielders must learn how to position themselves for relay throws from the outfielders in different situations (e.g., men on first and third and the ball hit to the center fielder either in the air or after a bounce). Similarly, the outfielders must learn where to throw to the cutoff man depending on different situations. Pitchers and catchers must learn to back up the plays depending on all these factors. Often these situations are presented in PowerPoint presentations after a practice, with the weary players expected to pick up the nuances.

"Death by PowerPoint" is an all too common experience for people in training. Often the slide shows are given out so that people can go through them repeatedly. Yet evidence shows that this form of study is ill-conceived and produces illusions of learning. That is, the trainees may know the information briefly, but they lose it quickly. Research shows that a much better technique for making the information stick for the long term is to practice retrieving it rather than simply being exposed to it repeatedly. That is, trainers should quiz trainees in the classroom and then put them in the practical situation where they need to perform and ask them to provide the answer; the trainee needs to practice retrieving or using the information to retain it for the long haul. Getting information out of memory is as critical to learning as is getting it into the memory system in the first place.

This section provides a quick overview of some of the topics in our chapter. The three principles we cover—spaced practice, interleaved practice, and retrieval practice—all produce durable and flexible learning. We now provide evidence to back up our claims. Although these principles apply across training situations—including training of first responders outside of the military—police, firefighters, and emergency medical technicians—we embed our principles in the context of problems that trainers confront in developing military personnel.

TESTING AS A LEARNING TOOL: THE POWER
OF RETRIEVAL PRACTICE

Tests are part and parcel of any educational system. Students stay up all night studying to earn a passing grade, instructors and universities base course grades largely on test results, and standardized tests dictate the direction of people's lives. Yet tests are typically viewed as a *measure* of learning or ability, not a method to enhance learning. This view is not altogether wrong; of course, tests are useful tools to assess what people do and do not know. However, tests are also a uniquely potent device to promote flexible use of knowledge and to entrench knowledge deeply.

Tests represent a good example of transfer-appropriate processing. In other words, tests create a good match between conditions of training and the conditions that may arise during future use of the trained knowledge and skills. Take, for example, students who read and re-read an assigned chapter prior to an exam. When they read it a second time, the material feels familiar and the reading fluent, and that familiarity and fluency may lead the student to a feeling of comprehension, as if they know the content; this is what we referred to earlier as an illusion of mastery. But assessment tests rarely provide students with chapters and ask, "Can you comprehend what this chapter says?" Instead, tests ask students to recall information, or to apply knowledge to solve problems. In other words, re-reading presents a poor match to the later method of assessment. Practice that requires retrieval—in other words, tests—is much better matched to conditions that arise during future use, including assessments (tests). It is for this reason that tests as learning devices can better be conceived of as *retrieval practice* because practicing retrieval is the appropriate method to prepare for the demands that arise during assessment tests—namely, retrieving knowledge and facts from memory. And in practical situations where learned information is to be used, it must be readily retrieved.

The beneficial effects of testing on retention was empirically demonstrated early in the twentieth century (Gates, 1917), but it was largely ignored as a learning tool until relatively recently. In one study, Roediger and Karpicke (2006) compared testing to repeated studying as a learning technique. They gave college students short passages to read about the sun and sea otters. In one experiment, students followed their initial study of the passage either with three additional study trials (SSSS, when including the initial study session) or they took three consecutive tests after initial study (STTT). The tests were difficult: in a form of testing called *free recall*, participants were told to recall everything they could from the passage they had read. To assess longer term learning, a final free recall test was given to both groups to assess memory for the material. Half of the students received this test 5 minutes after the last trial in the study schedule, whereas the other half of the students received their final test a week later. When tested soon after learning, students who studied the passage four times (SSSS) recalled about 12% more content than did the students who studied the passage once followed by three tests during learning (STTT), an advantage of repeated studying (see Figure 14.1). However, when this assessment test was given at a delay of 1 week, the pattern completely reversed: repeated testing (STTT) produced 21% greater recall than the repeated studying condition (SSSS).

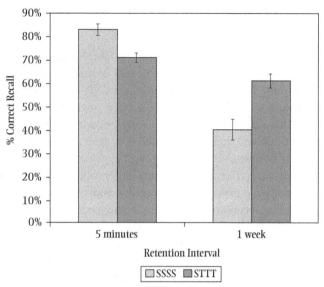

Figure 14.1 The results of Roediger and Karpicke (2006, Exp. 2). When tested 5 minutes after learning, students recalled more content from a text passage when they repeatedly studied (S) versus repeated testing (T); however, delayed recall was superior following repeated testing, demonstrating that tests enhance long-term retention. Error bars represent standard errors of the means and were recreated from the original figure. Adapted from H. L. Roediger & J. D. Karpicke, Test-enhanced learning: Taking memory tests improves long-term retention. *Psychological Science, 17,* 249–255, 2006.

This effect showing that cramming (repeated studying) produces rapid forgetting can be observed by comparing the 5-minute to the 1-week delayed tests in the figure: participants forgot nearly half of what they could recall when they initially studied four times (SSSS), but they only forgot about 14% of the content over a week when they studied once and took three tests during learning (STTT). The primary take-home from this experiment is that tests enhance long-term retention of information by slowing forgetting.

The enhanced retention following repeated retrieval practice is especially impressive given that the students spent considerably more time with the passage in the repeated study schedule than in the repeated testing schedule (i.e., studying four times compared to studying only once), so they had more opportunities in that condition to learn with the material right in front of them. Furthermore, students were unaware of the benefits of testing in this experiment. When asked how much of the passage they would remember in 1 week just after the learning phase of the experiment, the students who had studied four times (SSSS) predicted better delayed test performance than students who had studied once and taken three tests (STTT). Their predictions were exactly the opposite of the recall pattern on the tests given a week later. What went wrong? Perhaps learners are not skilled at predicting long-term forgetting, but instead make their predictions based on what they know when they make them. After all, their predictions were accurate regarding the tests given soon after learning. In other words, they mistook current performance to be an indicator of long-term learning, and it is this mistake that creates the illusion of mastery that is a hallmark of poor training techniques.

There are hundreds of experiments demonstrating advantages of retrieval practice with verbal materials like word lists, textbook chapters, vocabulary learning, and foreign-language acquisition (Adesope, Trevisan, & Sundararajan, 2017). We will limit our coverage, however, mostly to demonstrations of retrieval-enhanced learning in contexts we see as more fitting to military training.

All soldiers are trained on how to navigate terrain by using maps. As the following example reveals, tests during training enhance learning of maps. Carpenter and Pashler (2007) had students learn maps containing a dozen features such as roads, rivers, and buildings. Students attempted to learn the maps via a computer display either only through studying or through a combination of studying and testing. In the study-only condition, they simply viewed the map for 2 minutes. In the test-study condition, which also lasted a total of 2 minutes, they initially viewed the map with all 12 features in place for 20 seconds. After viewing the intact map for 20 seconds, they saw a version of the map with one feature missing, were asked to visualize the missing feature, and then were shown the missing feature along with the rest. They went through 12 trials like this, with each of the 12 features missing during one trial. Following the study-only and the test-study conditions of learning, students were asked to draw the maps from memory after a 30-minute delay. Students' drawings were more complete and more accurate following the test-study procedure than the study-only procedure, demonstrating that tests can enhance visual-spatial map learning.

Retrieval Practice Promotes Flexible Application of Learning

If the only benefit of retrieval practice was to enhance the durability of learning, we would still be advising its widespread use in education and training. We are especially strong advocates of the use of testing in training, however, because there are additional benefits beyond enhanced retention. One additional benefit is that testing often leads to greater flexibility of knowledge use.

Retrieval practice improves students' abilities to answer inference questions on assessment tests. Inference questions are test questions that require a student to use reasoning from the facts they learned as opposed to directly recalling the facts. For example, McDaniel, Howard, and Einstein (2009) had students initially study complex materials about the mechanical workings of brakes and pumps then gave them problem-solving questions that required the students to make inferences from the knowledge they gained during learning; they also received recall questions directly assessing individual fact retention. An example inference question was "What could be done to make brakes more effective, that is, to reduce the distance needed to stop?" The answer to this question was never directly presented in the text participants read; rather, they were required to piece together the answer from the facts they had learned. Students answered 14% more of these problem-solving questions correctly when they were tested during learning compared to when they only studied the material without tests. The benefit of retrieval practice was even larger for the recall of facts, demonstrating the typical direct benefit of testing.

Mechanical engineers in the military are responsible for designing and building complex machines like tanks and planes. Retrieval practice during training will enhance the retention and flexibility of their knowledge.

In another demonstration of flexible learning enhanced by testing—namely, transfer from one knowledge domain to another—Butler (2010) had students study text passages about one topic either by repeated reading or repeated testing, and then assessed their knowledge by giving them questions about a seemingly unrelated topic. For example, when an initial passage about bats included the fact that bat wings are more flexible than birds' wings, a transfer question was, "The US Military is looking at bat wings for inspiration in developing a new type of aircraft. How would this type of aircraft differ from traditional aircrafts like fighter jets?" (The answer: "Traditional aircrafts are modeled after bird wings, which are rigid and good for providing lift. Bat wings are more flexible, and thus an aircraft modeled on bat wings would have greater maneuverability"; Butler, 2010; p. 1127). Tests during learning were only about bats; the transfer questions were given on an assessment test 1 week after learning. Compared to the restudy condition, students who were repeatedly tested on their bat knowledge during learning answered the transfer questions correctly far more often than those who had re-read the material (68% vs. 44%, a whopping 24% difference).

Following up on the map-learning study just described (Carpenter & Pashler, 2007), Rohrer, Taylor, and Sholar (2012) found that tests enhance map learning involving novel tests of spatial knowledge. Briefly, they gave 4th and 5th grade children maps with 10 locations labeled. In a study-only condition, children labeled a paper map while viewing a screen with the labels in place (i.e., they simply copied the answers from the screen, which requires no retrieval from memory). In a test-study condition, they were given the name of a location and asked to identify it on a blank map, and then they were shown the correct answer on screen. In other words, they tried to retrieve the correct name and location before being shown the correct answer as feedback. One day later, they were then given a route to follow through the map, as if they were driving through the regions the map depicted, and asked to identify which locations they would "drive" through on their route. The test-study procedure during learning nearly doubled accuracy on this test relative to the study-only procedure.

Soldiers, like students, acquire knowledge in the classroom, but then they are required to apply that knowledge to novel problems that often occur in stressful, challenging situations. This type of flexible use of knowledge is critical to their success and survival. Retrieval practice during knowledge acquisition is a potent tool for enhancing the flexibility of knowledge use.

Additional Benefits of Testing

So far, we have outlined two benefits of retrieval practice: durability and flexibility of learning. Another benefit recently discovered is that retrieval practice guards against deleterious effects of stressful situations on memory (Smith, Floerke, & Thomas, 2016). Stress reduces memory retrieval (Gagnon & Wagner, 2016), a fact that can have disastrous consequences for soldiers. In the study by Smith and colleagues,

participants initially learned stimuli either via repeated studying or repeated retrieval practice. One day later, their memory was tested either without stress induction or after a stress induction episode that required participants to give speeches
and solve math problems in front of judges. The material learned under repeated
studying showed the typical detriments of stress: recall was worse after stress induction than without stress induction. What happened to the material that was learned
via repeated retrieval? In this case, stress did not decrease recall for the previously
tested material, and previously tested material was recalled better overall than previously restudied material, the typical benefit of testing. Although the stress of giving
a speech and solving math problems is not equivalent to the stress of jumping out
of an airplane into combat, this demonstration provides a promising avenue for a
method of reducing stress-induced retrieval failure.

Retrieval practice has a variety of additional benefits over nonretrieval methods
of learning. For example, tests can identify gaps in a learners' knowledge, which can
be useful for both trainees and trainers moving forward. Tests can also improve
learners' own judgments of their learning, thereby reducing the illusions of competence outlined earlier. Retrieval practice promotes organization of knowledge, can
facilitate retrieval of material that was not on the test, and can improve acquisition
of subsequent learning. To discuss each of these benefits in turn would require a
new chapter of its own, so we refer you to Roediger, Putnam, and Smith (2011),
who discuss these and other advantages of testing.

Two Tips for Implementing Retrieval Practice: Feedback and Repeated Testing

There are numerous considerations when thinking of how best to use tests during
training. What type of tests should one give? There are multiple-choice tests, essay
tests, true/false tests, and so on. When should tests be given? How often? This list
could be expanded. Here we suggest two best practices that we know make retrieval
practice particularly effective (see Putnam, Nestojko, & Roediger, 2016, for a discussion of test format and other related issues).

FEEDBACK

What happens when learners fail to recall the correct answer on a test question? At
best, they fail to learn that particular fact or skill. At worst, if they produced an incorrect answer on the test, they could retain that wrong answer as if it is the correct one
(Roediger & Marsh, 2005). An easy solution to this problem is to provide feedback
after tests. According to three recent meta-analyses of the research on testing, feedback generally boosts the benefits of retrieval-based learning (Adesope, Trevisan, &
Sundararajan, 2017; Rowland, 2014; Schwieren, Barenberg, & Dutke, 2017). The
type and timing of feedback are important, though.

Feedback following tests can take a few different forms. Two popular types of
feedback are verification feedback and answer feedback. Verification feedback
consists of telling students whether they were right or wrong on a specific test item
without providing the correct answer. There is evidence that this type of feedback
does not improve performance relative to tests without feedback (Fazio, Huelser,

Johnson, & Marsh, 2010; Pashler, Cepeda, Wixted, & Rohrer, 2005). In contrast, answer feedback consists of providing the correct answer after test trials, and this type of feedback enhances the benefits of retrieval practice (e.g., Butler, Godbole, & Marsh, 2013).

Another issue to consider is the timing of feedback. Instructors can opt to give feedback immediately after tests or even after each question on the test, as is done in intelligent tutoring systems. Alternatively, feedback might come later, such as when instructors give out corrected quizzes a day after they were taken in class. Early evidence suggested that immediate feedback was more useful to learners than delayed feedback (Kulik & Kulik, 1988). More recent research, however, suggests that delaying feedback by even a few seconds (or longer) improves retention relative to immediate feedback (e.g., Butler & Roediger, 2008; Mullet, Butler, Verdin, von Borries, & Marsh, 2014).

One caveat is warranted: this section regarding feedback is most relevant to verbal learning of the type that takes place in classrooms. There is in fact evidence that feedback provided too frequently during motor skill acquisition can be detrimental to transfer and long-term retention of learning (Schmidt, 1991), suggesting that there are limits to the dosage of feedback for some types of retrieval-based training.

Repeated Testing

Flashcards are sometimes used as a study strategy for students. When using flashcards, a student will read a question or prompt on one side of the card, attempt to recall the answer from memory, and then flip the card over to see if she got the answer right or wrong. Thus, flashcards afford a method of repeated retrieval practice with feedback, when used correctly. Unfortunately, students sometimes make the following mistake: the first time they correctly recall an answer, they place that card into a pile of "learned" content. This tactic is sometimes called the "drop" method because they drop cards once they get the answer right once (Karpicke, 2009). In fact, this strategy of recalling something correctly once (or maybe twice) is often built into the advice provided in instructions on how to use flashcards. The logic is that the correct answers show students they know the concept, so they should spend their time on concepts they do not yet know. However, as we have illustrated in this chapter, students often misinterpret current performance for evidence of lasting learning. The evidence to date suggests that multiple correct retrievals improve learning more than a single correct recall, which indicates that the flashcard-carrying student should put the correctly recalled card at the end of her study stack for additional practice.

In an experiment designed to examine whether dropping is, in fact, an efficient method of flashcard use or if it may be detrimental, Karpicke and Roediger (2008) had students learn 40 Swahili–English word pairs (e.g., mashua–boat, lesa–scarf) in one of four schedules of practice. In the study + test schedule, each pair received study and test trials (mashua–boat, then mashua–_____) in four cycles through the list of 40 pairs, regardless of performance on test trials. In the remaining three schedules, a pair was dropped fully or partially from subsequent practice once it was successfully recalled once. In the dropout schedule, a pair was dropped completely from subsequent cycles after one correct recall (no additional practice). In the repeated study only schedule, a pair would continue to be shown in all study trials (mashua–boat), but it was no longer tested after one correct recall. In the repeated retrieval only schedule, a pair would continue to be cued for all test trials (mashua–_____), but was not shown as study trials after one correct recall. All four schedules were followed by a test 1 week after practice. The first key finding was that the study + test schedule produced more than twice the rate of correct recall on this delayed test than did the dropout schedule (80% vs. 33%, respectively). The second key finding was dropping study trials but continuing retrieval practice (i.e., the repeated retrieval only schedule) did not harm recall relative to the study + test schedule, but that dropping test trials but continuing study trials (i.e., the repeated study only schedule) caused recall to be on par with the lowly dropout schedule (80% for repeated retrieval without restudying, vs. 36% for repeated studying without retrieval; see Figure 14.2). The take home: retrieval practice after successful recall greatly increased long-term retention, whereas additional studying after successful recall added no benefits to retention. When using flashcards—or any other method that involves retrieval practice—learners should recall information correctly more than once. Karpicke (2009) showed that, when left to their own devices, students often drop flashcards after only one or two correct recalls, but when students were held to a higher criterion of the number of correct recalls, they performed much better on delayed tests.

How many times should one recall something correctly before it has been mastered? Rawson and Dunlosky (2012) provide this advice, based on a combination of spacing (covered in the next section) and retrieval practice with

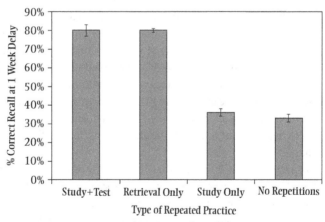

Figure 14.2 The results of Karpicke and Roediger (2008). Following one correct recall, students either continued both study and test trials (far left bar), selectively dropped either study trials (2nd from left) or retrieval trials (3rd from left), or dropped both study and retrieval trials (far right). The two schedules that contained continued retrieval practice (two left bars) produced much better long-term retention than the two schedules that did not incorporate repeated testing (two right bars). Error bars represent standard errors of the means and were recreated from the original figure.
Adapted from J. D. Karpicke & H. L. Roediger, The critical importance of retrieval for learning. *Science, 319,* 966–968, 2008.

feedback: learners should correctly recall content three times during initial acquisition, followed by three additional test trials with feedback spaced out over long periods of time. To keep some fact or concept or procedure at your mental fingertips, you should practice repeatedly at spaced intervals.

MASSED VERSUS SPACED PRACTICE

Learners as well as educators are typically aware that repetition leads to deeper, more lasting learning (Karpicke, Butler, & Roediger, 2009). Unfortunately, that repetition often takes the form of re-reading notes and book passages immediately before a test. In order to achieve the desired long lasting effects, however, learning must be repeated over a much longer period of time. The question that follows, of course, is when should repeated learning be used and how should it be scheduled? Below, we review research on spaced learning and offer guidelines for scheduling repeated learning sessions.

The Spacing Effect

The spacing effect, or the distributed practice effect (Cepeda, Pashler, Vul, Wixted, & Rohrer, 2006), refers to the finding that repeating study sessions spaced out over time result in better learning than repeated study sessions completed back to back. Spaced practice occurs when the study of a skill or piece of information is practiced with some amount of time between repetitions. Massed practice occurs when study of a skill or piece of information is practiced repeatedly with no time between repetitions. To return to our baseball example, the baseball player who practices hitting a curve ball repeatedly before switching to a fastball is using massed practice. Spacing can be achieved within one practice session (e.g., practicing hitting many different types of pitches each day at practice) or between different practice sessions (e.g., practicing batting on Monday, Wednesday, and Friday while practicing fielding on Tuesday and Thursday). Both within-session and between-session spacing create better learning than massed practice. Within-session spaced practice can be referred to as *interleaved practice* when the time between repetitions is filled by practicing different material. We expand on the benefits of interleaving later in this chapter.

The key to spacing research is that the distribution of time spent studying is manipulated while the total amount of time spent studying is held constant. The classic spacing effect literature involves participants memorizing a list of words to be recalled at a later test. Typically, some words are studied back to back (massed), whereas other words are studied once and then repeated at longer intervals. Then, both groups are tested after some delay. Distributed presentations of words lead to greater recall than massed presentations, and the greater the amount of time (or number of words) between repetitions, the better is later recall (e.g., Melton, 1970). The basic spacing design has been extended into classroom settings as well, with students learning material such as vocabulary definitions (Sobel, Cepeda, & Kapler, 2011) and US history facts (Carpenter, Pashler, & Cepeda, 2009) with the same positive impact.

As noted earlier in this chapter, massed practice typically feels more productive than spaced practice, especially in learning of skills. This may be due to the fact that massed practice allows learners to acquire knowledge more rapidly, even though the long-term retention for the knowledge is poorer (Son & Simon, 2012). Balota, Duchek, and Paullin (1989) found that when students were tested soon after the second study presentation, massed practice led to greater recall than did spaced practice. When tested after a delay, however, the spaced practice condition led to superior recall relative to massed practice. This may be why many students choose to cram for a test just before it. By using massed practice immediately before the test, students can recall the necessary information reasonably well (Roediger & Karpicke, 2006). If asked to recall the information a week (or more) later, however, those students would not have retained much of what they studied relative to spaced practice (or retrieval practice).

Generalization of Concepts

Spacing is effective for more than simply learning and repeating information. Several studies have used a spaced learning design to show improvements in students' abilities to generalize concepts to novel material. In a study by Gluckman, Vlach, and Sandhofer (2014), elementary school students learned about the food chain through lessons covering four different biomes. One group of students received all four biome lessons on the same day (massed condition), while another group learned about one biome each day for 4 days (spaced condition). Total time spent learning was held constant. Students were tested on their ability to recall facts from the lessons as well as on their ability to generalize concepts beyond what was taught in the lessons. Generalization questions were either simple (e.g., bigger animals usually eat smaller animals) or complex (e.g., for a given scenario involving insect population, "What do you think happens to the number of turtles in the swamp?" p. 269). The final test occurred 1 week after the final lesson. Fact questions were based on the biomes taught in the lessons, while the generalization questions were based on a biome that was not covered in the lessons. Thus, for the generalization questions, the students had to apply the principles they had learned to material they had never studied. On the final test, students in the spaced condition performed better on all three types of questions compared to those in the massed condition. They scored 13% higher on the fact questions, 16% higher on the simple generalization questions, and 21% higher on the complex generalization questions. Not only did the spaced schedule improve memory for facts, but it also enhanced the students' ability to transfer what they learned to new contexts.

Similarly, Bird (2011) used spaced practice to teach native Malay speakers English syntax in a college course, using two different levels of spacing of lessons (3 days vs. 14 days). The students practiced reading sentences on a worksheet and identifying errors in syntax. Students received worksheets either 3 days apart or 14 days apart. On a delayed test 60 days after the last study session, the students were asked to identify errors in syntax on novel sentences that had not been included in any previous practice session. Students who practiced identifying syntax errors 14 days apart performed 12% better on the final test of new sentences compared to the group who practiced 3 days apart. This study demonstrates that not only does spaced practice enhance the generalization of knowledge to new contexts, but also that the benefit can last for months following the final practice session. Furthermore, the greater the spacing, the better the long term retention.

Research in Skill Training

Research on the spacing effect has been well established in laboratory and classroom settings with verbal learning, but the benefits of spaced practice can be seen in skill training as well. For example, Moulton et al. (2006) studied medical students as they attempted to learn a difficult microsurgical technique to reattach tiny blood vessels. The lesson consisted of four sessions of instruction, which are usually given to medical students in 1 day. One group of students completed all four sessions in 1 day, as usual, whereas the other group of students completed the same set of lessons with 1 week between each session. When asked to perform the technique on rats 1 month after the fourth lesson, the students who learned in spaced lessons performed better than their peers who learned in the massed fashion. The spaced group took less time to complete the surgery, used fewer hand movements during surgery, and had more success reattaching the vessels. In fact, all the students in the spaced group completed their surgery while 16% of the students in the massed group damaged the vessels beyond repair and could not complete the surgery. Their rats died.

Heidt, Arbuthnott, and Price (2016) showed that spacing is effective in teaching the Enhanced Cognitive Interview (ECI) to police officers as well. The ECI is an interview technique used by the police to question eyewitnesses with as little interviewer bias as possible. The officers were given 2 hours of training. One group completed the training in 1 day (massed), while the other group completed the training in two sessions of 1 hour each with 1 week between sessions (spaced). Again, the spaced group outperformed their massed counterparts by using more open-ended questions as opposed to leading questions in their interviews.

The Right Amount of Spacing

Up to this point, we have reviewed the evidence that spaced practice results in better long-term learning than massed practice. But how much time should one place between practice sessions? Additional research on spacing has revealed that there is no one spacing interval that always works. For example, in one study students learned face-name pairs until they knew 70% of them. Then they received one final learning episode either 10 minutes or 24 hours later. When they were given a final test 1 day after their last study trial, there was no benefit of spaced presentation. In other conditions, however, students were tested after a week. Then the spacing effect emerged, with those having a spaced presentation after 24 hours recalling more word pairs than those who had only 10 minutes separating original learning from relearning (Pyc, Balota, McDermott, Tully, & Roediger, 2014). Figure 14.3 illustrates this pattern of results.

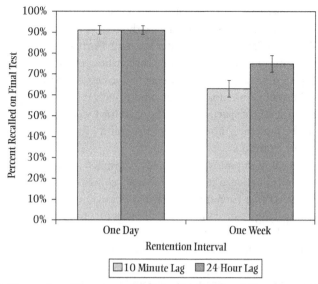

Figure 14.3 The results of Experiment 2b (left pair of bars) and Experiment 4 (right pair of bars) by Pyc, Balota, McDermott, Tully, and Roediger (2014). Participants studied face-name pairs in two separate study sessions either 10 minutes apart or 24 hours apart. When tested 1 day after the second study session, the groups showed no difference in performance. When tested 1 week after the second study session, the group that studied with 24 hours between sessions performed better than the group that studied with only 10 minutes between sessions. Error bars represent standard errors of the means and were recreated from the original figure.
Adapted from M. A. Pyc, D. A. Balota, K. B. McDermott, T. Tully, & H. L. Roediger, Between-list lag effects in recall depend on retention interval, *Memory & Cognition, 42,* 965–977, 2014, copyright 2014 by Psychonomic Society, Inc. Reprinted with permission of Springer.

The ideal interval for spacing likely depends on many different factors, but the factor identified in the Pyc et al. study (2014)—the retention interval between study and test—has been shown repeatedly to affect the success of spaced practice. Cepeda, Vul, Rohrer, Wixted, and Pashler (2008) provided a broad assessment of various spacing gaps and retention intervals. More than 1,000 people studied obscure trivia items in two sessions (initial study and review) with nine different spacing intervals ranging from 0 days (the massed condition) to spacing of up to 105 days between sessions. Participants were tested on the trivia 7, 35, 70, or 350 days after their review session. All the groups given spaced presentation outperformed the massed practice group. The most successful groups scored up to 64% higher than the massed practice group. But there was no best spacing interval for all conditions; rather each retention interval required a different spacing interval for best performance. For example, for those tested 350 days after their review session, the group with 21 days between sessions performed the best. For those tested 1 week after their last review session, the group that used 1 day of spacing performed the best. These results show that there is a balance to be struck between the spacing of practice sessions and the time until the final test. Using the longest spacing interval between practice sessions isn't always the best route to take, if the final assessment will occur relatively quickly after learning. Further research is required to determine the optimum spacing schedule for various retention intervals, but the research completed so far allows us to make educated estimates. After reviewing the available literature, Putnam, Nestojko, and Roediger (2016) suggested the following guideline: 1 day of spacing should be used for 1 week of retention, 1 week of spacing should be used for 2 months of retention, and 1 month of spacing should be used for 1 year of retention.

In general, the longer you would like to remember a topic or skill, the more spacing should occur between practice sessions. Practice sessions should not, however, be so far apart that forgetting effectively erases the benefits of the previous session. Often, spacing research involves simply presenting the information again. That works to a degree. However, if retrieval attempts are made before restudy in spaced conditions, the beneficial effect of spacing repetition is much greater (Agarwal, Finley, Rose, & Roediger, 2016). And, as noted in the previous section, to maintain knowledge for the long term, repeated practice sessions at widely spaced intervals are important. For example, if medical students know that a test of surgical techniques will occur at the end of the year (and will be needed in their practice), they are better off practicing those techniques once a month for the entire year than massing their study when the techniques are first taught.

Spacing requires planning, and such planning becomes increasingly important when one needs to complete multiple courses or learn multiple skills within the same time frame. In those cases, it becomes important to overlap spacing schedules. One might practice seven different skills each week, devoting 1 day to practicing each skill. That way, each skill is practiced with a 1-week spacing interval, but no days are wasted waiting for the next practice session. How time is spent during each practice session is equally important. Earlier in this section, we briefly mentioned a type of within-session spacing known as interleaving. In the following section, we will review the interleaving literature and provide examples of how an interleaved practice schedule can benefit learning in several different domains.

Spacing Suggestions for Operational Settings

Most training in all settings is massed, for reasons discussed earlier. Massed training leads to quick gains in learning and both students and trainers tend to favor it for this reason. Massed training, however, leads to rapid decay of knowledge and skills. The trainers of Navy SEALS worried about the massed nature of their training because training of critical skills (e.g., parachute jumping) is taught in a massed fashion. In the case of learning this skill, spacing of training after initial learning is difficult because training must involve coordination with other units that fly the airplanes (and getting the airplanes themselves to the SEAL base in Coronado, California). Thus, practical considerations can limit spaced training.

Because military training is composed of weeks (or more) of learning difficult skills in many different skill sets, spacing and interleaving should be worked into the training schedule whenever possible. In fact, there may already be areas of training that use spacing techniques. Military training incorporates huge amounts of repetition to instill necessary skills in the soldiers. Spacing those repetitions over time rather than running them back-to-back is a simple and straightforward way of employing the spacing effect. Drills that a soldier is expected to know by heart should be revisited every week or perhaps every month in order to prevent forgetting. The Jumpmaster school in the US Army, for example, is already using the principle of spacing by requiring their graduates to attend meetings and practice their skills periodically even after the formal classes are finished (Kienery & Lahr, personal communication, 2016). In addition to practicing drills, spacing can be employed in classroom settings. Revisiting important points each week in a class or having regular quizzes over recurring themes in the curriculum will help to reap the benefits of both the spacing effect and the retrieval practice effect. Taking the amount of instruction and practice that is already being used and rescheduling it so that consolidation can occur between lessons can go a long way to improve the efficiency and efficacy of existing military training programs.

One issue encountered in practical situations is when to introduce spaced practice. After all, some basic learning must occur before a trainee can practice at spaced intervals. This is particularly true for those skills that can result in severe injury or death when performed incorrectly. Although there is not much evidence yet to back up this recommendation, one practical solution is to have a bit of massed practice to gain a certain level of knowledge about each skill to be learned and then to begin to space out the sessions of practice on those skills.

INTERLEAVED PRACTICE

In our section on the spacing effect, we discussed the importance of organizing study and practice sessions over time. In this section, we review the research pertaining to the most effective ways to arrange individual practice examples within sessions. Mixing many different types of examples (interleaving) is far more effective for long-term learning than grouping together similar examples (blocking) within a practice session. The following section will provide guidance on how to design each practice session in order to achieve long-term retention.

Interleaving Versus Blocking

Let's revisit the baseball player example once more. On the days he practices batting, he needs to review curve balls, fastballs, and change ups (and possibly other pitches, but we'll stick with three for now). He can begin practice by hitting a curve ball many times in a row. Then he can move on to the fastball, then the change up. This type of practice schedule is referred to as blocking (a particular type of massed practice). Alternatively, he can mix up hitting all three pitches throughout the session. This type of practice schedule is referred to as interleaving. There is strong evidence that an interleaved practice schedule results in better long-term and flexible learning in at least three domains: motor skill learning, category learning, and mathematical problem-solving.

Much like in spacing research, a key principle of interleaving research is that the number of practice trials in a study session remains constant across groups. Only the organization of those trials is manipulated. The classic interleaving experiment typically involves asking participants to learn a set of related skills in a specific order, then testing those skills after some delay. Rohrer and Taylor (2007), for example, asked students to learn the proper equations used to calculate the volume of four solid three-dimensional shapes. One group of students followed a blocked schedule in which they practiced calculating the volume of one type of solid per session (much as occurs in classrooms). Another group of students followed an interleaved schedule in which they practiced calculating the volume of all four types of solids during every practice session. There were four practice sessions total, spaced 1 week apart. Both groups were then tested 1 week after the fourth practice session. During initial learning, the blocked group reached a higher level of performance than did the interleaved group. On the final test, however, the interleaved group calculated the volumes of the solids correctly 63% of the time, whereas the blocked group was only able to calculate the volumes correctly 20% of the time.

With such a dramatic difference in performance (43%!), why isn't interleaving a more widely used technique? As in our discussion of massed practice, blocked practice sessions feel more productive (Rohrer & Taylor, 2007) because initial learning is faster if the learning is blocked. In the experiment just described, students in the blocked group calculated the volumes of the solids more successfully than their interleaved peers *during* each practice session (89% compared with 60% accuracy overall). They learned the calculation more quickly and implemented them successfully, but they did not retain the knowledge after a week's delay. Why? Because with blocked practice, students know the type of solid they have and they know the formula for calculating its volume. So they just apply the one formula over and over. In the interleaved learning situation, however, they must determine what type of solid is being described, and they must then retrieve the appropriate equation for that volume. The final test on all four volumes requires the skill of determining what type of solid is being described and retrieving that equation. Students who learned by interleaving practiced this skill, whereas those learning through blocked practice never had to learn this discrimination. Thus, using a term from earlier in the chapter, interleaved learning leads to greater transfer-appropriate processing than does blocked learning because tests almost always require students to figure out what type of challenge they are facing.

Other interleaving experiments have obtained similar results. Kornell and Bjork (2008) had students learn some material on a blocked schedule and other material on an interleaved schedule so that all students experienced both types of practice sessions. After the final test, they asked students which schedule helped them to learn better. Even though test scores were much better for the material learned on an interleaved schedule, 78% of the students reported that they learned the blocked material as well as or better than the interleaved material. That is probably because blocked learning seems easier than interleaved learning.

In another study, a group of undergraduates were presented with an explanation of both blocked and interleaved study schedules. When asked to choose which would lead to better learning, more than 90% chose the blocked schedule (McCabe,

2011). Whether the reason for this preference is due to the typical structure of lesson plans and textbooks or due to the feeling of success achieved during blocked practice is unknown. Another possible reason is that interleaved learning feels hard and leads to more errors (a desirable difficulty). We will see that interleaving is also more successful in the learning of motor skills.

Research in Motor Skill Training

For decades, we have known that interleaved practice produces better long-term retention for motor skill learning. The first study to demonstrate the effect occurred nearly 40 years ago using patterned arm movements (Shea & Morgan, 1979). Since then, the literature has expanded to include studies in the domain of sports training, playing musical instruments, and surgical training. In each field of skill acquisition, the same patterns are observed: blocked practice leads to more rapid skill learning, but interleaved practice leads to better long-term retention and transfer to novel situations.

In a study by Goode and Magill (1986), college students with no prior experience were taught three types of badminton serves on either a blocked or interleaved practice schedule. For both schedules, students practiced 3 times per week for 3 weeks (9 sessions total). The blocked group practiced 36 short serves on one day, 36 long serves the next day, and 36 drive serves the following day. This schedule was repeated each week. The interleaved group practiced 12 serves of each type (short, long, and drive) in random order during every session. For both groups, the serves were practiced only on the right side of the court. One day after the last practice section, all students were tested on each of the three serves they had learned. Compared to the blocked group, the interleaved group was able to land more accurate serves not only from the right side of the court (where they had practiced) but also from the left side of the court (from which they had never served during the experiment). This study illustrates that interleaved practice leads to improved motor skill learning both in contexts that match the practice conditions and in new contexts where the learner must adjust their skills to the environment. Similar results have been found in studies on baseball batting (Hall, Domingues, & Cavazos, 1994), golf (Porter, Landin, Hebert, & Baum, 2007), and volleyball (Kalkhoran & Shariati, 2012).

The advantages of interleaved practice are not limited to novices. A study of formally trained piano players by Abushanab and Bishara (2013) demonstrated the same pattern of results. In this study, rather than learning how to play the piano, pianists learned to play new melodies with the goal of increasing their speed and accuracy on each melody. Each pianist practiced some melodies using a blocked schedule and other melodies using an interleaved schedule. During the practice session, the pianists were able to reach higher speeds on the melodies practiced on a blocked schedule compared to the interleaved schedule. When tested on the melodies 2 days later, however, melodies practiced using the interleaved schedule were played more quickly than those practiced using the blocked schedule. Accuracy was high for both groups during practice and test due to the fact that all the participants were experienced piano players. Unlike studies that typically use novices, this study illustrates that learners with prior experience can use interleaved practice to hone their existing skill sets. In military training, for example, each soldier needs to know what to do if the firing pin on their rifle gets jammed. By interleaving various rifle maintenance techniques during training, even experienced soldiers can shave precious seconds off the time required to recall the appropriate action and repair their rifle during a combat situation, where each second is critical.

Recently, Welsher and Grierson (2017) used interleaving to study a training task used to teach medical students specific hand movements within a confined space meant to imitate the conditions of a laparoscopic surgical procedure. The students had to pick up a bean with a surgical tool using their dominant hand, pass it to their nondominant hand, and then deposit the bean into a dish. The task was confined to a small box, which restricted the hand movements that the students could use to complete the task. In this study, medical students observed experts and novices as they completed the training task. The students also practiced the task themselves intermittently between observations. One group's observation was scheduled using a blocked format, while another group's observations were scheduled using an interleaved format. In the blocked schedule, students observed an expert completing the training task 20 times back to back and also observed a novice (one of their peers) completing the task 20 times back to back. In the interleaved schedule, the expert and novice alternated completing the training task until each had performed the task 20 times. For both groups, students attempted the task themselves after each set of 10 observations. At the end of the final observation, the students were tested on their ability to complete the training task. The following day, the students were tested on their ability to complete that task again by leading with their nondominant hand (all practice trials and tests had been lead with the dominant hand).

Interestingly, performance by both groups improved at the same rate during the observation and practice trials, and performance on the immediate test was also nearly identical for both groups. Differences between the groups emerged during the test using the nondominant hand. When leading with their nondominant hand, the blocked group produced more than 50% more errors than the interleaved group. The blocked schedule was far less successful when the students had to adjust their skills to a new procedure, even one that closely resembled what they had been practicing. Thus, the interleaved observation served to make learning more flexible and applicable to a new situation.

Research in Category Learning

Interleaving examples offer benefits to differentiating between categories within a group as well. Kornell and Bjork (2008), discussed earlier in this section, performed a well-known study of the interleaving advantage in category learning using painting styles. In this study, students were asked to learn the styles of 12 different artists by viewing 6 paintings done by each artist. For 6 of the artists, paintings appeared in a blocked format (all 6 paintings by one artist in a row). For the other 6 artists, paintings appeared in an interleaved format (no 2 paintings by the same artist were shown back to back). Fifteen minutes after the last painting was studied, students were shown new paintings (4 for each artist in random order) and asked to determine which artist created each painting. Students were better able to correctly identify the artist of the novel paintings when the work of that artist had originally been studied in the interleaved condition relative to the blocked condition (although students believed blocked learning led to better performance).

Kang and Pashler (2012) sought to determine why the interleaved schedule resulted in better category learning than the blocked schedule in the Kornell and Bjork (2008) experiments. In one of their new experiments, paintings by different artists were presented simultaneously (side by side) in addition to the interleaved and blocked schedules. They found that the simultaneous presentation resulted in learning that was just as good as the interleaved learning schedule (both were superior to blocked learning). This result suggests that the enhanced learning in the interleaved condition may be a product of students contrasting the styles of different artists. They learned what features differ between various styles more easily than in the blocked case. In the blocked case, people probably concentrate on the commonalities between different works by the same artist.

Interleaving benefits have been found in cases of auditory discrimination as well. Chen, Grierson, and Norman (2015) conducted a study in which nursing students were taught to discriminate between different respiratory and cardiac diagnoses by listening to internal body sounds through a stethoscope. The nursing students listened to recordings of 8 different diagnoses (4 respiratory disorders and 4 cardiac disorders). The students heard three example of each diagnosis using either a blocked or interleaved schedule. Immediately after studying the recordings, the students were tested on their ability to match the correct diagnosis with the recording. Half of the recordings on the test were taken directly from the study session while the other half were new recordings of the diagnoses they had studied. The students also took the same test 1 week later. Nursing students in the interleaved group outperformed the blocked group for both respiratory and cardiac disorder identification on both the immediate and delayed tests. The difference in performance was particularly dramatic for the new recordings. As you can see in Figure 14.4, the interleaved group scored somewhat higher than the blocked group on the recordings they had heard during study. For the new recordings, however, the difference in performance is much more striking. In fact, the interleaved group performed just as well on the new examples as the blocked group did on examples they had heard before. The field of medicine is rich with studies demonstrating the advantage of interleaved practice in category discrimination. Similar patterns of results have been found in psychiatric diagnoses (Zulkiply, McLean, Burt, & Bath, 2012) and electrocardiogram reading (Hatala, Brooks, & Norman, 2003), as well.

Research in Mathematical Problem-Solving

Doug Rohrer's work on interleaved practice in mathematical problem-solving makes up a substantial portion of the interleaving literature. We described one study earlier, the one involving solving for volumes of different kinds of solids. Through laboratory and classroom research, Rohrer and his colleagues have been able to dissect the interleaving advantage in order to understand the underlying patterns of performance within the field of mathematics. In one study, for example, Taylor and

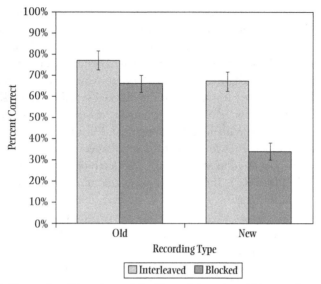

Figure 14.4 The results of Experiment 3 by Chen, Grierson, and Norman (2015). Nursing students tested on respiratory and cardiac disorder recordings performed better on immediate and delayed tests when study followed an interleaved schedule compared to a blocked schedule. When test performance was divided between old (previously studied) and new (previously unstudied) recordings (shown here), there was a greater difference in performance for new recordings than for old recordings.
Adapted from R. Chen, L. Grierson, & G. Norman. Manipulation of cognitive load variables and impact on auscultation test performance, *Advances in Health Sciences Education, 20,* 935–952, 2015, copyright 2014 by Springer Science+Business Media Dordrecht. Reprinted with permission of Springer.

Rohrer (2010) asked elementary school students to solve math problems involving prisms. Students had to determine the number of faces, corners, edges, and angles on various prisms. Each type of problem could be solved using a different formula, which the students learned how to apply. Students completed a series of practice problems in either a blocked or interleaved format. The following day the students took two tests. For both tests, all of the math problems were new cases of the types of problems they had studied. That is, none of the practice problems was included on either test. On the first test, no formulas were provided. Students had to recall and apply the appropriate formula for each problem. On the second test, the formula for each type of problem (face, corner, edge, and angle) was provided at the top of the page.

During the practice session, students in the blocked group performed much better than their classmates in the interleaved group. The blocked group got nearly every practice problem correct, while the interleaved group only got between 70% and 80% correct. On the first test, however, the interleaved group performed better than the blocked group. Interestingly, the interleaved group's performance stayed at roughly the same level it had been at during practice, 77%. The blocked group's performance suffered severely, dropping from near perfect during practice down to 38% on the test. On the second test, in which students were given the formulas and told which formula applied to which problem (e.g., "faces = b + 2," p. 842), the groups showed nearly no difference in performance. The blocked group returned to near perfect performance (90%) and the interleaved group achieved perfect performance (100%). This change in performance could either be because the blocked group couldn't remember the formulas they learned or because they were using the right formulas but on the wrong test problems.

Taylor and Rohrer (2010) addressed this issue by analyzing the types of errors made on the first delayed test. For both the interleaved and blocked groups they identified two types of errors: fabrication errors and discrimination errors. *Fabrication errors* were those in which the student used a formula that was not taught during the experiment. Fabrication errors included misremembered formulas and formulas learned in other units of the math class. Making a fabrication error would suggest that the student simply couldn't remember the correct formula. *Discrimination errors* were those in which the student used a formula taught during the experiment, but used it on the wrong type of problem (e.g., using the faces formula to calculate the number of edges on a prism). Making a discrimination error would suggest that the student couldn't remember how to apply the formulas they learned. Remarkably, the pattern of errors differed dramatically between the blocked and interleaved groups (see Figure 14.5). The interleaved group's errors were evenly split between fabrication and discrimination errors. The blocked group, however, made three times as many discrimination errors as fabrication errors. Additionally, the students in both groups made about the same number of fabrication errors. So, the students in the blocked group weren't having any more trouble remembering the formulas than their classmates in the interleaved group. Rather, the blocked group was having trouble knowing when to apply the formulas they had learned.

In his chapter on interleaving for classroom learning, Kang (2016) perfectly sums up the advantage of interleaved practice, "it is not sufficient to learn *how* to execute a strategy; one must also know *when* a particular strategy is appropriate" (p. 86). In each study described in this chapter, we discussed how interleaved practice led to a better ability to apply the skills learned to novel situations. Since no training program or classroom lesson can cover every instance where a skill might be needed, transfer of the skill to new contexts is crucial. For this reason, we endorse interleaved practice over blocked practice wherever it can reasonably be applied. Learning will be slower and more effortful, but will result in more long lasting, flexible understanding.

Interleaving Suggestions for Military Training

Interleaving has not yet been adopted in many instructional fields. Classrooms across the country teach their curriculums using subject units and assign homework in a blocked format. Similarly, in virtually all arenas of training of which we are aware (sports, music, business, and the military), blocked training is the norm. Yet, as we have described, the benefits of interleaving have been found in a diverse range of settings. Studies in education from elementary school and medical school, in sports, music, and art all benefit from interleaving. Military training is no different.

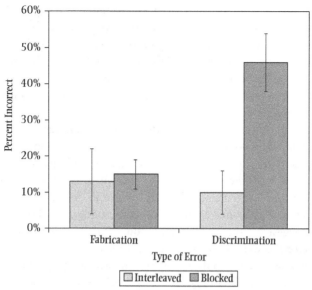

Figure 14.5 Errors made on the first test in the study by Taylor and Rohrer (2010), expressed as percent incorrect for two types of errors (fabrication and discrimination), plotted as a function of practice condition (interleaved vs. blocked). In this experiment, elementary school students learned formulas to solve four different types of math problems about prisms. Students practiced using the formulas one problem type per practice set (blocked) or all four problem types in each practice set (interleaved). They were tested the following day on a set of new problems that required them to recall and use the formulas they had learned the previous day. The interleaved group produced fewer errors over all (the sum of the two light gray bars), with significantly fewer discrimination errors than the blocked group. Error bars represent standard errors of the means and were recreated from the original figure.

Adapted from K. Taylor & D. Rohrer, The effects of interleaving practice. *Applied Cognitive Psychology, 24,* 837–848, 2010, copyright 2009 by John Wiley & Sons, Ltd. Reprinted with permission of John Wiley and Sons.

For example, a soldier in combat, and especially an officer in charge of directing soldiers, must know at a moment's notice which tactical formation is best for the given situation. Training programs cannot possibly be expected to run drills on every scenario that might occur in a combat setting; time is too limited and combat is too unpredictable. Instead, a training program should prepare soldiers to apply the principles they learn to novel situations, which is exactly what an interleaved practice schedule does. Much like spacing, interleaving can be achieved simply by rearranging the existing practice drills so that soldiers learn not only what to do in a particular formation, but also when that formation is more useful than another.

Interleaving can be useful outside of learning tactical formations as well. According to the US Army's *Soldier's Manual of Common Tasks: Warrior Skills Level 1* (2015), each army soldier must learn to "identify terrain features on a map" (p. 3–49). This type of learning is perfectly suited to interleaved practice, specifically as discussed in our section on category learning. A soldier could implement an interleaved practice schedule during his own individual study. By studying maps with different types of terrain in random order, the soldier would be able to differentiate between hills, saddles, and valleys (for example) more quickly and efficiently than a soldier who studied the same maps in a blocked schedule. Using the interleaved format would also result in a soldier who is able to quickly and accurately read a map that he or she has never seen before. Implementing interleaving across the various facets of military training will produce soldiers who can apply their diverse knowledge to any situation effectively.

CONCLUSION

To summarize, retrieval practice, spaced practice, and interleaved practice are each useful, scientifically backed methods to create long-term, flexible learning in a variety of settings with many different types of materials. Our review of the literature in this chapter has summarized research in laboratory, classroom, and professional settings. We have shown that the techniques we suggest are effective on materials as simple as lists of words and as complex as microsurgical procedures. It should come as no shock then that the best recommendation we can make to improve military training programs is to implement spaced, interleaved retrieval practice wherever possible. And although we have focused our attention on how these techniques relate to military training programs, they certainly apply in training personnel in other high-stakes settings. Agencies that train first responders—such as police officers, firefighters, and emergency medical technicians (EMTs)—will benefit from these techniques. We will close this chapter with a few recommendations on how to apply each of these principles.

Putting It All Together: Advice for Implementing These Principles

RETRIEVAL PRACTICE
Retrieval practice is already being used in military training extensively for skills training. For example, soldiers learn how to fire a weapon accurately and consistently by practicing often on firing ranges designed to mimic combat situations. Retrieval practice can be used in classroom settings as well by adding frequent, low-stakes quizzing to the existing curriculum. In this way, soldiers are required to recall and apply their training in every stage of learning throughout the program. Additionally, soldiers should be provided with feedback for incorrect answers or for errors, allowing them to identify and improve on weak areas for future tests. Finally, quizzes (as well as drill practice, weapons training, etc.) should be repeated frequently throughout the program. Retrieving knowledge from memory once is insufficient for long-term retention. A soldier should be required to retrieve the knowledge gained from his training repeatedly and throughout the course of training.

SPACED PRACTICE
We discussed the benefits of spaced learning over massed learning at length in this chapter. One simple way to use spacing is to take a lesson that is typically taught in

a day-long seminar and break it up into several smaller lessons spaced out a week apart. Reviews of the learned material (ideally through retrieval practice) should also be spaced out over time to prevent forgetting. The spacing schedule for any individual training program depends on the retention interval (the time until the final test). Longer retention intervals require longer spacing between sessions. In general, 1 day of spacing is useful for 1 week of retention, 1 week of spacing is useful for 2 months of retention, and 1 month of spacing is useful for 1 year of retention. Soldiers need training to last throughout their time in the military, so continual spaced refreshers for practicing critical skills should be implemented. A spacing schedule can expand as time goes on, to reflect the changing needs of the soldiers. Perhaps 1 day of spacing is needed while soldiers initially learn a new tactical formation. After they learn the basics, spacing can be increased to one training session per week, to find and correct weak areas or common errors. Finally, when the soldiers can routinely perform the formation correctly, spacing is increased to once per month, so that forgetting over time is minimized.

INTERLEAVED PRACTICE

Interleaving research has shown that simply mixing up the order in which skills are practiced can have dramatic effects on retention and flexibility of learning. A soldier who must learn to repair a machine or vehicle in the field, for example, would be better off if he or she practiced fixing many different mechanical issues in random order rather than practicing the same one over and over before moving on to the next issue. In the field, soldiers will rarely be told what is wrong before they start working. They will need to assess the situation to figure out which solution to apply and then apply that solution correctly, potentially under stressful conditions and time restraints. By mixing up practice during training, soldiers get the opportunity to learn what different issues look like and how to tell one issue from another, as is evidenced in the category learning literature. A soldier will also more easily remember which solutions to use in which situations, as discussed in the literature on mathematical problem-solving. Even if the soldier encounters a problem in the field that she had never seen during training, the soldier who practiced using an interleaved schedule would be best equipped to apply the principles she learned to the new situation successfully.

Automated Training Using These Principles

A major challenge in training is how to get thousands of people up to speed without spending too many resources. There is a long tradition of the military utilizing psychological tools and services en masse, from the intelligence tests and personnel tests used for recruitment and placement during World War I to the clinical treatment of soldiers returning from World War II (Fancher & Rutherford, 2012; Hilgard, 1987). A more recent development in this tradition is intelligent tutoring systems designed to train soldiers. For example, the Immersive Naval Officer Training System (INOTS) is an immersive environment for role-playing with virtual humans designed to train officers' interpersonal skills (Hays et al., 2012). At the same time the military has been developing virtual training environments for various skills, the education industry has been designing products aimed at college students and instructors to optimize learning in and out of the classroom (e.g., Assessment and LEarning in Knowledge Spaces, ALEKs; Falmagne, Cosyn, Doignon, & Thiéry, 2006).

We propose a convergence of these simultaneous developments. Specifically, we believe the military is uniquely situated to develop adaptive learning programs that utilize the cognitive principles outlined in this chapter. Such a learning system could provide individual soldiers with training tailored to their performance to optimize long-term retention and transfer of skills by implementing schedules of spaced, interleaved retrieval practice. Furthermore, this type of digital learning environment would be cost-efficient in the long run, given that classroom training costs time and money. Our idea is not, of course, completely novel. For example, the Air Force Research Laboratory has engaged with cognitive psychologists to develop and assess learning algorithms for intelligent tutoring systems (Jastrzembski, Gluck, & Gunzelmann, 2006). Our goal in discussing intelligent tutoring systems in this chapter is to encourage further development of these systems by the military, specifically focusing on implementing spacing, interleaving, and retrieval practice. If you want thousands of soldiers or emergency personnel to efficiently learn skills that will last, designing any learning environment—digital or traditional classroom and field training—with these principles in mind will certainly help.

REFERENCES

Abushanab, B., & Bishara, A. J. (2013). Memory and metacognition for piano melodies: Illusory advantages of fixed-over random-order practice. *Memory & Cognition, 41,* 928–937.

Adesope, O. O., Trevisan, D. A., & Sundararajan, N. (2017). Rethinking the use of tests: A meta-analysis of practice testing. *Review of Educational Research, 87*(3), 659–701.

Agarwal, P., Finley, J. R., Rose, N., & Roediger, H. L. (2017). Benefits from retrieval practice are greater for students with lower working memory capacity. *Memory, 25*(6), 764–771.

Balota, D. A., Duchek, J. M., & Paullin, R. (1989). Age-related differences in the impact of spacing, lag, and retention interval. *Psychology and Aging, 4,* 3–9.

Bird, S. (2011). Effects of distributed practice on the acquisition of second language English syntax. *Applied Psycholinguistics, 32,* 437–442.

Bjork, R. A. (1994). Memory and metamemory considerations in the training of human beings. In J. Metcalfe & A. Shimamura (Eds.), *Metacognition: Knowing About Knowing* (pp. 185–205). Cambridge, MA: MIT Press.

Brown, P. C., Roediger, H. L, & McDaniel, M. A. (2014). *Make It Stick: The Science of Successful Learning.* Cambridge, MA: Harvard University Press.

Butler, A. C. (2010). Repeated testing produces superior transfer of learning relative to repeated studying. *Journal of Experimental Psychology: Learning, Memory, and Cognition, 36,* 1118–1133.

Butler, A. C., Godbole, N., & Marsh, E. J. (2013). Explanation feedback is better than correct answer feedback for promoting transfer of learning. *Journal of Educational Psychology, 105,* 290–298.

Butler, A. C., & Roediger, H. L. (2008). Feedback enhances the positive effects and reduces the negative effects of multiple-choice testing. *Memory & Cognition, 36*, 604–616.

Carpenter, S. K., & Pashler, H. (2007). Testing beyond words: Using tests to enhance visuospatial map learning. *Psychonomic Bulletin & Review, 14*, 474–478.

Carpenter, S. K., Pashler, H., & Cepeda, N. J. (2009). Using tests to enhance 8th grade students' retention of US history facts. *Applied Cognitive Psychology, 23*, 760–771.

Cepeda, N. J., Pashler, H., Vul, E., Wixted, J. T., & Rohrer, D. (2006). Distributed practice in verbal recall tasks: A review and quantitative synthesis. *Psychological Bulletin, 132*, 354–380.

Cepeda, N. J., Vul, E., Rohrer, D., Wixted, J. T., & Pashler, H. (2008). Spacing effects in learning: A temporal ridgeline of optimal retention. *Psychological Science, 19*, 1095–1102.

Chen, R., Grierson, L., & Norman, G. (2015). Manipulation of cognitive load variables and impact on auscultation test performance. *Advances in Health Sciences Education, 20*, 935–952.

Couch, D. (2004). *The Finishing School.* New York: Three Rivers Press.

Couch, D. (2009). *The Warrior Elite: The Forging of SEAL Class 228.* New York: Three Rivers Press.

Falmagne, J. C., Cosyn, E., Doignon, J. P, & Thiéry, N. (2006). The assessment of knowledge, in theory and in practice. In R. Missaoui & J. Schmid (Eds.), *Formal concept analysis* (pp. 61–79). Berlin: Springer.

Fancher, R., & Rutherford, A. (2012). *Pioneers of Psychology: A History.* New York: W. W. Norton & Company.

Fazio, L. K., Huelser, B. J., Johnson, A., & Marsh, E. J. (2010). Receiving right/wrong feedback: Consequences for learning. *Memory, 18*, 335–350.

Gagnon, S. A., & Wagner, A. D. (2016). Acute stress and episodic memory retrieval: Neurobiological mechanisms and behavioral consequences. *Annals of the New York Academy of Sciences, 1369*, 55–75.

Gates, A. I. (1917). Recitation as a factor in memorizing. *Archives of Psychology, 40*, 1–124.

Gluckman, M., Vlach, H. A., & Sandhofer, C. M. (2014). Spacing simultaneously promotes multiple forms of learning in children's science curriculum. *Applied Cognitive Psychology, 28*, 266–273.

Goode, S., & Magill, R. A. (1986). Contextual interference effects in learning three badminton serves. *Research Quarterly for Exercise and Sport, 57*, 308–314.

Hall, K. G., Domingues, D. A., & Cavazos, R. (1994). Contextual interference effects with skilled baseball players. *Perceptual and Motor Skills, 78*, 835–841.

Hatala, R. M., Brooks, L. R., & Norman, G. R. (2003). Practice makes perfect: The critical role of mixed practice in the acquisition of ECG interpretation skills. *Advances in Health Sciences Education, 8*, 17–26.

Hays, M.J., Campbell, J.C., Timmer, M.A., Poore, J. C., Webb, A. K., Stark, C. & King, T. K. (2012, December). *Can role-play with virtual humans teach interpersonal skills?* Proceedings of the 34th Interservice/Industry Training, Simulation, and Education Conference, Orlando, FL.

Heidt, C. T., Arbuthnott, K. D., & Price, H. L. (2016). The effects of distributed learning on enhanced cognitive interview training. *Psychiatry, Psychology, and Law, 23*, 47–61.

Hilgard, E. R. (1987). *Psychology in America: A Historical Survey.* New York: Harcourt Brace Jovanovich.

Jastrzembski, T. S., Gluck, K. A., & Gunzelmann, G. (2006). Knowledge tracing and prediction of future trainee performance. In *The Proceedings of the Interservice/Industry Training, Simulation, and Education Conference*. Orlando, FL: National Training Systems Association (pp. 1498–1508).

Kalkhoran, A. F., & Shariati, A. (2012). The effects of contextual interference on learning volleyball motor skills. *Journal of Physical Education and Sport, 12*, 550–556.

Kang, S. H. K. (2016). The benefits of interleaved practice for learning. In J. C. Horvath, J. Lodge, & J. A. C. Hattie (Eds.), *From the Laboratory to the Classroom: Translating the Science of Learning for Teachers*. (pp. 79–93). Oxford: Routledge.

Kang, S. H. K., & Pashler, H. (2012). Learning painting styles: Spacing is advantageous when it promotes discriminative contrast. *Applied Cognitive Psychology, 26*, 97–103.

Karpicke, J. D. (2009). Metacognitive control and strategy selection: Deciding to practice retrieval during learning. *Journal of Experimental Psychology: General, 138*, 469–486.

Karpicke, J. D., Butler, A. C., & Roediger, H. L. (2009). Metacognitive strategies in student learning: Do students practice retrieval when they study on their own? *Memory, 17*, 471–479.

Karpicke, J. D., & Roediger, H. L. (2008). The critical importance of retrieval for learning. *Science, 319*, 966–968.

Kornell, N., & Bjork, R. A. (2008). Learning concepts and categories: Is spacing the "enemy of induction"? *Psychological Science, 13*, 585–592.

Kulik, J. A., & Kulik, C. C. (1988). Timing of feedback and verbal learning. *Review of Educational Research, 58*, 79–97.

McCabe, J. (2011). Metacognitive awareness of learning strategies in undergraduates. *Memory & Cognition, 39*, 462–476.

McDaniel, M. A., Howard, D. C., & Einstein, G. O. (2009). The read-recite-review study strategy: Effective and portable. *Psychological Science, 20*, 516–522.

Melton, A. W. (1970). The situation with respect to the spacing of repetitions and memory. *Journal of Verbal Learning and Verbal Behavior, 9*, 596–606.

Moulton, C.-A. E., Dubrowski, A., MacRae, H., Graham, B., Grober, E., & Reznick, R. (2006). Teaching surgical skills: What kind of practice makes perfect? A randomized, controlled trial. *Annals of Surgery, 244*, 400–409.

Mullet, H. G., Butler, A. C., Verdin, B., von Borries, R., & Marsh, E. J. (2014). Delaying feedback promotes transfer of knowledge despite student preferences to receive feedback immediately. *Journal of Applied Research in Memory and Cognition, 3*, 222–229.

Pashler, H., Cepeda, N. J., Wixted, J. T., & Rohrer, D. (2005). When does feedback facilitate learning of words? *Journal of Experimental Psychology: Learning, Memory, and Cognition, 31*, 3–8.

Porter, J., Landin, D., Hebert, E., & Baum, B. (2007). The effects of three levels of contextual interference on performance outcomes and movement patterns in golf skills. *International Journal of Sports Science and Coaching, 2*, 243–255.

Putnam, A. L., Nestojko, J. F., & Roediger, H. L. (2016). Improving student learning: Two strategies to make it stick. In J. C. Horvath, J. Lodge, & J. A. C. Hattie (Eds.), *From the Laboratory to the Classroom: Translating the Science of Learning for Teachers*. (pp. 94–121). Oxford: Routledge.

Pyc, M. A., Balota, D. A., McDermott, K. B., Tully, T., & Roediger, H. L. (2014). Between-list lag effects in recall depend on retention interval. *Memory & Cognition, 42*, 965–977.

Rawson, K. A., & Dunlosky, J. (2012). When is practice testing most effective for improving durability and efficiency of student learning? *Educational Psychology Review, 24*, 419–435.

Roediger, H. L., Gallo, D. A., & Geraci, L. (2002). Processing approaches to cognition: The impetus from the levels of processing framework. *Memory, 10*, 319–332.

Roediger, H. L., & Karpicke, J. D. (2006). Test-enhanced learning: Taking memory tests improves long-term retention. *Psychological Science, 17*, 249–255.

Roediger, H. L., & Marsh, E. J. (2005). The positive and negative consequences of multiple-choice testing. *Journal of Experimental Psychology: Learning, Memory, and Cognition, 31*, 1155–1159.

Roediger, H. L., Putnam, A. L., & Smith, M. (2011). Ten benefits of testing and their applications to educational practice. In J. Mestre & B. H. Ross (Eds.), *Psychology of Learning and Motivation: Advances in Research and Theory, Vol. 55* (pp. 1–36). Oxford: Elsevier.

Rohrer, D., & Taylor, K. (2007). The shuffling of mathematics practice problems improves learning. *Instructional Science, 35*, 481–498.

Rohrer, D., Taylor, K., & Sholar, B. (2010). Tests enhance the transfer of learning. *Journal of Experimental Psychology: Learning, Memory, and Cognition, 36*, 233–239.

Rowland, C. A. (2014). The effect of testing versus restudy on retention: A meta-analytic review of the testing effect. *Psychological Bulletin, 140*, 1432–1463.

Schmidt, R. A. (1991). Frequent augmented feedback can degrade learning: Evidence and interpretations. In G. E. Stelmach & J. Requin (Eds.), *Tutorials in Motor Neuroscience* (pp. 59–75). Dordrecht, The Netherlands: Kluwer.

Schwieren, J., Barenberg, J., & Dutke, S. (2017). The testing effect in the psychology classroom: A meta-analytic perspective. *Psychology Learning & Teaching, 16*(2), 179–196.

Shea, J. B., & Morgan, R. L. (1979). Contextual interference effects on the acquisition, retention, and transfer of a motor skill. *Journal of Experimental Psychology: Human Learning and Memory, 5*, 179–187.

Smith, A. M., Floerke, V. A., & Thomas, A. K. (2016). Retrieval practice protects memory against acute stress. *Science, 354*, 1046–1048.

Sobel, H. S., Cepeda, N. J., & Kapler, I. V. (2011). Spacing effects in real-world classroom vocabulary learning, *Applied Cognitive Psychology, 25*, 763–767.

Soderstrom, N. C., & Bjork, R. A. (2015). Learning versus performance: An integrative review. *Perspectives on Psychological Science, 10*, 176–199.

Son, L. K., & Simon, D. A. (2012). Distributed learning: Data, metacognition, and educational implications. *Educational Psychology Review, 24*, 379–399.

Taylor, K., & Rohrer, D. (2010). The effects of interleaving practice. *Applied Cognitive Psychology, 24*, 837–848.

US Department of the Army. (2015). Identify terrain features on a map. In *Soldier's Manual of Common Tasks: Warrior Skills Level 1* (pp. 3-49–3-57). Washington, DC: US Department of the Army.

Welsher, A., & Grierson, L. E. (2017). Enhancing technical skill learning through interleaved mixed-model observational practice. *Advances in Health Sciences Education, 22*(5), 1201–1211.

Zulkiply, N., McLean, J., Burt, J. S., & Bath, D. (2012). Spacing and induction: Application to exemplars presented as auditory and visual text. *Learning and Instruction, 22*, 215–221.

15

Examining the Influence of Adaptive Instructional Techniques on Human Performance for Tasks Conducted in Extremely Stressful Work Environments

ROBERT SOTTILARE AND STEPHEN GOLDBERG

INTRODUCTION

This chapter examines the potential benefits of adaptive instructional techniques on training for successful human performance during tasks conducted in extremely stressful work environments. Highly stressful work environments span civilian occupations as well as military combat and other dangerous operational settings including law enforcement, firefighting, and emergency medicine. Extreme work environments often include time and performance stressors, but some may also include safety hazards such as those experienced by working as a deck hand on a fishing boat off Alaska or hanging steel in the construction of skyscrapers. Regardless of the type of "extreme environment," the instructional designer must understand what should be represented in the training environment (e.g., simulation) in order to influence knowledge and skill acquisition to the point where the learner can successfully perform the expected tasks in the work environment regardless of the conditions.

A vivid example of the consummate operator in extreme environments is the fictional character James Bond, created by the novelist Ian Fleming. Bond always seems to be prepared for any situation. He understands the mission goal, the operating environment, available assets, and how to use them. This, combined with physical skills and quick thinking, allows Bond to not just survive any situation, but win. This example raises several questions. How did Bond reach this pinnacle of performance? Exposure in training and in operations to a variety of extreme situations allowed Bond to adapt and hone his strategies and his skills, but which attributes influenced his success most? Is triumph over adversity solely a matter of quick thinking and reflexes, or is there more to it? Is it realistic to think we can train people to this level of proficiency? How might a real-life operator learn to succeed in extreme environments with persistent stressors? An example of a persistent stressful environment is a team of astronauts on a mission to Mars (Petranek, 2015). The team's survival depends on the spacecraft and ground systems. There will be constant stress about system failures, isolation, and the lack of available help with the growing distance from Earth. The team will be isolated and will have to assess and solve problems. Both the James Bond and Mars mission examples will be used to illustrate concepts discussed throughout this chapter.

For the past 40 years, the primary adaptive instructional technology has been the intelligent tutoring system (ITS) which uses artificially intelligent, computer-based agents to monitor both the behaviors and physiology of the learner and the attributes of the training environment in real time. ITSs vary interaction and feedback for each learner and modify the difficulty level of the training environment based on the learner's capabilities, needs, and limitations during the training. Adaptive instructional technologies (tools and methods) tailor the training experience for each individual learner and for teams of learners in order to optimize their learning and resultant performance (Sottilare, Ragusa, Hoffman & Goldberg, 2013).

To better understand adaptive instruction in the context of extremely stressful work environments, we first define *stress*, then distinguish the characteristics of the stressful *work environment* from the *training environment*, and finally identify examples of *extremely stressful environments*.

Stress and Stressors

Extremely stressful environments usually have a negative impact on performance. However, stress at lower levels can work to facilitate improved performance. The Yerkes-Dodson law (Yerkes & Dodson, 1908) defines an empirical relationship between arousal and performance stress. Within the Yerkes-Dodson model, the performance of easy tasks improved with increasing stress, but, with more difficult tasks, an increase in stress results in an inverse U-shaped function with better performance within medium stress levels and declining performance within higher stress levels (Deffenbacher, 1983). Selye (1936) defined stress as "the nonspecific response of the body to any demand made on it" (p. 32). Stress is caused by a *stressor*, which Selye (1976) defined as any factor, event, or agent that threatens an organism's well-being and thereby initiates a stress response. For our purposes, we have divided stressors into two categories: physical (i.e., environmental and physiological stressors) and mental (i.e., cognitive and value-based stressors), which are described with respect to our learning effect model (LEM; Sottilare, Ragusa, Hoffman & Goldberg, 2013; Sottilare, 2012) in the discussion section of this chapter.

Stress can have both protective and damaging effects on the body. Under stress the body attempts to adapt by maintaining homeostasis and by reducing the long-term negative impact of stress (allostatic load) through a process of allostasis (McEwen, 2000). "Allostasis" (literally "maintaining stability, or homeostasis, through change") refers to the process of adaptation to acute stress involving the output of stress hormones which act in the ways just described to restore homeostasis in the face of a challenge (Sterling & Eyer, 1988). Selye modeled the interaction between stressors and the body using a three-stage model called the *general adaptation syndrome* (GAS; Selye, 1936). In the first stage, *alarm*, the body reacts to the stressor (e.g., threat). This is typically a fight (engage) or flight (withdraw) response. In our Bond example, James is more likely to engage because he is confident of a win, but in our Mars mission, the initial reaction could be to withdraw, but to where? In the second stage, *resistance*, the body compensates by focusing resources to deal with the stressor. Finally, in the third stage, *exhaustion*, stressors may continue beyond the body's capability to compensate and resources may be taxed or depleted. This is a likely scenario for our Mars mission, where a crew member has nowhere to escape the stressor. The body applies different resources depending on the type and persistence of the stressor. Given each of these models the impact of stress on the body and performance is related to its intensity and duration, the nature of the task, the experience base of the learner, and the learner's resilience to the effects of the stressor.

Work Versus Training Environments

While both the training and the work environment provide opportunities to acquire knowledge and skill, the work environment is distinguished from the learning environment in that it is the setting in which the learner will execute the task under actual (and sometimes unpredictable) conditions including stressors. The training environment is the setting in which the learner gains knowledge and practices the execution of the task under anticipated on-the-job conditions which may include stressors. For example, the training environment for a college football team is the practice field or the film room where the players learn about game situations and practice techniques to fulfill their individual and collective roles. Practice sessions consist of both individual drills to improve task competency (e.g., blocking tackling, kicking and passing) and partial and whole-team repetition of plays to improve team coordination and timing. Practice may be suspended by the coach to provide feedback and support during teachable moments.

The work environment for a college football team is the actual game, where nearly all the adaptation to change happens in real time and there is little opportunity to correct performance through performance feedback and repetition. Mistakes and poor performance (e.g., missed blocks or dropped passes) in the work environment are effectively permanent and may be more difficult to overcome than in the training environment where the situation can be reset. The permanence of work environment outcomes, in and of itself, contributes to a higher level of stress in the work environment than in the training environment.

Having identified differences between training and work environments, we are left to answer the question: Should every stressor represented in the work environment also be represented in the training environment? The goals of each environment are different. The work environment is about the participant performing necessary tasks as quickly and accurately as possible under a variety of conditions to meet the objectives of the job. The training environment is about the learner optimizing his acquisition of knowledge and skill under a variety of conditions to meet the learning objectives and prepare him to perform in the work environment. Kavanagh (2005) suggests that military training establishment "should focus on developing training that realistically represents the environment in which the soldier will be expected to perform." We argue that stressors represented in the work environment should be represented in the training environment only to the degree that they are necessary determinants of learning and the transfer of skills to the work environment. In other words, we don't need to represent every stressor in the training environment, only those stressors which have an effect on learning objectives which have been designed to meet performance objectives in the work environment. The "less than perfect" training strategy may be important from economic, safety, and efficiency perspectives.

- *Economics*: It may be too expensive to represent some stressors in the training environment, and the return on investment in terms of learning may not be realized.
- *Safety*: Representing some stressors may pose too great a risk to the trainee(s), with little return on investment with respect to learning.
- *Efficiency*: Implementing extraneous stressors may distract the learner from developing coping skills arising from germane stressors per the Cognitive Load Theory (Sweller, Van Merrienboer, & Paas, 1998; Sottilare & Goldberg, 2012).

Elements of Extremely Stressful Environments

If stress is the response of the body to any demand made on it, then extreme stress is the result of exposure to stressors beyond what is encountered in everyday life. Extreme stressors are different from everyday stressors in their intensity, frequency, and duration (Baum, Cohen & Hall, 1993). Extremely stressful environments often include situations where failure has a high cost (e.g., loss of life or severe injury). Examples of "in extremis" environments and situations follow.

Military personnel conduct vigilance tasks (e.g., guard duty or sensor-monitoring) during peace-time operations; however, such tasks have an added burden of stress when they are conducted without sleep over long periods of time (e.g., days) during combat operations. In these examples, the performer may or may not be in danger, but their degraded performance may endanger others. Vigilance tasks are stressful, and how quickly performance deteriorates demonstrates how hard it is to sustain attention over prolonged periods (Mackworth, 1948). The effect of sleep deprivation is well documented in the literature with respect to its negative impact on mood, cognitive performance, motor function, executive attention, and working memory (Durmer & Dinges, 2005). Diminished cognitive functioning that results from lack of sleep is evident in the significant decrement in performance of vigilance tasks. In an extremely stressful environment the consequences of failures in vigilance can include potential loss of life.

Another type of extremely stressful environment is one in which threats are of short duration but occur frequently. A participants' goal in such a situation is to accomplish the assigned mission while simultaneously surviving the threat. Firemen in a burning building where they experience searing temperatures, choking smoke, and danger from falling debris is one example. In our James Bond example, very few people would need the skills to cope with the variety and intensity of environments encountered by Bond. Therefore, the variety and intensity of his training must also be extreme to allow proper transfer of skills to the operational environment. Bond escaping from impossible situations illustrates the short and high-intensity threat.

A squad of soldiers conducting a reconnaissance mission in an urban environment where they encounter numerous insurgent groups is another example. Decisions on whether to care for wounded squad members versus defend their position might add to extreme stress in this environment.

Another example of an extremely stressful situation which could apply to both military and civilians is the mission of triage. In civilian life, an emergency room physician assesses and prioritizes the treatment of patients. The civilian physician's mission is roughly equivalent to the task of a military physician prioritizing the treatment of wounded soldiers. For these physicians, the goal is for each patient who needs care to receive that care in a timely manner. Physicians and medical resources are limited and decisions during triage regarding patients on either end of the injury spectrum (e.g., minor wounds or untreatable wounds) may be to withhold treatment in order to treat those in most need who can benefit from treatment. Decisions made during triage that result in the death of patients are examples of the stressful tradeoff doctors must make and could conflict with the physician's oath (World Medical Association): "I will maintain the utmost respect for human life" and be a source of inner conflict and stress.

Our Mars mission scenario illustrates a different kind of stress—persistent, but extreme. The crew going to Mars will be isolated for about 6 months in transit from Earth. Stress may be induced by separation from family or by interaction with a restricted group of people. There are few if any analogs for this situation, but some suggest this is "likely to have a significant impact on the outcome of long-duration missions in space" (Palinkas, 2007, p. 25). How will we train to mitigate this risk? What strategies or interventions might be needed when individual and personal interaction issues arise?

Leading people in extreme situations, where followers perceive their lives are in danger, has its own challenges, as described by Kolditz (2007) and Campbell (2012). For example, Ernest Shackleton led a doomed expedition to the Antarctic in 1914 that would ultimately fail but be lauded for their ability to survive against the odds in an extreme environment of freezing temperatures, gale force winds, and little or no food. After their ship, *Endurance*, was trapped in the pack ice and crushed, Shackleton and his crew were forced to live in the open, crossing the ice, and later in lifeboats reaching Elephant Island where they survived for 6 months. Finally, Shackleton and five men navigated 820 miles in an open boat from Elephant Island to South Georgia Island. Upon landing in South Georgia Island, they hiked across the interior of the island to a whaling station where he was able to organize a rescue mission for his crew left on Elephant Island. In the face of their hardships, Shackleton kept them focused on goals that would ultimately result in their survival.

So what attributes or advantages gave Shackleton the edge he needed to lead in this extreme environment and survive? First, this was not Shackleton's first expedition to the Antarctic, so he knew what to expect. Second, he had experience in various leadership roles prior to the *Endurance* voyage and, by all accounts, was an effective leader. According to Campbell (2012), "the essential consideration is whether threat expectation is chronic and continuous; or whether it is sporadic and episodic." The leadership capabilities required by each differ, but supportive leadership in both contexts is absolutely essential when threat is chronic and continuous, as it would have been during the months of hardship endured by Shackleton and his crew. Campbell, Campbell, & Ness (2008) highlight the significant role effective leadership has in creating resilience in the face of chronic and continuous threats. Based on this, it seems that experience, which could include training, plays a major role in performance in extreme environments.

Adaptive instructional techniques, including the introduction of appropriate stressors at appropriate levels during training, can positively affect the performance of the learner later in their work environment. This may be accomplished through gradual exposure to varying types of stressors and levels of stress throughout practice. Practicing under stressors similar to those in the work environment enables learners to develop solutions which aid them later in managing real world stressors. This was almost certainly the case with Shackleton who had extensive experience from previous expeditions and cold weather operations at sea and on land.

Vygotsky's *zone of proximal development* (ZPD; 1978), along with tutoring design principles developed by Anderson, Boyle, Farrell, and Reiser (1987) and later elaborated by Corbett, Koedinger, and Anderson (1997) and Sottilare and Goldberg (2012), envisioned that cognitive load (e.g., working memory) could be optimized by matching learners' domain competence with the difficulty/grain size of the problems presented to them. In other words, if instruction starts with easier, straightforward problems and scenarios for less skilled or less experienced learners, it can gradually escalate to more difficult and elaborate problems and scenarios as learners acquire the skills to cope with increased task difficulty along with the associated stressors. An important principle of adaptive training is to provide each learner with a clear picture of the results and consequences of his or her decisions and actions during and after training. Consistent feedback allows learners to adjust their mental models and alter their performance strategies between training events, which may result in higher probability of success.

DISCUSSION

The goal of this chapter is to evaluate how adaptive instructional techniques might be tailored to personalize training in real time to optimize human performance and build critical skills needed to succeed in extreme settings. The belief is that adaptive techniques can teach individuals and teams to learn skills while coping with stressors, even extreme stressors. This approach allows learners to focus on the critical behaviors that can result in lower error rates and more optimal decisions. Unlike adaptable technologies, which can be changed by the user to support their needs, adaptive technologies possess intelligence, which allows them to recognize learning opportunities and change their actions in response to the changing needs of the user and conditions in the environment (Oppermann, 1994). Adaptive instruction is provided by ITSs, computer-based instructors which guide learning experiences and tailor the presentation of content, feedback, guidance, and direction. They adapt instruction and guide the learner toward meeting established learning objectives based on their capabilities, needs, and limitations. Per Vygotsky (1978), ITSs may also drive changes in the training environment and optimize learning by more closely matching the domain competence (prior knowledge) of the learner with the challenge level of the training environment (e.g., problem difficulty or scenario complexity). As noted earlier, the training environment represents the work environment by including the essential elements of the work environment which may impact progress in reaching learning objectives to include representative stressors.

Representing Stressors from Work Environments During Training

Aspects of tasks that must be learned and performed successfully during training can be a source of stress to the learner. Task complexity, the training participant's prior knowledge of the task (domain competency), and the conditions and standards under which the task must be performed, may all contribute to stress. Conditions dictate when trainees perform tasks, and they also define the constraints under which they must be performed. Established standards define how well tasks must be performed to meet job demands. Stressors in the work environment can limit performance or cause workers to have to cope or adapt their behavior during task execution in order to meet performance standards. Stressors frequently limit the speed and accuracy of performance.

Consideration must be given to how stressors are introduced and implemented in training environments. Are they a critical part of the conditions under which the task is performed, and how are they reflected in the task's learning objectives? Stressors should contribute to learning or transfer of learning and be a relevant part of the training experience. When stressors are included in the training process, the trainer must decide when and to what degree and frequency they should be introduced. Often it is best for learners to conquer the rudiments of a task before performance is complicated by stressors (Friedland & Keinan, 1992). The ability to measure and control stressor levels in the training environment is a critical adaptation managed by ITSs in order to match learner competency level with scenario complexity. Judiciously exposing participants to increasing levels of stress during training until you reach levels similar to those in the workplace should result in better performance in the actual work environment.

The next step in making the case for adaptive instruction as a tool for developing competency in extremely stressful environments is understanding the capabilities and limitations of accurately representing physical (i.e., environmental and physiological) and mental (i.e., cognitive and value-based) stressors within training environments. This is also an important step toward the effective use of ITSs in preparing learners for work in stressful environments. Next we discuss the ability to represent various stressors during training. We chose to discuss these stressors in four separate chunks: environmental, physiological, cognitive, and value-based stressors.

Representing Environmental Stressors During Training

Environmental or external stressors include extremes in temperature (hot and cold), precipitation, noise, light, wind, dust and wind-blown particles, and vibration. Environmental stressors are rarely represented in virtual simulations. Some models of munition trajectory in virtual marksmanship simulations include the effect of wind, but not necessarily as a stressor. Not all stressors are critical to the learning objectives. For example, if the mission is primarily cognitive (e.g., planning, decision-making, or problem-solving), extreme temperatures in the training environment may not play a significant role in the training objectives unless the learner will be regularly performing these cognitive tasks under those extreme temperature conditions. However, if the task is more physical (e.g., reconnaissance in desert regions), exposure to temperature could be important in adapting one's work performance and acclimatizing one's body to stressors. However, it might not always be the goal of training to acclimate the trainee to environmental stressors. The goal may be to identify strategies to mitigate the effect of environmental stressors (e.g., regular rest and water intake during task execution in desert environments).

When implementing environmental stressors in the training environment, primary consideration should be given to the health of the trainees. For example, a combat scenario for a squad conducting a reconnaissance mission in a village in an arid climate might include elevated temperatures in the training simulation. However, elevated temperatures should be integrated with the training environment gradually over a series of training events in order to understand the limitations of trainees, acclimate them progressively to extremes, and establish standards for performance in the work environment.

Other environmental elements may also be required in training environments to duplicate the work environment and provide realism sufficient to support training objectives. For our reconnaissance mission, visual fidelity of the terrain is important to the learning objectives and should be sufficiently represented in the training simulation to allow soldiers to move, shoot, and communicate as they would on the actual terrain. Sound may or may not be a stressor, but its physical attributes (e.g., sources and reflection in the village) may also be important in either masking or supporting the location of weapons firing and create a stressor based on a feeling of vulnerability.

Representing Physiological Stressors During Training

Possible physiological or internal stressors include sleep deprivation, dehydration, fasting, and muscular and aerobic fatigue. It is understood that physiological stressors may be initiated and sustained by environmental stressors but that they may also lack a specific source and may be due to the overall effect of the task execution, the environment, and the experience of the learner. Depending on the duration of the physiological stressor, there may or may not be significant effect on higher cognitive functions. Sleep deprivation has a negative impact on mood, cognitive performance, and motor function (Durmer & Dinges, 2005). Even mild dehydration has a negative effect on cognitive performance (Wilson & Morley, 2003). Short-term fasting was shown to have a negative effect on problem-solving in children (Pollitt, Lewis, Garza, & Shulman, 1983). High-intensity aerobic exercise had gender-specific effects on cognition. It improved women's executive function performance and trail-making (a measure of cognitive flexibility tied to attention), visual search and scanning, sequencing and shifting, psychomotor speed, abstraction, flexibility, ability to execute and modify a plan of action, and ability to maintain two trains of thought simultaneously (Baker et al., 2010).

Due to the relatively short durations of most training exercises (30 minutes to 3 days), physiological stressors are the least represented stressors in training. The most frequently occurring physiological stressor is muscular and aerobic fatigue during live training events (real people on real terrain conducting real tasks), which, as noted, may have a positive effect on cognitive functions. However, physical task performance is also affected by fatigue, and muscular and aerobic endurance can be developed gradually over time.

REPRESENTING COGNITIVE STRESSORS DURING TRAINING

Examples of cognitive stressors include time limitations/pressures, uncertainty, ambiguity, information overload, information deprivation, isolation, task complexity, and cognitive workload. Cognitive stressors are the most prevalent work related stressors represented in the training environment. These stressors tend to be driven by the scenario and represented widely in both individual and team training systems.

A training scenario with cognitive stressors can be developed within the serious game platform, Virtual BattleSpace (VBS). VBS is a first-person interface which supports interaction between team members within a virtual environment. VBS plays on a desktop computer. An example of a possible scenario would begin with the trainee, a member of a US Army squad, receiving instructions from his sergeant to remain close to the unit as it patrols a small village. When the unit falls under attack, the trainee is faced with the decision to either treat casualties his squad has taken or to return fire and defend his position. If the trainee decides to treat casualties, his unit may be overrun by enemy forces. If he decides to defend his position, some or all of the members of his unit could die. The scenario contains several stressors including task complexity, time pressures created by the casualty situation, and a bit of information overload as the sergeant continues to bark out orders while the casualties scream for help and the enemy rains fire down on his position.

REPRESENTING VALUE-BASED STRESSORS DURING TRAINING

Value-based stressors are events that cause emotional reactions due to their conflict with the learner's value system. Emotional reactions could range from fear, anger, and anxiety to resentment, grief, loss of faith, and boredom. While long-term decisions to maintain a career with a specific organization may be driven by compatibility of values, highly stressful settings may present significant situational conflict between individual values and assigned goals or missions resulting in emotional distress, inaction, or both.

Value-based stressors are moderately represented in training, but their inclusion is growing as military forces increasingly take on roles that go beyond combat (e.g., sustainment and stability operations). In stability operations soldiers are interacting with people whose culture and values likely conflict with their own. Here again, the experience and competency the learner acquired through training plays a significant role in fostering success in real-world ambiguous situations. Soldiers who have not grown their competence to acceptable levels will likely make poor decisions, or, as a result of feelings of helplessness, fear, or overwhelming emotions, may do nothing at all. Training under these conditions could impede learning if emotions are not managed by the trainee. Managing emotional reactions is related to Goleman's (1995) concept of emotional intelligence (EI), which is the ability to perceive, understand, and manage one's emotions (and the emotions of others) to support one's goals (Salovey & Mayer, 1990). Representing value-based stressors in training is important to clearly align individual and organizational values and set organizational boundaries, especially when individual learners are expected to encounter highly stressful work environments.

Growing Desirable Skills in Stressful Domains Through Adaptive Instruction

This section (1) explores what the impact of including physical and mental stressors during training has on the development of desirable skills and characteristics (e.g., domain knowledge, task competency, resilience, perseverance, flexibility, collaboration, and critical thinking); and (2) demonstrates how an adaptive tutor might tailor physical and mental stressors to develop and maintain them.

STRESSORS AND PHYSIOLOGICAL RESPONSES

Next we discuss the relationship between exposure to extreme stressors and how they can be used in training to foster development of desirable skills and characteristics. Extreme stressors usually trigger a physiological response in those exposed to them. Exposure to stressors causes the body and the brain to respond by releasing hormones and neurotransmitters (Levy, 2014). This includes the primary stress hormone, cortisol, which directly affects the functioning of the heart, lungs, circulation system, metabolism, immune system, and skin. Extreme stressors can also be the cause that results in the release of neurotransmitters like dopamine, norepinephrine, and epinephrine (adrenaline). These chemicals activate the amygdala, which triggers a fear response. As a result of this flood of hormones and neurotransmitters, the brain releases neuropeptides, which increase alertness along with feelings of anxiety.

Brandon and Silke (2007) discuss the body's reactions to exposure to stressors (e.g., threatening or harmful events). Reaction to a single stressful event usually results in intense emotions which gradually *dissipate* over time. A second exposure to the same stressor could cause an even stronger response and higher intensity emotions. During heightened states of fear, anxiety, or vigilance, the subject may react with a more intense response than normal, referred to as *sensitization*. However, persistent exposure to a single stress-producing event might result in an individual *adapting to it*, which would delay the dissipation of intense emotions. Repeated exposure to a stressful event over time could result in *habituation*, where the subject experiences a progressively lower response to the event resulting from each exposure.

The following section provides insight into the relationship between stressors and fostering desirable learning outcomes such as knowledge acquisition, recall, and skill development, including problem-solving and collaborative and critical thinking skills. Furthermore, resilience and flexibility are traits that can lead to outcomes and characteristics which aid learners in coping with stressors.

DEVELOPING DESIRABLE SKILLS AND CHARACTERISTICS IN STRESSFUL ADAPTIVE TRAINING ENVIRONMENTS

The literature shows a clear negative relationship between long-term, persistent stressors and performance, and in fact defines a clear relationship between work-related stressors and mental disorders such as depression (Netterstrøm & Conrad, 2007). Nevertheless, there are effective ways of learning to cope with persistent stressors. For example, "stress inoculation" is a gradual exposure to increasing physical and mental stressors over a limited period of time during short training events. This technique provides the learner with an opportunity to develop coping mechanisms and viable solutions after repeated exposures (Saunders, Driskell, Johnston, & Salas, 1996). The following provides an argument for the relationship between exposure to stressors during training and the development of positive traits (e.g., resilience and flexibility), which, in the long run, may aid the learner by enhancing his or her performance in extremely stressful work environments.

As noted earlier, adaptive training techniques that use artificial intelligent, software-based agents have been used to monitor and act on both the learner and the learner's training environment. A goal of this interaction is to manage the flow and challenge level of the instruction so that it is neither too easy nor too difficult and is within the current capabilities of the learner. Adaptive training systems seek to maintain the learner in a ZPD (Vygotsky, 1978), where the difficulty level of instruction is appropriate to the learner's current skill level and state of knowledge (Csikszentmihalyi, 1990; Murray & Arroyo, 2003).

Goetzman (2012) notes four steps to produce deep learning that lasts. First, the instructor should anchor the content within the learner's experience. Anchoring knowledge and skills to learner's capabilities can serve as launch points to new learning. Second, the instructor adds new information. Next, the instructor provides opportunities for the learner to apply the new learning content in new ways or in differing situations. Finally, the instructor asks the learner to articulate how he will apply what he has learned in future scenarios.

The further the instructor progresses the learner from an anchor, the more stressful the experience may become, as the learner ventures into unknown learning territory. Adding new content too quickly could also cause stress. Bjork (1994) refers to stressors in training environments as *desirable difficulties*. He notes that instructional strategies that vary the conditions of learning and the associated stress can enhance learner comprehension and retention. Providing sufficient but not excessive levels of stress produces optimal learning. Too many stressors might result in learner states of confusion, frustration, or anger that could also limit engagement, flexibility, and cooperation, and increase anxiety and lower self-esteem. If there are insufficient stressors represented in the training environment, the learner may become bored and withdrawn, with the result being little or no learning. So, how much stress is the appropriate amount to foster learning? This largely depends upon the individual learner and his or her experience managing stress. However, in stressful working environments (where the cost of failure is high in terms of loss of life, injury, monetary, morale, or other consequences) learning under realistic levels of stress is important and can sometimes present significant challenges for learners.

The acquisition of knowledge or skills may be moderated (blocked or enhanced) by environmental effects like stressors, but Bjork (1994) finds that recall/retention may also be enhanced by the temporal proximity of learning events to stressors or desirable difficulties. The presence of extreme stressors can result in anxiety and declines in performance (Yerkes & Dodson, 1908), and the absence of stressors may result in anxiety or boredom. Both high and low stress levels can have negative effects on the learning process. As noted earlier, there are advantages to the presence of stressors in training. They contribute to the development of desirable skills and characteristics. A prime example of the benefits of stress is the development of coping behaviors that result in *resilience*.

Developing Resilience in Stressful Adaptive Training Environments

Resilience is defined as the capacity to recover quickly from difficulties (Merriam-Webster online dictionary) and maintain a positive outlook in pursuit of one's goals (e.g., health or success). Ong, Bergeman, Bisconti, and Wallace (2006) investigated the functional role of psychological resilience and the impact of positive emotions during stressful experiences. Their findings indicated that, over time, the experience of positive emotions contributes to the ability of highly resilient individuals to recover effectively from daily stressors.

While important to survival, extreme stress can inhibit learning. In clinical settings, patients' care is based on the decisions of physicians and nurses. For many clinicians, their work environment is also an on-the-job training environment that can cause high stress and anxiety. High levels of anxiety can affect learner's ability to acquire and recall knowledge, develop skills, and perform to expected levels (Moscaritolo, 2009). While some clinicians may not react well in extremely stressful environments, others thrive due in part to their ability to rapidly develop coping mechanisms and build resilience. Arnetz, Nevedal, Lumley, Backman, and Lublin (2009) studied the effect of resilience training methods on stress management and performance for police officers exposed to critical incident trauma (CIT) such as accidents, fires, riots, and violent crime scenes. The resilience training was delivered via a critical incident police work simulation. The results indicated statistically reliable reductions in negative mood, heart rate reactivity, cortisol, and self-reported stress, along with improved performance. As effective as this training approach was, it provided the same content and interaction for each learner regardless of his or her experience or associated knowledge within the domain. Understanding and acting on critical individual differences could have allowed tailoring of these CIT simulations to aid the learners in setting knowledge and skills that they could carry forward to other training and work experiences.

In other research on resilience training, Steensma, Den Heijer, and Stallen (2007) took a more direct approach to studying the effects of a resilience training program on former employees who suffered from prolonged illness due to workplace-induced stress. Nine coping methods, including meditation and rational insights, were used to strengthen trainee resilience and develop appropriate coping behaviors. Trainees demonstrated improved coping behaviors and reduced avoidance and passive reaction behaviors.

Both "stress in the workplace" examples demonstrate people's ability to develop coping skills and thereby build resilience to stress. These studies suggest that increased resilience can result from adapting the challenge level of the training environment (ala Vygotsky's ZPD) or through behavioral modification techniques (e.g., visualization, relaxation exercises) administered prior to exposure to highly stressful experiences.

Developing Cognitive Flexibility in Stressful Adaptive Training Environments

> *Cognitive flexibility* is the ability to transition thoughts between multiple
> concepts or perspectives. It also reflects one's ability to process multiple
> concepts simultaneously such as the color and shape of an object or
> perspectives of republicans and democrats. An individual who is able to
> switch quickly from thinking about one concept, characteristic, or perspective
> to another—would be said to possess a high degree of cognitive flexibility.
> —MENTAL HEALTH DAILY

Cognitive flexibility is important to learning and performance because it is associated with a superior ability to think abstractly, leading to improved analytical skills, comprehension, and coping strategies. Individuals with increased cognitive flexibility are able to link more sensory information during memory creation resulting in increased working memory and neural efficiency (*Mental Health Daily*, 2015).

Han et al. (2011) noted that better cognitive performances were correlated with lower perceived levels of stress and anxiety. In other words, high performers were able to manage their stress. These results suggest that cognitive flexibility could enhance human performance by modulating the development of anxiety and stress during stressful events. The development of cognitive flexibility skills may also aid learning in complex and ill-defined domains (Spiro, Coulson, Feltovich, & Anderson, 1988).

Cognitive Flexibility Theory (CFT) examines the manner in which knowledge representations are constructed by the learner so they can be easily restructured later to adapt to changing scenarios (Spiro et al., 1988). Developing the ability to construct and modify mental models may result from exposure to situations where there is a need to practice these skills. CFT suggests that learners may have greater opportunity to develop cognitive flexibility skills in adaptive training environments where there are multiple representations of instructional content, context-dependent knowledge, complex content, case-based instruction, and interrelated knowledge representations (Jonassen, Ambruso, & Olesen, 1992; Sottilare &

Goldberg, 2012). This seems to indicate that using adaptive training methods provides a means to expose learners to changing environments in order to develop and maintain cognitive flexibility skills.

Developing Problem-Solving Skills in Stressful Adaptive Training Environments

The ability to solve problems in stressful environments is similar to the development of resilience only with the added complexity of maintaining focus on the problem (i.e., attentional control). There are significant individual differences in ability to perform under stress. Beilock and DeCaro (2007) investigated how individual differences in "working memory" affected performance outcomes in solving math problems under low- and high-stress conditions. Individuals with more working memory tended to choose more complicated ways of solving the problems than the individuals with more limited working memory capacity, and their performance under low stress was superior.

While working memory capacity tends to be predictive of success in solving problems (Conway et al., 2005), this advantage for higher capacity individuals does not survive high-stress conditions (Beilock, Rydell, & McConnell, 2007). Under high stress, the higher working memory individuals tended to retreat to a more simplistic problem-solving approach and their performance suffered. While under high stress, low working memory individuals maintained the same performance they showed under low-stress conditions.

In a higher stress situation, the performer who normally selects a more memory intensive rule-based strategy may find that stress has limited his ability to recall those rules, while a learner with lower capacity of working memory may be able to perform more or less the same under varying levels of stress since he tends to use more simplistic problem-solving approaches that are not as susceptible to effects on his working memory. The ability to gauge one's reaction to stress may be trainable. The success of metacognitive instructional strategies (e.g., reflecting, summarizing, questioning, clarifying, and predicting) suggests this may be true. Brown, Palincsar, and Armbruster (1984) found learners who were taught basic metacognitive strategies and then reminded to use them improved their ability to monitor their own thinking. Once metacognitive strategies become automatic, learners were able to focus more of their working memory to the complex tasks of planning, generating, and reviewing. Similarly, metacognitive coaching strategies could be used to aid the learner in developing behaviors which enhance their ability to monitor and react to changes in their own cognitive processes.

Developing Collaborative Skills in Stressful Adaptive Training Environments

Salas and Cannon-Bowers (2001) report on research evaluating the use of stress-exposure training (SET) as a tool to prepare trainees to work in high stress environments. The SET approach is based on clinical research with a three phased stress inoculation procedure. The first phase provides trainees with "preparatory information that includes a description of which stressors are likely to be encountered in the environment and what the likely impact of those stressors will be on the trainee" (Salas & Cannon-Bowers, 2001, p. 483). The next phase focuses on the development of coping skills (behavioral and cognitive) to aid the learner in managing stress. Finally, in the third phase, the trainee is provided opportunities to apply and practice their learned coping skills under conditions of gradually increasing stress. SET has been shown to reduce the trainee's perceived level of stress while simultaneously improving performance.

The modeling of stress exposure within teams is more complex and less well understood since perceived stress is different for each individual within a team, and this perception is based largely on each individual's experience and coping skills. The application of stress exposure training is a common part of team training for critical missions where lives may be at risk. Teams training for military and space missions where high degrees of precision and skill are needed to be successful at highly interdependent tasks are likely to receive stress exposure training. It is routine for unexpected faults or changes in training scenarios to occur in order to create crises within the team. As with individual trainees, the training challenge level may (and should) be varied (ala Vygotsky) in order to maintain the engagement of the team and to inoculate them with the essence (if not the precise sources) of the stress they are likely to face in the work environment.

USING ADAPTIVE TECHNIQUES TO VARY STRESSORS AND DEVELOP DESIRABLE SKILLS AND CHARACTERISTICS

As noted in the preceding discussions, the need to maintain acceptable levels of performance under stressful environments may be the impetus for developing coping and problem-solving skills and enhancing characteristics such resilience, cognitive flexibility, and collaboration. Adaptation to varying stress levels may in fact be a pathway to providing the environment necessary to inoculate individual trainees to previously unknown stressors and create the conditions for development of coping skills that trainees may transfer to stressful work environments. Understanding the learner's characteristics that moderate development of coping skills is central to being able to intelligently adapt instruction to foster the growth of those skills.

Rus et al. (2013, p. 183) state that a learner model "is a central component to any tutoring system that also claims to be intelligent." A learner model is a set of learner states and traits that impact or describe the state of the trainee's or learner's learning and performance. It is important to understand what to include and not include in the learner model so it is efficient, supports general learning conditions, and, when stress is a performance condition, provides sufficient measures of stress for individual learners and teams. Measures must be sensitive to varying levels of stress and their effect on each trainee and team. As noted previously, previous exposure of individuals or teams to relevant stressors (or similar stressors) in the recent past, their success in coping with those stressors (e.g., the presence of coping skills), individual traits like flexibility, resilience (also known as grit), and their ability to think critically affect each learner's perception of stress. For teams, leadership qualities (e.g., ability to set goals, organize, and make progress toward goals) may be key to team satisfaction and viability in the presence of extreme stress.

APPLICATION OF ADAPTIVE TRAINING TO HUMAN PERFORMANCE OPTIMIZATION

As noted earlier, the ITS observes, develops strategies, and acts upon the learner and the training environment (e.g., virtual simulator or desktop serious game) with the goal of optimizing learning, performance, retention, and transfer of skills to the work environment. It is generally accepted that ITSs have four major components (Elson-Cook, 1993; Nkambou, Mizoguchi, & Bourdeau, 2010; Graesser, Conley, & Olney, 2012; Psotka & Mutter, 2008; Sleeman & Brown, 1982; VanLehn, 2006; Woolf, 2009): the learner model, the domain model, the instructional or pedagogical model, and a tutor–user interface. The learner model includes learning, performance, physical, cognitive, affective, motivational, and other psychological states that evolve during the course of learning. The domain model contains descriptions of the skills, knowledge, and strategies of the topic being tutored. It normally contains the ideal learner (also known as expert model) to which the learner's actions and performance are compared. The instructional model examines the output of the domain and learner models, selects tutoring strategies (plans for future actions), and then decides what to do next. Finally, the tutor–user interface interprets the learner's input through various input media (e.g., speech, typing, clicking) and produces output in different media (e.g., text, speech, diagrams, animations, agents) in response.

Careful selection of strategies and tactics by the tutor are aimed at optimizing the efficiency and effectiveness of adaptive training sessions by providing the learner with experiences tailored to match their current capabilities. Today, ITSs are adept at providing meaningful instruction in domains like mathematics, physics, chemistry, and other sciences where the process of learning is highly structured, and learning occurs in logical steps. As effective as adaptive training techniques are in these well-defined domains, there are some challenges to be overcome if they are to be just as successful in providing training for less structured domains such as those found in the military, commercial aviation, law enforcement, and medical fields.

Per the US Army's Combined Arms Center (October 2014), goals for human performance optimization (HPO) include *establishing cognitive dominance, executing realistic training*, and *driving institutional agility*. Each of these HPO thrusts are to be implemented at the individual, team, and institutional levels. *Cognitive dominance* (Matthews, 2014) is an "intellectual advantage over a situation or adversary that fosters proactive agility over reactive adaptation, facilitating the ability to anticipate change before it occurs." Training will be a key element in realizing cognitive dominance, and adaptive training will allow individual soldiers and teams to flex their mental muscles by building a variety of training experiences. The key challenge to realizing cognitive dominance is the ability to bring the cost of content generation down through the automation of authoring processes in adaptive training. To be adaptive, ITSs must have options to display alternate content/media. A concept that seeks to solve this issue is *evolutionary scenario generation* (ESG), where a single parent scenario can be used to automatically generate thousands of viable child scenarios thereby reducing the authoring load. Machine learning algorithms are being developed at the US Army Research Laboratory to support ESG, but it may be years before this concept can be generalized broadly across Army training domains. The good news is that ITS authoring tools are becoming easier to use (Ososky, Sottilare, Brawner, Long, & Graesser, 2015).

Realistic training encompasses soldiers operating as part of a team, as they do in their work environments, and the most effective way to develop cohesive teams is through trust. To be realistic, soldiers must experience "tough, ethically challenging, and rigorous training that not only fully replicates the physical stresses of combat, but the social and cultural aspects as well" (US Army Combined Arms Center, 2014, p. 15). This may be the most promising area for the use of adaptive training techniques. Most of this chapter has been dedicated to the proposition that individuals and teams can be successfully trained to adapt to stressors through exposure over time. The major challenges in realistic training are (1) deciding how much realism is necessary to efficiently train the task, (2) determining what methods are needed to accurately classify the learner's or team's states (e.g., performance, engagement) in real-time during training, and (3) determining what methods are needed to accurately select optimal instructional strategies (plans for action) and tactics (actions) based on the states of the learner and the conditions in the training environment.

Finally, *institutional agility* stresses the goal *to be superior in the art of learning and adaptation*. Institutional agility may also be advanced by adaptive training where the focus of the training scenarios is on the development of characteristics like critical thinking, cognitive flexibility, and cooperation instead of learning to perform a specific task. Exercising judgment/decision-making in simulated planning and execution of realistic scenarios with the critical stressors at hand will enable soldiers and civilians alike to develop institutional agility.

APPLICATION DOMAINS FOR ADAPTIVE INSTRUCTION

While today's ITSs have been applied primarily in science, technology, engineering, and mathematics domains, their capabilities continue to grow and diversify. There may be no limit to the task domains and scenarios which could be delivered by ITSs in the near future. For example, groundbreaking research in adaptive training led to the creation of the Generalized Intelligent Framework for Tutoring (GIFT; Sottilare, Brawner, Goldberg, & Holden, 2012), which is now being used to drive prototype adaptive scenarios in existing simulations (e.g., Virtual Battle Space). The ability to manage and adapt instruction in real time without a human in the loop in existing simulations is a giant leap forward in expanding the potential application domains for adaptive instruction. A standardized GIFT application interface is making integration with existing training systems and tools easier. Ongoing research is examining and overcoming barriers to the use of adaptive instruction in cognitive (e.g., problem-solving and decision-making), affective (e.g., moral dilemmas and judgment), psychomotor (e.g., sports, marksmanship, or assembly tasks in factories), and social domains (e.g., collaborative problem-solving or team-based tasks). If it is safe and practical to use a training methodology, then adaptive instruction will be able to manage and adapt the training experience.

CONCLUSION

Performance in extreme environments poses the most significant threat to operators. Their ability to manage their stress and perform their missions will provide the most significant return on investment (e.g., survival). This chapter provides guidelines to designing adaptive instruction as a means for training personnel to operate in these extreme environments. We began by introducing Ian Fleming's James Bond as the shining example of an operator who can succeed in the face of extreme danger during short, but intense scenarios, but we also examined scenarios where operators were exposed to stressors which were less intense but more persistent over a long period of time (e.g., a mission to Mars). As a goal for adaptive instruction, we identified five areas of focus to develop the learner's ability to cope with stressful environments: stress exposure or inoculation, exercising psychological resilience, promoting cognitive flexibility, enhancing problem-solving skills, and enhancing collaborative skills. Stress inoculation is a method of gradually exposing learners to increasing levels of stress over time so they can adapt and develop coping strategies. Psychological resilience might be exercised by gradually increasing the pace of change. Related to psychological resilience is the learner's ability to transition between multiple concepts or perspectives. Exercising the learner to change between moderate numbers of topics and gradually increasing to higher numbers of topics could result in the ability to better modulate anxiety during stressful events. Solving problems under stress might enhance the learner's ability to recognize their reaction to varying stress levels (e.g., emotional intelligence) and to develop coping mechanisms to deal with higher stress levels or cognitive dissonance (Graesser et al., 2006). Finally, exercising collaborative skills is important to recognizing stress reactions in others and learning to help manage them (Goleman, 1995).

Based on our findings, we provide four recommendations for the application of adaptive instruction to HPO in extreme environments. First, we advocate that stressors (their intensity and their duration) can and should be used by instructional designers to shape training, accelerate learning, and enhance transfer of skills from training to work or operational environments. While stressors are often viewed as moderators of negative behaviors and inhibitors of learning, an analysis of the literature also demonstrates the utility of stressors as motivators of behavioral change and learning. This chapter highlighted sources of stress (stressors) which may be easily and realistically represented in training simulations and scenarios in order to support opportunities for the development of trainee coping skills. There are significant opportunities to expand the role of adaptive instructional techniques in both military and civilian training using stressors as tools to influence learning outcomes. In extreme operational environments, adaptive training methods may be the difference between success and failure.

Second, we note that adaptive instruction in any environment is most effective when the tutor has a thorough understanding of the learners and their needs (Sottilare, Graesser, Hu, & Holden, 2013). Human tutors intervene with learners based largely on their observations of the learners and their understanding of each individual's learning habits and trends over time. The effectiveness of the computer-based tutor is also based on its knowledge of the learner, its ability to recognize learning opportunities, its ability to select optimal instructional strategies (e.g., prompt the learner for more information), and, finally, its ability to select optimal instructional tactics (e.g., manipulate the difficulty level in the training environment to keep the learner engaged or vary the pace and content of feedback to the learner). Based on this knowledge, we recommend "big data" approaches to understand learning trends for individuals and populations across training experiences. Continuous evaluation of the effectiveness of adaptive instructional techniques will evolve course content and interactions with the learner over time and thereby accelerate learning, reduce classroom instruction and associated infrastructure, and enhance transfer of skills to operations.

Our third recommendation is to expand adaptive instruction in extreme environments to team contexts. Stressors can play a major role in adapting the difficulty level of the training environment. The same principles noted earlier for individual training may also be applied to collective (team) training environments. While the modeling and optimization features needed to train teams are much more complex than for individuals, the potential payoff is also significantly higher. We also want to understand team strategies for coping with long-term stressors in team situations. This would be critical to assessing team states and remediating harmful states before they negatively impact the mission or result in loss of life.

Finally, our fourth recommendation is to expand the capabilities of ITSs to more task domains. Research is needed to understand how adaptive instruction might be used to develop attentional focus, rapid assessment, and faster decision-making in rapidly changing environments as well as those environments with persistent stressors. This would result in a set of best instructional practices which could be implemented broadly across training systems and ITSs and include strategies for optimizing human performance in extreme environments.

REFERENCES

Anderson, J. R., Boyle, C. F., Farrell, R., & Reiser, B. J. (1984). *Cognitive Principles in the Design of Computer Tutors* (No. TR-84-1-ONR). Pittsburgh, PA: Carnegie-Mellon University, Department of Psychology.

Arnetz, B. B., Nevedal, D. C., Lumley, M. A., Backman, L., & Lublin, A. (2009). Trauma resilience training for police: Psychophysiological and performance effects. *Journal of Police and Criminal Psychology, 24*(1), 1–9.

Baker, L. D., Frank, L. L., Foster-Schubert, K., Green, P. S., Wilkinson, C. W., McTiernan, A., . . . Duncan, G. E. (2010). Effects of aerobic exercise on mild cognitive impairment: A controlled trial. *Archives of Neurology, 67*(1), 71–79.

Baum, A., Cohen, L., & Hall, M. (1993). Control and intrusive memories as possible determinants of chronic stress. *Psychosomatic Medicine, 55*(3), 274–286.

Beilock, S. L., & DeCaro, M. S. (2007). From poor performance to success under stress: Working memory, strategy selection, and mathematical problem solving under pressure. *Journal of Experimental Psychology: Learning, Memory, and Cognition, 33*(6), 983.

Beilock, S. L., Rydell, R. J., & McConnell, A. R. (2007). Stereotype threat and working memory: Mechanisms, alleviation, and spill over. *Journal of Experimental Psychology: General, 136*, 256–276.

Bjork, R. A. (1994). Memory and metamemory considerations in the training of human beings. In J. Metcalfe & A. Shimamura (Eds.), *Metacognition: Knowing About Knowing* (pp. 185–205). Cambridge, MA: MIT Press.

Brandon, S. E., & Silke, A. P. (2007). Near and long-term psychological effects of exposure to terrorist attacks. *Psychology of Terrorism*, 175–193.

Brown, A. L., Palincsar, A. S., & Armbruster, B. B. (1984). Instructing comprehension-fostering activities in interactive learning situations. In H. Mandl, N. L. Stein, & T. Trabasso (Eds.), *Learning and Comprehension of Text* (pp. 255–286). Hillsdale, NJ: Lawrence Erlbaum.

Campbell, D. J. (2012). Leadership in dangerous contexts: A team-focused, replenishment-of-resources approach. In J. H. Laurence & M. D. Matthews (Eds.), *The Oxford Handbook of Military Psychology* (pp. 158–175). New York: Oxford University Press.

Campbell, D., Campbell, K., & Ness, J. W. (2008). Resilience through leadership. In *Biobehavioral Resilience to Stress* (pp. 63–94). CRC Press.

Conway, A. R. A., Kane, M. J., Bunting, M. F., Hambrick, D. Z., Wilhelm, O., & Engle, R. W. (2005). Working memory span tasks: A methodological review and user's guide. *Psychonomic Bulletin & Review*, 12, 769–786.

Corbett, A. T., Koedinger, K. R., & Anderson, J. R. (1997). Intelligent tutoring systems. In M. G. Helander, T. K. Landauer, & P. Prabhu (Eds.), *Handbook of Human-Computer Interaction* (pp. 849–874). New York: Elsevier.

Csikszentmihalyi, M. (1990). *Flow: The Psychology of Optimal Experience.* New York: Harper & Row.

Deffenbacher, K. A. (1983). The influence of arousal on reliability testimony. In S. M. A. Lloyd-Bostock & R. B. Clifford (Eds.), *Evaluating Witness Testimony: Recent Psychological Research and New Perspectives* (235–251). Chichester: Wiley.

Durmer, J. S., & Dinges, D. F. (2005). Neurocognitive consequences of sleep deprivation. *Seminars in Neurology* 25(1), 117–129.

Elson-Cook, M. (1993). Student modeling in intelligent tutoring systems. *Artificial Intelligence Review*, 7, 227–240.

Friedland, N. & Keinan, G. (1992). Training effective performance in stressful situations: Three approaches and implications for combat training. *Military Psychology*, 4(3), 157–174.

Goetzman, D. (2012). *Dialogue education step by step: A guide for designing exceptional learning events.* Retrieved from http://www.globallearningpartners.com/resources/books/dialogue-education-step-by-step

Goleman, D. (1995). *Emotional Intelligence.* New York: Bantam Books.

Graesser, A.C., Conley, M. & Olney, A. (2012). Intelligent tutoring systems. In K. R. Harris, S. Graham, & T. Urdan (Eds.), *APA Educational Psychology Handbook: Vol. 3. Applications to Learning and Teaching* (pp. 451–473). Washington, DC: American Psychological Association.

Graesser, A. C., McDaniel, B., Chipman, P., Witherspoon, A., D'Mello, S., & Gholson, B. (2006). Detection of emotions during learning with AutoTutor. In *Proceedings of the 28th Annual Meetings of the Cognitive Science Society* (pp. 285–290). Vancouver, British Columbia, Canada: Lawrence Erlbaum Associates, Inc.

Han, D. H., Park, H. W., Kee, B. S., Na, C., Na, D. H., & Zaichkowsky, L. (2011). Performance enhancement with low stress and anxiety modulated by cognitive flexibility. *Psychiatry Investigation*, 8(3), 221–6. doi:10.4306/pi.2011.8.3.221

Jonassen, D., Ambruso, D. & Olesen, J. (1992). Designing hypertext on transfusion medicine using cognitive flexibility theory. *Journal of Educational Multimedia and Hypermedia, 1*(3), 309–322.

Kavanagh, J. (2005). Stress and performance: A review of the literature and its applicability to the military. *Rand Corporation Technical Report.* ISBN 0-8330-3830-3

Kolditz, T. A. (2007). *In Extremis Leadership: Leading as If Your Life Depended on It.* San Francisco: Jossey-Bass.

Levy, L. (2014, October). How stress affects the brain during learning. *Edudemic.* Retrieved from http://www.edudemic.com

Mackworth, N. H. (1948). The breakdown of vigilance during prolonged visual search, *Quarterly Journal of Experimental Psychology, 1*, 6–21

Matthews, M. D. (2014). *Head Strong: How Psychology Is Revolutionizing War.* New York: Oxford University Press.

McEwen, B. S. (2000). Allostasis and allostatic load: Implications for neuropsychopharmacology. *Neuropsychopharmacology. 22*, 108–124. doi:10.1016/S0893-133X(99)0029-3

Mental Health Daily. (2015, June 26). *7 ways to increase your cognitive flexibility.* Retrieved from: http://mentalhealthdaily.com/2015/07/26/7-ways-to-increase-your-cognitive-flexibility/

Moscaritolo, L. M. (2009). Interventional strategies to decrease nursing student anxiety in the clinical learning environment. *Journal of Nursing Education, 48*(1), 17.

Murray, T. & Arroyo, I. (2003). Toward an operational definition of the zone of proximal development for adaptive instructional software. In R. Alterman & D. Kirsh (Eds.), *Proceedings of the 25th Annual Meeting of the Cognitive Science Society* (p. 1389). Cincinnati, OH: CogSci Society.

Netterstrøm, B. & Conrad, N. (2007). *The Relationship Between Work-Related Stressors and the Development of Mental Disorders Other Than Post-Traumatic Stress Disorder: A Reference Document on Behalf of the Danish Work Environment Research Fund.* Denmark: Clinic of Occupational Medicine, Hillerød Hospital.

Nkambou, R., Mizoguchi, R. & Bourdeau, J. (2010). *Advances in Intelligent Tutoring Systems.* Berlin: Springer-Verlag.

Ong, A. D., Bergeman, C. S., Bisconti, T. L., & Wallace, K. A. (2006). Psychological resilience, positive emotions, and successful adaptation to stress in later life. *Journal of Personality and Social Psychology, 91*(4), 730.

Oppermann, R. (1994). Adaptively supported adaptability. *International Journal of Human Computer Studies, 40*(3), 455–472.

Ososky, S., Sottilare, R., Brawner, K., Long, R., & Graesser, A. (2015). *Authoring Tools and Methods for Adaptive Training and Education in Support of the US Army Learning Model: Research Outline* (ARL-SR-0339). Aberdeen Proving Ground, MD: US Army Research Laboratory.

Palinkas, L. A. (2007). Psychosocial issues in long-term space flight: Overview. *Gravitational and Space Research, 14*(2).

Petranek, S. (2015). *How We'll Live on Mars.* New York: Simon & Schuster.

Pollitt, E., Lewis, N. L., Garza, C., & Shulman, R. J. (1983). Fasting and cognitive function. *Journal of Psychiatric Research, 17*(2), 169–174.

Psotka, J. & Mutter, S.A. (1988). *Intelligent Tutoring Systems: Lessons Learned.* Hillsdale, NJ: Lawrence Erlbaum Associates.

Merriam-Webster.com. (2018). Definition of resilience. In *Merriam-Webster's online dictionary*. Retrieved from: http://www.merriam-webster.com/dictionary/resilience

Rus, V., Baggett, W., Gire, E., Franceschetti, D., Conley, M., & Graesser, A. (2013). Towards learner models based on learning progressions (LPs) in DeepTutor. In R. Sottilare, A. Graesser, X. Hu, & H. Holden (Eds.) *Design Recommendations for Intelligent Tutoring Systems: Volume 1- Learner Modeling.* Orlando, FL: Army Research Laboratory. ISBN 978-0-9893923-0-3.

Salas, E., & Cannon-Bowers, J. A. (2001). The science of training: A decade of progress. *Annual Review of Psychology, 52*(1), 471–499.

Salovey, P., & Mayer, J. D. (1990). Emotional intelligence. *Imagination, Cognition and Personality, 9,* 185–211.

Saunders, T., Driskell, J. E., Johnston, J. H., & Salas, E. (1996). The effect of stress inoculation training on anxiety and performance. *Journal of Occupational Health Psychology, 1*(2), 170.

Selye, H. (1936). A syndrome produced by diverse nocuous agents. *Nature, 138,* 32.

Selye, H. (1976). *The Stress of Life* (Rev. ed.). New York: McGraw-Hill.

Sleeman D., & Brown, J. S. (Eds.). (1982). *Intelligent Tutoring Systems.* Orlando, FL: Academic Press.

Sottilare, R. (2012, September). Considerations in the development of an ontology for a Generalized Intelligent Framework for Tutoring. *International Defense & Homeland Security Simulation Workshop in Proceedings of the I3M Conference.* Vienna, Austria.

Sottilare, R. A., Brawner, K. W., Goldberg, B. S., & Holden, H. K. (2012). The Generalized Intelligent Framework for Tutoring (GIFT). Concept paper released as part of GIFT software documentation. Orlando, FL: US Army Research Laboratory–Human Research & Engineering Directorate (ARL-HRED).

Sottilare, R. & Goldberg, B. (2012). Designing adaptive computer-based tutors to accelerate learning and facilitate retention. *Cognitive Technology, 17*(1), 19–34.

Sottilare, R., Graesser, A., Hu, X., & Holden, H. (2013). Learner modeling preface. In R. Sottilare, A. Graesser, X. Hu, & H. Holden (Eds.), *Design Recommendations for Intelligent Tutoring Systems: Volume 1- Learner Modeling.* Orlando, FL: Army Research Laboratory. ISBN 978-0-9893923-0-3.

Sottilare, R., Ragusa, C., Hoffman, M., & Goldberg, B. (2013, December). Characterizing an adaptive tutoring learning effect chain for individual and team tutoring. In *Proceedings of the Interservice/Industry Training Simulation & Education Conference,* Orlando, Florida.

Spiro, R. J., Coulson, R. L., Feltovich, P. J. & Anderson, D. (1988). Cognitive flexibility theory: Advanced knowledge acquisition in ill-structured domains. In V. Patel (Ed.), *Proceedings of the 10th Annual Conference of the Cognitive Science Society.* Hillsdale, NJ: Lawrence Erlbaum Associates.

Steensma, H., Den Heijer, M., & Stallen, V. (2007). Research note: Effects of resilience training on the reduction of stress and depression among Dutch workers. *International Quarterly of Community Health Education, 27*(2), 145–159.

Sterling, P. & Eyer, J. (1988). Allostasis: A new paradigm to explain arousal pathology. In S. Fisher & J. Reason (Eds.), *Handbook of Life Stress, Cognition and Health* (pp. 629–649). New York: Wiley.

Sweller, J., Van Merrienboer, J., & Paas, F. (1998). Cognitive architecture and instructional design. *Educational Psychology Review, 10* (3), 251–296.

US Army Combined Arms Center (2014). The human dimension white paper: A framework for optimizing human performance. https://usacac.army.mil/publications/human-dimension-white-paper

VanLehn, K. (2006). The behavior of tutoring systems. *International Journal of Artificial Intelligence in Education. 16*(3), 227–265.

Vygotsky, L. S. (1978). *Mind in Society: The Development of Higher Psychological Processes.* Cambridge, MA: Harvard University Press.

Wilson, M. G., & Morley, J. E. (2003). Impaired cognitive function and mental performance in mild dehydration. *European Journal of Clinical Nutrition, 57,* S24–S29.

Woolf, B. P. (2009). *Building Intelligent Interactive Tutors.* Burlington, MA: Morgan Kaufmann.

Yerkes, R. M. & Dodson, J. D. (1908). The relation of strength of stimulus to rapidity of habit formation, *Journal of Comparative Neurology and Psychology, 18,* 459–482 doi:10.1002/cne.920180503.

16

Noncognitive Amplifiers of Human Performance

Unpacking the 25/75 Rule

MICHAEL D. MATTHEWS, RICHARD M. LERNER,
AND HUBERT ANNEN*

INTRODUCTION

For more than 100 years, psychologists have worked diligently to identify factors that contribute to human performance. World War I energized this work, as the military turned to psychologists to improve the assessment and classification of the millions of men who volunteered or were conscripted to serve in the various branches of the military. Led by then president of the American Psychological Association, Robert Yerkes, psychologists quickly developed intelligence and aptitude tests that form the basis of modern testing (Rumsey, 2012). In understanding human performance, much of the research over the past 100 years has continued to focus on the relationship of talent (intelligence, aptitude, and other cognitive constructs) to various aspects of human performance. And this research has been quite fruitful. Overall, measures of talent appear to account for about 25% of variation in human performance (Neisser et al., 1996). This represents a sizeable and important contribution to predicting such things as academic grades and job performance.

The finding that talent accounts for about 25% of performance is consistent enough that we refer to it as the "25/75 rule." This helps underscore something that should be obvious—if 25% of performance is accounted for by talent, then 75% is accounted for by other, noncognitive factors, and much of this variance remains unaccounted for. Given that the primary focus of psychology has been on talent, this gives rise to the idea that a more systematic focus on noncognitive factors might begin to add to the proportion of variability in human performance that may be accounted for through systematic study and observation. For instance, if the

---

*The views expressed herein are those of the author and do not reflect the position of the United States Military Academy, the Department of the Army, or the Department of Defense.

intelligence quotient (IQ) predicts 25% of variation in academic grades, and a combination of noncognitive factors are identified and explored that predict another 25% of variation in academic grades, then parents, students, and educators would be in a position to prepare and develop themselves or others more effectively to optimize the potential for academic success. Over time, the "leftover" variance, that which is left unexplained, would diminish.

The purpose of this chapter is to explore and describe a variety of noncognitive constructs that are emerging as important predictors of human performance. This emerging research represents a revolution in how psychologists go about predicting performance. To the extent that the study of noncognitive contributors to human performance is in its infancy, there exists the potential for a seismic increase in the understanding of how humans perform across a wide spectrum of domains. Identifying and understanding these noncognitive constructs should inform educators, employers, and others on strategies to optimize domain specific performance, from students learning more effectively in school, workers being more productive employees, to soldiers executing their missions with greater skill and success.

Specifically, this chapter looks at three different but related noncognitive factors that are emerging as critical to understanding how well people perform and how long they may sustain high performance. First, the constructs of grit and hardiness are discussed. This is followed by a more general discussion of the role of character in understanding human performance. Finally, the role of psychological resilience and resilience skills in sustaining and enhancing human performance is explored. Because the military is particularly interested in human performance optimization, a good deal of the research presented is conducted in a military context. That said, the reader should see obvious extrapolations from the military domain to other important educational and occupational contexts.

We refer to these noncognitive constructs collectively as "amplifiers" of human performance. The exact way that talent and noncognitive amplifiers may interact no doubt varies as a function of the specific construct, situation, and task. These amplifiers may be correlated with, or orthogonal to talent measures, depending on what is being studied.

To illustrate how noncognitive constructs may amplify performance, consider the case of very selective organizations composed of only the most talented individuals. Rhodes scholars, for instance, are at the apex of academic achievement, yet in each cohort of scholars, some will perform better than others. Professional sports teams comprise the very best athletes, and those who become "all stars" may possess the same talent as those who are not as successful. In the military, the most talented soldier is not always the one who performs the best under fire. In all of these cases, noncognitive factors amplify the potential and performance of individuals, proving to be the difference-maker in who succeeds at the highest levels.

GRIT AND HARDINESS

We begin our examination of noncognitive amplifiers by looking at two constructs that have been well researched in a variety of domains. *Grit*, the passionate pursuit of long-term goals, appears to be particularly important in amplifying talent to achieve the highest level of performance in challenging tasks and situations (Duckworth, 2016). Grit refers to the ability to persevere when most people would give up. *Hardiness* is a psychological construct that is related to the ability of individuals to thrive and succeed in challenging and sometimes adverse circumstances (Maddi, 2012). Both grit and hardiness seem particularly relevant to understanding the upper edge of human performance.

Grit

Duckworth, Peterson, Matthews, and Kelly (2007) describe the origin and initial validation of the grit construct. They trace the long history of the study of talent and achievement and the somewhat more recent study of personality and achievement. This review suggested that to understand high achievement, both talent and personality must be considered. The review also suggested that individuals who could sustain a prolonged and passionate effort toward important goals—essentially the definition of grit—achieved more than those who lack this ability. Moreover, Duckworth and her colleagues could not identify an existing instrument that adequately assessed this capacity. Accordingly, using a sample of 1,545 respondents to 27 candidate questions, a final grit scale comprising 12 items was developed, consisting of two subscales—consistency of interests ($\alpha = .85$) and perseverance of effort ($\alpha = .78$).

Duckworth et al. (2007) then assessed the relationship between grit and a variety of outcome measures. Grit was found to be positively correlated with educational attainment, with non–high school graduates having the lowest grit scores and college graduates the highest. Older respondents were found to be "grittier" than younger respondents. Among undergraduate psychology majors, higher grit scores were associated with higher grade point averages. A particularly interesting finding was that grit predicted advancement to higher rounds in the Scripps National Spelling Bee, whose contestants ranged in age from 7 to 15 years. From questionnaire data, it appeared that high-grit contestants studied longer than their lower grit counterparts.

Perhaps the most interesting results reported by Duckworth et al. (2007) involved the performance of cadets at the United States Military Academy, commonly known as "West Point." The concept of grit centers on the ability of people to achieve daunting goals, sometimes in adverse conditions. Merely being admitted to West Point probably requires a great deal of grit. Prospective cadets must achieve high academic performance, show a consistent pattern of leadership, and be in top physical shape. Not surprisingly, Duckworth et al. found that West Point cadets had the highest grit scores—by nearly a half standard deviation—of other populations sampled, scoring approximately a half standard deviation higher than Ivy League undergraduates.

Once admitted, new West Point cadets must complete Cadet Basic Training (CBT) before beginning West Point's rigorous undergraduate academic curriculum in the fall semester. In CBT, new cadets must learn military customs and traditions, basic soldier skills, and socialization into the military. Instruction includes challenging physical tasks including long road marches and daunting obstacle courses. They are awakened at 5:00 A.M. and are kept busy until taps at 10:00 P.M. Many are away from home for the first time, and they are allowed minimal contact with parents and friends. Training is designed to challenge each new cadet every day.

Duckworth and her colleagues (2007) assessed the grit of new cadets shortly after they arrived at West Point to begin their 47-month journey to graduation and commissioning as second lieutenants. It is worth noting that the cohorts studied entered West Point at the height of the Iraq and Afghanistan wars, thus adding to the weight of their choice to attend West Point. Duckworth et al. also gathered admissions data on the new cadets, including indexes of academic, leadership, and physical fitness potential. These were rolled into a composite score, called the Whole Candidate Score (WCS), that West Point uses to select applicants for admission.

The results were surprising. Grit proved to be the only statistically significant predictor of the successful completion of CBT. Academic potential had no relation in predicting which cadets completed CBT. Moreover, grit and the WCS were not correlated. Knowing a cadet's grit score provided no information on his or her WCS and vice versa. Additional analyses showed that while grit and the conscientiousness component of the Big Five personality measure were highly correlated, it demonstrated incremental variance over conscientiousness in success measures. In predicting academic grades of the cadet's first academic semester, WCS was the strongest predictor, but again, grit added incrementally to this prediction.

The West Point results are important because they show—in a large sample of people operating in a challenging institutional context—that grit is vital to success. Especially convincing are the CBT results. This daunting training period is more of a "gut check" than an experience based on high-aptitude test scores or being valedictorian of one's high school class. The failure of WCS and the success of grit in predicting CBT retention underscore that grit is especially vital in understanding achievement that is based on a basic refusal to give up.

While the implications for grit as an approach to optimizing human performance is clear, additional work must be done before it can be used in a practical way. First, the current measure of grit is transparent and easily prone to faking. So if grit was used to screen prospective college students or employees, candidates could easily mark their answers to falsely increase their grit score. Second, strategies for developing grit must be discovered. Duckworth (2016) offers clues on where to begin. She identifies four stages of the development of grit: interest, practice, purpose, and hope. For an institution like the military, increasing grit likely would require a multipronged strategy of selection, classification, and training/development. It is essential that prospective soldiers have a strong interest in the military. Once selected, they should be given ample opportunity to practice the skills needed for success. The overarching purpose and meaning of their profession should be explicitly reinforced. In addition, hope—which Duckworth (p. 169) defines as the expectation that one's own efforts will improve the future—must be instilled. In short, institutions striving for grittier members or employees must improve strategies for building all four components of grit.

Extending the concept of grit from an individual trait or characteristic to one that represents teams is essential. In military operations in particular, the basic functional unit is a small team. Do these small teams, in the military or in other venues, differ in group-level grit? Is team grit the summation of the grit of its individual members, or is it an emergent phenomenon, a case where the whole is greater than the sum of its parts? Currently, there is no metric for assessing team grit. Creating a tool for team grit assessment is necessary to better understand the nature of team grit and to find ways to develop and increase it.

Hardiness

Grit is linked to the ability of a person to doggedly pursue long-term goals, such as excelling in college and gaining admission to medical school, sticking with the hours of practice needed to attain elite status as an athlete or musician, or to endure the difficult challenges of military basic training. In contrast, hardiness addresses the ability of people to thrive in spite of difficult circumstances. A hardy plant may exist on a rocky, arid mountain. A hardy person, by analogy, endures and may even thrive in conditions that some may find unbearable, such as combat. Hardiness was first described by Suzanne Kobasa (1979) and elaborated on extensively by Salvatore Maddi (2012). Hardiness helps differentiate among people who succeed in high stress or dangerous situations from those who fail.

Hardiness consists of three subcomponents, often referred to as the "3 C's." The first, *commitment*, represents the ability of a person to remain engaged in goal-directed behavior despite high stress. This component has conceptual similarity to grit. *Challenge* is the second subcomponent of hardiness. This refers to the tendency for a person to frame a difficult task or set of circumstances as a challenge, perhaps a chance to grow, versus as a threat to his or her well-being. The third subcomponent of hardiness is *control*. Similar to self-efficacy, control represents the belief a person has that his or her actions are directly linked to outcome. To illustrate, a hardy salesperson would persist in efforts to sell a product even when sales occur infrequently (commitment), view a difficult sale as an opportunity to develop more effective sales techniques (challenge), and possess an unshakable belief that his or her skills and behavior directly influence the outcome of a sales pitch.

The military provides a good context in which to study hardiness. As Bartone (1999) observed, in writing about hardiness among military personnel, "Although previous studies show ill effects of stress on some of these personnel, few studies have sought to explain continued good health and resiliency maintained by the majority of veterans." Bartone studied the resilience and adaption of Army reserve soldiers who were activated for duty in the Gulf War I. In addition to exposure to the dangers of war, deployment involves a long period of separation from family and friends, and a host of other stressors. In this study, soldiers high in hardiness reported better adjustment than those lower in hardiness. In short, hardiness appeared to provide a protective factor against the adversity of a combat deployment.

Subsequent research on hardiness in military populations reinforced Bartone's (1999) findings. Kelly, Matthews, and Bartone (2005) and, more recently Maddi et al. (Maddi, Matthews, Kelly, Villarreal, & White, 2012), report that hardiness is linked to a variety of performance outcomes and retention in West Point cadets. And hardiness appears to have robust predictive validity over time. In a prospective study, Bartone, Kelly, and Matthews (2013) administered the hardiness scale to new cadets shortly after they arrived at West Point to begin their 47-month training and educational development. Bartone et al. followed those who graduated (about 80% of the original sample) 3 years into their careers as Army officers. At this time, the West Point Office of Institutional Research conducted a survey of the battalion commanders of these graduates, who were by this time first-lieutenants in the Army and most of whom had combat experience. The battalion commanders rated the leadership traits and competency of these lieutenants. It turned out that hardiness, assessed more than 7 years earlier, remained a significant predictor of leadership ratings. Former cadets who score higher in hardiness were rated as better leaders than those with lower assessed hardiness. Thus, high hardiness in small-unit leaders showed a secondary, beneficial effect in their followers.

Maddi (2012) presents a history and overview of the impact of hardiness in a wide range of populations, from school children to a variety of occupations. He also describes a validated approach to training hardiness, thus providing a tool that may be used to optimize human performance through increasing hardiness.

The Relationship Between Grit and Hardiness

Grit and hardiness are conceptually related to some degree. However, Maddi et al. (2012) report the correlation between the two measures in West Point cadets is .46. Although statistically significant, this suggests that the two constructs measure somewhat different things. Grit is designed to account for relentless pursuit of challenging, long-term goals. Grit, per se, is not directly linked to resilience or psychological well-being. Hardiness, in contrast, represents the ability of an individual to be resilient and to maintain psychological well-being in the face of adversity.

It follows, therefore, that both grit and hardiness are important in optimizing human performance. In some tasks, like completing a college degree or learning to play a musical instrument with a high level of expertise, grit may play a greater role. But for tasks that involve a threat to physical or emotional well-being, hardiness may be more relevant. For institutions that wish to optimize human performance, strategies to recruit, train, and maintain gritty and hardy individuals should be developed. And, similar to the preceding discussion about team grit, there may be strategies for enhancing both grit and hardiness at the small team or unit level. Additional research is needed to determine how to measure these constructs at the aggregate level, and if and how team level grit and hardiness can best be nurtured.

CHARACTER STRENGTHS

What Is Character?

There are a myriad of attributes of individuals that may be studied in order to identify the features of human behavior and development that, when present, will optimize human performance. However, for more than 2,000 years (at least since the time of Aristotle), one domain of attributes has drawn the attention of philosophers and scientists: character. Indeed, across history, people have sought to identify facets of human behavior and development that mark a thriving or flourishing person; that is, someone who acts in ways that reflect positively on both himself or herself and, at the same time, contribute reliably and effectively to other people and the community. Character may be the noncognitive attribute that maximizes the probability of such indications of optimal human performance (Callina et al., 2017; Lerner & Callina, 2014).

But why do researchers and practitioners have the common goal of wanting to understand how to enhance the character of individuals, perhaps especially young people on the path toward defining themselves and trying to discover how they will fit into their social world (Lerner, 2004)? Both sets of professionals agree that character development is an essential marker of a positively developing person and that people of good character are essential for the moral and ethical leadership of our nation and its institutions. Indeed, Nucci (2016, p. 4) has emphasized that "any meaningful notion of character has to place morality at the center. Other features of character such as grit, or social and emotional intelligence that can support morality, can also be directed at negative goals." Perhaps surprisingly, therefore, despite this agreement about the fundamental importance of character for positive human development and for the institutions of democracy and civil society, scholars and practitioners disagree about how to define character!

Berkowitz (2011, 2012) has described this diversity of definitions as reflecting a sort of Towel of Babel. Simply, there is a plethora of terms used by scholars and practitioners to describe character and its development. In addition to the term "character" itself, there is also widespread use of terms such as "socioemotional learning" (SEL), "positive youth development" (PYD), "virtues," "strengths," and, as well, "soft skills" and "noncognitive skills" (Farrington et al., 2012).

Across these terminological differences, however, contemporary scholars converge on a common depiction of the essential features of character. That is, as explained by Berkowitz, Bier, and McCauley (2016, p. 3), "character is the set of psychological characteristics that motivate and enable one to function as a moral agent, to perform optimally, to effectively pursue knowledge and intellectual flourishing, and to be an effective member of society." In other words, Berkowitz et al. indicate that, across the current literature discussing the structure and function of character, scholars point out that character has at least four facets: moral, performance, intellectual, and civic.

Current Ideas About the Content of Character

As Berkowitz et al. (2016) note, there may be different categories of actions reflecting character. For example, Lickona and Davidson (2005) identified character as being composed of strengths classifiable into two categories: moral virtues and performance character. Moral virtues reflect moral functioning (Berkowitz, 2012) and were conceptualized by Lickona and Davidson (p. 18) as involving "integrity, justice, caring, and respect—[which are] needed for successful interpersonal relationships and ethical behavior." In turn, performance character was thought to comprise attributes that reflect exemplary task performance; that is, "qualities such as effort, diligence, perseverance, a strong work ethic, a positive attitude, ingenuity, and self-discipline needed to realize one's potential for excellence in academics, co-curricular activities, the workplace, or any other area of endeavor."

A third possible component of character consists of attributes that involve contributions to civil society; that is, civic character comprises the knowledge, skills, and commitments involved in being an active and positively engaged citizen (Seider, 2012). In turn, Baehr (2013) proposed that character also involves intellectual attributes such as love of learning, seeking truth, creativity, and other attributes of cognition associated with leading a life devoted to "the pursuit of distinctively epistemic [knowledge-oriented] goods" (p. 1).

The Primacy of the Moral Dimension of Character

Although a person's character may indeed involve multiple facets or dimensions, morality is "first among equals." That is, what makes any behavior involving other hypothesized domains of character (e.g., performance, intellectual, or civic domains) indicative of character is that they "motivate and enable [a person] to act as a moral agent" (Berkowitz, 2012, p. 248). That is, whatever other facets of cognitive, emotional, or behavioral functioning may be thought of as being involved in character, these facets have to be integrated with moral agency in order for a person to authentically possess character. Nucci (2016, p. 5) reminds us that "performance qua performance is not a sufficient indicator of a person's character" and, because all facets of character must work as an integrated system to reflect character, authentic character can be seen as a fundamental strength of a person as he or she lives in and transacts with his or her world. Character strengths motivate and enable the person to "do the right thing" for self, others, and society across time and place.

Peterson and Seligman (2004) developed a widely regarded classification of human character strengths. Based on careful review of psychological research, the teachings of the world's major religions, and the insights of philosophers, Peterson and Seligman identified 24 strengths of character they believe are universal to humans. These strengths are thought to be valued by all humans, regardless of national origin, culture, or religious affiliation. They constitute strengths at different historical times and in different places. These 24 strengths are categorized into six "moral virtues." These six moral virtues, with their associated character strengths, are wisdom and knowledge (creativity, curiosity, judgment, love of learning, perspective); courage (bravery, persistence, integrity, vitality); justice (teamwork, fairness, leadership); humanity (capacity to love, kindness, social intelligence); temperance (forgiveness, modesty, prudence, self-regulation); and transcendence (appreciation of beauty, gratitude, hope/optimism, humor, and spirituality). Research on these character strengths continues as an active area of scholarship through this writing (e.g., McGrath, 2015).

In short, as Berkowitz, Althof, and Bier (2012, p. 72) explain, character represents the psychological attributes of people "that motivate and enable them to act in ethical, democratic, and socially effective and productive ways." In other words, character represents an asset, or strength, of both a person and of a society. People with character engage in mutually beneficial relations with their social world; by the dint of their character, they "do the right thing" for themselves and for society (Johnson et al., 2016). Indeed, if one's purpose in life is to act as a person of character, to model or to lead others through the strength of one's character, then such goals "provide meaning and direction to a person's life" (Nucci, 2016, p. 25; see also Damon, 2009; Damon & Colby, 2015).

Character as an Individual–Context Relational Process

All human life involves people's exchanges with the physical and social facets of their context. Indeed, the idea of adaptation is that the person has to adjust to the features and changes in his or her world in order to survive, and, in turn, the person must support the features of his or her world that enable his or her survival. All of life involves, then, the mutual regulation of person and context. These mutually influential relations can be represented as individual ↔ context relations. The bidirectional arrow in this representation signifies that people affect their contexts as their contexts affect them. When such mutually influential relations are also mutually beneficial, then adaptive developmental regulations exist (Brandtstädter, 1998).

Character is an attribute of human life that reflects a specific type of relationship individuals have with their world, one that *standardly* involves such mutually beneficial exchanges between a person and his or her environment or context. That is, because we have seen that the defining feature of character is moral agency aimed at contributing to both self and society, the mutually beneficial relations comprising character prototypically involve exchanges between an individual and other individuals in the life of a person; that is, individual ↔ individual relations. In other words, whereas the context can refer to the physical ecology of human life (e.g., water quality, the levels of pollution in his or her community), context can also refer to the other people in the individual's world (e.g., family members, classmates, teammates, or members of a unit he or she is commanding; e.g., Colby, 2008).

At its most general level, character involves a person acting on his or her world in ways that benefit it (e.g., improving the quality of the air or water in one's community) and, in turn, the world thereby providing benefits for the person (e.g., providing a healthier environment within which the person lives). However, even these individual ↔ context relations can be interpreted as serving (and, indeed, because of a person's moral agency, may in fact be intended to serve) the person's social world. Hence, mutually beneficial individual ↔ individual relations are the hallmark of character (Lerner & Callina, 2014).

Across time and place, then, a person's manifestation of "good" character, or a person whom we describe as showing strength of character, involves the person reliably and coherently contributing positively to the world—the institutions, settings, and people—that is supporting him or her (Lerner, 2004). Simply, a person of good character does "the right thing" in a particular setting, although the specific attribute of character required for such a contribution may change across situations or developmental periods. Good character involves coherence of acting in ways that reflect "doing the right thing," although what is right to do in a given situation may vary (Nucci, 2017; Lerner & Callina, 2014). Generosity may be needed in one setting, humility and forgiveness in another, and courage and integrity in still another.

In sum, character is not conceived as a global attribute of the person; that is, character is not just one thing. It involves many different instances of human cognitive, emotional, and behavioral functioning that can enable an individual to be involved in individual ↔ individual relations with others in his or her world that involve mutual benefits and reflect moral agency.

The Process of Character Development

Character, then, is an individual ↔ individual process that involves the person doing what is right, correct, or virtuous for both others and himself or herself. Sokol, Hammond, and Berkowitz (2010) emphasize that "a phenomenon like character, first and foremost, is seen as a dynamic process, and not a fixed feature of a person" (p. 584). If character functions as a dynamic process—that is, as a process involving changes in one part of the relationship (or system) influencing (and being influenced by) changes in another part of the relationship (or system)—then *character is a developmental phenomenon*.

In other words, character is not a fixed or static attribute of human functioning. It is not a hereditarily determined attribute or a feature of human life that exists as immutable in the face of environmental variation (i.e., it is not a "trait;" Costa, McCrae, & Siegler, 1999). Instead, character develops through the continuation across life of mutually beneficial individual ↔ context or individual ↔ individual relations.

Current evidence from the biological sciences supports the idea of the modifiability of character across the life span (e.g., Lester, Conradt, & Marsit, 2016; Meaney, 2010). For instance, evidence from the field of epigenetics demonstrates the power of the environment in regulating how genes are expressed. The structural features of genes (e.g., proteins) are affected by chemical processes (e.g., methylation) that moderate the function of these structures. These processes can alter whether a gene is turned off or on and, if turned on, to what degree. These epigenetic (i.e., meaning "beyond the gene") processes are affected by the individual's unique set of life experiences and the specific environments he or she encounters. These environments range from those involving cellular events through social interactions (Slavich & Cole, 2013). Moreover, the changes induced by the individual ↔ context process involved in epigenetics can be transmitted to offspring and to the offspring of offspring (i.e., to grandchildren; Lester et al., 2016; Misteli, 2013). Therefore, character can undergo relatively systematic changes (it can show "plasticity") across life and across generations.

What do this epigenetic process and the resulting phenomenon of human plasticity mean for character development? Simply, character is eminently mutable. Because character attributes are a joint function of "biopsychosocial" developmental history and current environment and experiences, they probably are not easily changed by a single experience, course of instruction, or other short-term intervention. But systematic efforts by an individual, especially in an environment specifically designed to promote character growth, have every possibility of being successful. For instance, Callina et al. (2017) have discussed how college changes people's values and character. So, too, does years of employment and, as well, military training and experience. But systematic character change requires mindful effort in a supportive organizational context. Leaders can mindfully seek opportunities to grow their own character. More importantly, perhaps, leaders can set the occasion for character growth in others. Change may not be quick or easy, but is clearly achievable.

In sum, the development of good character results from the individual ↔ individual relations we have described. As a consequence, programs aimed at developing character (i.e., character education programs) should focus on the process of assuring that relations among people (e.g., leaders and subordinates) are mutually beneficial. Indeed, Nucci and Narvaez (2008, p. 3) note that "all approaches to moral and character education recognize the importance of social interactions for students' moral growth."

Moral agency is vital in instantiating such interactions as instances of character, and other instances of noncognitive skills, for instance, intentional self-regulation (ISR) processes, can amplify the probability of actions reflective of moral agency (Lerner & Callina, 2014). Indeed, ISR represents one of a person's key noncognitive contributions to the individual ↔ context relations that moderate the course of character development (Nucci, 2017). With such self-governance skills, the person can do the right thing—show the attributes necessary to serve self and others in a mutually beneficial way—across different settings and, as well, across the life span (Elder, Shanahan, & Jennings, 2015).

Conclusions

Optimizing human performance can be achieved through many different means. However, when the goal of such optimization efforts is to maximize the probability that individuals will flourish in ways reflecting personal well-being *and* morally meaningful contributions to the institutions of civil society and democracy, then the target of one's work should be focused on character. When successfully promoted, no other noncognitive feature of human development may better amplify such individual and context outcomes of optimal human performance. Enhancing the character development of young people will develop citizens of civil society to be moral agents serving self and democratic institutions in mutually beneficial ways.

RESILIENCE

In recent times, resilience, commonly understood as the *ability to deal successfully with challenging situations and to carry on and persevere in the face of adversity,* has become a catchword. This is not surprising; on the one hand, everyday tasks, either at the workplace or in private, appear to be increasingly demanding and complex; on the other hand, people are confronted with media reports of accidents, shootings, terror attacks, and other threatening situations as natural disasters. Against this backdrop, a psychological construct that promises to have an answer to this unpredictable or even dangerous world finds a fertile soil. But no matter how welcome this may be, resilience cannot be the magic wand that provides a solution to every challenge or menace. In fact, in the context of human performance optimization, the analysis of its theoretical foundation and a consideration of recent and current research is necessary in order to understand this construct and to create the preconditions for its application. Therefore, this section investigates (a) the origin of the construct, (b) the approach of resilience as a personality trait, and (c) the possibilities and limitations of resilience training, and it emphasizes the relevance of a resilience-promoting environment.

A Bit of History

Initially, a pathogenic perspective—how diseases develop, appear, and could be cured—dominated the field of mental health. Basic questions addressed risk factors, vulnerabilities, and therapies. However, theories and models about emergence and treatment of diseases did not take into account the fact that most people, facing the same or similar circumstances, remain healthy. Only since the 1960s has this unbalanced pathogenic perspective been enhanced, with the introduction of the complementary notion of *salutogenesis*—the origins of health (Antonovsky, 1979). With the work of Werner in the early 1970s (Werner, Bierman, & French, 1971), the concept of resilience appeared more frequently in the relevant psychological literature. Antonovsky's insights were mainly influenced by survivors of the Holocaust who were able to leave behind their traumatic experiences and live a normal and healthy life. Werner investigated children who grew up in great poverty and heavily burdened social environments. She found that at least one-third of these children overcame these unfavorable conditions. Werner described them as *resilient.*

Subsequent research helped refine the notion of resilience as (a) the ability to *"bounce back,"* (b) the ability to continue forward and maintain equilibrium in the face of chronic adversity, (c) the ability to live with ongoing fear and uncertainty, and (d) the ability to adapt to difficult and challenging life experiences. In addition, this research delivered evidence that this is more the rule than the exception, more common than rare (Meichenbaum, 2013)—or, as illustrated with Masten's (2001) metaphor: "ordinary magic." Consequently, this raises the question about the essential components of this ordinary magic.

A Closer Look

Taking into account that resilience occurs on different levels—that is, from the individual level to the community level to whole populations or nations—and can be related to various thematic areas, such as environment or economy (see Lucini, 2014; Masten & Obradovic, 2008; Soucek, Ziegler, Schlett, & Pauls, 2016), the focus of the present section remains on *psychological resilience* on the *individual level.* Despite this narrowing of the research focus, numerous factors related to resilience are found in the literature, making a summary of the field difficult. In the framework of a RAND study Meredith et al. (2011) conducted a systematic review of the scientific literature on psychological resilience. Out of 270 relevant publications, they identified 20 evidence-informed factors associated with resilience. Of those, the following seven were assigned to individual-level factors: positive coping, positive affect, positive thinking, realism, behavioral control, physical fitness, and altruism. A recent meta-analytic study describes the psychosocial factors believed to be amenable to resilience development, including self-efficacy, optimism, social resources, and cognitive appraisal/coping (Vanhove, Herian, Perez, Harms, & Lester, 2015). From a practice-oriented perspective, the American Psychological Association names four factors related to resilience: the capacity to make realistic plans and take steps to carry them out, a positive view of yourself and confidence in your strengths and abilities, skills in communication and problem-solving, and the capacity to manage strong feelings and impulses.

The essence of these three investigations clearly reflect the following elements of resilience

- One needs a certain degree of intelligence or *cognitive skills* to detect the heart of a problem and the relevant steps toward the solution.
- Regarding the willingness to take these steps, *optimism* is needed, as well as trusting in one's own skills and abilities (*self-esteem, self-efficacy*).
- These situations can result in intense *emotions*, which must be reappraised and *regulated*.
- And, finally, overcoming a challenging situation often calls for social support, and, accordingly, the person involved needs *social resources* and the *communication* and *social skills* to activate them.

This demonstrates that the concept of resilience is related to other concepts. The most obvious connection is to *stress appraisal and coping strategies* and their effects on the primary and secondary prevention of stress (see Lazarus & Folkman, 1984). Thus, the difference between primary and secondary prevention can be seen as the major distinction between resilience and stress management. The latter emphasizes mitigating the negative effects of stress exposure, whereas the former is always forward-looking and aims to promote wellness and competence in order to prevent the negative effects of some future stressor. However, the protective factors developed as part of resilience-building programs overlap somewhat with those trained through stress management interventions, such as cognitive reappraisal and coping strategies.

Also worth mentioning is the proximity to the *sense of coherence* (SOC) construct—a generalized orientation toward the world, perceived on a continuum as comprehensible, manageable, and meaningful (Antonovsky, 1996). Confronted with a stressor, the person with a strong SOC will wish to and be motivated to cope, will believe that the challenge is understood, and will believe that resources to cope are available. SOC is, in effect, the operationalization of the *salutogenic* approach and differs from similar concepts, such as optimism, self-efficacy, or hardiness, in its unique combination of the cognitive, behavioral, and motivational factors.

Finally, one could argue that resilience is the end product of intuitive application of *positive psychology* to the management of personal adversity. Resilience training programs are often based on the theoretical framework of positive psychology, which emphasizes the identification and use of individual strengths, the cognitive reframing of activating events and respective beliefs, and the application of constructive and positive communication styles (see Reivich & Shatté, 2003).

There exists a vast literature on resilience and its components. Furthermore, it is closely related to other concepts. As things stand, resilience programs are prevention-oriented: the salutogenic approach serves as ideological orientation and reflects the shift from "fix what's wrong" to "build what's strong," and positive psychology provides the primary theoretical foundation for resilience training. As will be discussed in the following section, more insights about relevant factors of resilience come to the fore when reviewing the instruments intended to measure resilience.

Resilient by Nature

Although resilience emphasizes adaptive coping with demanding situations, it's often operationalized as a stable personality trait (Pangallo, Zibarras, Lewis, & Flaxman, 2015). The assumption that resilience is a specific disposition of a person, an ability to deal with precarious and dangerous life circumstances, can be traced to the work of Werner et al. (1971) and Antonovsky (1979). This determination facilitates the classification of resilience similar to other aspects of personality as well as its operationalization following the established methodology on research on personality traits (Schumacher, Leppert, Gunzelmann, Strauss, & Brähler, 2004). Several studies suggest a respective genetic disposition, and, although this cannot be the whole picture, one can at least state a certain *potential* of resilience.

On the basis of this assumption, it makes sense to implement resilience measures in personnel selection procedures, specifically in high-reliability organizations (Weick & Sutcliffe, 2007) such as firefighting teams, healthcare centers, police forces, air control centers, and the military. Not surprisingly, considerable efforts were undertaken to operationalize and measure resilience, focusing on promoting attributes and similar protective factors that support and maintain well-being or work performance even under difficult circumstances. Such factors are typically treated as independent variables or predictors of some dependent variable representing successful adaptation (King & King, 2013).

In 2011, Windle, Bennett, and Noyes conducted a quantitative methodological review, with the goals of (a) identifying useful resilience measurement scales and their target population, (b) assessing the psychometric rigor of measures, and (c) detecting implications for research and practice. Their analysis of a large number of potential papers eventually yielded 15 measures. Subsequently, these measures were assessed for psychometric properties such as internal consistency, content, criterion and construct validity, reliability, responsiveness, and interpretability. As a result, the following three scales received the highest ratings:

- *Connor-Davidson Resilience Scale* (CD-RISC; Connor & Davidson, 2003): The authors defined resilience as a general ability to cope with stress, and then identified qualities of resilient individuals (e.g., hardiness, self-esteem, problem-solving, faith) to guide item development, which resulted in 25 items grouped in five factors (personal competence, trust/tolerance/

strengthening effects of stress, acceptance of change and secure relationships, control, spiritual influences). This instrument is one of the most widely used measures of resilience (King & King, 2013).

- *Resilience Scale for Adults* (RSA; Friborg, Hjemdal, Rosenvinge, & Martinussen, 2003): Based on longitudinal research to identify some of the key features of resilient people, the authors used family support and cohesion, external support systems, and dispositional attitudes and behaviors to define the items. The resulting 37 items are grouped in five factors (personal competence, social competence, family coherence, social support, and personal structure).
- *Brief Resilience Scale* (BRS; Smith et al., 2008): The authors suggest that assessing the ability to recover in individuals who are ill is important, and, by developing this 6-item scale, they maintained a specific focus on bouncing back from stress.

Windle et al. (2011) indicated that all the measures tested (including those just mentioned) had some missing information regarding the psychometric properties and, when considering all criteria, also the quality of the questionnaires with the highest ratings appear to be only moderate. They conclude that making recommendations about the use of resilience scales is difficult due to the lack of psychometric information and that consideration should be given to the goal of the measurement (i.e., "what do you want to use it for?"). Thus, with regard to the military context, King and King (2013) suggest two additional scales to consider.

- *Dispositional Resilience Scale* (DRS-15; Bartone, 1995): This measure centers on the construct of hardiness, which is defined as a generalized style of healthy functioning with cognitive, emotional, and behavioral elements. It comprises 15 items split into three factors (sense of control of one's life, commitment in terms of the meaning ascribed to new experience, and openness to viewing change as a challenge).
- *Response to Stressful Experiences Scale* (RSES; Johnson et al., 2011): Item selection and validation of this self-report measure were accomplished using samples drawn from military units that had been deployed to the Iraq or Afghanistan theater of operations. Factor analysis of the resulting 22-item scale suggested five resilience-promoting factors (meaning making and restoration; active coping; cognitive flexibility; spirituality; self-efficacy).

Finally, the *Resilience Scale* (RS; Wagnild & Young, 1993) should not be forgotten. It attempts to assess an individual's capacity to live a life worth living. In its initial version, the 25-item scale measures five personal concepts including equanimity, perseverance, meaningfulness, self-reliance, and existential aloneness. Subsequent factor analysis yielded a two-dimensional structure, consisting of personal competence and acceptance of self and life. In the course of the construction of a German version of the RS, a one-dimensional solution became apparent (Schumacher et al., 2004), which eventually resulted in a short version (RS-11). The RS-11 proved to be a reliable, valid, and, above all, an economic instrument to measure psychological resilience as a trait. As such it is widely used in German-speaking countries; for instance, in the context of a comprehensive study on stress in the Swiss Armed Forces, it was the most significant predictor regarding the attrition rate in basic military training (Wyss & Annen, 2011).

Considering the various resilience scales just described, they all represent the attempt to assess an array of mostly global personal characteristics and social factors that may promote resilience. This raises questions about the extent to which resilience researchers are measuring resilience or an entirely different experience (Windle et al., 2011). For example, a study by Robins, John, Caspi, Moffitt, and Stouthamber-Loeber (1996) demonstrates that the "resilient type" was characterized by above-average scores on all dimensions (neuroticism reverse coded) of the Five-Factor model (FFM; Costa & McCrae, 1992). In a recent study Waaktaar and Torgersen (2010) showed that FFM added more to the explained variance in adolescents' adaptive behaviors than did certain resilience scales. Therefore, it remains the question whether resilience should be assessed within the framework of, for instance, the well-known dimensions of the FFM of general personality or whether resilience as a personality characteristic would be more efficiently assessed with a specialized instrument like a resilience scale.

Furthermore, resilience is not a simple or static construct. An individual may be resilient in one domain of their life (e.g., work life) but not in another (e.g., family life), during one phase of their life (e.g., middle age) but not during a different phase (e.g., adolescence) and in response to one type of trauma but not another (Masten, 2001). So the scope of the application of resilience measures has to be clearly defined, and the detection of longitudinal patterns of growth or decline in an individual's standing on a relevant attribute has to be taken into account. Here, the object is to observe and quantify resilience as individual differences in the intraindividual (within-person) change process (King & King, 2013).

To sum up, research suggests that resilience is not only an inherent immovable trait of individuals, but a modifiable construct (Leppin et al., 2014), and various personal examples (see Reivich & Shatté, 2003) show that people are able to personally grow during or in the aftermath of challenging, stressful, or even traumatic experiences. It is thus clear that people have different starting positions when they face challenges or threats, but the respective disposition is not cast in stone; it can rather be developed and the respective development process can be sped up and reinforced by specific training methods.

Resilience Can Be Trained

In the past decade, organizations have increasingly sought to adopt resilience-building programs to prevent absenteeism, counterproductive work behavior, and other stress-related issues. To date, the overall effect of such programs was rather small (Vanhove et al., 2015), but even small effects when applied to large numbers of individuals may result in significant economic and societal benefits. Thus, the Comprehensive Soldier and Family Fitness (CSF2) program of the US Army (Cornum, Matthews, & Seligman, 2011), which is to our knowledge the largest project in this vein, serves as a perfect example for the relevant issues relating to resilience training.

CSF2 consists of three components. The first is the Global Assessment Tool (GAT), a specifically developed psychometrically valid assessment tool that, when administered online, is a time-efficient way of measuring an individual's fitness in the four dimensions of psychological fitness (emotional, social, family, spiritual; see Peterson, Park, & Castro, 2011, for details). This provides service members with individualized feedback that can guide self-paced training, which is the second main element of the program. Depending on their relative psychological strengths identified on the GAT assessment, soldiers receive a selection of appropriate self-development opportunities. The third pillar is the training of master resilience trainers (MRT) for the delivery of resilience training within their units on ways that service members can bolster core resilience competencies such as self-awareness, self-regulation, optimism, mental agility, strength of character, and connection (see Reivich, Seligman, & McBride, 2011, for details).

This resource-intensive initiative is evaluated constantly—to date, four technical reports have been published. The third report shows that soldiers who received resilience training improved their GAT score more than those soldiers who did not attend the training; the training appears to be more effective for soldiers between the ages of 18 and 24 years than for older soldiers; and, finally, the training is more effective when commanders ensure that training is properly scheduled, when commanders select confident junior leaders to serve as trainers, and when the trainers feel that their commanders support them (Lester, Harms, Herian, Krasikova, & Beal, 2011). The fourth report assessed whether training impacted actual behavioral health diagnoses across a 15-month period and led to two key findings: (1) units that received MRTs at the company level had 60% fewer diagnoses of drug and alcohol abuse compared to units without MRTs, and (2) units that received MRTs at the company level had 13% fewer diagnoses of anxiety, depression, and PTSD compared to units without MRTs (Harms, Herian, Krasikova, Vanhove, & Lester, 2013). Furthermore, Griffith and West (2013) published their results based on an online survey among National Guard soldiers and civilians about their resilience training experience: 92% of the respondents indicated the training was helpful and improved resilience competencies that enhanced coping with stressful circumstances; 97% stated that these competencies were subsequently used in their military and civilian jobs. In addition, a measure of resilience competencies showed self-reported changes largely pertained to increased self-awareness and strength of character, including improved optimism, mental agility, and connection with others. Self-reported change in resilience competencies was associated with fewer behavioral health symptoms, especially for those reporting more current stressful events (buffering effect). The study of Carr et al. (2013) is the first of its kind reporting descriptive assessment of the delivery of resilience training in a deployed environment. Among other inventories, the CD-RISC was administered before and after resilience training for all personnel assigned to a military facility in Afghanistan. Results reveal that, despite the training, resilient thinking was observed to decline across the deployment period. However, given that there was no comparison group, the respective results can't be seen as an evaluation of the training program. So, the principal value in this descriptive study is to inform expectations of military commands in their use of MRT and similar programs.

Since the scientific research on MRT is still sparse, a look at a recent meta-analytic study of resilience-building program effectiveness (Vanhove et al., 2015) is helpful. Based on a literature search the authors extracted 42 independent samples (i.e., resilience training programs). Its systematic examination showed that participants in resilience-building programs improved scores on performance and well-being outcomes and reduced scores on outcomes reflecting psychosocial deficits upon post-training assessment; however, results suggest that the effect of resilience-building diminishes over time. In terms of the occupational setting, resilience trainings caused a positive and significant impact in both military and nonmilitary settings. However, findings regarding the effects of targeted versus universal programs as well as the method of program delivery (i.e., computer-based; group-based; classroom; one-on-one; train-the-trainer) are less clear. First, differential effects associated with targeted and universal programs were observed as a far stronger distal effect was associated with targeted programs. Second, one-on-one delivery formats appear to have had the strongest effect, but since the vast majority of programs used group-based classroom formats, and effects associated with the remaining delivery formats stem from very few studies, this findings should be interpreted with great caution.

Altogether, an increase in efforts to promote resilience can be stated and considerable financial, material, and human resources are invested in mechanisms aimed at facilitating and bolstering resilience of service members, but there still seems to be an imbalance between this heavy investment and evidence-based documentation of the beneficial effects of these efforts. Specifically in a practice-oriented environment such as the military, facts and figures have to be delivered in order to gain and sustain the commitment of commanders and to prevent the outcome reported by Carr et al. (2013) in which the program was made voluntary for one unit and, when made voluntary, saw no participation. Thus, in addition to the pursuing efforts in evaluating the effects of resilience training, preferably conducting randomized control studies using rigorous designs, the expectations, attitudes, or even prejudices of the persons involved should be considered.

Building a Culture of Resilience

Any efforts toward enhancing resilience of individuals or groups must be accompanied with measures that create, facilitate, and maintain a resilience-promoting culture on the organizational as well as on the individual level. Previous experience with the CSF2 program made clear that a buy-in on all levels is indispensable. In this particular case the US Army Chief of Staff wanted to start this program and ensured his support (Casey, 2011). Furthermore, a strong strategic communication was necessary to win the commitment of leaders at all levels, but also of all the stakeholders in the military, media, and politics. In fact, it has been demonstrated that this is a selling point with the soldier's parents—they see that CSF2 trains the soldiers with the kinds of skills that will make them not just better soldiers but will also help them become better people (Cornum, 2012). However, the program must also guard against unrealistic expectations; it should rather promote a positive attitude toward psychological aspects and interventions.

For instance, despite considerable efforts such as the CSF2 program, mental health stigma continues to be a significant barrier to seeking help by service members (Bryan & Morrow, 2011). Resilience-engendering programs must still take this factor into account and consider ways to reduce those barriers. Measures such as emphasizing personal strengths—instead of trying to eliminate the weaknesses—and practical opportunities to improve them as well as situating the program close to physical training appear to be promising; in addition, practical barriers regarding leave, transportation, and child care, and the like must be reduced.

Mental barriers, which relate to the specific culture of the military or similar high-reliability organizations and the particular personality of its members are more difficult to address. For instance, organizations such as the military tend to overestimate planning and corresponding regulations. They foster a primarily zero-defect culture and therefore create plans to prepare for the inevitable, preempt the undesirable, and control the controllable. As rational this may sound, routine can't handle novel events, and human fallibility is like gravity, weather, and terrain—just another foreseeable hazard (Reason, 1997). Systems and organizations often respond to such disturbances with new rules and prohibitions designed to prevent the same disruption from happening in the future. But this kind of response reduces flexibility to deal with subsequent unpredictable changes. So, a resilient system, either an individual or an organization, bears the marks of its dealings with the unexpected not in the form of more elaborate defenses but in the form of more elaborate response capabilities (Sutcliffe & Vogus, 2003). In particular, this requires a *commitment* to resilience, where it is accepted that one will be surprised, so that persons concentrate on developing general resources to cope with and change swiftly. This commitment is difficult to sustain because one must keep learning without knowing in advance just what one will be learning and how it will be applied. However, this understanding of resilience does not ignore foresight and anticipation, but is mindful of its limitations (Weick & Sutcliffe, 2007), and leaders must be aware of these limitations.

Emotions are an integral part of resilience training since they are key for enhancing one's self-regulation competency. But traditionally military personnel have been encouraged and often trained to set emotions aside in the midst of the stressors of military life in general and even more so in deployment (Griffith & West, 2013). This is, therefore, another mental barrier to deal with, and, not surprisingly, resilience trainings contains several methods to detect, control, and use emotions in favor of the mission and the social environment.

In general, we have the tools to bolster resilience and to design bespoke trainings for organizations, groups, and individuals. Ordering resilience-building programs is the first step, but this first step will address mainly the participant's extrinsic motivation, and its effects might disappear quickly after the course ends. Therefore, the planning of such trainings should also focus on creating meaning, changing attitudes, and ensuring intrinsic motivation. To aid in this, Dweck's (1999) studies on performance versus mastery-goals offer a promising point of view. She demonstrated that people approaching a task with the attitude that intelligence is modifiable and that mistakes are a source for development, perform better than people who view intelligence as unchangeable and consider mistakes a relevant sign of one's performance capability. In brief, the inner attitude with which a person faces a challenge has a fundamental impact on the measurable result. As a consequence, besides the common routine of setting behavior-oriented goals, such as SMART goals (Locke & Latham, 1990), a general attitude, mainly driven by affects, should be considered. Although the statement "being resilient is important" is supported by most people and is cognitively connected with a positive attitude, this doesn't automatically result in resilient-promoting behavior. It is rather the affective attitude that stands for the power of a goal. So, it is of utmost importance that a person accepts the goal personally, and, accordingly first of all, the attitude has to be addressed. Only when on this level an affectively positive connoted goal exists should the relevant behavior be defined (Storch, 2009). In order to achieve the required positive affect, so-called *motto-goals* (Storch & Faude-Koivisto, 2014) have to be created. These are characterized as images, metaphors, or specific role models, and they help connect the conscious with the subconscious levels of the mental system as well as the extrinsic with the intrinsic motivation. Whenever resilience-building programs are applied, not only behavior-oriented SMART goals and "what if" plans have to be discussed, but also and above all motto-goals, which ensure a positive affective attitude regarding resilience.

To conclude, resilience is not only the sum of a disposition and the accumulation of trained behaviors but a specific *mindset* that impacts everyday decisions and actions.

And the Future?

Science rarely delivers clear results. The lack of an unequivocal measure of resilience and clear proof of the efficacy of resilience training should not be taken as an excuse for doing nothing. With its orientation on people's strengths, dealing with resilience takes us in the right direction and should always be considered in the realm of human performance optimization. Valid measuring instruments currently exist and can be used as a part of selection procedures, as a basis for self-reflection in the context of courses and trainings, or as a tool to evaluate the mental state of individuals or groups before, during, and after challenging experiences such as military deployment. Further research is needed specifically regarding the incremental validity of resilience measures in order to narrow down the construct of resilience more precisely or to better define which aspect of resilience should be measured in a given situation.

As the example of the US Army's Master Resilience Training shows impressively, there exist a plethora of theoretically well-founded training methods. However, the comparison with physical training speaks for itself: these methods are based on a long tradition of research in sports science and experiences in countless competitions on different levels; nevertheless, the outcome of physical training differs considerably since it depends on the individual's talent and disposition, the general motivation, the current health and mental state, and various environmental factors. Therefore, the expectations for the impact and effectiveness of resilience training should remain realistic. Applied to a large number of persons and as part of a prevention program, its economical balance might be preferable compared with the diagnosis–treatment approach. But this general assumption won't be sufficient to justify personal, financial, and temporal resources needed for such programs. Accordingly, in order to evaluate the impact of resilience, alternative methods and measures should be taken into account. For example, instead of comparing the well-being or optimism of participants before and after the training, which depends on several uncontrollable factors and/or reflects a general, rather vague mental state, one could focus on the reaction in relevant stress situations: a standardized stress test is administered prior to the resilience training where subjective (e.g., perceived stress, affectivity) as well as objective (e.g., heart rate variability, salivary α-amylase) stress measures are collected; after the resilience training the participants are exposed to the same stress test again and the application of the same measurement methods. They are then compared with a control group to determine how the resilience training could improve the stress reaction (see Annen & Boesch, 2014; La Marca et al., 2012).

Using the best measurement instruments and trainings methods won't elicit the desired effects when the organization and its members aren't ready to appreciate the value in dealing with resilience. Any intervention to implement resilience must be accompanied with actions which help to foster a beneficial culture in terms of resilience. This ranges from informing the executive level of the organization with the aim to ensure their goodwill and support of resilience-building programs to building an adequate attitude and mindset in individuals, which requires realistic expectations as well as visible and perceptible results.

With particular regard to human performance optimization there are additional fields of study worth considering. Due to its expected multiplication effect, the resilience of leaders should become a focus of attention. Whereas individual resilience can be reactive and doesn't always include social interaction, a leader must be proactive, especially in times of stress, and communication is one of his or her most important tools. This example suggests that the resilience of leaders has specific characteristics which should be addressed in research and practice, especially in high-reliability organizations.

FUTURE DIRECTIONS IN NONCOGNITIVE PERFORMANCE AMPLIFIERS

Given the complexity of human behavior, particularly so in challenging and dangerous situations, an expanded focus on noncognitive amplifiers in optimizing human performance offers the opportunity to more fully understand human behavior in high-threat, high-stakes settings. More than a century of research reliably shows that about 25% of human behavior may be attributed to talent, broadly defined. The research reviewed in this chapter represents advances that contribute toward identifying the factors that account for the remaining 75% of variation in performance. We do not propose that grit, hardiness, character strengths, and resilience are the only constructs that are relevant. Instead, we see a need for systematic research aimed at discovering and understanding the myriad of noncognitive contributors to human performance.

We also recognize a need for both basic and applied research in this area. For example, additional basic research on grit may clarify its genetic basis, how trainable it may be, and produce a reliable metric of team grit. Although a variety of character measures exist, they do not seem sensitive to developmental influence and can easily be faked. Similar to grit, more research is needed to fully identify how malleable character is and just what conditions set the occasion for meaningful character growth. Resilience is difficult to define and much is yet to be learned about its genetic, biological, cognitive, and social determinants.

Large-scale, integrative research projects are needed. At West Point, a 5-year longitudinal study of character assessment and development, called Project *Arete*, has been recently launched (Callina et al, 2017). Conducted by scientists from Tufts University, West Point, and a variety of other institutions, Project *Arete* will allow researchers to systematically explore the measurement and development of character in a sophisticated, longitudinal design. Similar studies conducted in other institutions and contexts are needed to better understand how to measure character and how to design educational systems to enhance it.

The potential of leveraging noncognitive factors to optimize human performance is largely untapped. And its impact may be substantial. Duckworth (2016) suggests that grit, for example, may "count" twice, compared to intelligence, in determining performance. It may also turn out that noncognitive factors are more malleable than intelligence, and through additional basic and applied research, new ways of optimizing individual and team performance may allow organizations to develop more effective strategies for improving and optimizing the performance of their workforces.

REFERENCES

American Psychological Association. (n.d.). *The Road to Resilience*. Retrieved from http://www.apa.org/helpcenter/road-resilience.aspx

Annen, H., & Boesch, M. (2014, October). Resilience as a predictor for military training outcomes. Presentation at the 56th Annual Conference of the International Military Testing Association, Hamburg, Germany.

Antonovsky, A. (1979). *Health, Stress and Coping*. San Francisco: Jossey-Bass.

Antonovsky, A. (1996). The salutogenic model as a theory to guide health promotion. *Health Promotion International, 11*, 11–18.

Baehr, J. (2013). Educating for intellectual virtues: From theory to practice. *Journal of Philosophy of Education, 47*, 248–262.

Bartone, P. T. (1995, July). *A short hardiness scale*. Paper presented at the annual convention of the American Psychological Society, New York, New York. Retrieved from http://www.dtic.mil/cgi-bin/GetTRDoc?AD=ADA298548

Bartone, P. T. (1999). Hardiness protects against war-related stress in Army reserve forces. *Consulting Psychology Journal: Practice and Research, 51*, 72–82.

Bartone, P. T., Kelly, D. R., & Matthews, M. D. (2013). Hardiness predicts adaptability in military leaders. *International Journal of Selection and Assessment, 21*, 200–210.

Berkowitz, M. W. (2011). What works in values education. *International Journal of Educational Research, 50*(3), 153–158.

Berkowitz, M. W. (2012). Moral and character education. In K. R. Harris, S. Graham, & T. Urdan (Eds.), *APA educational psychology handbook: Vol. 2. Individual differences and contextual factors* (pp. 247–264). Washington, DC: American Psychological Association.

Berkowitz, M. W., Althof, W., & Bier, M. C. (2012). The practice of pro-social education. In P. Brown, M. Corrigan, & A. Higgins-D'Alessandro (Eds.), *The Handbook of Prosocial Education: Volume 1* (pp. 71–90). Lanham MD: Rowman & Littlefield.

Berkowitz, M. W., Bier, M. C., & McCauley, B. (2016, July). *Effective features and practices that support character development.* Paper presented at the National Academies of Sciences, Engineering, and Medicine Workshop on Approaches to the Development of Character, Washington, D.C.

Brandtstädter, J. (1998). Action perspectives on human development. In R. M. Lerner (Ed.), *Handbook of Child Psychology* (5th ed., Vol. 1, pp. 807–866). New York: Wiley.

Bryan, C. J. & Morrow, C. E. (2011). Circumventing mental health stigma by embracing the warrior culture: Lessons learned from the Defender's Edge program. *Professional Psychology: Research and Practice, 42,* 16–23.

Callina, K. S., Ryan, D., Murray, E. D., Colby, A., Damon, W., Matthews, M., & Lerner, R. M. (2017). Developing leaders of character at the United States Military Academy: A relational developmental systems analysis. *Journal of College and Character, 18,* 9–27. doi:10.1080/2194587X.2016.1260475

Carr, W., Bradley, D., Ogle, A. D., Eonta, S. E., Pyle, B. L., & Santiago, P. (2013). Resilience training in a population of deployed personnel. *Military Psychology, 25,* 148–155.

Casey Jr., G. W. (2011). Comprehensive Soldier Fitness: A vision for psychological resilience in the US Army. *American Psychologist, 66,* 1–3.

Colby, A. (2008). Fostering the moral and civic development of college students. In L. Nucci & D. Narvaez (Eds.), *Handbook of Moral and Character Education* (pp. 391–413). Oxford: Routledge.

Connor, K. M., & Davidson, J. R. T. (2003). Development of a new resilience scale: The Connor-Davidson resilience scale (CD-RISC). *Depression and Anxiety, 18*(2), 76–82.

Cornum, R. (2012). "Does it really help . . . ?"—Resilience training in the US Army. In H. Annen (Ed.), *Psychische Widerstandskraft—Wesentliche Faktoren und Konsequenzen für die militärische Ausbildung und Führung* [Mental resilience—Relevant factors and consequences for military training and leadership]. *MILAK Schrift Nr. 14.* (pp. 81–89). Birmensdorf, Switzerland: Militärakademie an der ETH Zürich.

Cornum, R., Matthews, M. D., & Seligman, M. E. (2011). Comprehensive soldier fitness: Building resilience in a challenging institutional context. *American Psychologist, 66,* 4–9.

Costa, P. T., & McCrae, R. R. (1992). Normal personality assessment in clinical practice: The NEO Personality Inventory. *Psychological Assessment, 4,* 5–13.

Costa, P. T., Jr., McCrae, R. R., & Siegler, I. C. (1999). Continuity and change over the adult life cycle: Personality and personality disorders. In C. R. Cloninger (Ed.), *Personality and Psychopathology* (pp. 129—154). Washington, DC: American Psychiatric Press.

Damon, W. (2009). *The Path to Purpose: How Young People Find Their Calling in Life.* New York: Simon and Schuster.

Damon, W., & Colby, A. (2015). *The Power of Ideals: The Real Story of Moral Choice.* New York: Oxford University Press.

Duckworth, A. (2016). *Grit: The Power of Passion and Perseverance.* New York: Scribner.

Duckworth, A. L., Peterson, C., Matthews, M. D., & Kelly, D. R. (2007). Grit: Perseverance and passion for long term goals. *Journal of Personality and Social Psychology, 92,* 1087–1101.

Dweck, C. (1999). *Self-Theories: Their Role in Motivation, Personality, And Development.* Philadelphia: Psychology Press.

Elder, G. H., Shanahan, M. J., & Jennings, J. A. (2015). Human development in time and place. In M. H. Bornstein and T. Leventhal (Eds.), *Handbook of Child Psychology and Developmental Science, Volume 4: Ecological Settings and Processes* (7th ed., pp. 6–54). Editor-in-chief: R. M. Lerner. Hoboken, NJ: Wiley.

Farrington, C. A., Roderick, M., Allensworth, E., Nagaoka, J., Keyes, T. S., Johnson, D. W., & Beechum, N. O. (2012). *Teaching Adolescents to Become Learners. The Role of Noncognitive Factors in Shaping School Performance: A Critical Literature Review.* Chicago: University of Chicago Consortium on Chicago School Research.

Friborg, O., Hjemdal, O., Rosenvinge, J. H., & Martinussen, M. (2003). A new rating scale for adult resilience: What are the central protective resources behind healthy adjustment? *International Journal of Methods in Psychiatric Research, 12,* 65–76.

Griffith, J. & West, C. (2013). Master Resilience Training and its relationship to individual well-being and stress buffering among Army National Guard soldiers. *The Journal of Behavior Health Services & Research, 40,* 140–155.

Harms, P. D., Herian, M. N., Krasikova, D. V., Vanhove, A., & Lester, P. B. (2013). *The Comprehensive Soldier Fitness Program Evaluation. Report #4: Evaluation of Resilience Training and Mental and Behavioral Health Outcomes.* Monterey, CA: Research Facilitation Team (RFT).

Johnson, D. C., Polusny, M. A., Erbes, C. R., King, D., King, L., Litz, B. T., . . . Southwick, S. M. (2011). Development and initial validation of the Response to Stressful Experiences Scale. *Military Medicine, 176,* 161–169.

Johnson, S. K., Buckingham, M. H., Morris, S. L., Suzuki, S., Weiner, M. B., Hershberg, R. M., . . . Lerner, R. M. (2016). Adolescents' character role models: Exploring who young people look up to as examples of how to be a good person. *Research in Human Development, 13*(2), 126–141.

Kelly, D. R., Matthews, M. D., & Bartone, P. T. (2005). Hardiness and adaptation to a challenging military environment. *Proceedings of the International Applied Military Psychology Symposium.* Washington, DC: Walter Reed Army Institute of Research.

King L. A., & King, D. W. (2013). Measuring resilience and growth. In B. A. Moore & J. E. Barnett (Eds.), *Military Psychologists' Desk Reference* (pp. 301–305). New York: Oxford University Press.

Kobasa, S. C. (1979). Stressful life events, personality, and health-inquiry into hardiness. *Journal of Personality and Social Psychology, 37,* 1–11. doi:10.1037/0022-3514.37.1.1. PMID 458548

La Marca, R., Bösch, M., Sefidan, S., Annen, H., Wyss, Th., Mäder, U., Roos, L., & Ehlert, U. (2012). A decrease in perceived social support during military service is associated with a concomitant increase in baseline and decrease in stress reactivity levels of salivary alpha-amylase. *European Journal of Psychotraumatology (Suppl 1)*, 109.

Lazarus, R. S., & Folkman, S. (1984). *Stress Appraisal and Coping.* New York: Springer.

Leppin, A. L., Bora, P. R., Tilburt, J. C., Gionfriddo, M. R., Zeballos-Palacios, C., Dulohery, M. . . . Montori, V. M. (2014). The efficacy of resiliency training programs: A systematic review and meta-analysis of randomized trials. *PLOS ONE, 9*(10). doi:10.1371/journal.pone.0111420

Lerner, R. M. (2004). *Liberty: Thriving and Civic Engagement Among American Youth.* Thousand Oaks, CA: Sage.

Lerner, R. M., & Callina, K. S. (2014). The study of character development: Toward tests of a relational developmental systems model. *Human Development, 57*(6), 322–346.

Lester, B. M., Conradt, E., & Marsit, C. (2016). Introduction to the special section on epigenetics. *Child Development, 87* (1), 29–37.

Lester, P. B., Harms, P. D., Herian, M. N., Krasikova, D. V., & Beal, S. J. (2011). *The Comprehensive Soldier Fitness Program Evaluation. Report #3: Longitudinal Analysis of the Impact of Master Resilience Training on Self-Reported Resilience and Psychological Health Data.* Washington, DC: Department of the Army.

Lickona, T., & Davidson, M. (2005). *Smart and Good High Schools: Developing Excellence and Ethics for Success in School, Work and Beyond.* Cortland, NY: Center for the 4th and 5th Rs (Respect and Responsibility).

Locke, E., & Latham, G. (1990). *A Theory of Goal Setting and Task Performance.* Englewood Cliffs, NJ: Prentice Hall.

Lucini, B. (2014). *Disaster Resilience from a Sociological Perspective.* Heidelberg, Germany: Springer.

Maddi, S. R. (2012). *Hardiness: Turning Stressful Circumstances into Resilience Growth.* New York: Springer.

Maddi, S. R., Matthews, M. D., Kelly, D. R., Villarreal, B., & White, M. (2012). The role of hardiness and grit in predicting performance and retention of USMA cadets. *Military Psychology, 24,* 19–28.

Masten, A. S. (2001). Ordinary magic: Resilience-processes in development. *American Psychologist, 56,* 227–238.

Masten, A. S., & Obradovic, J. (2008). Disaster preparation and recovery: Lessons from research on resilience in human development. *Ecology and Society, 13* (1), 9.

McGrath, R. E. (2015). Integrating psychological and cultural perspectives on virtue: The hierarchical structure of character strengths. *The Journal of Positive Psychology, 10,* 407–424.

Meaney, M. J. (2010). Epigenetics and the biological definition of gene x environment interactions. *Child Development, 81*(1), 41–79.

Meichenbaum, D. (2013). Ways to bolster resilience across the deployment cycle. In B. A. Moore & J. E. Barnett (Eds.), *Military Psychologists' Desk Reference* (pp. 325–328). New York: Oxford University Press.

Meredith, L. S., Sherbourne, C. D., Gaillot, S., Hansell, L., Ritschard, H. V., Parker, A. M., & Wrenn, G. (2011). *Promoting psychological resilience in the US Military.* Santa Monica, CA: RAND Corporation.

Misteli, T. (2013). The cell biology of genomes: Bringing the double helix to life. *Cell, 152*(6), 1209–1212.

Neisser, U., Boodoo, G., Bouchard Jr, T. J., Boykin, A. W., Brody, N., Ceci, S. J., . . . Urbina, S. (1996). Intelligence: Knowns and unknowns. *American Psychologist, 51,* 77–101. doi: 10.1037/0003-066X.51.2.77

Nucci, L. (2016, July). *Character: A multi-faceted developmental system.* Paper presented at the National Academies of Sciences, Engineering, and Medicine Workshop on Approaches to the Development of Character, Washington, DC.

Nucci, L. (2017). Character: A multifaceted developmental system. *Journal of Character Education, 13*(1), 1–16.

Nucci, L. & Narvaez, D. (2008). Introduction and overview. In L. Nucci & D. Narvaez (Eds.), *Handbook of Moral and Character Education* (pp. 1–7). Oxford: Routledge.

Pangallo, A., Zibarras, L., Lewis, R., & Flaxman, P. (2015). Resilience through the lens of interactionism: A systematic review. *Psychological Assessment, 27*, 1–20.

Peterson, C., Park, N., & Castro, C. A. (2011). Assessment for the US Army Comprehensive Soldier Fitness program: the Global Assessment Tool. *American Psychologist, 66* (*1*), 10–18.

Peterson, C., & Seligman, M. E. P. (2004). *Character Strengths and Virtues: A Handbook and Classification*. Washington, DC: American Psychological Association.

Reason, J. T. (1997). *Managing the Risks of Organizational Accidents*. Brookfield, VT.: Ashgate.

Reivich, K., & Shatté, A. (2003). *The Resilience Factor*. New York: Broadway Books.

Reivich, K. J., Seligman, M. E. P., & McBride, S. (2011). Master Resilience Training in the US Army. *American Psychologist, 66*, 25–34.

Robins, R. W., John, O. P., Caspi, A., Moffitt, T. E., & Stouthamber-Loeber, M. (1996). Resilient, overcontrolled, and undercontrolled boys: Three replicable personality types. *Journal of Personality & Social Psychology, 70*, 157–171.

Rumsey, Michael G. (2012). Military selection and classification in the United States. In J. H. Laurence & M. D. Matthews (Eds.), *The Oxford Handbook of Military Psychology* (pp. 129–147). New York: Oxford University Press.

Schumacher, J., Leppert, K., Gunzelmann, T., Strauss, B., and Brähler, E. (2004). *Die Resilienzskala—Ein Fragebogen zur Erfassung der psychischen Widerstandsfähigkeit als Personmerkmal* [The resilience scale—A questionnaire to measure mental resilience as a personality trait]. Retrieved from the European Network for Mental Health Promotion: http://www.mentalhealthpromotion.net/resources/resilienzskala2.pdf

Seider, S. (2012). *Character Compass: How Powerful School Culture Can Point Students Toward Success*. Cambridge, MA: Harvard Education Press.

Slavich, G. M., & Cole, S. W. (2013). The emerging field of human social genomics. *Clinical Psychological Science, 1*(3), 331–348.

Smith, B. W., Dalen, J., Wiggins, K., Tooley, E., Christopher, P., & Bernard, J. (2008). The brief resilience scale: Assessing the ability to bounce back. *International Journal of Behavioral Medicine, 15*, 194–200.

Sokol, B. W., Hammond, S. I., & Berkowitz, M. W. (2010). The developmental contours of character. In T. Lovat, R. Toomey, & N. Clement (Eds.), *International Research Handbook on Values Education and Student Wellbeing* (pp. 579–603). Dordrecht, Netherlands: Springer.

Soucek, R., Ziegler, M., Schlett, C., & Pauls, N. (2016). Resilienz im Arbeitsleben—Eine inhaltliche Differenzierung von Resilienz auf den Ebenen von Individuen, Teams und Organisationen [Resilience in the working life—A differentiation of resilience on the individual, team, and organizational level]. *Gruppe. Interaktion. Organisation, 47*, 131–137.

Storch, M. (2009). Motto-Ziele, S.M.A.R.T.-Ziele und Motivation [Motto-Goals, S.M.A.R.T.-Goals, and Motivation]. In B. Birgmeier (Ed.), *Coachingwissen: Denn sie wissen nicht, was sie tun?* (pp. 183–205). Wiesbaden, Germany: Verlag für Sozialwissenschaften.

Storch, M., & Faude-Koivisto, T. (2014). Ressourcen aktivieren mit Mottozielen [Activating resources with motto-goals]. In A. Ryba, D. Pauw, D. Ginati, & S. Rietmann (Eds.), *Professionell coachen* (pp. 334–347). Weinheim, Germany: Beltz.

Sutcliffe, K. M., & Vogus, T. J. (2003). Organizing for resilience. In K. S. Cameron, J. E. Dutten, & R. E. Quinn (Eds.), *Positive Organizational Scholarship* (pp 94–110). San Francisco, CA: Berrett-Koehler.

Vanhove, A. J., Herian, M. N., Perez, A. L. U., Harms, P. D., & Lester, P. B. (2015). Can resilience be developed at work? A meta-analytic review of resilience-building programme effectiveness. *Journal of Occupational and Organizational Psychology, 89,* 278–307.

Waaktaar, T., & Torgersen, S. (2010). How resilient are resilience scales? The Big Five scales outperform resilience in predicting adjustment in adolescents. *Scandinavian Journal of Psychology, 51,* 157–163.

Wagnild, G. M., & Young, H. M. (1993). Development and psychometric evaluation of the Resilience Scale. *Journal of Nursing Measurement, 1,* 165–177.

Weick, K. E., & Sutcliffe, K. M. (2007). *Managing the Unexpected: Resilient Performance in an Age of Uncertainty* (2nd ed). San Francisco, CA: Jossey-Bass.

Werner, E. E., Bierman, J. M., & French, F. E. (1971). *The Children of Kauai: A Longitudinal Study from the Prenatal Period to Age Ten.* Honolulu: University of Hawaii Press.

Windle, G., Bennett, K. M., & Noyes, J. (2011). A methodological review of resilience measurement scales. *Health and Quality of Life Outcomes, 9:8.* doi:10.1186/1477-7525-9-8

Wyss, T. & Annen, H. (2011). *PROGRESS—Einfluss von progressiv aufgebauter körperlicher Belastung, Sport und Führungsstil auf Fitness, Verletzungen, Austritte, militärische Leistungsfähigkeit, Stress und Motivation bei Schweizer Rekruten* [PROGRESS—The impact of progressive increased physical strain, sport, and leadership styles on fitness, injuries, attrition, military performance, stress, and motivation in Swiss Army recruits]. Magglingen/Birmensdorf: Interne Studie BASPO/MILAK.

17

Leading Teams to Optimize Performance

LISSA V. YOUNG

INTRODUCTION

This chapter examines how human performance can be influenced, both negatively and positively, by teams. Individuals often choose to engage in extreme settings as a way of conquering a challenge or satisfying a calling. In the history of the human endeavor toward greatness, humans often form teams to achieve outrageous goals. Ancient mariners sailed ships into the vast unknown together. Eskimos journeyed across the continental icepack as collections of villages. Astronauts catapulted toward the cosmos in teams. Rarely have humans achieved greatness alone. Almost every monumental achievement has resulted from the carefully coordinated efforts of many. This chapter discusses key elements of team performance by way of deconstructing them into their component parts and then examining how those parts can be put together through performance optimizing processes. This chapter suggests ways a leader can deliberately design teams to optimize human performance.

This book considers both the cognitive and the neurological aspects of human performance, both of which are influenced by the social psychological aspects of being a team member. This chapter is a practitioner's guide to understanding how that influence takes place. Leaders who better understand those influence pathways are more able to create the conditions for optimal team performance.

All leaders are concerned with their organization's overall effectiveness. Organizational effectiveness is a product of the complicated interplay of the organization's members in their subunits. Teams comprise many of these subunits and, as such, are critical to organizational performance. Therefore, leaders must focus their team leading efforts on optimizing both individual *and* team performance. Leaders must be able to create the capacity for greatness in their teams. Additionally, leaders must be able to launch, lead, and disband teams, as the situation requires. These tasks depend on a sophisticated understanding of teams as theoretical and practical organizational entities.

In many ways, "team life" has become synonymous with "organizational life." Given the ubiquity of teams and their importance to organizational performance, it is essential to understand how they work and how they are affected by the dynamic landscape of organizational and interpersonal relationships. Although we value diversity in team composition, that diversity comes with its own challenges for interpersonal relations and, therefore, the team's performance. Of specific interest are the ways in which leaders can optimize team performance by understanding and managing team dynamics.

The following factors and processes have been shown to enhance team performance:

1. Teams as open systems
2. Team composition
3. Team norms
4. Team member roles and status
5. Team processes
6. The importance of effective socialization on teams
7. The delicate relationship between developing highly cohesive teams, and managing intergroup conflict
8. The dynamics of group decision-making
9. The team's effects on individuals
10. Team performance

The process of understanding and influencing individual behavior, even in isolation, is difficult and complex. In our roles as team leaders, we rarely lead individuals, but rather groups of individuals. These groups can develop and exhibit behavioral patterns that may not be inferred by the characteristics of individuals alone. For example, a decision-making team formed of members with very diverse backgrounds, ages, and experiences may be very good at solving complex problems, but may experience constant conflict among members when the group confronts simple or routine tasks (Ancona & Caldwell, 1992; Mannix & Neale, 2005).

In a highly cohesive unit, the group as a whole may be able to accomplish what the individuals by themselves could not. However, an organization's leadership faces great challenges when confronted with a highly cohesive group that has goals and norms that are incongruent with those of the organization. In each of these cases, we must understand and manage group processes in order to satisfy individual, group, and organizational expectations.

Effective leaders must be capable of pulling together individuals of diverse backgrounds, personalities, abilities, training, and experience and molding them into a cohesive, high performing team. The challenge is to bring all of the unique contributions of people together in such a way that the whole will equal more than simply the sum of the parts. Ardant Du Picq (1921/1987) best captures this notion: Four brave men who do not know each other will not dare to attack a lion. Four less brave men, but knowing each other well, sure of their reliability and consequently of mutual aid, will attack resolutely.

With the implementation of the cohesion, operational readiness, and training (COHORT) manning system in the mid-1980s, the Army made great strides in providing the resources and policies that support team formation and development. However, policies and raw materials alone were not enough. Research from the field indicated that one of the key factors in determining effectiveness among COHORT units was the unit leader's ability to understand and harness the power of groups.

The following passage from D. H. Marlow (1987) of the Walter Reed Army Institute of Research highlights this finding:

> Interviews and observations summarized in this report repeatedly come back to company/battery (leadership) policies and practices which either enhance or inhibit the potential of COHORT (cohesion, operational readiness, and training). The COHORT process cannot substitute for good leadership but may, to a limited degree, compensate for leadership deficiencies. (p. 2)

Part of the answer to why some COHORT commanders could better harness the potential assets of their units may lie in their own ability to fully grasp and take advantage of the dynamic process of how groups form, develop, and perform.

In this chapter, I discuss four theories of group behavior. The first two are based upon bonds that develop among group members. These bonds exist both horizontally among peers and vertically between superiors and subordinates. The third theory deals with problems that arise when the bonds among subgroups decay. When this occurs, specific strategies can be employed to restore those disintegrating bonds. Last, I introduce models of individual and group decision-making and how these can affect group dynamics.

This chapter examines a variety of perspectives that help explain the influence of Group Processes on individual behavior and vice versa. At the conclusion of this chapter, you should have a better understanding of how the different elements of groups and teams influence each other and develop the synergy that is characteristic of effective group functioning.

Teams are often touted as a way to increase or enhance organizational performance and yet both research and anecdotal evidence suggest that they often fail to do so. While there are a number of reasons why teams may not succeed in producing optimal performance, one particularly salient issue is the underutilization of team members' knowledge and skills (Hackman, 2002). It is well documented that team members are often unable to capitalize fully on the team's collective knowledge due to members' inability see beyond each other's specific *status characteristics* (such as gender, race, or social status) to leverage each other's task-relevant knowledge, skills, and abilities (Foschi, Warriner, & Hart, 1985). This oversight can leave much of the team's talent untapped, potentially hindering the team's performance (Kochan et al., 2003).

Although this tendency of team members to focus more on colleagues' demographics than potential intellectual contributions abounds, researchers tend to promote the virtues of team diversity while overlooking the ways that these cognitive classifications (i.e., "stereotypes") can potentially undermine the benefits that diverse teams may offer. One exception comes from status characteristics theory, in which Berger, Cohen, and Zelditch (1972) offer an account of how biased evaluations can occur in team settings. Their theory explores how group members use status differences to determine perceived competence, as well as expectations for the performance abilities of fellow team members. These performance expectations, in turn, affect the power and prestige orders of these groups (Berger, Norman, Balkwell, & Smith, 1992; Berger, Ridgeway, Fisek, & Norman, 1998; Foschi, 1992, 2000), and these critical group dynamics impact the team's performance. Hence, status characteristics theory offers a compelling, but arguably somewhat inadequate, lens through which to examine the impact of diversity on teams. Despite its contributions, status characteristics theory, like many traditional approaches to studying team diversity, tends to limit its focus to single diversity attributes.

In reality, diversity is both multidimensional and complex (i.e., people hold and represent multiple identities simultaneously, and others experience these identities in different ways). This suggests a need for a theory and analytic approach that can address this complexity (Garcia-Prieto, Bellard, & Schneider, 2003). However, in much of the research on stereotyping and team performance, social scientists tend to examine specific sources of bias independently (Bantel & Jackson, 1989; Chatman, Polzer, Barsade, & Neale, 1998; Apesteguia, Azmat, & Iriberri, 2012; Newhesier & Dovidio, 2012). Some researchers suggest this trend is a logical extension of the way that prominent empirical work on diversity has been framed (Alise & Teddlie, 2010; Bryman, Collinson, Grint, Jackson, & Uhl-Bien, 2011). A vast majority of research on stereotyping and prejudice in teams is based in social identity and social categorization theories, both of which presuppose readily detectable diversity such as sex, race, and age. This has created a strong theoretical rationale for focusing on independent, category-specific sources of diversity (Brewer & Pierce, 2005; Wells & Aicher, 2013; Williams & O'Reilly, 1998).

Although it makes sense conceptually that individual diversity attributes influence team outcomes, they do not act in isolation and, because of this, there is a need to empirically assess the multidimensionality of diversity (Jackson, Joshi, & Erhardt, 2003). People have multiple identities operating simultaneously (Garcia-Prieto et al., 2003), and, because of this, the total impact of different sources of stereotyping on team performance is different from that of just a single individual. By focusing on the whole of a variety of sources of interpersonal bias, we can obtain a more realistic view of its impact on team performance.

A TAXONOMY OF TEAMS

Understanding teams and team processes is extremely difficult. A taxonomy or framework helps isolate the complexities of teams so that the informed and reflective leader can accurately determine how to use the team's capabilities to optimize performance and, therefore, best benefit the organization.

An open systems model views teams as living, dynamic systems that take inputs (people and situations), process them (through team structural dimensions), and produce outputs (performance, effects on individuals, and effects on the team). Refer to Figure 17.1 and Figure 17.2. Figure 17.1 is the framework that informed the development of Figure 17.2. Both provide excellent graphical representations of the architecture of teams. These frameworks help us better understand the individual elements and interactions within teams, which influence their performance. Within these frameworks, the team inputs consist of both situational and individual characteristics. The throughput processes comprise two key elements. The first is the

The Conditions for Team Effectiveness

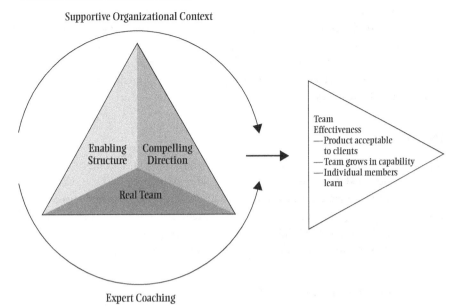

Figure 17.1 A taxonomy of teams.
Reprinted from J. Richard Hackman, *Leading Teams: Setting the Stage for Great Performances*. Harvard Business Press Books, 2002, all rights reserved.

An Open Systems Model of Groups

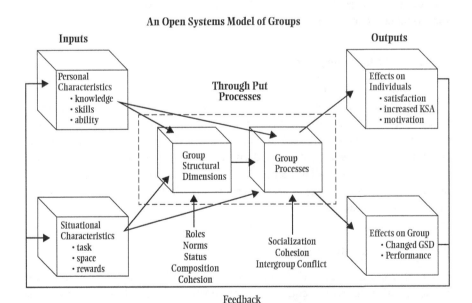

Figure 17.2 A model for groups as open systems.
Image created by the members of the Department of Behavioral Sciences and Leadership, United States Military Academy, West Point, NY, 1996.

team's structural dimensions, which are the team's composition, the team's formal and informal norms, individual team member status, and various team member roles. The second element of the team's throughput process is the team processes. These processes consist of the ways the team members interact with one another. Team processes include socialization, cohesion, and interteam conflict. This framework and its dimensions help us understand how teams function, make decisions, and maintain themselves.

INPUTS

Inputs to the team's throughput processes are those factors relevant to each team member's personal characteristics, including what they bring to the team in terms of personality, knowledge, skills, abilities, and qualities. The situation faced by the team is another input. This refers to environmental factors such as the nature of the team's task and the helpfulness of the team's workspace, as well as motivational factors such as the absence or presence of punishments and rewards.

Personal Characteristics

The inputs of this framework consist of the personal characteristics of the individual team members. Personal or individual characteristics include the individual strengths and weaknesses (knowledge, skills, abilities, biases, values, and beliefs) that people bring to the team. The caliber of the team's inputs has a tremendous impact on the team's performance outcomes. It is generally easier to achieve top team performance when you start with superior team inputs.

Situational Characteristics

The second aspect of the inputs to the teams as open systems model is the situational characteristics. From the physical surroundings to the size of the team itself, many factors influence how teams behave. In this model, these characteristics consist of the team's task, the physical space in which the team operates, and the reward system that is leveraged to incentivize teams. Consider the critical impact that the nature of the task itself has on teams. A competitive cycling team that is highly successful at accomplishing its racing strategies might fail miserably at the task of completing a crossword puzzle.

THROUGHPUT PROCESSES

The next major dimension of the open systems model of teams is the throughput processes. This dimension consists of two constructs internal to team dynamics. The first is the team's structural dimensions, such as the team members' roles, team norms, team members' status, team composition, and team cohesion. The second dimension is the team's processes. These consist of socialization, cohesion, and intergroup conflict management. When orchestrated effectively, these elements combine to optimize any team's performance.

Group Structural Dimensions

A single dimension by itself does not always spell success or failure for a team. High cohesion can have both positive and negative effects on team processes and performance, and these can be moderated by the team's cohesion and norms. Low performance norms combined with high cohesion typically can mean complications for a leader, while high cohesion and high-performance norms usually lead to high performing teams (Evans & Davis, 2005). Structural dimensions have an impact on performance because they affect the intervening variable called *group processes*.

Group Processes

Group processes influence a team's dimensions regardless of how mature the team is. Team members might interact with each other inconsistently, stable communication patterns form that may or may not reflect formal organizational lines, informal leaders emerge, cliques may form, some people on the team may become more powerful. Teams themselves may become major sources of rewards or punishments for individual members. These are all examples of group processes. Each example in turn may have either a positive or a negative effect on whether the team succeeds in its organizationally appointed mission.

Group processes evolve and change over the life of the team. What is an important issue early in the life of a team might be a "non-issue" at some later point. As teams mature, they pass through somewhat predictable stages of development. Knowing where a team is in its development helps leaders understand what is needed to help the team progress to more mature stages. However, it is difficult to understand what stage a team is in without first understanding the basic building blocks of teams: *group structural dimensions*.

Team structural dimensions and team processes form the center of this group system. They are interdependent, and a small change in one can have a major impact on the other. For example, certain subgroups within a team may constantly argue or compete with each other in a manner that is dysfunctional to the team's overall mission. From this observation of group process, an observer could infer that this team's problems might be due to low cohesiveness and dysfunctional norms about competition and cooperation. Altering group structural dimensions to fix this problem can potentially make the group processes support the mission instead of hindering it.

The third major dimension of the open systems model of teams is in the outputs that follow from the team's processes. As the model illustrates, there are two categories of outputs. These outputs follow directly from our definition of organizational effectiveness. We are concerned with the effect the group has on individual members and the effect the group has on the organizational mission because leaders must close the gap between individual and organizational needs. Members often join teams voluntarily because membership fills an individual need or desire (Hackman, 2002). These members will not hesitate to quit a club or informal group that becomes a burden or is dissatisfying. Some will quit mentally or psychologically if the team no longer meets their needs. Therefore, team leaders must be concerned with the team's impact on member growth and satisfaction. In addition to satisfaction, groups can either enhance or attenuate individual member knowledge, skills, and abilities. Many teams form primarily for these reasons (Hackman, 2002). Fitness groups, chess clubs, and study groups are examples of these types of groups. On the other hand, you have probably belonged to at least one team where you could not seem to live up to your potential or where you were stifled, bored, or frustrated. Good team leaders strive to meet the needs of their team members so that they in turn can live up to their potential.

On the other side of the leadership gap is the organization's mission. Some teams are not formed for fun and fellowship; they are organized, equipped, and trained to accomplish an assigned task. Therefore, the process of effective leadership is about influencing the team to accomplish its assignment to the highest possible standards of performance. Related to the accomplishment of the task, one effect that groups have through structure and process are changes to the group itself. New norms form over time. Status in the organization may shift as members spend more time together. Roles are altered and adjusted (perhaps in response to personnel turbulence). These outputs are evaluated and fed back into the team. The parent organization might reward high rates of success. These rewards are perceived as a change in the team's situational characteristics. If one output from the team is the production of better, smarter, more technically competent team members, then, when considering the group over time, the individual inputs may have shifted dramatically. This feedback process is what makes groups dynamic and is fundamental to their growth and development over time.

Research on team dynamics has identified patterns of team interaction that can be used to chart and forecast a team's development. These patterns involve the resolution of issues associated with engaging in the team's work and getting along with others (Mannix & Neale, 2005). In the study of the stages of team development, we learn how to recognize these patterns. The better our understanding of the issues that arise at the various stages of team development, the more effective our leader actions will be in addressing team issues. Be cautious in making a general classification of a team based on this framework because different subteams within your organization may be at different stages of development. Additionally, a fully formed and mature team may experience different stages of development depending on the task they are assigned.

SOCIALIZATION

Socialization is a complex and critical task for organizational leaders. Socialization is the process of teaching members of a group or organization what they need to know in order to maintain team membership. It is the process through which an individual is prepared to meet the requirements demanded by members of the team or organization. Socialization processes affect values, needs and drives, social roles and identities, self-conception, and the general manner in which business is conducted in teams. Socialization is the acquisition by individuals of a considerable range of qualities that guide their behavior in group and organizational contexts.

Moreland and Levine (1982) suggested that there are three basic reciprocal processes occurring in group socialization: evaluation, commitment, and role transition. Evaluation involves the group and the individual appraising each other.

Commitment involves how strongly tied the individual is to the group and how strongly tied the group is to its individual members. Finally, all group members have roles within the group. The group and the individuals negotiate the role that each member plays in the group. In role transition, Moreland and Levine examine how the group and its group members negotiate three type of roles: nonmembers, quasi-members, and full members. Nonmembers constitute anybody not part of the group, such as former members and prospective members. "Quasi-members occupy a role that lies at the margins of the group, for they have either not yet been granted full membership or are being pushed out of the group by the others" (Forsyth, 2009, p. 95). Full members have all the rights and responsibilities associated with the group.

Three processes are used to explain the socialization process for a new member.

Investigation Stage

In this stage, newcomers are engaged in reconnaissance. They are trying to decide which group fits their individual needs. There are various ways newcomers can learn about a particular group: they can talk to current or former members or read available literature on the group. If group members engage in recruitment, they are trying to decide which newcomers should be invited into the group. There are many possible recruitment techniques, such as inviting newcomers for an interview or talking to other group members who know the newcomers. If this stage is successful then the newcomers moves from a non-member status to becoming a quasi-member (i.e., a new member). This point is called *entry* (Moreland & Levine, 1982).

Socialization begins well before members enter a particular group. In the investigation stage of socialization, members are receiving information about the group's norms, history, culture, and structure. This information, accurate or not, is often the basis from which new members create their own expectations about entry into the organization. Good organizations select sponsors to serve as role models for new members, helping to ensure that the prospective member has accurate information about the new organization. The role models also ease the member's transition and reduce the natural feelings of stress and anxiety of team entry.

Socialization Stage

Two main processes occur in the socialization stage: assimilation and accommodation. In assimilation, newcomers learn and accept the "norms, values and perspectives" (Forsyth, 2009, p. 97) of the group. In accommodation, the group adjusts itself to fit the needs of the newcomers. The amount of accommodation and assimilation that occurs in a group need not be an even trade. There are many circumstances in which a group demands a great deal of assimilation but produces very little accommodation and vice-versa. For example, a military basic training platoon demands a great deal of assimilation of its new recruits and offers very little accommodation for them. On the other hand, a high school acting club is very accommodating of its new members and demands far less assimilation. If the newcomers and group members agree on the appropriate amounts of assimilation and accommodation, then the newcomers move from quasi-members to full members. This point is called *acceptance*.

New team members must be oriented to organizational goals and priorities. If applicable, the assigned individual sponsor can accomplish much of this. However, key organizational leaders should give some type of formal in-briefing to new members. Periodic information briefings should also be conducted to ensure that new and senior members of the organization understand current priorities. Leaders must also facilitate mutual acceptance by both the individual and the group. This can be accomplished through several methods, including a social activity to welcome newcomers, an introduction of the newcomer to the group, an indoctrination period, or an acceptance/initiation or induction ceremony.

Maintenance Stage

Once a newcomer has become a full member, the role negotiation process begins. In role negotiation, group members "negotiate the nature and quantity of each member's expected contribution to the group" (Forsyth, 2009, p. 97). For example, group members must negotiate who will lead and who will follow. In some organizations, this negotiation is less apparent because they have highly formalized hierarchical structures that dictate who leads and who follows. However, there are always informal and emerging leaders within these structured groups. Many group members stay in the maintenance stage the entire time they are in a group. For example, a basketball player may stay with a team for his or her entire career. However, sometimes a tension builds in the maintenance stage because role negotiation has not been accomplished. For example, a person who wishes to lead might be assigned a follower's role. Perhaps team members are not following the norms and values of the group and therefore are engaging in inappropriate behavior. When this occurs, a full member may move back to a point of being a quasi-member (i.e., marginal member). This point is called *divergence*.

Resocialization Stage

Once a group member reverts to being a quasi-member, two possible courses of action can occur. *Convergence* happens when, through the process of accommodation and assimilation, the group members and the quasi-member resolve their issues. Alternatively, when the group and the quasi-member are unable to resolve the problems, the final transition point of *exit* is reached.

Remembrance Stage

The remembrance stage encompasses two possible processes: *tradition* and *reminiscence* (Moreland & Levine, 1982). In *tradition*, the group members discuss the person who left the group, including the topics of the former member's contribution to the group and why he or she left. If the person left because of a failure to be resocialized, then this tradition process can take on a negative tone. In *reminiscence*, the group members who left think about their contributions to the group and the reasons why they left.

Socialization also occurs when members leave the organization. Are these departing members recognized for their achievements? This is often done at a farewell party or ceremony. Are the departing members afforded the opportunity to communicate to the organization whatever lessons, problems, and insights they gleaned while in the organization? This is often accomplished by an out-briefing to the organizational leader. Or are departing members treated like "lame ducks" and not afforded the opportunity to pass on their perspectives? Are they recognized for their contributions? The answers to these questions may shed light on the effectiveness of the organization's socialization processes and how such processes can affect members of the group, the group itself, and the accomplishment of the group's goals.

COHESION

Carl von Clausewitz wrote in his classic, *On War* (1873):

> An army that maintains its cohesion under the most murderous fire; that cannot be shaken by imaginary fears and resists well-founded ones with all its might; that is proud of its victories . . . whose physical power, like the muscles of an athlete, has been steeled by training in privation and effort; a force that regards such efforts as a means to victory rather than a curse on its cause; that is mindful of all these duties and qualities. . . such an army is imbued with the true military spirit. (p. 255)

Extensive research concludes that leaders' understanding of cohesion and its outcomes is central to effective and sustained organizational performance (Wageman, Nunes, Burruss, & Hackman, 2008). Therefore, a more complete understanding of groups requires a closer examination of those factors that both contribute to and detract from cohesion and the effects that cohesion has on the organization, its members and their performance.

The degree to which members are attracted to and remain in a group is often called *cohesion*. In other words, cohesion is the strength by which a group is "glued together." We should expect that highly cohesive teams would show greater levels of mutual respect, trust, confidence, and understanding. These intangibles are difficult to observe and measure. However, since a highly cohesive group is one that is "glued" tightly together, we should observe members showing greater care about the group and stronger commitment to it. From this, we would expect that these members place more energy, both physical and psychological, into group activities. With more energy from members, these teams will have more collective resources to devote to team activities, efforts and goals. Out of these observations are derived the common indicators of group cohesion (Moreland & Levine, 1982).

Greater Interaction and Communication

We expect that members of a close-knit group would communicate more with each other. Because they value the group, they are more willing to take part in the group's efforts and activities, and this causes more interaction (although this is task-dependent). It has been shown that the greater the cohesion, the greater the communication activity between members in the group. Cohesive groups also meet more, and this naturally adds to the communication and interaction of members (Aries, 1976).

In highly cohesive groups, all members participate more. The quality of communication is characterized by greater cooperation and friendliness and is oriented toward keeping the group together. In low-cohesive groups, members are less cooperative, tend to keep comments that relate to group performance to themselves, and are more aggressive in the way they respond to group interaction. There is a reciprocal relationship between a group's communication and interaction processes. The more cohesive a group is, the greater the quantity and quality of its communications, and this builds even greater cohesion (Aries, 1976).

Power of the Team over Its Members

When members are committed to their group, they are more willing to make personal changes, and even sacrifices, to remain an active part of the group (Moreland & Levine, 1982). This allows the group to have power over the opinions and behavior of its members. Highly cohesive groups exert strong pressure on group members to conform to the group's opinions, attitudes, and behaviors.

Another interesting facet of the group's power over its members is that highly cohesive groups increase their members' ability to resist external pressures as well as internal pressures placed on them. When a team is very cohesive, it can tolerate more resistance, stress, and even internal rebellion without risking disintegration. Less cohesive teams disintegrate more quickly under both internal and external scrutiny. In highly cohesive groups, members value their belonging to the group to the point of a great willingness to change themselves and tolerate others to remain in the group (Moreland & Levine, 1982).

Goal Attainment

It is somewhat intuitive that highly cohesive groups will be more successful at directing group efforts and energy toward attainment of group goals. Experience in athletic competition tells us that a team's cohesiveness can make the difference between winning and losing. That is why one of the fundamentals of team training is building teamwork (Stout, Salas, & Fowlkes, 1997).

However, teams do not always set goals that the organization desires. If a highly cohesive group sets productivity and successful organizational performance as its goals, then these goals will attain more than low-cohesive groups. However, leaders must be wary of cohesive groups that choose dysfunctional norms and eschew performance standards that are aligned with their organization's goals. A leader's greatest challenge may be redirecting a highly cohesive group with dysfunctional performance norms toward organizationally desired goals and objectives.

Member Satisfaction

When there is much interaction and cooperative communication among group members, there is bound to be a sense of member satisfaction from being part of the group. In those moments of triumph when we belong to a team in which everybody pulls together to accomplish some difficult mission, there is indeed great satisfaction.

Team Loyalty and Identification

Teams that offer satisfaction and invoke power over members' opinions and actions also inspire greater loyalty from their members. This in turn leads the group to spend less effort in maintaining its membership (effort that in turn can be directed toward goal accomplishment). Military history is full of examples of soldiers from highly cohesive units fighting tenaciously because of their unit's lineage and tradition. At the battle of Rorke's Drift in 1879 (Zulu–British War), in which 11 Victoria Crosses were awarded (Britain's highest award for combat bravery), 139 British soldiers withstood and defeated a Zulu force of more than 4,000 warriors. During the battle, the British colors were the rallying point for the small surrounded British garrison, and many soldiers gave their lives keeping the colors up in plain view on the battlefield.

Elaborate Norms and Practices

When a group achieves high cohesion, we begin to see extensive behavioral routines and practices that members perform together to express their group uniqueness and identification. Examples might be informal initiations such as the famous *Prop Blasts* that military airborne units conduct for their new officers, or even simple inside jokes and ways of kidding one another. Often there are enigmatic rituals and symbols that group members adopt to represent themselves. These norms and practices help members to establish a psychological "we–they" boundary between themselves and the rest of the world. In the common indicators of cohesion there is a circular, mutually reinforcing relationship. As a group becomes more cohesive, it creates and develops these unique norms and practices, and these practices in turn fuel cohesion (Hogg & Terry, 2000).

INTERGROUP CONFLICT MANAGEMENT

One of the goals of leaders is to build cohesive, high-performing teams. Competition between functional groups can benefit the overall organization, but competition becomes conflict when it is dysfunctional (i.e., when it impacts negatively upon performance). Sometimes units within an organization develop differing views on what is and is not important to success. Most of the time the problem is not a villainous scheme to subvert the organization, but an honest difference in what is seen to be the best way to get the job done. In order to avoid this type of calamity, it is important to identify present and potential sources of conflict, as well as strategies that can be used to prevent or recover from dysfunctional conflict.

The symptoms of conflict are sometimes blatant and obvious, such as physical fights or arguments between individuals or groups. It can also be subtler. When one work unit sabotages the work of another, then intergroup conflict has become dysfunctional. In each case, the leader must find a way to manage conflict.

There are seven sources of intergroup conflict identified in the literature on teams (Fischer, 2006; Associates, the Department of Behavioral Sciences and Leadership, 1988). The first is called *goal orientation*. When teams focus on different end-states, they can often come into conflict with one another. In a resource-constrained environment, which leaders often face, it is imperative that teams align themselves toward a single goal, or at least mutually reinforcing goals, so that resources can be expended prudently. In this way, an organization does not have to expend precious resources toward bifurcated goals which do not move the organization toward its desired end-state (Associates, the Department of Behavioral Sciences and Leadership, 1988).

The second source of intergroup conflict is *time orientation*. This type of conflict can occur when teams experience different levels of urgency and are operating under different deadline conditions. If one team is operating under a short suspense and another team is not, and additionally, if those two teams need to share resources, then they will inevitably come into conflict (Associates, the Department of Behavioral Sciences and Leadership, 1988).

The third source of intergroup conflict is *physical separation*. This happens when teams are not co-located in the same building or geographic region. This condition can sometimes occur with "distributed teams." These teams are deployed to different geographic regions and therefore have little opportunity to interact and socialize. This lack of contact can lead to a loss of intimacy and shared understanding, which eventually degrades team cohesion. Distributed teams do not experience the same working environments and are not exposed to the same leadership and therefore may develop entirely different cultures. They can often drift apart and not appreciate the other's perspective. When these teams are asked to come together to accomplish a task for the larger organization, they are likely to clash before they meld (Associates, the Department of Behavioral Sciences and Leadership, 1988).

The fourth source of intergroup conflict is *infrequent interaction*. This is a predictable outcome of teams experiencing physical separation and the same principles apply. The challenge for the leaders of teams that have infrequent interaction is to attempt to compensate for that lack of interaction by creating conditions that require the disparate teams to interact. Leaders can do this by assigning projects across team boundaries, which require the cooperation and skill integration of the separated units. If physical proximity is not an option, then the leader can create opportunities for interstation travel as well as frequent and iterative video-teleconferences focused on the assigned projects. Ultimately, if a leader cannot physically co-locate his or her teams, then they must create opportunities for them to work together and leverage that work using the gifts of modern technology. Only when human beings on teams interact with other human beings on other teams can the true magic of cooperation and cohesion be created (Associates, the Department of Behavioral Sciences and Leadership, 1988).

The fifth source of intergroup conflict is the *nature of the work* assigned to teams. If a leader assigns one of her teams a very tangible task, such as clean the break room by Friday, and then she assigns another one of her teams something less tangible, such as improve the morale of the administrative staff in the company, then those two teams may experience some conflict. The members of both teams will dutifully pursue their assigned tasks but will not understand the other's frustrations if they meet with failure in tending to their different duties. Leaders should be mindful of the nature of the tasks assigned to different groups in their organizations. If the nature of the tasks is consistently different, then intergroup conflict will likely occur (Corsaro, Cantù, & Tunisini, 2012).

The sixth source of intergroup conflict has been discussed previously as an aspect of both physically separated teams as well as teams with different goal orientations. The key to this source of conflict is *scarce resources*. If teams compete for scarce resources, there will be conflict (Corsaro et al., 2012). Leaders must ensure that their teams have equal access to the same resources. However, this is not always possible. Leaders may find that one team is disadvantaged by the excesses of another team. In these rare cases, it is imperative that leaders try to keep this from leading to intergroup conflict, and the best way to do this is to secure resources for all teams, as best they can. If they cannot do this, and one or more of their teams must operate with less, then the leader must be creative in how he or she ensures that the team continues to work hard and not focus on its shortfalls. Often these disparities in resources are short-lived and cyclical, and soon enough each of a leader's teams will be afforded the same resource-rich opportunities. The hallmark of great team leadership is the ability to mask the fluctuation in resources.

The seventh and final source of intergroup conflict is something known as *ambiguous work assignments*. This can manifest when team members do not fully comprehend who is responsible for what tasks in a team's assignment. It is important for the leader to ensure role clarity in the team's structure and task assignments. Another way to ensure intergroup conflict is to assign two different teams similar, but not well-defined tasks. If there is any overlap, the teams will, more than likely, clash. A leader should avoid such situations. Only when there is clarity of work assignments can leaders ensure that they avoid intergroup conflict of this nature.

There are many ways to generate intergroup conflict, wittingly or not, but there are also many ways to manage intergroup conflict. There are five ways a platoon leader can avoid or mitigate intergroup conflict. The first is to *establish superordinate goals*. These are goals that the teams recognize as more important than the issues they are facing currently. If a leader can lift the heads of his or her team and get their team members to focus on something "bigger," then they have gone a long way in facilitating the deconstruction of intergroup conflict (Deutsch, Coleman, & Marcus, 2006).

The second key strategy is to "take charge" and *force* teams to overcome their differences. This may not be the best way to mitigate conflict, but it may be the only way, depending on the conditions faced by the conflicting teams. Sometimes teams mired in conflict need the forcing function of a supervisor demanding a change in behavior. Sometimes a leader may be faced with this awkward but necessary task (Eisenhardt, Kahwajy, & Bourgeois, 1997).

The third strategy for overcoming intergroup conflict is to engage the warring factions in *problem-solving activities*. If a leader demands the constituents devote themselves to cooperative problem-solving then he or she will find that a lot of energy will be devoted to finding the best, right answer. This strategy engages teams in constructive solution-making and is usually successful. This strategy also degrades the sources of conflict experienced by the factions prior to this forced cooperation (Deutsch et al., 2006).

The fourth strategy is to *create liaisons* that can see the problem from both sides. These liaisons are critical in the process of creating a common understanding of the underlying issues in conflicting groups. Liaisons can help groups truly understand their opponents' perspective, which is a critical first step in deflating the tensions driving intergroup conflict. If leaders can get liaisons in place and deploy them effectively, then they can truly dismantle dysfunctional conflict across teams (Deutsch et al., 2006).

The last and least effective method of managing intergroup conflict is *avoidance*. Although this might feel like the safest method, it is rarely effective. A leader is responsible for creating and nurturing a functional organizational culture that focuses workers on task accomplishment, and so avoidance is never a first option. There might be times when avoidance is the best course of action, but the conditions that determine that are exceptional. Typically, avoidance leads to escalation, which can cause a complete deconstruction of the functional group dynamics that a leader has worked to develop. It is generally the better course of action to intervene in intergroup conflict on behalf of intergroup harmony (Eisenhardt et al., 1997).

In this section, we examined the center components of the taxonomy of teams, the Group Processes. These elements, if understood and leveraged by a team leader and the team members themselves, can have considerable impact on the ability of the team to optimize its performance, not only as a group, but likewise can enhance the ability of each of its individual members. These are critical components of optimizing performance in extreme environments and cannot be understated. The next section examines the actual outputs of teams, tracing the precedent components of this team model and discussing the impacts on the team's performance (outcomes).

GROUP OUTPUTS

A team's processes results in the team's output. These outputs are in the form of the impact on the group, as well as the impact on the individuals who compose that group.

Effects on the Individual

We can start by outlining the possible effects on an individual as a result of being a member of a particular team or group. Membership on a team influences an individual's level of satisfaction, which may be driven by that person's experience of their own altered (improved) knowledge, skills, and abilities. Presumably, functional teams will increase their members' individual knowledge, skills, and abilities, which will in turn improve their satisfaction with being a member of that team. Satisfied members will more likely choose to remain on the team, and therefore the team benefits from their contributions. This dynamic is essential to realizing a team's overall potential and leads to higher levels of team and individual performance. This can, in turn, impact the psychological states of individual team members, as well as the overall heartiness of the team as a group. The cycle of benevolence is prodigious.

Effects on the Group

A second aspect of the effects of group outputs is their effects on the groups itself. Specifically, as a result of the team's functioning, teams should experience changes in elements of their Group Structural Dimensions, such as more effective socialization and increased cohesion, as well as role clarity. And, finally, there may be reduced intergroup conflict. Another and some would argue more important outcome of a group is the group's performance. By this, we mean does the team perform at its best? Do these processes contribute to the improvement of the team's performance? Some argue that this is all that matters in examining a group's processes. Learning how to optimize a team's performance is a critical component of ensuring success in extreme settings.

CONCLUSION

Understanding how to optimize human performance in teams is a critical core competency for leaders and is the requisite for optimizing not only the team's performance, but also that of each individual on the team. It is imperative that leaders understand the inputs, throughput processes, and outputs of teams so they can manage all aspects of team dynamics in extreme environments. If a leader can take deliberate charge of each of these key elements that make up their teams, then they can and should shape them, which will ultimately lead to the highest levels of team performance. For leaders in extreme environments, this may ensure survival and could be considered a moral imperative.

Directions for Future Research

Given the modern, distributed nature of virtual teams, research can be leveraged to examine the impact of those specific conditions on team processes and outcomes. It would enhance our understanding of teams in general if we examined the effects of leadership, composition, configuration, and distance in distributed teams. This would lay the foundation for our understanding of teams in the modern work world. Additionally, given that this distribution of teams is occurring globally, the nuances of intercultural communication and cohesion come to the fore as critical aspects of team performance. Research in this domain would also reveal elements that would help leaders be more effective and efficient when composing, developing, motivating, and communicating with their work teams.

"Diversity" is a team component whose definition keeps expanding. We are moving well beyond our traditional focus on demographic diversity and its impact on team dynamics and performance. Diversity in decision-making styles, human capital status, extroversion, intelligence, and a host of additional dimensions all lend themselves to research that can provide us insights into more effectively forming and leading teams. Recent years have seen a burgeoning interest in the ways that teams share information and the effects that has on team performance. The awareness of a need to share and the timing of the decision to share information has complex effects on how teams solve problems. These kinds of variables are driving insightful research on team dynamics (Chatman et al., 1998).

Other team "hygiene" factors are also of interest. For example, research into team resilience is emerging and informing the ways that we understand teams working in extreme conditions, such as search and rescue, firefighting, and military operations (Bartone, 2003). Additionally, the collaborative proclivity of teams impacts how well they operate interprofessionally, and this is important for understanding how teams are engaging today. The list of potentially interesting dimensions is exhaustive; I provide a few ideas here:

1. Cross-cultural communication and cognitive styles, and their impact on transactive memory and willingness to share information.
2. The impact on willingness to "speak up," of the anonymity provided by digital communication channels.
3. The effects of leveraging artificial intelligence on team decision-making effectiveness.
4. The flat organization and how team performance is affected by organizational structure.
5. The effects of age disparity (intergenerational team composition) on team dynamics and performance.
6. What variables affect a team's ability to learn?
7. What variables can influence a team's ability to innovate?

REFERENCES

Alise, M. A., & Teddlie, C. (2010). A continuation of the paradigm wars? Prevalence rates of methodological approaches across the social/behavioral sciences. *Journal of Mixed Methods Research, 4*(2), 103–126. doi:10.1177/1558689809360805

Ancona, D. G., & Caldwell, D. F. (1992). Demography and design: predictors of new product team performance. *Organization Science, 3*(3), 321–341.

Apesteguia, J., Azmat, G., & Iriberri, N. (2012). The impact of gender composition on team performance and decision making: Evidence from the field. *Management Science, 58*(1), 78–93.

Aries, E. (1976). Interaction patterns and themes of male, female and mixed groups. *Small Group Behavior, 7*(1), 7–18. doi.org/10.1177/104649647600700102

Associates, the Department of Behavioral Sciences and Leadership, United States Military Academy, West Point, New York. (1988). *Leadership in Organizations.* Garden City Park, NY: Avery.

Bantel, K. A., & Jackson, S. E. (1989). Top management and innovations in banking: Does the composition of the top team make a difference? *Strategic Management Journal, 10*(S1), 107–124.

Bartone, P. (2003). Hardiness as a resiliency resource under high stress conditions. In D. Paton, J. M. Violanti, & L. M. Smith (Eds.), *Promoting Capabilities to Manage Posttraumatic Stress: Perspectives on Resilience* (pp. 59–73). Springfield, IL: Charles C. Thomas.

Berger, J., Cohen, B. P., & Zelditch, M. (1972). Status characteristics and social interaction. *American Sociological Review, 37*(3), 241–255.

Berger, J., Norman, R. Z., Balkwell, J. W., & Smith, R. F. (1992). Status inconsistency in task situations. *American Sociological Review, 57*(6), 843–855.

Berger, J., Ridgeway, C. L., Fisek, M. H., & Norman, R. Z. (1998). The legitimation and delegitimation of power and prestige orders. *American Sociological Review, 63*(3), 379. doi:10.2307/2657555

Brewer, M. B., & Pierce, K. P. (2005). Social identity complexity and outgroup tolerance. *Personality & Social Psychology Bulletin, 31*(3), 428–37. doi:10.1177/0146167204271710

Bryman, A., Collinson, D., Grint, K., Jackson, B., & Uhl-Bien, M. (Eds.). (2011). *The SAGE Handbook of Leadership.* Los Angeles, CA: Sage.

Chatman, J. A., Polzer, J. T., Barsade, S. G., & Neale, M. A. (1998). Being different yet feeling similar: the influence on demographic composition and organizational culture on work processes and outcomes. *Administrative Science Quarterly, 43*(4), 749–780.

Clausewitz, Carl von (1873). *On War: Volumes 1–3.* London: N. Trubner & Co.

Corsaro, D., Cantù, C., & Tunisini, A. (2012). Actors' heterogeneity in innovation networks. *Industrial Marketing Management, 41*(5), 780–789. doi: 10.1016/j.indmarman.2012.06.005

Deutsch, M., Coleman, P. T., & Marcus, E. C. (2006). *The Handbook of Conflict Resolution: Theory and Practice.* San Francisco: Jossey-Bass.

Du Picq, A. (1921/1987). Battle studies: ancient and modern battle. Reprinted in *Roots of Strategy, Book 2.* Harrisburg, PA: Stackpole Books.

Eisenhardt, K. M., Kahwajy, J. L., & Bourgeois, L. J. (1997). How management teams can have a good fight. *Harvard Business Review, 75,* 77–86.

Evans, R. W., & Davis, W. D. (2005). High-performance work systems and organizational performance: The mediating role of internal social structure. *Journal of Management, 31*(05), 758–775. doi: 10.1177/0149206305279370

Fischer, M. (Oct. 2006). Civil society in conflict transformation: Ambivalence, potentials and challenges. *Berghof Handbook for Conflict Transformation.* Retrieved from http://image.berghof-foundation.org/fileadmin/redaktion/Publications/Handbook/Articles/fischer_cso_handbookII.pdf

Forsyth, D. (2009). *Group Dynamics.* Belmont, CA: Cengage Learning.

Foschi, M. (1992). Gender and double standards for competence. In C. L. Ridgeway (Ed.), *Gender Interactions and Inequality* (pp. 181–207). New York: Springer.

Foschi, M. (2000). Double standards for competence: theory and research. *Annual Review of Sociology, 26*(1), 21–42. doi: 10.1146/annurev.soc.26.1.21

Foschi, M., Warriner, G. K., & Hart, S. D. (1985). Standards, expectations, and interpersonal influence. *Social Psychology Quarterly, 48*(2), 108–117.

Garcia-Prieto, P., Bellard, E., & Schneider, S. C. (2003). Experiencing diversity, conflict, and emotions in teams. *Applied Psychology, 52*(3), 413–440. doi:10.1111/1464-0597.00142

Hackman, J. R. (2002). A real team. In J. R. Hackman (Ed.), *Leading Teams: Setting the Stage for Great Performances* (pp. 36–60). Boston, MA: Harvard Business School Press.

Hogg, M. A., & Terry, D. J. (2000). Social contextual influences on attitude-behavior correspondence, attitude change, and persuasion. In M. A. Hogg & D. J. Terry (Eds.), *Attitudes, Behavior, and Social Context: The Role of Norms and Group Membership* (pp. 1–9). London: Lawrence Erlbaum Associates.

Jackson, S. E., Joshi, A., & Erhardt, N. L. (2003). Recent research on team and organizational diversity: SWOT analysis and implications. *Journal of Management, 29*(6), 801–830. doi:10.1016/S0149-2063

Kochan, T., Bezrukova, K., Ely, R. J., Jackson, S. E., Joshi, A., . . . Thomas, D. (2003). The effects of diversity on business performance: Report of the diversity research network. *Human Resource Management, 42*(1), 3–21. doi:10.1002/hrm.10061

Mannix, E., & Neale, M. A. (2005). What differences make a difference: the promise and reality of diverse teams in organizations. *Psychological Science in the Public Interest, 6*(2), 31–55. doi:10.1111/j.1529-1006.2005.00022.

Marlow, D. H. (1987). *New Manning System Field Evaluation* (Technical Report No. 5). Washington, DC: Walter Reed Army Institute of Research.

Moreland, R. L., & Levine, J. M. (1982). Socialization in small groups. *Advances in Experimental Social Psychology, 15,* 137–192.

Newhesier, A., & Dovidio, J. F. (2012). Individual differences and intergroup bias: Divergent dynamics associated with prejudice and stereotyping. *Personality and Individual Differences, 53,* 70–74.

Stout, R. J., Salas, E., & Fowlkes, J. E (1997). Enhancing teamwork in complex environments through team training. *Group Dynamics: Theory, Research, and Practice, 1*(2), 169–182.

Wageman, R., Nunes, D. A., Burruss, J. A., & Hackman, J. R. (2008). *Senior Leadership Teams: What It Takes to Make Them Great.* Boston, MA: Harvard Business Press.

Wells, J. E., & Aicher, T. J. (2013). Follow the leader: A relational demography, similarity attraction, and social identity theory of leadership approach of a team's performance. *Gender Issues, 30,* 1–14. doi:10.1007/s12147-013-9112-8

Williams, K. Y., & O'Reilly, C. A. (1998). Demography and diversity in organizations: A review of 40 years of research in organizational behavior. In B. M. Staw & L. L. Cummings (Eds.), *Research in Organizational Behavior* (Vol. 20, pp. 77–140). Greenwich, CT: Jai Press.

18

The Ethics of Human Enhancement

An Overview and Framework

JANICE H. LAURENCE AND JOSHUA A. CARLISLE

Gentlemen, we can rebuild him. We have the technology.

We have the capability to make the world's first bionic man.

Steve Austin will be that man. Better than he was before.

Better. Stronger. Faster.

— OSCAR GOLDMAN, *The Six Million Dollar Man*[1]

INTRODUCTION

So went the opening voice-over for the mid-1970s television series, *The Six Million Dollar Man*. Following a test-flight crash, astronaut Steve Austin was barely alive. A top secret agency used bionic parts—right arm, both legs, left eye—to rebuild Austin in exchange for his willingness to carry out intelligence missions that were beyond the capabilities of a normal man. Words that once set a tone of fantastical science fiction now describe a developing reality for soldiers and others who serve the public under extreme conditions. Indeed, our capabilities to rebuild humans, to make ourselves stronger, faster—"better"—continue to grow at a rapid pace.

This volume has highlighted scientific breakthroughs and future possibilities for human optimization. Many of these possibilities have the potential to impact the well-being of humans, reshape our social arrangements, or change our fundamental understanding of our own nature and limitations. Technological and bionic devices as well as pharmaceutical and surgical enhancements are exciting innovations that may well serve national security needs. Improving cognitive function, vigilance, attention capacity, and decision-making speed and accuracy would come in handy in the fog of war or even civil emergencies. Likewise, decreasing the need for sleep and negating the deleterious effects of stress and trauma could be decisive on the battlefield or in other extreme environments. Compensating for the limitations of the human weapon system sounds promising for national security (Krishnan, 2014). We have the technology to do these things, or we soon will. But should we? One might think that the virtues of human enhancement (HE) are self-evident. If good is good, then isn't better better? If we have the means to improve people's lives, why wouldn't we? But no change so profound could be so simple. What are the potential negatives to human optimization? This chapter raises some key ethical issues surrounding HE and proposes a framework for evaluating interventions so as to keep moral concerns central to the ongoing development of biotechnological enhancements.

The ethics of HE has been described recently as "one of the most important topics in bioethics" (Menuz, 2015, p. 61) and "the most significant area of bi-oethical interest in the last twenty years" (Harris, 2011, p. 102). But the concept of HE, as such, came to the forefront of bioethics relatively recently. A 1993 lecture by LeRoy Walters on the future of enhancement reverberated widely, leading 5 years later to one of the first book-length, philosophical treatments of the topic, *Enhancing Human Traits*, edited by Erik Parens (Bateman & Gayon, 2015, p. 20). This controversial topic reached a wider audience the following decade, with the publication of a report by The President's Council on Bioethics in 2003 (Menuz, 2015, p. 60). Over the past decade, numerous governmental and nongovernmental agencies have dedicated resources to investigating the ethics of HE. These include The Hastings Center, The President's Council on Bioethics, the Oxford Uehiro Centre for Practical Ethics, The European Commission for Ethics in Public Policy Making, the SATORI project, the European Parliament Science and Technology Options Assessment, and many other organizations and universities across the world. In addition, the number of academic journal articles and books on the topic of HE continues to grow exponentially.

Despite—or perhaps because of—this burgeoning of the field, there remains much debate regarding the moral permissibility of enhancement as well as the appropriate terms and frameworks to define such debate. The topic of HE is complex because, in a very direct manner, it gets to the heart of what we take to be the central concerns of ethics, involving concepts such as human nature, identity, fairness, dignity, virtue, and duties to our offspring and fellow beings (Lin & Allhoff, 2008).

Beyond implicating these moral concepts, HE has the potential to challenge their basic foundations. Consider our views of the Olympic Games, for example. We typically celebrate athletes for what they are able to do through hard work and training. Might there come a time when we see the athletes only as biotechnological vessels who (that?) showcase what the scientists from the competing nations can accomplish? Some philosophers have expressed concern that enhancements might become so pervasive that individual dignity could be undermined (Sandel, 2002, 2009). If human dignity depends, at least in part, on what we make of ourselves—that is, what we make of our given nature—then what becomes of dignity when we are made by drugs or technology instead?

Our initial normative question when contemplating the improvement of Steve Austin, the Six Million Dollar Man, was simply, "should we do it?" That basic question masks the complexity of questions to be asked about HE and the spectrum of people and groups who ask them. Researchers want to know that their work is going to benefit the world. Policymakers want to regulate or deregulate in a responsible manner. Practitioners want to act in the best interests of their patients and according to the best standards of their professions. Individuals want to know that they are doing the right things for themselves—or for those children or loved ones for whom they are responsible—while not negatively impacting their fellow human beings. Beyond these people for whom the question of enhancement may come up explicitly, we must also consider what impact a given intervention might have in the future and on the rest of the world, to include humans, animals, the environment, and so on.

Examples from a military context can bring into focus the scope of potential consequences. Vigilance, fatigue and stress relief, improved decision-making, and emotion regulation may win the war but forestall peace or well-being in the future. The long-term effects of psychopharmacological substances, especially when used in off-label ways, is unknown (Agrid et al., 2013). Lack of certainty regarding possible risks does not mitigate the need to thoroughly evaluate the likelihood and severity of potential harms (Douglas, 2015). The risk of addiction and irreversible brain damage must be assessed regardless of how difficult it is to do so. Given that entering soldiers are typically teenagers, the potentially harmful effects on the developing brain require grave consideration, as do potential risks to future generations (Gupta, Fischer, & Frewer, 2015). The consequences of biological, chemical, and cognitive interventions may not emerge while in service but rather when enhanced soldiers become veterans. Support for veterans who suffer from service-related deleterious health effects including suicide risk and trauma is often inadequate (Morin, 2011; Ryan & Burrell, 2012). One might well expect the inadequacies and costs of long-term care to be even greater for preventing or negating the negative effects of HE.

Effects of enhancement on human emotion carry potentially large-scale implications. Although reducing empathy in drone pilots (Agrid et al., 2013) or even ground forces may seem wise, it may be detrimental during missions such as counterinsurgency where emotion intelligence, prosocial behavior, and cultural competence are key (Damasio, 2007; Laurence, 2011). Imagine the ill effects of acquired sociopathy for civil policing. Military and police missions are not just about engaging the enemy or deadly perpetrators but also about nation-building, disaster relief, and community interaction to counter criminals and terrorists. Reducing the psychological costs of harming others might well enable one to avoid posttraumatic stress, but it could also lead to atrocities (Douglas, 2015).

In addition to societal consequences are personal and familial ones. Alert, perceptive, and fearless soldiers, unfazed by stress, unburdened by empathy, and who can go for prolonged periods without food or sleep may find it hard to adjust to the mere mortal world. Undermining psychological responses such as empathy, sympathy, and moral reasoning is likely to have far-reaching negative impacts upon mental health (Douglas, 2015). A person altered in these areas is no longer the same and may confront potential loss of a sense of self and self-acceptance (Agrid et al., 2013). Physical interventions pose similar risks and problems. Therapeutic procedures such as hand and facial transplantations are controversial because of the psychological and social obstacles they introduce. Adjustment for the patient and family members to an altered identity is difficult, and thus pre- and post-counseling is extensive not only for the treated individuals but also for their families (Black, 2010; Freeman & Jaoudé, 2007). The potential ramifications of enhancements outside of the rehabilitative realm deserve as much, if not more, consideration.

Reintegration with family and with the civilian world is often tumultuous for today's soldiers (Booth & Lederer, 2012; Ryan & Burrell, 2012) and others who serve in extreme settings. After deployment and even separation from service, those who hang up their uniform—and their families—often continue to deal with combat injuries and mental health problems. Although this is nothing new and not unique to biological and cognitive enhancement, what may be exacerbated are problems with social and family relationships owing to the long-term effects of suppression of emotions and modification of the prefrontal cortex (Damasio, 2007). Imagine a spouse, child, or other family member coping with someone who has been enhanced to the point of becoming an ever alert, emotionless, or detached automaton. Or consider the repercussions of amplifying the family friction between a cognitively enhanced soldier and a spouse who has taken care of family responsibilities and decisions in the soldier's absence. Domestic violence and divorce are potential consequences with profound costs.

In addition to the perspectives of affected individuals and communities, we must also consider the contexts in which these questions will continue to arise. Since the early publications in the 1990s and 2000s mentioned earlier, the debate about the ethics of HE has occurred largely at the highest level of abstraction, considering primarily how to define HE and whether it is permissible at the overall level. Some have argued that this is the wrong approach and that, instead, permissibility should be addressed on a case-by-case basis. Many of the stakeholders will not be theorists or policymakers at a large scale; they will be making discrete, real-world ethical decisions. Nonetheless, the philosophers working in this area will provide invaluable tools in the form of conceptual analysis and argumentation that will enable decision-making at the ground level.

A framework for discussing the ethics of HE must be able to accommodate all of these things: the existing scholarship, the conceptual complexities, the numerous stakeholders, and the wide-ranging ethical implications. Thus, the aim of this chapter is to propose such a framework, one that will serve both as a structure for understanding the current issues and debates and as a guide for stakeholders to use in making decisions about the ethics of particular HE interventions. In doing so, we will borrow from an adjacent field of applied ethics, Just War Theory.

Clarifying Definitions

Defining the terms of the HE debate proves uniquely difficult. Gyngell and Selgelid (2016) note that "the lack of consensus regarding how best to understand 'enhancement' has long been cited as a factor impeding ethical debate about enhancement technologies" (p. 111). Other scholars have opined that "the definition, scope and limits of HE are as vague as the term is salient" (Bateman, Gayon, Allouche, Goffette, & Marzano, 2015, p. 1). To appreciate the ethical complexity involved, one need only consider the ambiguity of the compound term itself: "HE." If our project is to enhance humans, do we mean to enhance all humans? A particular human? A particular group of humans? Who is enhanced and why? These questions prompt concerns over social justice and fairness. Furthermore, even after answering the question of scope, there is some ambiguity remaining between the evaluative and biological senses of the word "human" (Juengst & Moseley, 2015). That is, are we to understand "human" primarily as a species with a certain genetic make-up or are we to understand "human" to designate a particular type of being that has moral worth of some sort?

The word "enhancement" is similarly ambiguous. For a given human whom we aim to enhance, are we trying to enhance them in an overall manner related to health or well-being? Or are we trying to enhance them along a particular mode or capacity, perhaps in cognitive performance such as memory, focus, or attention, or perhaps in terms of physical performance such as strength, stamina, or speed? There will inevitably be tradeoffs between general and specific aims. While some capacity-focused enhancing interventions might increase the overall well-being of the enhanced people, others might come at a cost to well-being. For example, drugs such as amphetamines or Modafinil are used to increase the alertness and vigilance of pilots, soldiers, surgeons, and professionals in other demanding fields. Such interventions might increase cognitive capacity in the intended way while at the same time producing in the user negative consequences such as nervousness, loss of appetite, and problems with sleep (Cornum, Caldwell, & Cornum, 1997).

In the other direction, there might be interventions aimed at increasing well-being through capacity-focused disenhancements. The "blind chicken problem" describes the "dumb-down" approach to animal disenhancement in which "researchers identify the genetic or neurological basis for certain characteristics or abilities, and produce animals that lack them by removing or otherwise disabling them either genetically or through nano-mechanical intervention in cellular and neurological processes" (Thompson 2008, p. 308). In the case of hens, such practices aim to improve the hens' quality of life by making them less aggressive in temperament or less likely to feel stress in a crowded environment. Such examples show that the locus of enhancement can be narrow or wide in scope and that enhancements in one particular domain of life might count as disenhancements when evaluated from another perspective. These questions prompt concerns over how we define ourselves as individuals and groups and how we understand what it means to flourish as such.

Having discussed these conceptual problems with defining *enhancement*, we must also mention that many authors in this collection discuss not HE but rather human *performance optimization*. Is there any difference between these two concepts? First, the goal of enhancing *humans* suggests a generality that optimizing *performance* lacks; the latter seems to focus attention more on already existing practices. However, it must be determined which categories of performance are to be optimized, and such categories could span the entire range of human activities. Thus, for practical or theoretical purposes, "human performance" and "human" seem to be extensionally equivalent. At the same time, whereas "human performance" seems to push in a more conservative direction, potentially limiting the range of intervention, "optimization" seems to push in the opposite, more liberal direction, suggesting that the targets of intervention are not merely enhanced but optimized. Where the concept of enhancement raises questions of "how far" and "in what directions," the concept of optimization risks overlooking such questions and the unintended consequences they might reveal. Such conceptual risks can be managed, and we are not recommending that the literature be altered to fit the terminology here.

Nonetheless, one might think that the distinction between "performance optimization" and "enhancement" is a morally significant one. Gyngell and Selgelid (2016) note that when the concept of enhancement was first introduced in the bioethics literature, it was thought to describe a domain of practices that were inherently morally problematic. However, that definitional approach risks begging the question in the debate. This is, in part, what led Parens (1998) to note that many believed the term "enhancement" to be "so freighted with erroneous assumptions and so ripe for abuse that we ought not even use it" (p. s1). Much of the past debate on the ethics of HE has relied on definitions that inevitably tilt the argument to one side or the other. Gyngell and Selgelid (2016) surveyed the history of enhancement definitions and distilled those into seven main types: the Constructivist Approach, the Normal Functioning Approach, Beyond Species Typical Approach, Beyond Species Maximum Approach, Welfarist Conception, the Modern Welfarist Approach, and the Functional Approach. The details of each type are beyond the scope of our chapter. It is important to note, however, that the authors present the definition types not as contributions to the debate over which definition is correct, but as tools that can be used to clarify discussions about the ethics of HE. It might be that, instead of arriving at any consensus about a general definition for enhancement, we come to accept a variety of enhancements as potential interventions, none of them being deemed permissible or impermissible right out of the conceptual gate, but each requiring individualized ethical scrutiny in a given case. Gyngell and Selgelid themselves argue that none of the seven types of enhancement comes with an inherent moral polarity. Contrary to what some have argued (Earp, Sandberg, Kahane, & Savulescu, 2014), this is not a reason to abandon the general concept of enhancement or any of these more specific conceptual types. Even though the conceptual definitions themselves may not answer the moral questions we are asking, they can be useful in drawing our attention to morally relevant features of a proposed HE intervention.

Though we recommend that a definition of enhancement be clearly identified when considering specific interventions, we need to have a working definition with which to start. Gyngell and Selgelid (2016) note that enhancement "is perhaps most commonly conceived as the non-therapeutic beneficial alteration (of capacities) that does not involve treating or preventing disease" (p. 112). Forsberg, Shelley-Egan, Thorstensen, Landeweerd, and Hofmann (2017) provide the following definition: "Human enhancement (HE) is the common denominator for applications or activities that are designed to temporarily or permanently improve human beings in different ways, as opposed to merely repairing damages" (p. 1). These broad definitions reflect the foundational literature in the ethics of HE and direct our attention to a morally relevant domain of activity—one of beneficial alteration or improvement. As we present a framework for conceptualizing the ethics of HE and evaluating the justness of particular interventions, we recommend that the reader keep in mind the general definition of enhancement provided here while realizing that a thorough application of the framework to a given case will require more specificity in practice.

Why Just War Theory as a Framework?

Two major thinkers in the field of HE ethics draw attention to a growing "biopolitical fault line developing between pro-enhancement and anti-enhancement groupings" (Bostrom & Savulescu, 2009, p.1). They note that while the terms of this disagreement are being debated, there remains an "opportunity open for academic bioethicists to influence the shape and direction of this debate before it settles into a fixedly linear ideological tug-of-war" (2009, p. 2). Their description of the situation is telling in terms of the tone and focus of the HE debate and the lack of a defined, agreed-upon framework to guide it.

As noted, the debate regarding enhancement is largely occurring at the highest level of abstraction. Most arguments presented in the literature aim at answering the basic question: Is HE morally permissible? While we agree that this is the fundamental question in the field, the internal academic dialogue does not always answer the needs of the various stakeholders. As Savulescu remarked in an interview, the first cloning of an animal—the sheep, Dolly—happened while the bioethicists were still debating about how to proceed with the debates. Focusing too exclusively on this high level risks putting HE ethics in the same situation, behind the emerging biotechnology it exists to guide.

The gulf between theory and practice deepens where, in order to make the moral problems stand out clearly, the theoretical debates often gravitate toward fringe cases. This is a useful method to tease out intuitions and to hone in on the key moral features at play, but it can become detached from reality. Thus, there has been much criticism that the HE debates are not well-grounded in what is currently scientifically and technologically feasible. While the fundamental ethical inquiry must continue, it is important that other dialogues more practical in nature progress in a parallel—but also intersecting—manner, so that decision-makers have the best existing tools to support their judgments. We believe that there is not only an opportunity to shape the current debate, but also a need to expand the scope of the dialogue across all implicated sectors. It is here that Just War Theory (JWT) provides a useful model.

In the field of armed conflict, JWT accomplishes the theoretical and practical aims of a moral framework while satisfying the three criteria essential to HE ethics: comprehensiveness, transparency, and user-friendliness (Forsberg et al., 2017). In their review and evaluation of ethical frameworks related to the field of human cognitive enhancement (HCE), Forsberg and colleagues (2017) argue that these three criteria are essential to ensure the quality of an ethical framework for the particular domain of HE they consider. A comprehensive framework will incorporate a broad inclusion of perspectives and values. A transparent framework will be straightforward to all stakeholders and will explain clearly how it supports judgements about the morality of given enhancements. Relatedly, to be user-friendly, an ethical framework should be relatively easy to follow across various circumstances and from various worldviews.

There are several positive reasons to adopt the JWT framework and apply it within HE debates. First, there is a great deal of overlap in concepts and concerns across the two fields. Each places a high value and focus on the rights of those affected by the actions and the consent of those people involved in the enterprises. Each requires careful attention to the relationships between individual rights and governmental rights and powers. The two fields involve human conflict and competition over goods and resources. Furthermore, discussions of both just war and HE implicate global issues and concerns.

In addition to this overlap, JWT has a well-established footing in the international community. Discussions about the ethics of biotechnological advances in HE require a framework that can be easily conceptualized and applied to a variety of cases. Furthermore, we agree with the view that an "ethical framework that is to be useful for a variety of decision-makers in liberal societies should not require the user to subscribe to any particular substantive moral approach" (Forsberg et al., 2017, p. 31). The JWT framework fulfils this requirement in that the rules it contains can both accommodate and be explained through various moral lenses. The framework not only maps onto existing academic discourses in practical ethics—allowing for potential sharing of research and insights—but also is relatively well understood and accepted by nonacademic stakeholders such as governmental officials.

Despite these reasons that speak for the aptness of the JWT framework, one might nevertheless argue that adopting the analogy would stack the deck against HE. That is, one might claim that, instead of making the world more just, JWT paved the way for rationalizing unjust wars. If there are aspects of modern JWT that have increased injustice, these can be considered as the ethics of HE advances. We contend that, when seen as a general framework to evaluate the permissibility of war, JWT has at the very least the potential to do more good than harm.

Just Enhancement Theory: The Spectrum

Is war morally permissible? That is the fundamental question of JWT. The analogous question for HE becomes: Is HE morally permissible? The literature in both fields gives three basic answers to these questions: no, yes, and the question is misleading or illegitimate. In JWT, the first answer, "no," is represented by Pacifism, the view that war is never morally permissible. The third answer is represented by the position of Realism, the view that the concept of morality does not apply to war. The space between those two poles accommodates theories of just war, theories that argue—by means of various lines of reasoning—for the criteria of war's permissibility.

Within the existing HE literature, there are various labels for these three basic positions. We agree with Giubilini and Sanyal (2015) that many of these labels are misleading or ill-fitting to the topic. They write, for example, that Roache and Clark (2009, pp. 1–2) use the labels *bioconservative* to refer to positions that restrict HE, the label *biomoderate* to refer to positions that are cautious but vary in terms of restricting or permitting HE based on different factors, and the label *bioliberal* to refer to positions on the permissive end of the spectrum (2015, p. 234). Furthermore, they write, "Jonathan Moreno uses 'bioconservative' to refer to anti-enhancement positions on both the political right (stemming from a concern for the loss of traditional values and dignity) and political left (stemming from worries about social inequality and ecological problems) (Moreno, 2011, 121)" (2015, p. 234). Giubilini and Sanyal concur with Ruth Macklin's assertion that such terms, imported as they are from political thought, do not help progress arguments in the field of bioethics. For similar reasons, Arthur Caplan (2009) avoids these terms, opting instead for the labels of *meliorists* (for proponents of enhancement) and *anti-meliorists* (for those who oppose enhancement; Giubilini & Sanyal, 2015, p. 234). Giubilini and Sanyal (2015) themselves refer to the three basic positions above as *conservative, restrictive,* and *permissive,* respectively (p. 233).

While agreeing with Giubilini and Sanyal, we do not adopt these labels here, for a few reasons. First, though they present good arguments for the relevance of the term "conservative"—e.g., that many such positions trace ideologically back to Burkean conservatism—the term "conservative" nonetheless suffers from possibly misleading political connotations. Furthermore, the three terms direct attention not to the content of the philosophical positions themselves, but rather to the groupings in which those positions find themselves. To avoid these problems, we present here our own more intensionally focused labels for these positions, modeled on the corresponding concepts from JWT: Pacifism, Realism, and JWT itself. We will call the position that HE is never morally permissible Enhancement Abstentionism. The position at the other end of the spectrum—that the question itself is ill-formed—we will call Enhancement Non-Conceptualism. The intervening space between those two poles we will label as Just Enhancement Theory (JET).

Enhancement Abstentionism is the position that HE is never morally permissible and, thus, that humans should abstain from enhancement. To understand or formulate such positions clearly, it is critical to identify how each such view defines enhancement and then to explain what, according to that particular view, makes enhancement wrong. The grounds for the wrongness determines the form of abstentionism. There are four basic forms such positions might take: (1) Religious Abstentionism (RA), (2) Virtue Abstentionism (VA), (3) Consequentialist Abstentionism (CA), and (4) Deontological Abstentionsism (DA).

As the name implies, RA claims that HE is wrong because it runs counter to the will of God, violates religious doctrine, or conflicts with some other religious tenet(s). Sometimes this takes the form of a "playing god" criticism. However, though the vocabulary of religion is invoked here, theological views do not seem to be the most common source of this criticism. Weckert (2016) notes that secular versions of the "playing god" argument are now more common than religious ones (p. 87). Some have argued that many of the standard arguments in this area not only do not rely upon religious doctrine but are inconsistent with mainstream theological views (Bostrom & Savulescu, 2009; Coady, 2009; van den Belt, 2009; Giubilini & Sanyal, 2015). Thus, what seems like an RA position might turn out to be another form of enhancement abstentionism. For example, some anti-enhancement arguments suggest that, unlike God, humans are not all-knowing, and our hubristic attempts to remold nature are likely to unleash unforeseen, disastrous consequences. Such arguments, while appealing to God for comparison, ultimately rely on consequences to explain why intervening in nature would be wrong. Other arguments might, instead of relying upon consequentialist reasoning, explain the wrongness of enhancement through virtue-based concerns. Thus, while a particular anti-enhancement view might seem to be religious in nature, its form will be determined by how it explains the ultimate grounds for wrongness. Given that RA views depend on substantive religious beliefs, theology is the proper place to debate those particular views. To consider philosophically grounded views, we turn our attention to the other three abstentionist positions corresponding to the moral theories of Consequentialism, Deontology, and Virtue Ethics.

CA is the view that enhancement is wrong because the bad consequences will outweigh the good. One such view is the consequentialist form of the "playing god" objection just mentioned; namely, no matter what good intentions we may have, altering human nature is bound to end in disaster (Sandel, 2002, p. 287). Another CA position is that the resources used to pursue enhancement could more effectively help mankind if they were allocated to traditional medical research aimed at treating and preventing diseases (Selgelid, 2014, p. 11). CA is a theoretically unstable position, however, in that it rests on the claim that enhancement interventions will always result in more bad than good or be less effective at increasing well-being than other available options. This claim is more convincing if we view enhancement as a monolithic concept. If, instead, we view enhancement as a collection of disparate possible interventions, the permissibility of a particular enhancement will be an open question to be answered by calculating the likely consequences in a specific context—where some consequences will be unknowable. For that reason, while CA arguments might be presented as if they were categorical and firmly planted at one end of the spectrum, their consequentialist foundations involve contingencies that do not fit well with the strong claims of abstentionism.

DA claims that enhancement is wrong because it infringes on people's rights or violates principles of liberty or equality (Giubilini & Sanyal, 2015). For example, Jurgen Habermas (2003) argues that some forms of genetic enhancement might violate the principle of rational consent. He contrasts the possibility of future generations being able to accept or reject certain aspects of culture that are passed down to them, an ability they might use deliberately, with their possible inability to consent to large-scale modifications of the gene pool. Another deontological concern is that enhancements might become so common that people would essentially be required to enhance themselves to maintain their jobs, social status, and the like. Such concerns arise in the domain of sports, where athletes might feel coerced to take performance-enhancing drugs to remain competitive. Similarly, those who do not take cognitive-enhancing drugs could find themselves left behind in school or the workplace. In such cases, DA can claim that enhancements are morally impermissible because they create inequality or coerce people, undermining their autonomy.

VA claims that enhancement is inconsistent with human character, nature, excellence, or flourishing. For example, Francis Fukuyama (2002) writes that human nature "has provided a stable continuity to our experience as a species" and that it is "conjointly with religion, what defines our most basic values" (p. 7). Similarly, Sandel (2009) argues that enhancements "diminish our humanity" and threaten aspects of "human freedom" and "human flourishing" (p. 24). Furthermore, he argues that enhancement could undermine the role of "giftedness" in our lives, the idea that much of our moral worth comes from what we make of the lives we are given. Creating our own nature, he argues, could destabilize this essential aspect of what it means to be human.

At the other end of the spectrum is HE Non-Conceptualism. Such positions go beyond the idea that HE could be morally permissible to claim instead that there are no unique moral questions to be answered about HE, per se. Thinkers on this end of the spectrum are sometimes labeled "bioliberals," "transhumanists," or even "posthumanists," though these terms are not equivalent. As discussed, such positions sometimes define enhancement in such a way as to argue that such activities have no inherent moral polarity. Giubilini and Sanyal (2015) categorize the "welfarist" view of enhancement as one example (p. 234). According to that view, to enhance is to increase a person's chances of living a good life, all things considered. This definitional move undercuts distinctions that opponents of HE typically introduce, usually by claiming that enhancement goes beyond medical treatment or what is normal for humans. It is important to note that while HE Non-Conceptualists claim that there are no good reasons to be opposed to HE in principle, almost all of them reserve the right to make moral judgments about particular cases of intervention. Claiming that there is nothing morally exceptional about HE, per se, is not the same as claiming that all instances of HE are permissible. For such thinkers, when a given intervention is wrong, it is wrong for reasons that other sorts of actions might be wrong. Thus, while abstentionist positions—because they represent different explanations of why HE is always wrong—can be seen as a closed point at one end of the spectrum, non-conceptualist views are not so tidy. In fact, they represent more of an open point on the line because, instead of claiming that HE is always morally permissible, they make the modest claim that HE is at least sometimes morally permissible.

Once again, our framework is not meant to be static. It is to be used to evaluate an argument after identifying the particular definition of enhancement on which that argument relies. When so applied, the spectrum we describe might seem to perpetuate a problem mentioned at the beginning of the chapter. Namely, there has been too much focus on the overarching question of the permissibility or impermissibility of HE and too little focus on the specific application of theories to individual instances of HE. Thus, in the next section, we will introduce the practical use of our theoretical framework.

Just Enhancement Theory Framework

This ethical groundwork leads to the more practical project of this chapter, which is to borrow and apply a theoretical framework from JWT to help evaluate the morality of specific HE cases. JWT is divided into three categories that map onto the three basic domains of moral evaluation of war: (1) *jus ad bellum*, or the justice of going to war; (2) *jus in bello*, the justice of conduct in war; and (3) *jus post bellum*, the justice of postwar conditions. Our aim here is not to argue that HE is analogous to JWT in a larger sense, but rather that categories developed in JWT can be useful in organizing positions within the enhancement debate and in systematically evaluating proposed interventions along moral lines.

The core proposition of JWT is that it is sometimes morally permissible for a state to go to war (Orend, 2013, p. 33). To support the claim that a state's resorting to war was just, one must show that the war was begun, executed, and concluded in a just fashion. To claim that a war was just in an overall sense, it must be shown to have been just at each of these stages. There are good reasons to think that these categories are not independent. That is, it might be impossible to satisfy the rules of *jus in bello* if the resort to war itself was unjust. Theorists may disagree about claims about justice at one stage or another, but they agree about the usefulness of the categories themselves as ways of looking into the ethics of armed conflict.

Analogously, the core proposition of JET is that HE is sometimes morally permissible. To argue that a particular intervention or class of interventions is permissible, one must show that: (1) there is a morally acceptable reason for the intervention, (2) the intervention is brought about in a just way, and (3) the post-enhancement environment preserves and respects human rights and does not produce negative consequences that outweigh the positive ones.

JAE: JUSAD ENHANCEMENT

According to JWT, a state is just in resorting to war only when it meets all six rules of *jus ad bellum*: Just Cause, Proportionality, Right Intention, Public Declaration by Proper Authority, Last Resort, Probability of Success (Orend, 2013, p. 33). Of these, the last two rules are superfluous—they are covered more clearly and systematically by the Proportionality rule (see Hurka, 2005). We will adapt and define the other four rules to determine that a given enhancement intervention is just only when it meets the four rules of *jus ad enhancement* (JAE).

Just Cause. The just cause rule asks whether there is a morally acceptable reason for pursuing the enhancement. As stated previously, there are various ways of using the proposed framework. If we are using the framework to understand a theoretical argument about enhancement, in applying the just cause rule we would be looking into what the theorist considers to be good or bad reasons for enhancement. Alternately, if we are applying the framework in the context of a proposed enhancement, in applying the just cause rule we would be evaluating the reasons for and against the enhancement in the particular case at hand.

Once again, the moral theoretical approaches can help us locate or explain reasons that would support an enhancement intervention in a given case. There are consequentialist concerns related to happiness, well-being, and the like. For example, Fröding (2011) discusses a study which indicates that "different forms of the AVPR1A gene are associated with variations in pair bonding and relationship quality" and that such genetic research might be used to support "enhancements which could boost love and attachment in relationships" (p. 223). For example, Bostrom and Sandberg (2009) cite a number of studies to support their claim that "even small improvements in general cognitive capacities can have important positive effects," such as increased health and income for individuals as well as likely downstream improvements across a society's economy, technology, and culture (p. 330). Thus, enhancements might be pursued at various scales from individuals to larger populations in order to increase general well-being, resiliency, and social functioning.

There might be deontological concerns related to duties, rights, and fairness relevant to an enhancement intervention. For example, we might consider a previously oppressed population that has been systematically denied equal opportunity to education and, as a result, falls below the societal average for success in school and the workforce. Research has shown that social interventions such as early childhood education have beneficial impacts on disadvantaged populations and that the positive effects of such programs exceed their costs (Elango, Garcia, Heckman, & Hojman, 2015). However, it is conceivable that through biomedical enhancements it might be possible to achieve even greater results at lower costs. So, the deontological argument goes, such enhancements would be permissible. Some might argue that, all else being equal, given the decision to intervene either socially or biomedically, the latter would not be merely permissible but would be obligatory. After all, to choose the less effective method would be a misuse of taxpayers' money and would be unfair to those who potentially benefit.

There might also be concerns of virtue related to preserving or enhancing human nature, flourishing, or valued practices (de Sio, Robichaud, & Vincent, 2014, p. 181). For example, some researchers have suggested that biomedical interventions might be able to greatly increase impulse control (Savulescu, Douglas, & Persson, 2014). This would give people more agency in developing themselves and shaping their own characters. Another type of enhancement that has recently come to the forefront of HE debates is moral enhancement. Among others, Walker (2010) has advocated for the construction of an interdisciplinary program, one he calls the Genetic Virtue Program (GVP), aimed at "enhancing the biological aspects of virtue" (p. 90).

These lines of reasoning are not mutually exclusive. It is likely that any of these potential interventions would have implications that could be classified as consequentialist, deontological, or virtue-based. Such reasons could reinforce and support each other or, in some cases, speak against each other. This leads to the second rule of JAE.

Proportionality. Identifying a good reason for the intervention is only the first step. After finding a just cause—the reasons that speak for the intervention—we must also identify those reasons that speak against the enhancement. The rule of Proportionality asks whether the good results we seek to achieve through the enhancement outweigh (or at least equal) the bad results. Considering once again the case of a biomedical enhancement aimed at increasing intelligence, we must weigh the potential benefits of the enhancement against the universal costs that come with it. At this stage, it might become apparent that different types of enhancements that aim at the same result (or are done for the same reason) would nevertheless differ in terms of their moral permissibility because of other factors such interventions would introduce. For example, in the case at hand, we might consider intervening through genetic engineering, nanotechnology, or drugs. Genetic engineering could introduce additional ethical concerns such as the right of potential offspring to rationally consent to such a permanent measure. The use of nanotechnology such as implanting chips into brains, in addition to the likely health risks at large scales, might introduce concerns about personal identity. Furthermore, such interventions might be too "effective," introducing greater intelligence differences across society. It could be that the pharmaceutical intervention would be less permanent, thus somewhat mitigating the concerns over risks and rational consent. However, if the drug were to alter brain chemistry in a more radical way, these mitigating features would recede. According to the rule of proportionality, the right action would be the one—among those possible actions satisfying the just cause criteria—that results in the greatest good measured in benefits minus costs.

Right intention. The rule of right intention asks: Does the intervention aim specifically at achieving the just cause and not at achieving some sort of "back door" or "off-label" purpose? Assessing an agent's intentions can be difficult, but it is not impossible. A pattern of actions or the lack of mitigating actions will often make clear an agent's aims. The rule, however, is useful not only as a guide to assess others, but, more importantly, as a check on one's own practices. Thus, it is important for stakeholders contemplating enhancements to design and plan them in ways that narrowly achieve their aims and avoid bringing about otherwise impermissible effects.

The overlap between HE and armed conflict is an especially problematic area in this regard. Enhancements that might seem permissible when viewed narrowly could become impermissible when viewed from a broader perspective. Given the demands placed on soldiers, it seems prima facie permissible—if not obligatory— to find ways to mitigate the myriad negative effects of combat on their bodies and minds. As such, research programs continue to seek ways to reduce fatigue, emotional stress, and fear. In the original Star Trek series of the late 1960s, an episode entitled "A Taste of Armageddon" depicted a computer-simulated war between two neighboring planets. Although the computer simulation results in no human bloodshed or physical ruins, citizens are required to report to disintegration booths for execution so as to meet the calculated casualty counts.[2] By relieving fatigue, emotional stress, or empathy, HE might lower the costs of war. But if those enhancements are used to promote an unjust war, they may become impermissible.

Pacemakers to regulate heart rate as well as bowel and bladder control can compensate for human limitations (Moore, 2013). Orthotic exoskeletons can enhance strength and endurance (Tennison & Moreno, 2012). Pharmacological agents can speed up recovery and rehabilitation thus allowing personnel to resume their duties as quickly as possible and contribute to missions longer (Tracey & Flower, 2014). However, one could argue that war, policing, and other high-risk professions cannot and should not be practiced by dampening empathy or leaving no trace of traumatic events (Tennison & Moreno, 2012). Even assuming this concern could be mitigated, enhancements such as these would make wars less costly and abhorrent to the nations that wage them. The increased efficiencies of soldiers would likely reduce manpower requirements and costs, and the increased resiliency and ability of soldiers would reduce the repugnancy of war in the eyes of policymakers and the broader public, making states more likely to resort to war when they would not have otherwise done so. Given that some wars are unjust and that, even in just wars, unjust actions are committed, the otherwise permissible enhancement of soldiers might be outweighed by the second- and third-order negative effects. Moreover, once the enhancements are developed and made available in the international community, some states might enhance soldiers to intentionally wage unjust wars. Whether unintentional or intentional, the downstream effects of enhancement must be comprehensively evaluated when contemplating the initial narrowly construed aims. In addition, such concerns can be applied beyond the domain of war, such as to sports and academics.

It is not enough that one not explicitly aim at the secondary negative effects that enhancement interventions might bring about; one must also take active steps to identify potential negative effects and then to avoid and mitigate them. The next rule of JAE is useful in this regard.

Publicity. In JWT, the principle of Public Declaration aims to "inform the target, or enemy, country that they now face war and its substantial hazards" and to give them a last chance to capitulate to a peaceful process (Orend, 2013, p. 50). In JAE, the rule of Publicity serves both an ethical and an epistemological purpose. Fulfilling this rule ensures that the agent presents all reasons for and against the proposed action as well as an account of how those reasons relate to and balance with each other; the agent "must be able to show exactly how one goes from the reasons to the conclusion" (Forsberg, 2007, p. 461). This prevents people from being able to shift their explanations for their actions in response to objections or questions. Such public information—because it identifies positive and negative aspects of the situation—also makes it easier for stakeholders, to cultivate the good features and mitigate the bad ones.

The second, epistemological function of the publicity requirement recognizes that HE interventions are likely to have complex effects not easily identifiable from any one given perspective. Making the justificatory argument public ensures that it is "transparent and open for criticism" (Forsberg, 2007, p. 462). This enables discussion among all affected parties and dialogue with the larger philosophical and scientific community. The publicity requirement cannot be fulfilled in a perfunctory manner, however, by simply making an announcement and allowing stakeholders to "be heard." Instead, it should be viewed as an iterative process; though the public debate will have a peak point, the dialogue has no theoretical endpoint, given that the overall context may change at a later time. In practice, there are various methods to meet this requirement, depending on the circumstances. Researchers will publish articles, government agencies will publish op-eds or hold public forums, and ethics committees will convene. This concern for ongoing sensitivity to the overall system in which enhancements will take place leads naturally to the next category of JET.

JIE: JUS IN ENHANCEMENT

In JWT, whereas *jus ad bellum* refers to the justice of resorting to war, *jus in bello* requires that a war be fought justly, that the rights of stakeholders on all sides are respected. Likewise, the domain of JIE includes all of the requirements to research and implement HE in an ethical manner.

The selection of individuals for enhancement can stand as an illustration of this domain and, again, the military context brings key ethical concerns into view. Military orders and a sense of duty may diminish autonomy and preclude truly voluntary submission to off-label drugs, transcranial biosensors, technical devices, and the like (Illes & Bird, 2006). Enhancements in the form of steroids or even caffeine and nicotine may pale in comparison to medically condoned pharmacological agents. Coercion, either implicit or explicit, is a concern. Will soldiers and first responders be explicitly required to accept enhancement? If not, will implicit pressure to achieve peak performance serve as the coercive mechanism? Beyond coercion, there are also epistemic challenges to consent. The full extent and risk of the enhancement may not be clear to those who receive them. Although soldiers and others who serve in extreme settings may be afforded little privacy while deployed, brain–computer interfaces may go a step further. There is potential for misuse of technology that analyzes and controls brain states (Moore, 2013; Parashar, 2014). Grappling with issues of autonomy and coercion is necessary (Douglas, 2015; Krishnan, 2014).

Opportunity as well as consent is an ethical issue in selection. Will all soldiers and police be enhanced, or only select Special Operations Forces and elite law enforcement members? If cost is part of the equation, not all will be slated for optimization. The conundrum here is that this option might well deny life-saving benefits to most of those serving in dangerous conditions. Just as there were outcries in the early years of the Iraq War regarding shortages of body armor (Farley, 2008), limitations on access to enhancements sound alarms. Claims of coercion and denial of benefits reveal the double-edged sword of neuroscientific advances.

In matters of bioethics, ethical concerns involved in implementation overlap with the requirements of institutional review boards (IRBs). As readers of this volume are most likely well-versed in this realm, we will not treat this topic at length. We will, however, follow Orend's model of JWT in noting that the domain of JIE has two sets of rules: one set covering responsibility to those directly involved in or affected by the research or implementation of HE and one set covering the larger society beyond those directly involved. While IRBs cover most of the terrain for the first set of rules, a full consideration of all potentially affected parties requires a broader analysis. In this respect, tools such as those proposed by Forsberg et al. should be adopted and adapted. After surveying six of the main ethical assessment tools in the field of HCE, the authors recommend the ethical matrix and the ethical impacts assessment (2017, p. 61). Incorporating such frameworks will enable thorough consideration of the morally relevant features surrounding HE interventions and will assist decision-makers across various contexts in coming to well-informed judgments regarding HE. These frameworks will help ensure that the rules of JAE are fully considered and satisfied, as well. Their incorporation across the spectrum of HE stakeholders will also contribute to meeting requirements in the last category of JET: jus post enhancement.

JPE: JUS POST ENHANCEMENT

The domain of JPE focuses on the state of affairs post-intervention. The basic requirement is that the object of the intervention—the individual enhanced—should be better off as a result of the enhancement and that the rest of society should be no worse off. Such calculation raises the question: What do we mean by the individual being "better off?" It is not inherent in most definitions of enhancement that the individual be made better off as a whole. In a liberal society, we generally give people free rein to decide what to do with their lives, even when we think such decisions are not in their best interest as viewed from the outside. We would typically not bar someone from pursuing what we see as a pipe dream to become a professional athlete even when we know that they have almost no chance at achieving their athletic goals and that such pursuit leaves their aptitudes in other fields unrealized. In the case of enhancements, then, we might find ourselves faced with the prospect of people seeking to improve themselves along single dimensions of their lives at the cost of their overall flourishing, happiness, or rational capacity. Thus, a complete account of JPE must account for "irrational" enhancement.

In this respect, it is important to keep clear the distinction between individual morality, moral value at the societal level, and law. It may be, for example, that morality would dictate that an individual should forgo an enhancement because that particular instance of enhancement might make things worse for them, their family, or even wider society. Permitting such enhancements on a broad scale, however, might ultimately result in more good than bad, thus constituting a reason for regulatory or legal permissions for that type of enhancement. Likewise, it might be that a given professional code could allegedly narrow the focus and responsibility of a researcher or practitioner. However, a complete ethics of HE needs to take into account the overall context and the likely effects that the development of enhancement technologies and actual interventions might have on the broader scale.

CONCLUSION

In the field of HE ethics, numerous definitions of HE have been offered and debated. As a general starting point, we conceive of HE as denoting activities that aim to permanently or temporarily improve humans, as opposed to merely repairing or preventing damages. Given a specific definition of HE, theories that deny the permissibility of HE can be classified as abstentionist. At the other end of the spectrum, those that deny any inherent moral significance in the concept of HE can be classified as HE non-conceptualist positions. JET comprises the spectrum outside the closed point of abstentionism, embracing the central tenet that HE is sometimes morally permissible.

We proposed the JET framework, borrowed from JWT, to organize thoughts on the topic of HE ethics and as a tool for stakeholders to use when assessing potential HE interventions. According to JET, for an HE intervention to be just, it must satisfy the criteria of all three categories below:

1. *JAE—jus ad enhancement.* A given HE intervention is pursued justly only when it meets the four rules of JAE:
   Just Cause. Identify a morally acceptable reason for the HE intervention. Ensure that the permissibility of the reason is not undermined by its subsumption under a primary, impermissible cause (e.g., making soldiers stronger is prima facie permissible but may become impermissible when done only for the sake of waging an unjust war; this relates to the rule of right intention, below).
   Proportionality. Ensure the good results sought through the enhancement outweigh (or at least equal) the bad results. In a situation in which there are

multiple ways to pursue or implement an HE intervention, choose the one that will result in the greatest good overall.

Right Intention. Ensure that the HE intervention aims narrowly and specifically at the just cause for the intervention and not at a back-door or off-label use. Identify potential negative effects and take active steps to avoid and mitigate them.

Publicity. Publicly present all of the reasons for and against the proposed action as well as an account of how they relate to and balance with each other, thoroughly showing how one gets from the reasons to the conclusion. Ensure a transparent and open dialogue across all stakeholders to comprehensively consider all viewpoints and objections while guaranteeing an ongoing sensitivity to moral features of the overall context.

2. *JIE—jus in enhancement.* Research and implement HE interventions in an ethical manner, ensuring that the rights of the enhanced individuals and the larger population are preserved and respected. Follow the procedures outlined by IRBs as well as ethical tools such as the ethical matrix and ethical impact assessment.

3. *JPE—jus post enhancement.* Ensure that the enhanced individuals and the larger society are not worse off due to the HE intervention. Use the tools recommended in JIE to maintain an ongoing awareness of and sensitivity to the moral features of the HE context and to intervene when necessary to guarantee the preservation of human rights, dignity, equality, and flourishing.

This general JET framework leaves room for additional debate and supplementation. Nonetheless, it takes advantage of a well-researched and applied framework from an adjacent and related field of applied ethics. Adopting and applying such a framework could enable a better shared understanding of the terms of the debate and could help stakeholders navigate the complexities of the moral terrain as they make important decisions and contributions in this emerging field.

National and civil security are important. Those who sign on to do our nation's bidding in dangerous environments are deserving of our gratitude along with state-of-the-art training and technology. However, we should not be blinded by the allure of neuroscience such that we trample over ethics and fail to consider second- and third-order effects. Neuroscience shows great promise for military and other dangerous operations. But we must weigh human dignity and humanitarian principles against military necessity.

The ends may not justify the means. Just as ethical and cultural considerations keep the United States from engaging in torture, illegal search and seizure, and the like, we must be cautious of the potential threats enhancement brings. If one can escape the horrors of war with a pill, does that really constitute improvement of the species? Protecting soldiers and first responders is noble. But we cannot afford a purely reductionist view of human beings (Kato, 2009). We must ensure that the benefits outweigh the harms, heavily weighing the potential psychological and social consequences (Gupta et al., 2015) and ensuring that we preserve our human dignity, extend fairness and virtue, and fulfill our duties to our fellow beings.

In closing, the following quotes from a great soldier and a great scientist offer wisdom. Let us heed their advice as we evaluate the ethics of enhancing human performance in extreme settings.

I would never trust a man who didn't cry; he wouldn't be human.

—Norman Schwarzkopf

It has become appallingly obvious that our technology has exceeded our humanity.

—Albert Einstein

NOTES

1.   http://www.imdb.com/title/tt0071054/quotes
2.   See https://en.wikipedia.org/wiki/A_Taste_of_Armageddon

REFERENCES

Agrid, Y., Ansermet, F., Benmakhlouf, A., Bousser, M., Dickele, A., Gerard, A., . . . Weil, B. (2013). *The use of biomedical techniques for "neuroenhancement" in healthy individuals: Ethical issues* (Opinion No. 122). Retrieved from National Consultative Ethics Committee for Health and Life Sciences website: http://www.ccne-ethique. fr/fr/publications/recours-aux-techniques-biomedicales-en-vue-de-neuro-amelioration-chez-la-personne-non#.WeomeGhSyM8

Bateman, S., Gayon, J., Allouche, S., Goffette, J., & Marzano, M. (2015). *Inquiring into Human Enhancement*. Houndmills, UK: Palgrave Macmillan.

Bateman, S., & Gayon, J. (2015). The concept and practice of HE: What is at stake? In S. Bateman, J. Gayon, S. Allouche, J. Goffette, & M. Marzano (Eds.), *Inquiring into Human Enhancement* (pp. 19–37). Houndmills, UK: Palgrave Macmillan.

Black, R. (2010, April 24). Experts discuss psychological aspects of face transplants following first full operation in Spain. *NY Daily News*. Retrieved from http://www. nydailynews.com

Booth, B., & Lederer, S. (2012). Military families in an era of persistent conflict. In J. H. Laurence & M. D. Matthews (Eds.), *The Oxford Handbook of Military Psychology* (pp. 365–380). New York: Oxford University Press.

Bostrom, N., & Roache, R. (2008). Ethical issues in Human Enhancement. In J. Ryberg, T. Petersen, & C. Wolf (Eds.), *New Waves in Applied Ethics* (pp. 120–152). Basingstoke, UK: Palgrave Macmillan.

Bostrom, N., & Sandberg, A. (2009). Cognitive enhancement: methods, ethics, regulatory challenges. *Science and Engineering Ethics, 15*(3), 311–341.

Bostrom, N., & Savulescu, J. (2009). Introduction—Human enhancement ethics: The state of the debate. In J. Savulescu & N. Bostrom (Eds.), *Human Enhancement* (pp. 1–22). New York: Oxford University Press.

Coady, T. (2009). Playing god. In J. Savulescu & N. Bostrom (Eds.), *Human Enhancement* (pp. 155–80). New York: Oxford University Press.

Cornum, R., Caldwell, J., & Cornum, K. (1997). Stimulant use in extended flight operations. *Air & Space Power Journal, 11*(1), 53.

Damasio, A. (2007). Neuroscience and ethics: Intersections. *The American Journal of Bioethics, 7*(1), 3–7. doi:10.1080/15265160601063910

Douglas, T. (2015). The harms of enhancement and the conclusive reasons view. *Cambridge Quarterly of Healthcare Ethics, 24*, 23–36.

Earp, B. D., Sandberg, A., Kahane, G., & Savulescu, J. (2014). When is diminishment a form of enhancement? Rethinking the enhancement debate in biomedical ethics. *Frontiers in Systems Neuroscience, 8*.

Elango, S., García, J. L., Heckman, J. J., & Hojman, A. (2015). *Early childhood education* (NBER Working Paper No. 21766). Retrieved from the National Bureau of Economic Research website: http://www.nber.org/papers/w21766

Farley, R. (2008, February). 50,000 started war without body armor. *Politifact.* Retrieved from http://www.politifact.com/truth-o-meter/statements/2008/feb/04/hillary-clinton/50000-started-war-without-body-armor/

Forsberg, E. M. (2007). Pluralism, the ethical matrix, and coming to conclusions. *Journal of Agricultural and Environmental Ethics, 20*(5), 455–468.

Forsberg, E. M., Shelley-Egan, C., Thorstensen, E., Landeweerd, L., & Hofmann, B. (2017). *Evaluating Ethical Frameworks for the Assessment of Human Cognitive Enhancement Applications.* Heidelberg, Germany: Springer.

Freeman, M., & Jaoudé, P. A. (2007). Justifying surgery's last taboo: The ethics of face transplants. *Journal of Medical Ethics, 33*, 76–81. doi:10.1136/jme.2006.016865

Fröding, B. E. E. (2011). Cognitive enhancement, virtue ethics and the good life. *Neuroethics, 4*(3), 223–234.

Fukuyama, F. (2002). *Our Posthuman Future.* New York: Farrar, Straus and Giroux.

Gupta, N., Fischer, A. R. H., & Frewer, L. J. (2015). Ethics, risk and benefits associated with different applications of nanotechnology: A comparison of expert and consumer perceptions of drivers of societal acceptance. *Nanoethics, 9*, 93–108. DOI 10.1007/s11569-015-0222-5

Gyngell, C., & Selgelid, M. J. (2016). Clarity and moral significance. In S. Clarke, J. Savulescu, C. A. J. Coady, A. Giubilini, & S. Sanyal (Eds.), *The Ethics of Human Enhancement: Understanding the Debate* (pp. 87–99). Oxford: Oxford University Press.

Giubilini, A., & Sanyal, S. (2015). The ethics of human enhancement. *Philosophy Compass, 10*(4), 233–243.

Habermas, J. (2003). *The Future of Human Nature* (W. Rehg, M. Pensky, & H. Beister, Trans.). Cambridge, MA: Polity.

Harris, J. (2011). Moral enhancement and freedom. *Bioethics, 25*(2), 102–111. https://doi.org/10.1111/j.1467-8519.2010.01854.x

Hurka, T. (2005). Proportionality in the morality of war. *Philosophy & Public Affairs, 33*(1), 34–66.

Illes, J., & Bird, S. J. (2006). Neuroethics: A modern context for ethics in neuroscience. *Trends in Neurosciences, 29*(9), 511–517.

Juengst, E., & Moseley, D. (2015). Human enhancement. In E. N. Zalta (Ed.), *The Stanford Encyclopedia of Philosophy* (2015 Edition). Retrieved from https://plato.stanford.edu/entries/enhancement/

Kato, Y. (2009). Elaborating the list of nanotech-related ethical issues. *Journal of International Biotechnology Law, 6*, 150–155.

Krishnan, A. (2014, November). From psyops to neurowar: What are the dangers? Paper presented at the ISAC-ISSS Conference, Austin, TX.

Laurence, J. H. (2011). Leading across cultures. In P. Sweeney, M. Matthews, & P. Lester (Eds.), *Leadership in Dangerous Situations: A Handbook for the Armed Forces, Emergency Services, and First Responders* (pp. 291–310). Annapolis, MD: Naval Institute Press.

Lin, P., & Allhoff, F. (2008). Untangling the debate: The ethics of human enhancement. *NanoEthics, 2*(3), 251.

Menuz, V. (2015). Why do we wish to be enhanced? In S. Bateman, J. Gayon, S. Allouche, J. Goffette, & M. Marzano (Eds.), *Inquiring into Human Enhancement* (pp. 19–37). Houndmills, UK: Palgrave Macmillan.

Moreno, J. (2011). *The Body Politic.* New York: Bellevue Literary Press.

Moore, B. E. (2013). The brain computer interface future: Time for a strategy (Technical report). Maxwell Air Force Base, AL: Air War College Air University. Retrieved from http://www.dtic.mil/docs/citations/AD1018886

Morin, R. (2011). *For many injured veterans, a lifetime of consequences.* Retrieved from Pew Research Center website: http://www.pewsocialtrends.org/2011/11/08/section-1-the-consequences-of-serious-injuries/

Orend, B. (2013). *The morality of war* (2nd ed.). Peterborough, Canada: Broadview Press.

Parashar, S. (2014). Neuroscientific technologies in security and defense strategies. *Penn Biothics Journal, 7*(i), 23–27.

Parens, E. (1998). Special supplement: Is better always good? The Enhancement Project. *The Hastings Center Report, 28*(1), S1–S17. doi:10.2307/3527981

Roache, R., & Clarke, S. (2009). Bioconservatism, bioliberalism, and the wisdom of repugnance. *Monash Bioethics Review, 28,* 1–21. https://doi.org/10.1007/BF03351306

Ryan, D. M., & Burrell, L. M. (2012). What they deserve: Quality of life in the US military. In J. H. Laurence & M. D. Matthews (Eds.), *The Oxford Handbook of Military Psychology* (pp. 381–399). New York: Oxford University Press.

Sandel M. J. (2002). What's wrong with enhancement. President's Council on Bioethics, Washington, DC. Retrieved from https://bioethicsarchive.georgetown.edu/pcbe/background/sandelpaper.html

Sandel, M. J. (2009). *The Case Against Perfection.* Cambridge, MA: Harvard University Press.

Santoni de Sio, F., Robichaud, P., & Vincent, N. (2014). Who should enhance? Conceptual and normative dimensions of cognitive enhancement. *HUMANA.MENTE Journal of Philosophical Studies, 7*(26), 179–197. http://www.humanamente.eu/index.php/HM/article/view/121

Savulescu, J., Douglas, T., & Persson, I. (2014). Autonomy and the ethics of biological behaviour modification. In A. Akabayashi (Ed.), *The Future of Bioethics: International Dialogues* (pp. 91–112). New York: Oxford University Press.

Selgelid, M. J. (2014). Moderate eugenics and human enhancement. *Medicine, Health Care and Philosophy, 17*(1), 3–12.

Tennison, M. N., & Moreno, J. D. (2012). Neuroscience, ethics, and national security: The state of the art. *PLoS Biology, 10*(3), e1001289.

Thompson, P. B. (2008). The opposite of human enhancement: Nanotechnology and the blind chicken problem. *Nanoethics, 2*(3), 305–316.

Tracey, I., & Flower, R. (2014). The warrior in the machine: Neuroscience goes to war. *Nature Reviews Neuroscience 15,* 825–834. doi:10.1038/nrn3835

Van den Belt, H. (2009). Playing God in Frankenstein's footsteps: synthetic biology and the meaning of life. *Nanoethics, 3*(3), 257.

Walker, M. (2010). In defense of the Genetic Virtue Program: A rejoinder. *Politics and the Life Sciences, 29*(1), 90–96.

Weckert, J. (2016). Playing god: What is the problem?. In S. Clarke, J. Savulescu, C. A. J. Coady, A. Giubilini, & S. Sanyal (Eds.), *The Ethics of Human Enhancement: Understanding the Debate* (pp. 87–99). Oxford: Oxford University Press.

19

Human Performance Optimization

Synthesis and Integration

MICHAEL D. MATTHEWS AND DAVID M. SCHNYER*

INTRODUCTION

The purpose of this book is to explore scientifically grounded approaches to optimizing human performance. While the impetus for this work came from a study sponsored by the US Army (Bolduc, Davis, Gallus, Green, & Matthews, 2015), the strategies for enhancing human performance contained in this volume have wide applicability across many types of organizations. In particular, organizations whose employees work in dangerous, unpredictable, and high-stakes settings should find the ideas discussed in this book to be particularly relevant. In addition to the military, such organizations include law enforcement agencies, fire departments, first responders, healthcare providers, high-risk corporations, and humanitarian relief agencies, just to name a few. The common denominator in these organizations is the need for individual members and teams to sustain high levels of performance under demanding conditions and often for prolonged periods. The focus of this book is how can this best be accomplished with the hope for minimal adverse long-term mental or physical consequences.

The scope of this inquiry is broad and includes many dimensions of human performance. In accordance with the Army study of human performance optimization (HPO), the topics included in this book focused on the cognitive, social, and physical aspects of human performance. In reviewing the concepts and ideas covered in this volume, it is apparent that some HPO strategies could be implemented without a great deal of additional research and development. Other promising approaches require more research and development, but might offer means to enhancing performance within the next few years. Organizations like the military, that have the requisite resources, may use the information summarized in this book to prioritize

---

*The views expressed herein are those of the author and do not reflect the position of the United States Military Academy, the Department of the Army, or the Department of Defense.

future research and development in HPO, and to shape current efforts in achieving this goal.

There is a veritable explosion in basic behavioral and neuroscientific research that may bear on HPO. However, there is always concern that the science of HPO may outpace the development of ethical constraints when applied to improving human performance. The editors underscore the vital importance of the ethical considerations provided by Laurence and Carlisle in Chapter 18. Ethical guidelines and restraints are absolutely necessary when applying emerging brain and behavioral sciences to modifying the behavior or potential of real people because second- and third-order effects—on the individual, the organization, and society—are sure to occur. Therefore, Chapter 18 should be considered essential reading to any organization contemplating applying basic science to achieve HPO.

WHAT ARE THE IMMEDIATE AND LONG-TERM TAKEAWAYS FROM THIS BOOK?

Organizations could immediately choose from a number of currently well-understood approaches that are safe, effective, and ethical and that could clearly enhance the performance of individual workers and teams. A unified and comprehensive approach that addresses the full spectrum of human performance—cognitive, physical, and social—is likely to be more effective in achieving human performance optimization than a piecemeal approach that focuses on only select aspects of performance. Moreover, it is critical that the focus on improving performance be genuinely tied to improving the quality of life for workers and not just as an expedient means to win battles (in the case of the military) or increase profits (in the private sector). Furthermore, organizations that absorb the philosophy of enriching worker's well-being and improving performance into their organizational culture and values will be more likely to achieve success than organizations that implement performance-enhancing strategies that are divorced from these organizational values.

With these points in mind, based on the content of this book, here are some steps that organizations may implement that should both improve worker's well-being and enhance job performance. Depending on an organization's mission, some methods may be more appropriate than others. These recommendations are grounded in scientific research, but the focus of this brief review is on specific actions organizations may adopt. The reader should refer back to the appropriate chapters to review in depth the empirical basis for the recommendations.

Currently Attainable Strategies

PHYSICAL DOMAIN

Friedl and Grate (Chapter 2) highlight the advances being made in metabolic enhancement of the human brain. It is clear in their review that brain health can be optimized by a number of relatively simple (in theory) but sometimes difficult to implement (in practice) strategies. These include balanced nutrition, adequate sleep, and encouraging a non-sedentary lifestyle. Interestingly, Friedl and Grate recommend behavioral measures to mitigate against stress that cross over into recommendations (see later discussion) from other domains. This could include adopting evidence-based methods such as hardiness training (see Chapter 16) and improved leadership and organizational climate (Chapter 17). They also point to the effectiveness of meditation and mindfulness training that, as they point out, are associated with positive changes in brain function associated with greater life satisfaction.

Gaffney-Stomberg and McClung (Chapter 3) focused much of their review specifically on nutrition and performance. While they point out that short-term nutritional deficits do not have significant impacts on cognitive performance, longer lasting deprivations significantly impair multiple aspects of cognition. The remedy goes beyond getting enough calories, and they provide evidence that people who must perform in physically demanding and stressful conditions may benefit from carbohydrates when their performance begins to wane. In such environments and conditions, it is important to ensure that iron levels are adequate, and this can be achieved by dietary supplements or eating foods rich in iron such as leafy green vegetables. Because calcium loss and attendant stress fractures are common in physically demanding training and work settings, it is important to optimize calcium and vitamin D intake. Promoting and providing a healthy diet may seem obvious, but the amount of lost productivity that is linked to the cognitive and physical deficits caused by poor diet are substantial and often overlooked. Given individual differences in physiology and metabolism, organizations would benefit from developing individualized nutrition plans for their employees and providing the resources to implement them.

Tharion et al. (Chapter 7) present another physically based approach to optimizing human performance. This involves using person-specific physiological monitors to help individual workers avoid states that impair performance or acutely threaten their health, such as hyperthermia. There is a rapidly growing commercial marketplace of physiological monitors that are readily obtainable, tracking such things as physical activity, sleep, and biometrics such as heart rate, respiration, and skin temperature. Some are even beginning to measure stress hormone release through the skin. When paired with computational algorithms and translated into easy and meaningful feedback through cell phones or tablets, these devices can serve to motivate wearers to meet daily exercise and sleep goals. Given the overarching role of adequate sleep and exercise, as seen in various chapters in this volume, this represents a highly desirable method of enhancing performance by improving overall worker wellness. It may be that organizations that provide workers with these devices and implement effective approaches of encouraging workers to use and pay attention to them may quickly recoup the associated costs through increased productivity and decreased healthcare outlays. Moreover, feedback from these devices can be summed to provide information about a team of individuals or group health and wellness.

Ness and Wojciechowski (Chapter 9) provide an interesting perspective to mitigating against stress. Taking a behavior genetics perspective, they argue that, rather than trying to optimize behavioral phenotype through difficult and potentially damaging pharmacological or physiological interventions, it is more productive to focus on devising strategies that optimize behaviors in the normal range of capabilities (what geneticists call the "wild type"). Ness and Wojciechowski argue that the fundamental strategy to achieving HPO is to create a strong environment that "pervasively and repeatedly prompts and reinforces particular biobehavioral attributes and discourages other attributes and associated behaviors" (Chapter 9, p. 186). An example is military service academies, where cadets are provided with regular and salient cues that guide their development and day-to-day behavior. Sports teams provide another example, where athletes are regularly monitored and provided with the resources and tools needed to excel. High-stakes corporations could benefit by providing a stronger environment to support institutional goals. Too often, workers are supplied with vague objectives and little feedback. Arguably, effective corporate organizations do provide a strong environment through establishing clear organizational mission statements and values, clearly defining individual and team goals, and actively developing leaders who understand team dynamics and cohesion. From a different perspective, Young (Chapter 17) also addresses this issue.

Sleep represents perhaps the most researched basic system wide biobehavioral function, both in terms of its biological basis and strategies to improve work performance and brain health by optimizing sleep behavior. Shattuck and colleagues (Chapter 10) thoroughly explore this topic with a focus on human performance, health, and well-being, as well as the best countermeasures to combat fatigue. It is well known that adequate sleep is necessary for optimal performance, but the issue for high-stakes organizations is that there are times when individuals and teams must perform under conditions of circadian stress and/or greatly restricted sleep. Under these conditions, short-term solutions may include pharmacologically based countermeasures that range from mild central nervous system stimulant drugs (a notable example is caffeine) to napping strategies. As they emphasize, organizations must establish policies that support obtaining adequate sleep, especially given poor sleep's increasingly well-established link to mental illness.

COGNITIVE DOMAIN

With considerable research and commercial resources being directed to "brain training," Chapman and colleagues (Chapter 12) describe specific research and application efforts being done by the Brain Performance Institute, which is part of the Center for BrainHealth at the University of Texas at Dallas. These efforts take basic neurocognitive research and from that derive effective strategies to optimize cognitive performance. One of their most promising interventions is called Strategic Memory Advanced Reasoning Training (SMART). SMART includes several modules of training aimed at improving attention, improving integrative reasoning, and enhancing mental flexibility and innovative thinking. The SMART training protocols have been used in a variety of populations, including children in a learning environment, posttraumatic stress disorder (PTSD) and head-injured patients, elderly individuals, and a variety of military populations including West Point intercollegiate athletes. Results indicate that SMART is associated with reliable and substantive improvements in cognitive function. SMART shows potential, both as a therapeutic strategy to restore cognitive function and as a performance enhancement strategy among nonclinical populations that can easily be applied in any institutional or organizational context.

Another immediately applicable approach to enhancing cognitive performance is described in Chapter 14 by Roediger and his colleagues. They present strong evidence that retrieval practice enhances cognitive performance. In typical classroom settings, students are presented with material to read and study and, after a period of time, are given an exam to assess their mastery of the material. Roediger et al. show that repeated testing during the learning process, prior to the formal assessment exam, yields much better and more persistent learning. This not an entirely new idea, and the authors trace components of this approach back more than 100 years. Interestingly, this approach captures the essence of the "Thayer-method" of instruction used for more than 200 years at West Point. With this method, cadets must orally recite and be tested on material every lesson, not just at the time of an exam. Roediger et al. review research showing the effectiveness of this approach for many different populations, ranging from college students to Navy Seals. The approach is easily learned and integrated into educational and training protocols and they have created a manualized approach for easy implementation.

Rapid advances in simulation technology have given rise to intelligent instructional systems (Sottilare & Goldberg, Chapter 15). Intelligent tutoring systems are designed to provide individualized training tailored around a given user's current state of knowledge and learning style. For students of the history of psychology, current intelligent tutoring systems are reminiscent of B. F. Skinner's "teaching machines" (Skinner, 1958). Sottilare and Goldberg argue that intelligent tutoring systems are especially relevant to training skills required in dangerous and high stakes settings. Emergency room medical personnel or field medics must make decisions quickly, and their decisions have tangible life or death consequences. Traditionally, these skills were acquired by classroom instruction and considerable on-the-job training. The latter, however, can be costly when mistakes may worsen a patient's condition. Using intelligent tutoring systems to supplement classroom and live-practice training may significantly improve the readiness of workers in such occupations to perform effectively and safely, and with fewer errors than traditional methods alone. As Sottilare and Goldberg maintain, these systems are presently attainable and can be developed for a myriad of occupations and training needs.

Thus far in the cognitive domain, the focus has been on improving basic cognitive skills—memory, attention, decision-making—or, more broadly, learning. Matthews et al. (Chapter 16) introduce the idea of "noncognitive amplifiers" of human performance. These include specific traits or skills that interact with cognitive capabilities to enhance performance. Character strengths of various types, such as grit and hardiness, as well as resilience skills, all contribute to optimizing performance but are often ignored by trainers and developers. A variety of training protocols now exist that may enhance these noncognitive skills and traits in workers. Since only about 25% of the variation of human performance is attributable to cognitive factors (Chapter 16, p. 356), training workers to be grittier, hardier, and more resilient, and teaching them how to leverage different identified character strengths to achieve goals and maintain psychological health should be a pillar of any organization's strategy to achieve HPO.

SOCIAL DOMAIN

Much of the focus of this book is on neurocognitive components of human performance optimization, but two chapters deal with topics that fit more securely in the social domain. In Chapter 16, Matthews and his associates review the concept of resilience. A number of empirically derived approaches exist to improve resilience. The Army's Comprehensive Soldier Fitness (CSF) program includes a metric for assessing fitness/resilience, a train-the-trainer protocol to ensure that qualified fitness coaches are available throughout the organization, and a series of exercises designed to enhance personal resilience, many of which can be completed online. Organizations should be able to tailor this approach to fit their own culture and needs. Another promising method, ready for immediate application, is mindfulness training (Cahn, Goodman, Peterson, Maturi, & Mills, 2017).

Chapter 16 also describes character—another aspect of leadership and social functioning that plays an important role in shaping individual behavior. At the organizational level, high-performing organizations should have a clear vision statement and a developmental plan that emphasizes the importance of character. Selecting individuals of high character, removing those who fail to meet standards, and having a plan to inculcate character in new and existing employees will lead to a more resilient and effective organization.

Finally, Young (Chapter 17) discusses how leadership and team dynamics affect individual performance. Team structure and group dynamics are an integral part of enhancing both individual and organizational effectiveness. The recommendations presented in this chapter provide a blueprint for how organizations can develop a plan to enhance performance by improving team cohesion and dynamics. Given that the interaction between leadership and team dynamics that results in cohesive activity does not necessarily come "naturally" to teams and organizations, a systematic effort toward this end is necessary to achieve success.

Future Strategies

PHYSICAL DOMAIN

The pace of innovation in cognitive neuroscience is such that other approaches to HPO may emerge rather quickly, some within the next decade. Several chapters suggest advances focusing on genetic/epigenetic manipulations (see Friedl & Grate, Chapter 2; Gaffney-Stomberg & McClung, Chapter 3; Sitaram et al., Chapter 6; and Martindale, Chapter 13). Epigenetics involves the modification of the genetic code through environmental interactions. When scientists fully understand how to change the expression of genes by exogenous manipulation, many doors to HPO may open. For instance, soldiers, law enforcement personnel, firefighters, and others employed in risky occupations are regularly exposed to situations that may induce a chronic and debilitating stress response that could result in PTSD. Not all people are equally vulnerable to stress; in fact, the large majority do not develop a pathological response. This may be due to genetically based, individual differences in vulnerability to stress. It is conceivable that vulnerable individuals could be screened and identified prior to stress exposure and then an epigenetic-based intervention could be administered that improves their resistance to severe stress. Such a strategy awaits considerable further scientific research and medical and ethical considerations need to be explored, but, in principle, such effects should be achievable.

Other future HPO interventions may involve alteration of brain function. Friedl and Grate (Chapter 2), Sitaram et al. (Chapter 6), and Chang et al. (Chapter 8) provide detailed analyses of different approaches to optimizing brain function to improve performance. A day may come when implanted electrical circuitry (i.e., brain chips) may improve memory and attention or help maintain arousal. Brain–machine interfaces (BMI) involve directly connecting external devices, including prosthetics, with the brain. It is easy to envision the use of cochlear implants to improve hearing and retinal implants to improve seeing not only for impaired individuals but in the future to "augment" an individual's normal functioning. BMIs may also be used to improve the motor control of prosthetic limbs, and recent advances in prosthetics design provide sensory feedback from a gloved interface on a normal individual or through an artificial prosthetic for someone who has lost a limb. It is easy to extrapolate these advances to a future of "super human" performance where a human operator could be "wired in" to robotic devices controlled by the operator's brain. The operator could then interact with the world through the BMI to allow these platforms to conduct dangerous missions or activities without direct danger to the operator. Imagine a robot that, to the uninformed observer, could move, operate, and perhaps communicate in ways indistinguishable from a real human. Such a platform could search a building for a bomb or operate in outer space or in a radioactive environment as a proxy for the human operator.

Tharion and colleagues (Chapter 7) discuss the next generation of wearable monitors (that far exceed the current scope and accuracy of feedback) that can be used to monitor, regulate, and enhance the performance of the wearer or teams of wearers. When the engineering challenges of power supply, reliability, durability, and weight constraints are resolved, these monitoring systems may provide a means to exponentially improve human performance. Similarly, as Trujillo (Chapter 5) explores, practical methods of directly monitoring brain function through improved and deployable EEG monitors can be incorporated into human monitoring/feedback systems.

Chottekalapanda, Greengard, and Sagi (Chapter 4) discuss their groundbreaking research on the molecular and cellular components of mood disorders. Their work on the protein p11, an important factor in mediating depressive responses in animal studies of depressive pathology and a precursor to serotonin receptor signaling, is promising. As they summarize, other research establishes a relationship between increased p11 effects and decreased vulnerability to stress, with important implications for moderating the mental effects of stress on an individual. Interestingly, as they point out, decreased p11 levels and serotonin receptor activity are associated with depressive behavior both in experimental studies of mice and in humans diagnosed with major depressive disorder. Resilient responses and adjustment are associated with higher p11 and serotonin receptor activity. This suggests that p11 levels may provide a potential biomarker for vulnerability to stress. If current and future research confirms that the nexus between p11 and vulnerability or resilience is reliable in humans, then it may someday be possible to screen or monitor individuals who seek to work in high-risk occupations for vulnerability to stress-induced depressive disorder. This would represent a significant advance in the selection and assignment of people to dangerous and threatening occupations and assignments. For example, a police department could screen applicants partially on the basis of p11 and thereby reduce not only healthcare costs, but also improve police community relations, to the extent that depression-free police officers are less likely to engage in negative and sometimes violent interactions with citizens.

Finally, Agarwal and Deshpande (Chapter 11) review state-of-the-art research in the development and deployment of exoskeletons. While the idea of exoskeletons as a means of enhancing load-bearing capability and other abilities of humans dates back several decades, rapid developments in engineering and computer sciences bring exoskeletons closer to practical daily application. In highly demanding work situations, such systems could serve to augment the physical capabilities of individuals in ways that greatly increase their power and efficiency, and also that of the team. Infantry soldiers, for instance, would be able to more effectively carry heavy loads of ammunition, protective gear, and food and water over longer distances, thus putting less strain on logistical support. Firefighters would benefit in a similar fashion, being able to carry and deploy firefighting implements for longer periods before needing to rest. These technologies, while not presently commonly useable, may become so in the relatively near future.

COGNITIVE DOMAIN

An advantage of the HPO strategies in the cognitive domain is that they are largely based on noninvasive training and educational strategies and that they are, for the most part, currently implementable. Additional research may refine and expand methods to achieve cognitive HPO. Most likely, emerging brain science may produce methods of directly altering brain functions that serve to further enhance cognitive function by improving and sustaining attention and memory or improving metacognitive skills.

For noncognitive amplifiers, additional research on how to measure and train grit may provide a powerful tool in helping people attain long-term goals. In addition, grit may be construed as a small-team trait, not just an individual trait. Research is needed to determine how to define, measure, and train team-level grit. Similar to comments on cognitive skills, future psychologically based resilience training may be supplemented by direct brain interventions to reduce vulnerability or improve resilience in the face of adversity. At present, while the importance of character is recognized in regulating human performance, not so much is known on how to systematically nurture and develop it.

SOCIAL DOMAIN

Matthews and his associates (Chapter 16) describe Project *Arete*, an ongoing study of character assessment and development at West Point. The results of this 5-year longitudinal study should reveal new strategies and best practices for achieving HPO through nurturing and developing positive character traits among employees. One of the biggest needs, one that is not yet achieved, is an objectively valid and reliable measure of character. In short, to develop character a reliable metric of character must exist. Most current measures are either too easily faked or lack psychometric validity. Future efforts aimed at developing a better measure of character will provide the tools that organizations must have in order to assess applicants and new hires in this area and to evaluate the effectiveness of training and developmental strategies aimed at growing character.

In resilience, we anticipate future approaches that are more brain-based than training-based. Here, Chapter 16 intersects with a variety of other topics in the book. Brain implants, manipulating brain chemical function, or stimulating brain regions may in theory improve resilience. Epigenetics offers the very real possibility of very soon altering the expression of genes that mediate the stress reaction. While these and many other brain-based strategies may emerge, these should be approached with caution for a host of ethical reasons, as noted in Chapter 18.

At the team and organizational level, Young (Chapter 17) suggests that teams may someday leverage artificial intelligence systems to improve decision-making and perhaps other aspects of individual and team performance. As with resilience, brain-based strategies may come about in the future that may stimulate greater team or social bonding.

A FURTHER COMMENT ON ETHICS

Throughout history, tension has always existed between science and ethics. This may be particularly true where science and military science intersect. The relationship between science and the military may be described as symbiotic in nature, with advances in one domain feeding further developments and applications in the other. As Matthews (2014) discusses, the advent of the United States' entry into World War I necessitated a new approach to selecting and classifying large numbers of recruits into a variety of military jobs. To meet this need, the emerging science of psychology stepped up and quickly advanced the science and application of aptitude testing. In addition, chemistry and physics in the early twentieth century produced nerve gas and the atomic bomb, both of which represent examples of scientific advances with direct application in weapons development, but that also created significant ethical questions with respect to their use as a tool of warfare.

The application of scientific advances to alter normal human behavior is especially problematic from an ethical perspective. Thus, Laurence and Carlisle's thoughts (Chapter 18) on ethical considerations in human performance optimization are especially relevant. Just because science and engineering *can* produce a method for achieving HPO does not mean that method *should* be used. The editors and authors of this volume urge restraint and caution in the process of transitioning the ideas in this book from the laboratory to the workplace. This is particularly true for HPO protocols that directly impact brain or other physiological functioning.

CONCLUSION

There are many steps that organizations might undertake at present to enhance individual and team performance. Challenges to achieving this goal include

(a) establishing HPO as a salient organizational goal, (b) developing a strategy that effectively reaches all levels of an organization, and (c) designing an approach that is relevant and suitable to the needs of the organization. Not all of the presently attainable approaches included in this book are appropriate for every organization. The needs of the military differ from those of a fire department, and these in turn differ from those of a multinational corporation. However, regardless of the application, the approaches reviewed in this book should prove valuable.

It is important that organizations base their HPO strategies on scientifically valid principles of human behavior and function. There is an abundance of flashy, popular approaches that look good during a "sales pitch" but in the end do not change behavior. Steps that are simple yet validated in sound research could represent the best strategy. Hypothetically, if an organization wanted to achieve HPO, a conservative approach that implements better learning and training strategies coupled with validated methods of improving resilience would be a sound start.

In the same vein, organizations should not ignore the HPO technologies that are being developed and will be deployed in the coming years. If deemed safe, effective, and ethical, brain- or genetic-based strategies that improve attention or other cognitive skills, enhance physical strength, or make workers less vulnerable to physical and mental stress should be considered. For organizations that can afford it, research and development dollars should be dedicated to developing these technologies and sorting potentially useful ones from those that are not effective or are harmful. We believe that this volume can provide a timely roadmap to our current state of knowledge and art in HPO, but, more importantly, we hope that it will also provide a vision of the potential future.

REFERENCES

Bolduc, D. R., Davis, C. Z., Gallus, J., Green, R. L., & Matthews, M. D. (2015, June). *Chief of Staff of the Army Strategic Studies Group Human Performance Optimization Concept Team Final Report*. Arlington, VA: CSA SSG.

Cahn, B. R., Goodman, M. S., Peterson, C. T., Maturi, R., & Mills, P. J. (2017). Yoga, meditation, and mind-body health: Increased BDNF, cortisol awakening response, and altered inflammatory marker expression after a 3-month yoga and meditation retreat. *Frontiers in Neuroscience, 11*, 1–13.

Matthews, M. D. (2014). *Head Strong: How Psychology Is Revolutionizing War*. New York: Oxford University Press.

Skinner, B. (1958). Teaching machines. *Science, 128*(3330), 969–977. Retrieved from http://www.jstor.org/stable/1755240

Index

Tables and figures are indicated by an italic *t* and *f* following the paragraph number